THE GREENWOOD GUIDE TO AMERICAN POPULAR CULTURE

THE GREENWOOD GUIDE TO AMERICAN POPULAR CULTURE

Volume I

Edited by M. Thomas Inge and Dennis Hall

GREENWOOD PRESS
Westport, Connecticut • London

Library of Congress Cataloging-in-Publication Data

The Greenwood Guide to American popular culture / edited by M. Thomas Inge and Dennis Hall.
    p.   cm.
    Includes bibliographical references and index.
    ISBN 0–313–30878–0 (set : alk. paper)—ISBN 0–313–32367–4 (v. 1 : alk. paper)—
    ISBN 0–313–32368–2 (v. 2 : alk. paper)—ISBN 0–313–32369–0 (v. 3 : alk. paper)—
    ISBN 0–313–32370–4 (v. 4 : alk. paper)
    1. Popular culture—United States.   2. Popular culture—United States—History—Sources.
    3. Popular culture—United States—Bibliography.   I. Inge, M. Thomas.   II. Hall, Dennis.
E169.1.H2643   2002
306.4'0973—dc21   2002071291

British Library Cataloguing in Publication Data is available.

Library of Congress Catalog Card Number: 2002071291
ISBN: 0–313–30878–0 (set)
        0–313–32367–4 (v. 1)
        0–313–32368–2 (v. 2)
        0–313–32369–0 (v. 3)
        0–313–32370–4 (v. 4)

First published in 2002

Greenwood Press, 88 Post Road West, Westport, CT 06881
An imprint of Greenwood Publishing Group, Inc.
www.greenwood.com

Printed in the United States of America

∞

The paper used in this book complies with the
Permanent Paper Standard issued by the National
Information Standards Organization (Z39.48–1984).

10 9 8 7 6 5 4 3 2 1

For
Donária Carvalho Inge
and
Susan Hall

They stood by their men.

CONTENTS

Contents

Contents

PREFACE

The Greenwood Guide to American Popular Culture is a revision, expansion, and modification of the reference work formerly known as the *Handbook of American Popular Culture*. In the beginning, that project was intended as a single volume providing bibliographic and practical access to starting points for the study of the major areas of popular culture—hence the term "handbook." That volume appeared in 1978, but so many topics were excluded for lack of space that second and third volumes were published in 1980 and 1981. The continuing expansion of academic interest in popular culture called for a second edition, which was done in two stages. Ten revised and five new chapters on genres of literature were brought together in the *Handbook of American Popular Literature* in 1988. This was followed in 1989 by the revised and expanded second edition of the *Handbook of American Popular Culture* in three volumes, which covered another forty-seven topics excluding those in the literature volume.

All of the topics have now been reunited in the current guide with some modifications. Scholarship has expanded so rapidly and in such volume in advertising, detective and mystery fiction, and gender studies that the researcher can turn to entire sections of reference works and bibliographies on the shelves of libraries, not to mention the Internet, so they have been excluded. A few other chapters have been deleted because of diminished scholarly interest. Several new topics have been added, however: amusement parks, do-it-yourself and home improvement, housing, living history and reenactments, museums and collecting, and New Age movements. The introduction to the second edition of the handbook has been retained because of its historic interest, and an entirely new chapter on the study of popular culture by Michael Dunne appears at the beginning.

As was true in earlier versions, each chapter, prepared or revised by authorities on the subjects, provides a brief chronological survey of the development of the medium or topic; a critical guide in essay form to the standard or most useful reference works, bibliographies, histories, critical studies, and journals; a description of existing research centers or collections of primary and secondary sources when relevant; and a checklist of works cited in the text. With this guide, the student, scholar, librarian, or general reader can easily locate the kind of information needed to complete a research project, answer a question, build a basic library, or read about a topic or personality as a matter of interest.

The coeditors wish to express their appreciation to the contributors to this and the earlier editions of the *Handbook*. Without them, this literally would not have been possible. Inge wishes to thank Nancy B. Newins and Cynthia L. Hartung for their interlibrary loan efforts, Michael P. Bradenham and Donna Lira for their keen proofreading skills, as well as Susan G. Timberlake and Diana L. Lewis for their secretarial support at Randolph-Macon College. The faithful material and moral support of the administration, President Roger H. Martin and Dean Robert Holyer, as always is greatly appreciated. Donária makes all things possible and sets the music of the spheres to a samba beat. Hall wishes to thank the Department of English, University of Louisville, for its generous support, particularly in assigning graduate service assistants to this project: Steve Wexler, Michael Fox, Clark Pollitt, and especially Sarah Croy. Colleagues in the Ekstrom Library provided daily help, as did many with skills in computer technology, most notably, Mark Crane. Special thanks to the spirits of the garden and to Susan.

M. Thomas Inge
Dennis Hall

INTRODUCTION

M. Thomas Inge

The development of the field of popular culture as a legitimate subject of critical scrutiny and scholarly investigation in America began with the declaration of Gilbert Seldes in his audacious and groundbreaking book published in 1924, *The 7 Lively Arts*, where he asserted that

> entertainment of a high order existed in places not usually associated with Art, that the place where an object was to be seen or heard had no bearing on its merits, . . . and that a comic strip printed on newspulp which would tear and rumple in a day might be as worthy of a second look as a considerable number of canvasses at most of our museums.[1]

While the guardians of high culture and the New York critics looked on in disbelief, Seldes issued a series of propositions that threatened the foundations of the intellectual establishment. Among them were the following:

> That there is no opposition between the great and the lively [i.e., popular] arts.
> That except in a period when the major arts flourish with exceptional vigour, the lively arts are likely to be the most intelligent phenomenon of their day.
> That the lively arts as they exist in America today are entertaining, interesting and important.
> That with a few exceptions these same arts are more interesting to the adult cultivated intelligence than most of the things which pass for art in cultured society.[2]

While outrage met his propositions, Seldes established the point of view that twentieth-century America had an artistic tradition of its own different from, but no less respectable than, the European, and most of the work done in the study of popular culture since is but an extrapolation of ideas expressed in his book. Not until the 1950s, however, did serious discussion begin, with such critics as Henry Nash Smith, who looked to the popular literature of the dime novel as a way of understanding American culture in *Virgin Land* (1950), and Dwight MacDonald's several essays, later collected in *Against the American Grain* (1962), in which he expressed alarm over what he saw as the trivialization of American culture through the mass media. Critics of the 1960s—Leo Lowenthal, Marshall McLuhan, Benjamin DeMott, Susan Sontag, Leslie Fiedler, and Tom Wolfe among them— approached popular culture in a variety of ways, distinctive but nearly always for reasons that had little to do with a proper appreciation for the subject. Then in the 1970s criticism of the popular arts matured with such standard works as Russel B. Nye's comprehensive history *The Unembarrassed Muse* (1970) and John Cawelti's definitive study of formula in Western fiction and film, *The Six-Gun Mystique* (1971).

Academic study of popular culture began with early investigations within the established disciplines, such as sociologists who examined the mass media for what they revealed about social attitudes and mores and English teachers who turned to film when they discovered that some of the same critical tools applied to literature could also be used in an appreciation of the motion picture. Likewise, those engaged in research in folklore, history, mass communications, and anthropology often found it profitable to include popular culture in their purview.

The development of popular culture as a separate field began with the establishment of the *Journal of Popular Culture* in the summer of 1967 and the founding of the Popular Culture Association in 1969, both through the leadership of Ray B. Browne and the support of such scholars as Russel B. Nye, John Cawelti, Carl Bode, and Marshall Fishwick. Also in 1969 Ray B. Browne established the Center for the Study of Popular Culture at Bowling Green State University in Ohio, which coordinates archival and research activities and the publication of books and several journals and supports degree-granting programs in the Department of Popular Culture. The Popular Culture Association, as an affiliate organization, supports scholarly sessions at the national and regional meetings of the Modern Language Association and the American Historical Association, as well as other professional societies, and has held its own national convention on a regular basis since 1971. There are also eleven regional and state associations that meet regularly, and there are a Canadian Popular Culture Association and a Japanese Popular Culture Association, which were developed with the assistance of the American association.

All of this scholarly study has had its impact on curriculum. In a survey published in 1980, *Currents of Warm Life: Popular Culture in Higher Education*, Mark Gordon and Jack Nachbar reported that almost 2,000 courses in popular culture were then being offered in the United States among 260 four-year colleges and universities surveyed, and on the basis of the data gathered, they projected the actual existence of nearly 20,000 courses throughout the nation. The seven most frequently offered subjects were popular literature (especially detective and science fiction), film, mass media, ethnic studies, television and radio, history and popular culture, and popular music. These courses were most commonly offered by departments of English, speech/communications, sociology, history, journalism,

American studies, ethnic studies, and art (in descending order of frequency). While the growth and expansion of courses have been remarkable, only one other school besides Bowling Green State University has developed a degree program in popular culture—Morgan State University in Baltimore—but then all humanities and liberal arts programs have experienced little growth under the economic conditions of the last few decades in higher education.

The serious and systematic study of popular culture may be the most significant and potentially useful of the trends in academic research and teaching in the last half of the twentieth century in the United States. Scholarly study in this area helps modern society understand itself better and provides new avenues and methods of bringing to bear on contemporary problems the principles and traditions of humanism. It is no longer necessary to justify the study of popular culture by an alliance with some other social or cultural purpose. We have come to recognize that each form or medium of expression has its own aesthetic principles, techniques, and ways of conveying ideas. Each has been subject to misuse and ineptitude, but each has witnessed levels of artistic accomplishment remarkable by any measure, although finally each must be evaluated within and by its own self-generated set of standards and objectives. This last may be the most immediate task ahead for those who wish to fulfill the vision and propositions of Gilbert Seldes offered over seventy-five years ago.

WHY STUDY POPULAR CULTURE?

Why is it important that we study popular culture? Because there is no more revealing index to the total character and nature of a society than an examination of its popular arts and the way it spends its leisure time. Norman F. Cantor and Michael S. Werthman have put it most aptly:

> Play is not frivolous; it is a serious matter centering on how men treat one another, a reflection of man's needs, aspirations, and nature. The rules which regulate the games people play differ from those prescribed for most human activities inasmuch as a man may choose to play or be a spectator or absent himself altogether. These choices are not open in the larger, more public game of life that depends on political and economic compulsion. The quality of volition therefore informs the whole history of popular culture. In that history is described what men have done and are doing with their capabilities, and further, it measures human potentiality not by showing what man can be forced to do, but by demonstrating what he can do when left to his own devices, free to follow the inclinations of his mind and spirit.[3]

In other words, popular culture shows people at their best, at their most capable and creative, and in their most liberated state. Thus, the health of a society is directly reflected in the liveliness and quality of its entertainment.

Popular culture is also the place to look for the emerging art forms of the future. Drama and poetry have been with us since classical times and earlier, while the novel in the West developed in the eighteenth century and came to flower in the nineteenth and twentieth centuries. Painting and sculpture have lengthy pedigrees in Western civilization, while the print and the graphic arts came into being with the invention of printing. In this century, however, a great variety of new forms has come into being for creative expression. At least one of them, film, has in a very short time matured and become in the eyes of many a fine art, as has photography. Jazz has been acclaimed as well as a distinctive form of American art. Other examples of new art forms developed within the last 100 years include radio drama, television drama, comic strips and comic books, animated films, docudramas, and many varieties of popular music. None of these have quite achieved the maturity found in film, but each has the potential of becoming the focus for creative energy and striking accomplishment. Some of these will drop from view, undoubtedly, but others may not fully blossom until sometime in the twenty-first century. In any case, there are a large number of cultural possibilities available to the artist, more than ever before in the known history of civilization.

Finally, Americans in particular should study their popular arts to understand themselves better. The media inform their environment, make suggestions to people about ways to view themselves, provide role models from infancy through old age, give information and news as they happen, provide education, influence their opinions, and open up opportunities for creative expression. Culture emanates from society, voices its hopes and aspirations, quells its fears and insecurities, and draws on the mythic consciousness of an entire civilization or race. It is an integral part of life and a permanent record of what we believe and are. While future historians will find the accumulated popular culture invaluable, the mirror is there for us to look into immediately. America's popular culture is known throughout the world and serves as a silent ambassador. We should know what it says about us.

THE DEFINITION OF POPULAR CULTURE

What exactly is popular culture? So varied are its forms and so diverse its implications that most definitions are either too narrow or too inclusive. Ray B. Browne's definition may be both the briefest and the broadest: "all the experiences in life shared by people in common, generally though not necessarily disseminated by the mass media."[4] While the qualifying phrase helps, the term "experience" seems much too general and the meaning of "people in common" too vague. (How many people must share the experience before it becomes common enough to be popular?)

The British critic C.W.E. Bigsby probes at the ambiguities inherent in two words, the adjective "popular" and the noun "culture":

Part of the difficulty over the meaning of the term "popular culture" arises from the differing meanings attributable to the word "popular" itself, for as the OED [*Oxford English Dictionary*] makes evident it can mean both "intended for and suited to ordinary people," or "prevalent or current among, or accepted by, the people generally." The latter includes everyone; the former excludes all but the "ordinary." Hence popular culture is sometimes presented as that which appeals only to the community ("mass culture") or to the average ("middlebrow"), thus confirming the social fragmentation of society, and sometimes as a phenomenon cutting across class lines. For some, therefore, it is a simple opiate, for others a subversive and liberating force, linking those of differing social and educational background.

There is further difficulty still in that the word "culture" is susceptible both of a general and a specialized meaning. In the former sense it implies the attitudes and values of a society as expressed through the symbolic form of language, myths, rituals, life-styles, establishments (political, religious, educational); in the latter it is closer to the meaning implied by Matthew Arnold and defined by the OED as "the training, development, and refinement of mind, taste, manners: the condition of being thus trained and refined, the intellectual side of civilization." . . . Thus, by analogy, popular culture is sometimes defined as the attitudes and values of those excluded from the intellectual elite and expressed through myths, rituals and lifestyles specific to this excluded group, and sometimes as the popular, as opposed to the intellectual arts.[5]

What is useful here is the identification of culture as "language, myths, rituals, life-styles, establishments," all symbolic forms for the expression of the attitudes and values of society. But this seems to suggest that culture is somehow automatic and unconscious, not a willful expression of a person's creative urges, as it has been in the post-industrial society.

Michael J. Bell has suggested a useful definition that pays attention simultaneously to purpose, form, and function:

At its simplest popular culture is the culture of mass appeal. A creation is popular when it is created to respond to the experiences and values of the majority, when it is produced in such a way that the majority have easy access to it, and when it can be understood and interpreted by that majority without the aid of special knowledge or experience.[6]

This may be the most serviceable of the definitions reviewed so far, except for the repetition of the problematic word—"majority." Are we speaking of the majority of the people on the face of the earth, in one nation, among one ethnic group, within one economic class, or what? What constitutes a majority?

Perhaps the most useful definition has been offered by the historians Norman F. Cantor and Michael S. Werthman:

Man's culture is the complex of all he knows, all he possesses, and all he does. His laws and religious beliefs, his art and morals, his customs and ideas are the content of his culture. . . . And cutting across cultural and subcultural boundaries is the fundamental distinction between work and play: between what is done of necessity and what is done by choice.

George Santayana, writing about the distinctions between work and play, indicated the importance of the things men do when they are not engaged in the fight for survival or the avoidance of pain. He said:

We may measure the degree of happiness and civilization which any race has attained by the proportion of its energy which is devoted to free and generous pursuits, to the adornment of life and the culture of the imagination. For it is in the spontaneous play of his faculties that man finds himself and his happiness. Slavery is the most degrading condition of which he is capable, and he is as often a slave to the niggardliness of the earth and the inclemency of heaven, as to a master or an Institution. He is a slave when all his energy is spent on avoiding suffering and death, when all his action is imposed from without, and no breath or strength is left him for free enjoyment. . . . Work and play here take on a different meaning and become equivalent to servitude and freedom. . . . We no longer mean by work all that is done usefully, but only what is done unwillingly and by the spur of necessity. By play, we are designating no longer what is done fruitlessly, but whatever is done spontaneously and for its own sake, whether it have or not an ulterior utility.

Popular culture may be seen as all those things man does and all those artifacts he creates for their own sake, all that diverts his mind and body from the sad business of life. Popular culture is really what people do when they are not working: it is man in pursuit of pleasure, excitement, beauty, and fulfillment.[7]

I would refine this definition for my purposes one step further: popular culture is what we do by choice to engage our minds and our bodies when we are not working or sleeping. This can be active—playing baseball, driving an automobile, dancing—or passive—watching television, sunbathing, or reading a book. It can be creative—painting a portrait, writing a poem, cooking a meal—or simply responsive—playing a game, watching a circus, or listening to music. While highly inclusive and perhaps imprecise, such a definition allows for the great diversity of form and the wide degree of latitude for engagement of mind and body necessary for any discussion of popular culture in this century.

HIGH CULTURE AND POPULAR CULTURE

In the effort to define popular culture, nearly all commentators have assumed that there are clear distinctions to be made between high or elite culture and popular or mass culture. For those trained in the traditional methods of cultural analysis, it is easy to draw up a list of seemingly opposite distinctions in form, function, and methods of evaluation. I mention here only the most obvious.

Form

High culture is generally thought to be fairly exclusive in its style and content, the individual and subjective expression of an artist who aims to be different and daring in his or her approach, with the intention of stretching the boundaries and limitations of the form of art practiced. A premium is placed on originality and novelty; the work is often complex and intricate in its structure, the end result often being mystification and a recognition of the refusal of existence to answer to a person's rational categories. Form, then, is but an extension of a philosophical attitude that recognizes mutability, temporality, and free will as influential factors in the scheme of things and the universe.

Popular culture, however, is thought to be comprehensive or relevant to a large part of the population in its style and content. It is often an anonymous or seemingly objective product of a team or an individual creative technician who follows traditional or tried-and-true approaches to the material. The patterns tend to be highly formulaic, occasionally with a different twist for surprise effect but nothing radical to disturb expectations. Situations and moral dilemmas are often oversimplified so that no mistake can be made about right and wrong, and complex questions are made easy by clarifying them in terms of standard theological categories. Mystery and the irrational have little place here since everything can ultimately be explained or has a rational basis. Form, then, reflects an attitude that embraces stability, security, and even determinism as essential factors in human existence.

Function

The function of high culture is to validate the experience of the individual. Creation is a purely aesthetic act in pursuit of truth and beauty and, that being so, is therefore self-justifying. "Art for art's sake" is a phrase generally applied to allow for creations that are non-representational and totally without use or even meaning. Whether or not the object answers our efforts to understand it, it is assumed that enlightenment is the artist's purpose, that we are better educated for having been exposed to the artist's vision, no matter how solitary or absurd. The art piece is designed aggressively to confront us, to challenge our assumptions and beliefs about art and life, and to identify the unanswered questions about existence. Rather than provide answers, it poses the questions and posits irresolvable conflicts and dilemmas.

Popular culture, on the other hand, validates the common experience of the larger part of the population. The creative act is a social act with clear economic or political consequences. It is "art for society's sake," with explicit functions to fulfill in addressing a social problem, supporting a political attitude, or selling a product that answers a psychological need, such as supporting our self-confidence. While a kind of subtle instruction or subliminal suggestion is going on, the primary purpose is to entertain us, to cause us to relax and escape the pressures of our jobs, our problems, and our personal relationships. We want to laugh and forget, not be reminded of the tragedies and injustices of the world. We also seek in popular culture to have our attitudes and biases confirmed, to know that there are others just like us with the same thoughts, and to be encouraged to believe that everything will come out right in the end. By providing a vicarious outlet for our emotional tendencies and a safety valve for our aggressions, the cultural act has a therapeutic effect and makes us feel better physically and psychologically. The answers to questions are given, and every situation has a happy ending.

Evaluation

In our efforts to appreciate and evaluate high culture, we have developed a carefully formulated, if not entirely agreed-upon, set of critical standards designed as measures against which each piece of art of its kind can be compared and found worthy or lacking. In many forms—and certainly this seems true of literature—the standards derive from the classical principles set down by the Greek critics and thinkers, and a special premium is placed on the longevity of an idea or technique, as if age were a sign of validity. Some would argue, in fact, that only with the passage of time can a piece of art be properly evaluated as it gains in reputation among the cultural arbiters of an age. Its final value, then, derives from the respect that it garners among critics, the body of commentary and appreciative criticism that gathers around it. Since high culture appeals to the intellect and the noble aspirations of people, it is to be cherished and protected against the ravages of time and the whims of changing social and political systems.

Popular culture, designed to appeal to the common person and the largest part of the population, is to be evaluated only by the personal taste of the individual consumer. Its success and reputation are based on how widely distributed it is or how many people it reaches. Sales charts and the money earned by the creators are the only methods of determining its value. Because it appeals to our emotions and panders to our needs, it satisfies the baser side or nonintellectual part of human nature. Ultimately, therefore, it may be debasing, corrupting, and potentially evil, even though it never challenges the mores or principles of the larger society. Perhaps there is some of the Puritanic in this attitude—if it's fun, it must be sinful.

While such an elaborate listing of comparative features between high and popular culture would seem reflective of a substantial body of empirical data and scientifically verifiable theory, the fact is that the whole thing is an elaborate fiction, an intellectual concoction generated by the American academy and critical establishment (with the help of the British). So effectively have these arguments and points of cultural theology been preached by the critical priesthood of scholars and teachers that we are inclined to agree with them without reservation. Yes, we agree, there is a vast difference between Shakespeare and Neil Simon, forgetting in the face of cultural authority that both directed their plays to the widest possible audiences, that both addressed the basic human problems of their societies, and that both are enormously popular on the commercial stage with or without the approval of the priesthood. Shakespeare has not survived because of the enormous body of criticism generated by scholars of his work (enough to fill entire buildings) but because of the actability, durability, and continuing appeal of his plays to people of all nations and cultures.

In his influential sociological study *Popular Culture and High Culture*, Herbert J. Gans accepts the two as given separate phenomena but goes on to argue in behalf of cultural pluralism:

> I believe both to be cultures and my analysis . . . rests on two value judgements: (1) that popular culture reflects and expresses the aesthetic and other wants of people (thus making it culture and not just commercial menace); and (2) that all people have a right to the culture they prefer, regardless of whether it is high or popular.[8]

Ray B. Browne has suggested that perhaps the best metaphorical figure to describe all art and culture is that of a flattened ellipse or lens:

In the center, largest in bulk and easiest seen through is Popular Culture, which includes Mass Culture. On either end of the lens are High and Folk Cultures, both looking fundamentally alike in many aspects and both having a great deal in common, for both have keen direct vision and extensive peripheral insight and acumen. All four derive in many ways and to many degrees from one another, and the lines of demarcation between any two are indistinct and fluid.[9]

I wish to go one step further than both Gans and Browne. What I wish to argue is that there are *no* distinctions between what we call high culture and popular culture, at least not in the twentieth and the twenty-first centuries in the United States, which have witnessed the deep social changes wrought by industrialism, technology, and democracy. What we have is simply American culture. In the mass society in which we live, the older cultural distinctions make no sense, and we must seek new ways to understand the forms, functions, and ways of evaluating our arts and creative achievements. Then Americans might stop apologizing for the fact that our only indigenous art forms seem to have been jazz and the comics and that primarily in film have we had an international cultural impact. In fact, we might then begin to take pride in those particular accomplishments.

Where would Americans go if they wished to participate in highbrow culture? To the art gallery, the museum, the opera, the symphony concert, or the ballet? If they attended any of these in Washington, D.C., for example, say, at the Kennedy Center, would they find themselves rubbing shoulders with the cultural elite? A few scholars might be present from one of the local universities, a few wealthy patrons of the arts, an ambassador or two, some political figures, and the critic from the *Washington Post*, but the vast majority of those attending are government white-collar workers, young executives and lawyers, American and foreign students, tourists, and other middle-class people—well educated perhaps, even some Ph.D.s among them, but by and large a typical cross-section of the American populace of all ages, classes, and ethnic groups. Such cultural events are open to, and attended by, all Americans, who by no stretch of the imagination could be called cultural elites. They may discuss the performance or exhibition, sometimes knowledgeably and sometimes on the basis of individual taste, but they do not constitute any sort of select society. In the United States, wealth has never gone hand in hand with sophistication or education, so except for a handful of philanthropists, we have had few patrons of the arts in the original sense. The patrons are the thousands of ordinary people who pay the price of admission or the taxes to subsidize the museum or program.

The extent to which high and popular culture merge in America was illustrated by a magazine called *Connoisseur*. According to a promotional flyer sent to thousands of homes in the United States, *Connoisseur* was a "clear and comprehensive guide for people 'in the know' about enduring values of art and beauty." The audience was identified in this way: "If you are classic and aristocratic in your tastes, but democratic and modern in their application [never mind the inherent contradictions here], you are the best of the breed—a contemporary connoisseur." The magazine promised to introduce the reader to the finest hotels and restaurants in the world, the loveliest precious stones, secrets of successful bidding at art auctions, how to select an architect or a decorator, or how to find a trustworthy art dealer to assess the value of his or her collection of paintings. Advertisements in selected issues promoted Ming dynasty ceramics, rare works of art, antiques, horses, and exclusive hotels.

While much of this was merely Madison Avenue rhetoric and advertising hype, are we to assume that the readers of this magazine were the highbrows who supported high culture? Were they a small and select group of the tasteful and wealthy? According to the statement of ownership and circulation required by the U.S. Post Office to be published in all magazines once a year to maintain fourth-class mailing privileges, on October 1, 1987, over 374,600 copies of *Connoisseur* were printed, sold, and distributed that month. According to the Internal Revenue Service tax returns, in the latest year for which the information was available, only about 17,266 people in the United States annually earned $1 million or more. So, who were all the current and potential readers? They were the middle-class people who used *Connoisseur* magazine as a wish book or enjoyed the status of having a copy on display on the coffee table. The audience of connoisseurs, which their subscription campaign sought to expand, was a fantasy, a nonexistent group. For only $9.99 a year, the reader could be included among "those who are confident that they know the best and are proud of it." The inexpensive price of the magazine and the mass mailing of subscription appeals were indicators of its actual market—the aspiring American middle class, not the actual connoisseurs, who would hardly need a magazine to tutor them in taste.

There are simply too many examples of high and popular art that cross the boundaries to argue with any conviction that a firm line of demarcation exists. Such pieces of popular art as the film *Citizen Kane*, the comic strips *Krazy Kat* and *Little Nemo in Slumberland*, or the comedy of Charlie Chaplin have come to be recognized as classics in their own right, and each has inspired large quantities of critical commentary. On the other hand, such examples of high art as Shakespeare's *Hamlet*, Picasso's *Guernica*, or da Vinci's *Mona Lisa* have entered the popular consciousness and would be promptly recognized, and to a large extent even understood, by just about everyone. Valid aesthetic distinctions may be made between Tolstoy's *War and Peace* and Margaret Mitchell's *Gone with the Wind*, yet both have been profoundly influential in shaping the attitudes of Americans toward the events that they portray and the meaning of history. Which of the two has been read by more people? Mitchell's extremely popular novel, of course, not to mention the countless millions who have seen the motion picture version, which has never ceased to be shown in some part of the world since it was first released over sixty years ago.

It would seem to make better sense to describe all that we have been discussing—high culture, low culture, mass media, popular culture, or whatever—as simply culture. Culture is a creative response to our environment, an effort to make sense out of disorder, a desire to discover beauty and meaning in the ugliness and absurdity of our world. Whether it be simple or complex, elite or democratic, individually crafted or mass-produced, we should drop the adjectives "high" and "popular" and address ourselves to the total culture of twenty-first-century-American society without maintaining false distinctions that have no reality in the modern world. Until that time comes, however, it will continue to be necessary to use the term "popular culture" as in the title of this reference work in the traditional sense.

M. Thomas Inge

NOTES

1. Gilbert Seldes, *The 7 Lively Arts*, rev. ed. (New York: Harper and Brothers, 1957), p. 3.

2. Ibid., pp. 294–95.

3. Norman F. Cantor and Michael S. Werthman, *The History of Popular Culture to 1815* (New York: Macmillan, 1968), pp. xxiii–xxiv.

4. Ray B. Browne, *Popular Culture and the Expanding Consciousness* (New York: Wiley, 1973), p. 6.

5. C.W.E. Bigsby, *Approaches to Popular Culture* (London: Edward Arnold, 1976), pp. 17–18.

6. Michael J. Bell, "The Study of Popular Culture," in *Concise Histories of American Popular Culture*, ed. M. Thomas Inge (Westport, Conn.: Greenwood Press, 1982), p. 443.

7. Cantor and Werthman, pp. xxi–xxii.

8. Herbert J. Gans, *Popular Culture and High Culture* (New York: Basic Books, 1974), p. vii.

9. Ray B. Browne, *Popular Culture and Curricula* (Bowling Green, Ohio: Bowling Green University Popular Press 1972), p. 10.

THE STUDY OF POPULAR CULTURE

Michael Dunne

"The study of popular culture" is a topic that can best be approached by asking two interrelated questions: What is (was) popular culture? How have we (how should we) study it? Each element of this interrogative equation has attracted considerable, sometimes acrimonious attention over the years. Since these discussions have usually emerged from the mixture of disinterested intellectual analysis and professional self-interest that often attends academic debate, the answers proposed have turned out to be almost as various as the scholars who have proposed them.[1] Much of the contention centers, naturally enough, on the first question since we must identify our field of inquiry before we can discover anything useful to say about it. So we should begin with the question: Just what *is* popular culture anyhow?

Faced with an equally challenging question in the Hollywood musical *The Band-wagon* (1953), Arthur Schwartz and Howard Dietz define the amorphous subject identified in the title of their song "That's Entertainment" by providing a series of examples, including "the clown with his pants falling down" and the "great Shakespearean scene where a ghost and a prince meet and everyone ends in mince-meat." Since the song itself is entertaining, it enacts the very quality that it claims to be defining. The song also models exemplification as a useful approach to the problem of defining other complex entities such as "popular culture." Thus, in this chapter I engage in the study of popular culture even as I attempt to define it through examples.

Movies are an important part of popular culture, of course. One need only think about the several stages of *Star Wars* hysteria to see *how* important. But even before George Lucas first went off to kindergarten, Humphrey Bogart was up on the screen teaching a lot of men how to smoke with the correct manly squint, and Clark Gable was showing them how to do without undershirts. In the same way, Grace Kelly showed many women the advantages of putting their hair in a French twist, and Katharine Hepburn showed everyone what an independent woman looked and sounded like. Obviously, movies have been a significant influence on American culture. Some commentators have even held John Wayne responsible for American involvement in the Vietnam War.[2] If we add Saturday afternoon matinees to these examples of cinematic influence—along with Elvis movies, screwball comedies, quirky history lessons from Spike Lee and Oliver Stone, and the usual assortment of musicals, biblical epics, and two-handkerchief "weepies"— we end up with a provisional list that shows just how significantly movies have influenced the development of American popular culture, at least in the twentieth and twenty-first centuries.

Popular music has also been indispensable to this development, as the term itself implies. Minstrelsy, silver band music, college and club songs, patriotic ditties, spirituals and hymns—all contributed to the emerging culture of eighteenth- and nineteenth-century America. In the twentieth century, ragtime, jazz, swing, bebop, Broadway show tunes, radio broadcasts, movie themes, *Your Hit Parade*, rhythm and blues, country music, soul, hip-hop, heavy metal—even Musak—appeared, found their initial audiences, spread, evolved, mixed with other forms, and temporarily disappeared—but only temporarily. Today, every historical form of music is probably available on compact disc (CD) in the larger urban "record" stores or from an on-line service. Anyone who has bought even a single CD from a catalog can attest to the monthly avalanche of other catalogs offering unimaginable collections of inspiring World War II ballads, hits by the Doors, and Pavarotti's favorite arias. As in the better "record" stores, these catalogs offer classical music right down the aisle from reggae and jazz. Popular music has been, is, and apparently ever shall be, part of popular culture.

Years ago, when people were not walking down the street plugged into earphones, radio supplied much of our popular music. First as an outlet for the kinds of big bands led by Tommy Dorsey and Glenn Miller and for popular singers like Bing Crosby and Johnny Mercer and later as the primary venue for rock and soul records, radio connected Americans to the popular music of the day. Even today, when the radio market is so narrowly divided into highly specific musical formats, radio can figure prominently in promoting songs and launching new musical careers, especially in the country music field. Stopped in our cars at traffic lights, we can listen to the musical preferences of the driver waiting next to us. The music may be coming from an automotive tape- or CD-player, but it is just as likely to be blasting out of a car radio. By the same token, the car radio is just as likely to be blasting out no kind of music at all, but the outraged protest of someone calling in to a talk-radio program. This might remind us that even during the heyday of the big-band broadcasts, the most popular radio shows were not musically oriented but were comedies like *Amos and Andy* and *Fibber Magee and Molly* or dramas like *One Man's Family* and *Gangbusters*. Like television later on, radio once sought to be all things to all people, and also like television, radio continues to be a crucial element of American popular culture.

Various print media have long been recognized as significant contributors also. In fact, we might credit Johannes Gutenberg's perfection of the printing press in the mid-fifteenth century with originating the whole concept of the popular since the reproduction of identical print texts inevitably created a diffusion of cultural access. Or we might see the developments of newspapers in the eighteenth century and of inexpensive pulp books and magazines in the late-nineteenth and twentieth centuries as the crucial events. Practically universal in all histories of popular culture, however, is some acknowledgment that the proliferation of printed texts has contributed incalculably to its development. Even if we concede what many see as a real decline today in the appeal of print culture, the influence of print media on the development of American popular culture should be clear. It has become standard practice, for example, to begin college anthologies of American literature with Renaissance explorers' exaggerated accounts of the physical bounty of the Americas, accounts intended to lure new settlers to these shores.[3] Benjamin Franklin launched his career early in the eighteenth century by writing anonymous columns for his brother's newspaper, the *New England Courant.*[4] Abraham Lincoln is popularly believed to have greeted Harriet Beecher Stowe as "the little woman who wrote the book [*Uncle Tom's Cabin* (1852)] that made this great war."[5] The popular novels of success written by Horatio Alger Jr. (1832–1899) obviously lurk in the backgrounds of the real-life achievements of celebrities including George M. Cohan, J. Edgar Hoover, and Ronald Reagan[6] and of highly respected novels such as *The Great Gatsby* (1925) by F. Scott Fitzgerald, *A Cool Million* (1933) by Nathanael West, and *Invisible Man* (1948) by Ralph Ellison. *The Man Nobody Knows* (1924), Bruce Barton's book about Jesus, the greatest salesman ever, Irma Rombauer's irreplaceable *The Joy of Cooking* (1931), Dale Carnegie's *How to Win Friends and Influence People* (1936), Grace Metalious' "scandalous" novel *Peyton Place* (1956)—all of these works enjoyed fabulous popularity, ran through multiple printings and/or later editions (sometimes screen adaptations), and in the process significantly helped shape American popular culture.[7]

Adding comic books like *Superman* and *Archie* and comic strips like *Bringing Up Father* and *Doonesbury* to this brief list of best-sellers helps us realize that popular culture would not be popular culture without sizable infusions of ink. Still today, when the last days of print culture have supposedly arrived, newsmagazines and morning television shows annually provide lists of the season's hottest new books for consumers on the lookout for Christmas gifts. Even members of the culture uninterested in buying the self-help books and tell-all celebrity autobiographies that top most best-seller lists can get their print fix at the supermarket check-out counters, where the most recent issues of the *Star* and *National Enquirer* deliver much the same raw data in slightly different configurations, and this survey has not so far mentioned the devoted readers of the paperback mysteries, romances, thrillers, westerns, and science fiction that are probably displayed on shelves located in supermarkets and drugstores not far from the tabloids. In short, print has played, and continues to play, a major role in American popular culture.

Recognizing the marketability of various forms of print should remind us of another essential constituent of this culture. Objects of all sorts, from toys and "collectibles" to cars and guns, also play very prominent roles. Barbie must have at least some influence on the little girls who play with her, just as shoeboxes full of matchbox cars must have at least some influence on the boys. Of course, cross-gender play probably takes place, strengthening the suspicion that the cultural influence of objects is mutual and influential rather than gender-specific and deterministic. Perhaps this is how the McGuffey *Readers* influenced Americans of earlier generations. No matter what influences whom, however, there can be little doubt that American popular culture has been shaped in various ways by Buicks, lava lamps, backpacks, cigarettes, sunglasses, and pink flamingo yard sculptures.

What we eat also falls under the heading of popular culture: fast food highly advertised along interstate highways and on television, Aunt Sally's "famous" green bean casserole, the canned fruitcake that family members have been passing back and forth as a Christmas gift for years, the Pillsbury bake-off. Popular sports and leisure activities are also important. March Madness, the World Series, the Superbowl, the Kentucky Derby, the Boston Marathon, bass fishing, tennis, stock car racing, golf at the local country club, all the ways in which we imagine our relationships to supposedly healthy competition—these are also constituents of popular culture. Just as important is what we wear on these and other occasions: logoed knit shirts in this year's new "fashion" colors, faded Levis, incredibly expensive running shoes, prom dresses, T-shirts associating the wearer with *South Park* or exotic branches of the Hard Rock Café. It is unsurprising, then, that how we think about our bodies should also be understood to be part of popular culture. Just as significant is how we think about other people's bodies: their tans, mustaches, breasts, buffed and chiseled torsos, bouncin' and behavin' hair, and—the ultimate determinant—their possession or lack of thinness.[8] By noting these objects and practices, we have naturally anticipated another central element of American popular culture: advertising. As many commentators have explained, the thousands of sales pitches that we cannot help encountering every day are not really about cars or soft drinks or dandruff but about freedom and prestige and sexual desirability.[9] That is, these advertisements are about how we have been taught to think about ourselves in America today. In this respect, advertising offers perhaps the most revealing picture of our culture, skewed admittedly by the seller's profit motive and the tricks of the advertising trade but a highly revealing picture nevertheless. To study our ads is to study our popular culture.

There is no better place to study our ads than on television. Whether through the fabulously expensive spots for beverages, cars, and fast food featured on the annual Superbowl broadcasts or through low-rent, late-night infomercials for amazing health-and beauty-enhancing products, the television screen clearly shows us what we are supposed to want to be. The same screen also provides most of us with comedy and drama, with documentaries about wild animals and World War II, with what we know about local, national, and international news, and with all the ingredients of celebrity culture. What is more, television does this always and everywhere. Most American homes contain more than one television set, and the people living there have these sets turned on for approximately seven hours a day.[10] Bars have long made it a practice to keep the tube always turned on, and restaurants are increasingly following suit. Gyms and health spas display banks of television screens over their stationary bicycles and treadmills. Places where we have to wait for anything—doctors' waiting rooms, airport lounges, automobile dealers' repair rooms, rent-a-car offices—usually have a television set on. As cable networks proliferate in breathtaking numbers, these countless hours of television time are certain to be filled with something for nearly everyone: cooking and decorating shows, rebroadcasts of "historic" sporting events, evangelistic religious services, music videos of all sorts, romantic movies, cartoons, lost episodes of *Mr. Ed* and *The Honeymooners*. About television today we might reiterate John Dryden's amazed remark about the works of Geoffrey Chaucer: "here is God's plenty."[11] Therefore, even though most of us have probably echoed the complaint in Bruce

Springsteen's song "57 Channels (and Nothin' on),"[12] we cannot avoid the conclusion that contemporary American popular culture flourishes on television.

Television allows us to see ads, commodities, and bodies for ourselves, and so television also allows (alerts) viewers to discern the (usually) unstated myths, narratives, and cultural values that support and animate the whole panorama. As several of the examples already cited have suggested, American popular culture also consists of how we think about ourselves and others, about gender, race, and class, how we see our roles in our families, communities, and the nation, how we see America in relation to the rest of the world, how we relate our personal experience to the possibility of the spiritual, and what we think about money.[13]

In light of all these factors, we may provisionally answer the question of just what popular culture is by concluding that popular culture is everything that we have or want right here, right now, and most of what we have had or wanted before. Formerly, as the collections of essays cited in the notes demonstrate, it was a necessary part of all inquiries into the nature of popular culture to distinguish among high and low, demotic and hieratic,[14] or popular, elite, and folk cultures. In the present cultural environment, such distinctions seem less valuable for several reasons. For one thing, all definitions of the sort tend to valorize the side of the binary distinction associated with evening clothes and European accents, even when this valorization is contrary to the author's original intentions. In the process, such distinctions end up conceding actual existence to "high" or "elite" culture, even though the very idea probably started out as a merely provisional category of inquiry, an example of Saussurean "difference."[15] It is also true that contemporary attitudes toward race, class, ethnicity, and gender tend to reject any categorical distinctions that may result in (even unintentional) hierarchies. Perhaps, finally, the methods of production, distribution, and consumption operating in what Fredric Jameson calls "late capitalism" tend to erase what in earlier times might have seemed to be permanent cultural patterns and thus to make such distinctions merely moot.[16] For whatever reasons, then, the time to drop these labels seems to have arrived.[17] Today, popular culture is the sea in which we, as Americans, are born, swim, nourish ourselves, grow, perhaps mate, reproduce, and die.

One might naturally—and correctly—assume that a phenomenon so widespread and various as American popular culture would have attracted a great deal of scholarly analysis and commentary in years past. Surveys of this literature usually begin by noting that official academic study of popular culture should probably be dated by the founding either of the *Journal of Popular Culture* in 1967 or of the Popular Culture Association in 1969, both events largely superintended by Professor Ray B. Browne. It is equally customary, however, to note that earlier writers and scholars prepared the ground for these events, even if they were unaware of doing so.

The 7 Lively Arts (1924) by Gilbert Seldes is nearly always singled out for mention in this regard, probably because Seldes so clearly anticipates principles central to most serious studies of American popular culture produced in the 1970s and beyond. In summary, Seldes says that he was moved to write the book by his recognition that "[w]e are the inheritors of a tradition that what is worthwhile must be dull; and as often as not we invert the maxim and pretend that what is dull is higher in quality, more serious, 'greater art' in short than whatever is light

T. S. Eliot. Courtesy of the Nobel Foundation

and easy and gay" (265–66). One thinks of the irreverent Groucho Marx and W. C. Fields as Seldes' allies in these culture wars, as well as of Jiggs sneaking out on his wife, Maggie, at the symphony in order to play poker at Dinty Moore's saloon.[18] All of these pictures suggest that we may actually be capable of deciding for ourselves both how to spend our time and whether these decisions result in real pleasure. In consequence of his basic assumptions, Seldes rejects the common practice of "the grading of the arts and placing some of them forever at the lower table" (3). In place of a strategy likely to result in the (inevitable) elevation of opera and ballet and the (consequent) demotion of movies and comic strips, Seldes seriously discusses and praises slapstick film comedy, pop songs, ragtime, jazz, popular magazine humor, Ziegfeld reviews, Jerome Kern's songs, one-man shows by Eddie Cantor, Ed Wynn, Al Jolson, and Fanny Brice, burlesque comedians, comic strips (especially *Krazy Kat*), vaudeville, tap dancing, newspaper columnists, and circus clowns. Returning to his material thirty-three years later, Seldes writes that he is sorry only that he underestimated the importance of radio.

The other side of the debate over popular culture can be understood by observing that so many of Seldes' contemporaries simply and automatically assumed premises contrary to his. In the "Statement of Principles," introductory to *I'll Take My Stand* (1930) by Twelve Southerners, for example, John Crowe Ransom writes confidently: "We have more time in which to consume, and many more products to be consumed. But the tempo of our labors communicates itself to our satisfactions, and these also become brutal and hurried. The constitution of the natural man probably does not permit him to shorten his labor-time and enlarge his consuming-time indefinitely. He has to pay the penalty in satiety and aimlessness" (xlii). The phrase *popular culture* does not appear in Ransom's introductory remarks or elsewhere in *I'll Take My Stand*, but it is apparent from the overall tenor of the book that the adjectives *popular* or *lively* could not be linked positively to the noun *culture* by any of the twelve contributors. The same can be easily assumed about T. S. Eliot on the evidence of the social criticism that he produced during the 1930s. In his *After Strange Gods* (1934), delivered originally as lectures to a suitably genteel audience at the University of Virginia, Eliot recognizes that "the aim of the 'neo-agrarians' in the South will be qualified as quixotic, as a hopeless stand for a cause which was lost long before they were born," but he still encourages his audience to hope that "tradition" can triumph over contemporary materialism because "the aim is a good aim, and the alternatives intolerable" (17–18). In *The Idea of a Christian Society* (1939), Eliot further develops these ideas by warning against the lowering of cultural standards likely to come about in industrial or "mass" society:

> But what is more insidious than any censorship, is the steady influence which operates silently in any mass society organized for profit, for the depression of standards of art and culture. The increasing organization of advertisement and propaganda—or the influencing of masses of men by any means except through their intelligence—is all against them. The economic system is against them; the chaos of ideals and confusion of thought in our large-scale mass education is against them; and against them also is the disappearance of any class of people who recognize public and private responsibility of patronage of the best that is made and written. (39–40)

Eliot's language—"mass society," "class of people," "responsibility of patronage"—might give most of us pause today, and not only those of us contemplating careers as MTV veejays. Yet, Eliot's assumptions about a preferable, attainable alternative to the market-driven culture of twentieth-century America are commonplace in the discursive community to which his lectures—and this chapter—belong.

A somewhat less provocative voice may serve better to clarify the point. In a frequently cited essay, "Masscult and Midcult" (1960), former Trotskyite and Yale graduate Dwight Macdonald writes, "For about two centuries Western culture has in fact been two cultures: the traditional kind—let us call it High Culture—that is chronicled in the textbooks, and a novel kind that is manufactured for the market. This latter may be called Mass Culture, or better Masscult, since it really isn't culture at all. Masscult is a parody of High Culture" (3). Since his essay was originally published in *Partisan Review*, Macdonald can hardly be lumped in with Ransom and Eliot as an agrarian or Anglican reactionary, and yet his easy use of the term *mass* and his fondness—contra Seldes—for "the grading of the arts and placing some of them forever at the lower table" allow us to see the common ground between Macdonald and the more right-wing critics of popular culture. Comments like the following make the recognition even easier: "As I have already noted in this essay, the separation of Folk Art and High Culture in fairly watertight compartments corresponded to the sharp line once drawn between the common people and the aristocracy. The blurring of this line, however desirable politically, has had unfortunate results culturally" (34). Like Ransom and Eliot—and unlike Seldes—Macdonald believes that he knows what is good for us better than we do ourselves. Apparently, old Eli trumps Trotsky!

Liberal political affiliations are, of course, no guarantee that a critic will become an advocate for popular culture. Herbert Marcuse, for example, stridently opposes the popular in his highly influential *One-Dimensional Man*, published four years after Macdonald's essay. In a typical passage, Marcuse adds his voice to those of other intellectuals eager to save us from ourselves:

> No matter how much such needs [our needs "to relax, to have fun, to behave and consume in accordance with the advertisements, to love and hate what others love and hate"] may have become the individual's own, reproduced and fortified by the conditions of his existence; no matter how much he identifies himself with them and finds himself in their satisfaction, they continue to be what they were from the beginning—products of a society whose dominant interest demands repression. (5)

From the right and from the left, then, many elitist critics of the time inveighed against the popular in order to valorize some other form of art. That the alternative proposed by these critics is sometimes the traditionally canonical and sometimes the wildly avant-garde suggests that the negative pole of popular culture is probably more significant in these discussions than the positive one.

It is important to note that Macdonald and Marcuse were writing in the early 1960s, when the *Saturday Evening Post* and *Life* magazine were still major factors in the culture wars. Perhaps the facts of life determining print culture at the time help to explain Macdonald's aggrieved tone: "Today, in the United States, the demands of the audience, which has changed from a small body of connoisseurs into a large body of ignoramuses, have become the chief criteria of success" (18). Looking back from the perspective of four more decades, it is possible even for "a large body of ignoramuses" to understand that Jacqueline Kennedy was soon to invite Pablo Casals and Robert Frost to the White House, that *Life* and the *Post* would eventually cease publication, and that Macdonald's judgment of American popular music—"The only major form of Folk Art that still persists in this country is jazz, and the difference between Folk Art and Masscult may be most readily perceived by comparing the kind of thing heard at the annual Newport Jazz Festivals to Rock 'n' Roll. The former is musically interesting and emotionally real; the latter is not" (14)—would come to seem absurd. Absurd judgments notwithstanding, Macdonald's assumptions about high culture would continue to resonate in works like *The Closing of the American Mind* (1987) by Allan Bloom and *The Book of Virtues* (1993) by William J. Bennett, neither of whom has much politically in common with Herbert Marcuse.

Around the same time that Macdonald and Marcuse were feeling so pessimistic about the popular cultural landscape, Susan Sontag was able to find considerable cause for optimism. Especially in her essay "One Culture and the New Sensibility" (1966), Sontag seems fairly sanguine about the cultural and economic developments that distressed some of the critics already cited:

The distinction between "high" and "low" (or "mass" or "popular") culture is based partly on an evaluation of the difference between unique and mass-produced objects. In a era of mass technological reproduction, the work of the serious artist had a special value simply because it was unique, because it bore his personal, individual signature. The works of popular culture (and even films were for a long time included in this category) were seen as having little value because they were manufactured objects, bearing no individual stamp—group concoctions made for an undifferentiated audience. But in the light of contemporary practice in the arts, this distinction appears extremely shallow. (297)

Sontag's parenthetical comment that "even films" had been snobbishly denigrated in the past is probably evidence enough that she was seeing things differently than did Ransom, Eliot, Marcuse, and Macdonald, but as further evidence we can also note her approval of mid-1960s America for its "abandonment of the Matthew Arnold idea of culture" (302). Sontag explains that she has in mind here the dimension of Arnold's cultural criticism in which art is intended primarily to offer "a criticism of life" (299–300), a tendency that she associates with didactic "interpretations." Putting aside the question of how accurately Sontag was reading Arnold, her own practice might be seen actually to ally her with Arnold's definition of criticism in his famous essay "The Function of Criticism at the Present Time" (1864): "It obeys an instinct prompting it to try to know the best that is known and thought in the world, irrespectively of practice, politics, and everything of the kind" (18). This is clear when Sontag concludes her essay by writing, "From the vantage point of this new sensibility, the beauty of a machine or the solution of a mathematical problem, of a painting by Jasper Johns, of a film by Jean-Luc Godard, and of the personalities and music of the Beatles is equally accessible" (304). Although Sontag had other intentions in adopting "One Culture" as her title, her version of the public's relations with cultural products tempts me to align her title with my views in this chapter.

Sontag's work can be seen as a definite sign that the supposedly unbridgeable gap between true "culture" and popular mediation was closing for at least some critics and scholars in the 1960s. Usually, Marshall McLuhan also receives considerable credit for bridging this gap because of his books *Understanding Media* (1964) and (chiefly) *The Medium Is the Message* (1967). In the earlier work McLuhan pursues his now-famous distinction between the "hot" and the "cool" by referring to, among others, Plato, John Donne, William Shakespeare, Perry Como, Al Capp, *Mad* magazine, Paddy Chayefsky's film *Marty*, Margaret Mead, and Oswald Spengler. In *The Medium Is the Message*, McLuhan's punning title is reinforced by his unconventional (for 1967) use of graphics and typefaces, his provocative paradoxes, and his striking assortment of references. As in his earlier book—and in so many texts by other writers today—McLuhan deliberately mixes and matches diverse referential fields to support his arguments. Thus, *Alice in Wonderland* collides with Plato, Marilyn Monroe with John Cage, Bob Dylan with A. N. Whitehead, and the Beatles with James Joyce. Resulting is a sense of all-enveloping popular culture rather like the one proposed in this chapter.

Despite the unquestionable contributions of critics like Sontag and McLuhan, however, the most vital developments in the establishment of popular culture

Marshall McLuhan. © Bettman/CORBIS

studies as a recognized field of intellectual inquiry occurred, as noted before, toward the end of the 1960s. The *Journal of Popular Culture* began publication under the editorship of Ray B. Browne at Bowling Green State University in Ohio in 1967, and the Popular Culture Association (PCA) began in 1969, in large part to offer a more vital alternative to the young, but increasingly stodgy, American Studies Association. Both of these institutions of popular culture continue to prosper today. As Gary Hoppenstand reports in his essay on Ray and Pat Browne in *Pioneers in Popular Culture Studies*, "From its modest beginning of 200 members, the PCA has grown into a vibrant organization of 3500 scholars, and the national PCA meeting alone draws 1500–2000 participants annually" (44).[19] Surely a great many educational, economic, and demographic changes have helped to make the critical study of popular culture a legitimate—in fact, a necessary—component of intellectual life in America today, but the journal and the scholarly association begun by Ray Browne should receive the lion's share of the credit for the explosion of "popular culture studies."

An early ally of Ray Browne and the first president of the Popular Culture Association, Russel B. Nye, also contributed greatly to the advancement of this overall project with his much-admired book *The Unembarrassed Muse: The Popular Arts in America* (1970). In the words of his Preface, Nye operates under the premise that "*[p]opular* is interpreted to mean 'generally dispersed and approved'—descriptive of those artistic productions which express the taste and understanding of the majority and which are free of control, in content and execution, from minority standards of correctness." This premise is developed in Nye's historically inflected studies of popular fiction and poetry, theater, dime novels and comics, mysteries, science fiction, westerns, popular music, movies, radio, and television. Nye's admirable intention throughout the book is, as he writes, "[t]o erase the boundaries, created by snobbery and cultism, that have so long divided the arts" (420), but his focus on print culture and (perhaps) his adoption of the term *arts* in his subtitle demonstrate that the cultural field that he was surveying differs decisively from ours today. Like Seldes, Nye sees his determined opponents to be the enormous body of snobs rigidly upholding the standards of "high" culture against the encroachments of the popular. Today, however, these elitists seem to be ghettoized into the confines of PBS fund-raisers and snootier charitable events. It is significant that, although culture wars continue to enlist the energies of academics on the cultural right and left, practitioners of popular culture seldom make bluenoses and poseurs even objects of satire in today's films and television programs. Roles for actors like Margaret Dumont and Gale Gordon thus seem to be growing scarcer and scarcer. Although many factors have brought about this change, the pioneering efforts of committed scholars such as Browne and Nye have been highly influential.

Valuable support for these efforts came from many directions, as in the debate between David Manning White and Bernard Rosenberg over the nature and value of popular culture published under the title *Mass Culture Revisited* (1971). At one point in the book, White asks, and answers, a question that has troubled thinkers as different as John Crowe Ransom and Herbert Marcuse:

> So why doesn't the average man avail himself of his ever-increasing leisure to study Bach's two-part inventions or attend lectures on the Postimpressionists at his local museum of fine arts? Why, in other words, does he choose to sit passively in front of the television set night after night? Why are the mass media so seductive of his hard-won leisure hours? Perhaps, because the seductee is getting what he has always craved—a partial, palatable answer to the questions all men ask themselves, whether they are philosophers or coal-miners: Who am I, why am I here, what is the meaning of my life vis-a-vis the universe? (15–16)

White's willingness to accept that people may actually be getting what they want out of popular culture accords with the assumptions governing many other discussions of this topic in the early 1970s. Equally symptomatic of these changed intellectual assumptions is White's view of the consumers of popular culture, significantly different from Dwight Macdonald's perception of the supposedly undifferentiated integers composing Masscult: "Audiences consist of individuals, who even when they share common viewing or reading experiences, use the media to satisfy their own particular purposes. A so-called 'audience of fifty million' is a statistical amalgam that indiscriminately lumps together fifty million distinct individuals, each concerned with fulfilling his own needs, goals, and expectations" (18). Later critics—most notably, perhaps, John Fiske—have pushed these assumptions further and teased out their implications more searchingly, but it is clear that statements like White's in the early 1970s were already pointing the way for these critics.

Probably better known than White's work, *Popular Culture and High Culture: An Analysis and Evaluation of Taste* (1974) by Herbert J. Gans also contributed usefully to a growing interest in the audience's interactions with popular culture and with the agencies of its production. As Gans wisely observes,

> The mass media, and perhaps all of commercial popular culture, are often engaged in a guessing game, trying to figure out what people want, or rather, what they will accept, although the game is made easier by the fact that the audience must choose from a limited set of alternatives and that its interest is often low enough to make it willing to settle for the lesser of two or three evils. Still, the media executives who become successful by guessing correctly can often sense what an audience will accept, and frequently they are so firmly embedded themselves in the popular culture to which they are adding that they are "representatives" of the audience, even if they may also be tough-minded and cynical businessmen and women at the same time. (ix)

Later studies using more sophisticated demographic tools and critical tools like Mikhail Bakhtin's theory of dialogics have succeeded in drawing more precise and challenging conclusions than Gans', but his assumptions are obviously still in tune with many later developments in the field.

Even more exciting, perhaps, than the ongoing critical discussions of the nature and power of popular culture were many books published during the 1970s that simply took for granted that popular culture was a significant force in contemporary American life. Many of these books still appear in scholarly bibliographies today, testimony both to their continuing value as research tools and to their influence on later scholars. A review of some of the more prominent of these books and of the studies that have followed in their wake down through the 1990s should indicate how and why we should continue to study popular culture.

In 1972 Arlene Croce published *The Fred Astaire & Ginger Rogers Book*, a happy combination of text and photographs whose subject should be apparent. Also apparent is the assumption that many people, other than Arlene Croce, want to know more about "Fred and Ginger." One reason for this interest is suggested in Croce's comment about the 1935 Astaire/Rogers film *Top Hat*: "In the class-conscious Thirties, it was possible to imagine characters who spent their lives in evening dress—to imagine them as faintly preposterous holdovers from the Twenties, slipping from their satin beds at twilight, dancing the night away and then stumbling, top-hatted and ermine-tangled, out of speakeasies at dawn" (56). The economic/romantic fantasy that Croce describes surely helps us to think more provocatively about America in the 1930s, but this fantasy's continuing power in the 1970s, in which Croce was writing, and even today helps us to see how popularly dispersed cultural artifacts such as films can reflect elements of the national soul. When Mia Farrow's character, Celia, indulges in this fantasy while watching *Top Hat* in Woody Allen's 1985 film *The Purple Rose of Cairo*, the connections between past and present in this respect are especially clear.

In the same year that Croce published her study of Astaire and Rogers, Roger Kahn published his highly successful *The Boys of Summer*. Using the Brooklyn Dodgers baseball team of the early 1950s merely as his point of departure, Kahn combines the topics of sports, race, urban life, gender, journalism, and the physical ravages of time into a lively and probing analysis of American culture in the 1950s and the 1970s. Kahn writes, "As many ball players, officials, umpires and journalists envisioned it, the entity of baseball rose in alabaster, a temple of white supremacy" (xvi), and it is easy to conclude that his remarks have much broader cultural applications. Jackie Robinson's integration of major league baseball in 1947 thus becomes in this book an issue of national identity rather than of mere sports:

> Everywhere, in New England drawing rooms and on porches in the South, in California, which had no major league baseball teams, and in New York City, which had three, men and women talked about the Jackie Robinson Dodgers, and as they talked they confronted themselves and American racism. That confrontation was, I believe, as important as *Brown vs. Board of Education of Topeka*, in creating the racially troubled hopeful present. (xvii)

In the present of which Kahn writes, the Dodgers of the 1950s have grown prematurely aged—as often happens to athletes—and have had to confront the problems of typical middle-aged mortals. Because of Kahn's artistic sympathies, these confrontations become ours, resulting in a highly complex view of our common culture. Another consequence of Kahn's vision is a succession of other books about sports in America that take it for granted, as Kahn does, that individual sports and sporting events provide windows into the larger culture. Even the shortest list of such books would include *Five Seasons* (1977) by Roger Angell, *The Breaks of the Game* (1981) by David Halberstam, and *Take Time for Paradise: Americans and Their Games* (1989) by A. Bartlett Giamatti. Giamatti's book is especially illustrative of this trend since he brings his experience as a former professor of English at Yale and as the then current commissioner of major league baseball to bear on questions regarding the relations of professional sports to American culture. Like Kahn, Giamatti is struck by the pathos involved in an athlete's not dying young. "Former professional athletes . . . never grow up in any real sense," he writes, "because they were meant always to be young and strong and special, somewhere in late adolescence in fact, and that expectation was one they shared. They are profoundly innocent" (58–59). Giamatti is like Kahn also in extending his challenging insights beyond the immediate case: "Baseball fulfills the promise America made itself to cherish the individual while recognizing the overarching claims of the group" (103). In other words, just as we are invited to see ourselves dancing on the screen by *Top Hat*, we are equally invited to see ourselves hitting the game-winning homer, acing a serve at Forest Hills, slam-dunking the winning goal, finishing the Boston Marathon. At least since the 1970s, these dreams have been given legitimacy as parts of our common culture.

Arthur Asa Berger's *The Comic-Stripped American* (1973) also assumes both the presence and the importance of popular culture, as his subtitle makes clear: *What Dick Tracy, Blondie, Daddy Warbucks, and Charlie Brown Tell Us about Ourselves.* Berger's premise should sound familiar on the basis of what we have been discussing so far: "If we accept the hypothesis that our popular arts mirror our culture, that somehow they are tied to our concerns and based upon widespread assumptions, then the study of our popular culture becomes an important means of understanding our society" (6–7). Berger's own study progresses from *The Yel-*

low Kid, *The Katzenjammer Kids*, and *Krazy Kat*, through *Little Orphan Annie*, *Superman*, and *Pogo*, to the underground "comix" of the 1960s. By applying the ideas of thinkers as varied as Boccaccio, Marshal McLuhan, Mircea Eliade, and Northrop Frye to his material, Berger brings out both the technical strategies and the thematic emphases of this popular art form. Thus, while he explains technically that "The language [of *Flash Gordon*] is purple and overly dramatic, the figures tend to be uni-dimensional, and [Alex] Raymond's use of science might be rather simple-minded" (137), Berger is also comfortable in claiming thematically that "[t]he final irony of *Pogo* is the final irony of our democracy" (180). More recently, a considerable number of insightful studies of the comics have advanced our knowledge of both the technique of comic artists and their thematic projects vis-à-vis American culture more generally, the work of M. Thomas Inge being especially noteworthy. In his *Comics as Culture* (1990), for example, Inge brings together new and previously published material to demonstrate that "[t]he comics are well and deservedly loved, but they should be respected for what they have contributed to the visual and narrative arts of the world" (xxi). Wide-ranging analyses of comic style, language, narrative structure, and social influence appear in the chapters that follow, as well as specific discussions of *Little Nemo*, *Krazy Kat*, *Snuffy Smith*, and *Peanuts*. Inge also examines relations between comics and William Faulkner, Charlie Chaplin, and modern art, as well as institutional comic influences such as *The New Yorker* and *EC Comics*. Here and in other book-length works including *The American Comic Book* (1985), *Great American Comics: 100 Years of Cartoon Art* (1990), and *Anything Can Happen in a Comic Strip: Centennial Reflections on an American Art Form* (1995), Inge devotes the same scholarly attention and professional integrity to analyses of comic books and comic strips that he elsewhere devotes to the works of American literary giants like Melville and Faulkner. What we can know and say about American popular culture is surely broadened and deepened by the work of critics like Berger and Inge.

We may say the same about Richard Slotkin's revolutionary study *Regeneration through Violence: The Mythology of the American Frontier, 1600–1860* (1973). Following in the footsteps of earlier practitioners of American studies such as Henry Nash Smith, whose *Virgin Land: The American West as Symbol and Myth* (1950) mapped out the territory ahead for later scholars of the American West, Slotkin investigates the connections among historical events on the American frontier, popular conceptions of these events, American literature, and contemporary American culture. Slotkin's involvement in the larger project of American culture should be evident in remarks like the following: "The voluminous reports of presidential commissions on violence, racism, and civil disorder have recently begun to say to us what artists like Melville and Faulkner had earlier prophesied: that myths reach out of the past to cripple, incapacitate, or strike down the living" (5). It seems to me significant that, although the project begun by Smith has unquestionably developed by Slotkin's day, the evidence educed is still derived from print culture. Thus, while critics like Kahn and Berger were reading American culture through its most popular products, highly influential scholarly books of the times were often focused largely on belletristic texts. By the time of Jane Tompkins' *West of Everything: The Inner Life of Westerns* (1992), though, the western has taken on transgeneric significance with a structure that is recognizable despite the medium in which it is incarnated. As Tompkins writes, "[W]hen you read a Western novel or watch a Western movie on television, you are in the same world no matter what the medium: the hero is the same, the story line is the same, the setting, the values, the actions are the same" (7). Therefore, as Garry Wills explains in *John Wayne's America* (1997), "The Western can deal with the largest themes in American history—beginning with the 'original sin' of our country, the seizing of land from its original owners" (313). It is unsurprising, therefore, that books about the western frontier appeared in the early stages of popular culture studies and that they continue to appear today.

Another inevitable development is illustrated by Molly Haskell's 1975 study *From Reverence to Rape: The Treatment of Women in the Movies*. Haskell begins by assuming that while "[m]ost of the popular novels, plays, short stories of the twenties, thirties, forties, and fifties have all but disappeared, . . . the films based on them have survived to tell us more vividly than any old or new journalism what it was like, or what our dream life was like, and how we saw ourselves in the women of those times" (xiv). This assumption obviously accords with what other critics of the 1970s were saying about other forms of American popular culture. Haskell's book introduces another note, however, when she draws upon more personal experience such as the following: "My own split, between the way I saw myself (as a free agent) and the way I was expected to behave (as a lady, deferential to authority), was reflected, as such things often are, in the movies and in the parallel split in the movie heroines" (viii). This is to say that in addition to its aptness as a barometer of popular cultural studies in the mid-1970s, Haskell's *From Reverence to Rape* can be seen as striking evidence that the thematic project of feminism would increasingly play a role in the ongoing discourse of these studies.

The historical evidence makes it clear that Haskell's approach as well as her subject were in tune with the intellectual spirit of the times. Emily Toth reports in her essay on Susan Koppelman in the *Pioneers in Popular Culture Studies* collection that the first women's studies session at PCA took place in 1972 at only the second annual conference (147)—five years before the official establishment of the National Women's Studies Association.[20] Koppelman's essay on Toth in the same collection emphasizes the contributions of both of these feminist scholars to the evolving field of popular culture studies. As in Haskell's book, personal experience alternates with the customary dates, titles, and footnotes to ground this criticism in the felt experience of American culture.

It is unsurprising, then, that Haskell's later work has continued to contribute to the conversation that she helped get started. Her place in this conversation seems clear in light of remarks like the following, from *Holding My Own in No Man's Land: Women and Men and Film and Feminists* (1997): "My approach, for someone teaching a gender-related course, has been idiosyncratic, to say the least. Though there's plenty to object to in the representation of women in the male-dominated art form of the twentieth century, I've increasingly come to look for and cherish the heroic or contrary images of women that go against the grain of oppression" (4). To illustrate this program, we might consider Haskell's typically incisive judgment that in his 1964 comedy *Man's Favorite Sport?* director Howard Hawks "gives us Rock Hudson and Paula Prentiss as primordial man and woman, Adam and Eve in the lush, hazardous Eden of a hunting and fishing resort. But an Adam and Eve saddled with a bitter, comical heritage of sexual distrust, bravado, and fear, archetypes that are infinitely closer to the American experience than such articulate *angst*-mongers as Jeanne and Monica and Marcello and Max and Harriet and Jean-Paul (Sartre or Belmondo)" (118). These comments throw light on this unquestionably minor piece of cinematic fluff even as they illuminate some more significant cultural issues involved in how we think about gender in America. Like other wide-ranging feminist critics such as Jane Tompkins and Naomi Wolf, Haskell combines the personal and the academic to establish a third form of cultural criticism. In the process, Haskell enriches our own form of cultural studies with observations of this sort: "The *Iliad* spends pages describing the way the different warriors dress for battle, details upon details of colors and fabrics, the design and metal of armor and swords; just such an epic could be written about women painstakingly assembling their faces in the battle dress of lipstick and mascara" (186). Maybe so! we probably say when reading this sentence, and isn't that the whole point of cultural studies after all?

Even as popular cultural studies of film and fiction were being enriched by feminist insights, the study of popular music was also beginning to grow in sophistication in work such as Greil Marcus' *Mystery Train; Images of America in Rock 'n' Roll Music* (1975). Although the largest portion of *Mystery Train* consists of highly specific studies of the music produced by the Band, Sly Stone, Randy Newman, and Elvis Presley, Marcus early announces that his book is more generally "an attempt to broaden the context in which the music is heard; to deal with rock 'n' roll not as youth culture, or counter culture, but simply as American culture" (4). Like the film and comics critics already discussed, Marcus uses the particular example of a single popular phenomenon to authorize an analysis of the larger culture, who *we* are and how *we* sometimes think and feel. Thus, while discussing Randy Newman's possible relations to popular stardom, Marcus instances the recent blockbuster hit movie *The Godfather* to establish a broader point:

> In one way or another we are all affected by hits, and are forced to define ourselves in terms of our response to them, just as we are all, for good or ill, affected by the romantic heroism of the Westerns, and not necessarily by, say, the chaotic heroism that is the subject of Orson Welles' movies. Certainly we are caught up in these things that impelled Welles, but his version of them, the shape of his vision, has not inevitably become part of us; we don't have to live in the world as he tried to define it, as we helplessly live out and respond to the nostalgia of John Ford or Howard Hawks. (129–30)

Over twenty years later, Marcus is still working to broaden the cultural contexts of rock criticism and still making valuable discoveries. Thus, he writes in *Invisible Republic: Bob Dylan's Basement Tapes* (1997), "More than its own art movement, its own social movement, or its own fact, the folk revival [of the early 1960s] was part of something much bigger, more dangerous, and more important: the civil rights movement" (22). As he did earlier with *The Godfather*, Marcus also uses popular films [e.g., *Bonnie and Clyde*,] in *Invisible Republic* to anchor an analysis of far-reaching cultural forces: "On the screen hundreds of rounds smashed into metal and bone. In the theater you could hear every one of them, and with the sounds bouncing off the datelines of the newspaper you carried in your head you could hear every echo: Newark, Detroit, Saigon, Hanoi" (140). Popular music criticism of this sort has been produced by many critics for several decades now, enriching our cultural discourse in all sorts of ways, and whenever we get around to distributing the credit, Marcus certainly deserves a large share of it.

In terms of the development of popular culture studies as an academic discipline, however, the most significant book published in 1976 was assuredly *Adventure, Mystery, and Romance: Formula Stories as Art and Popular Culture* by John G. Cawelti. Just as critics including Haskell and Marcus were enriching the thematic dimensions of the discipline (McLuhan's "message"), Cawelti brought increased sophistication to bear on the stylistic/structural dimension. Beginning with a commitment to analyzing "popular story formulas, those narrative and dramatic structures that form such a large part of the cultural diet of the majority of readers, television viewers, and film audiences," Cawelti proposes to "deal with the phenomenon in relation to the cultural patterns it reveals, and is shaped by, and with the impact formula stories have on culture" (2). In pursuit of these aims, Cawelti addresses himself cheerfully to the print culture that engaged the energies of earlier critics such as Russel Nye, but he also recognizes the evolution of contemporary mediation by analyzing films like *Scarface* and *The Ox Bow Incident* and television series including *Mannix* and *Gunsmoke*. He is willing to do so, as he writes, because Cawelti is comfortable in rejecting the purely hieratic aesthetic standards promulgated by many earlier critics: "The trouble with this sort of [hieratic] approach is that it tends to make us perceive and evaluate formula literature simply as an inferior and perverted form of something better, instead of seeing its 'escapist' characteristics as aspects of an artistic type with its own purposes and justification" (13). Escape is necessary, Cawelti argues, from "the ennui and boredom that are particularly prevalent in the relatively secure, routine, and organized lives of the great majority of the contemporary American and Western European public. At the same time, we seek escape from our consciousness of the ultimate insecurities and ambiguities that afflict even the most secure sort of life: death, the failure of love, our inability to accomplish all we had hoped for, the threat of atomic holocaust" (16–17). Here is an even clearer answer to the question posed earlier by David Manning White: "Why, in other words, does [the average man] choose to sit passively in front of the television set night after night? Why are the mass media so seductive of his hard-won leisure hours?" The answer is that the "average" man or woman is dealing with the inescapable facts of life by escaping through the formula "convention plus invention." Or, as Cawelti explains the process:

> In general, the escapist aspect of formulaic art makes it analogous to certain kinds of games or play. In fact, if we look at television schedules, we find they contain a predominance of spectator sports and formulaic stories. Like such games as football or baseball, formulaic stories are individual versions of a general pattern defined by a set of rules. While the rules remain the same, the highly varied ways in which they can be embodied in particular characters and actions produce a patterned experience of excitement, suspense, and release that, as in the case of the great games, can be perennially engrossing no matter how often the game is played. In the formula world, as in play, the ego is enhanced because conflicts are resolved and inescapable tensions and frustrations temporarily transcended. (19–20)

With the arrival of Cawelti's book, we may observe in retrospect, the most important tools for a productive era of thematic and stylistic popular culture studies were already in place.

One reason for the immediate critical acceptance of Cawelti's book—in addition to his excellent analyses of a wide variety of texts—was the contemporary expectation that theories of "structure" might be capable of yielding benefits even beyond those already demonstrated by anthropologists. Like many developments in postwar cultural analysis, this interest in "structures" originally developed abroad, the key text probably being the 1970 English translation of Roland Barthes' *Mythologies*. Using the linguistic distinction between "signifier" and "signified" pioneered by Ferdinand de Saussure, Barthes' essays in this collection offered semiological analyses of wrestling, cooking, photography, automobile advertising, army recruiting posters, sci-fi spaceships, striptease acts, and numerous other phenomena of French culture. The lesson for English-speaking—especially American—critics was clear. Though not specifically "structuralist" or dependent on Barthes' work, numerous works of popular cultural criticism began to assume—along with Barthes and Cawelti—that a common structure could be usefully discerned beneath many supposedly unique cultural products. David Grote (1983) and Lawrence E. Mintz (1985), for example, both assume that a typical episode of a television situation comedy follows a predictable plot development. E. Ann Kaplan (1987) makes similar assumptions about music videos. As we have seen, Jane Tompkins applies the method to westerns. Apparently, actual practitioners often shared these critical assumptions, as Arthur Kempton explains in his analysis of Berry Gordy's formula for an extraordinary string of popular Motown record hits: "a verse, another verse, a bridge, a chorus, back to the verse, one more chorus and out" (50). Whether specifically structuralist in inspiration or not, the discovery of such patterns has been the enabling force in many studies of popular culture.

As we might perhaps expect, however, not everyone was swept up into a frenzy of enthusiasm for the popular. In illustration, we might consider the cultural ground contested in the discourse involving several influential books published during the 1980s: *What Was Literature? Class, Culture, and Mass Society* (1982) by Leslie Fiedler, *Reading the Romance: Women, Patriarchy, and Popular Literature* (1984) by Janice Radway, *The Closing of the American Mind* (1987) by Allan Bloom, and *Highbrow/Lowbrow: The Emergence of Cultural Hierarchy in America* (1988) by Lawrence E. Levine. Fiedler's (characteristically) provocative title promises that he has moved beyond what we have learned to call the "canon" of elite literature to embrace more popular forms. Fiedler "feel[s] the need to take the first steps—outside the academy as well as in, on the lecture platform or the 'tube,' wherever anyone will listen to me—toward creating a new kind of literature" (115). In this book, Fiedler takes several steps in this direction by writing sympathetically about such uncanonical texts as *Uncle Tom's Cabin*, *Gone with the Wind*, and *Starsky and Hutch*. Radway seems to have already arrived at the point Fiedler aspires to by choosing romance novels as her subject in the first place and by concluding:

Commodities like mass-produced literary texts are selected, purchased, constructed, and used by real people with previously existing needs, desires, intentions, and interpretive strategies. By reinstating those active individuals and their creative, constructive activities at the heart of our interpretive enterprise, we avoid blinding ourselves to the fact that the essentially human practice of making meaning goes on even in a world increasingly dominated by things and by consumption. (221)

To Bloom, critical judgments like Fiedler's and Radway's are symptomatic of the social malaise that we may join the Marxists in calling "commodity culture." In contrast to Fiedler and Radway, Bloom believes that "[c]ulture refers to art, music, literature, educational television, certain kinds of movies—in short, everything that is uplifting and edifying, as opposed to commerce" (187). Popular songs of the sort admired by Greil Marcus are even worse than popular narratives in Bloom's opinion, since they are based on "three great lyrical themes: sex, hate, and a smarmy, hypocritical version of brotherly love" (74). Aside from the implicit moral decay associated with these songs, there is also a failure in communication: "With rock, illusions of shared feelings, bodily contact and grunted formulas, which are supposed to contain so much meaning beyond speech, are the basis of association" (75). So much for "the essentially human practice of making meaning," at least where the "common" man or woman is concerned! Things were not always thus, according to Bloom: "Thirty years ago . . . university students usually had some early emotive association with Beethoven, Chopin and Brahms, which was a permanent part of their makeup and to which they were likely to respond throughout their lives. This was probably the only regularly recognizable class distinction between educated and uneducated in America" (69). Aha! proponents of demotic culture can exclaim; we knew class had to come in somewhere! In fact, this is just the problem, as Levine explains in his critique of Bloom's book: "There is, finally, the same sense that culture is something created by the few for the few, threatened by the many, and imperiled by democracy; the conviction that culture cannot come from the young, the inexperienced, the untutored, the marginal; the belief that culture is finite and fixed, defined and measured, complex and difficult of access, recognizable only by those trained to recognize it, comprehensible only to those qualified to comprehend it" (252). Levine shares the views of several critics quoted earlier that the cultural divisions postulated by thinkers like Bloom need not always pertain: "Evidence of what appears to be a growing cultural eclecticism and flexibility is everywhere at hand" (243). As evidence, "[W]e gradually come to the realization that Fred Astaire was one of this century's fine dancers, Louis Armstrong one of its important musicians, Charlie Chaplin one of its acute social commentators" (234), irrespective of class labels. The battles over high school reading lists, general education requirements in universities, and public funding for the arts that erupt with predictable frequency demonstrate that the conflicts encapsuled in these quotations continued to flare throughout the 1990s.

Since American popular culture has increasingly saturated the cultures of other nations in the 1960s and beyond, it is only to be expected that criticism of American popular culture would move beyond disputes like those just discussed to take on an increasingly international favor. Thus, many—perhaps the majority of— articles in journals such as *Studies in Popular Culture* and *Journal of Popular Culture* today may be expected to contain references to continental critics such as Barthes, Mikhail Bakhtin, Jean Baudrillard, and Umberto Eco. Baudrillard's primary thesis, for example, is that American capitalism has succeeded in substituting "simulations" for "reality," seducing the consumers of American popular culture into a false state of consciousness in which they can no longer distinguish the true from the false. As Baudrillard writes in his influential essay "Simulacra and Simulations" (1981), "It is no longer a question of a false representation of reality (ideology), but of concealing the fact that the real is no longer real, and thus of saving the reality principle" (172). This is also Eco's point in his much wittier study *Travels in Hyperreality* (1986), where he describes the quintessential American wax museum, which "shows Brigitte Bardot with a skimpy handkerchief around her loins, it rejoices in the life of Christ with Mahler and Tchaikovsky, it reconstructs the chariot race from *Ben Hur* in a curved space to suggest panoramic Vista Vision, for everything must equal reality even if, as in these cases, reality was fantasy" (15). For both critics, it is necessary to postulate levels of "reality" in which some objects (usually continental, such as red wine, unfiltered cigarettes, and cathedrals) are more "real" than others (usually American, such as Gap jeans, Kellogg's Fruit Loops, and Yankee Stadium). Readers reluctant to accept distinctions of this sort may suspect that traces of Sausurrean "difference" taint the theories of Baudrillard and Eco, reminiscent of the valorizations of high culture at the expense of low culture in years gone by. Since echoes of thinkers like Herbert Marcuse linger in the pronouncements of these recent continental critics, such suspicions are probably well grounded.

Bakhtin's theories seem more congenial to many contemporary thinkers, perhaps because his books do not directly address the American scene. Therefore, it is easier to exempt Bakhtin from the indictment of epistemological elitism attached to the likes of Baudrillard and Eco. As Maria Shevtsova (1992) affirms in a typically positive judgment, "Bakhtin's theory of culture is, above all, also a theory of popular culture—people's culture or folk culture" (749). Bakhtin's own comments, as in this "Response to a Question from the *Novy Mir* Editorial Staff," lend credence to such affirmative assessments: "The powerful deep currents of culture (especially the lower popular ones), which actually determine the creativity of writers, remain undisclosed, and sometimes researchers are completely unaware of them" (*Speech Genres* 3). These currents circulate primarily in terms of the social force that Bakhtin calls "carnivalization." Especially in his book *Rabelais and His World*, Bakhtin proposes the carnival spirit as a form of demotic social energy engaged in a "dialogic" contest with the designs of "monologic," hegemonic culture. In Bakhtin's world it is unlikely that the powers-that-be could successfully impose very much—not even very clever simulations—on the populace, at least not for very long. Chief among the weapons available to "popular" or "folk" culture is acceptance of what Bakhtin calls "the grotesque body of the world." As he explains in his book on Rabelais:

> Contrary to the modern canons, the grotesque body is not separated from the rest of the world. It is not a closed, completed unit; it is unfinished, outgrows itself, transgresses its own limits. The stress is laid on those parts of the body that are open to the outside world, that is, the parts through which the body itself goes out to meet the world. This means that the emphasis is on the apertures or the convexities, or on various ramifications and offshoots: the open mouth, the genital organs, the breasts, the phallus, the potbelly, the nose. (26)

Inspired by such Bakhtinian affirmations, many other critics have gone on to emphasize the creative energies of American popular culture. As we might expect of a theoretical project that arose in Stalinist Russia, however, Bakhtin's "dialogical" strategies must, first of all, assume the existence of a powerful adversarial force in hegemonic capitalism.

The same may be said of the "cultural studies" approach of John Fiske, imported from England. Fiske is like Bakhtin (and other critics, including David Manning White and Janice Radway) in assuming that members of any audience retain considerable power as individuals. In *Television Culture*, for example, Fiske writes, "The hegemony of the [television] text is never total, but always has to struggle to impose itself against the diversity of meanings that the diversity of readers will produce" (93). Moreover, a more advanced television program—which Fiske calls a "producerly" television text by analogy to Roland Barthes' category of the "writerly" print text[21]—allows for subjective responses and filling-in of the textual blank. In other words, such a program "treats its readers as members of a semiotic democracy, already equipped with the discursive competencies to make meanings and motivated by pleasure to want to participate in the process" (95). Fiske's audience is thus rather like Bakhtin's, a collection of semifree individual subjects; however, as in Bakhtin's theory, this collection of individuals must engage endlessly in a struggle against hegemony, or monologism, or just plain "them." In this respect, even these more positive theories of how audiences interact with mediated texts assume some form of class conflict. Perhaps it will be ever thus in popular culture studies.

After all this exemplification, listing, citing, and analysis, we are probably left with still another question: Where does all this leave us in terms of "the study of popular culture"? In one sense, the study of popular culture is going forward with great enthusiasm. The annual international meetings of PCA are well attended, and so are meetings of the regional chapters. Journals publishing articles focused on the study of popular culture flourish. Consider only the most obvious titles: *Journal of Popular Culture, Studies in Popular Culture, Mid-Atlantic Almanack, Popular Culture Review, Popular Music and Society, The Journal of Popular Film and Television*, and *Clues*. Most academic quarterlies and film journals also publish at least some articles that can easily be identified as popular cultural studies. Newsmagazines regularly wrinkle their editorial brows while producing glossy analyses of where we are pop-culturally and where we are going. Web sites for performers, television series, collectible objects, and film genres proliferate. Some cable channels show only old television shows or cartoons. Reruns run rampant.[22]

Yet, a newspaper headline that someone taped to the door of my office says, "Clinton Blasts Pop Culture." After the 1998 PCA convention in Orlando, Florida, Eric L. Wee archly reported in the *Washington Post* that "as incredible as it seems," the study of popular culture, "once the kooky idea of a few people at a backwater college called Bowling Green State University in Ohio" may actually be "the future" (F1). Wee did not seem particularly overjoyed at the prospect. During the 1992 presidential campaign, J. Danforth Quayle, vice president of the whole United States, blamed the *Murphy Brown* sitcom for the lamentable state of the American family. Following the 1999 high school shooting disaster in Littleton, Colorado, and elsewhere, leading congressional Republicans blamed the teenagers' deadly use of automatic weapons on rampant representations of violence in television, films, and video games.[23] In a spirit of true political nonpartisanship, Senator Joseph I. Lieberman, Democratic candidate for vice president in the 2000 elections, continually excoriated television as a violent wasteland, even while accepting generous campaign contributions from media sources.[24] Exactly what all of this tells us in terms of the questions proposed at the beginning of this chapter is thus somewhat problematic. That there has been considerable change in the intellectual climate of American academic scholarship seems clear, but that this change has met firm resistance in some quarters seems equally clear. While French cultural critics might be inclined to observe of this situation, *plus ca change, plus c'est la meme chose*, the more optimistic American "take" on the matter might be better articulated by two previously unmentioned cultural authorities, Sonny and Cher, who said memorably, "The beat goes on."

NOTES

1. One sampling of such opinion—by Ray Browne, Russel B. Nye, and Herbert Gans— appears in *The Popular Culture Reader* (3d ed., 1983), edited by Christopher D. Geist and Jack Nachbar; another, edited by Roger B. Rollin with the title "Understanding Popular Culture: A Symposium," appears in *Studies in Popular Culture* 6 (1983), with contributions by Gary L. Harmon, Dennis R. Hall, Lawrence E. Mintz, and Marilyn Sherman, and Rollin.

2. For a discussion of John Wayne's possible "responsibility" for the Vietnam War, see Tom Englehardt, *The End of Victory Culture*, 175–80; and Garry Wills, *John Wayne's America*, 12–14.

3. See the early pages of, for example, *The Norton Anthology of American Literature* (1999), edited by Nina Baym et al.; and *The Harper American Literature* (1999), edited by Donald McQuade et al.

4. Franklin recounts his early forays into print in his *Autobiography*, 40ff.

5. Regarding the Lincoln/Stowe incident, see Alfred Kazin's introduction to *Uncle Tom's Cabin*, by Harriet Beecher Stowe, ix.

6. On Alger's readers, see Gary Scharnhorst and Jack Bales, *The Lost Life of Horatio Alger, Jr.*, 149–56.

7. For more information on Barton's and Carnegie's best-sellers, see *Golden Multitudes: The Story of Best Sellers in the United States* by Frank Luther Mott. For *The Joy of Cooking*, see *Stand Facing the Stove: The Story of the Women Who Gave America* The Joy of Cooking by Anne Mendelson. Regarding *Peyton Place*, see *The Unembarrassed Muse* by Russel Nye.

8. Body images are the subject of *The Beauty Myth* (1991) by Naomi Wolf and *Am I Thin Enough Yet?* by Sharlene Hesse-Biber, among many other recent works.

9. Concerning the focus of advertisements on "an audience's psychological needs, its attitudes and anxieties," see, for example, *Popular Writing in America* (1993), ed. Donald McQuade and Robert Atwan, 2–8.

10. According to the 1998 Economic Review provided on the Motion Picture Association of America Web site, the "U.S. Average Hours of TV Usage Per Household" total is seven hours and fifteen minutes per day.

11. John Dryden, "Preface to Fables Ancient and Modern" (1700), 161.

12. Even though Springsteen's character has cable television and a satellite dish, he and his baby are distressed to discover that there's "nothin' on." She is so disappointed by this that she walks out on him, and he is so disappointed in turn that he shoots out his television set with a .44 magnum.

13. Jack Nachbar and Kevin Lause provide a useful survey of these abstract forces in

their introductory essay, "Songs of the Unseen Road: Myths, Beliefs and Values in Popular Culture," in *Popular Culture: An Introductory Text*, 82–109.

14. Northrop Frye introduces the terms *demotic* and *hieratic* in this sense to clarify a similar point (pp. 94–95) about literary styles in *The Well-Tempered Critic* (1963).

15. Concerning "difference," see, for example, this explanation by J. Douglas Kneale in *The Johns Hopkins Guide to Literary Theory and Criticism*: "[W]ords acquire value or identity not through any natural correspondence between signifier and signified but through each word's opposition to every other word within a system of interdependence in which both signifiers and signifieds are defined in terms of what they are not, that is, in terms of simultaneous linguistic presence and absence, or what Saussure calls 'difference' " (186).

16. See Jameson's *Postmodernism, Or, The Cultural Logic of Late Capitalism* (1991).

17. M. Thomas Inge proposed in the second edition of the *Handbook of American Popular Culture*, "It would seem to make better sense to describe all of this we have been discussing—high culture, low culture, mass culture, mass media, popular culture, or whatever—as simply culture. . . . Whether it be simple or complex, elite or democratic, individually crafted or mass produced, we should drop the adjectives 'high' and 'popular' and address ourselves to the total culture of twentieth-century American society without maintaining false distinctions that have no reality in the modern world" (xxxi).

18. Lawrence Levine discusses the Marx Brothers in this cultural context and adds Charlie Chaplin to the list in *Highbrow/Lowbrow: The Emergence of Cultural Hierarchy in America*, 135.

19. In addition to the International Popular Culture Association, several regional organizations flourish in the United States. These are the Far West, Great Plains, Mid-Atlantic, Midwest, North East, Pacific, Southwest/Texas, Superior Region, and the South.

20. For more information on the National Women's Studies Association, see the organization's Web site: http://www.nwsa.org/about.htm.

21. Barthes draws his "readerly/writerly" distinction in *S/Z* (1974).

22. In David Marc's *Comic Visions: Television Comedy and American Culture*, he writes wittily about the likelihood that an inveterate channel-switcher might encounter "dueling Lucies" on competing channels, 204.

23. See, for example, "House Undertakes Days-Long Battle on Youth Violence," *New York Times*, June 17, 1999: A1+.

24. See, for example, Dana Calvo's article, "Lieberman Waxes Nostalgic for Good Old Days of Broadcasting Television," *Los Angeles Times*, September 20, 2000: 1F.

BIBLIOGRAPHY

Angell, Roger. *Five Seasons*. New York: Simon & Schuster, 1977.

Arnold, Matthew. "The Function of Criticism at the Present Time." *Essays in Criticism: First Series*. London: Macmillan, 1903, 1–44.

Bakhtin, Mikhail. *Rabelais and His World*. Trans. Helene Iswolsky. Bloomington: Indiana University Press, 1984.

———. *Speech Genres and Other Late Essays*. Trans. Vern W. McGee. Austin: University of Texas Press, 1986.

Barthes, Roland. *Mythologies*. Trans. Annette Lavers. New York: Hill and Wang, 1970.

———. *S/Z*. Trans. Richard Miller. New York: Hill and Wang, 1974.

Baudrillard, Jean. "Simulacra and Simulations." 1981. Trans. Paul Foss, Paul Patton, and Philip Beitchman. *Selected Writings*. Ed. Mark Posner. Stanford, Calif.: Stanford University Press, 1988, 166–84.

Baym, Nina, et al., eds. *The Norton Anthology of American Literature.* Shorter 5th ed. New York: Norton, 1999.

Berger, Arthur Asa. *The Comic-Stripped American: What Dick Tracy, Blondie, Daddy Warbucks, and Charley Brown Tell Us about Ourselves.* New York: Walker, 1973.

Bloom, Allan. *The Closing of the American Mind.* New York: Simon and Schuster, 1987.

Browne, Ray B. "Popular Culture—New Notes toward a Definition." Geist and Nachbar, eds., 13–20.

Browne, Ray B., and Michael Marsden, eds. *Pioneers in Popular Culture Studies.* Bowling Green, OH: Bowling Green State University Popular Press, 1999.

Calvo, Dana. "Lieberman Waxes Nostalgic for Good Old Days of Broadcasting Television." *Los Angeles Times,* September 20, 2000: 1F.

Cawelti, John G. *Adventure, Mystery, and Romance: Formula Stories as Art and Popular Culture.* Chicago: University of Chicago Press, 1976.

Croce, Arlene. *The Fred Astaire & Ginger Rogers Book.* New York: Outerbridge and Lazard, 1972.

Dryden, John. "Preface to Fables Ancient and Modern, Translated into Verse from Homer, Ovid, Boccaccio, and Chaucer, with Original Poems." *Literary Criticism of John Dryden.* Ed. Arthur C. Kirsch. Lincoln: University of Nebraska Press, 1966, 147–70.

Eco, Umberto. *Travels in Hyperreality: Essays.* Trans. William Weaver. New York: Harcourt, 1986.

Eliot, T. S. *After Strange Gods: A Primer of Modern Heresy.* London: Faber and Faber, 1934.

———. *The Idea of a Christian Society.* London: Faber and Faber, 1939.

Englehardt, Tom. *The End of Victory Culture: Cold War America and the Disillusioning of a Generation.* New York: Basic Books, 1995.

Fiedler, Leslie A. *What Was Literature? Class, Culture, and Mass Society.* New York: Simon and Schuster, 1982.

Fiske, John. *Television Culture.* London and New York: Routledge, 1987.

Franklin, Benjamin. *The Autobiography.* Ed. with intro. Louis P. Masur. Boston: Bedford, 1993.

Frye, Northrop. *The Well-Tempered Critic.* Bloomington: Indiana University Press, 1963.

Gans, Herbert J. *Popular Culture and High Culture: An Analysis and Evaluation of Taste.* New York: Basic Books, 1974.

———. "Popular Culture's Defects as a Commercial Enterprise." Geist and Nachbar, eds., 30–40.

Geist, Christopher D., and Jack Nachbar, eds. *The Popular Culture Reader.* 3d ed. Bowling Green, Ohio: Bowling Green University Popular Press, 1983.

Giamatti, A. Bartlett. *Take Time for Paradise: Americans and Their Games.* New York: Summit, 1989.

Grote, David. *The End of Comedy: The Sit-Com and the Comedic Tradition.* Hamden, Conn.: Archon, 1983.

Halberstam, David. *The Breaks of the Game.* New York: Knopf, 1981.

Hall, Dennis R. "The Study of Popular Culture: Origin and Developments." *Studies in Popular Culture* 6 (1983), 16–25.

Harmon, Gary L. "On the Nature and Functions of Popular Culture." *Studies in Popular Culture* 6 (1983), 3–15.

Haskell, Molly. *From Reverence to Rape: The Treatment of Women in the Movies.* New York: Penguin, 1975.

———. *Holding My Own in No Man's Land: Women and Men and Film and Feminists.* New York: Oxford University Press, 1997.

Hesse-Biber, Sharlene. *Am I Thin Enough Yet?: The Cult of Thinness and the Commercialization of Identity.* New York: Oxford University Press, 1996.

Hoppenstand, Gary. "Ray and Pat Browne: Scholars of Everyday Culture." Browne and Marsden, eds., 33–65.

I'll Take My Stand: The South and the Agrarian Tradition. By Twelve Southerners. 1930. Intro. Louis D. Rubin Jr. Baton Rouge: Louisiana State University Press, 1980.

Inge, M. Thomas. *The American Comic Book.* Columbus: Ohio State University Libraries, 1985.

———. *Anything Can Happen in a Comic Strip: Centennial Reflections on an American Art Form.* Jackson: University Press of Mississippi/Ohio State University Libraries, 1995.

———. *Comics as Culture.* Jackson: University of Mississippi Press, 1990.

———. *Great American Comics. 100 Years of Cartoon Art.* Washington, DC: Smithsonian Traveling Exhibition Services, 1990.

———. Introduction. *Handbook of American Popular Culture.* 2d ed. Westport, Conn.: Greenwood, 1989.

Jameson, Fredric. *Postmodernism, or, The Cultural Logic of Late Capitalism.* Durham, N.C.: Duke University Press, 1991.

Kahn, Roger. *The Boys of Summer.* New York: Harper and Row, 1972.

Kaplan, E. Ann. *Rocking around the Clock: Music Television, Postmodernism, and Consumer Culture.* London: Methuen, 1987.

Kazin, Alfred. Introduction. *Uncle Tom's Cabin.* By Harriet Beecher Stowe. New York: Bantam, 1981, vii–xv.

Kempton, Arthur. "The Fall of the Black Empires." *The New York Review of Books,* June 10, 1999: 50–56.

Kneale, J. Douglas. "Deconstruction." *The Johns Hopkins Guide to Literary Theory and Criticism.* Ed. Michael Groden and Martin Kreiswirth. Baltimore: Johns Hopkins University Press, 1994, 185–92.

Koppelman, Susan, and Emily Toth. "Emily Toth: Ms. Mentor Meets Kate Chopin." Browne and Marsden, eds., 207–20.

Levine, Lawrence E. *Highbrow/Lowbrow: The Emergence of Cultural Hierarchy in America.* Cambridge: Harvard University Press, 1988.

Macdonald, Dwight. "Masscult and Midcult." 1960. *Against the American Grain.* New York: Random House, 1962, 3–75.

Marc, David. *Comic Visions: Television Comedy and American Culture.* Boston: Unwin Hyman, 1989.

Marcus, Greil. *Invisible Republic: Bob Dylan's Basement Tapes.* New York: Henry Holt, 1997.

———. *Mystery Train; Images of America in Rock 'n' Roll Music.* New York: Dutton, 1975.

Marcuse, Herbert. *One-Dimensional Man: Studies in the Ideology of Advanced Industrial Society.* Boston: Beacon Press, 1964.

McLuhan, Marshall. *Understanding Media: The Extensions of Man.* New York: McGraw-Hill, 1964.

McLuhan, Marshall, and Quentin Fiore. *The Medium Is the Message.* Coord. Jerome Angel. New York: Random House, 1967.

McQuade, Donald, et al., eds. *The Harper American Literature.* 3d ed., single vol. New York: Longman, 1999.

McQuade, Donald, and Robert Atwan, eds. *Popular Writing in America: The Interaction of Style and Audience.* 5th ed. New York: Oxford University Press, 1993.

Mendelson, Anne. *Stand Facing the Stove: The Story of the Women Who Gave America* The Joy of Cooking. New York: Henry Holt, 1996.

Mintz, Lawrence E. "Notes toward a Methodology of Popular Culture Study." *Studies in Popular Culture* 6 (1983), 26–34.

———. "Situation Comedy." *TV Genres: A Handbook and Reference Guide.* Ed. Brian Rose. Westport, Conn.: Greenwood, 1985, 107–29.

Mitchell, Alison, and Frank Bruni. "House Undertakes Days-Long Battle on Youth Violence." *New York Times,* June 17, 1999: A1+.

Motion Picture Association of America Web site: http://www.mpaa.org/useconomicreview/1998/sld038.htm

Mott, Frank Luther. *Golden Multitudes: The Story of Best Sellers in the United States.* New York: Bowker, 1947.

Nachbar, Jack, and Kevin Lause, eds. *Popular Culture: An Introductory Text.* Bowling Green, Ohio: Bowling Green State University Popular Press, 1992.

National Women's Studies Association Web site: http://www.nwsa.org/about.htm

Nye, Russel. "Notes on a Rationale for Popular Culture." Geist and Nachbar, eds., 21–29.

———. *The Unembarrassed Muse: The Popular Arts in America.* New York: Dial, 1970.

Radway, Janice. *Reading the Romance: Women, Patriarchy, and Popular Literature.* Chapel Hill: University of North Carolina Press, 1984.

Scharnhorst, Gary, and Jack Bales. *The Lost Life of Horatio Alger, Jr.* Bloomington: Indiana University Press, 1985.

Schwartz, Arthur, and Howard Dietz. "That's Entertainment." *The Band Wagon.* RHI 72253, 1996.

Seldes, Gilbert. *The 7 Lively Arts.* 1924. New York: Sagamore Press, 1957.

Sherman, Marilyn R., and Roger B. Rollin. "Opportunities for Research and Publication in Popular Culture." *Studies in Popular Culture* 6 (1983), 35–46.

Shevtsova, Maria. "Dialogism in the Novel and Bakhtin's Theory of Culture." *New Literary History* 23 (1992), 747–63.

Slotkin, Richard. *Regeneration Through Violence: The Mythology of the American Frontier, 1600–1860.* Middletown, Conn.: Wesleyan University Press, 1973.

Smith, Henry Nash. *Virgin Land: The American West as Symbol and Myth.* Cambridge, MA: Harvard University Press, 1950.

Sontag, Susan. "One Culture and the New Sensibility." *Against Interpretation and Other Essays.* New York: Farrar, Straus, and Giroux, 1966, 293–304.

Springsteen, Bruce. "57 Channels (and Nothin' On)." *Human Touch*. 1992 Sony, B0000028 SR.

Tompkins, Jane. *West of Everything: The Inner Life of Westerns*. New York: Oxford University Press, 1992.

Toth, Emily, and Susan Koppelman. "Susan Koppelman: Diva of the Short Story." Browne and Marsden, eds., 137–56.

Wee, Eric L. "Pop Goes the Culture; These Professors Study the Philosophy of Captain Kirk and the Poetry of R.E.M. Sure, It's Fun. But Is It Academic?" *Washington Post*, April 19, 1998: F1+.

White, David Manning, and Bernard Rosenberg, eds. *Mass Culture Revisited*. Intro. Paul F. Lazarfeld. New York: Van Nostrand, 1971.

Wills, Garry. *John Wayne's America: The Politics of Celebrity*. New York: Simon and Schuster, 1997.

Wolf, Naomi. *The Beauty Myth: How Images of Beauty Are Used against Women*. New York: Morrow, 1991.

ALMANACS

Robert K. Dodge

Americans today are only vaguely aware of the importance of almanacs during the first 250 years of American history. Most of us can quote a few of Poor Richard's sayings and associate them with an almanac; most of us probably remember the story of Abraham Lincoln and his use of an almanac to prove the innocence of a client; and many of us may remember reading in our history books that a Bible and an almanac constituted the only reading matter for most of our pioneers.

Anything else we remember about early American almanacs is probably associated with a sense of the quaint, of people who spelled with a final "k" and who attempted to predict the weather a year in advance.

Almanacs were much more than quaint. They were the forerunners of modern magazines and city directories. They served as calendars and road maps. They helped to publicize the U. S. Constitution. They served as vehicles for advertising and for politics and religion, and they spread humor throughout the country. They provide us an important source of information about American life and attitudes in the seventeenth, eighteenth, and nineteenth centuries.

HISTORIC OUTLINE

In 1639 Stephen Daye printed America's first almanac in Cambridge, Massachusetts. For the next two and a half centuries and longer, almanacs constituted an important part of American life.

Most seventeenth-century almanacs appear quite modest. Almost all of them are sixteen-page pamphlets. A few extended to twenty-four or even thirty-two pages, beginning the gradual but steady tendency of American almanacs to lengthen. The sixteen-page almanacs devoted a separate page to each month. (Some of today's "factual" almanacs of a thousand or more pages devote fewer pages to the calendar.) Another page was often used to introduce the calendar and to give information concerning the dates of eclipses. Two of the three additional pages consisted of the front and back covers. The remaining page, usually the inside of the back cover, was sometimes used for advertisements, sometimes to provide information on events of the coming year, and sometimes to present an essay on the science of astronomy.

The calendar, considered the heart of the almanac, contained such information as the time of sunrise and sunset, the beginning date of each season (under the old-style calendar more variable than today), the phases of the moon, and usually some astrological information as well. If the intended readership included commercial fishermen or shippers, the calendar would include information on tides. The longer almanacs often allotted two pages to each month, although at least one twenty-four-page almanac included a nine-page explanation of its twelve-page calendar.

In the eighteenth century the almanac industry became more competitive. After all, the printing of an almanac had become a very profitable sideline for many American printers. They had a guaranteed market among farmers, commercial fishermen, and sailors. Naturally each almanac maker wanted to capture as large a share of the market as possible. It was perhaps competition more than any other influence that led to the changes in the eighteenth-century almanac, changes that make them more interesting to the student of American popular culture than are the majority of the almanacs from the seventeenth century.

Early competition concentrated on the accuracy of the calendar. Almanac makers extolled the virtues of their own calendars and often pointed out real or imagined inaccuracies in their competitors'. Sometimes a free errata sheet for the calendar of a major competitor was offered with the purchase of an almanac.

Another form of competition involved piracy. One of the reasons that bibliographies list so many editions of such popular titles as Thomas Greenleaf's and Abraham Weatherwise's almanacs appears to be that some of the editions were piracies. In at least one case the piracy had more involved motives, at least if Nathaniel Ames, publisher of one of America's first bestselling almanacs, was correct in his assessment of the competition. Ames complained that his competitors had banded together to produce a fraudulent and inaccurate almanac under his name in order to discredit him and his calendars.[1]

Ames and James Franklin can be credited with beginning to change the rules of almanac competition. They realized that the accuracy of a calendar as a sales inducement could be pushed only to a certain point, and they began the process of including other material to sell their almanacs. Ames often included short paragraphs on current events and on morality in general. James Franklin invented the character of Poor Robin, who gave his readers the sayings of Poor Robin.

While Ames and James Franklin began the process of changing the rules of competition, it was Benjamin Franklin who carried the process to its completion. Benjamin Franklin's first almanac burst upon the Philadelphia scene with the creation of Poor Richard and the prediction of the death of Titan Leeds, at the time the most popular almanac maker in the city.

Both the sayings of Poor Richard and the prediction, to which Leeds foolishly responded, helped Franklin's almanac to capture the attention of Philadelphia, and as Franklin saw the popularity of Poor Richard's sayings grow, he increased their number. The idea for the prediction, like the idea for the sayings, was borrowed: the prediction from Jonathan Swift's satire of the astrologer John

Poor Richard's Almanac. Courtesy of the Library of Congress

Partridge in *The Bickerstaff Papers* (1708); the sayings from his brother. But, while Franklin treated the prediction almost exactly as Swift had, he developed the sayings far beyond what his brother had done.

Other almanac makers soon accepted the idea that material other than the calendar could make their almanacs sell. In the decades following the introduction of Poor Richard, almanacs grew longer and longer as publishers competed to include more and more material that the public would buy. It is such material that makes eighteenth- and nineteenth-century almanacs so interesting to the student of American popular culture.

For example, historians of farming in early America will find hundreds of "valuable receipts" for improving soil, increasing crop yields, and curing diseases in livestock. Many of the recipes appear to be based on superstition, and a few appear to be based on even less than that, but many more seem to represent a real interest in the establishment of an empirical science of farming. Two of the better suggestions include the use of lime as a fertilizer (useful only when the soil is acidic) and the addition of green organic material to the soil.

Other recipes offered cures for various human ailments. The gout, bloody flux, toothache, and nosebleed are provided with "sure and certain" cures. The science of medicine appears even less advanced than that of agriculture, but a trial-and-error methodology was beginning here as well.

Some almanacs included recipes for the preparation and preservation of food. Such recipes impress the modern reader with their emphasis on preservation and with the large quantities they were intended to serve. Measurements tended to be imprecise.

Many of the almanacs contained descriptions of American customs. One almanac printed an essay in favor of the New England custom of bundling. According to the essay, bundlers were almost always pure, and that newfangled innovation, the sofa, was far more dangerous to a woman's chastity. A long poem against bundling appeared in one of the Andrew Beers almanacs for 1793. Unlike the essay, the moralistic poem includes much detail about what its author thought took place in the bundling bed. One quatrain describes a man and a woman who had bundled together, each wearing a full set of clothing and wrapped in a separate sheet. The man, however, caught the itch from the woman, and she caught a bastard from him.[2]

Other described customs included bees and peddling. A few publishers, most notably Robert Thomas of *The (Old) Farmer's Almanack*, opposed the custom of social gatherings known as bees as wasteful of time and property. Thomas believed that a family had plenty of time during the long winter to husk its corn as it became necessary without the expense of entertaining all of the neighbors. Most almanac makers, however, considered bees of all kinds to be either harmless entertainment or positive ways for neighbors to help each other.

Peddlers constituted an important method of distribution for the almanac industry. Other media might criticize the peddler and, perhaps, deservedly so, but, as many of today's newspapers romanticize the newsboy, so did almanacs tend to romanticize the peddler.

Judging from what was printed in almanacs, early Americans must have liked to read about the exotic and the horrible. Indian captivity narratives and other stories of Indian cruelty abound, as do stories of Indian stoicism. Stories of cannibalism in America and Africa are common. Some almanacs described exotic animals, such as the giraffe and the elephant. The myth of the elephant's memory was demonstrated. Sentimental stories were popular as well. Some of the sentimental stories appear grotesque, at best, to the modern reader, but they do represent one form of popular story for the time.

By the last half of the eighteenth century, many of the almanacs had begun to provide pure information in the style of the present *World Almanac and Book of Facts* or the other large present-day almanacs familiar to most of us. The information was usually local, but a selection of almanacs would provide such information for most of the United States. What clubs existed in a particular city? What were the roads and their condition? Who were the political officers? What were the churches, and who were the clergymen? Most localities had one or more almanacs that attempted to answer such questions. A few even attempted to name every family in the locality.

Other kinds of information dealt with current events, including politics. The first balloon ascension was noted in many almanacs and even inspired the publication of the *Balloon Almanac*. The settlement of the frontier was a popular topic, as was the American Revolution and later the adoption of the Constitution. Laws and tariffs were reprinted. George Washington's "Farewell Address" was widely reprinted, as were many of the writings of Benjamin Franklin.

Another topic that must interest the student of popular culture is humor. Comic almanacs flourished in the nineteenth century. The David Crockett almanacs are probably the best known, but Josh Billings (Henry Wheeler Shaw), Commodore Rollingpin (John Henton Carter), and others produced comic almanacs. *All-My-Nack*, *Allminax*, and *Allmaniac* were among the comic misspellings. In addition, many of the serious almanacs contained comic material, much as *Reader's Digest* and other magazines do today. Such comic material constitutes one of the few sources of early popular humor still available to us. Between 1776 and 1800, for example, more than 1,500 comic items were published in serious American almanacs. Certainly much of the comedy was literary rather than popular, and much of it was not even very comic. In some cases the comic items seem to have been copied directly from British sources. Nevertheless, this body of humor is worthy of study simply because it does constitute almost the only source of written popular humor before the *Spirit of the Times* and its competing journals, and the almanac remained an important source even after that.

The nineteenth century saw the development of advertising almanacs, especially those advertising patent medicines. Milton Drake says that about fifty patent medicine almanacs were published in the century, many of them in continuous publication for several years.[3] Many other groups used almanacs for advertising in the nineteenth century. Drake lists religious groups, uplift groups, political groups, labor and professional groups, fraternal groups, and pressure groups, as well as straightforward sales-related advertisers such as those printing and distributing almanacs in this century. The *Christian Almanac*, one of the religious almanacs, grew to have a circulation of 300,000 in 1850.[4]

The twentieth century brought about additional changes in U.S. almanacs. The almanac of pure information certainly became the dominant form. For some publishers, the word *almanac* has come to mean any yearly compilation of information and statistics, whether in a particular field (for example, the *Nurse's Almanac* and the *Standard Educational Almanac*) or more general (the *World Almanac and Book of Facts*). The calendar, if it exists at all, has been relegated to a very minor role. In the case of a few publications, such as *The People's Almanac* by David Wallechinsky and Irving Wallace, even the characteristic of yearly publication has been dropped. A few old-time or family almanacs are still published. Most prominent among them is the *Old Farmer's Almanac*, a direct descendant of Robert B. Thomas' *Farmer's Almanac*. Its appeal to a sense of nostalgia and quaintness had gained it a circulation of 2 million in 1970.

Scholars interested in American ethnic groups will find that U.S. almanacs have been published in at least twenty languages including twelve European languages and six American Indian languages.

REFERENCE WORKS

Two bibliographies are essential to the study of American almanacs. The first, *American Bibliography* by Charles Evans, is a fourteen-volume work that claims to be a dictionary of all "books, pamphlets and periodical publications" printed in America before 1821. Before his death, however, Evans had carried the bibliography only through part of 1799. The American Antiquarian Society (AAS) finished 1799, 1800, and the index, which has a separate heading for almanacs. The Evans-American Antiquarian Society publication lists more than 5,000 almanacs as having been printed in America before the end of 1800. It is somewhat confusing that these listings include almanacs published *for* 1801. With few exceptions almanacs were published in the fall or winter of the year preceding the year of their calendar.

Evans's entries, some of which were taken from advertisements and other sources, contain some ghosts. In at least one case an almanac appears to be listed under two different titles. Nevertheless, Evans' bibliography is important for at least two reasons. Evans and the American Antiquarian Society were among the first to consider the almanacs an important scholarly resource. Besides, this bibliography and its supplement provide access to *Early American Imprints*, a Readex Microprint Edition edited by Clifford K. Shipton and published by the American Antiquarian Society.

Any library with a set of these microcards and the later supplement, also edited by Shipton, holds a representative collection of seventeenth- and eighteenth-century American almanacs. It may appear that the collection is biased toward almanacs published in the Northeast, but it must be remembered that by far the majority of almanac publishers, especially in these two centuries, were located in the Northeast.

Access to the supplement to *Early American Imprints* is provided by the two-volume *Supplement to Charles Evans' American Bibliography* by Roger P. Bristol, which has a separate heading for almanacs in the index. The index lists nearly a thousand almanacs not included in *American Bibliography*.

From 1958 to 1966, Ralph Shaw and Richard Shoemaker published twenty-two additional volumes of *American Bibliography* on a less comprehensive plan than that of Evans. Their work is subtitled *A Preliminary Checklist for 1801–1819*, and they call it "a preliminary step in filling the gap in American bibliography."[5] Like the Evans-AAS volumes, the Shaw–Shoemaker volumes locate entries whose locations are known, but, because there is no separate listing for almanacs in the index, it is necessary to search each volume in order to find all of the almanacs.

In 1967, Richard Shoemaker again began expanding *American Bibliography* by publishing *A Checklist of American Imprints*. Beginning with 1820, that series now extends through 1833. In addition to Shoemaker, Gayle and M. Frances Cooper and Scott and Carol Bruntjen have worked as compilers. There are comprehensive title and author indexes for 1820 to 1829, but, as with the Shaw–Shoemaker volumes of *American Bibliography*, the student of almanacs must search each volume or read through the entire title index. These volumes provide locations. Most useful for the almanac researcher, then, are the Evans-AAS volumes and the supplement, which have a more usable index and provide access to the AAS microcard collection.

The second indispensable bibliography is Milton Drake's two-volume *Almanacs of the United States*, which attempts to list and locate all American almanacs published before 1850. In addition, for some states, notably those in the Confederacy and some of the western states, Drake carries the list into the 1870s. Drake's work contains 14,385 entries and locates nearly 75,000 copies. Drake canvassed 558 libraries and read about "four hundred bibliographical works in search of defunct issues."[6] Drake believes that he has, in fact, listed 85 percent or more of the almanacs published before 1850. As a bibliography of almanacs, Drake obviously supersedes Evans. Evans, however, is still essential to most almanac researchers for the access that it gives to the AAS microcard collection.

In addition to his list, Drake provides an interesting and informative introduction. We learn, for example, that the old story of Lincoln's saving a client with an almanac is supported by Illinois court records of an account of a British lawyer who had earlier used a fraudulent almanac to save his client in the same way. Drake also includes a list of American towns and cities where almanacs were published and the date of the earliest listed almanac for each town. He lists about 350 such cities and towns. Finally, Drake includes a bibliography of secondary source material, most of which his work has superseded.

To seek out almanacs published after 1850 is much more difficult because there is no specialized almanac bibliography such as Drake's, and many of the compilers of general bibliographies did not consider almanacs worthy of inclusion. Those general bibliographies that do include almanacs often seem to include too few. *The American Catalogue* is one of only a few general bibliographies that list almanacs. For the period from 1895 to 1900 it lists only forty almanacs and forty-seven calendars and yearbooks. *The American Catalogue*, founded by F. Leypoldt and continued by Lynds E. Jones and R. R. Bowker, lists books in print from 1876 to 1910. Its subject index has a heading for almanacs and another for calendars and yearbooks. *The Catalogue of Public Documents* put out by the Superintendent of Documents lists calendars and nautical almanacs published by agencies of the U.S. government.

RESEARCH COLLECTIONS

The first library to collect almanacs aggressively was that of the American Antiquarian Society under the direction of Clarence Brigham. Consequently, the AAS has perhaps the largest collection of early American almanacs of any library. It is this collection that formed the basis for the almanac representation in their microcard edition of *Early American Imprints*.

The holdings of the AAS are so great that when Milton Drake began work on his *Almanacs of the United States*, he believed that a canvass of the AAS holdings together with those of the Library of Congress, the New York Public Library, Rutgers University, the New York Historical Society, "and a scattering of others" would serve to find "everything that matters."[7] That search did net Drake 10,000 entries and located 20,000 copies, but his expansion of the search to more than 500 libraries netted an additional 4,000 entries and 55,000 located copies.

Most of the almanacs of early America were produced for a specific locality. It may be expected that state and local libraries will provide good sources for almanacs originally published within the locality or state that they serve and that they will, perhaps, hold copies not found in such giant collections as the AAS and the Library of Congress.

It is no surprise, then, that researchers interested in almanacs published in early Virginia will find copies, often unique, in the College of William and Mary, the Colonial Williamsburg Library, and the Virginia Historical Society Library, as well as in the Library of Congress. It is somewhat surprising that for very early Virginia almanacs the Huntington Library in San Marino, California, is an important source, as is the Washington State Historical Library and the William L. Clements Library in Ann Arbor, Michigan. The Huntington Library has collected many of the earliest almanacs from several of the states that have a colonial history. It owns the only extant copy of *An Almanack* for 1646, published in Cambridge, Massachusetts, by Stephen Daye. According to Drake, it is the earliest almanac still extant.

For almanacs published in Alabama, the important local libraries include the University of Alabama and the Alabama Department of Archives and History in Montgomery; for those published in California, the important local libraries are the Bancroft Library and the University of California Library in Berkeley, the California State Library in Sacramento, the California Historical Society in San Francisco, and, somewhat less important, the University of California at Los Angeles.

For Connecticut, the following local libraries have important holdings: the Connecticut Historical Society and the Connecticut State Library in Hartford, Yale University in New Haven, and local historical societies in New Haven, Litchfield, and New London. The Western Reserve Historical Society in Cleveland, Ohio, also has several Connecticut almanacs.

For Delaware, the Henry Francis DuPont Winterthur Museum in Winterthur has an important collection of early almanacs. The University of Delaware in Newark has a collection of nineteenth-century almanacs. The Pennsylvania Historical Society Library in Philadelphia appears to have a larger collection than either of the in-state libraries.

For the District of Columbia, the best local resources are, of course, the Library of Congress and the Public Library of the District of Columbia.

The De Renne Georgia Library in Athens is the best in-state source for almanacs published in Georgia. Emory University in Atlanta and the Georgia Historical Society in Savannah as well as the Atlanta Public Library have some holdings.

For Illinois, the Newberry Library and the Chicago Historical Society in Chicago and the Illinois Historical Library in Springfield provide the best local sources for almanac research.

For Indiana, consult the Indiana Historical Society and the Indiana State Library in Indianapolis, as well as Earlham College in Richmond and Indiana University in Bloomington. The Ohio State Historical Society in Columbus, Ohio, also has several Indiana almanacs.

The Kentucky Historical Society in Frankfort, the Louisville Free Public Library, the Lexington Public Library, and the University of Kentucky Library in Lexington have holdings of almanacs published in Kentucky, as do the Indiana Historical Society and the Washington State Historical Society.

Of the almanacs published in Louisiana, only a few are listed by Drake as being

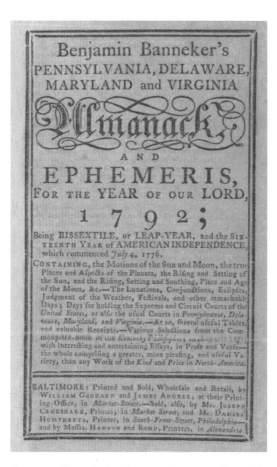

Benjamin Banneker's Almanac. Courtesy of the Library of Congress

held in Louisiana libraries. The Howard-Tilton Memorial Library at Tulane University in New Orleans has all of them.

For Maine, the important in-state sources include the Maine Historical Society and Longfellow House in Portland as well as the Bowdoin College Library in Brunswick and the Bangor Public Library.

For Maryland there are two important local libraries: the Enoch Pratt Library and the Maryland Historical Society, both in Baltimore.

Massachusetts, along with Pennsylvania and New York, was one of the top three almanac-producing states. There are many libraries with important holdings of almanacs published in Massachusetts. Probably the most important in-state library for Massachusetts is the American Antiquarian Society Library in Worcester, but the Massachusetts Historical Society and the Boston Public Library in Boston and Harvard University in Cambridge rival it as far as in-state almanacs are concerned. In addition, both the New York and Pennsylvania historical societies have significant holdings of Massachusetts almanacs, and many libraries throughout the state have some almanacs. The *(Old) Farmer's Almanack* was originally published in Massachusetts and appears to be the most widely collected of all American almanacs. Drake lists eighty libraries in twenty-four states holding copies of the 1850 edition of this Boston almanac.

Few almanacs were published in Michigan. Consult the Burton Historical Collection and the Detroit Public Library in Detroit as well as the Michigan State Library in Lansing. Even fewer were published in Minnesota, and there are no significant in-state holdings of Minnesota almanacs. The only significant in-state holdings of Mississippi almanacs are at the State Department of Archives and History in Jackson. For Missouri, the most significant holdings are at the Missouri Historical Society in St. Louis, but the Missouri State Historical Society in Columbia and the Mercantile Library Association in St. Louis are worth consulting.

For New Hampshire, whose presses produced about 500 almanacs, the most important in-state library is that of the New Hampshire Historical Society in Concord. The State Library in Concord and the Dartmouth College Library are also important.

New Jersey has two important libraries of almanac holdings: Rutgers University in New Brunswick and the New Jersey Historical Society in Newark.

New York produced far more almanacs than any other state. Several libraries hold significant numbers of New York almanacs, including the New York Public Library, the New York Historical Society, the Long Island Historical Society, and the Pierpont Morgan Library, all of New York City, and the New York State Library in Buffalo. In addition to the national collections, such out-of-state libraries as the John Carter Brown Library in Providence, Rhode Island, the Pennsylvania Historical Society, the American Philosophical Society, and the Rosenbach Foundation of Philadelphia, and the Huntington Library have collections that are significant.

In North Carolina, the University of North Carolina at Chapel Hill and Duke University at Durham have the two largest collections. The North Carolina Historical Commission and the State Library in Raleigh have smaller collections.

Several Ohio libraries have significant holdings of Ohio almanacs. They are the Ohio State Library in Columbus, the Public Library of Cincinnati and Hamilton County, the Historical and Philosophical Society of Ohio, which is also in Cincinnati, the Western Reserve Historical Society in Cleveland, the Dayton Public Library, and Marietta College.

Few almanacs were published in Oregon. The Oregon Historical Society in Portland has most of them. The Library Association of Portland and the University of Oregon in Eugene also have holdings.

Pennsylvania is the third largest almanac-producing state. The Historical Society of Pennsylvania and the American Philosophical Society, both in Philadelphia, have large holdings of Pennsylvania almanacs. Each has some unique copies, as does the Library Company of Philadelphia. The Rosenbach Foundation of Philadelphia has several almanacs, at least one of which is unique, as do the New York Historical Society and the John Carter Brown Library.

The Rhode Island Historical Society has large holdings of Rhode Island almanacs as does the John Carter Brown Library. Both are in Providence. For South Carolina, the most significant in-state holdings are in the Charleston Library and the South Carolina Historical Society. Both are located in Charleston. The South Carolina State Library in Columbia also has some almanacs.

The Tennessee State Library in Nashville has succeeded in collecting most of the almanacs published in that state. All but one of the few almanacs published in Utah are held by the Library of the Church of Jesus Christ of Latter-day Saints in Salt Lake City. In-state libraries that have collected Vermont almanacs include the Vermont State Library and the Vermont Historical Society in Montpelier and the University of Vermont in Burlington.

Apart from the five national collections already listed and the in-state collections, some libraries have significant national or regional holdings, although they are not comparable to those of the AAS or the Library of Congress. Such historical societies as the Western Reserve, the Washington State, the Massachusetts, and the Pennsylvania have collected actively both inside and outside their states. The Harvard, Yale, Indiana, Brown, and Texas university libraries have also accumulated large holdings of out-of-state almanacs, as have the American Philosophical Society and the Huntington Library.

Any scholar interested in examining American almanacs should realize how very spread out they are. To be sure, they are concentrated in the Northeast, from Washington, D.C., to Boston, but many unique copies can be found in California and throughout the state libraries. A scholar should probably begin by consulting a copy of Drake's bibliography, from which much of the preceding information has been taken, deciding which almanacs he or she needs to examine, and planning a reasonable travel schedule. He or she should also bear in mind that many U.S. libraries have several thousand copies of almanacs published before 1801 available on microcard.

HISTORY AND CRITICISM

Like many other articles of popular culture, almanacs have too often been considered beneath the efforts of scholarship. Aside from biographers of Franklin, few scholars gave much attention to American almanacs until George Lyman Kittredge wrote *The Old Farmer and His Almanack* and Clarence Brigham began his efforts to build up the AAS collection of almanacs.

The Old Farmer and His Almanack deals with the almanacs of Robert B. Thomas. Kittredge brilliantly discusses the divisions of Thomas' almanac, including the Farmer's Calendar, the letters to the editor, the sayings, and the anecdotes. Kittredge's best chapters deal with Thomas' folk wisdom, the characters he created for the Farmer's Calendar, and the letters. Perhaps the most significant aspect of Kittredge's book, however, was that it gave a certain respectability to the study of almanacs. If the great scholar of Shakespeare and early British literature considered almanacs important enough to devote an entire book to one almanac, then perhaps other almanacs deserved a closer look.

Samuel Briggs' *The Essays, Humor and Poems of Nathaniel Ames, Father and Son, of Dedham, Massachusetts from Their Almanacks, 1726–1775* reprinted much of the Ames almanacs, omitting the calendars. It also contains several essays by Briggs: "Almanacks," "The Rise of the Almanack in America," "The Ames Family, and the Town of Dedham," "The Old Tavern," "Notes on Each Almanack." Of the essays, "The Rise of the Almanack in America" is one of the most interesting.

Richard M. Dorson edited *Davy Crockett: American Comic Legend*, which contains material on the Crockett almanacs. Joseph Leach's *The Typical Texan: Biography of an American Myth* is important as a scholarly book on a subject other than almanacs that uses almanacs as an important source of material.

Milton Drake's *Almanacs of the United States* has already been fully discussed under the Reference Works section. It is an essential book for anyone who wants to study American almanacs.

Robb Sagendorph's *America and Her Almanacs: Wit, Wisdom and Weather* is less a scholarly book than an exercise in nostalgia. At the time he wrote *America and Her Almanacs*, Sagendorph had been editor of the *Old Farmer's Almanac* for thirty-one years. He claims, with some accuracy, that "reading the early almanacs is the only way to see into the heart of Colonial America." It may not be the only way, but it is an excellent way, and Sagendorph's book provides a great deal of almanac material to read and more than 200 woodcuts reproduced from the almanacs. One chapter is devoted to *Poor Richard*.

In 1970 Henry Wheeler Shaw's *Josh Billings' Farmers' Allminax* was reprinted in a volume called *Old Probability: Perhaps Rain—Perhaps Not. Old Probability* is nothing more than a reprint of the Josh Billings' almanacs.

Marion Barber Stowell's *Early American Almanacs: The Colonial Weekday Bible* may be the most important almanac book since Drake's bibliography. *Early American Almanacs* is one of only a few books that attempt to deal with the entire spectrum of American almanacs for a specific period. Stowell studied some 450 almanacs of the seventeenth and eighteenth centuries. She described many of the almanac makers and provided many examples from the almanacs. It is possible that she could have been more successful in her immense task if there had been a larger body of competent scholarship preceding her. She does succeed in showing the importance of almanacs to early America and in creating the first systematic, broadly based study of early American almanacs that is not primarily bibliographical.

Clarence Brigham wrote two articles for the *Proceedings of the American Antiquarian Society*, "An Account of American Almanacs and Their Value for Historical Study" and "Report of the Librarian," which contains a summary of the AAS collection of American almanacs. Both articles helped encourage the use of almanacs as documentary sources. The AAS had already begun using its *Proceedings* to encourage almanac study. As early as 1907 Victor Hugo Paltsits had published "The Almanacs of Roger Sherman, 1750–1761," and in 1914 George Emery Littlefield published "Notes on the Calendar and the Almanac" in the *Proceedings*.

Bernard S. Capp's *English Almanacs, 1500–1800: Astrology and the Popular Press* deals entirely with almanacs published in Britain. It serves, however, to provide a general view of the background out of which American almanacs grew.

Robert K. Dodge's *Early American Almanac Humor* is a selection of humorous items drawn from the almanacs of the early American republic (1776–1800). Dodge claims to have found early examples of Yankee trickster stories, of American tall tales, and of other stories that entered the mainstream of American humor. Dodge also completed two books about almanacs published by Greenwood Press.

Both Tanis Thorne and Robert Dodge have published articles making the case for the study of almanacs. Thorne's "The Almanacs of the San Francisco Bay Region, 1850–1861: A Neglected Historical Source" appeared in 1978. Dodge's "Access to Popular Culture: Early American Almanacs" was published in 1979.

A number of articles have dealt with the almanacs of one publisher or of one author. Alfred B. Page covered the almanacs of John Tulley from 1687 to 1702, and Frank H. Severance published "The Story of Phinney's Western Almanack, with Notes on Other Calendars and Weather Forecasters of Buffalo." Jasper Marsh wrote "Amos Pope and His Almanacs," and Arthur D. Graeff published a series of articles in volumes 5 and 6 (1938 and 1939) of the *American-German Review*. The articles, seldom more than two pages long, are entitled "Pennsylvania German Almanacs." F. G. Woodward published "An Early Tennessee Almanac and Its Maker: Hill's Almanac 1825–1862," and Robert T. Sidwell wrote "An Odd Fish: Samuel Keimer and a Footnote to American Educational History." Keimer was a publisher of an almanac in Philadelphia, but Sidwell deals with him primarily as an educator.

In 1968 two articles were published dealing with John Henton Carter, the author of *Commodore Rollingpin's Almanac*. John T. Flanagan's "John Henton Carter, Alias 'Commodore Rollingpin'" and James T. Swift's "From Pantry to Pen: The Saga of Commodore Rollingpin" both concentrate on the man as well as his work.

Another article that deals with comic almanacs is David Kesterson's "Josh Billings 'Defolks' Rural America," in which Kesterson compares Billings' parody with the farmer's almanac tradition that inspired it. Nancy Merrill's "Henry Ranlet: Exeter Printer" deals with an important almanac maker and printer of the early republic.

Also of interest are articles that use almanacs as source material. Chester E. Eisinger's "The Farmer in the Eighteenth Century Almanac" uses almanacs to determine the strength of the agrarian view of life in eighteenth century America. Elsie H. and Curtis Booker's "Patent Medicines before the Wiley Act of 1906" uses almanac advertising as a source. Robert Dodge's "Didactic Humor in the Almanacs of Early America," "The Irish Comic Stereotype in the Almanacs of the Early Republic," and his two notes and short article on Americanisms in *American Speech* also use almanacs as sources. Giles E. Gobetz's "Slovenian Ethnic Studies" and Jon Stanley Wenrick's "Indians in Almanacs, 1783–1815" find almanacs to be sources for ethnic studies.

Marion Barber Stowell's excellent work "The Influence of Nathaniel Ames on the Literary Taste of His Time" serves as a model of the kind of article for which almanacs can serve as sources. Three other important works include Maxine Moore's *That Lonely Game: Melville, Mardi, and the Almanac*, Allan R. Raymond's "To Reach Men's Minds: Almanacs and the American Revolution, 1760–1777," and Rose Lockwood's "The Scientific Revolution in Seventeenth-Century New-England," which sees the almanacs as one of the battlegrounds between the Puritans' belief in a finite and largely Ptolemaic universe and the astronomers' scientific belief in an infinite Copernican universe. Dick Goddard's "Six Inches of Partly Cloudy" focuses on methods of predicting the weather before the development of meteorology.

NOTES

1. Samuel Briggs, *The Essays, Humor and Poems of Nathaniel Ames, Father and Son, of Dedham, Massachusetts from Their Almanacks, 1726–1775* (Detroit: Singing Tree Press, 1969), 372.

2. "A Song upon Bundling," *Beers's Almanac for 1793* (Hartford, Conn.: Hudson and Goodwin, 1792), 26–27.

3. Milton Drake, *Almanacs of the United States* (New York: Scarecrow Press, 1962), 1; xiii.

4. Drake, p. x.

5. Ralph R. Shaw and Richard H. Shoemaker, *American Bibliography: A Preliminary Checklist for 1801* (New York: Scarecrow Press, 1958), iii.

6. Drake, 1; xv.

7. Drake, 1; xv.

BIBLIOGRAPHY

Booker, Elsie H., and Curtis Booker. "Patent Medicines before the Wiley Act of 1906." *North Carolina Folklore* 18 (November 1970), 130–42.

Briggs, Samuel. *The Essays, Humor and Poems of Nathaniel Ames, Father and Son, of Dedham, Massachusetts from Their Almanacks, 1726–1775.* Cleveland: Western Reserve Press, 1891. Reprint. Detroit: Singing Tree Press, 1969.

Brigham, Clarence. "An Account of American Almanacs and Their Value for Historical Study." *Proceedings of the American Antiquarian Society*, n.s. 34 (October 1925), 3–28.

———. "Report of the Librarian." *Proceedings of the American Antiquarian Society*, n.s. 35 (October 1926), 190–218.

Bristol, Roger P. *Supplement to Charles Evans' American Bibliography.* Charlottesville: University Press of Virginia, 1970.

Capp, Bernard S. *English Almanacs, 1500–1800: Astrology and the Popular Press.* Ithaca, NY: Cornell University Press, 1979.

Danforth, Samuel. *An Almanack for the Year of Our Lord 1646. . . .* Cambridge, Mass.: Printed by Stephen Daye, 1646.

Dodge, Robert. "Access to Popular Culture: Early American Almanacs." *Kentucky Folklore Record* 25 (January–June 1979), 11–15.

———. "Damn Yankee." *American Speech*, 57 (Fall 1982), 240.

———. "Didactic Humor in the Almanacs of Early America." *Journal of Popular Culture*, 5 (Winter 1971), 592–605.

———. *Early American Almanac Humor.* Bowling Green, Ohio: Bowling Green University Popular Press, 1987.

———. "Four Americanisms Found in Early Almanacs." *American Speech*, 60 (Fall 1985), 270–71.

———. "The Irish Comic Stereotype in the Almanacs of the Early Republic." *Eire-Ireland*, 19 (Fall 1984), 111–20.

———. *A Tale Type and Motif Index of Early U.S. Almanacs.* Westport, CT: Greenwood Press, 1991.

———. *A Topical Index of Early U.S. Almanacs, 1776–1800.* Westport, CT: Greenwood Press, 1997.

———. "Twistical." *American Speech*, 56 (Fall 1981), 218.

Dorson, Richard M. *Davy Crockett: American Comic Legend.* New York: Spiral Editions, 1939.

Drake, Milton. *Almanacs of the United States.* 2 vols. New York: Scarecrow Press, 1962.

Eisinger, Chester E. "The Farmer in the Eighteenth Century Almanac." *Agricultural History*, 28 (July 1954), 107–12.

Evans, Charles. *American Bibliography*. 14 vols. Worcester, Mass.: American Antiquarian Society, 1903–1955. Reprint. New York: Peter Smith, 1941–1967.

Flanagan, John T. "John Henton Carter, Alias 'Commodore Rollingpin.' " *Missouri Historical Review*, 63 (October 1968), 38–64.

Gobetz, Giles E. "Slovenian Ethnic Studies." *Journal of Ethnic Studies*, 2 (Winter 1975), 99–103.

Goddard, Dick. "Six Inches of Partly Cloudy." *Inland Seas*, 41 (Winter 1985), 244–54.

Graeff, Arthur D. "Pennsylvania German Almanacs." *American-German Review*, 5 (April–May 1939), 4–7, 36; 5 (June–July 1939), 30–33, 37–38; 5 (August–September 1939), 24–29; 6 (October–November 1939), 10–12, 40; 6 (December 1939–January 1940), 12–19; 6 (April–May 1940), 10–13, 37; 6 (June–July 1940), 9–12; 6 (August–September 1940), 10–14.

Kesterson, David. "Josh Billings 'Defolks' Rural America." *Tennessee Folklore Society Bulletin*, 41 (1975), 57–64.

Kittredge, George Lyman. *The Old Farmer and His Almanack*. Cambridge: Harvard University Press, 1920. Reprint. New York: Benjamin Blom, 1967.

Leach, Joseph. *The Typical Texan: Biography of an American Myth*. Dallas: Southern Methodist University Press, 1952.

Leypoldt, F., Lynds E. Jones, and R. R. Bowker. *The American Catalogue*. New York: Bowker, 1880–1911. Reprint. New York: Peter Smith, 1941.

Littlefield, George Emery. "Notes on the Calendar and the Almanac." *Proceedings of the American Antiquarian Society*, n.s. 24 (October 1914), 11–64.

Lockwood, Rose. "The Scientific Revolution in Seventeenth-Century New-England." *New England Quarterly*, 53 (Spring 1980), 76–95.

Marsh, Jasper. "Amos Pope and His Almanacs." *Danvers Historical Society, Historical Collections*, 10 (1922), 93–114.

McDowell, Marion Barber (now Marion Barber Stowell). "Early American Almanacs: The History of a Neglected Literary Genre." Ph.D. diss., Florida State University, 1974.

Merrill, Nancy. "Henry Ranlet: Exeter Printer, 1762–1807." *History of New Hampshire*, 37 (Winter 1982), 250–82.

Moore, Maxine. *That Lonely Game: Melville, Mardi, and the Almanac*. Columbia: University of Missouri Press, 1975.

Page, Alfred B. "The Almanacs of John Tulley: 1687–1702." *Publications of the Colonial Society of Massachusetts*, 13 (July 1912), 207–23.

Paltsits, Victor Hugo. "The Almanacs of Roger Sherman, 1750–1761." *Proceedings of the American Antiquarian Society*, n.s. 18 (April 1907), 213–58.

Raymond, Allan R. "To Reach Men's Minds: Almanacs and the American Revolution, 1760–1777." *New England Quarterly*, 51 (Fall 1978), 370–95.

Rowland, Howard S., and Beatrice Rowland. *The Nurses' Almanac*. Germantown, Md.: Aspen Systems, 1978.

Sagendorph, Robb. *America and Her Almanacs: Wit, Wisdom and Weather*. Boston: Yankee-Little, Brown, 1970.

Severance, Frank H. "The Story of Phinney's Western Almanack, with Notes on

Other Calendars and Weather Forecasters of Buffalo." *Buffalo Historical Society Publications*, 24 (December 1920), 343–58.

Shaw, Henry Wheeler. *Old Probability: Perhaps Rain—Perhaps Not*. New York: G. W. Carleton, 1876. Reprint. Upper Saddle River, N.J.: Literature House/Gregg Press, 1970.

Shaw, Ralph R., and Richard H. Shoemaker. *American Bibliography: A Preliminary Checklist for 1801–1819*. 20 vols. New York: Scarecrow Press, 1958–64.

Shipton, Clifford K. *Early American Imprints, 1639–1800*. Worcester, Mass.: American Antiquarian Society, 1956–1964.

———. *Early American Imprints, 1639–1800. Supplement*. Worcester, Mass.: American Antiquarian Society, 1966–68.

Shoemaker, Richard, et al. *A Checklist of American Imprints, 1820–1833*, yearly. Metuchen, N.J.: Scarecrow Press, 1964–   .

Sidwell, Robert T. "An Odd Fish: Samuel Keimer and a Footnote to American Educational History." *History of Education Quarterly*, 6 (Spring 1966), 16–30.

The Standard Education Almanac. Los Angeles: Academic Media, 1968–   .

Stowell, Marion Barber. *Early American Almanacs: The Colonial Weekday Bible*. New York: Burt Franklin, 1977.

———. "The Influence of Nathaniel Ames on the Literary Taste of His Time." *Early American Literature*, 18 (Summer 1983), 127–45.

Superintendent of Documents. *The Catalogue of Public Documents*. Washington, D.C.: Government Printing Office, 1896–1941. Reprint. New York: Johnson Reprint/Kraus Reprint, 1963.

Swift, James T. "From Pantry to Pen: The Saga of Commodore Rolling-pin." *Missouri Historical Bulletin*, 24 (January 1968), 113–21.

Throne, Tanis. "The Almanacs of the San Francisco Bay Region, 1850–1861: A Neglected Historical Source." *Journal of the West*, 17 (Summer 1978), 36–45.

Wallechinsky, David, and Irving Wallace. *The People's Almanac*. Garden City, N.Y.: Doubleday, 1975.

Wenrick, Jon Stanley. "For Education and Entertainment—Almanacs in the Early American Republic, 1783–1815." Ph.D. diss., Claremont Graduate School, 1974.

———. "Indians in Almanacs, 1783–1815." *Indian Historian*, 8 (Winter 1977), 36–42.

Woodward, F. G. "An Early Tennessee Almanac and Its Maker: Hill's Almanac 1825–1862." *Tennessee Folklore Society Bulletin*, 18 (March 1952), 9–14.

The World Almanac and Book of Facts. New York: Press Publishing (1868–1923), New York World (1924–1931), New York World-Telegram (1932–1966), and Newspaper Enterprise Association (1967–   ).

AMUSEMENT PARKS AND FAIRS

Judith A. Adams-Volpe

Nineteenth-century America engendered a form of popular entertainment that diverged from other developing amusements such as the theater and the circus due to its essential participatory nature. Amusement parks and fairs demand full ambulatory engagement by all of their "audiences." In fact, the audience becomes an integral part of the performance experience. As in the European tradition, the earliest American fairs were market fairs with a preponderance of agricultural goods. The American amusement park evolved from the market fair tradition and from late nineteenth-century pleasure parks at the end of trolley lines. Its early development as raucous midways in urban settings, where the operating force was chaos and all social groups mingled, was transformed in the last quarter of the twentieth century into enclosed, precisely planned and engineered theme parks where protection is the organizing principle and technology creates a temporal paradise.

Social, economic, and cultural factors that have shaped the American experience also influenced the emergence and forms of amusement parks and fairs for more than a century. The essential American dream of a perfect world, the waves of immigrants, the rise of mechanization and corporate culture, a growing need for escapism, the expansion of education, and the harnessing of nature by technology-driven innovation are all mirrored in our fair and amusement park venues, as they evolved from agricultural market displays and sylvan parks, to "pyrotechnic insanitariums," to Disney's utopian "World."

HISTORICAL OUTLINE

Amusement Parks

From the early carousel and roller-coaster manufacturers and the pleasure parks of the mid-nineteenth century, the American amusement park industry reached a

Lakeside Amusement Park, Denver, Colorado, 1909. Courtesy of the Denver Public Library

zenith of around 2,000 amusement parks in 1920, then declined precipitously to only approximately 250 parks by 1940. Demographics and economic and social conditions coincided with the creation of Disneyland Park in 1955 to spark a resurgence and restructuring in the form of the theme park. The business grew to a $6 billion annual enterprise in the late 1990s.

Integral elements of the American amusement park germinated from medieval trade fairs in Europe, especially in England. Bartholomew Fair in London, first held in the twelfth century, combined trade and commerce with the stimulation of uninhibited behavior. Wares such as cloth, leather, metalware, and livestock were exhibited and bartered, but by the Elizabethan period entertainment elements dominated. Pleasure-seekers enjoyed jugglers, puppet shows, freaks, dancers, actors, and plenty of liquid spirits. A 1729 poem by George Alexander Steven depicts the revelry:

> The tap house guests roaring and the mouth pieces bawling;
> Pimps, paunbrokers, strollers, fat landladies, sailors,
> Bawds, bailies, jilts, jockeys, thieves, tumblers, and tailors;
> Here's Punch's whole play of the Gunpowder Plot,
> Wild beasts all alive, and peas-pudding all hot. . . .
> (quoted in Samuel McKechnie. *Popular Entertainments through the Ages*, p. 45)

By the middle of the nineteenth century, the fair was overrun by the criminal element and unruly mobs. The last Bartholomew Fair was held in 1855. The attraction of amusement enterprises to unsavory and criminal elements would persist as a formative factor in the development of the industry.

The chaotic, dangerous, and often transitory fairs were countered by the creation of "pleasure gardens," beginning as spas or appendages to taverns or inns and becoming sylvan preserves in the urban landscape. London's Vauxhall Gardens (est. 1661) and Ranelagh Gardens (est. 1742) were the paramount examples of these pleasure resorts. Vauxhall's walks, arbors, roses, cherries, and nightingales moved many contemporary observers to describe it in Edenic terms. Eighteenth-century literary figures, such as Swift, Walpole, Johnson, Boswell, Fielding, and Burney, immortalized its gardens, spectacular illuminations, and entertainments. Thousands of glimmering lamps, an exotic central entertainment structure, and the opportunity of contact with the titled class heightened the sense of wonder. Ranelagh Gardens boasted an exquisite rotunda, 555 feet in circumference, built by William Jones, architect to the East India Company. Crystal chandeliers lit the gilded interior, and a painted rainbow encircled the ceiling. The upper classes were eager to pay to promenade their fine fashions in this pleasure dome. Ranelagh's fame is based on its entertainments, which included eight-year-old Wolfgang Amadeus Mozart and George Frederic Handel, as well as a simulated volcano exhibition complete with flames and "lava." Like the fairs, Vauxhall was eventually plagued by rowdies, thieves, and hooligans who terrorized people on the grounds. Despite adding elaborate fireworks displays, balloon ascents, and dramatic reenactments of historical events, such as the Battle of Waterloo, Vauxhall lost its appeal and closed in 1859. Ranelagh's tenure was much shorter, closing in 1803.

One more major influence on the development of amusement parks was the Prater park in Vienna. Joseph II opened his former hunting grounds as a park for the Viennese public in 1766. Extensive landscaping joined entertainment structures, refreshments, puppet shows, and primitive rides such as swings and hand-driven carousels. With his democratic desires, Joseph envisioned the Prater as an area where all classes would mingle. When Franz von Gerstner built the first railroad in Austria in 1823, he placed his experimental railroad in the Prater so that the public could experience it as a ride attraction, thus using the amusement setting to acclimate the public to a new, initially fearsome technology.

Mechanized thrill machines are central components that transformed sylvan pleasure gardens into amusement parks. The most enduring of the mechanical rides, the carousel and the roller coaster, hold a powerful grasp on the human psyche, achieving the status of icons of fun, thrills, and escape. The carousel originates in twelfth-century war games, and the French added a ring-spearing tournament. Servants or animals served as the energy source to turn a round platform with wooden horses ridden by young noblemen in training. In 1867 Gustav A. Dentzel redesigned his Philadelphia cabinetmaking shop to accommodate the manufacture of carousels operated by steam engine. Alan Herschell and his North Tonawanda, New York, firm, Armitage-Herschell Co., developed a carousel that rotated on a track instead of a central post, and he added an organ. His merry-go-rounds were portable, facilitating travel to small villages beyond the cities. By 1891, Herschell was manufacturing a carousel per day. The later Herschell-Spillman Co. was the largest manufacturer of carousels in America. Herschell carousels are preserved at the Herschell Carrousel Factory Museum in North Tonawanda and at the Henry Ford Museum in Dearborn, Michigan. Another major firm was the Philadelphia Toboggan Company, established in 1903 by Henry Auchy and Chester Albright. For twenty-five years the company built exquisitely decorated carousels for major amusement parks such as Elitch Gardens, Euclid Beach, Riverview Park, and Luna Park at Coney Island. William Mangels, author of *The Outdoor Amusement Industry from Earliest Times to the Present*, and a carousel manufacturer, patented the device that imparted a smooth, galloping motion to the horses. The allure of the carousel results from its elegant, prancing steeds, its mirrors, lights, gilt, and carvings, and its nostalgic organ music. It creates an atmosphere of romance, relaxation, and elegance in the midst of a frenetic amusement environment.

Adding to the noise, chaos, and intense physical sensations of the traditional amusement park is the roller coaster. Perhaps originating in seventy-foot-high sledding inclines popular in seventeenth-century Russia, the first wheeled coaster was built in 1804 in Paris. Consisting of an artificial hill constructed of timber over which small-wheeled carriages ran on a track, the speed caused many accidents. In 1817 an improved coaster was constructed in the Parisian Jardin Beaujon. It included a guardrail and was circular so that cars would return to the starting point. Despite numerous patents, no further advances are evident until Richard Knudsen of Brooklyn patented a coaster called an "inclined-plane railway." The device consisted of two parallel tracks with undulating hills on which coaster cars holding four passengers each ran by gravity. At the end, a lift mechanism raised the cars back to the higher level and into place for another ride. Although Knudsen never articulated his plans into an operating coaster, La Marcus Adna Thompson used Knudsen's system to build the first coaster at Coney Island in 1884. His Switchback Railway cars held ten passengers each, and at a nickel a ride, his receipts exceeded $600 a day. By 1888, he had built nearly fifty coasters in the United States and Europe. Thompson's invention of automatic cable grips, allowing emergency stops, and Philip Hinckle's development of a chain system to convey cars up long initial inclines sparked the emergence of the giant thrill machine coasters that dominate today's parks as they combine the appearance of danger with actual safety.

John A. Miller is generally considered to be the father of the modern roller coaster and holds over 100 patents. He started the trend to higher, steeper, and more terrifying speeds in the coasters that he built beginning in the early 1900s. The Roaring Twenties became the golden age of the roller coaster. The scream machines built in this decade marvelously reflected the reckless excitement and sensual thrill-seeking of the epoch. Vernon Keenan and Harry Baker built the famous "Cyclone" at Coney Island in 1927. Harry Traver and Frederick Church built "extreme machines," "the Bobs" at Riverview Park in Chicago, and the "Aero-Coaster" in Playland at Rye Beach, New York. The Great Depression and World War II brought a sudden end to these massive "woodie" coasters and to the traditional amusement park, as well. A rebirth "coaster boom" began in 1972 with John Allen's "Racer" at the King's Island theme park in Cincinnati. New technologies of computers, tubular steel, and plastics, joined with multidisciplinary teams of engineers, were embraced by developers of the megacoaster terror rides of the 1980s and 1990s, such as the "Magnum XL 200" at Cedar Point in San-

Coney Island, New York, 1910. Courtesy of the Library of Congress

dusky, Ohio. The roller coaster is a vigorous reflection of the American spirit, dreams driven by speed and a focus on the future, and our demand for unfettered release from all constraints.

Considered by many historians to be the greatest of all international expositions, the World's Columbian Exposition of 1893 in Chicago introduced most of the essential elements of American amusement parks from Coney Island to Walt Disney World. This plaster actualization of a prophetic New Jerusalem rising from the swamplands at the edge of the frontier celebrated the 400th anniversary of Columbus' discovery of the New World. The "White City" of ornate neoclassical alabaster buildings, golden statuary, and reflecting canals signaled America's coming-of-age. The architecture imitated the classicism and culture of Europe, yet the new technologies of steam, steel construction, and electricity demonstrated the power, utility, magnificence, and service potential of America's burgeoning industrial drive. The World's Columbian Exposition gave us the midway and the Ferris wheel, a heavenly dream world within an enclosed site, the harnessing of technologies for the purposes of fun and spectacle, and a sectored environment carefully merging entertainment, landscape architecture, engineering, and education. It is significant that Walt Disney's father worked as a construction laborer at the exposition, although before the amusement tycoon's birth.

Daniel Burnham and Frederick Law Olmsted were responsible for the architectural style and the landscape design of the exposition. The planning effort was unprecedented in its scope, detail, and mass publicity. It was designed to show America that its collective aspirations were "progressive," that its stature was nearing preeminence, and that a New Jerusalem was within its grasp. The gigantic Manufactures and Liberal Arts Building was the largest building built to date, with forty-four acres of floor space, and the steel arched-truss frame roof was considered the greatest engineering feat on the grounds. The Westinghouse Company won the lighting contract, which resulted in the nationwide use of alternating current, as opposed to Thomas Edison's direct current. The exposition's spectacular illumination, use of electricity to power the elevated trains, moving sidewalk, and nearly everything else proved this mysterious form of energy to be safe, a servant rather than a master to humans, and a source of marvelous pleasure.

As a venture to generate revenues at the exposition, the planners established a separate amusement and entertainment strip nearly a mile long, which became known as the Midway Plaisance. Entrepreneur Sol Bloom took charge of the midway and created a hodgepodge of reproductions of exotic villages from around the world. Even the midway cleverly mirrored the "educational" aspirations of the planners of the exposition. Streets of Cairo commingled with Blarney Castle, Bedouin tents, a Moorish café, Old Vienna, an African Dahomey village, and a Javanese South Sea village. Three hundred natives performed as exhibits, which emphasized the quite evident racial and ethnic prejudice permeating the exposition. At the far end of America's first midway was the incomparable Ferris wheel.

Young George Washington Gale Ferris, accepting Burnham's challenge to create something "novel" and "daring" for the exposition, comparable to Paris' Eiffel Tower, designed a stupendous, 264-foot-high steel wheel (three times larger than the largest wheel in history to date). Actually, the structure was two concentric wheels from which thirty-six pendulum cars hung, each with a capacity of sixty passengers. It represented the first large-scale harnessing of technology solely for the purpose of fun. The axle was the largest single piece of forged steel manufactured to date, weighing over forty-five tons. Powered by two 1,000-horsepower engines, the mammoth ride could carry 2,160 riders. Part of its appeal was the impression of danger, but the elevation of the ride gave fairgoers an unprecedented bird's-eye view of the entire exposition and environs. The Ferris wheel had a perfect safety record with its air brakes and its ability to absorb both winds up to 100 miles per hour and lightning bolts. Ferris' giant wheel is considered to be responsible for the exposition's thin profit margin. The construction cost of $350,000 was recovered within weeks; 1,453,611 customers rode it for the exorbitant charge of fifty cents, and the gross take was $726,805.50. After 1893 Ferris himself and his wheel did not fare well. Refusing to sell the wheel to interested amusement entrepreneurs, his own small park in Chicago was not successful, and he died in depression and bankruptcy in 1896. The original Ferris wheel entertained fairgoers at the Louisiana Purchase Exposition in St. Louis in 1904, but it was finally dynamited in 1906. The Ferris wheel at the Prater park in Vienna is the only surviving massive wheel of this kind with passenger cabs of nearly railroad-car size.

Product firsts at the Columbian Exposition include the electric-powered elevated train (the main transportation medium for the fair and harbinger of Chicago's "El" system and Disney's monorail), a moving sidewalk (precursor of the moving walkways that we see in airports and other places where efficient movement of crowds is necessary), elevators, Cracker Jacks, Aunt Jemima, the zipper, and mass marketing. Underlying its beauty and magnificence, the exposition highlighted the products of American industry. All of the goods on display were presented as manifestations of "progress" and of a prosperous, glorious future.

The exposition perfectly integrated three concepts: unity, magnitude, and illusion, the formative factors in all of the coming century's amusement ventures. Historian Alan Trachtenberg sums up the exposition's impact: "For a summer's moment, White City had seemed the fruition of a nation, a culture, a whole society: the celestial city of man set upon a hill for all the world to behold" (1982). Our fantasy amusement retreats in the succeeding century, no matter how futurist or fantastic or what technologies create our wonders, are all essentially offspring of Chicago's glorious White City.

During the final decade of the nineteenth century, electric trolley lines were developed in most larger American cities. Street railway owners, recognizing an ingenious way to increase ridership in the slower summer months, built pleasure parks at the end of the lines. Beginning as shady picnic groves, often near water, the parks quickly added and expanded with mechanical amusements, dance halls, sports fields, boat rides, restaurants, and more. The parks instantly became financial bonanzas for the transit companies. By the early 1900s every major city boasted one or more trolley parks: Boston's Revere Beach, Cleveland's Euclid Beach, Palisades Park near New York City, Chicago's Cheltenham Beach, Denver's Manhattan Beach, Pittsburgh's Kennywood Park, St. Louis' Forest Park Highlands, the Chutes in San Francisco, and the premier Willow Grove Park near Philadelphia.

The development and form of all of these parks, however, were essentially influenced by the most famous park of the period, Coney Island, which in its beginnings was the terminus of a horse-drawn streetcar line from Brooklyn. By the

1870s steamboats carried visitors from Manhattan to Coney. But the development that turned Coney Island from a relatively sedate, if rather unsavory, seaside resort area into a "pyrotechnic insanitarium" was the completion of the Prospect Park & Coney Island Railroad in 1875. The railroad allowed Coney's clientele to explode from the thousands to the millions. The criminal element also discovered Coney Island with gamblers, con artists, gangsters, and prostitutes establishing themselves largely in the western portion of the area. Their activities were tolerated for a fee by "boss" John Y. McKane, who served as a one-man government holding the posts of police chief, town supervisor, head of the board of health, and even superintendent of Sunday schools. The flamboyant McKane, who influenced even presidential elections through ballot-box stuffing, finally was indicted for attacking state election poll watchers and was sent to Sing Sing in 1894. The departure of McKane and some extensive fires opened up the beach area for legitimate forms of entertainment.

The era of mass entertainment began in 1897, when George Cornelius Tilyou opened his Steeplechase Park. Visiting the World's Columbian Exposition on his honeymoon, Tilyou was entranced by the Ferris wheel and eagerly tried to purchase it, without success. Tilyou had also witnessed the success of early mechanical amusement devices such as LaMarcus Thompson's Switchback Railway and merry-go-rounds. He was influenced by Paul Boyton's modest Sea Lion Park established at Coney in 1895, the first enclosed amusement park with an admission fee. Tilyou recognized the value of creating an enclosed amusement enterprise that could keep out much of the rowdy criminal element with a "pay-one-price" entrance fee.

Tilyou's incredible success was based on his understanding of the needs of Coney's visitors. New York's burgeoning immigrant population needed opportunities for assimilation, relief from dingy, crowded living arrangements and work that was tedious and repetitive, and also a chance to escape the repressive sexual mores of the period. Every element of Steeplechase Park was designed to sweep away restraints and propel the crowds into extroverted, intense activity. Many of Coney's revelers were young, single, and seeking to mingle with others. Tilyou designed mechanical contrivances that threw young bodies into intimate, but innocent, contact or lifted long skirts to reveal shapely legs never glimpsed on a city street. Steeplechase, the "Funny Place," promised and delivered irresponsible and rather diabolical fun. The fifteen-acre park included the namesake Steeplechase mechanical horse-race ride, "blowholes" of compressed air that sent skirts flying, distortion mirrors, exotic architecture simulating European venues, and rides such as the "human roulette wheel," where motion threw bodies in all directions and control of one's limbs was lost. The patrons were definitely the show at Steeplechase Park as social proprieties were shattered, flesh was exposed, and strenuous physical activity led to a tremendous sense of release. Steeplechase made people "take the brakes off." Tilyou also engaged Frederic Thompson and Elmer "Skip" Dundy to permanently locate in Steeplechase their "Trip to the Moon," America's first illusion ride created for the Pan American Exposition in Buffalo in 1901. The lure of Tilyou's "sanitized sex," sanctioned by the public nature of his amusement park, was irresistible to turn-of-the-century New Yorkers, and its lure remained vigorous for decades. Steeplechase Park survived devastating fires, the Great Depression, two world wars, and radical cultural change. When Tilyou died in 1914, his son took over management of the park, and it remained in operation into the 1960s. Tilyou was an entertainment genius whose vision remains a preeminent formative factor in American amusement. As such, he can be considered to cast his shadow even on Walt Disney, who spectacularly augmented but essentially built on Tilyou's foundation of enclosure and exclusion, psychological insight of the desires of his clientele, and the merger of technology and fun.

In the summer of 1903, Frederic Thompson and Skip Dundy left Steeplechase and opened their own lavish, twenty-two-acre, million-dollar amusement center, Luna Park. Thompson, once an architecture student, abandoned all restraint and created a sumptuously ornamental dreamscape with swirling pinwheels and crescents, blazing spires and turrets, minarets, sculpted fantastic animals, and shows featuring strange peoples and lands, and, most impressive of all, everything was ablaze with 250,000 electric lights, the greatest concentration of electric power ever attempted. Thompson and Dundy appealed to desires for unrestrained extravagance, the wonder of the fantastic, and the vitality of ceaseless motion, illumination, and sound. Historian John Kasson, in his wonderful study of Coney Island, *Amusing the Million*, vividly describes Luna as "Super-Saracenic or Oriental Orgasmic." Thompson used the same plaster staff utilized to make the magnificent facades of the World's Columbian Exposition to produce marvelous curving structures and dynamic, exotic illusion. He also strove to re-create the midway, with an Eskimo village, canals of Venice, a Dutch windmill, and a Japanese garden. Illusion rides included his "Trip to the Moon" and "Twenty Thousand Leagues under the Sea."

Luna was the place where millions of city dwellers from drab tenements, dulled by the thrift, plainness, and drudgery of daily life and made tense by mechanized work, could indulge themselves in opulent splendor while being constantly bombarded by the bizarre and fantastic. Thompson, like Tilyou, actively sought to exclude the sordid or criminal element. He advertised Luna as "the place for your mother, your sister, and your sweetheart." He and Dundy added live entertainment shows limited to brief durations, including the repeated simulated burning of a four-story apartment building, re-creations of the Johnstown and Galveston floods, the eruption of Mt. Vesuvius, and the fall of Pompeii. These shows and the Thompson-Dundy illusion rides were the conceptual harbingers of virtual extravaganza rides, such as "Earthquake: The Big One" and "Jurassic Park" at Universal Studios.

In just its second year, 4 million visitors paid for the Luna experience, and attendance continued to climb for the rest of the first decade of the new century. In 1907 Dundy died, and Thompson no longer had his partner to curb his drinking tendencies. He died an alcoholic in 1919, and those who took over Luna Park failed to reinvest money for standard upkeep. Luna, built of flimsy staff (plaster and fiber), paint, wood, and light bulbs, quickly crumbled and lost its fiery glitter. Despite renovations in 1935 and 1941, Luna ended in a devastating fire in 1946.

Dreamland, Coney's most extravagant park in terms of costs to build and use of 1 million electric lights, is important for its failure. Built by William H. Reynolds in 1904, Dreamland was classic in style, nearly all white, and featured a quasi-religious show, "The Creation." Reynolds attempted to create a park with a veneer of culture. Cashier booths and many concessions were run by young girls in white college gowns and mortar boards. It did include an immense, extravagant ballroom. But the Coney Island crowd was not intrigued or impressed with cultural pretense. They wanted fun and chaos, not refinement. Dreamland did ultimately provide perhaps Coney's greatest spectacle when on May 27, 1911, a pot of tar in the park's "Hell's Gate" ride sparked a conflagration that engulfed most of Coney's entertainment strip, destroying Dreamland and many other attractions. On this night, Coney was truly a "pyrotechnic insanitarium" with crazed lions running in the streets with burning manes, animals screaming in cages where they burned to death, and flames leaping higher than any of Coney's towers. Of course, nearly the entire population of New York came out to the beach the next day to witness the ruins.

Coney Island's huge crowds mirrored the unprecedented population growth of New York City during Coney's heyday in the early decades of the twentieth century. From 1850 to 1940 the city's population grew from 700,000 to 7.5 million, largely the result of the great waves of immigrants. Coney's parks were also designed to appeal to the largest segment of the population, fifteen to thirty-year-olds. In contrast, by 1950, when Coney was clearly well in decline, the dominant population group had become those aged twenty-five to fifty-four years. Industrialization and organized labor achieved a ten-hour reduction in the workweek between 1890 and 1925, thus giving Coney's revelers more time for leisure activities and a bit more discretionary income. In 1920, the subway extended to Coney Island, turning the millions into tens of millions of visitors. Paradoxically, those arriving at Coney on a nickel subway ride demanded their amusement at subway prices. Decline became inevitable, due to the changing social and economic patterns that resulted in the demise of most of the traditional urban amusement parks throughout the United States. In its heyday, however, Coney Island was an intoxicant that turned the values of its time upside down. Coney's amusement shattered all expectations of normalcy and turned engines of industry into joy machines and spectacle. While the World's Columbian Exposition made America *look* good, Coney Island made America *feel* good.

The years following World War I marked the zenith of the traditional amusement park in America, with around 2,000 parks in 1920 located in or near most cities in all areas of the country. The 1920s was also the epitome of mechanical rides, particularly the roller coaster, with giant, bumpy, lightning-fast, and fearsome "woodies" dominating the landscape of most parks. Among the most famous of the urban traditional parks were Cincinnati's own Coney Island, Electric Park in Kansas City, Elitch Gardens in Denver, Euclid Beach in Cleveland, Forest Park Highlands in St. Louis, Glen Echo in Washington, D.C., Olympic Park in Irvington, New Jersey, Palisades Park in Fort Lee, New Jersey, Playland at the Beach in San Francisco, Revere Beach in Boston, and Riverview Park in Chicago. These parks generally shared such characteristics as location on urban transportation systems, focus on mechanized amusement rides, especially large roller coasters, intense use of electric lights, dedicated renovation and upkeep during their heyday, music and ballroom dancing, games of chance, and more tranquil picnic groves. Riverview Park was the testing ground for scream machine "woodie" roller coasters with the major coaster builders John Miller, Harry Traver, Frederick Church, and Fred Pearce all establishing offices in the park. There were as many as eleven and no fewer than six leviathan coasters in the park during most of its existence. The most famous were "The Bobs," built by Church, Traver, and Thomas Prior in 1924, featuring a first hill of eighty-seven feet and a savage, reported sixty-seven-degree drop; and the "Blue Streak," later renamed the "Fireball," with a terrorizing drop of ninety feet burrowing beneath the ground and a speed of sixty-five miles per hour, which exceeded that of most contemporary coasters.

With the advent of extended public transportation and the automobile, amusement parks in suburban settings also flourished. Among the most famous are Cedar Point in Sandusky, Ohio; Crystal Beach in Crystal Beach, Ontario, near Buffalo, New York; Dorney Park in Allentown, Pennsylvania; Hershey Park in Hershey, Pennsylvania; Kennywood Park near Pittsburgh; Pacific Ocean Park in Long Beach, California; Playland in Rye, New York; Rockaway's Playland in Rockaway Beach, New York; Rocky Glen Park near Scranton, Pennsylvania; and Venice Amusement Park in Venice, California. These parks were less vulnerable to urban rowdy elements as well as urban development pressures. Most of them carefully balanced the sylvan grove element with the excitement of rides and entertainment. Cedar Point and Kennywood can boast over a century of existence. These two amusement enterprises have made the successful transformation from a traditional park to a modern "theme" park. Both embraced continuous appearance of major roller coasters, among them the "Jack Rabbit," "Racer," and "Thunderbolt" at Kennywood and the "Corkscrew," "Gemini," "Iron Dragon," and "Magnum XL-200" at Cedar Point. Kennywood cleverly used the emergence of television to its advantage, running advertising spots on local stations and presenting television stars in appearances at the park, such as Captain Video, the Howdy Doody show stars, Captain Kangaroo, the Cisco Kid, and Zorro. Both parks owe their success to dedicated, attentive management with exceptional constant capital expenditure programs. Both parks have also wisely preserved and still feature some of the nostalgic elements of their distant history, creating an intriguing blend of gentler times with the intense technology of today.

With a few notable exceptions, traditional amusement parks went into rapid decline starting with Prohibition and the Great Depression. This was accelerated by World War II and the selling of many of the parks by the transportation companies to private individuals or business groups. In the 1940s and 1950s, the affluent urban population fled to the suburbs, to be replaced by people with severely limited incomes and with racial tensions. Urban property became increasingly valuable, making park acreage much desired for industry, retail, and housing. The urban parks could not expand, not even to create parking lots for automobiles. In the 1950s the television set invaded households, quickly transforming the living room into a preferred center of entertainment. Most of the parks mirrored the depressing fate of Riverview Park, where in 1967 all of the rides, including the unparalleled roller coasters, were reduced to mournful piles of broken wood and steel by bulldozers, to be replaced with a shopping center, a factory, and parking lots.

In July 1955 a new era in America popular culture emerged from the orange groves of Anaheim, California, as Disneyland Park opened, created from the imagination and psyche of Walter Elias Disney. This place of fantasy would become, as Sergei Eisenstein perceptively stated, a compelling vision of "paradise regained" for the American public in the latter half of the twentieth century. Fortified against the intrusion of the real world by a massive earth barrier and admission gates, Disneyland Park actualizes a perfect world of pleasure where electronics, plastics, and subtle crowd manipulation are harnessed for fun and escape. Disney ingeniously juxtaposed advanced and new technologies with an atmosphere of nostalgia to achieve an ideal vision of American history.

Disney's own childhood was harsh, threatening, and filled with toil. He was born in 1901 in Chicago, the fourth son of Elias and Flora Disney. Elias was an itinerant worker who had been lured from the Kissimmee area of Florida (ironically, where Walt Disney World would later be built) for work in the construction boom associated with the World's Columbian Exposition. Walt's father was cold, stern, and excessively frugal. In 1906 he moved the family to a small farm in Marceline, about 100 miles from Kansas City and near the main line of the Atchison, Topeka & Santa Fe Railroad. The two older bothers returned to Chicago almost immediately, and Walt, his brother Roy, and sister Ruth Flora were left with large responsibilities to keep the farm running. Farm animals became Walt's only playmates as well as his distraction from his despotic and forbidding father and overweary mother. Marceline's Main Street would later be idealized as Main Street, U.S.A., the entrance to Disneyland. These years were brutally hard for the family, enduring crop failure, swine fever, and typhoid. By 1910, the farm was lost, and the family moved to Kansas City. Walt's adolescence was a time of constant work, dragged out of bed at 3:30 A.M. for his extensive paper route and ruled by an increasingly cruel father who was incapable of love or affection. While Kansas City was extremely conservative during the period 1910–1920, with a recreation superintendent who strictly regulated all types of amusement with a puritanical vigor, Walt and his brother Roy must have occasionally escaped to Kansas City's two amusement parks, Forest Park and Electric Park. Walt tasted freedom for one summer as a candy clerk on the Santa Fe Railroad. For this young boy, whose life had been dominated by backbreaking work and no affection, the steam railroad quickly became splendid and romantic.

Walt's career began as an apprentice in an advertising agency in Kansas City, where he met Ub Iwerks, who would become a premier animator. The two moved to a company making one-minute animated cartoon advertisements for local theaters. Through the Kansas City Public Library, Disney became familiar with the work of Georges Melies, who first merged live actors and sketched backgrounds in a 1902 film, and with newspaper cartoonist Winsor McCay, whose 1909 cartoon "Gertie the Dinosaur" ran in Kansas City theaters. Soon, Disney and Iwerks were making their own cartoons in Disney's garage. In the summer of 1923, the twenty-two-year-old Disney boarded a train for Los Angeles, where his brother Roy was then living. His first successful venture was a series of "Alice" cartoons blending a real-life child with animated cartoon animals and backgrounds.

Disney and Iwerks created Walt Disney Studio around 1925, and their early productions centered on a perky rodent created by Walt. *Plane Crazy*, *Gallopin' Gaucho*, and *Steamboat Willie* launched Mickey Mouse as a cultural icon of innocence, pep, good humor, daring, and also sexual neutrality. The company made other cartoons, but the studio's fortunes took a preeminent turn with the groundbreaking animated feature film *Snow White and the Seven Dwarfs*, three years in the making and debuting on December 21, 1937.

World War II slowed work at the studio, and Disney engaged in a field survey of amusement parks in the United States and abroad. He was especially impressed with Tivoli Gardens in Copenhagen and Greenfield Village, a historical park in

Dearborn, Michigan, that celebrates American entrepreneurial ingenuity. Walt's brother Roy would not back his brother's plans for the development of an amusement park, so Walt financed the new WED Enterprises with his own resources in 1952. He established a small staff of designers whom he immediately dubbed "imagineers." In this period, Disney's only other major project was the animated film *Peter Pan* (1953), in which a perpetual boy's enchanted Never-Never Land is an isolated island where no one grows up and one adventure leads to another.

Disney and his crew developed the basic design elements for his amusement park: a single entrance; a coherent, sequenced layout; wide, leisurely walkways; extensive landscaping; plenty of food and entertainment; attractions unique to Disney; efficient, high-capacity operations. The projected Santa Ana Freeway would make the Anaheim property a half-hour drive from Los Angeles, yet out of the range of mass public transportation, thus not accessible to the poorer population and unsupervised adolescents. In a truly inspired move, Disney turned to the television networks, specifically, the then-fledgling American Broadcasting Company, to provide financial backing to build the park. He promised to produce a weekly hour-long television program, *Disneyland*, in return for ABC's financial investment. Thus, from the beginning, this amusement park was essentially linked with the new cultural giant, television. Together they would establish the dominant outdoor entertainment venue of the twentieth century.

Disneyland Park encompassed fifty-five acres and a $17 million investment. Its opening day of July 17, 1955, was not picture-perfect, and an exceptional heat wave almost dried up the cash reserves, but within six months, over 1 million "guests" had entered the magic land. In its second year, 4 million people came through the gates. Disney quickly moved to a one-price admission charge and dropped separate pricing for rides. Within ten years, the fifty-millionth guest made attendance equal a quarter of the population of the United States.

Disneyland's entrance, Main Street, USA, is an idealized caricature of small-town America painted in soothing tones and free of any disorder, decline, or even mud. Its architecture, however, has been as influential as the park itself. It has inspired the design of the historic restoration of countless town centers, shopping malls, and even such urban projects as Baltimore's Harborplace and Boston's Faneuil Hall Marketplace. The original succeeding sectors of the park, Fantasyland, Adventureland, Frontierland, and Tomorrowland, embody total control of space, movement, and mood to create a succession of visual stereotypes so profound in effect that they achieve the status of national popular images. They represent our aspirations of adventure, freedom, the harnessing of technology for human purposes, daring, and the enduring appeal of legend, myth, and illusion. Disneyland is a paradise for America's democratic citizens. It glorifies small-town America, our frontier heroes, and our technological tinkerers and geniuses. Disney at least visually dismisses elitism and an aristocratic class, thus elevating the democratic spirit. Like Chicago's White City of 1893, however, Disneyland enshrines Anglo-American imagery to the exclusion of ethnic infusions. Its values are those of commercialism, civic rule, and technology while it totally forgets the spiritual and personal growth. It exudes prosperity and shuns diversity. It is the dream world of predominantly white, corporate America. Disneyland uses the technologies of plastics and computer electronics, instead of Coney Island's steel, steam, and elec-

Disney World's Magic Kingdom, Orlando, Florida. © Painet

tricity, to achieve its wonders. Almost everything inside Disneyland is man-made and programmed. The only human sense that can destroy the illusion is touch.

Beyond the genius of Walt Disney, just as for Coney Island, part of Disneyland's success belongs to demographics and economic trends. The post–World War II baby boom changed the age group configuration of the United States. Between 1940 and 1965, the number of children under fifteen years of age increased from 33 million to 59 million, an increase of 80 percent. At the same time, per capita personal income increased between 1940 and 1970 by nearly 500 percent, thus greatly enhancing discretionary income available for entertainment. Disney recognized these trends as well as the decline of the traditional amusement park due to the public's fears of safety and displeasure at the decaying infrastructure of most of the parks. Disneyland is always immaculate, totally captivating, generating amazement, and its location and cost ensure exclusivity. When demographics shifted after 1960 with a marked decrease in the birthrate, Disneyland was well positioned since the strongest appeal of the park has always been to adults. As families became smaller, they possessed more disposable income, and they continued to flock to Disneyland, with adult admissions consistently outnumbering those for children at a rate of four to one.

Entrepreneurs were not quick to copy the Disneyland success. There were several newsworthy and expensive failures in the succeeding decade, all generated by investment groups. Denver's Magic Mountain was aborted just before opening, Pleasure Island near Boston, built at a cost of $4 million, was unsuccessful until it scaled down to a small traditional park. Pacific Ocean Park, a $14 million investment on Santa Monica pier, had such high overhead costs that routine maintenance was neglected, and it was closed by bankruptcy after a decade. Freedomland USA, built in the middle of Bronx, New York, in 1960 at a then-fabulous cost of $33 million and designed by a former Disneyland planner, emphasized education over fun and excitement. Besides lacking thrill rides, its crucial flaw was inattention to media exposure. It operated in the red for three years and brought in thrill rides in desperation, but it quietly closed in 1964. Besides its shortcomings, its urban location was an insurmountable burden because it could not guarantee the safety, cleanliness, and order by then required for family entertainment.

Despite a rocky start, corporate ownership, rather than the dedicated genius of individuals, finally did emerge as the means to the development of outdoor entertainment enterprises in the last quarter of the twentieth century. Six Flags over Texas, between Dallas and Fort Worth, opened in 1961 with six themed areas, many thrill rides, and a multitude of shows and performers. Its success led the corporate backers to gamble on their formula by starting a chain, Six Flags, Inc., with new parks near Atlanta and St. Louis. These parks were located outside the cities on the interstate highways, distant from mass transportation, thus encouraging the patronage of families. The Six Flags parks emphasized thrill rides from the start, especially extravagant roller coasters. They also demanded constant attention to cleanliness and meticulous maintenance. The themed sectors, like at Disneyland, are exotic and dominated by easily understandable sensory images. The success of these enterprises set the stage for the burgeoning of the theme park industry in the 1970s.

The approximate $50 million investment required for the development of a major theme park in the 1970s necessitated corporate or conglomerate ownership. The two dozen theme parks appearing in the 1970s shared design and content elements: total pleasure zones completely engineered and planned to the smallest detail; location resulting from detailed market studies and land acquisition dealings; safe and controlled leisure environments cloistered by distance and physical barriers from the chaotic and dangerous cities; four to six themed sectors connected by a unifying idea; architecture, landscaping, shows, and attractions coordinated to create a relatively brief "experience"; megascale thrill rides; and design to promote family patronage. The segmented structure of these parks, like Disneyland, is a reflection of the nature of television entertainment in which half-hour or hour programming provides a series of distinctly different settings and situations each evening. The lackluster exterior shells and vegetative buffer zones of the parks do nothing to lure customers or build excitement. Those who visit the parks are well aware of the attractions through mass advertising, especially via television.

Five corporate enterprises dominated theme park development in the 1970s and 1980s. Taft Broadcasting built Kings Island near Cincinnati, Kings Dominion near Richmond, Virginia, and Canada's Wonderland near Toronto. The parks utilized the Hanna Barbera cartoon characters owned by Taft. Marriott Corporation entered the theme park industry in 1976, opening two identical Great America parks in Santa Clara, California, and in Gurnee, Illinois. These historic-themed parks celebrate nineteenth-century American values of frontier, agriculture, and commerce. Rising capital expenditures and declining corporate interest in its fantasy worlds led to Marriott's selling of the parks in 1984, the same year that Taft divested itself of its theme park enterprises. Anheuser-Busch expanded its Tampa Busch Gardens into a wildlife park and built a new park, the Old Country, in Williamsburg, Virginia. In 1989 Anheuser-Busch purchased four Sea World attractions from Harcourt Brace Jovanovich and continually expanded these parks as their signature attractions in the 1990s. The Anheuser-Busch parks became the most successful theme parks in the late 1990s, other than the Disney parks, due to their spectacular entertainment offerings, unique atmosphere, willingness to continually invest substantial resources to maintenance and capital improvements, and appeal to all age groups, especially the rapidly growing aging population.

Bally Manufacturing Corporation acquired all Six Flags parks in 1982. Bally also opened the 1,500-acre Great Adventure park in Jackson, New Jersey, in 1974. This enterprise, comparatively large in size, approaching the scale of the Disney parks, suffered for years due to a fatal fire in 1984. Despite its diversity of large thrill rides, wild animals, and lush landscaping, it never realized its expected potential due to planning mistakes, lack of crowd control, and high cost of food and soft drinks. Bally bought the Great America park in Gurnee, Illinois, in 1984 and was then operating seven theme parks, including Six Flags Magic Mountain near Los Angeles. However, in 1987 Bally sold all of its amusement park holdings to Wesray Corporation. Under Wesray, the individual parks had more independence in management and operation. In the 1990s, Time Warner acquired all Six Flags parks as well as many other parks, which then were placed under the Six Flags organization, including Elitch Gardens, Astroworld, Great America, Magic Mountain, Great Adventure, Great Escape, and Darien Lake—a total of seventeen parks. MCA, Inc., the motion picture and entertainment giant, operates the two Universal Studios parks in Orlando and Hollywood, opening in 1988 and 1990, respectively. These parks emphasize the virtual experiential attractions such as "Twister," "Earthquake: The Big One," and "Terminator 2: 3-D Battle." Initially scooped by Disney's addition of MGM Studios within Walt Disney World, Universal Studios in Orlando has successfully increased its market share and appeal through integration of fast-paced, intense, high-technology attractions. By 2000, it had become a major rival and near equal of Disney World in terms of attracting the public and dominating the psyche of vacationers.

Two parks owned by nonconglomerates are notable for their stunning success, Knott's Berry Farm in Buena Park, California, and Cedar Point in Sandusky, Ohio. Walter Knott started his enterprise as a berry farm, gift shop, and museum in the 1940s. He began to move historic gold-mining structures and ghost town buildings to his farm, opened the Chicken Dinner Restaurant, and eventually added thrill rides to his "farm." He added the world's first "Corkscrew" looping roller coaster in 1975 and created several core theme areas, including a "Kingdom of the Dinosaurs" and a "Wild Water Wilderness." Knott's Berry Farm grew by serendipity, contrary to the planned, contained creation of the theme parks of the 1970s. It remained one of the top five attractions in terms of attendance in the 1990s. Cedar Point is one of the few traditional parks to make the transition to a successful theme park. Its location on a small peninsula surrounded on three sides by Lake Erie makes it expansive and alluring as compared to the usual barrier-surrounded, enclosed theme parks. Over a century old, Cedar Point has been fortunate in its owners, who have consistently invested capital funds in new attractions and maintenance. The park wisely integrated many of its historical features, including the grand Hotel Breakers, now on the National Register of Historic Places, with a large number of spectacular roller coasters boasting state-of-the-art technology and maximum thrills.

Frustrated by the lack of space in the 160-acre Disneyland Park, which quickly became surrounded by tacky suburban development, in the mid-1960s Walt Disney quickly began to purchase swampland and citrus groves in central Florida. By 1965 he had secured forty-three square miles, at a total cost of only $5 million. He had also secured a deal with the Florida state government for absolute control over the vast tract of land. Thus, Disney created a kind of Vatican City dominion in central Florida. Appropriately, the developing Walt Disney World would replace the spiritual as our collective dream of a "Perfect World," our twentieth-century Garden of Eden.

Walt Disney World's rise from the Florida swamps would be an unprecedented engineering feat, developing new technologies of construction engineering, water management, energy generation, waste management, transportation, and environmental control. Through the independent Reedy Creek Improvement District, the Disney enterprise has complete control and authority to develop, own, and operate utility, flood control, drainage systems, and building codes. Walt Disney conceived of a complete vacation destination with themed attractions, hotels and resorts, and recreational facilities for boating, tennis, golf, and more. He also articulated his treasured dream, the Experimental Prototype Community of Tomorrow (EPCOT), a utopian, futuristic city of tomorrow complete with a permanent resident population, industry, schools, and research facilities. He believed that the Walt Disney World resort would easily pay for this dream metropolis.

But on December 15, 1966, Walt Disney died of lung cancer, six months before the first earth-moving equipment would begin the creation of the Magic Kingdom. Disney's plans for the Magic Kingdom were meticulously followed by the Disney organization, then led by his brother Roy. Walt Disney World, first comprising the Magic Kingdom and some resort areas, opened on October 23, 1971. This initial $400 million investment continues to grow and change as the world's premier entertainment destination and enterprise. EPCOT Center opened on October 1, 1982, at a cost of over $900 million. While it barely resembles Disney's vision of a domed city of 20,000 inhabitants, EPCOT mirrors and permanently re-creates the great world industrial expositions that were temporary entertainments and wonders, generally existing only for a fleeting summer. Like the expositions, EPCOT celebrates American technological ingenuity, corporate enterprise, and international cultures and images. Continual expansion of the Disney World complex includes the theme entertainment venues Disney-MGM Studios, Discovery Island, Blizzard Beach, Typhoon Lagoon, River Country, Animal Kingdom, and the Pleasure Island nightclub complex for adults. Many resort complexes have also been added, all with themed environments. Walt Disney World continues to draw over 30 million people each year, and revenues reach multiple billions.

The Walt Disney World infrastructure is powered by computer technology and formed by plastics. These are as central to its function as electricity and plaster "staff" were to the World's Columbian Exposition and Coney Island. Most structures are made of forms of plastics for durability, ease of maintenance, flexibility in design, and continuity in environmental effect. Rocks, trees, mountains, and Victorian shops are all plastic, but only a touch can reveal the absence of natural products. Computers run everything from the still-futuristic monorail, rides, audioanimatronic shows and devices, food preparation, all entertainment shows, and multimedia events such as the fireworks and laser extravaganzas, to the environmental control devices, waste processors, utilities, services, fire-sensing apparatus, and ticket machines.

Visitors to Walt Disney World are predominantly upper-middle-class, with demographic statistics indicating that 75 percent of the adults are professionals, technical personnel, or managers. Only 2 percent are laborers, 3 to 5 percent are blacks, and 2 percent are Hispanic. Most guests travel from outside Florida, and the resort is completely dependent on airlines and the interstate highway system. In the late 1990s, admission rose to approximately forty dollars per person, with alternatives for four- or five-day tickets. Thus, Walt Disney World is clearly inaccessible to the poor. Disney's worlds reflect corporate managerial structures, the creation of safe, isolated, and technologically dependent resort zones, an emphasis on visual learning and constant sensory stimulation, unquestioned dependence on, and faith in, technologies, and a detachment from social problems.

EPCOT Center is primarily a showcase for American corporate culture. Just like the World's Columbian Exposition, the EPCOT fair glorifies and advertises American technology. Corporate sponsors funded the building and development of the major pavilions in Future World: Bell System, Exxon, General Electric, General Motors, Kodak, Kraft, United Technologies, Metropolitan Life, AT&T, Sperry, Coca-Cola, and American Express. The World Showcase, too, devoted to exotic country pavilions, is largely a display of products and foods, along with easily associated and recognized architectural forms.

Attracting more than 30 million people a year, Walt Disney World is the world's pilgrimage center. Just as a journey to Mecca, Canterbury, or Rome once sanctified a pilgrim as a member of a holy community, a visit to Disney World brings the traveler to a luxurious and safe haven of entertainment where today's pilgrim reaffirms faith in the scripture of progress through technology, control through managerial hierarchy, and consumerism. The atmosphere of corporate achievement and control through careful management is a dream world for the white-collar professional. In our postmodern world, play, leisure, and mythic values of American culture are our American dream. The cult of technology and illusion has largely replaced the archaic rituals and scriptures of organized religion. The "Perfect World" of Disney is our paradise. The Disney cathedral surrounds us with rosy vistas in which we see the perfectibility of humans through democracy and technology. But it is a limited view that excludes social reality and the challenges that we can overcome with personal growth. It glorifies a selective American history by ignoring our problems, failures, and shortcomings. Through the Disney illusory world, we repress the unattractive and difficult.

Walt Disney World's grand scale and ability to totally immerse its visitors in programmed experience have eclipsed and threatened nearly all outdoor amusement enterprises. In the late 1990s, theme parks were struggling and closing. Some notable exceptions such as Universal Studios and the Sea Worlds present very distinctive experiences that are doing well in a culture that values leisure as renewal and as an energizing force. The Sea World parks appeal to the dominant age group now—the aging baby boomers. Universal Studio's appeal is more limited and emphasizes intense sensory attack rather than leisure. Walt Disney World's continued dominance could be in jeopardy as ethnic demographics dramatically change in the coming decades. Even Disney executives recognize that a saturation point seems to have been reached regarding its appeal—in the late 1990s attendance became static, and some public boredom with the Disney venues became evident. In the third millennium, technology has become closely associated with work, pressure, and a loss of leisure time. We increasingly want to escape its influence and demands on us. It becomes harder to view or experience it as fun and as spectacle. Our amusement enterprises may need to change their major focus from technology to the serenity of relaxation and escape from the encompassing scope of our information and communication technologies, experiencing instead natural beauty, endeavors demanding personal skills, and precious time for attention to our own individual growth. In the 1920s we wanted to be titillated; in the 1950s we wanted to be protected and amazed; in the 1970s we wanted to be sensually bombarded and technically engaged; in the 1990s we wanted to be pampered and indulged as members of the social elite; in the new millennium will we need to escape, having given up societal and corporate quests for our personal dreams?

Fairs

Cattle and hog fairs held by Dutch immigrants in the Manhattan area in the mid-1600s emphasized trading of produce but also included entertainment such as puppet shows, tightrope dancing, clowns, and music, as well as contests, competitions, and races. The agricultural fair quickly became the dominant type of fair in America, and it remains so today. Throughout their history, these fairs have struggled with the balance between agricultural education and popular merriment and amusement. From the beginnings, the agricultural fairs tried to keep entertainment at a minimum, but they were never successful. Critics from the nineteenth century to the present have chastised the fairs for too much vulgarity, frivolity, games of chance, races, and other amusements that draw attention away from the educational programs that were the original motivators of the events. However, in order to exist at all, the fairs need the monetary support of the revelers who come to have fun and to be entertained.

Thomas Coke of Holkham, England, developed a model for the agricultural fair tradition. In the late eighteenth century, he offered festive sheep-shearings on his estate during which agricultural knowledge was dispensed, along with trials of improved implements and sale of livestock. There were also feasts and cash prizes. Some people from America attended Coke's festivals, among them George Washington Custis, who owned an extensive farm in Arlington, Virginia. Custis' land is now Arlington Cemetery. Beginning in 1803, Custis began his own festive sheep-shearing events, which offered many prizes for superior sheep, wool, and domestic manufactures, largely textiles. Such events were also held around the turn of the century in Philadelphia and New York. They formed the basis for the modern American agricultural fair, now mostly recognizable as county and state fairs.

Elkanah Watson of Albany, New York, is generally regarded as the father of American agricultural fairs. Descended from a respectable Plymouth, Massachusetts, family, Watson was not the common rural farmer that he claimed to be when teaching agricultural improvement to his numerous audiences. He learned the merchant trade, then traveled widely in America and France, established an import trade in French textiles during the Revolutionary War, and then returned to the United States to teach his economic development ideas almost like an itinerant preacher. Settling in Albany, he pressed for a canal to link Albany and the eastern part of the state to Lake Erie on the western border. He personally explored a possible route for the canal and published a book about his observations on the deficiencies of agriculture and economic development in western New York around 1790. His drive was impressive—to remake the nation in his own entrepreneurial image. Losing patience with the Dutch lack of interest in innovations and improvements, he bought a farm over the state line in Berkshire County, Massachusetts. On October 1, 1810, he organized an ambitious exposition to display animal stock, plows, and other agricultural equipment. There were also music bands and competitions complete with prizes. This was the first of the Berkshire County Fairs. In 1811 the Berkshire Agricultural Society was formed, the first American "practical society" created to organize annual exhibitions and shows. The Berkshire fairs gradually grew with more prizes, and women were soon encouraged to attend and enter their textiles, culinary creations, and other wares in the competitions.

The county fair, as developed in Massachusetts, was of significant benefit to the farmers, and it also provided a yearly entertainment and social event. These fairs soon became prevalent throughout the East and Midwest. They all generally included public exhibits, educational lectures, competitions with judging and awarding of prizes, meetings of the sponsoring society, a religious ceremony, and social pleasures such as dances. The invention of the McCormick reaper, first exhibited and demonstrated in 1831, and John Deere's steel plow, developed in 1837, sparked significant growth of local fairs. From the 1830s through the 1860s American agriculture experienced a golden age of innovation, increased productivity and prices, and widespread commerce with international scope. Beginning with New York, many eastern states began to provide grants for annual agricultural exhibitions. The first state fair was held in Syracuse, New York, in 1841. New Jersey, Michigan, Pennsylvania, Ohio, Oregon, Wisconsin, Indiana, Illinois, and Iowa followed suit and established their state fairs by 1854. By 1858 there were at least 912 county and state agricultural societies in the United States, most of them sponsoring fairs. By 1913, the Department of Agriculture identified 2,740 societies sponsoring fairs. Throughout the twentieth century, fairs proliferated most in the heartland midwestern states. The South was much slower to show interest in the development of fairs. The antebellum South was steeped in tradition with little interest in innovation. No public support was established as in eastern and midwest states, and political divisiveness hampered any initiatives. There were a few exceptions. John C. Calhoun established an agricultural society in Pendleton, South Carolina, in 1815, and Col. Lewis Sanders started a cattle show in Lexington, Kentucky, the following year. Kentucky fairs gained popularity with the more socially elite, and by 1856 there were twenty-one fairs throughout the state, generally including impressive social events displaying blooded stock and "blueblood" owners.

Besides state allocations, state fairs were also boosted by the growth of the railroads in the mid-nineteenth century. Because of the availability of railroad travel, the large state fairs created permanent structures for the annual events. The zenith of the state and county fairs was the period 1850–1870. At this time, the fairs were the primary source for intellectual and social activities for the farm population. During these midcentury years, the fairs were dedicated to their educational and commercial missions, so that amusement remained secondary. The St. Louis Agricultural and Mechanical Association initiated a huge and elaborate fair in 1856 that drew hundreds of thousands of visitors each year. It was considered the largest and most beautiful of the fairs, with extensive landscape architecture, as well as elaborate permanent buildings and sculptures. The St. Louis fair continued into the 1890s, when its sponsoring society went bankrupt through mismanagement and competition from Chicago's World's Columbian Exposition. Following its ending, the legislature established the Missouri State Fair in 1901, which continues to the present.

The World's Columbian Exposition in 1893 caused grave problems for most fairs that year and in subsequent years. Using railroad transportation and lured by the grandeur and spectacle of this first world's fair in America, people made the trip to Chicago and ignored their state and county fairs. Many fairs skipped 1893 altogether, and many others should have followed suit. In the ensuing years, American tastes for spectacle, dazzle, and magnitude had been whetted, and expectations for fairs and entertainment could not be met on the local level.

The entertainment and amusement aspects of fairs were always integral to their success; however, these factors have progressively assumed a greater proportion of the overall fair experience. The most popular events at nineteenth-century fairs generally were the horse races. Even during the zenith years of 1850–1870, agricultural journalists were constantly complaining about the dominant influence of entertainment at the fairs, which drew people away from educational programs. The fairs needed very large gate receipts in order to remain viable. Money was needed for contest prizes and to build and maintain permanent fairgrounds, including first-class racetracks and grand buildings. Thus, in order to offer the educational and commercial venues of the fairs, more and more entertainment and fun were necessary. The success of fairs has always been measured by gate receipts.

Throughout the nineteenth century, the educational and social needs of racial minorities were generally ignored by fairs. Southern fairs were quite strictly segregated, and even the World's Columbian Exposition treated blacks as well as unfamiliar ethnic groups as "curiosities." Negro fairs appeared in the South in the late nineteenth century in North and South Carolina and were started by Booker T. Washington at the Farmer's Institute at Tuskegee, Alabama, in 1898. His events were imitated throughout the South. The Indian International Fair began in Muskogee, Indian Territory (now Oklahoma), in 1874. First organized by Creek and Cherokee leaders, it later incorporated Cheyenne, Arapaho, Comanche, and Kiowa organizers. Horse racing was a major draw for the Indian Fair, contributing to its continuance into the 1890s. A Navaho Nation Fair began in 1938 in Window Rock, Arizona. Still strong at present, it now claims to be "the world's largest American Indian Fair."

The Order of the Patrons of Husbandry, the Grange, founded in 1867, continuously tried to minimize the amusement and frivolous nature of the fairs in order to return the events to their original purposes. They started their own fairs with generally no success and also created special events at state and local fairs, such as picnics featuring equipment displays. However, by the beginning of the twentieth century most observers thought that the fairs were largely entertaining people uninterested in farming. County fairs seemed in jeopardy but gained interest and viability because the automobile made local travel easy, as well as the development of the 4-H youth movement and the Future Farmers of America. The county fairs received new vigor as a mode for competition and display of local youth accomplishment and talents.

Traveling midway carnivals now provide much of the entertainment and amusement venues for county and state fairs. While nineteenth-century traveling carnivals were largely unsavory and included the criminal element, several reliable and successful businesses emerged to dominate this industry. Carl J. Sedlmayr created his Royal American Shows in 1921. It has grown to travel with eighty double-length railroad cars and offers over fifty rides and attractions. His career is documented in the movie *King of the Carnival*. The James E. Strates show boasts a mile-long midway. Both of these organizations are under second-generation leadership. Other traveling midways are Amusements of America, the Coleman Brothers Shows, Goodings Million Dollar Midway, and the Mighty Thomas Carnival. These carnival elements, including amusement rides, games of chance, trinket vendors, food concessions, and some sideshows, now form the core of the fair experience.

While the future of the American fair seems gloomy to many observers, fair attendance today is high, and some state fairs are booming. The big fairs are no longer tied to agriculture, yet there is enough of the farm experience to promote nostalgia and to satisfy the curiosity of today's urban population. There is a widespread desire to have more understanding of food production and to recognize the process that results in jugs of milk, cellophane-wrapped meat, and frozen vegetables. In addition, recent writings on fairs emphasize the importance of participation in fair contests as a means to exhibit accomplishments representing personal merit and the beauty of crafted products. We continue to patronize our county and state fairs in search of simpler times, to encounter experiences and values that are submerged by our technologically driven environments, to view and experience personal accomplishments, to lose our pretenses and cares in simple pleasures as elementary as a snow cone, and to encounter the rarity of participatory entertainment.

REFERENCE WORKS

William F. Mangels, a carousel manufacturer and author of the major historical text *The Outdoor Amusement Industry from Earliest Times to the Present*, developed a large and important collection of artifacts, memorabilia, and literature related to amusement parks and the industry. His collection is now held at the Circus Hall of Fame in Sarasota, Florida. The Brooklyn Public Library and the Kansas City Public Library are noteworthy for their historical collections related to amusement parks in those areas. The Museum of the City of New York contains materials related to Coney Island.

Don Wilmeth's chapter on "Outdoor Amusements" in his *Variety Entertainment and Outdoor Amusements: A Reference Guide* remains a major overview of amusement parks and fairs with historical and bibliographic essays. He also covers "Outdoor Entertainment," including amusement parks and fairs, in his chapter "Circus and Outdoor Entertainment," in the 1989 edition of the *Handbook of American Popular Culture*.

Several publications in the Vance Bibliographies series address amusement parks: Glenna Dunning's *The American Amusement Park: An Annotated Bibliography*, focusing on planning and management issues; James C. Starbuck's *Theme Parks: A Partially Annotated Bibliography of Articles about Modern Amusement Parks*; and Anthony G. White's *Amusement Parks: A Selected Bibliography*. Walt Disney receives book-length bibliographic treatment in *Walt Disney: A Guide to References and Resources*, by Elizabeth Leebron and Lynn Gartley. John E. Findling and Kimberly D. Pelle have edited the *Historical Dictionary of World's Fairs and Expositions, 1851–1988*. The World's Columbian Exposition receives extensive bibliographic study in *The World's Columbian Exposition: A Centennial Bibliographic Guide* by David Bertuca, Donald Hartman, and Sue Neumeister.

Some directories provide information on individual amusement parks in specific years or at a certain time period. In 1994, John and Joann Norris produced *Amusement Parks: An American Guidebook*. Tim O'Brien's *The Amusement Park Guide* appeared in 1991. Jeff Ulmer compiled *Amusement Parks of America: A Comprehensive Guide* in 1980. In 1978, James W. Reed prepared *The Top 100 Amusement Parks of the United States: The 1978 Guidebook to Amusement Parks*; and Tom Onosko produced *Funland U.S.A.: The Complete Guidebook to 100 Major Amusement and Theme Parks*. Reed updated his work in 1982 and 1987 in his *Amusement Park Guidebook*. The *National Directory of Theme and Amusement Parks* is published on an irregular basis by Pilot Books. *Funparks & Attractions* is published annually by BPI Communications. A previous title of this directory was *Funparks Directory*.

A purely statistical research study, *An Economic and Cultural Impact Study of the Amusement Park and Attraction Industry*, was prepared in 1977 by Shiv K. Gupta of the Wharton Applied Research Center for the International Association of Amusement Parks and Attractions. Although dated now, it addressed income sources, expenditures, revenues, attendance, advertising, employment, characteristics of families attending, and more.

HISTORY AND CRITICISM

Amusement Parks

The literature related to amusement parks is abundant and intriguing. Many of the studies of the historical antecedents are strong, scholarly works, while treatments of the parks largely lack scholarly rigor until recent years. Much historical material relates to specific parks, and now publications on Walt Disney and the Disney enterprise dominate the literature.

The origins of the American amusement park in fairs and pleasure gardens are well documented in significant studies. T.F.G. Dexter's *The Pagan Origin of Fairs* and H. W. Waters' *History of Fairs and Expositions* set the essential background. English fairs are examined in works that hold the status of classic studies: Thomas Frost's *The Old Showmen and the Old London Fairs*; Henry Morley's *Memories of Bartholomew Fair*; Ian Starsmore's *English Fairs*; and William Addison's *English Fairs and Markets*. Broader studies of note are David Braithwaite's *Fairground Architecture: The World of Amusement Parks, Carnivals, and Fairs* and Samuel McKechnie's *Popular Entertainments through the Ages*. There are numerous important studies of the pleasure gardens. Warwick Wroth provides the most comprehensive examinations in *The London Pleasure Gardens of the Eighteenth Century* (with Arthur Edgar Wroth), and *Cremorne and the Later London Gardens*. Another substantial work is Edwin Beresford Chancellor's *The Pleasure Haunts of London during Four Centuries*. Vauxhall Gardens has received much scholarly attention, chiefly in W. S. Scott's *Green Retreats, The Story of Vauxhall Gardens, 1661–1859*; and James Granville Southworth's *Vauxhall Gardens: A Chapter in the Social History of England*. Ranelagh is covered by Mollie Sands in *Invitation to Ranelagh, 1742–1803*. In another study, she concentrates on *The Eighteenth-Century Pleasure Gardens of Marylebone, 1737–1777*. A broader study that includes the pleasure gardens is Max F. Schulz's *Paradise Preserved: Recreations of Eden in Eighteenth- and Nineteenth-Century England*. While pleasure gardens in America have not received careful attention beyond scattered journal articles, some information is available in O. G. Sonneck's *Early Concert Life in America (1731–1800)* since he gives significant attention to concerts performed in pleasure gardens of the period.

World's fairs and international expositions played a leading formative role in the architectural styles, activities, environment and management of American amusement parks. Paul Greenhalgh's excellent volume *Ephemeral Vistas: The Expositions Universelles, Great Exhibitions, and World's Fairs, 1851–1939* covers these events in Europe and America. Robert W. Rydell provides a perceptive analysis of world's fairs held in America in *All the World's a Fair: Visions of Empire at*

American International Expositions, 1876–1916. Edo McCullough presents a fascinating and nostalgic history of American fairs with a focus on the midway in *World's Fair Midways: An Affectionate Account of American Amusement Areas from the Crystal Palace to the Crystal Ball*. As a dominant cultural influence in America for our amusement enterprises and our wider culture, the World's Columbian Exposition has received extensive scholarly investigation and analysis. The previously mentioned *The World's Columbian Exposition: A Centennial Bibliographic Guide* by Bertuca, Hartman, and Neumeister is a comprehensive and invaluable resource for study of all aspects of the exposition. The most respected and scholarly investigations are Reid Badger's *The Great American Fair: The World's Columbian Exposition and American Culture*; David F. Burg's *Chicago's White City of 1893*; and Alan Trachtenberg's treatment of the Columbian Exposition in his *The Incorporation of America: Culture and Society in the Gilded Age*. Arnold Lewis focuses on the cultural effect of the architecture in his *An Early Encounter with Tomorrow: Europeans, Chicago's Loop, and the World's Columbian Exposition*. Some valuable materials produced at the time of the exposition are Daniel Hudson Burnham's *World's Columbian Exposition: The Book of the Builders*; John J. Flinn's two-volume *Official Guide to the World's Columbian Exposition*; Benjamin C. Truman's *History of the World's Fair*; Rossiter Johnson's four-volume *A History of the World's Columbian Exposition Held in Chicago in 1893*, a key comprehensive resource; Trumbull White and William Iglehart's *World's Columbian Exposition, Chicago, 1893: A Complete History of the Enterprise*; and Harry Gardner Cutler's *The World's Fair: Its Meaning and Scope*. Also published at the time of the exposition and of more limited scope are J. P. Barrett's extensive and comprehensive *Electricity at the Columbian Exposition* (Barrett was responsible for everything related to electricity at the fair); and Halsey C. Ives' *The Dream City: A Portfolio of Photographic Views of the World's Columbian Exposition*. The photography of Charles Dudley Arnold, which very deliberately fostered imagery of authority and grandeur for the exposition, is analyzed in Peter B. Hales' 1984 study *Silver Cities: The Photography of American Urbanization, 1839–1915*. Pamela Potter-Hennessey has produced a three-volume Ph.D. dissertation at the University of Maryland on "The Sculpture at the 1893 World's Columbian Exposition: International Encounters and Jingoistic Spectacles."

Recreation and outdoor entertainment in America were surveyed and analyzed in several landmark studies in the first half of the twentieth century. Chief among these are Foster Rhea Dulles' *America Learns to Play: A History of Popular Recreation, 1607–1940*; Richard Henry Edwards' 1915 social and moral investigation which includes amusement parks, *Popular Amusements*; Joe McKennon's *Pictorial History of the American Carnival*; and Rollin Lynde Hartt's *The People at Play: Excursions in the Humor and Philosophy of Popular Amusements*. Hartt's study is an exhaustive analysis of American culture as it relates to leisure time, the impact of the automobile, and urban and rural recreations. A more recent study is David Nasaw's perceptive and extensively researched *Going Out: The Rise and Fall of Public Amusements*, which covers urban entertainments from "concert saloons" through amusement parks, baseball, and motion pictures. The architecture of amusement parks and fairs prior to the emergence of theme parks is discussed by David Braithwaite in *Fairground Architecture: The World of Amusement Parks, Carnivals, and Fairs*. A collection edited in 1995 by William L. Slout, *Popular Amusements in Horse &*

Buggy America: An Anthology of Contemporaneous Essays, includes numerous nineteenth-century writings on exhibitions, amusement "for the poor," summer resorts, amusement parks, and the circus.

Still serving as a standard source on the history of amusement parks in America is William F. Mangels' *The Outdoor Amusement Industry from Earliest Times to the Present*. While not especially scholarly in its presentation, this study is quite comprehensive and contains much special knowledge from the author, who was a carousel manufacturer, a wonderful collector, and a charming narrator. His study covers historical antecedents to amusement parks, early American parks, carnivals, Coney Island, historical surveys of the roller coaster, carousel, Ferris wheel, and other mechanical devices. Published in 1952, Mangels does not cover the contemporary amusement enterprise. Judith A. Adams provides a more up-to-date, scholarly study in *The American Amusement Park Industry: A History of Technology and Thrills*. This volume covers influences, chiefly the World's Columbian Exposition, and spans from Coney Island to theme parks and the Disney enterprises through 1990. She analyzes amusement parks as affected by American social and economic trends and how the parks themselves reflect and influence American culture and values. Other valuable historical surveys of American amusement parks are Gary Kyriazi's wonderfully illustrated *The Great American Amusement Parks: A Pictorial History*, covering from Coney Island through the emergence of theme parks; and Al Griffin's *Step Right Up, Folks!*, focusing on the traditional parks and rides. "The American Amusement Park," an in-depth section in the *Journal of Popular Culture* (Summer 1981), is edited by Margaret J. King and is a valuable resource with scholarly articles on the appeal of the amusement/theme park, Cedar Point park, the Marriott Great America parks, the roller coaster as architectural symbol, and three articles on the symbolism and cultural influence of the Disney parks.

Coney Island had received more scholarly and nostalgic attention than any other amusement area until the large number of publications on the Disney enterprises. The first place to begin for any study or interest in Coney Island is John F. Kasson's perceptive, yet relatively brief, *Amusing the Million: Coney Island at the Turn of the Century*. Kasson most effectively analyzes the meaning of Coney, its cultural influence, and its effects on its millions of visitors. The most extensive and useful histories are Edo McCullough's *Good Old Coney Island* and Oliver Pilat and Jo Ranson's *Sodom by the Sea: An Affectionate History of Coney Island*. Richard Snow's brief volume, *Coney Island: A Postcard Journey to the City of Fire*, illustrates the atmosphere of Coney in its heyday. Another collection of illustrations is Harvey Stein's *Coney Island*. An investigation of Coney's unique architecture and its relationship to the city is included in Rem Koolhaas' *Delirious New York*. Artists Reginald Marsh, Joseph Stella, and Robert Riggs found Coney Island to be a favorite subject, depicting the sensuality and the strong physical nature of the Coney experience. The work of these artists is illustrated in Lloyd Goodrich's *Reginald Marsh*, Norman Sasowsky's *The Prints of Reginald Marsh*, Irma Jaffe's *Joseph Stella*, and a lengthy article, "To Heaven by Subway," in *Fortune* magazine (August 1938), which contains illustrations by Robert Riggs that depict the sensual ambience of Steeplechase Park. This article remains a superb resource on Coney Island. Two other article-length studies are of significant value to an understanding of Coney Island. Robert E. Snow and David E. Wright's "Coney Island: A Case Study of Popular Culture and Technical Change," in the *Journal of Popular*

Culture, sparked most recent attention to Coney. The most in-depth discussion to date of George Cornelius Tilyou, developer of Steeplechase Park, is Peter Lyon's "The Master Showman of Coney Island," in *American Heritage* in 1958. The later history of Steeplechase Park is minutely chronicled in James J. Onorato and Michael Paul Onorato's four-volume *Steeplechase Park, Coney Island, 1928– 1964: The Diary of James J. Onorato*. Wonderful articles written in the early years of the century truly depict the Coney experience. Edward F. Tilyou's "Why the Schoolma'am Walked into the Sea," in *American Magazine* (July 1922), is a delightful analysis of the effects of Coney on its visitors, by the son of Steeplechase's founder. Frederic Thompson, co-owner of Luna Park, wrote "Amusing the Million" for *Everybody's Magazine* in 1908. Richard LeGallienne's "Human Need of Coney Island," in *Cosmopolitan* in 1905, explains the lure of the mecca by the sea.

Other seaside resorts with significant amusement park venues have also received attention. Richmond Barrett's *Good Old Summer Days* is a wide-ranging study. American and British resorts are included in Sarah Howell's *The Seaside*. Atlantic City, New Jersey, in its seaside resort days prior to casino gambling, is remembered in Charles F. Funnell's *By the Beautiful Sea: The Rise and High Times of That Great American Resort, Atlantic City*; Vicki Gold Levi and Lee Eisenberg's *Atlantic City: 125 Years of Ocean Madness*; William McMahon's *So Young . . . So Gay*; and Bill Kent's *Atlantic City: America's Playground: An Illustrated History of Atlantic City*. Other useful general studies are Sean and Robert Manley's *Beaches: Their Lives, Legends, and Lore*; and Frank Butler's *Book of the Boardwalk*.

Amusement rides, particularly the carousel and roller coaster, have received a good deal of attention. The standard, well-researched, and beautifully illustrated study of the carousel is Frederick A. Fried's *A Pictorial History of the Carousel*. Nina Fraley presents a brief, perceptive introduction in *The American Carousel*. Carousel animals and figures as well as midway show fronts are included in Fred and Mary Fried's *America's Forgotten Folk Arts*. The art of carousel animals is also the focus of Tina Gottdenker's *Carvers and Their Merry-Go-Rounds*, William Manns' *Painted Ponies*, and Roland Summit's *Flying Horses*. In a recent study, Carrie Papa presents *The Carousel Keepers: An Oral History of American Carousels*. The two major studies and pictorial archives on the roller coaster are Robert Cartmell's *The Incredible Scream Machine: A History of the Roller Coaster* and Herma Silverstein's *Scream Machines: Roller Coasters Past, Present, and Future*. Also useful is Todd H. Throgmorton's *Roller Coasters: An Illustrated Guide to the Rides in the United States and Canada, with a History*.

The history of many traditional amusement parks has been chronicled in works that are not especially scholarly in nature but that provide accurate historical records, memoir information, generally extensive historical illustrations, and a fine understanding of the atmosphere of the specific parks and chronicle the economic and social forces that influenced the development and often the decline of the enterprise. Among the best park histories are Lee Bush et al.'s *Euclid Beach Is Closed for the Season* and *Euclid Beach Park: A Second Look*; David W. and Diane De Mali Francis' *Cedar Point: The Queen of American Watering Places*; Charles J. Jacques Jr.'s *Kennywood: Roller Coaster Capital of the World* and *More Kennywood Memories*; Alan A. Siegel's *Smile: A Picture History of Olympic Park, 1887–1965*; Chuck Wlodarczyk's *Riverview: Gone but Not Forgotten. A Photo History, 1904– 1967*; and Paul Ilyinsky and Dick Perry's memoir of Cincinnati's Coney Island park, *Goodbye, Coney Island, Goodbye*. Also of interest is Rob Lewis' largely pictorial review *Rhode Island Amusement Parks*, covering five traditional parks.

The Disney parks and their founder are the subjects of a growing body of literature that is scholarly, detailed, and evaluative. The most important and influential biographical studies of Walt Disney are Richard Schickel's *The Disney Version: The Life, Times, Art, and Commerce of Walt Disney*, which is balanced and critical as well as authoritative; Leonard Mosley's *Disney's World: A Biography*, perhaps the most extensive biography and analysis of Disney's direct involvement in the planning and management of his enterprises; and Bob Thomas' *Walt Disney: An American Original*. The design of the parks and specific buildings is discussed in *Walt Disney Imagineering: A Behind the Dreams Look at Making the Magic Real*. Disneyland Park is thoroughly chronicled, with an emphasis on its development and problems at its opening, in Randy Bright's *Disneyland, Inside Story*. Bob Schlinger provides *The Unofficial Guide to Disneyland*. Walt Disney World is receiving continuing scholarly attention, which tends to integrate the social and cultural influence of this dominant amusement enterprise. Studies include Richard R. Beard's *Walt Disney's EPCOT Center: Creating the New World of Tomorrow*; John Taylor's business/finance/corporate takeover analysis, *Storming the Magic Kingdom: Wall Street, the Raiders, and the Battle for Disney*; and Eric Smoodin's *Disney Discourse: Producing the Magic Kingdom*. Both parks receive serious sociological study in *Disney and His Worlds*, by Alan Bryman. A valuable journal article written by the chief environmental engineer for Walt Disney World provides detailed information on the engineering projects and innovations developed for the park and resort: Arthur Bravo's "Environmental Systems at Walt Disney World," in the *Journal of the Environmental Engineering Division, Proceedings of the American Society of Civil Engineers*. Both parks receive extensive pictorial treatment in Valerie Childs' *The Magic of Disneyland and Walt Disney World*. Tokyo Disneyland is chronicled and discussed by Aviad E. Raz in *Riding the Black Ship: Japan and Tokyo Disneyland*. The many forms of Disney's art are documented in Christopher Finch's *The Art of Walt Disney: From Mickey Mouse to the Magic Kingdoms*. Also intriguing and full of perceptive commentary on all aspects of Disney's work is *Eisenstein on Disney*, edited by Jay Leyda, a compilation of Soviet filmmaker Sergei Eisenstein's analysis and reaction to Disney in writings and letters. Eisenstein made the striking comment that "the epos of Disney is 'Paradise Regained.' "

Attention to theme parks as an amusement park form has been scanty in terms of analysis and interpretation, other than in Adams' *American Amusement Park Industry*. *Theatre Crafts* journal devoted an issue to "Theme Parks USA" in Spring 1977. The ten essays look at the rise and fall of the traditional park, "scream machine" rides, ride background surround-sound systems, safety of rides, the Disney parks, and more. Architecture and design of theme parks and application to nonamusement venues are treated with professional detail in Louis Wasserman's *Merchandising Architecture: Architectural Implications and Applications of Amusement Theme Parks*. Anthony and Patricia Wylson study the design of largely outdoor entertainment in their *Theme Parks, Leisure Centers, Zoos, and Aquaria*. Knott's Berry Farm, one of the most popular and successful theme parks, receives focused treatment in Stephen Gould's short *Walter Knott and His Knott's Berry Farm*.

Academic journals publishing significant articles dealing with American amusement parks and fairs are *World's Fair*, the *Journal of Popular Culture*, and the

Journal of American Culture. National Amusement Park Historical News and its continuation, *NAPHA News*, provide informative, yet brief, discussions of a wide range of topics. The major trade magazine is the weekly *Amusement Business. Funworld* is published monthly by the International Association of Amusement Parks and Attractions, and *At the Park* also covers the industry. The fan group American Coaster Enthusiasts produces the quarterly publication *Roller Coaster!*

Fairs

The American county and state fair tradition has received little scholarly attention, especially in regard to encompassing historical or contemporary studies. Donald B. Marti's *Historical Directory of American Agricultural Fairs* describes 205 events, including date spans, features, and major sources of information. Marti also provides an excellent and lengthy historical survey. George K. Holmes' *List of Agricultural Fairs and Exhibitions in the United States* begins with a valuable historic essay with emphasis on the geographic spread of fairs. Information on arts and crafts fairs is available in Frances Shemanski's *A Guide to Fairs and Festivals in the United States. Amusement Business* publishes the *Directory of North American Fairs, Festivals and Expositions.*

Lila Perl's *America Goes to the Fair: All about State and County Fairs in the USA* is useful for its factual content, although it is written for a younger audience. In addition to its historical content, Perl gives attention to entertainment components of the midway. Other books for a more juvenile audience are helpful especially for their illustrations: Audree Distad's *Come to the Fair;* Steve Lesberg and Naomi Goldberg's *County Fair;* and Jack Pierce's *The State Fair Book.*

The standard history of agricultural fairs through the first quarter of the twentieth century is Wayne Caldwell Neely's *The Agricultural Fair.* He focuses on patterns of development. Helen Auger's broad historical survey *The Book of Fairs* is an impressionistic overview from the earliest fairs through the world fairs held in San Francisco and New York in the late 1930s. Researchers should turn to studies of agriculture in specific states or of individual fairs themselves and agricultural societies to locate detailed information and scholarship. Books written by Elkanah Watson, regarded as the father of American agricultural fairs, are valuable for their depiction of farming practices and the economic environment in the early nineteenth century: *History of the Rise, Progress, and Existing Condition of the Western Canals in the State of New York;* and *History of Agricultural Societies on the Modern Berkshire System.* Interesting for its documentation of the form of fairs in the 1930s is *The Fundamental Principles of Successful County and State Fairs,* edited by George Jackson. A primary source for history of agriculture in America is Liberty Hyde Bailey's monumental *Cyclopedia of American Agriculture,* first published in 1907. Histories of agriculture in states or regions are also useful for information on fairs and the emergence of societies. Among the most valuable are Robert Leslie Jones' *History of Agriculture in Ohio to 1880;* Ulysses Prentice Hedrick's *A History of Agriculture in the State of New York;* Clarence A. Day's *A History of Maine Agriculture 1604–1860;* Lewis C. Gray's *History of Agriculture in the Southern United States to 1860;* Steven Whitcomb Fletcher's *Pennsylvania Agriculture and Country Life 1840–1940;* Willard Range's *A Century of Georgia Agriculture, 1850–1950;* Thomas D. Clark's *Agrarian Kentucky;* and Hubert G. Schmidt's *Agriculture in New Jersey, A*

Three-Hundred Year History. Histories of agricultural societies are important since the societies initially developed most of the local and state fairs. See especially John Hamilton's *Agricultural Fair Associations and Their Utilization in Agricultural Education and Improvement.* Also valuable are Simon Baatz's *"Venerate the Plough": A History of the Philadelphia Society for Promoting Agriculture 1785–1985*; Chalmers S. Murray's *This Our Land, the Story of the Agricultural Society of South Carolina*; and Darwin S. Hall and R. I. Holcombe's *History of the Minnesota State Agricultural Society.* Researchers must also give attention to the official publications of state historical societies and agricultural societies and boards, often published as "Transactions" or "Memoirs."

There are a number of book-length histories and studies of individual state fairs. Two titles of special note are Ray P. Speer and Harry J. Frost's *Minnesota State Fair: The History and Heritage of 100 Years* and John W. Ryan's *The Wisconsin State Fair, Its Modern Role and Objectives.* Also of interest are *Maryland State Fair—100 Years*, edited by Paul E. Carre, and Nancy Wiley's *Great State Fair of Texas.*

Leslie Prosterman's valuable study, *Ordinary Life, Festival Days: Aesthetics in the Midwest County Fair* provides a combination of academic field observation, interviews, and personal reactions with an emphasis on competitions and judging. Two other books on New England fairs are important for their memoir quality, providing individualistic impressions of the rural fair experience. Phil Primack, in his *New England Country Fair*, contrasts several fairs and provides wonderful photographs that capture the charm as well as the tawdriness of the fairs. Charles Fish's *Blue Ribbons and Burlesque: A Book of Country Fairs* is a written and photographic memoir of three Vermont fairs. He emphasizes the centrality of racing and the importance to fair contestants of exhibiting their accomplishments and displaying the beauty of their art.

A couple studies provide histories and information on the influence of national agricultural organizations. *Rich Harvest: A History of the Grange, 1867–1900*, by Dennis Swen Nordin, includes discussion of the largely unsuccessful attempts by Grange organizations to develop their own fairs dedicated to education and largely devoid of entertainment. The youth organizations 4-H and Future Farmers of America are covered in Thomas and Marilyn Wessel's *4-H: An American Idea*; Franklin M. Reck's *The 4-H Story: A History of 4-H Club Work*; and A. Webster Tenney's *The FFA at 50.*

Three books on major Canadian fairs are quite useful for their analysis of the impact of these events on national and local culture. Most important is Keith Walden's extensive study *Becoming Modern in Toronto: The Industrial Exhibition and the Shaping of a Late Victorian Culture.* James Lorimer's smaller volume, *The Ex: A Picture History of the Canadian National Exhibition*, looks at the same national exhibition and provides much more pictorial coverage. David Breen and Kenneth Coates' study *Vancouver's Fair, an Administrative and Political History of the Pacific National Exhibition* focuses on the cultural trends that led to its growth and eventual decline.

Most state historical journals give significant coverage to the history of agriculture and occasional historical studies of the development and influence of fairs. The major source of information on the contemporary commercial aspects of fairs and events is *Amusement Business.* The most important historical journals often publishing studies of state, county, and local fairs are *Agricultural History, New*

York History, Indiana Magazine of History, Chronicles of Oklahoma, Nebraska History, and journals beginning around the mid-nineteenth-century, *New England Farmer, American Agriculturist,* and *Rural New-Yorker*. Researchers must also examine the "Transactions," "Proceedings," and "Memoirs" of state historical societies and agricultural societies.

BIBLIOGRAPHY

General Sources

Braithwaite, David. *Fairground Architecture: The World of Amusement Parks, Carnivals, and Fairs*. New York: Praeger, 1968.

Wilmeth, Don B. "Circus and Outdoor Entertainment." In *Handbook of American Popular Culture*, ed. M. Thomas Inge. New York: Greenwood Press, 1989, 173–203.

————. *Variety Entertainment and Outdoor Amusements: A Reference Guide*. Westport, Conn.: Greenwood Press, 1982.

Amusement Parks

Adams, Judith A. *The American Amusement Park Industry: A History of Technology and Thrills*. Boston: Twayne, 1991.

Addison, William. *English Fairs and Markets*. London: B. T. Batsford, 1953.

Badger, Reid. *The Great American Fair: The World's Columbian Exposition and American Culture*. Chicago: Nelson Hall, 1979.

Barrett, J. P. *Electricity at the Columbian Exposition*. Chicago: R. R. Donnelley and Sons, 1894.

Barrett, Richmond. *Good Old Summer Days*. Boston: Houghton Mifflin, 1952.

Beard, Richard R. *Walt Disney's EPCOT Center; Creating the New World of Tomorrow*. New York: Abrams, 1982.

Bertuca, David J., Donald K. Hartman, and Sue M. Neumeister. *The World's Columbian Exposition: A Centennial Bibliographic Guide*. Westport, Conn.: Greenwood Press, 1996.

Bravo, Arthur. "Environmental Systems at Walt Disney World." *Journal of the Environmental Engineering Division, Proceedings of the American Society of Civil Engineers* 101, no. EE6 (December 1975), 887–95.

Bright, Randy. *Disneyland, Inside Story*. New York: Abrams, 1987.

Bryman, Alan. *Disney and His Worlds*. London and New York: Routledge, 1995.

Burg, David F. *Chicago's White City of 1893*. Lexington: University Press of Kentucky, 1976.

Burnham, Daniel Hudson. *World's Columbian Exposition: The Book of the Builders: Being a Chronicle of the Origin and Plan of the World's Fair: Of the Architecture of the Buildings and Landscape: Of the Work of Construction: Of the Decorations and Embellishments: And of the Operation*. Chicago: Columbian Memorial Publication Society, 1894.

Bush, Lee, et al. *Euclid Beach Is Closed for the Season*. Cleveland: Dillon/Liederback, 1977.

———. *Euclid Beach Park: A Second Look*. Mentor, Ohio: Amusement Park Books, 1979.

Butler, Frank. *Book of the Boardwalk*. Atlantic City, N.J.: The 1954 Association, 1953.

Cartmell, Robert. *The Incredible Scream Machine: A History of the Roller Coaster*. Bowling Green, Ohio: Bowling Green State University Popular Press; Fairview Park, Ohio: Amusement Park Books, 1987.

Chancellor, Edwin Beresford. *The Pleasure Haunts of London during Four Centuries*. 1925. Reprint. New York: Benjamin Blom, 1971.

Childs, Valerie. *The Magic of Disneyland and Walt Disney World*. New York: Mayflower Books, 1979.

Cutler, Harry Gardner. *The World's Fair: Its Meaning and Scope*. Chicago: Star, 1891.

Dexter, T.F.G. *The Pagan Origin of Fairs*. Perranporth, Cornwall, England: New Knowledge Press, 1930.

Dulles, Foster Rhea. *America Learns to Play: A History of Popular Recreation, 1607–1940*. New York: Appleton-Century, 1940.

Dunning, Glenna. *The American Amusement Park: An Annotated Bibliography*. Architecture Series Bibliography A1318. Monticello, Ill.: Vance Bibliographies, 1985.

Edwards, Richard Henry. *Popular Amusements*. 1915. Reprint. New York: Arno Press, 1976.

Finch, Christopher. *The Art of Walt Disney: From Mickey Mouse to the Magic Kingdoms*. New York: Abrams, 1975.

Findling, John E., ed., and Kimberly D. Pelle, asst. ed. *Historical Dictionary of World's Fairs and Expositions, 1851–1988*. New York: Greenwood Press, 1990.

Flinn, John J., ed. *Official Guide to the World's Columbian Exposition*. 2 vols. Chicago: N. Jaul, 1894.

Fraley, Nina. *The American Carousel*. Berkeley, Calif.: Redbug Workshop, 1979.

Francis, David W., and Diane De Mali Francis. *Cedar Point: The Queen of American Watering Places*. Canton, Ohio: Daring Books, 1988.

Fried, Frederick A. *A Pictorial History of the Carousel*. New York: Barnes, 1964.

Fried, Frederick, and Mary Fried. *America's Forgotten Folk Arts*. New York: Pantheon Books, 1978.

Frost, Thomas. *The Old Showmen and the Old London Fairs*. 1881. Reprint. Ann Arbor, Mich.: Gryphon Books, 1971.

Funnell, Charles F. *By the Beautiful Sea: The Rise and High Times of That Great American Resort, Atlantic City*. New York: Alfred A. Knopf, 1975.

Funparks & Attractions. Annual. Nashville, Tenn.: BPI Communications, 1994–   .

Goodrich, Lloyd. *Reginald Marsh*. New York: Harry N. Abrams, 1972.

Gottdenker, Tina Cristiani. *Carvers and Their Merry-Go-Rounds*. West Babylon, N.Y.: Second Annual Conference Committee, NCR, 1974.

Gould, Stephen. *Walter Knott and His Knott's Berry Farm*. Fullerton, Calif.: RB Productions, 1998.

Greenhalgh, Paul. *Ephemeral Vistas: The Expositions Universelles, Great Exhibitions, and World's Fairs, 1851–1939*. Manchester, England: Manchester University Press, 1988.

Griffin, Al. *Step Right Up Folks!* Chicago: Henry Regnery, 1974.

Gupta, Shiv K. *An Economic and Cultural Impact Study of the Amusement Park and Attraction Industry*. Philadelphia: Wharton Applied Research Center, University of Pennsylvania, 1977.

Hales, Peter B. *Silver Cities: The Photography of American Urbanization, 1839–1915*. Phildelphia: Temple University Press, 1984.

Hartt, Rollin Lynde. *The People at Play: Excursions in the Humor and Philosophy of Popular Amusements*. Boston: Houghton Mifflin, 1909.

Howell, Sarah. *The Seaside*. London: Studio Vista, 1974.

Ilyinsky, Paul, and Dick Perry. *Goodbye, Coney Island, Goodbye*. Englewood Cliffs, N.J.: Prentice-Hall, 1972. (Coney Island park in Cincinnati.)

Ives, Halsey C. *The Dream City: A Portfolio of Photographic Views of the World's Columbian Exposition*. St. Louis: N. D. Thompson, 1893.

Jacques, Charles J., Jr. *Kennywood: Roller Coaster Capital of the World*. Vestal, N.Y.: Vestal Press, 1982.

———. *More Kennywood Memories*. Jefferson, Ohio: Amusement Park Journal, 1998.

Jaffe, Irma. *Joseph Stella*. Cambridge: Harvard University Press, 1970.

Johnson, Rossiter. *A History of the World's Columbian Exposition Held in Chicago in 1893*. 4 vols. New York: Appleton, 1897–1898.

Kasson, John F. *Amusing the Million: Coney Island at the Turn of the Century*. New York: Hill and Wang, 1978.

Kent, Bill. *Atlantic City: America's Playground: An Illustrated History of Atlantic City*. Encinitas, Calif.: Heritage Media Corp., 1998.

King, Margaret J., ed. "The American Amusement Park." In-depth section. *Journal of Popular Culture* 15 (Summer 1981), 56–179.

Koolhaas, Rem. *Delirious New York: A Retroactive Manifesto for Manhattan*. New York: Oxford University Press, 1978.

Kyriazi, Gary. *The Great American Amusement Parks: A Pictorial History*. Secaucus, N.J.: Citadel, 1976.

Leebron, Elizabeth, and Lynn Gartley. *Walt Disney: A Guide to References and Resources*. Boston: G. K. Hall, 1979.

Le Gallienne, Richard. "Human Need of Coney Island." *Cosmopolitan* 39 (July 1905), 239–46.

Levi, Vicki Gold, and Lee Eisenberg. *Atlantic City: 125 Years of Ocean Madness*. New York: Clarkson N. Potter, 1979.

Lewis, Arnold. *An Early Encounter with Tomorrow: Europeans, Chicago's Loop, and the World's Columbian Exposition*. Urbana: University of Illinois Press, 1997.

Lewis, Rob. *Rhode Island Amusement Parks*. Charleston, S.C.: Arcadia, 1998.

Leyda, Jay, ed. *Eisenstein on Disney*. London: Methuen, 1988.

Lyon, Peter. "The Master Showman of Coney Island." *American Heritage* 9 (June 1958), 14–21, 92–95.

Mangels, William F. *The Outdoor Amusement Industry from Earliest Times to the Present*. New York: Vantage, 1952.

Manley, Sean, and Robert Manley. *Beaches: Their Lives, Legends, and Lore*. Philadelphia and London: Chilton Book, 1968.

Manns, William. *Painted Ponies*. Millwood, N.Y.: Zon International, 1987.

McCullough, Edo. *Good Old Coney Island*. New York: Scribner, 1957.

————. *World's Fair Midways: An Affectionate Account of American Amusement Areas from the Crystal Palace to the Crystal Ball*. New York: Exposition Press, 1966. Reprint. New York: Arno Press, 1976.

McKechnie, Samuel. *Popular Entertainments through the Ages*. London: Samson Low, Marston, 1931. Reprint. New York: Benjamin Blom, 1969.

McKennon, Joe. *Pictorial History of the American Carnival*. Sarasota, Fla.: Carnival, 1972.

McMahon, William. *So Young . . . So Gay*. Atlantic City, N.J.: Atlantic City Press, 1970.

Morley, Henry. *Memories of Bartholomew Fair*. 1880. Reprint. Detroit: Singing Tree Press, 1969.

Mosley, Leonard. *Disney's World: A Biography*. New York: Stein and Day, 1985.

Nasaw, David. *Going Out: The Rise and Fall of Public Amusements*. New York: Basic Books, 1993.

National Directory of Theme and Amusement Parks. New York: Pilot Books, 1978– .

Norris, John, and Joann Norris, eds. *Amusement Parks: An American Guidebook*. Jefferson, N.C.: McFarland, 1994.

O'Brian, Tim. *The Amusement Park Guide: Fun for the Whole Family at More than 250 Amusement Parks from Coast to Coast*. Chester, Conn.: Globe Pequot Press, 1991.

Onorato, James J., and Michael Paul Onorato. *Steeplechase Park, Coney Island, 1928–1964: The Diary of James J. Onorato*. 4 vols. Bellingham, Wash.: Pacific Rim Books, 1997.

Onosko, Tom, ed. *Funland U.S.A.: The Complete Guidebook to 100 Major Amusement and Theme Parks*. New York: Ballantine Press, 1978.

Papa, Carrie. *The Carousel Keepers: An Oral History of American Carousels*. Blacksburg, Va.: McDonald and Woodward, 1998.

Pilat, Oliver, and Jo Ranson. *Sodom by the Sea: An Affectionate History of Coney Island*. Garden City, N.Y.: Doubleday, 1941.

Potter-Hennessey, Pamela. "The Sculpture at the 1893 World's Columbian Exposition; International Encounters and Jingoistic Spectacles." 3 vols. Ph.D. diss., University of Maryland, College Park, 1995.

Raz, Aviad E. *Riding the Black Ship: Japan and Tokyo Disneyland*. Cambridge: Harvard University Asia Center, 1999.

Reed, James W. *Amusement Park Guidebook*. Quarryville, Pa.: Reed, 1982.

————. *Amusement Park Guidebook*. New Holland, Pa.: Reed, 1987.

————. *The Top 100 Amusement Parks of the United States: The 1978 Guidebook to Amusement Parks*. Quarryville, Pa.: Reed, 1978.

Rydell, Robert W. *All the World's a Fair: Visions of Empire at American International Expositions, 1876–1916*. Chicago: University of Chicago Press, 1984.

Sands, Mollie. *The Eighteenth-Century Pleasure Gardens of Marylebone, 1737–1777*. London: Society for Theatre Research, 1987.

————. *Invitation to Ranelagh, 1742–1803*. London: John Westhouse, 1946.

Sasowsky, Norman. *The Prints of Reginald Marsh*. New York: Clarkson N. Potter, 1976.

Schickel, Richard. *The Disney Version: The Life, Times, Art, and Commerce of Walt Disney*. New York: Simon and Schuster, 1968.

Schlinger, Bob. *The Unofficial Guide to Disneyland*. Rev. ed. Englewood Cliffs, N.J.: Prentice-Hall, 1985.

Schulz, Max F. *Paradise Preserved: Recreations of Eden in Eighteenth- and Nineteenth-Century England*. Cambridge: Cambridge University Press, 1985.

Scott, W. S. *Green Retreats, The Story of Vauxhall Gardens, 1661–1859*. London: Odhams Press, 1955.

Siegel, Alan A. *Smile: A Picture History of Olympic Park, 1887–1965*. Irvington, N.J.: Irvington Historical Society, 1983.

Silverstein, Herma. *Scream Machines: Roller Coasters Past, Present, and Future*. New York: Walker, 1986.

Slout, William L., ed. *Popular Amusements in Horse & Buggy America: An Anthology of Contemporaneous Essays*. San Bernardino, Calif.: Borgo Press, 1995.

Smoodin, Eric, ed. *Disney Discourse: Producing the Magic Kingdom*. New York: Routledge, 1994.

Snow, Richard. *Coney Island: A Postcard Journey to the City of Fire*. New York: Brightwaters Press, 1984.

Snow, Robert E., and David E. Wright. "Coney Island: A Case Study of Popular Culture and Technical Change." *Journal of Popular Culture* 9 (Spring 1976), 960–75.

Sonneck, O. G. *Early Concert Life in America (1731–1800)*. Leipzig: Breitkopf and Hartel, 1907.

Southworth, James Granville. *Vauxhall Gardens: A Chapter in the Social History of England*. New York: Columbia University Press, 1944.

Starbuck, James C. *Theme Parks: A Partially Annotated Bibliography of Articles about Modern Amusement Parks*. Exchange Bibliography 953. Monticello, Ill.: Council of Planning Librarians, 1976.

Starsmore, Ian. *English Fairs*. Levittown, N.Y.: Transatlantic Arts, 1976.

Stein, Harvey. *Coney Island*. New York: W. W Norton, 1998.

Summit, Roland. *Flying Horses*. Rolling Hills: Flying Horses, 1970.

Taylor, John. *Storming the Magic Kingdom: Wall Street, the Raiders, and the Battle for Disney*. New York: Knopf, 1987.

"Theme Parks USA." Special issue. *Theatre Crafts* 11 (September 1977), 27–103.

Thomas, Bob. *Walt Disney: An American Original*. New York: Simon and Schuster, 1976.

Thompson, Frederic. "Amusing the Million." *Everybody's Magazine* 19 (September 1908), 378+.

Throgmorton, Todd H. *Roller Coasters: An Illustrated Guide to the Rides in the United States and Canada, with a History*. Jefferson, N.C.: McFarland, 1993.

Tilyou, Edward F. "Why the Schoolma'am Walked into the Sea." *American Magazine* 94 (July 1922), 18–21, 86, 91–92, 94.

"To Heaven by Subway." *Fortune Magazine* 18 (August 1938), 60–68, 102–4, 106.

Trachtenberg, Alan. *The Incorporation of America: Culture and Society in the Gilded Age*. New York: Hill and Wang, 1982.

Truman, Benjamin C. *History of the World's Fair: Being a Complete and Authentic Description of the Columbian Exposition from Its Inception*. Philadelphia: H. W. Kelley, 1893. Reprint. New York: Arno Press, 1976.

Ulmer, Jeff. *Amusement Parks of America: A Comprehensive Guide*. New York: Dial Press, 1980.

Walt Disney Imagineering: A behind the Dreams Look at Making the Magic Real. Imagineers Group, Walt Disney Co. New York: Hyperion, 1996.

Wasserman, Louis. *Merchandising Architecture: Architectural Implications and Applications of Amusement Theme Parks.* Sheboygan, Wis.: Privately printed, 1978.

Waters, H. W. *History of Fairs and Expositions.* London, Ontario: Reid, 1939.

White, Anthony G. *Amusement Parks: A Selected Bibliography.* Architecture Series Bibliography A1052. Monticello, Ill.: Vance Bibliographies, 1983.

White, Trumbull, and William Igleheart. *World's Columbian Exposition, Chicago, 1893: A Complete History of the Enterprise: A Full Description of the Buildings and Exhibits in All Departments: And a Short Account of Previous Expositions.* . . . Philadelphia: C. Foster, 1893.

Wlodarczyk, Chuck. *Riverview: Gone but Not Forgotten. A Photo History, 1904–1967.* Chicago: Riverview, 1977.

Wroth, Warwick. *Cremorne and the Later London Gardens.* London: Elliot Stock, 1907.

Wroth, Warwick, with Arthur Edgar Wroth. *The London Pleasure Gardens of the Eighteenth Century.* London: Macmillan, 1896. Reprint. Hamden, Conn.: Archon, 1979.

Wylson, Anthony, and Patricia Wylson. *Theme Parks, Leisure Centers, Zoos, and Aquaria.* New York: Wiley, 1994.

Fairs

Auger, Helen. *The Book of Fairs.* New York: Harcourt, Brace, 1930.

Baatz, Simon. *"Venerate the Plough": A History of the Philadelphia Society for Promoting Agriculture 1785–1985.* Philadelphia: The Society, 1985.

Bailey, Liberty Hyde. *Cyclopedia of American Agriculture.* 4 vols. New York: Macmillan, 1907.

Breen, David, and Kenneth Coates. *Vancouver's Fair: An Administrative and Political History of the Pacific National Exhibition.* Vancouver: University of British Columbia Press, 1982.

Carre, Paul E. *Maryland State Fair—100 Years.* Timonium, Md.: The Fair, 1981.

Clark, Thomas D. *Agrarian Kentucky.* Lexington: University Press of Kentucky, 1977.

Day, Clarence A. *A History of Maine Agriculture 1604–1860.* Orono: University of Maine Press, 1954.

Directory of North American Fairs, Festivals, and Expositions. Annual. Nashville: Amusement Business, 1986– .

Distad, Audree. *Come to the Fair.* New York: Harper and Row, 1977.

Fish, Charles. *Blue Ribbons and Burlesque: A Book of Country Fairs.* Woodstock, Vt.: Countryman Press, 1998.

Fletcher, Steven Whitcomb. *Pennsylvania Agriculture and Country Life 1840–1940.* Harrisburg: Pennsylvania Historical and Museum Commission, 1955.

Gray, Lewis C. *History of Agriculture in the Southern United States to 1860.* Washington, D.C.: Carnegie Institution, 1933.

Hall, Darwin S., and R. I. Holcombe. *History of the Minnesota State Agricultural Society.* St. Paul: The Society, 1910.

Hamilton, John. *Agricultural Fair Associations and Their Utilization in Agricultural*

Education and Improvement. U.S. Department of Agriculture, Office of Experiment Stations, Circular 109. Washington, D.C.: Government Printing Office, 1911.

Hedrick, Ulysses Prentice. *A History of Agriculture in the State of New York.* Albany: New York State Agricultural Society, 1933.

Holmes, George K. *List of Agricultural Fairs and Exhibitions in the United States.* U.S. Department of Agriculture, Bureau of Statistics, Bulletin 102. Washington, D.C.: Government Printing Office, 1913.

Jackson, George, ed. *The Fundamental Principles of Successful County and State Fairs.* Lincoln, Nebr.: Wekesser-Brinkman, 1939.

Jones, Robert Leslie. *History of Agriculture in Ohio to 1880.* Kent, Ohio: Kent State University Press, 1983.

Lesberg, Steve, and Naomi Goldberg. *County Fair.* New York and London: Peebles Press, 1978.

Lorimer, James. *The Ex: A Picture History of the Canadian National Exhibition.* Toronto: James Lewis and Samuel, 1973.

Marti, Donald B. *Historical Directory of American Agricultural Fairs.* New York: Greenwood Press, 1986.

Murray, Chalmers S. *This Our Land, the Story of the Agricultural Society of South Carolina.* Charleston, S.C.: Carolina Art Association, 1949.

Neely, Wayne Caldwell. *The Agricultural Fair.* New York: Columbia University Press, 1935.

Nordin, Dennis Sven. *Rich Harvest: A History of the Grange, 1867–1900.* Jackson: University Press of Mississippi, 1974.

Perl, Lila. *America Goes to the Fair: All About State and County Fairs in the USA.* New York: William Morrow, 1974.

Pierce, Jack. *The State Fair Book.* Minneapolis: Carolrhoda Books, 1980.

Primack, Phil. *New England Country Fair.* Chester, Conn.: Globe Pequot Press, 1982.

Prosterman, Leslie. *Ordinary Life, Festival Days: Aesthetics in the Midwestern County Fair.* Washington, D.C.: Smithsonian Institution Press, 1995.

Range, Willard. *A Century of Georgia Agriculture, 1850–1950.* Athens: University of Georgia Press, 1954.

Reck, Franklin M. *The 4-H Story: A History of 4-H Club Work.* Ames: Iowa State College Press, 1951.

Ryan, John W. *The Wisconsin State Fair, Its Modern Role and Objectives.* Madison: University of Wisconsin Research and Advisory Service, Bureau of Government, Report NS2, February 1960.

Schmidt, Hubert G. *Agriculture in New Jersey, A Three-Hundred Year History.* New Brunswick, N.J.: Rutgers University Press, 1973.

Shemanski, Frances. *A Guide to Fairs and Festivals in the United States.* Westport, Conn.: Greenwood Press, 1984.

Speer, Ray P., and Harry J. Frost. *Minnesota State Fair: The History and Heritage of 100 Years.* St. Paul: Argus, 1964.

Tenney, A. Webster. *The FFA at 50.* Alexandria, Va.: Future Farmers of America, 1977.

Walden, Keith. *Becoming Modern in Toronto: The Industrial Exhibition and the Shaping of a Late Victorian Culture.* Toronto: University of Toronto Press, 1997.

Watson, Elkanah. *History of Agricultural Societies on the Modern Berkshire System.* Albany: D. Steele, 1820.

———. *History of the Rise, Progress, and Existing Condition of the Western Canals in the State of New York.* Albany: D. Steele, 1820.

Wessel, Thomas, and Mary Wessel. *4-H: An American Idea.* Chevy Chase, Md.: National 4-H Council, 1982.

Wiley, Nancy. *Great State Fair of Texas.* Dallas: Taylor, 1985.

Periodicals

Agricultural History. Berkeley, Calif., 1927– .

American Agriculturalist. Poughkeepsie, N.Y., 1842–1964.

Amusement Business. Nashville, 1961– .

At the Park: A Journal for the Amusement Park Industry. Chicago, 1990– .

Chronicles of Oklahoma. Oklahoma City, 1921– .

Funworld. Alexandria, Va., 1986– .

Indiana Magazine of History. Bloomington, Ind., 1905– .

Journal of American Culture. Bowling Green, Ohio, 1978– .

Journal of Popular Culture. Bowling Green, Ohio, 1967– .

National Amusement Park Historical News. Mt. Prospect, Ill., 1978–1988. Continued by *NAPHA News.* Mt. Prospect, Ill., 1989– .

Nebraska History. Lincoln, Nebr., 1918– .

New England Farmer. Boston, 1822–1913.

New York History. Albany, 1932– .

Roller Coaster! Chicago, 1979– .

Rural New-Yorker. New York, 1879–1964.

World's Fair. Corte Madera, Calif., 1981–1995.

Silver Lake, Ohio. Courtesy of the Library of Congress

Loop the Loop, Coney Island, New York. Courtesy of the Denver Public Library

Santa Monica Pier, California. Photo by Harry M. Rhoads. Courtesy of the Library of Congress

Scene from the 1977 film, *Rollercoaster*. Kobal Collection/Universal

Lakeside Amusement Park, Colorado. Courtesy of the Denver Public Library

Father with children on rollercoaster at state fair,
St. Paul, Minnesota. © Skjold Photographs

Busch Gardens, Tampa, Florida. © Painet

ANIMATION

Maureen Furniss

Animation has been an integral part of American popular culture since at least the 1600s, when animated imagery of various types was created with optical toys and projecting devices. After motion pictures were first screened to the public, in 1895–1896, live-action and animated films soon became immensely popular and commercially successful forms of entertainment worldwide. Filmmaking centers developed within many countries, with France, Germany, England, and the United States all vying for the biggest shares of this lucrative business.

However, American productions—both live-action and animated—eventually dominated commercial production worldwide and now can be said to "define" the practices in the minds of most viewers. American live-action and animated cinema began to achieve international domination during World War I, when European countries were affected greatly by the conflict. But it was not until the 1930s, after the "coming of sound" to motion pictures, that animation from the Walt Disney, Warner Bros., MGM, and other studios solidified into what is now known as the "golden age" of classical Hollywood animation. Through the 1930s and 1940s, American animation experienced a vitality that produced the bulk of great films now known as "classics" of the industry. This golden age lasted until the early 1950s, when changes in film exhibition patterns led to the closure of theatrical animation units at Hollywood studios, while the growth of television lured animators into a new medium. With various lulls and surges, the American animation industry continued on through the next several decades; generally, the 1960s through the early 1980s are seen as a period that produced little remarkable production. However, since the late 1980s, there has been another period of great growth and creative activity in the American industry and, indeed, worldwide.

During the same period, the late 1980s to the present, animation also has become the focus of in-depth study by scholars. During the 1990s, in particular, valuable books and other publications were produced in the emerging field of animation studies. The growth in research has been accompanied by a parallel increase in the availability of animation in various home-entertainment formats. As a result, we are now able to see and read about a wide range of animated productions. After a brief historical outline, this review will covers reference books; books on history and theory; journals; and other literature that will be of interest to individuals conducting research in the area of animation studies.

HISTORICAL OUTLINE

Long before 1895, when a motion picture was screened publicly for the first time, models for both live-action and animated films had been established by optical toys and various forms of projected images involving sequential movements. Among these "cinematic precursors" are the painted and photographed glass slides of magic lantern shows, which date back to the mid-seventeenth century, as well as several kinds of entertainments that have been popular since the early- to mid-1800s, for example, the two-state animated images of the thaumatrope, the cyclical multistep animation produced for a phenakistiscope wheel, and the cyclical multistep animation produced from the linear strips of paper used in a zoetrope. Equally interesting in terms of cinematic models are the motion studies conducted by Englishman Eadweard Muybridge in the United States and Frenchman Jean Etienne Marey in his own country, which allowed scientists as well as artists to better understand the dynamics of human and animal movement.

Eventually, technology was developed that allowed the recording of sequential images on a flexible film base. The French brothers Auguste and Louis Lumière, using their versatile cinématographe camera/developer/projector, were the first to screen films publicly in 1895, but it did not take long for others to join them, resulting in the development of what shortly would become a major industry. During the first twenty years of film history (1895–1915), film production also sprang up in the United States, England, Italy, Germany, Japan, and other countries. Although the United States was the largest consumer of motion pictures during these early years, it did not dominate in terms of production. Rather, France was the world's leading producer of films.

The domination of the French film company Pathé Frères was aided by the American Thomas Edison. Since the 1890s, Edison had been a leading force in American film development. In 1908, Edison established the Motion Picture Patents Company (MPPC) as an alliance among major American film production companies; these companies pooled their patents to many essential processes and technologies and effectively limited the ability of "outsiders" to do business. When Edison granted Pathé Frères the rights to use these patents, he helped the French production company by limiting competition from most other foreign filmmakers. The only other foreign company licensed by Edison was that of perhaps the most popular filmmaker in the world at that time, Georges Méliès; actually, that license was granted to Méliès' American office, which was run by his unscrupulous brother, Gaston.

Though the power of the MPPC was waning by 1914, the American film industry was moving forward as a whole. Within a few years, it began to dominate world production. As noted, World War I weakened the producing power of European filmmaking nations; the German national film industry was the only one to emerge from the war in a relatively strong position, but its power was hindered by a number of restrictions enacted by American distributors. During the war, American studios restructured their distribution methods, developing domestic distribution channels so that they would not have to rely on distributors located in London. England had been the major world trade center prior to the war and therefore was a logical choice for distributing American films to the European continent. With its own distribution channels in place, the American film industry had much more control over pricing and other important matters.

After it became the world power in filmmaking and distribution, the technical, formal, and thematic content of American productions significantly impacted the creation of conventional standards across the world. Though individual countries have developed their own styles of filmmaking throughout history, American live-action cinema has remained commercially dominant on an international level, continuing to set aesthetic norms for viewers. In terms of animation, the situation has been similar. American—that is "Hollywood"—animated productions have continued to be very popular with foreign audiences; today the Disney studio, for one, makes its animated feature films in a number of languages, anticipating widespread international release.

By the mid-1910s, animation production in the United States already was dominated by the techniques of two-dimensional animation, specifically paper and later cel, which developed into the conventional narrative storytelling tradition associated with studios such as Disney and Warner Bros. However, when the film industry was in its infancy, three-dimensional techniques, such as the use of objects, clay and puppets, also appeared with some frequency. Though some Americans employed 3-D, many animated films of this type came from European sources.

In his 3-D animations, pioneering French filmmaker Georges Méliès used stop motion—that is, stopping the camera, then adding or removing an object and starting the camera again—a practice that silent film scholar Donald Crafton considers to be a technical predecessor of regular frame-by-frame animation. Méliès' most famous film is *Voyage dans la lune* (Trip to the Moon, 1902), in which aggressive moon inhabitants (called Selenites) burst into flames and "disappear" after being hit by the umbrellas of explorers from earth.

By 1907, the Spaniard Segundo de Chomón, who worked for French and Italian production companies under the name of Chomont, had created his popular *El hotel eléctrico* (The Electric Hotel). This film and many others, including American J. Stuart Blackton's *Haunted Hotel* (1907), played on the novelty of "spooky" or "haunted" surroundings, wherein objects seemed to move of their own accord or due to the forces of some evil spirit.

Clay, cutouts, and puppets appeared in various animated films made during the early years of film history. For example, puppets were animated in the 1907 film *The Teddy Bears*, directed by the American Edwin Porter. Blackton worked with clay animation in the 1910 film *Chew Chew Land*. American Willis O'Brien, who became famous for his special effects animation in the features *The Lost World* (directed by Harry Hoyt, 1925) and *King Kong* (directed by Merian C. Cooper, 1933), was doing object animation in the mid-1910s in short works such as *The Dinosaur and the Missing Link* (1915). The Russian-born filmmaker Ladislas Starewicz also had a long career animating objects, including extremely realistic-looking insect models in *Mest' Kinomatograficheskogo Operatora* (The Cameraman's Revenge, 1912).

Historical and industrial factors helped determine that cels—and not clay or puppets, for instance—quickly would become the dominant technique of commercial animation production. Among them is the fact that, in the 1910s, the mode of film production in America moved from an individual and small-group process toward an assembly-line method employing large numbers of people in narrowly defined job classifications. This reorganization was influenced by a set of principles known generally as Taylorism, named for a pioneer in management theory, Frederick W. Taylor.

A significant reason that paper-based and then cel animation came to dominate the American industry during the early years of film history is that these techniques lend themselves to an assembly-line method of production. Whereas clay or puppet animation is most labor-intensive during the shooting stage, when objects must be manipulated in front of the camera by a small crew of people, paper and cel animation tends to be most labor-intensive during the production stage, when a large number of people can work on drawing and coloring the thousands of images that will be filmed. The distribution of labor that can be achieved with drawn animation allows key creative individuals to do initial design work on a project, while less skilled (and lower-paid) workers complete the more repetitive tasks, allowing the key creators to move on to another project. Because animation is such a labor-intensive process, the American industry could not have flourished as it did without finding a means of cutting costs and speeding up production: an assembly-line method of production employing 2-D animation proved to be effective.

During the 1910s and 1920s, various 2-D production methods were in use, including "retracing" and the "slash system." Retracing, which requires each element of a piece of art to be drawn over and over again, is perhaps the most basic method used to create animation. This method was used in the work of influential animators Emile Cohl, from France, who created *Fantasmagorie* (1908) and many other films, and Winsor McCay, from the United States, who created *Little Nemo* (1911) and *Gertie the Dinosaur* (1914), among others. Significant changes to the retracing system were introduced by Canadian Raoul Barré, who generally is credited with making two major contributions to animation production: the slash system (also called "slash and tear") and the "perf and peg" alignment system. Using the slash system, an individual was freed from tedious retracing: the artist drew one background and laid it over another sheet containing the moving elements, cutting out a space so that images on the underlying sheet of paper could be seen. Barré's standardized perf and peg system, variations of which are still in use today, involves the use of punched holes at the bottom (or top) of animation paper (or cels) and a similarly designed peg-bar that holds sheets for drawing or shooting, all of which allows for precise registration of images.

The invention that has had the largest impact on the animation industry is the clear, flexible sheet of drawing material generally known as a cel (also spelled "cell," especially during the early years of film history). Moving images are drawn onto a cel, which can be layered and placed over a background drawing or painting. This system was invented and patented by animator Earl Hurd in 1914. Until

1950, animation cels—like 35mm film stocks—were made with a nitrate base that was quite flammable and deteriorated relatively easily.

At first, the development of the cel system was hampered by the fact that any studio wishing to use it had to pay royalties to the Bray-Hurd Patent Company (Earl Hurd went into business with another animation pioneer, John Randolph Bray), increasing the expense of an already expensive system. As production time became an increasingly significant consideration, more and more studios began using cels. Still, it was not until 1932, when the patent came into the public domain, that cel animation really became the industry norm. To make the system more affordable during its early years, studios saved money by reusing cels. This could be done by cycling motions (repeating a set of movements, as in a "walk cycle") in a film, reusing actions or backgrounds in several films, or washing the cels and repainting them for future productions, typically up to six times.

During the 1920s, there were a number of successful animation companies in the United States. Among them were studios run by Pat Sullivan, who produced the "Felix the Cat" series; Max Fleischer, who produced the "Out of the Inkwell" films starring Ko-Ko the Clown; and Walt Disney, who produced the "Alice Comedies." These filmmakers' works all were distributed by Margaret J. Winkler, a female whose great success distributing short animated and live-action series made her a novelty within the male-dominated motion picture industry. Until relatively recently, it was very difficult for women to find work in creative or executive positions within the field of animation; most were employed as inkers, painters, and color key artists (assisting with the color design of films).

While the "Felix the Cat" films did not make the transition to sound very well, both the Fleischer and Disney studios continued to battle for popularity during the 1930s, amid a growing field of animation studios. Fleischer's "Betty Boop" and "Popeye" series were successful properties, but in the long run nothing compared to the success of Disney's character Mickey Mouse, who was introduced to the public in a 1928 film, *Steamboat Willie*. During the 1930s, the Disney studio released two series, the "Mickey Mouse" films, which employed a growing cast of starring characters, and the "Silly Symphony" films, a series of "one-shot" shorts (no repeating characters or related plots) that provided a place to test new technology. Other American animation studios to appear on the scene during the late 1920s and 1930s included Terrytoons, Walter Lantz, Van Buren, Ub Iwerks, Screen Gems, Warner Bros., and MGM.

Despite the popularity of various series at these studios, Disney managed to capture a great deal of attention with its many achievements, along with its careful marketing strategies, which were implemented worldwide by the early 1930s. Among the studio's most publicized achievements was the release of its first feature, *Snow White*, in 1937. Although it was not the first feature-length animated film to be produced (e.g., the German Lotte Reiniger completed her film *Prince Achmed* in 1926), it did mark a great achievement in terms of classical Hollywood animation.

A turning point for the Disney studio came during the early 1940s, when dissent set in among its employees. During the depression years, the Disney studio had taken in many new artists in order to produce *Snow White*. As the economy improved and workers began demanding changes in employment practices, including shorter hours and higher pay, union membership grew. A strike occurred at the

Scene from *Anchors Aweigh*, 1945. The Kobol Collection/MGM

Disney studio in 1941, and arbitrators were called in to settle the dispute. Eventually, many of Disney's best animators either left or were fired. Some animators left for political reasons, but others departed because of World War II, which America entered late that year.

A number of artists from various studios went to the army's First Motion Picture Unit in Culver City, to create animated maps and other materials for the war effort. After the war, some of them—including a handful of ex-Disney employees who had been involved with the strike—banded together with other progressively minded artists to create an extraordinary studio that, while relatively short-lived, continues to have great influence on animation aesthetics today: United Productions of America (UPA). Founders Stephen Bosustow, Zachary Schwartz, and David Hilberman initially began the company under the name Industrial Film and Poster Service. They first designed posters but soon began making films, including two shorts for the United Auto Workers Union, *Hell Bent for Election* (1944) and *The Brotherhood of Man* (1946). Eventually, UPA became known for an array of stylish short films, such as *Gerald McBoing-Boing* (1951), *Rooty-Toot-Toot* (1952), *Madeline* (1952), and *The Tell Tale Heart* (1953), as well as the "Mr. Magoo" series.

UPA's aesthetic came to be known as a "limited animation" style, which can be contrasted with the style of "full animation" generally employed in the classical animation of Disney or Warner Bros., for example. Limited animation is driven more by sound and dialogue than movement, which is the foundation of full animation. In the case of UPA, its designs were influenced by modern art aesthetics. However, limited animation as it was applied during subsequent years by the American animation industry was not always so successful. As a result, the term "limited animation" has acquired a negative connotation.

Like many other Hollywood studios, UPA was phased out during the mid-1950s. Many of its artists, such as Bill Hurtz (perhaps best known for his work on Jay Ward's "Rocky and Bullwinkle" series), went into television production. Some of the significant studios to develop during the late 1950s, 1960s, and 1970s, as a result of the expansion of made-for-television animation, were Jay Ward, Hanna-Barbera, Filmation, DePatie-Freleng, and Ruby Spears. At that time, a lot of animation work for American series began to be shipped "offshore" (mostly to a variety of Asian countries), where labor costs were lower. The fast pace and lower budgets of television production encouraged the use of a limited animation style for economic reasons—because it employs so little movement, it saves time in the rendering of images and, therefore, costs less than full animation. However, much of the work produced was poorly conceived. Artists had little opportunity to develop stories or correct errors, partly because the animation was being finished overseas, far from its American studio. Bold, solid colors had to be employed so that images could be identified despite the poor resolution of television screens (in comparison with projected film); as a result, made-for-television animation looked a lot cheaper than its theatrical counterparts. In fact, it really was.

The Disney studio continued to produce animated features during the 1960s and 1970s, some of which were quite profitable, and it had little competition from other theatrical films. A few notable exceptions exist in the British feature *Yellow Submarine* (released in 1968 by Apple Films and King Features) and the work of Ralph Bakshi, who created the X-rated *Fritz the Cat* in 1972 and a number of other adult-oriented animated features.

During the 1960s, the programming of "Saturday morning cartoons" was begun as television networks realized the profit potential created by blocks of children's animation airing on weekend mornings; advertisers targeting young consumers were easily attracted. The first year that all three networks at the time (ABC, CBS, and NBC) offered a Saturday morning lineup was 1966. At about the same time, a number of special interest groups began to question the ethics of made-for-television animation. One of the most vocal of these groups was Action for Children's Television (ACT), which helped create reforms leading to more educational programming and less advertising. The success of the Children's Television Workshop's *Sesame Street*, which first aired in 1968, convinced some skeptics that educational programming could attract viewers.

While the majority of children's animation appearing during the early 1970s fell into the categories of male-oriented superhero action/adventures, animated remakes of live-action television shows, or comedies generally involving adventure and/or music performances (Hanna-Barbera's *Scooby-Doo*, which first aired in 1969, and *Josie and the Pussycats*, which first aired in 1970, serve as examples), educational or "prosocial" programming did appear. One of the best examples is the series *Fat Albert and the Cosby Kids*, created in conjunction with Bill Cosby and a panel of educators and produced by Filmation; it first aired in 1972. This series was progressive not only in its inclusion of positive role models and behaviors for children but because it helped redress the racism that characterized the content of much golden age animation. Naturally, the fact that golden era animation was managed and designed predominantly by a white male population affected its content; white women and people of color rarely were depicted as the interest center of an animated work and generally were portrayed in a stereotypical manner. Efforts by stereotyped groups to criticize the animation industry generally resulted in the removal of sensitive images rather than the creation of more carefully balanced diversity. For example, as protests about the depiction of African Americans grew through the 1940s and 1950s, one finds that black images become much more scarce in American animation.

Despite the work of industry reformers during the 1970s, the changing political climate of the early 1980s brought deregulation of the industry. With it came the sanctioning of "program-length advertising," or animated series that essentially were developed around commercial products (i.e., toys) that children could purchase. An example is Filmation's *He-Man and Masters of the Universe*, first aired in 1985. Educational programming once again became a low priority as executives based decisions on profitability rather than community welfare (much less aesthetic concerns). Already, many of the leading animation studios had been purchased by corporate entities as part of a general trend toward conglomeration in the film and television industries. The new management at this time was much less knowledgeable (or concerned) about animation in particular than the workings of industry on a larger scale.

Some of the most interesting animation being created during the 1980s occurred within television advertising, which always had welcomed animated imagery. Studios such as Kurtz & Friends, R. O. Blechman, Ink Tank, Duck Soup, and many others specialized in, and had great success with, this form of animation. Advertising studios primarily used traditional 2-D techniques, then began embracing the developing techniques of computer animation, particularly for television station identifications and program logos and in product ads. The Will Vinton Studio, which produced a series of popular commercials featuring dancing "California Raisins," helped to again popularize 3-D animation through its studio's Claymation technique.

Another area of growth during the 1980s was within the realm of independent animation production. Actually, this area had been developing since the 1960s, when a number of animation courses began to be taught throughout American universities. Programs at Harvard University, the University of California at Los Angeles, New York University, California Institute of the Arts, and other universities began to turn out animation artists who worked commercially by day and did personal projects by night or experimenters who found employment teaching at universities that could lend support to the production of independent projects. Women, who previously had found few creative opportunities within the realm of animation, found that college programs allowed them to direct and animate works; their films often explored the experience of being female, influenced by the growth of women's studies and gender studies, as well as feminism in general. Film festivals sponsored by ASIFA (l'Association Internationale du Film d'Animation, an international animation society) or independent promoters developed worldwide, providing regular showcases for independent work.

Scene from *Cool World*, 1992. The Kobol Collection/Paramount

During the mid- to late 1980s, a series of developments in the American animation industry signaled that changes were occurring within the commercial realm as well. First, there were big changes in store for the Disney company when, in 1984, Frank Wells was brought in as president and Michael Eisner became the new chief executive officer; they brought in other associates to create a new Disney image, including Jeffrey Katzenberg. The success of Disney's animated features, beginning with the live-action and animation combined *Who Framed Roger Rabbit*, released in 1989, revealed that animation could attract a broad range of viewers, both adults and children. The phenomenal popularity of *The Little Mermaid* in 1990 and plans for a line of animated features in subsequent years indicated that Disney was very optimistic about the profitability of animated productions.

An equally strong message was sent to the industry with the 1990 debut of *The Simpsons* series in a prime-time slot on the newly launched Fox television network (characters in the series first appeared on the network's *The Tracey Ullman Show* series, as bumpers around commercial breaks). *The Simpsons* proved that the public was willing to embrace something other than full-animation made by Disney. In doing so, it greatly invigorated made-for-television animation production and encouraged the production of various styles and techniques. MTV, Nickelodeon, and other cable television networks began their own successful animation series, many oriented toward adult viewers, and alternatives to Disney cel-animated features began appearing in theaters. Most notable was the feature *Beavis and Butt-Head Do America* (1996, based on MTV's popular television series), which earned box-office records. The creator of Beavis and Butt-Head, Mike Judge, created another successful television series, *King of the Hill*, which the Fox Network debuted in a prime-time slot after *The Simpsons*.

During this time of prosperity, Disney itself diversified in its animation technique, producing a 3-D feature, *The Nightmare before Christmas* (1993), and the first completely computer-generated film, *Toy Story* (1995). Another new direction was taken by Dreamworks with its 1998 release of *The Prince of Egypt*, the biblical story of Moses, a definite departure from the musical comedies constituting Disney's primary focus.

A great deal of research and development continues to be poured into computer-generated imagery (CGI) because it seems to represent the future of animated production. Already, many 2-D animated series appearing on television are finished using ink-and-paint programs, plus 3-D animation is used extensively to create special effects in live-action features. The first completely CGI series made for television were *Les fables géometriques* (Geometric Fables, beginning in 1989) and *Insektors* (beginning 1993), both released through the French production house Fantôme Animation, and *Reboot* (released in 1994), by the Canadian production house Mainframe Entertainment. Animated CGI features such as *Antz* (produced by Dreamworks) and *A Bug's Life* (produced by Pixar and Disney), both released in 1998, reflect the limitations of the technology in representing human subjects or hair and fur of any kind; insects and toys are used as subjects because the computer excels at creating hard, shiny surfaces. Motion capture is another technique currently undergoing testing; it bases animation on the performance of a human actor who is linked electronically to a computer, theoretically saving time in the animation process.

The future of animation seems optimistic, but it is difficult to tell the direction that it will take during the next few years. What seems certain is that new technologies will continue to play a significant role, both as production tools and as "delivery systems" for animated imagery, by way of software, animated games, and Internet sites. Although the next generation of animation artists can expect to work on computers, studios still are stressing the need for traditional animation training, including extensive life drawing skills. Clearly, some combination of traditional aesthetics and new technologies will carry animation into the twenty-first century.

REFERENCE WORKS

Of the relatively early reference works, Thomas W. Hoffer's *Animation: A Reference Guide*, published by Greenwood Press in 1981, is among the most useful. In the book, the author himself describes the work as "an encyclopedic survey and guide to the animation literature in cel, stop-action, drawing-on-film, experimental, and computer graphic modes." In addition to a historical overview, the book contains seven appendixes about major research centers, a chronology, sources for collectors, and annotated listings from the trade press.

Through Scarecrow Press, George Woolery published another useful series of reference works during the 1980s, including two titles related to animation: *Children's Television: The First Thirty-Five Years, 1946–1981, Part I: Animated Cartoon Series*, published in 1983, and *Animated TV Specials: The Complete Directory to the First Twenty-Five Years, 1962–1987*, published in 1988. The *Children's Television* book contains series synopses, complete production credits, and broadcast schedules for every animated television series from 1946 to 1981. *Animated TV Specials* contains the broadcast history, principal characters and voices, and synopsis of shows aired on networks or in syndication on American television between 1962 and 1987. Generally it does not include any program identified initially as being a theatrical film. Its appendixes include "Most Frequently Aired/Longest Running Network Animated TV Specials," "TV Specials Utilizing Stop-Motion Animated Puppets," "Holiday and Topical Animated TV Specials," and "Animated TV Specials Series." It also contains a "Name Index" to producers, directors, filmmakers, writers, musicians, lyricists, and voices and a "Selected Subject Index" to studios, production companies, and distributors.

More recently, a number of other animation-related reference guides have been published. Among them is John Lent's 1994 book, *Animation, Caricature, and Gag and Political Cartoons in the United States and Canada—An International Bibliography*, which is part of the Greenwood Press series, "Bibliographies and Indexes in Popular Culture." One chapter focuses on "U.S. Animation," containing coverage of such categories as legal issues, animation studios, children's press, and syndication.

Denis Gifford's *American Animated Films: The Silent Era, 1897–1929*, published by McFarland in 1990, provides details on the films themselves. It references productions chronologically by 140 series titles, beginning with Blackton Cartoons (1897), Vitagraph Cartoons (1900–1909), and Winsor McCay Cartoons (1911–1918) and running through the two Mickey Mouse cartoons of 1928 originally recorded as silent films, *Plane Crazy* and *The Gallopin' Gaucho*. Included with each entry, when applicable, are alternative and British titles, production company name, production credits, distributor, length of film, changes in titles or distributors, and other significant information.

A larger period of time is covered in McFarland's 1998 publication *Film Cartoons: A Guide to 20th-Century American Animated Features and Shorts*, written by Douglas L. McCall. This book is divided into three sections, the first of which covers 180 animated feature films, mostly American but also some films produced outside the country. It includes general information, notes, production and voice credits, and in some cases awards and other information. Part 2 deals with fifty-eight feature-length, live-action/animation combination films; it lists the titles and year of release for each film, plus a description of the animation contained in it. Part 3 covers 1,500 animated shorts with brief notes, which include title, year of release, director, studio, various production credits, and in some cases synopses, notes, and awards. These shorts are mainly productions of major Hollywood studios. A variety of animation studios is covered in an appendix; they are both large and small and mostly American, though a few studios from Canada and England are included. Entries in this book are very uneven in their content, with some being relatively full and others including very little information.

More consistently useful entries can be found in Hal Erickson's *Television Cartoon Shows: An Illustrated Encyclopedia 1949 through 1993*, published by McFarland in 1995; this book is among the best resources available for made-for-television animation, at least in respect to American exhibition. A forty-two-page history of television introduces the volume, which contains the titles, networks, air dates, production credits, synopses, and related information (often quite useful) for every animated production aired on American broadcast and cable networks during the forty-four-year period. The book concludes with an eight-page chapter on voice artists, covering significant considerations related to the profession as well as a number of individuals who are well known in the field.

Two "popular" reference books were revised by their author, Jeff Lenburg, during the early 1990s: *The Encyclopedia of Animated Cartoons* and *The Great Cartoon Directors*. The *Encyclopedia*, originally published by Facts on File, contains "A Nutshell History of the American Animated Cartoon." This overview is followed by a synopsis, production credits, air dates, and, when applicable, episode titles for silent cartoon series, theatrical sound cartoon series, full-length animated features, animated television specials, and television cartoon series. A list of awards and honors is also included, along with a bibliography. *The Great Cartoon Directors*, published by Da Capo in 1993, includes profiles and a filmography for nine of Hollywood's most famous animation directors—Friz Freleng, Ub Iwerks, Chuck Jones, William Hanna, Joseph Barbera, Bob Clampett, Tex Avery, Walter Lantz, and Dave Fleischer. The filmographies contain titles and release dates for each production.

A focus on Warner Bros. shorts, in particular, can be found in Jerry Beck and Will Friedwald's 1988 reference book *Looney Tunes and Merry Melodies: A Complete Illustrated Guide to the Warner Bros. Cartoons*, which contains a chronological filmography of over 900 shorts produced by the studio, as well as listings for its network television series, specials, feature-length films, and government-sponsored cartoons. Entries include release date, main characters, writers, producers, and lead animators. Kathy Merlock Jackson's *Walt Disney: A Bio-Bibliography*, published by Greenwood Press in 1993, is an objective, evenhanded reference listing important sources for Disney information in all media, a variety of interviews, articles and speeches given by Disney, and filmographies, award lists, production credits, and other information pertaining to both Disney and his company. The book contains information on the impact of Disney on American culture, including extensive material on the theme parks.

A lot of reference information about the Disney studio has been produced under the company's own publishing label, Hyperion. As might be expected, these books tend to present a positive spin on all details, treading lightly over or ignoring controversial areas; nonetheless, Hyperion books provide varied and useful resources for many applications. Hyperion books include the 608-page *Disney A to Z: The Updated Official Encyclopedia*, written by Disney archivist Dave Smith and published in 1998. It contains more than 6,500 entries covering noteworthy company employees and visitors, Disney films and television shows, theme parks, and various other Disney ventures. Designed to be an aid for answering common questions asked of the archivists, the book offers short passages containing factual information and bits of trivia as well as air dates and limited production credits.

Leonard Maltin's *The Disney Films* was published by Hyperion in a third edition in 1995. It focuses primarily on the live-action and animated features produced under Walt Disney's supervision, from *Snow White* (1937) to *The Luckiest Millionaire* (1967). Production credits and a review are provided for each of these films, which are illustrated with one or more photos. Other features are discussed in essays constituting two additional chapters, one focusing on the years 1967 to 1984 and the other continuing until 1994 (the division resting on the 1984 formation of Touchstone Pictures and the changing Disney image as executives were brought in from "the outside" to turn around the company's relative stagnation). Although the 1995 film *Pocahontas* is mentioned in an essay, the "selected credits" listed for all the later features run only through 1994 (excluding that film). Final chapters include essays on the Disney shorts and made-for-television productions (the latter being quite brief); lists of titles by year also are included. A more recent book published by Hyperion, Joe Grant's 1997 *The Encyclopedia of Walt Disney's Animated Characters*, provides information related to the studio's short and feature-length productions. It is divided into three parts, covering shorts, television series, and features, and includes Disney stars as well as generic characters (e.g., Satan and Neptune). Some descriptions are brief, while others, such as Donald Duck (who receives eight pages), are quite lengthy; discussion of voice artists and a filmography are included in some cases.

Researchers wishing to locate specific animated films can consult David Kilmer's *The Animated Film Collector's Guide: Worldwide Sources for Cartoons on Videotape and Laserdisc*, published by John Libbey in 1997. This reference contains a list of useful books; listings of films by title, author, character, and studio; information on compilations of short films; names of distributors and resources; a worldwide list of chapters of ASIFA (the international animation society); an "honor roll" of award-winning films; and a review of a series of animated films released by Pioneer on laser disc. Although this book is international in its scope, it does not include information on "*anime*," or popular Japanese animation, which the author feels is handled sufficiently in other reference guides. Kilmer indicates that some of the titles that he includes can be found on film as well as video and laser disc.

The Whole Toon Catalog is a useful resource for individuals wishing to purchase a broad range of animated titles on video and laser disc, as well as audio and books. A Chicago-based, nonprofit arts organization and distributor, Facets Multimedia, publishes this general animation catalog in addition to a special catalog devoted to only Japanese animation. It can be ordered free of charge by calling the company's toll-free phone number, 1–800–331–6179 (see http://www.facets. org).

Collectors of animation art will find two books by Jeff Lotman of interest: *Animation Art: The Early Years, 1911–1953*, published in 1995, and *Animation Art: The Later Years, 1954–1993*, published in 1996, both by Schiffer. Containing thousands of examples of art, these books provide information on fair market prices for various types of animation art.

Individuals interested in college animation programs can consult Ernest Pintoff's *The Complete Guide to Animation and Computer Graphics Schools*, published by Watson-Guptill Publications in 1995. In addition to lists of schools by state (including addresses, curricular emphases, and general synopses of programs), the book contains one- to two-page statements (largely pertaining to education) made by fifty-seven accomplished educators, businesspeople, and artists in the field of animation. Another source of general information on schools, as well as animation equipment suppliers, film festivals, distributors of animated films, periodicals, and animation literature, is the American Film Institute's *Factfile #9: Animation*, compiled by Lucinda Travis and Jack Hannah in 1986.

HISTORY AND CRITICISM

The original publication of Donald Crafton's *Before Mickey: The Animated Film 1898–1928*, by the Massachusetts Institute of Technology in 1982, signaled a change in the nature of American animation scholarship (the book was reprinted by MIT in 1984 and 1987). By focusing on not only the silent era but also animation in Europe, this book went beyond the core of "golden age" Hollywood studios and even the few prominent experimental animators that had constituted the focus of most previous animation scholarship. Delving into the theory of animation in terms of self-figuration (the tendency for animation artists to render an element of themselves in their work), Crafton's book became part of the foundation of the emerging area of animation studies. Significant topics dealt with in this volume include the genre of "haunted hotel" trick films; the relationship between vaudeville and early animation practice; the pioneering animators Emile Cohl and Winsor McCay; John Randolph Bray, the studio system, and the influence of Taylorist management principles; commercial animation in Europe; the development of genre and narrative conventions; and Felix the Cat. Incidentally, in 1990 Crafton published an in-depth study of *Emile Cohl, Caricature and Film*, through Princeton University Press. Another example of excellent scholarship, this book examines Cohl as a link between the cinema and the field of popular graphic humor (he gained fame as a cartoonist).

Two books by John Canemaker provide in-depth studies of other silent-era legends. *Winsor McCay: His Life and Art*, published by Abbeville in 1987, includes well-researched historical information, as well as numerous illustrations and a bibliography. The same description can be used to characterize Canemaker's 1996 book, *Felix: The Twisted Tale of the World's Most Famous Cat*, published by Da Capo. Its selected filmography contains only titles and years. Both books are based in part on Canemaker's interviews and personal contact with family members, production personnel, and collectors who have allowed him to reproduce photos and memorabilia in the books.

Another landmark in the development of animation studies was the publication of Giannalberto Bendazzi's book, *Cartoons: One Hundred Years of Cinema Animation*, by John Libbey in 1994 (it previously had been published in Italian- and French-language versions). The most comprehensive study of its kind to date, *Cartoons* provides an encyclopedic history of animation produced worldwide, both at major studios and on a smaller scale. Bendazzi did much of his research at international animation festivals, probably the only place where one could find some of the marginal works that he discusses, such as Mongolian animation; to give an idea of the extent of his coverage, the influential Disney studio takes up only 10 of the book's 444 pages of text. Bendazzi covers the period between 1888 and 1990 in five sections, with additional sections devoted to new technologies (10 pages), a bibliography (including national publications and resources related to characters, filmmakers, education, aesthetics, and other topics), and indexes to names and titles. As the book's title suggests, filmed animation is of central concern in this book; made-for-television animation and other forms are not given much attention.

A wider view of formats is covered in Charles Solomon's *History of Animation: Enchanted Drawings*, first published in 1989 and reprinted by Wings Books in 1994. Beginning with a look at the silent era, Solomon's book then proceeds to cover Disney, 1928–1941; the studio cartoon, 1929–1941; wartime animation, 1941–1945; various studios of the period 1946–1960; the "silver age" of Disney, 1945–1960; UPA and the graphic revolution, 1943–1959; television animation; and changes within the industry, 1960–1994. The scope of coverage is broad, encompassing independent work and advertising, along with the "standards" of animation histories. Particularly noteworthy is Solomon's discussion of made-for-television animation. Though it is not exhaustive, it is far more detailed than most other accounts, which are few.

Earlier books that take a relatively wide view of animation history include Bruno Edera's *Full Length Animated Feature Films*, published by Hastings House in 1977, and John Halas' *Masters of Animation*, published by Salem House in 1987. Edera's book includes an overview of animation techniques, some general information related to production costs across the world, and discussion of feature films made in various regions. Chapters include pioneers 1916–1945; America (Disney); Middle East, Asia, and Australia; Eastern Europe; and Western Europe. A catalog published in the book contains many films, including some future productions, listing English and original titles, year of release, country of origin, running time, technique, basic production credits, and a synopsis. Halas' book covers general historical information, as well as brief overviews of national contexts and the "modern age" of animation (including computers, television and advertising). The majority of the book is devoted to several "masters" of animation from across the world. Four Americans are discussed: Walt Disney, Chuck Jones, and John and Faith Hubley. *Masters of Animation* was created in conjunction with a television series produced by the BBC in England.

For many years, the standard text of animation history courses was Leonard Maltin's *Of Mice and Magic: A History of American Animated Cartoons*, a well-illustrated, somewhat popular account of animation history. After an overview of the silent era, its content is organized by chapters on various studios: Disney, Fleischer, Terrytoons, Walter Lantz, Ub Iwerks, Van Beuren, Columbia, Warner Bros., MGM, Paramount/Famous, and UPA. Made-for-television animation is discussed briefly but, on the whole, discounted in its importance to the field. Maltin's approach is reflective of attitudes toward television work in the 1980s, prior to the second "golden age" of animation following the success of *The Simpsons* and the growth of made-for-television animation during the 1990s.

A new contribution to American studio animation history is Michael Barrier's *Hollywood Cartoons: American Animation in Its Golden Age*, published by Oxford University Press in 1999. This book, which focuses on short works produced between 1928 and 1966, is based on more than 200 interviews conducted by Barrier and animator Milton Gray beginning in 1969. A substantial portion of the text focuses on the Disney studio; Barrier notes that most of his primary research took place at the Disney archives due to the accessibility of their research materials, though he viewed thousands of films from all the major Hollywood studios in preparing to write the book. Warner Bros. also receives a significant amount of attention, with MGM and UPA each receiving a chapter (other studios are discussed in more generally focused chapters). Most of this book's 600-plus pages are text; there are few illustrations.

An earlier collection of essays on animation history was provided by Danny and Gerald Peary, editors of *The American Animated Cartoon: A Critical Anthology*, which was published by Dutton in 1980. This book contains essays (organized into chapters) dealing with a wide variety of historical issues, including six on early animation history; six on Disney; seven on Warner Bros.; five on other studios, including UPA; and seven on characters. The section on Disney includes his testimony before the House Committee on Un-American Activities, while a final chapter of the book contains writing on a variety of subjects, including interviews with Ralph Bakshi and Bill Hanna. Each chapter in the book is followed by a bibliography.

A few years later, the American Film Institute published two more anthologies that offer a variety of historical essays in animation studies. The first, *The Art of the Animated Image: An Anthology*, edited by Charles Solomon and published in 1987, contains essays on J. Stuart Blackton; Winsor McCay and personality animation; the Disney multiplane camera; the Walter Lantz Studio (a personal account by Leo Salkin); Norman McLaren; fine art animation; women animators; television and child audiences; and computer animation. The second anthology, *Storytelling in Animation: The Art of the Animated Image*, edited by John Canemaker and published in 1988, includes essays on nonobjective and nonlinear animation; animation writers; a personal statement on independent animation by Shamus Culhane; Caroline Leaf and her film *The Street*; computer animation; studio approaches to story; Disney storytelling; the visual nature of animation; and four Disney films: *Pigs Is Pigs*, *Who Framed Roger Rabbit*, *Snow White and the Seven Dwarfs*, and *Peter Pan*.

The reference books on Disney previously mentioned constitute only a small portion of the literature focused on this company. Although some of these books (too many to list here) are promotional efforts produced by the company itself or intended to appeal to fans of Disneyana (i.e., Disney lore and fantasy), recent years have seen the publication of scholarship on various facets of the Disney enterprise. A cross-section of them is mentioned in following paragraphs.

A useful place to begin is Russell Merritt and J. B. Kaufman's *Walt in Wonderland: The Silent Films of Walt Disney*, published first in combined English and Italian by Le Giornate del Cinema Muto and La Cineteca del Friuli in 1993 (a later edition in English only was published by Johns Hopkins University Press). This carefully researched study was groundbreaking in its discussion of the Disney studio's output prior to its "Mickey Mouse" films beginning in 1928; early histories of Disney tend to begin with Mickey Mouse, as if Disney never suffered the trials of his early years in business. The extensively illustrated book covers Walt Disney's early years in Kansas City, his early series, the development of the successful "Alice Comedy" and "Oswald" series in the 1920s, and events leading up to the arrival of "Mickey Mouse." A filmography provides credits, synopses, print sources, and other information.

Bob Thomas' *Walt Disney: An American Original* is a studio-authorized biography of the company's founder, a true icon of American culture. Thomas' reporting is fairly evenhanded; he contends that he was given full access to archives and not censored by the studio in any way. His account of Disney's life briefly extends beyond 1966, the year of his death, to document some of the final accomplishments of his brother Roy, who died in 1971. Thomas' book was first published in 1976 but reprinted by Hyperion in 1994. It was written in part to counteract negative depictions of Disney's life in analyses such as Richard Schickel's *The Disney Version: The Life, Times, Art and Commerce of Walt Disney*, originally published 1968 and reprinted by Ivan R. Dee in 1997.

A deeper look into the Disney company occurs in several anthologies. Eric Smoodin's *Disney Discourse: Producing the Magic Kingdom*, published by Routledge in 1994, combines some reprints of noncritical articles from the 1940s with recent critical essays. The latter include work on Disney's business history; its relationship with Technicolor; the development of EPCOT Center; Tokyo Disneyland; Latin American themes in films; and merchandising to children. *From Mouse to Mermaid: The Politics of Film, Gender and Culture*, edited by Elizabeth Bell and others, examines live-action and animated films produced by the Disney studio from a number of theoretical positions, including feminist, Marxist, poststructuralist, and cultural studies. It was published by Indiana University Press in 1995. Animation-related chapters cover such topics as adaptation in Disney's *Snow White* and *Pinocchio*; the development of female character types; depictions of nature in *Bambi*; masculinity in *Beauty and the Beast*; voice and body in *The Little Mermaid*; and EPCOT Center. A fascinating Marxist reading of a Disney character, though in the context of print cartoons, occurs in *How to Read Donald Duck: Imperialist Ideology in the Disney Comic*, written by Ariel Dorfman and Armand Mattelhart and published by International General in 1975.

Multiple facets of the Disney company are investigated in *Inside the Mouse: Work and Play at Disney World*, a 1995 book by the Project on Disney members Karen Klugman, Jane Kuenz, Shelton Waldrep, and Susan Willis. It is published by Duke University Press. This book contains ten essays written over a period of three years, combining personal responses to experiences in the park with more objective scholarly criticism. Essays ranging from employment policies to postmodern architecture result in a work that is not specifically related to animation and yet sheds light on the larger system of operation of one of the world's most influential animation studios. A study of this type also appears in Christopher Anderson's *Hollywood TV: The Studio System in the Fifties*, published by the University of Texas Press in 1994. His chapter on "Disneyland" documents the efforts of the Disney studio in combining the company's theme park with a popular television program, a crucial element in the immense success of the company in the post–World War I era.

Several books have documented the art of Disney animation. These include Robert D. Field's *The Art of Walt Disney*, published in 1942 by Macmillan, and Christopher Finch's *The Art of Walt Disney: From Mickey Mouse to the Magic Kingdom*, published by Harry N. Abrams in 1973 and reprinted in 1983. For another take on Disney's art, *The Art of Mickey Mouse*, a 1995 book edited by Craig Yoe and Janet Morra-Yoe and published by Hyperion, illustrates the many ways in which Disney's most famous character has been incorporated into the work of artists across the world. After a critical introduction by John Updike and a short forward by the editors, over 100 full-color artworks are published without commentary (artist name, title, year, media, and size are included).

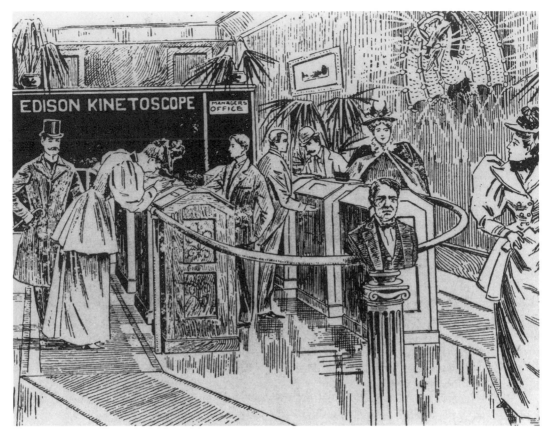

Edison Kinetoscope. The Kobol Collection

While a number of fine artists have been influenced by Disney art, the studio's aesthetics have had an even greater impact on the look of animation across the world. One of the most notable books to document the studio's style is *Disney Animation: The Illusion of Life*, by veteran Disney animators Frank Thomas and Ollie Johnson. Published by Abbeville in 1984, the book is part instructional text and part a history of the evolution of Disney's style.

Individuals looking for more instruction on how to create animation can find useful information in such publications as Kit Laybourne's *The Animation Book*, published by Crown in 1979; Richard Taylor's *The Encyclopedia of Animation Techniques*, published by Running Press in 1996; and Shamus Culhane's *Animation: From Script to Screen*, published by St. Martin's Press in 1988, which also contains a fair amount of Culhane's personal philosophy of artistic production. Roger Noake's *Animation: A Guide to Animated Film Techniques*, published by Macdonald Orbis in 1988, is a book on the production process, covering a wide range of techniques and featuring illustrations of both experimental and more commercial films from a number of countries. Peter Lord and Brian Sibley's *Creating 3D Animation: The Aardman Book of Filmmaking*, published by Harry Abrams in 1998, contains an overview of animation history plus a general introduction to the process of making three-dimensional animation. The authors are animators at Aardman, which is located in Bristol, England; included in their book is information on the making of the studio's "Wallace and Gromit" series. *Puppet Animation in the Cinema: History and Technique* is the focus of a 1975 book by L. Bruce Holman, published by A. S. Barnes. Sections on history and technique are followed by filmographies listing representative films from across the world and the work of seven puppet animators: George Pal, Bretislav Pojar, Ladislas Starevitch, Jirí Trnka, Hermina Tyurlová, Zenon Wasilewski, and Karel Zeman. Michael O'Rourke's *Principles of Three-Dimensional Computer Animation: Modeling, Rendering & Animating with 3D Computer Graphics*, revised in 1998 and published by Norton, is an instructive text suitable for college students wanting to learn how to create 3-D images with a computer.

To understand the complexity of the production process, one must be familiar with the many individuals who contribute to it. John Canemaker's *Before the Animation Begins: The Art and Lives of Disney Inspirational Sketch Artists*, published by Hyperion in 1996, sheds light on the complexity of the design process, focusing on the early 1930s through Disney's death in 1966. This extensively illustrated book constitutes original research on an important and largely overlooked area of the creative process, one of the few realms of the Disney studio open to women as well as men. Canemaker documents the work of Bianca Majolie, Sylvia Moberly-Holland, and Mary Blair, as well as several male artists, including Albert Hurter and Ken Anderson. A final chapter of the book overviews recent inspirational artists who have influenced Disney animation such as *The Lion King*, *Pocahontas*, and *Hercules*.

Walt Disney's direction of the studio's features, from *Snow White* to *The Jungle Book* (1967), is the subject of Robin Allan's book *Walt Disney and Europe: European Influences on the Animated Feature Films of Walt Disney*, published by John Libbey in 1999. It is based on primary sources, including archival research and interviews with individuals who worked closely with Disney, and also is well illustrated, many images coming from private archives and never before published.

While Disney has attracted a great deal of attention, a lot of writers, other individuals, and studios have constituted the focus of some study throughout the years—most of it popular rather than scholarly. Leslie Carbaga's *The Fleischer Story* provides a fairly anecdotal account of the studio that competed with the Disney studio during the 1920s and 1930s, when it produced the "Ko-Ko the Clown," "Betty Boop," and "Popeye" cartoon series, the feature *Gulliver's Travels*, and other animated productions. Carbaga's book, first published in 1976 and republished by Da Capo in 1988, overflows with illustrations, including photos, film stills, and production materials. A filmography listing titles and release dates is included as well. Fred M. Grandinetti's *Popeye: An Illustrated History of E. C. Segar's Character in Print, Radio, Television and Film Appearances, 1929–1993* focuses on one of the Fleischer studio's most popular stars. A wide variety of illustrations provides examples for each of the four chapters suggested by the book's title. A survey of characters associated with "Popeye" in its many forms, as well as an episode guide to animated productions (including title, year of release, and a brief synopsis) and various lists of trivia. Selected scripts from animated cartoons appear in the book's appendix. Grandinetti's book was published by McFarland in 1994.

A number of other directors and studios has been the focus of various publications written in a relatively popular format. For example, Joe Adamson has documented the histories of two legends of animation in *Tex Avery: King of Cartoons*, published by Popular Library in 1975 (reprinted by Da Capo in 1985), and *The Walter Lantz Story, with Woody Woodpecker and Friends*, published by G. B. Putnam's in 1985. John Cawley has written on *The Animated Films of Don Bluth* in a 1991 book by Image Publishing.

Several animators have taken to the keyboard and published their own life and career stories. Chuck Jones' *Chuck Amuck—The Life and Times of an Animated Cartoonist*, published by Farrar, Straus, and Giroux in 1989, is one of the best-known autobiographies in the field of animation. Bill Hanna's *A Cast of Friends* (written with Tom Ito) provides insight into the career of this animator and producer; it also constitutes one of the few histories focusing (in large part) on the made-for-television animation industry, generally, and his own influential company, Hanna-Barbera Productions, specifically. Shamus Culhane's *Talking Animals and Other People: The Autobiography of a Legendary Animator* originally was published in 1986, though it was reprinted by Da Capo in 1998; following this animator's diverse career, it includes information on the Fleischer, Iwerks, Disney, Lantz, and other studios.

Live-action and animation director Frank Tashlin is the subject of *Frank Tashlin*, an anthology edited by Roger Garcia with the assistance of Bernard Eisenschitz and published in 1994 by Éditions du Festival international du film de Locarno in collaboration with the British Film Institute. A fair number of photos, film stills, production materials, and drawings illustrate the eleven critical essays, commentary (by Robert Benayoun, Peter Bogdanovich, and Joe Dante), reprinted writing by Tashlin, and notes on films that fill this 240-page book. It is capped by a chronology, filmography (including uncredited and unrealized work), and bibliography, making it an indispensable resource for anyone writing on Tashlin.

Reading the Rabbit: Explorations in Warner Bros. Animation, edited by Kevin S. Sandler, focuses on another of the legendary animation studios of the classical era. The book was published by Rutgers University Press in 1998. Its essays focus on a diverse range of topics, including the influence of Charlie Thorson; caricature and parody; hillbilly and African American images; cross-dressing; merchandising; and fan culture. The specific topic of Warner Bros. music is covered in an essay by Scott Curtis, "The Sound of the Early Warner Bros. Cartoons," which appears in *Sound Theory/Sound Practice*, edited by Rick Altman and published by Routledge in 1992.

Throughout the golden era of the 1930s and 1940s, the dominant form of American animation was two-dimensional, specifically, cel animation. During the second "golden age" of the 1990s, animation blossomed in many forms. *Clay Animation*, a book by Michael Frierson, published by Twayne in 1994, documents the long history of this three-dimensional animation technique. It overviews the process of clay animation, as well as the invention of plasticine (the material used to create "clay" animation) and early clay films, including the work of Willie Hopkins and Helena Smith Dayton. Chapter highlights include clay animation during the 1920s and 1990s, as well as the work of Leonard Tregillus, Art Clokey (and the "Gumby" series), Will Vinton (and "Claymation"), Bruce Bickford (known for his work with musician Frank Zappa), and David Daniels (and his stratacut technique).

Some of the best-known three-dimensional animation is found in horror films featuring models of monsters. Paul M. Jensen's *The Men Who Made the Monsters*, published by Twayne in 1996, includes chapters on animators Willis O'Brien (probably best known for his work on the 1925 film *The Lost World* and the 1933 film *King Kong*) and Ray Harryhausen (known for his work on the 1963 film *Jason and the Argonauts* and numerous other productions), as well as live-action directors James Whale, Terence Fisher, and Freddie Francis. Most of Jensen's information seems to be culled from secondary sources, making this book useful for general information on the subjects but of less interest to advanced researchers. Ending the book is a selected bibliography, including writing by the subjects themselves, and a filmography, including title, production company, year of release, production credits, and running time.

Frank Thompson's *The Film, the Art, the Vision: Tim Burton's Nightmare before Christmas*, published by Hyperion in 1993, documents the production process of the influential puppet animation directed by Henry Selick. It reveals how the characters were created and moved before the camera, providing insight into the aesthetics of the film. Although it is certainly a "picture book," many of its illustrations offer very useful images of set and character construction. Images of replacement heads and eyes, shot breakdown sheets, and set devices are very helpful for understanding the aesthetics of the film. A related approach is used in a 1996 publication by Hyperion, written by Lucy Dahl, *James and the Giant Peach: The Book and Movie Scrapbook*. Taking a much smaller, more personal approach, this book contains several images of production materials and set photos that reveal insight about the film adaptation (also directed by Henry Selick), as told by the daughter of the book's author. However, it is primarily a novelty book.

The aesthetics of CGI is the subject of *Industrial Light & Magic*, written by Mark Cotta Vaz and Patricia Rose Duignan and published by Ballantine in 1996, explaining the company's groundbreaking special effects work in such films as *Terminator 2: Judgment Day* (1991). Jeff Kurtti's coffee-table book, *A Bug's Life: The Art and Making of an Epic of Miniature Proportion*, published by Hyperion in 1998, is certainly promotion and intended for a wide range of readers. However, its sketches, stills, and text reveal important considerations in the making of the film and the current state of CGI. For example, one chapter discusses the use of wide-screen space, while another discusses the design of bugs to overcome the "ick factor" that most people experience when confronted by insects.

A general overview of aesthetic issues can be found in Maureen Furniss' book, *Art in Motion: Animation Aesthetics*, published by John Libbey in 1998. This book, which is designed to be an introductory college course book, is broken into two parts. The first part contains information on animation studies in general; the foundations of studio practices; 2-D alternatives to cel animation; elements of mise-en-scène, sound, and structural design; the classical-era Disney studio; full and limited animation; 3-D animation; and new technologies. The second part of the book contains studies in animation aesthetics focusing on institutional regulators, animation audiences, issues of representation, and form in abstract animation.

More advanced readings on animation aesthetics can be found in a book edited by Jayne Pilling and published by John Libbey in 1997: *A Reader in Animation Studies*. It contains twenty-one essays divided into five sections: "New Technologies" (three essays), "Text and Context: Analyses of Individual Films" (eight essays), "Contemporary Cartoons and Cultural Studies" (two essays), "Theoretical Approaches" (four essays), and "(Rewriting) History" (four essays). Six essays deal with the Disney studio in some respect, while the rest cover a wide range of animated productions from around the world; topics related to American animation include the Bros. Quay (Americans whose studio is located in England), Susan Pitt, Joanna Priestley, the Fleischer Studio and clay animation, Jules Engel, and the "Ren & Stimpy" series.

Two books deal more directly with theoretical elements of animation. Paul Welles' *Understanding Animation* includes discussions of the evolution of animation; narrative strategies; the construction of comic events (including a "typology" of twenty-five gag sequences); the representation of race and gender; and the nature of animation audiences. He includes numerous case studies employing animation produced in the United States and elsewhere. Welles' book was published by Routledge in 1998. Alan Cholodenko's *The Illusion of Life: Essays on Animation*, published by Power Publications in 1991, contains essays presented at the Illusion of Life conference held in Sydney, Australia, in 1988. Aside from a transcribed speech by Chuck Jones that begins the volume, essays in the book rely heavily on poststructuralist and postmodernist critiques of French film theory employing semiology, Althusserian Marxism, and Lacanian psychoanalysis. Subjects covered include the animation of sound, violence in animation, the notion of the uncanny, and the concept of animation as monstrosity, the bringing to life of dead matter.

The aesthetics and theory of experimental animation are discussed in William C. Wees' book *Light Moving in Time: Studies in the Visual Aesthetics of Avant-Garde Film*, published in 1992 by the University of California Press. Individuals such as Jordan Belson and James Whitney, who employ frame-by-frame animation and real-time techniques, are discussed alongside live-action filmmakers Paul Sharits, Michael Snow, Kenneth Anger, and Stan Brakhage (whose work employs direct on-film animation techniques). Wees explores the relationship between actual vision and the cinematic form in these artists' works. He discusses operational and metaphorical similarities between the eye/brain and film/camera modes of seeing; although not overly technical, this material will appeal to those readers who have an interest in physiological and mechanical processes.

For many years, one of the only sources for information on "fine art" animated works was Robert Russett and Cecile Starr's *Experimental Animation: Origins of a New Art*, a revised book published by Da Capo in 1988 (originally published by Litton Educational Publishing in 1976). After an introduction to some new faces and technologies affecting independent animation, a series of short essays and interviews covers twenty-eight individuals considered to be groundbreaking contemporary imagists or pioneers in one of the following categories: abstract and "pictorial" animation in Europe, abstract animation in America, experimental animated sound, or new technologies. A separate chapter overviews the work of Norman McLaren and the National Film Board of Canada. Other artists covered include Lotte Reiniger, Len Lye, Oskar Fischinger, Mary Ellen Bute, Harry Smith, Larry Jordan, John and James Whitney, Stan VanDerBeek, Peter Foldes, and Ed Emshwiller. Its chapters sometimes are composed of interviews. Overall, the book is well illustrated—a necessity, due to the relative difficulty of seeing some of these artists' works, particularly at the time the book was published (the growth of home entertainment formats has made some of them more accessible).

Other sources for information on avant-garde animators include P. Adams Sitney's *Visionary Film: The American Avant-Garde 1943–1978*, originally published by Oxford University Press in 1974 and since reprinted, and David James' *Allegories of Cinema: American Film in the Sixties*, published by Princeton University Press in 1989. Both these books deal with animation in a relatively marginal way. Other articles on experimental animation can be found in a variety of publications produced by Anthology Film Archives in New York; for example, its recent anthology, *First Light*, edited by Robert Haller and published in 1998, includes writing on Jordan Belson, Oskar Fischinger, Marie Menken, Hans Richter, James Whitney, and others. Malcolm Le Grice's book *Abstract Film and Beyond*, published by the Massachusetts Institute of Technology in 1977, provides a history of abstract film and a discussion of its interrelation with other arts.

Experimental animator John Whitney's book *Digital Harmony: On the Complementarity of Music and Visual Art* notes the influence of such figures as Pythagoras (with his theories of harmony) and Arnold Schoenberg (with his twelve-tone compositions) on his creative process and output as an abstract filmmaker. It was published by McGraw-Hill in 1980. Whitney's detailed description of the design components of *Arabesque* (1975) and other films is potentially of great value but is too technical for all but the most musically and technologically literate readers. Of course, much of the book's technical information is outdated; still, it provides an interesting look at some groundbreaking work in computer animation and a relatively rare examination of the use of music in animation.

One of the most infamous experimental animators of the American avant-garde is Harry Smith. Although he was reclusive and secretive in life, friends of his were able to piece together a book overviewing his life and work posthumously. *American Magus: Harry Smith, a Modern Alchemist*, edited by Paola Igliori and published by Inanout Press in 1996, contains essays, interviews (mostly conducted between 1993 and 1995), reprints of primary documents, photographs, and a research guide that provides an appropriately diverse overview of this enigmatic musicologist, anthropologist, painter, filmmaker, occultist, and intellectual.

The variety of independent animation produced during the 1970s can be seen in *Frames: A Selection of Drawings and Statements by Independent American Animators*, which was self-published by animator George Griffin in 1976. This hard-to-find book contains illustrations and writing submitted by seventy artists, including Jane Aaron, Robert Breer, John Canemaker, Larry Cuba, Jules Engel, Candy Kugel, Caroline Leaf, Frank Mouris, Eliot Noyes, Pat O'Neill, Sara Petty, Maureen Selwood, Stan VanDerBeek, and James Whitney. The book also contains a list of names and addresses for the contributors.

Jayne Pilling's *Women in Animation: A Compendium*, published by the British Film Institute in 1992, provides another list of animators, in this case, women working internationally, both as pioneers and in recent years. This list—which contains for each name a country of origin, a summary of the woman's style (including, in some cases, quotes), and a list of films with dates of release—caps off a selection of critical essays, interviews, and illustrations related to a wide range of female artists. Some subjects include Lotte Reiniger, Mary Ellen Bute, Faith Hubley, Evelyn Lambart, Sayoko Kinoshita, Candy Kugel, Leeds Animation, Caroline Leaf, Sally Cruikshank, Joanna Priestley, Jane Aaron, Suzan Pitt, Kathy Rose, Ruth Hayes, Mary Beams, Monique Renault, Alison de Vere, Joanna Quinn, Candy Guard, Vera Neubauer, Joanna Woodward, Sarah Kennedy, Karen Watson, Joan Stabely, Nina Sabnani, and Nina Shorina. Their countries of origin or artistic practice include the United States, Canada, France, England, Wales, India, and Russia; Australian animation also is discussed.

Another volume edited by Jayne Pilling focuses on the relationship between *Cartoons & the Movies*; it was published by Dreamland in 1997 in conjunction with a retrospective at the Annecy International Animation Festival. Part theory and part history, this book contains nine essays covering such subjects as film titles; cross-media references (in the work of Frank Tashlin and in general); and the work of Everett Peck (creator of "Duckman"), Aardman Animation, and Tim Burton. This book represents one of several projects aimed at contextualizing the production of animation within a larger cultural setting, in this case, the film industry as a whole.

Eric Smoodin has conducted another analysis of cultural context in his book *Animating Culture: Hollywood Cartoons from the Sound Era*, published by Rutgers University Press in 1993. In this book, Smoodin employs various primary documents, such as copyright materials, film bills, and even Federal Bureau of Investigation records to fill in gaps in our understanding of animation history. One chapter examines the press's response to racism and eroticism in Disney's South American themed live-action/animation features. Other chapters address the links between culture, commerce, and government policy; the relationship between cartoons and features on a film bill; the workings of the government's "Private Snafu" series; and the effects of censorship on animation (a limited discussion, focusing primarily on one magazine article published in 1939).

The subject of censorship in animation is examined much more thoroughly in Karl Cohen's *Forbidden Animation: Censored Cartoons and Blacklisted Animators in America*. Covering both theatrical and made-for-television animation, Cohen investigates the subjects of racist imagery, blacklisting, and so-called uncensored, adult-oriented animation and how studios have responded to censorship pressures placed upon them by various institutions. His findings, which were published by McFarland in 1997, primarily are based on anecdotal information, interviews with historians, and textual analysis; primary documentation in this area can be difficult to come by.

Like Smoodin and Cohen, Michael S. Shull and David E. Wilt are interested in the relationship between the animation industry and other American institutions. In *Doing Their Bit: Wartime American Animated Short Films, 1939–1945*, published by McFarland in 1987, these researchers have focused their attention on the World War II era. Their book provides a content analysis of wartime cartoons released by major American studios, reflecting the way in which war themes were handled in this form of popular culture. Richard Shale's *Donald Duck Joins Up*, published by UMI Research Press in 1982, provides an account of Disney's production of World War II propaganda.

Part of the reason that animation has been of concern to various American institutions is that it, like other forms of media, can be a powerful tool for influencing public opinion. This very notion is expressed in *Drawing Insight: Com-*

municating Development through Animation, edited by Joyce Greene and Deborah Reber, a book published by Southbound in 1996. Growing out of special United Nations International Children's Emergency Fund (UNICEF) projects involving animated programming, this anthology is composed of essays written by industry leaders, development specialists, and animators on the subject of how animation can contribute positive messages in the areas of health and social change. Essay topics include approaches to creating early childhood development materials, merchandising program management, the Adolescent Girl Communication Initiative of Eastern and Southern Africa, the Street Kids International project, the training of animators in developing countries, the work of the Children's Television Workshop (producers of the *Sesame Street* series), and African animation.

Although *Drawing Insight* refers to a wide range of animated programming, most resources in the realm of animation studies relate primarily to theatrical animation. Made-for-television animation has been the subject of far less study. While popular television series generally become the subjects of trivia books or other popular literature, only occasionally does one find a publication such as *The World of Hanna-Barbera Cartoons*, which was published by the Museum of Radio and Television in 1995, for an exhibit held there June 23–September 24 of that year. Although composed primarily of production art, the book nonetheless provides a useful document of the many series that have emanated from Hanna-Barbera throughout its history.

The bulk of books focusing on made-for-television animation has been in the form of audience studies or theoretical discussions of spectator issues. Marsha Kinder's *Playing with Power in Movies, Television, and Video Games: From Muppet Babies to Teenage Mutant Ninja Turtles*, published by the University of California Press in 1991, serves as an example. Using psychoanalytic models of spectatorship and cognitive theory, she examines the manner in which children are positioned as both passive consumers and interactive participants. Her examination is not specific to animation but rather addresses media within a broader context; it is more concerned with content than form.

A few books treat animation as a subject related to merchandising and licensing. For example, both Cy Schneider's *Children's Television: The Art, the Business, and How It Works*, published by NTC Business Books in 1987, and Ellen Seiter's *Sold Separately: Parents & Children in Consumer Culture*, published by Rutgers University Press in 1995, treat animation in this manner. Tom Engelhardt's essay "The Shortcake Strategy," from the anthology *Watching Television*, which he edited with Tod Gitlin and published with Pantheon in 1986, is another oft-quoted resource for information on licensing and children's television (again, animation is treated within this context). *The ACT Guide to Children's Television*, written by Evelyn Kane and published by Beacon Press in 1979, provides insight into the organization's point of view and its recommendations for programming.

A number of periodicals have devoted themselves to the general topic of animation history, theory, aesthetics, and business practices. Among them are *Animato!*, *Animation Magazine*, and *Funnyworld*. *Animation World Magazine*, an electronic publication, is published on-line at http://www.awm.com; each of its monthly issues focuses on a different topic. More in-depth, researched articles on animation are presented in *Animation Journal*, published twice a year, which is the only peer-reviewed journal devoted to animation, and *Animatrix*, a publication of the University of California, Los Angeles (UCLA) graduate animation workshop that comes out more or less once a year. In the spring of 1994, *Animation Journal* published a special issue on women in animation; otherwise, its content, like that of *Animatrix*, is varied in each issue.

Worth noting, too, is *Film Culture*, which includes animators among the avant-garde filmmakers who constitute its focus. For example, its 1974 issue (nos. 58–60) contains a large article on "The Films of Oskar Fischinger," written by William Moritz, who single-handedly took on the task of excavating the extensive and largely dilapidated work of this master of abstract animation, assuring his rightful place in history. A number of *Film Culture* essays have been collected in P. Adams Sitney's *Film Culture Reader*, published by Praeger in 1970; it includes writing by Hans Richter, Parker Tyler, Stan Brakhage, P. Adams Sitney, Gene Youngblood, and many others.

Throughout history, periodicals devoted to film or media, in general, have at times published special issues related to animation. The first issue of *Hollywood Quarterly*, which was dated 1945–1946, while not a special issue, contains essays related to animation; for example, music and the animated cartoon, by Chuck Jones; UPA's film *The Brotherhood of Man*, by Ring Lardner Jr., Maurice Rapf, John Hubley, and Phil Eastman; and puppets and George Pal and his film on John Henry, by Sondra Gorney.

A December 1988 issue of *Griffithiana* contains three essays, "The Fantasia That Never Was," by John Canemaker; "Interview with Friz Freleng," by Reg Hartt; and "Mythic Mouse," chronicling the development of the Mickey Mouse character, by Karen and Russell Merritt. *The Velvet Light Trap* put out a special issue on animation in the fall of 1989 (no. 24). It contains interviews with Fleischer animator Myron Waldman and independent animators Paul Glabicki and Robert Breer, as well as essays on the Fleischer's "Popeye" series; Disney's *Peter Pan*; structure in American studio cartoons; theory and animation; and MTV and postmodernism.

The winter 1992 (vol. 3; no. 4) issue of *Screen* contains two animation-related essays, Mark Langer's "The Disney-Fleischer Dilemma: Product Differentiation and Technological Change" and David Forgacs "Disney Animation and the Business of Childhood." Paul Welles edited a special issue of *Art and Design* (May 1997, vol. 53), which included essays on dance animation, documentary aesthetics, the adaptation of Alice in Wonderland, and the Disney Studio (an interview including animators Zach Schwartz and Bob Godfrey). A special issue of *Film History* from 1993 (vol. 5, no. 2), edited by Mark Langer, contains essays on the subjects of the "Ren & Stimpy" series; early clay animation films; Disney's move into feature filmmaking; phenakistoscopes; the investigation of communism in the animation industry; caricature and parody in Warner Bros. cartoons; and Disney's *Cinderella*.

A special animation issue published by *The Hollywood Reporter* every year in winter (e.g., in 1999 it was the January 26 issue) presents articles on the current state of the animation industry in terms of economics, business practices, works in progress, studio personnel, and so forth. *The Hollywood Reporter* also published a "Careers in Animation" special issue in 1998, dated August 14–16.

ANTHOLOGIES AND REPRINTS

The reprint of Edwin G. Lutz's book *Animated Cartoons: How They Are Made, Their Origin and Development* (originally published in 1920 by Charles Scribners Sons), by Applewood in 1998, is generally of interest to researchers working on Disney, since this is the book that the young Walt used to learn the basic principles of the animation process. The book overviews processes and techniques in use during the 1910s, in addition to providing practical information on principles of movement.

Also related to Disney is a collection of essays by Russian theorist and filmmaker Sergei Eisenstein. *Eisenstein on Disney*, edited by Jay Leyda and published by Methuen in 1988, contains essays in which he discusses his concepts of metamorphosis and explains his theories of "attraction" in animated work. In addition, a range of illustrations is reproduced in the book, including a number by Eisenstein himself.

BIBLIOGRAPHY

Books and Articles

Adamson, Joe. *Tex Avery: King of Cartoons*. 1975. New York: Da Capo, 1985.

———. *The Walter Lantz Story, with Woody Woodpecker and Friends*. New York: G. B. Putnam, 1985.

Allan, Robin. *Walt Disney and Europe: European Influences on the Animated Feature Films of Walt Disney*. London: John Libbey, 1999.

Anderson, Christopher. *Hollywood TV: The Studio System in the Fifties*. Austin: University of Texas Press, 1994.

Barrier, Michael. *Hollywood Cartoons: American Animation in Its Golden Age*. New York: Oxford University Press, 1999.

Beck, Jerry, and Will Friedwald. *Looney Tunes and Merry Melodies: A Complete Illustrated Guide to the Warner Bros. Cartoons*. New York: Henry Holt, 1988.

Bell, Elizabeth, Lynda Haas, and Laura Sells, eds. *From Mouse to Mermaid: The Politics of Film, Gender and Culture*. Bloomington: Indiana University Press, 1995.

Bendazzi, Giannalberto. *Cartoons: One Hundred Years of Cinema Animation*. London: John Libbey, 1994.

Canemaker, John. *Before the Animation Begins: The Art and Lives of Disney Inspirational Sketch Artists*. New York: Hyperion, 1996.

———. *Felix: The Twisted Tales of the World's Most Famous Cat*. New York: Da Capo, 1996.

———. *Winsor McCay: His Life and Art*. New York: Abbeville, 1987.

———, ed. *Storytelling in Animation: The Art of the Animated Image*. Los Angeles: American Film Institute, 1988.

Carbaga, Leslie. *The Fleischer Story*. 1976. New York: Da Capo, 1988.

Cawley, John. *The Animated Films of Don Bluth*. New York: Image, 1991.

Cholodenko, Alan, ed. *The Illusion of Life: Essays on Animation*. Sydney: Power, 1991.

Cohen, Karl. *Forbidden Animation: Censored Cartoons and Blacklisted Animators in America*. Jefferson, N.C.: McFarland, 1997.

Crafton, Donald. *Before Mickey: The Animated Film, 1898–1928*. 1982. Cambridge: MIT Press, 1987.

———. *Emile Cohl, Caricature and Film*. Princeton, N.J.: Princeton University Press, 1990.

Culhane, Shamus. *Animation: From Script to Screen*. New York: St. Martin's, 1988.

———. *Talking Animals and Other People: The Autobiography of a Legendary Animator*. 1986. New York: Da Capo, 1998.

Curtis, David. *Experimental Cinema*. New York: Universe, 1971.

Curtis, Scott. "The Sound of the Early Warner Bros. Cartoons." In *Sound Theory/ Sound Practice*, ed. Rick Altman. New York: Routledge, 1992, 191–203.

Dahl, Lucy. *James and the Giant Peach: The Book and Movie Scrapbook*. New York: Hyperion, 1996.

Dorfman, Ariel, and Armand Mattelhart. *How to Read Donald Duck: Imperialist Ideology in the Disney Comic*. New York: International General, 1975.

Edera, Bruno. *Full Length Animated Feature Films*. New York: Hastings House, 1977.

Eisenstein, Sergei. *Eisenstein on Disney*. Ed. Jay Leyda. Trans. Alan Upchurch. London: Methuen, 1988.

Engelhardt, Tom. "The Shortcake Strategy." In *Watching Television*; Tod Gitlin and Tom Engelhardt. New York: Pantheon, 1986, 68–110.

Erickson, Hal. *Television Cartoon Shows: An Illustrated Encyclopedia 1949 through 1993*. Jefferson, N.C.: McFarland, 1995.

Field, Robert D. *The Art of Walt Disney*. New York: Macmillan, 1942.

Finch, Christopher. *The Art of Walt Disney: From Mickey Mouse to the Magic Kingdom*. New York: Abrams, 1973.

Frierson, Michael. *Clay Animation: American Highlights 1908 to the Present*. New York: Twayne, 1994.

Furniss, Maureen. *Art in Motion: Animation Aesthetics*. Sidney: John Libbey, 1998.

Garcia, Roger, and Bernard Eisenschitz, eds. *Frank Tashlin: A Retrospective*. Locarno: Locarno Film Festival, 1994.

Gifford, Denis. *American Animated Films: The Silent Era, 1897–1929*. Jefferson, N.C.: McFarland, 1990.

Gitlin, Tod and Tom Engelhardt, eds. *Watching Television*. New York: Pantheon, 1986.

Grandinetti, Fred M. *Popeye: An Illustrated History of E. C. Segar's Character in Print, Radio, Television and Film Appearances, 1929–1993*. Jefferson, N.C.: McFarland, 1994.

Grant, Joe. *The Encyclopedia of Walt Disney's Animated Characters*. New York: Hyperion, 1997.

Green, Joyce and Deborah Reber, eds. *Drawing Insight: Communicating Development through Animation*. Penang: Southbound, 1996.

Griffin, George. *Frames: A Selection of Drawings and Statements by Independent American Animators*. New York: George Griffin, 1976.

Halas, John. *Masters of Animation*. Topsfield, Mass.: Salem House, 1987.

Haller, Robert, ed. *First Light*. New York: Anthology Film Archives, 1998.

Hanna, Bill, and Tom Ito. *A Cast of Friends*. Dallas, Tex.: Taylor, 1996.

Hoffer, Thomas W. *Animation: A Reference Guide.* Westport, Conn.: Greenwood, 1981.

Holman, L. Bruce. *Puppet Animation in the Cinema: History and Technique.* South Brunswick, N.J.: A. S. Barnes, 1975.

Hubley, John, and Zachary Schwartz. "Animation Learns a New Language." *Hollywood Quarterly* 1 (1945–1946), 360–63.

Igliori, Paola, ed. *American Magus: Harry Smith, a Modern Alchemist.* New York: Inanout, 1996.

Inge, M. Thomas. *Perspectives on American Culture: Essays on Humor, Literature, and the Popular Arts.* West Cornwall, Conn.: Locust Hill, 1994.

Jackson, Kathy Merlock. *Walt Disney: A Bio-Bibliography.* Westport, Conn.: Greenwood, 1993.

James, David. *Allegories of Cinema: American Film in the Sixties.* Princeton, N.J.: Princeton University Press, 1989.

Jensen, Paul M. *The Men Who Made the Monsters.* New York: Twayne, 1996.

Jones, Chuck. *Chuck Amuck—The Life and Times of an Animated Cartoonist.* New York: Farrar, Straus, and Giroux, 1989.

Kane, Evelyn. *The ACT Guide to Children's Television.* Boston: Beacon Press, 1979.

Kilmer, David. *The Animated Film Collector's Guide: Worldwide Sources for Cartoons on Videotape and Laserdisc.* Sidney: John Libbey, 1997.

Kinder, Marsha. *Playing with Power in Movies, Television, and Video Games: From Muppet Babies to Teenage Mutant Ninja Turtles.* Berkeley: University of California Press, 1991.

Kurtti, Jeff. *A Bug's Life: The Art and Making of an Epic of Miniature Proportion.* New York: Hyperion, 1998.

Laybourne, Kit. *The Animation Book.* New York: Crown, 1979.

Le Grice, Malcolm. *Abstract Film and Beyond.* Cambridge: MIT Press, 1977.

Lenburg, Jeff. *The Encyclopedia of Animated Cartoons.* New York: Facts on File, 1991.

———. *The Great Cartoon Directors.* New York: Da Capo, 1993.

Lent, John, comp. *Animation, Caricature and Gag and Political Cartoons in the United States and Canada—An International Bibliography.* Westport, Conn.: Greenwood, 1994.

Lord, Peter, and Brian Sibley. *Creating 3D Animation: The Aardman Book of Filmmaking.* New York: Harry Abrams, 1998.

Lotman, Jeff. *Animation Art: The Early Years, 1911–1953.* Atglen, Pa.: Schiffer, 1995.

———. *Animation Art: The Later Years 1954–1993.* Atglen, Pa.: Schiffer, 1996.

Lutz, Edwin G. *Animated Cartoons: How They Are Made, Their Origin and Development.* 1920. Bedford, Mass.: Applewood, 1998.

Maltin, Leonard. *The Disney Films.* New York: Hyperion, 1995.

———. *Of Mice and Magic: A History of American Animated Cartoons.* 1980. New York: Plume, 1987.

McCall, Douglas L. *Film Cartoons: A Guide to 20th-Century American Animated Features and Shorts.* Jefferson, N.C.: McFarland, 1998.

Merritt, Russell, and J. B. Kaufman. *Walt in Wonderland: The Silent Films of Walt Disney.* Pordenone: Le Giornate del Cinema Muto/La Cineteca del Friuli, 1993.

Moritz, William. "The Films of Oskar Fischinger," *Film Culture* 58–60 (1974), 37–188.

Noake, Roger. *Animation: A Guide to Animated Film Techniques*. London: Macdonald Orbis, 1988.

O'Rourke, Michael. *Principles of Three-Dimensional Computer Animation: Modeling, Rendering & Animating with 3D Computer Graphics*. 1995. New York: Norton, 1998.

Peary, Danny and Gerald Peary, eds. *The American Animated Cartoon: A Critical Anthology*. New York: Dutton, 1980.

Pilling, Jayne, ed. *Cartoons & the Movies*. Paris: Dreamland, 1997.

———. *A Reader in Animation Studies*. Sydney: John Libbey, 1997.

———. *Women in Animation: A Compendium*. London: BFI, 1992.

Pintoff, Ernest. *The Complete Guide to Animation and Computer Graphics Schools*. New York: Watson-Guptill, 1995.

Project on Disney. *Inside the Mouse: Work and Play at Disney World*. Durham, N.C.: Duke University Press, 1995.

Renan, Sheldon. *An Introduction to the American Underground Film*. New York: E. P. Dutton, 1967.

Russett, Robert, and Cecile Starr. *Experimental Animation: Origins of a New Art*. 1976. New York: Da Capo, 1988.

Sandler, Kevin S. *Reading the Rabbit: Explorations in Warner Bros. Animation*. New Brunswick, N.J.: Rutgers, 1998.

Schickel, Richard. *The Disney Version: The Life, Times, Art and Commerce of Walt Disney*. 1968. Chicago: Ivan R. Dee, 1997.

Schneider, Cy. *Children's Television: The Art, the Business, and How It Works*. Chicago: NTC Business Books, 1987.

Seiter, Ellen. *Sold Separately: Parents & Children in Consumer Culture*. New Brunswick, N.J.: Rutgers University Press, 1995.

Shale, Richard. *Donald Duck Joins Up*. Ann Arbor, Mich.: UMI Research Press, 1982.

Shull, Michael S. and David E. Wilt. *Doing Their Bit: Wartime American Animated Short Films, 1939–1945*. Jefferson, N.C.: McFarland, 1987.

Sitney, P. Adams. *Visionary Film: The American Avant-Garde 1943–1978*. 1974. Oxford: Oxford University Press, 1979.

———, ed. *Film Culture Reader*. New York: Praeger, 1970.

Smith, Dave. *Disney A to Z: The Updated Official Encyclopedia*. New York: Hyperion, 1998.

Smoodin, Eric. *Animating Culture: Hollywood Cartoons from the Sound Era*. New Brunswick, N.J.: Rutgers, 1993.

———, ed. *Disney Discourse: Producing the Magic Kingdom*. New York: Routledge, 1994.

Solomon, Charles. *History of Animation: Enchanted Drawings*. 1989. New York: Wings Books, 1994.

———, ed. *The Art of the Animated Image: An Anthology*. Los Angeles: American Film Institute, 1987.

Stauffacher, Frank, ed. *Art in Cinema: A Symposium on the Avantgarde Film Together with Program Notes and References*. San Francisco: San Francisco Museum of Art, 1947.

Taylor, Richard. *The Encyclopedia of Animation Techniques*. London: Running Press, 1996.

Thomas, Bob. *Walt Disney: An American Original*. 1976. New York: Hyperion, 1994.

Thomas, Frank, and Ollie Johnston. *Disney Animation: The Illusion of Life*. New York: Abbeville, 1984.

Thompson, Frank. *The Film, the Art, the Vision: Tim Burton's Nightmare before Christmas*. New York: Hyperion, 1993.

Travis, Lucinda, and Jack Hannah, comps. *Factfile #9: Animation*. Los Angeles: American Film Institute, 1986.

Tyler, Parker. *Underground Film: A Critical History*. New York: Grove, 1969.

Vaz, Mark Cotta, and Patricia Rose Duignan. *Industrial Light & Magic*. New York: Ballantine, 1996.

Wees, William C. *Light Moving in Time: Studies in the Visual Aesthetics of Avant-Garde Film*. Berkeley: University of California Press, 1992.

Welles, Paul. *Understanding Animation*. London: Routledge, 1998.

Whitney, John. *Digital Harmony: On the Complementarity of Music and Visual Art*. Peterborough, N.H.: McGraw-Hill, 1980.

The Whole Toon Catalog. Chicago: Faccts Multimedia, various dates.

Woolery, George. *Animated TV Specials: The Complete Directory to the First Twenty-Five Years, 1962–1987*. Metuchen, N.J.: Scarecrow, 1988.

———. *Children's Television: The First Thirty-Five Years, 1946–1981, Part I: Animated Cartoon Series*. Metuchen, N.J.: Scarecrow, 1983.

The World of Hanna-Barbera Cartoons. New York: Museum of Radio and Television, 1995.

Yoe, Craig, and Janet Morra-Yoe, eds. *The Art of Mickey Mouse*. New York: Hyperion, 1995.

Youngblood, Gene. *Expanded Cinema*. New York: E. P. Dutton, 1970.

Periodicals

Animation Journal, 1992– .
Animation Magazine, 1987– .
Animato!, ca. 1980– .
Animatrix, 1984– .

ARCHITECTURE

Richard Guy Wilson and
Dale Allen Gyure

Architecture is the most conspicuous "art" that makes up our world. You can turn off the radio, refuse to watch *ER*, ignore the latest political scandal, and be revolted by Big Macs, but unless you become a hermit and retire to the mythical cave, the man-made environment intrudes. Buildings, whether they serve work, play, or sleep, reveal personal and cultural values; they are records, and, properly understood, they are our permanent diaries. William Morris, the English designer, poet, and revolutionary, observed in 1881: "Architecture embraces the consideration of the whole external surroundings of the life of man; we cannot escape from it if we would so long as we are part of civilization, for it means a moulding and altering to human needs of the very face of the earth itself, except in the outermost desert."[1] Morris saw architecture as virtually everything, not simply the top 5 percent of high design. Today that includes both the homes of the wealthy and ranch houses, courthouses and fast-food outlets, sculpture in public places and the real sculpture of our world, plastic flamingos in the front yard and superhighway interchanges, designer furniture and Ethan Allen "Olde Colonial" or "Arts and Crafts."

Since the mid-1970s, architecture has risen considerably in popularity. As an academic "growth industry," it has reached the status of "edutainment," or a field in which avocational interest is merged with scholarly vocation. There have been many public and cable television programs devoted to American architecture, such as "Pride of Place" and "America's Castles," and we are promised more. Architectural "superstars" such as Frank Gehry and Richard Meier grace the covers of magazines, and a sure sign of approval can be found in the countless articles that have appeared in airline magazines. Museums have discovered architecture, and while collecting entire buildings is generally hard—Old Sturbridge Village or the Ford Greenfield Village are the examples—a museum or gallery can show architectural drawings, photographs, fragments of buildings, and furniture. Tours are popular, from a day with the garden club, to a coach tour of the remains of old

Frank Lloyd Wright's Robie House. Courtesy of the Library of Congress

U.S. 1. Where in the early 1960s only one newspaper, the great, venerable *New York Times*, had a critic of architecture, now there are many. Architectural book publishing has flourished; books of all types, from studies of fast-food architecture, to the most recondite subjects, have appeared. Since the last edition of this chapter ten years ago, a plethora of books has appeared, and articles on diners, drive-in theaters, and roadside stands appear with frequency in places as diverse as the *Smithsonian* and the local op-ed page.

Popular architecture (or, alternatively, modern vernacular) constitutes at least 95 percent of our built surroundings. There is a need to understand this environment in all its aspects, not simply the current "in" subjects of fast-food palaces and the strip but also urban sprawl, shopping centers, ranch-style homes, and the symbolic meanings that people ascribe to, or invest in, their construction. Since the late eighteenth century and the development of a modern consciousness, most historians have felt that buildings are concrete expressions of a culture and a worldview. While this is perhaps more easily acceptable in terms of such public or semipublic monuments as the Getty Museum in Los Angeles or St. Peter's Cathedral, to take two extremes, there have been other views. Richard Oliver and Nancy Ferguson, writing about fast-food restaurants, diners, gas stations, and historical villages in the late 1970s, claim that "by their very familiarity, they can and do act as mirrors of our culture."[2] The profound shifts created by the Industrial Revolution have affected the built environment in many ways, most of which have been ignored. A radical discrepancy exists between the tastes, needs, and preferences of professionals—historians, critics, architects, urban designers, and planners and the decision makers whose policies they inform—and the people whose lives they influence.

Popular architecture, like all architecture, generally fulfills two functions: first, it allows some type of activity, and second, it communicates. The methods of communication through different signs and symbol systems are at the core of the study of popular architecture. The physical elements of coach lanterns and shutters on a house, the twisting nudes in front of Caesar's Palace in Las Vegas, and the giant Golden Arches convey messages of social status, association with the past, and information. To understand popular architecture, one must look at it not as simply an art of building but as a tangible expression of a way of life.

HISTORICAL OUTLINE

In the West before the late eighteenth century nearly all architecture was of two basic types: either folk (or vernacular or traditional) or academic high art. By folk architecture is meant buildings of a preindustrial society, houses, shops, or barns based on one or a very few types that admit only a few individual variations. In the vernacular traditions, the specialized architect or a designer did not exist; the building type was carried in the collective consciousness of the culture. Construction took place either by the final consumer or by a tradesman not far removed from the consumer, and the materials used were local. Academic high art architecture refers to specialized buildings, each one an original or unique creation (self-consciously in a "style"); the designer is a professional or an amateur who specializes in or has aspirations to the creation of significant monuments.

Popular architecture emerged with the Industrial Revolution. With popular architecture production is changed; building materials and even entire buildings are produced on a mass scale by a team or teams of specialists who are generally far removed from the ultimate consumer. Instead of one prevailing building type, there are many, with innumerable variations within each. The forms, plans, and images of buildings are products of fashion and are acquired through popular magazines, trade journals, books, governmental agencies, travel, and the media. The images refer to history, high art, technology, status, patriotism, and individual fantasies. Popular architecture is fashion- or style-conscious, and its symbols are generally chosen for their immediate impact.

Who designs popular architecture? The answer is, many people. Buildings by academically trained architects are not necessarily examples of high art, and in fact architects have been responsible for the mass-produced Mobil service station, ranch-style houses, and Miami Beach hotels. There is hardly a building activity of the modern age that architects have not participated in; they serve on the design staffs of many major corporations like Holiday Inn, Disney World, and Wal-Mart. But others, such as industrial designers, have also designed mass-produced commercial buildings. The profession did not emerge until the 1930s, but they quickly became the heroes of the new technological mass-production age. Walter Dorwin Teague, one of the first, designed the enamel-paneled, machinelike Texaco service station, reproduced in over 20,000 units. Another source for the designs of popular architecture is the builder or contractor. The increasingly technological nature of building precludes much design by actual workers, an old and honored tradition; instead, buildings today are increasingly prefabricated or come from kits. Finally, the consumer who decides to add a clip-on mansard to his storefront or put a French Provincial door on her ranch house and a plastic deer in the front yard is also a designer.

Between popular architecture and high art architecture the relationship has never been stable, and in spite of the elitist "trickle-down" theory that high art always informs low art or that popular architecture "rips off" high art architecture, the reverse is often true. Taste that used to be a sign of class and wealth is no longer an operable guide. Who or what actually informs the taste and the processes by which it trickles down, up, or sideways must always be considered in any study of popular architecture. Plans, forms, and images constantly shift from one level to another. Beginning in the 1980s, there has been a great spurt of interest by academic high art architects in the archetypal image of the 1930s and 1940s, the sleek, shiny, streamlined diners. As they were passing out of existence to be replaced by colonial- and Mediterranean-style diners, they were discovered and appropriated. A number of "postmodern" architects actually designed "new diners," and at least one of the original manufacturers is providing replicas of the 1940s–1950s diners. Or one can look at materials such as shingles, which have moved over the years from a vernacular exterior covering into the range of high art, back into the hands of the builder and Levittown, and once again back to becoming a chic material.

The emergence of postmodernism in the mid-1970s (though its roots can be traced back to the mid-1960s; see R. G. Wilson, "Abstraction versus Figuration") blurred some of the distinctions between high art architecture and popular architecture. With the advent of architectural modernism in the 1920s many architects consciously eschewed historical images and embraced abstract art as a source. Such abstract modernism was never the exclusive property of high art architecture; indeed, many contemporary strip and shopping malls owe a great deal to this source. Within high art architecture a shift began in the 1960s, when the pop art movement of Andy Warhol, Roy Lichtenstein, and others, along with Susan Sontag's concept of "camp," was picked up by Charles Moore and Robert Venturi. Architecturally, this meant an interest in, and an appropriation of, the imagery and symbolism of popular architecture for the purposes of high art. Consequently, much of the interest in popular architecture in the last two decades has been seen through a postmodernist sensibility of irony, wit, and condescension. This development has been coupled with a nostalgia craze for the most arcane bits of the popular past (i.e., Big Little Books, diner food, and 1950s tail fins). Yet, as at least one critic (Tom Wolfe in *From Bauhaus to Our House*) has claimed, the postmodernist architectural sensibility has retained an elitist code accessible only to the initiated.

The styles and motifs of popular architecture are communicated by one of two methods: experientially through observation and travel or secondhand through books, magazines, and trade journals. The first, of course, is nebulous and depends on study of specific individuals; the second has left a more tangible record.

Media influence can be followed by looking briefly at the development of the

American house. The ideal of the single-family house available to all classes of citizens is one of the unique aspects of American architecture. During the nineteenth century in the United States books began to appear intended for mass circulation that spread knowledge of stylistic details. The earliest were builders' guides such as Asher Benjamin's *The American Builder's Companion* and Minard Lafever's *The Modern Builder's Guide*. The contents were plates illustrating details of ornament and construction, with possibly a few elevations and plans of complete buildings. They helped spread the fashion for first Federal, then Greek Revival, and finally Gothic Revival styles to builders, carpenters, and, of course, consumers. Their continuation in print, in some cases nearly thirty years after first publication, accounts for the backward appearance of some buildings in more provincial areas. About midcentury a new type of publication appeared, the house pattern book, filled with plans and designs of complete buildings. The most popular of these were Andrew Jackson Downing's *Cottage Residences* and *The Architecture of Country Houses*. In these books, along with large, pretentious homes, there were "working men's cottages," "laborer's cottages," and small houses, along with details that would allow anybody with either skills or some funds to update his or her home. This type of publication continued throughout the nineteenth century in a virtual flood of titles and editions, such as George Woodward's *Woodward's National Architect*, E. C. Gardner's *Homes and How to Make Them*, and the Palliser Company's *New Cottage Homes and Details*. These books served as dream manuals for the masses. House details could be adapted from them by a local builder or architect, and in many cases complete sets of plans could be purchased at a nominal cost, such as those of the Palliser Company. The men responsible for these books were a varied lot; a few had some architectural background, but many were simply glorified carpenters who adopted aspects of high art styles for mass consumption.

Another method of communication was through magazines. *Godey's Lady's Book* published, between 1846 and 1892, 450 house designs. In the 1860s several magazines, such as the *American Builder* and the *Architectural Review and American Builder's Journal*, came into being that were directed specifically at the builder and carpenter. The first professional architectural magazine in the United States, the *American Architect and Building News*, was not founded until 1876. While magazines for professional architects always carry house designs, far more important were periodicals such as Gustav Stickley's *Craftsman* (1901–1916) and Henry L. Wilson's *Bungalow Magazine* (1909–1918), which actively promoted the low-slung, middle-class house. Both Stickley and Wilson collected their designs in book format.

With small modifications these same media patterns persisted into the 1990s. Certainly, one of the greatest influences on home design has been the mass-circulation homemaker magazine. A study of these magazines, which advocate different approaches to architectural style, interior furnishings, and gardens, is essential to any understanding of the popular culture of the home. Some at times advocated strong points of view. *The House Beautiful* in its early years supported the art and crafts movement and bungalow design. More famous was the *Ladies Home Journal*, which at the turn of the century sponsored home design by architects such as Frank Lloyd Wright. Through Wright's designs in the *Journal*, many builders and homeowners learned to imitate his work. Other *Journal* architects were more conservative and advocated styles ranging from colonial to Mediterranean. Other magazines such as *Early American Homes* have been almost single-minded in their sponsoring of "colonial" as the fit style for Americans. Today two strong directions can be seen in homemaker magazines such as *Better Homes and Gardens*: the first is a natural trend, and the second a rich eclecticism.

Tangential to the homemaker magazines are how-to-do-it magazines such as *Colonial Homes, Old House Journal, Victorian Homes*, and even *Martha Stewart Living*, which are filled with nostalgia for the good old days. These reflect any number of styles, but most frequently in the Stockcade and Cape Cod.

Specialized trade journals were probably the major new contribution of the twentieth century. Professional architectural magazines such as *Progressive Architecture* and *Architectural Record* have minimally affected popular taste, but they are important for tracing ideas. Far more important are magazines such as *Qualified Remodeler* and *Professional Builder and Apartment Business*, which are directed at the construction industry. They deal with such topics as "Bathroom Design: The Opulent Look" and "How to Facelift Old Buildings without Losing Their Charm."

Books or specialized issues of magazines devoted to home design had a long history in the twentieth century. Most were on the order of the house pattern books and presented images and ideas that could be adapted or copied at will. Collections of designs by architects such as *The Architectural Record Book of Vacation Houses* or *A Treasury of Contemporary Houses* are important since a vast range of styles, from radical to conservative, is shown. *The Building Guide* of *House and Garden* magazine for 1963–1964, for example, offered forty houses and plans ranging from the "contemporary" to the "traditional" and included designs such as "A Combination of Ranch and Colonial" and "The Plantation House in Miniature." Some, such as *The Book of Houses* by John F. Dean and Simon Breines, convey conventional wisdom, advising in a chapter entitled "What Price Style?" that "style, of course, is a subjective factor and if a family is emotionally drawn toward a 'Cape Cod' or a 'Georgian,' serious consideration should be given to a home of that type."

Also a creature of the media were the catalogs issued by house manufacturers. These catalogs paraded a variety of house sizes and styles in varying price ranges that the public could purchase in the form of kits. Perhaps the most important were published by companies such as the Aladdin Concrete Home Company of Bay City, Michigan, and Sears, Roebuck and Company of Chicago. The Sears designs accounted for nearly 100,000 homes in the years 1908–1940. Their designs have been collected in K. C. Stevenson and H. W. Jande, *Houses by Mail: A Guide to Houses from Sears, Roebuck and Company*. Individual Sears house catalogs from 1910 and 1926 have been reprinted by Dover.

Images of other building types are communicated in much the same manner. There are specialized trade journals of industries such as service stations and restaurants. The impact of fast food can be felt in many magazines such as *Restaurant Business* and *Nation's Restaurant News*. Many feature articles on designs and images of the fast-food industry. Books on office design and shopping centers abound, though they are, of course, directed at the professional in the field rather than at the public. But books such as Architectural Record's *Motels, Hotels and Restaurants* have influenced buildings around the world.

While popular architecture began to emerge in the eighteenth century with the Industrial Revolution, it and the associated components in the man-made environment have not been the subject of serious study until very recently. Among architects and historians the reasons are fairly obvious: popular architecture was not serious and lacked the imprint of *Kultur*. The study of architecture, whether historical or contemporary, has usually been confined to monuments: churches, temples, memorials, theaters, forums, palaces, homes of the elite, and buildings designed by architects that aspire to greatness. As a result of Germanic pedantic scholarship and English dilettantism, architecture is usually studied chronologically with concentration on critical and evaluative analysis of the styles, forms, plans, ornament, and details. While sometimes the cultural context and the purpose of a building are noted, in general the building is seen as existing independently in space and time. The preoccupation from the 1930s onward in both the United States and Europe with "modern architecture" led to a further separation from the field of popular architecture. Concerned with totally abstract designing in modern materials and techniques and completely removed from historical recall, nostalgia, or recognizable motifs, modern architecture developed its own language. While the historians of modern architecture have paid some attention to issues of prefabrication and industrial warehouses and factories, still it has been largely a history of designs by major architects. In these studies, as in the more traditional historical studies, the appearance of a Howard Johnson's, a Cozy Cape Cod Cottage from Mount Vernon Estates, or an entryway to Forest Lawn Cemetery in southern California would be only in the most negative of terms.

Variations from the study of certifiable monuments can be seen in the interest in American and vernacular architecture. Early American architecture is basically preindustrial vernacular, and the study of both this and nineteenth-century vernacular has grown spectacularly in recent years. The Vernacular Architecture Forum, an association of scholars, publishes a semiannual, *Perspectives in Vernacular Architecture*. An introductory book edited by Dell Upton is *America's Architectural Roots: Ethnic Groups that Built America*, which is a sort of style manual for vernacular buildings. A good example of a specific study is Sally McMurry's *Families & Farmhouses in 19th Century America*, which looks at the design changes in rural farmhouses as an index to larger societal issues. The most provocative author in the area of vernacular architecture, Henry Glassie, comes from a folklore background; his major works are *Pattern in the Material Folk Culture of the Eastern United States* and *Folk Housing in Middle Virginia*. In the latter book Glassie applies the structuralism of Claude Levi-Strauss and Noam Chomsky to vernacular houses, and while the results are dense and open to question, he offers suggestions for the study of popular architecture that have influenced a new generation of architectural historians.

Along with the other revolutions of the 1960s, a sense of crisis in the architectural and design world led in the 1970s and 1980s to a greater recognition of popular architecture and the necessity of understanding the entire man-made environment. One significant change was a sense of the failure of modern architecture that the brave new world envisioned in the 1930s, where "total design" could improve people's lives, was a hoax. Most consumers disliked, if not downright hated, modern buildings, not only for their sterile quality and uncomfortable feeling but also because they simply did not work well. Urban renewal, a product of modern architectural city planning, proved to be worse than the illness that it was supposed to correct. Jane Jacobs' book *The Death and Life of Great American Cities* was viewed as heretical for her celebration of the messy vitality of the street when published in 1961. Today it is the received orthodoxy. While many architects and critics still profess an admiration for modern architecture, the continuous bombardment of questions and alarming failures has opened the doors for some recognition of popular architecture.

The Museum of Modern Art in New York, the citadel of avant-garde modern chic, provided several new directions in the mid-1960s. In 1964 the exhibit *Architecture without Architects* by Bernard Rudofsky (after a book of same name) presented the thesis that centuries-old buildings executed by common men without the aid of designers could present eternal themes of architecture. Shown were not only homes and temples of primitive peoples but also granaries and fertilizer bins. Rudofsky went on to exploit this unself-conscious theme in *The Prodigious Builders*. In 1966 the Museum of Modern Art published Robert Venturi's *Complexity and Contradiction in Architecture*, the first openly critical look at the theories of modern architecture.

The leaders of postmodernism, Venturi and Moore, helped to spur the study of popular architecture in the 1960s and 1970s. Venturi's *Complexity and Contradiction* was concerned primarily with a rather obtuse design philosophy and, except for the notorious phrase "Main Street is almost alright," was not really concerned with popular architecture. The book that Venturi produced with Denise Scott Brown and Steven Izenour, *Learning from Las Vegas*, focused on popular architecture and argued that architects should look at the strip, for in spirit, if not style, it approached the grandeur of the Roman Forum, or "Las Vegas is to the strip what Rome is to the piazza." Charles Moore's writings were felicitous, with significant comments on suburban and motel culture. Moore's *Home Sweet Home: American Domestic Vernacular Architecture* (with Kathryn Smith and Peter Becker) is a wonderful collection of essays based on a series of southern California exhibitions in 1983–1984. Another harbinger of the change was Peter Blake. In 1964 he published *God's Own Junkyard*, a great diatribe against popular architecture. But within ten years he was writing admiring articles on the virtues of Disney World and the strip. *Progressive Architecture* magazine, once the high church of modern architecture but now sadly defunct, devoted its June 1978 issue to "Taste in America"; it contained articles on McDonald's design evolution and suburbia.

The other critical shift that began in the 1960s and still continues is the burgeoning historic preservation movement. Historic preservation as a movement can be traced back to the mid-nineteenth century in the United States and abroad. Up until the 1960s it was generally viewed as elitist and concerned with historic houses and re-creations of olden time in Williamsburg and other museum villages. But in the 1960s historic preservation became more populist in outlook, less concerned with the individual high art buildings and more with entire neighborhoods. Nods of approval have been given to lesser classes of structures; service stations, billboards, and diners now appear on the National Register of Historic Places. The Rhode Island Historical Preservation Commission has registered seventeen Quonset huts located at the U.S. Navy air station at Quonset, Rhode Island. The championing by preservationists of the large hillside sign for Hollywood and many other less prestigious sites is an indication of a changing climate toward popular architecture. Preservation studies have been carried out on working-class neigh-

Caesar's Palace, Las Vegas. © Painet

borhoods such as the Old West Side in Ann Arbor, Michigan, a blue-collar German enclave.

Others in the last few years, such as architectural and art historians, sociologists, planners, and anthropologists, have produced a wide variety of papers, articles, and books that have contributed to knowledge in the area. However, while some research is under way on such diverse topics as gas stations, fast-food restaurants, and amusement parks, the field is still virtually wide open. Most of the publications on these and similar topics tend toward the simplistic, emphasizing photographs and catalogs. Basic research needs to be done in every area, and methodological approaches need to be discussed. Societies dealing with different aspects of popular architecture have been founded, including the Society for Commercial Archaeology and the Society for Industrial Archaeology.

REFERENCE WORKS

There are no major reference works devoted specifically to popular architecture, and here, as elsewhere, one has to make piecemeal use of other sources. Among dictionaries, the *Dictionary of Architecture and Construction*, edited by Cyril M. Harris, is undoubtedly the best and most complete. Well illustrated with abundant references, it is directed at the professional. Harris has also produced two other useful works, aimed at a nonprofessional audience: *The Illustrated Dictionary of Historic Architecture* and *American Architecture: An Illustrated Encyclopedia*.

To be able to understand properly the allusions and references that popular architecture makes, identification of the style or styles of a building has a place. For the United States many books are available; representative examples are Marcus Whiffen's *American Architecture since 1780: A Guide to the Styles* and *What Style Is It?* by John Poppeliers et al. While recognition of a building's style is important, the problem with both of these books is the implication that style and how accurately a building falls within stylistic perimeters are the important questions. Obviously, buildings have other elements.

Biographical information on American architects can be found in Withey's *Biographical Dictionary of American Architects (Deceased)*. All levels of architects are included, but it is by no means complete. Also of use is Columbia University's *Avery Obituary Index of Architects and Artists*, which includes even more obscure figures. Finally there is the *Macmillan Encyclopedia of Architects*, edited by Adolf Placzek; however, it is exclusively concerned with high art architects.

For access to periodicals the major work is the *Avery Index to Architectural Periodicals*, produced by the staff at the Avery Architectural Library at Columbia University. This is a retrospective index of most English-language architectural periodicals and selected foreign and other periodicals. It is updated daily with supplements every few years and is now available on CD-ROM and on-line for research library groups. While primarily concerned with architectural periodicals, the *Avery Index* contains a vast gold mine of information that is conveniently indexed not only under authors, architects, and locations but also under subject headings such as "Diners," "Fast Food Restaurants," "Gasoline Stations," "Motels," and "Billboards."

There is no comprehensive bibliography of American architectural books. Though limited in scope, Henry-Russell Hitchcock's *American Architectural Books:*

A List of Books, Portfolios, and Pamphlets on Architecture and Related Subjects Published in America before 1895 is the best for the period. It does contain a comprehensive listing of builders' guides and pattern books, which are a major source for studying the dissemination of popular architectural idioms.

RESEARCH COLLECTIONS

Architecture by its very nature is generally a static entity, and while one can point to mobile homes and the ephemeral creations of the strip, most architecture is hardly collectible. Most research on architecture can be divided into two aspects: actual fieldwork and collection data and library or archival work where drawings, plans, photographs, magazines, and books devoted to buildings as well as materials devoted to their creators can be perused. While the collecting of architectural records and drawings (both presentation and working drawings) has grown in recent years, there is no collection specifically devoted to popular architecture. Many university libraries are avidly pursuing collections for their local areas, but storage and study space for the bulky materials are always a problem. The Committee for the Preservation of Architectural Records, located at the Prints and Photographs Division, Library of Congress, Washington, D.C. 20540, acts as a clearinghouse for information and infrequently publishes a free newsletter that contains information and research queries. Some states also have their own associations for the preservation of architectural records. A new form of research guide containing lists of local depositories has been produced by committees in Philadelphia, New York, Chicago, and other cities.

Most collections of architectural records tend to emphasize the unique architect, and the depositing of materials relating to popular creations is not common. The major collections are in the Avery Architectural Library at Columbia, the Smithsonian Institution's National Museum of American History in Washington, the Cooper-Hewitt Museum in New York, the Library of Environmental Design at the University of California, Berkeley, the Architectural Drawings Collection at the University of California, Santa Barbara, the Kahn Archives at the University of Pennsylvania, and the Northwest Architectural Archive at the University of Minneapolis. These collections may have materials that are related to popular architecture. Guides exist for some collections.

Much documentation on popular architecture remains in the hands of the original owners or patrons. Large corporations such as Mobil Oil, Sunoco, McDonald's, and White Tower have opened their files to qualified researchers in the past, but the major home builders, like the former Jim Walter Corporation, and smaller local builders should be contacted (see Housing chapter).

For extensive collections of books and periodicals that relate to popular architecture, the Avery Architectural Library at Columbia is easily the best in the United States, if not the world. Other extensive collections are the architectural or design libraries at the University of California, Berkeley, the University of Michigan, and the University of Virginia.

Photographs are, of course, one of the primary records of architecture and the sometimes transient creations of popular architecture. Local collections in libraries, newspapers, and museums should always be consulted. Undoubtedly, the major national collection is at the Library of Congress, Prints and Photographs

Art deco building, Miami Beach, Florida. © Painet

Division. Photographs of all types, from amateur to professional, including the Farm Security Administration's records of the 1930s, are deposited there. A wealth of material on the popular landscape waits to be used.

Also housed in the photographic division at the Library of Congress are the deposited records of the Historic American Buildings Survey (HABS). A division of the National Park Service, HABS was founded during the depression as an attempt to record through field research, photographs, and scale drawings many of the fast-disappearing creations of the built environment. After a hiatus HABS was refounded in 1957 and continues today to send field teams throughout the United States and territories to record architecture. While much of the focus of HABS has been on high art architecture, attention in recent years has been paid to movie theaters, service stations, and middle-class housing. As projects are completed, the records, along with drawings, photographs, and negatives, are deposited in the Library of Congress. In 1995, HABS published *America Preserved: A Checklist of Historic Buildings, Structures and Sites*, which contains a complete index (to that time) of HABS. An updated index can be found at the HABS site on the World Wide Web. In recent years catalogs for individual states, cities, and special subjects have been issued. In 1969 the Historic American Engineering Record (HAER) was established; it performs essentially the same function as HABS but is more concerned with bridges, locks, railroad stations, piers, and factories. While HAER has not published an index, it also has a searchable database on its Web site.

Finally, the National Register of Historic Places, also in the National Park Service, and the various state preservation agencies, while not officially research collections, frequently contain significant amounts of information and materials on both common and extravagant structures. The 1966 Historic Preservation Act mandated that every state have a historic preservation office and the methods of accomplishing a statewide survey of notable structures.

The explosion of the Internet in recent years has provided a forum for popular architecture enthusiasts and organizations. *Roadside Magazine*, a publication devoted to diners, and the *Movie Palace Resource Page*, operated by the League of Historic American Theatres, are but two of many Web sites that may be of interest. As with all Internet sites, quality control and scholarly rigor vary among these offerings; factual information should be carefully scrutinized. More important, however, are the databases now available to the public. The HABS/HAER projects and the National Register of Historic Places have searchable databases that provide invaluable opportunities for research. The Avery Index can also be accessed through the Getty Center for Art. The Society of Architectural Historians home page provides links to other interesting sites. Other archival materials are becoming available daily; an excellent recent example is "Research Materials for Architecture and the Built Environment Located in Washington, D.C." Internet addresses for these sites are provided at the end of the bibliography.

HISTORY AND CRITICISM

Because so little research has been done on popular architecture, there are no books devoted specifically to the topic as a whole. To gain a perspective on popular architecture, one has to refer to a wide range of books and articles.

Writings on the theory and methodology of the study of popular architecture are few. Smatterings of ideas can be found in older essays by J. Meredith Neil, Marshall Fishwick, and Dennis Alan Mann, and one can turn back to the standards on popular culture, such as works by Herbert J. Gans. Probably, though, the most important search for a methodology has been done by Alan Gowans, first in his *The Unchanging Arts*, which, while devoted largely to the other arts, does have some comments on architecture, and then in his rather ponderously titled *On Parallels in Universal History Discoverable in Arts and Artifacts*. This last, subtitled *An Outline Statement*, is a theory that what is art has changed over time, that the arts must be interpreted in their historic terms, and that "taste is determined by ideology." The implications for popular architecture are manifest, and while much needs to be fleshed out, it is an important beginning. George Kubler's *The Shape of Time: Remarks on the History of Things* has a somewhat different emphasis and argues that all man-made things can be viewed as art existing in a linked succession. As indicated earlier, the works by Henry Glassie offer several possibilities, and one should also look at Amos Rapoport's *House: Form and Culture*, which, while devoted to the building of primitive peoples, offers many suggestions.

Theoretical fads such as structuralism or semiotics come and go in architecture. In the 1970s, semiotics, or the application of linguistic theory of signs, developed by Ferdinand de Saussure and C. S. Pierre, was the hot topic. Most of the writing was jargon-ridden and obscure, but it demonstrated that all buildings and their furnishings carry meanings, intended or not. The most understandable introduction is Geoffrey Broadbent's article, "A Plain Man's Guide to the Theory of Signs in Architecture." One should also look at Charles Jencks and George Baird's collection of essays *Meaning in Architecture* and a three-part essay by Jencks in *Architecture and Urbanism*. Structuralism found surprisingly few adherents. Glassie's book on Virginia houses cited earlier is perhaps the most important example. After structuralism, the rather slippery notion of postmodernism came into vogue, with its witty and often ironic references to the historical past. Venturi's *Complexity and Contradiction in Architecture* was the point of departure. Again, Jencks provides one of the more readable treatments in *What Is Post-Modernism?* Today, deconstructionism and hermeneutics have their current advocates; however, no attention has focused on popular architecture.

Another area for the student to be aware of is the actual impact of the intangibles of space and form on humans. This is also an undeveloped field, surprisingly little research having been done on perception and cultural usages of space. Beginnings have been made by anthropologists such as Edward T. Hall in *The Hidden Dimension* and by psychologists such as Robert Sommer in *Personal Space: The Behavioral Basis of Design* and *Design Awareness*. Kent Bloomer and Charles Moore's *Body, Memory and Architecture*, which is written from an architect's point of view, while slim, offers some important insights. Christian Norberg-Schulz, in works like *Architecture: Meaning and Place*, and Gaston Bachelard's *The Poetics of Space* are characteristic of the impact of phenomenology on recent architectural theory. There are numerous other technical articles and research reports that the student can pursue if needed.

Another recent trend in architectural circles that considers cultural contexts and local identity and therefore has consequences for popular architecture is "critical regionalism." Kenneth Frampton's essay "Prospects for a Critical Regionalism" in

Perspecta is a useful introduction. The full implications of such an approach for popular architecture have yet to be explored.

The book that comes the closest to a general history of American architecture and pays some attention to popular culture is Alan Gowans' *Styles and Types of North American Architecture: Social Function and Cultural Expression*. While Gowans' concentration is on high art architecture, he does include a chapter on popular architecture and furniture from the 1940s to the 1980s. James Marston Fitch's *American Building: The Historical Forces That Shaped It*, while a general history, focuses more on physical and technological factors. He is very good for the period prior to the twentieth century. Again the focus is almost completely on high art. John Kouwenhoven's *Made in America: The Arts in Modern Civilization*, while published in 1948, is the only book that has seriously attempted to take a fresh look at American artifacts and study their uniqueness as typically American. His comments on the vernacular tradition are still worth reading.

Technological or construction history is a separate category from architecture due to its specialized nature. The best overall study of the American contribution is Carl Condit's two-volume work, *American Building Art*, which was condensed and revised into one volume, *American Building: Materials and Techniques from the Beginning of the Colonial Settlements to the Present*. A virtue of these pioneer attempts is that Condit understands technical language but can write literate English. James Marston Fitch has made a contribution here with his second study, *American Building: The Environmental Forces That Shaped It*. A physiological study of the different sensory elements that make buildings, it is an important work. The title of Sigfried Giedion's *Mechanization Takes Command: A Contribution to Anonymous History* is self-explanatory; it is the first serious attempt to trace many contributions to modern life such as bathtubs, kitchen ranges, and heating. Reyner Banham's *The Architecture of the Well-Tempered Environment* is more narrowly focused and deals with the period from the late nineteenth century to the 1960s and with the uses that high art architects have made of air conditioning, dropped ceilings, fluorescent lighting, and forced-air heating. Critical and prescriptive in nature, Banham's hero, if he has one, is Willis Carrier, inventor of air conditioning. However, Banham's perceptions are astute, and his thinking, as always, is original. The book is a must.

Books on furniture, interiors, and the decorative arts proliferate and encompass everything from how to collect Victorian to serious studies of specific furniture types. All are of some value, but for the student looking for a broad overview, there is little. Russell Lynes' *The Tastemakers*, published in 1954, is dated, but it is a popular history of American interior design that pays considerable attention to mass taste. Jan Jennings and Herbert Gottfried's *American Vernacular Interior Architecture, 1870–1940*, a catalog of interior details, is a step in the right direction. The term "interior design" indicates status, while the terms "interior decoration" and "decorator" are generally avoided by high art architects and decorators. As the title of Allen Tate and C. Ray Smith's *Interior Design in the Twentieth Century* indicates, the concern is exclusively with name designers and high-style furniture makers; the popular styles—French Provincial, Early American—receive little coverage. Far too rare are studies that attempt to interpret individual tastes in interior decoration. M. H. Harmon's *Psycho-Decorating: What Homes Reveal about People*, is based on interviews with 100 middle-income women who have decorated their

own homes. Extremely limited and filled with unsupportable interpretive gener-
alizations, still it indicates a direction that should be investigated. See also *Dining
in America*, edited by Kathryn Grover. Not strictly concerned with decorative arts
and far more inclusive and yet a book that must be mentioned is *I'll Buy That!
Fifty Small Wonders and Big Deals That Revolutionized the Lives of Consumers*, by the
editors of *Consumer Reports*. While the fifty wonders deal with everything from
"the Pill," to automobiles, to Levittown, the major portion of the book is devoted
to appliances and home goods. This is a book that no student of popular culture
can afford to be without.

The recent revival of interest in art deco or moderne of the 1920s and 1930s
has resulted in several books that deal with the decorative arts from a popular
point of view. Bevis Hillier's *Art Deco Style* (with Stephen Escritt) and his essay
in the Minneapolis Institute of Art's *The World of Art Deco* introduced a broad
range of objects; a more recent book with Stephen Escritt updates Hillier's earlier
work. The best coverage of the decorative arts, including mass-produced objects,
is in Dianne Pilgrim's essay in Richard Guy Wilson, Dianne Pilgrim, and Dickran
Tashjian, *The Machine Age in America, 1918–1941*. A collection of 1930s and 1940s
decorative trivia can be found in Lester Glassner and Brownie Harris, *Dime Store
Days*.

Hillier's book *The Decorative Arts of the Forties and Fifties: Austerity/Binge* is
mainly devoted to England, but the parallels with the United States are close
enough for it to be of value. This is an attempt to deal with what is jokingly
known in the trade as "Art Yucko." Filled with illustrations is *Fifties Style: Then
and Now* by Richard Horn.

The role of the industrial designer has been assessed in books such as Donald
Bush, *The Streamlined Decade*; Jeffrey L. Meikle, *Twentieth Century Limited: Industrial Design in America, 1925–1939*; Arthur Pulos, *American Design Ethic: A History of Industrial Design to 1940* and *The American Design Adventure, 1940–1975*;
and Wilson, Pilgrim, and Tashjian, *The Machine Age in America, 1918–1941*. Contemporary accounts by the designers themselves include Raymond Loewy's *Industrial Design*, Walter Dorwin Teague's *Design This Day*, and Harold Van Doren's
Industrial Design.

The history of the American landscape, urban, suburban, and rural, and how to
analyze it has a significant number of books of some importance. John Reps' *The
Making of Urban America: A History of City Planning in the United States*, while
focusing on the more formal or designed creations, includes everything from garden cities to railroad speculator towns. It is very good and has plenty of illustrations. For a wider view of the landscape in all its guises, John Brinckerhoff Jackson
is clearly superior. In books like *Landscapes, Discovering the Vernacular Landscape*,
and *A Sense of Time, a Sense of Place*, as well as old copies of *Landscape* magazine,
Jackson demonstrates his insight and intelligence. A good history that reflects
Jackson's wide perspective is John R. Stilgoe's *Common Landscape of America, 1580
to 1845*. Stilgoe later covered the development of the suburb in *Borderlands: Origins
of the American Suburb, 1820–1939*. An incomparable source for the historical study
of the landscape is the WPA Guide Series to the different states. A compilation
by Bernard A. Weisberger can be found in *The WPA Guide to America*. Another
class of books is the critical-analytical studies that generally contain some history
along with a methodology of how to look at the landscape. Most of them preju-

dicially call the popular environment "goop" and "crap" and contain prescriptive remedies; however, used with care, they are important. Examples are Kevin Lynch, *The Image of the City*; Donald Appleyard, Kevin Lynch, and John R. Myer, *The View from the Road*; Ian Nairn, *The American Landscape: A Critical View*; Richard Saul Wurman, *Making the City Observable*; and Grady Clay, *Close-up: How to Read the American City*. Clay's book contains an extensive analysis of the strip.

There are many books on American cities, but the best one from a visual point of view is Harold M. Mayer and Richard C. Wade's *Chicago: Growth of a Metropolis*. Attention is paid to the everyday realities of common buildings. The series of *New York* books by Robert Stern et al. are rather dense but do contain valuable information on the development of the city. The WPA Guide Series devoted several books to cities that should be looked at. Quite clearly the entry point for the study of popular architecture in a city should be Tom Wolfe's seminal essay on the "Versailles" of Las Vegas in *From Bauhaus to Our House*. Following this there is the previously mentioned work by Venturi, Brown, and Izenour, *Learning from Las Vegas*. This is written from an architect's and urban planner's point of view and provides an insightful look at all the elements of the American strip, gas stations, signs, parking lots, and "ugly and ordinary architecture." The actual history is slim, but the interpretation is challenging.

If Las Vegas is the Versailles of popular architecture, then Los Angeles is the Holy City. Reyner Banham's *Los Angeles: The Architecture of Four Ecologies* is every bit as important as *Learning from Las Vegas* and probably offers a more profound interpretation. Banham's book is a mix between high art and popular architecture, and he identifies as the four ecologies the oceanfront, the foothills, the Plains of Id, and the freeway world or autotopia. An Englishman, he appreciates the American scene as only an outsider can. Also to be looked at concerning Los Angeles is David Gebhard and Harriette Von Brenton's *L.A. in the Thirties, 1931–1941*. While containing many examples of high art architecture, it also looks at the early drive-ins, freeways, and movie lots.

Several exhibits have led to some rather ephemeral documents on popular architecture. *Signs of Life: Symbols in the American City* is a slim catalog of an important exhibit organized by Venturi and Brown and others at the Renwick Gallery of the Smithsonian Institution in 1976. The exhibit documented popular taste in the American home, strip, and street. An earlier catalog for the Institute for Contemporary Art in Philadelphia, *The Highway*, contains essays by Venturi and Brown. In 1978 the Cooper-Hewitt branch of the Smithsonian held an exhibit on architectural packaging and looked at four popular American building types; fast-food restaurants, diners, gasoline stations, and museum-village restorations. An article by Richard Oliver and Nancy Ferguson, the curators of the exhibit, appeared in *Architectural Record* for February 1978 and also as a reprint catalog. Finally, an excellent 1995 National Building Museum exhibition on the postwar housing boom produced *World War II and the American Dream: How Wartime Building Changed a Nation*, edited by Donald Albrecht.

One area of popular architecture studies that has received a great deal of attention has been the American penchant for movement and travel, specifically, the highway. Of course, Americans moved by other means before the automobile—and indeed they continued to in the twentieth century—but in general canals and railroads have been overlooked. The vast area of railroad buffdom includes

Hollywood sign. © Painet

thousands of books on virtually every aspect of trains, but these are generally very specialized. The best book that transcends the rail fan's narrow focus is Stilgoe's *Metropolitan Corridor: Railroads and the American Scene*. Stilgoe treats the period 1880–1930 and deals with the railroad as a cultural phenomenon. Attention is paid to the structures that used to border the right-of-way and the industrial scene.

However, the twentieth-century American highway has inspired most of the studies of popular architecture. The model study is Thomas J. Schlereth's *Reading the Road: U.S. 40 and the American Landscape*, which covers only the state of Indiana. He pays attention to the pre-twentieth-century road and covers paving and grading changes extensively as well as service stations, diners, and roadside structures. Jeff Brouws, Bernd Polster, and Phil Patton tread the line between scholarship and entertainment in *Highway: America's Endless Dream*; the book includes a catalog of "road movies." A far less scholarly and more openly nostalgic book is Phil Patton's *Open Road: A Celebration of the American Highway*. Older and written from the point of view of a professional landscape architect (and indeed an award-winning designer) is Lawrence Halprin's *Freeways*. He deals with the aesthetics of freeway design and its many images. David Brodsly's *L.A. Freeway: An Appreciative Essay* expands upon some of the observations of Reyner Banham noted earlier and gives a history of the mecca of freeways. The odd and frequently overscaled sculptures that one finds alongside the road have been analyzed—not very perceptively—by Karal Ann Marling in *The Colossus of Roads: Myth and Symbol along the American Highway*. The book is devoted to Minnesota and has a lot of footnotes and poor illustrations, but it is an opening gambit in a neglected area. Billboards are architecture and also art, but they have received scant attention from historians. *Billboard Art* by Sally Henderson and Robert Landau provides some history, though the concentration is on the recent past (i.e., post-1960) and California. James Fraser's *The American Billboard: 100 Years* attempts a more comprehensive history. One of the great designers of billboards, Otis Shepard, is barely known today; the only treatment of him is in Steve Strauss, *Moving Images*. The world of tourist attractions, from giant rattlesnakes to twine balls, is humorously told in Jack Barth, Doug Kirby, Ken Smith, and Milk Wilkins' *Roadside America*. A more analytical view but just as entertaining can be found in Umberto Eco's essay *Travels in Hyperreality*. Chester Liebs' *Main Street to Miracle Mile: American Roadside Architecture* is an ambitious attempt to deal with several types of structures. Unfortunately, the book becomes something of a catalog. Certainly the most entertaining is John Baeder's *Gas, Food and Lodging*, which is something of a personal memoir. Baeder is a contemporary painter infatuated with the relics of the road as well as postcards. The book is an interesting attempt to "do" history from postcards and succeeds very well.

Highway or roadside architecture has been the great growth area of popular architecture studies in recent years. Liebs' book *Main Street* is the starting point with his chapters on drive-in theaters, motels, gas stations, and other kinds of architecture. *California Crazy: Roadside Vernacular Architecture* by Jim Heimann and Rip Georges is primarily photographs of oversized flower pots and pigs acting as buildings. It does have an introduction by architectural historian David Gebhard that contains valuable information on designs found in the U.S. Patent Office. Daniel I. Veyra's *"Fill'er Up": An Architectural History of America's Gas Stations* is primarily pictures, though it does have an important listing of source materials. Michael Karl Witzel's *The American Gas Station* is a more in-depth study, but also filled with illustrations. For a full scholarly treatment of the topic, see *The Gas Station in America* by John Jakle and Keith Sculle. Master's theses from the many graduate programs in architectural history and historic preservation undoubtedly provide information in many of these areas; one example is Gary Wolf's on the Sunoco station. John Margolies is a noted photographer who has concentrated in the area; a collection of his photographs with minimal text is *The End of the Road: Vanishing Highway Architecture in America*. Also, the Society for Commercial Archeology publishes a journal that addresses all types of roadside architecture.

A very good book on the early history of roadside accommodations is Warren James Belasco's *Americans on the Road: From Autocamp to Motel, 1910–1945*. The book is carefully researched and documented, and the conclusions are sound. Margolies' *Home Away from Home: Motels in America* is an entertaining look at this vanishing icon. Jakle and Sculle, along with Jefferson Rogers, have tackled the same topic on a deeper level in *The Motel in America*.

The proliferation of "entertainment restaurants" like Planet Hollywood is beginning to draw attention. These restaurants often provide the whimsy of old-time roadside architecture in an urban or suburban setting, though many come off as overly artificial. A survey by category can be found in Michael Kaplan's *Theme Restaurants*.

Surprisingly, the auto-directed shopping mall or shopping center has received little academic study until recently. Richard Longstreth, an American architectural historian, is leading the investigation into this neglected area. His *City Center to*

Regional Mall: Architecture, the Automobile and Retailing in Los Angeles, 1920–1950 is a history of the southern California shopping center and the most comprehensive example to date. Longstreth has also published articles on community shopping centers in general and the Country Club Plaza in Kansas City, an important source for American shopping center design. Also to be looked at is Meredith L. Clausen, "Northgate Regional Shopping Center—Paradigm from the Provinces."

The subspecialty of roadside food buildings has attracted a lot of interest. Many of the previously mentioned books by Margolies, Liebs, Schlereth, and others deal with the subject. Richard Gutman has been the historian of the diner, first with an article and then with a book, *American Diner*, coauthored by Elliott Kaufman. Gutman's *American Diner: Then and Now* contains more text and fewer photographs than the earlier version. John Baeder, a popular contemporary painter, has collected his paintings of them in a book, *Diners*. *Roadside Magazine* continually publishes articles on diners and updates on preservation efforts. Alan Hess has written *Googie: Fifties Coffee Shop Architecture*, which is an interesting story of a California specialty that went nationwide. Actually, the original name of the restaurant was Googie's; it was designed by a high art architect named John Lautner, a follower of Frank Lloyd Wright. The exuberant image of Googie's caught on and led to a nationwide architectural phenomenon. Two employees of Robert Venturi, Paul Hirshorn and Steven Izenour, have written *White Towers*, which chronicles with excellent photographs the chain that began in the 1920s. Warren Belasco has written an article on the Howard Johnson's chain. Jim Heimann's *Car Hops and Curb Service: A History of American Drive-In Restaurants 1920–1960* is broader than most studies. There has also been a nostalgic interest in the food of the roadside, as exemplified by Tabori and Chang Stewart's *Roadside Food*. The best book overall on the subject of roadside food architecture is Philip Langdon's *Orange Roofs, Golden Arches*, which, as the title indicates, covers the subject in an engaging manner, with plenty of illustrations.

There is a sub-subspecialty in this area, and that is—as might be expected—McDonald's. Langdon is good on it; in addition, there are histories and cultural considerations of the company, such as John F. Love's *McDonald's: Behind the Arches*; Marshall Fishwick, "The World of Ronald McDonald," *Journal of American Culture*; and, of course, *Grinding It Out*, the memoirs of Ray Kroc, who founded the company—or perhaps more accurately, who made it into a national institution. In 1984 the American press was consumed by reports that the original McDonald's was closing. At the time, this was reported to be a stand in Des Plaines, Illinois, constructed in 1955. Alan Hess has put the story right; the first McDonald's was in San Bernardino, California, while the first of the eye-catching stands was designed by Stanley Meston and erected in Phoenix in 1953. That one has been demolished, but the second McDonald's has been lovingly restored to near-mint condition in Downey, California. See Hess' article in the *Journal of the Society of Architectural Historians*. Finally, one should look at the thesis by Abbott and Grosvenor on McDonald's.

Movie theaters are also attracting more attention. There is a Theater Historical Society—headquartered in Notre Dame, Indiana—which publishes a newsletter titled *Marquee* and holds conventions. There is also a League of Historic American Theatres, which maintains the "Movie Palace Resource Page" on the Internet.

Simon Tidworth's *Theatres: An Architectural and Cultural History* and Dennis Sharp's *The Picture Palace and Other Buildings for the Movies* offer an English picture of the history of movie palaces. The best American book is Maggie Valentine's *The Show Starts on the Sidewalk: An Architectural History of the Movie Theatre*. Less rigorous are two books, both conspicuously illustrated and popularly written: Ben Hall, *The Best Remaining Seats*, and David Naylor, *American Picture Palaces*. The outdoor movie theater, now almost extinct, has been entertainingly covered by Don and Susan Sanders in *The American Drive-In Movie Theater*.

The house as popular architecture is only begining to receive serious study. The extensive background of original sources that one might use for such a history has been outlined earlier in this chapter. The best book from an American point of view is Clifford Clark's *The American Family Home, 1800–1960*; it is comprehensive in that all types of houses, from architect-designed to pattern book and Levittown, are included. Clark attempts to see the family house as a social institution and also as architecture. Gwendolyn Wright's *Building the Dream: A Social History of Housing in America* is also important but marred by an excessive zeal to prove that the single-family, middle-class house is wrong and that everybody should live in apartments. The history of the type of housing popular at the turn of the century is surveyed in Robert Winter, *The California Bungalow*. Alan Gowans in *The Comfortable House: North American Suburban Architecture, 1890–1930* has some important information, though he tries to prove that all modern houses are bad and has a tendency to catalog. Some preliminary information on trailers and the mobile home industry can be found in Carlton M. Edwards, *Homes for Travel and Living*. Along this line, Robert Landau and James Phillippi's *Airstream* is unacademic but entertaining. Unfortunately, the history of the modern ranch burger, or the Cape Cod, still remains to be written.

There are numerous books on foreign housing; among them, Maurice W. Barley, *The House and Home*, covers 900 years of England, while Martin Pawley, *Architecture versus Housing*, treats the large housing block and is polemical in outlook. Also, Robin Boyd's *Australia's Home* should be looked at.

Some other areas suggestive of future examination are indicated by Alan Crawford and Robert Thorne's pamphlet *Birmingham Pubs, 1890–1930*. The architecture of amusement parks and recreation has similarly received little attention in the United States. A good history of the industry as a whole can be found in *The American Amusement Park Industry: A History of Technology and Thrills* by Judith A. Adams. Critical articles abound on Disneyland/World and others; they can be located through the periodical indexes. A recent exhibition on Disney architecture produced a book of perceptive essays entitled *Designing Disney's Theme Parks: The Architecture of Reassurance*, edited by Karal Ann Marling. There is also a picture book: Gary Kyriazi's *The Great American Amusement Park*.

Ten years ago, this chapter reported that the study of popular architecture was still in its infancy; sadly, the same can be said a decade later. Many of the previously noted books suffer from a lack of perspective and sound scholarship with regard to notes, research, and methodology and too frequently disintegrate into a nostalgic cry for the past. Others are excessively polemical or simply picture books. While there are good scholarly studies of some aspects of popular architecture, there is room for plenty of work!

ANTHOLOGIES AND REPRINTS

There has been little anthologization of literature on popular architecture. About the only anthologies have been those issued from the Popular Culture Press at Bowling Green University. *Popular Architecture*, edited by Marshall Fishwick and J. Meredith Neil, collects articles dealing with a variety of subjects, some appropriate, such as those by Neil, Brown, Attoe and Latus, Gowans, and others, but some far afield from the subject. Other essays on popular architecture subjects have appeared in *The Arts in a Democratic Society*, edited by Dennis Alan Mann, and *Icons of America*, edited by Ray B. Browne and Marshall Fishwick. A more difficult recent book attempting to address some of the issues is *Architecture of the Everyday*, edited by Steven Harris and Deborah Berke.

Reprints have proven to be the major source of builder's guides and house pattern books. The major publishers in this line have been Dover Publications and Da Capo Press. The list would be very long if the hundred or so reprinted were noted. Instead, reprinted works that have been referred to earlier are so noted in the bibliography at the end of this chapter.

NOTES

1. William Morris, "The Prospects of Architecture in Civilization," in *The Collected Works of William Morris*, ed. May Morris (London: Longmans, Green, 1910–1915), vol. 22, 120.

2. Richard Oliver and Nancy Ferguson, "Place, Product, Packaging," *Architectural Record* 163 (February 1978), 116.

BIBLIOGRAPHY

Books and Articles

Abbott, James G., and John R. Grosvenor. "Corporate Architecture and Design Theory: A Case Study of McDonald's." M.A. thesis, Miami University, 1976.

Adams, Judith A. *The American Amusement Park Industry: A History of Technology and Thrills.* Boston: Twayne, 1991.

Albrecht, Donald, ed. *World War II and the American Dream: How Wartime Building Changed a Nation.* Cambridge: MIT Press, 1995.

Appleyard, Donald, Kevin Lynch, and John R. Myer. *The View from the Road.* Cambridge: MIT Press, 1964.

Architectural Record. *The Architectural Record Book of Vacation Houses.* New York: McGraw-Hill, 1977.

———. *Motels, Hotels and Restaurants.* 2nd ed. New York: F. W. Dodge, 1960.

———. *A Treasury of Contemporary Houses.* New York: F. W. Dodge, 1954.

Bachelard, Gaston. *The Poetics of Space.* Trans. Maria Jolas. Boston: Beacon Press, 1969.

Baeder, John. *Diners.* New York: Harry N. Abrams, 1995.

———. *Gas, Food and Lodging.* New York: Abbeville Press, 1982.

Banham, Reyner. *The Architecture of the Well-Tempered Environment*. Chicago: University of Chicago Press, 1969.

———. *Los Angeles: The Architecture of Four Ecologies*. New York: Harper and Row, 1971.

Barley, Maurice W. *The House and Home: A Review of 900 Years of House Planning and Furnishing in Britain*. Greenwich, Conn.: New York Graphic Society, 1971.

Barth, Jack, et al. *Roadside America*. New York: Simon and Schuster, 1986.

Belasco, Warren J. *Americans on the Road: From Autocamp to Motel, 1910–1945*. Cambridge: MIT Press, 1979.

———. "Towards a Culinary Denominator: The Rise of Howard Johnson's, 1925–1940." *Journal of American Culture* 2 (Fall 1979), 508–12.

Benjamin, Asher. *The American Builder's Companion*. 6th ed. 1827. New York: Dover, 1969.

Blake, Peter. *God's Own Junkyard: The Planned Deterioration of America's Landscape*. New York: Holt, Rinehart, and Winston, 1964.

Bloomer, Kent C., and Charles W. Moore. *Body, Memory and Architecture*. New Haven, Conn.: Yale University Press, 1977.

Boyd, Robin. *Australia's Home: Its Origins, Builders and Occupiers*. Carlton, Victoria: Melbourne University Press, 1987.

Broadbent, Geoffrey. "A Plain Man's Guide to the Theory of Signs in Architecture." *Architectural Design* 47 (July–August 1977), 474–82.

Brodsly, David. *L.A. Freeway: An Appreciative Essay*. Berkeley: University of California Press, 1981.

Brouws, Jeff, Bernd Polster and Phil Patton. *Highway: America's Endless Dream*. New York: Stewart, Tabori, and Chang, 1997.

Browne, Ray B., and Marshall Fishwick, eds. *Icons of America*. Bowling Green, Ohio: Bowling Green University Popular Press, 1978.

Bush, Donald J. *The Streamlined Decade*. New York: George Braziller, 1975.

Clark, Clifford Edward, Jr. *The American Family Home, 1800–1960*. Chapel Hill: University of North Carolina Press, 1986.

Clausen, Meredith L. "Northgate Regional Shopping Center—Paradigm from the Provinces." *Journal of the Society of Architectural Historians* 43 (May 1984), 144–61.

Clay, Grady. *Close-up: How to Read the American City*. New York: Praeger, 1973.

Columbia University. *Avery Index to Architectural Periodicals*. 2nd ed. 15 vols. plus supplements. Boston: G. K. Hall, 1973.

———. *Avery Obituary Index of Architects and Artists*. 2nd ed. Boston: G. K. Hall, 1980.

Committee for the Preservation of Architectural Records. *Architectural Research Materials in New York City: A Guide to Resources in All Five Boroughs*. 2 vols. New York: Committee for the Preservation of Architectural Records, 1977.

Condit, Carl W. *American Building Art*. 2 vols. New York: Oxford University Press, 1960, 1961.

———. *American Building: Materials and Techniques From the Beginning of the Colonial Settlements to the Present*. 2nd ed. Chicago: University of Chicago Press, 1982.

Crawford, Alan, and Robert Thorne. *Birmingham Pubs, 1890–1930*. Birmingham,

England: Center for Urban and Regional Studies, University of Birmingham and the Victorian Society, Birmingham Group, 1975.

Cruickshank, Dan, ed. *Sir Banister Fletcher's A History of Architecture.* 20th ed. Oxford and Boston: Architectural Press, 1996.

Dean, John F., and Simon Breines. *The Book of Houses.* New York: Crown, 1946.

Downing, Andrew Jackson. *The Architecture of Country Houses.* 1850. Reprint. New York: Dover, 1969.

———. *Cottage Residences.* 1842. Reprint. Watkins Glen, N.Y.: Library of Victorian Culture, 1967.

Eco, Umberto. *Travels in Hyperreality.* Trans. William Weaver. San Diego, New York, and London: Harcourt, Brace, 1986.

Editors of Consumer Reports. *I'll Buy That! Fifty Small Wonders and Big Deals That Revolutionized the Lives of Consumers.* Mount Vernon, N.Y.: Consumer Reports Books, 1986.

Edwards, Carlton M. *Homes for Travel and Living: The History and Development of the Recreational Vehicle and Mobile Home Industry.* Lansing, Mich.: Carl Edwards and Associates, 1977.

Fishwick, Marshall, ed. "The World of Ronald McDonald." *Journal of American Culture* 1 (Summer 1978), 336–471.

Fishwick, Marshall, and Meredith Neil, eds. *Popular Architecture.* Bowling Green, Ohio: Bowling Green University Popular Press, [1975].

Fitch, James M. *American Building: The Environmental Forces That Shaped It.* Boston: Houghton Mifflin, 1972.

———. *American Building: The Historical Forces That Shaped It.* Boston: Houghton Mifflin, 1966.

Frampton, Kenneth. "Prospects for a Critical Regionalism." *Perspecta: The Yale Architectural Journal* 20 (1983), 147–62.

Fraser, James H. *The American Billboard: 100 Years.* New York: Harry N. Abrams, 1991.

Gans, Herbert J. *Popular Culture and High Culture.* New York: Basic Books, 1975.

Gardner, Eugene C. *Homes and How to Make Them.* Boston: J. B. Osgood. 1885.

Gebhard, David, and Harriette Von Brenton. *L.A. in the Thirties, 1931–1941.* Layton, Utah: Peregrine Smith, 1975.

Giedion, Sigfried. *Mechanization Takes Command: A Contribution to Anonymous History.* New York: Oxford University Press, 1948.

Glassie, Henry. *Folk Housing in Middle Virginia: A Structural Analysis of Historic Artifacts.* Knoxville: University of Tennessee Press, 1975.

———. *Pattern in the Material Folk Culture of the Eastern United States.* Philadelphia: University of Pennsylvania Press, 1968.

Glassner, Lester, and Brownie Harris. *Dime Store Days.* New York: Viking Press, 1980.

Gowans, Alan. *The Comfortable House: North American Suburban Architecture, 1890–1930.* Cambridge: MIT Press, 1986.

———. *Images of American Living: Four Centuries of Architecture and Furniture as Cultural Expression.* Philadelphia: J. B. Lippincott, 1964.

———. *On Parallels in Universal History Discoverable in Arts and Artifacts: An Outline Statement.* Watkins Glen, N.Y.: Institute for the Study of Universal History, 1974.

————. *Styles and Types of North American Architecture: Social Function and Cultural Expression*. New York: HarperCollins, 1992.

————. *The Unchanging Arts: New Forms for the Traditional Functions of Art in Society*. Philadelphia: J. B. Lippincott, 1971.

Grief, Martin. *Depression Modern: The Thirties Style in America*. New York: Universe Books, 1975.

Grover, Kathryn, ed. *Dining in America, 1850–1900*. Amherst: University of Massachusetts Press, 1987.

Gutman, Richard J. S. *American Diner: Then and Now*. New York: HarperPerennial, 1993.

Gutman, Richard J. S., and Elliott Kaufman. *American Diner*. New York: Harper and Row, 1979.

Hall, Ben M. *The Best Remaining Seats*. New York: Clarkson N. Potter, 1961.

Hall, Edward T. *The Hidden Dimension*. Garden City, N.Y.: Anchor Books, 1969.

Halprin, Lawrence. *Freeways*. New York: Reinhold, 1966.

Harmon, M. H. *Psycho-Decorating: What Homes Reveal about People*. New York: Wyden Books, 1977.

Harris, Cyril M. *The Illustrated Dictionary of Historic Architecture*. New York: Dover, 1977.

Harris, Cyril M., ed. *American Architecture: An Illustrated Encyclopedia*. New York: W. W. Norton, 1998.

————, ed. *Dictionary of Architecture and Construction*. 2nd ed. New York: McGraw-Hill, 1993.

Harris, Steven, and Deborah Berke, eds. *Architecture of the Everyday*. New York: Princeton Architectural Press and Yale Publications on Architecture, 1997.

Heimann, Jim. *Car Hops and Curb Service: A History of American Drive-In Restaurants 1920–1960*. San Francisco: Chronicle Books, 1996.

Heimann, Jim, and Rip Georges. *California Crazy: Roadside Vernacular Architecture*. San Francisco: Chronicle Books, 1980.

Henderson, Sally, and Robert Landau. *Billboard Art*. San Francisco: Chronicle Books, 1980.

Hess, Alan. *Googie: Fifties Coffee Shop Architecture*. San Francisco: Chronicle Books, 1985.

————. "The Origins of McDonald's Golden Arches." *Journal of the Society of Architectural Historians* 45 (March 1986), 60–67.

Hillier, Bevis. *The Decorative Arts of the Forties and Fifties: Austerity/Binge*. London: Studio Vista, 1975.

Hillier, Bevis, and Stephen Escritt. *Art Deco Style*. London: Phaidon, 1997.

Hirshorn, Paul, and Steven Izenour. "Learning from Hamburgers." *Architecture Plus* 1 (June 1973), 46–55.

————. *White Towers*. Cambridge, MA: MIT Press, 1979.

Historic American Building Survey. National Park Service. *Historic American Building Survey*. Washington, D.C.: Department of the Interior, 1941.

Hitchcock, Henry-Russell. *American Architectural Books: A List of Books, Portfolios, and Pamphlets on Architecture and Related Subjects Published in America before 1895*. New York: Da Capo Press, 1975.

Horn, Richard. *Fifties Style: Then and Now*. New York: Beech Tree Books, 1975.

House and Garden. *Building Guide, Fall–Winter, 1963–64*. New York: Conde Nast, 1963.

Institute for Contemporary Art. *The Highway*. Philadelphia: Institute for Contemporary Art, 1970.

Jackson, John Brinckerhoff. *Discovering the Vernacular Landscape*. New Haven, Conn: Yale University Press, 1984.

———. *Landscapes: Selected Essays*. Ed. Irvin H. Zube. Amherst: University of Massachusetts Press, 1970.

———. *A Sense of Time, A Sense of Place*. New Haven, Conn., and London: Yale University Press, 1994.

Jacobs, Jane. *The Death and Life of Great American Cities*. New York: Random House, 1961.

Jakle, John A., and Keith A. Sculle. *The Gas Station in America*. Baltimore and London: Johns Hopkins University Press, 1994.

Jakle, John A., Keith A. Sculle, and Jefferson S. Rogers. *The Motel in America*. Baltimore and London: Johns Hopkins University Press, 1996.

Jencks, Charles. "The Architectural Sign." *Architecture and Urbanism* 78 (April, May, June 1978), 3–10, 70–78, 1–8.

———. *What Is Post-Modernism?* 4th ed. London: Academy Editions, 1996.

Jencks, Charles, and George Baird, eds. *Meaning in Architecture*. New York: George Braziller, 1970.

Jennings, Jan, and Herbert Gottfried. *American Vernacular Interior Architecture, 1870–1940*. New York: Van Nostrand Reinhold, 1988.

Kaplan, Michael. *Theme Restaurants*. New York: PBC International, 1997.

Kouwenhoven, John. *Made in America: The Arts in Modern Civilization*. New York: W. W. Norton, 1948.

Kroc, Ray, with Robert Anderson. *Grinding It Out*. Chicago: Contemporary Books, 1977.

Kubler, George. *The Shape of Time: Remarks on the History of Things*. New Haven, Conn.: Yale University Press, 1962.

Kyriazi, Gary. *The Great American Amusement Park: A Pictorial History*. Secaucus, N.J.: Citadel Press, 1976.

Lafever, Minard. *The Modern Builder's Guide*. New York: Sleight, 1833.

Landau, Robert, and James Phillippi. *Airstream*. Salt Lake City, Utah: Peregrine Smith, 1984.

Langdon, Philip. *Orange Roofs, Golden Arches: The Architecture of American Chain Restaurants*. New York: Alfred A. Knopf, 1986.

Liebs, Chester. *Main Street to Miracle Mile: American Roadside Architecture*. Boston: New York Graphic Society, 1985.

Loewy, Raymond. *Industrial Design*. Woodstock, N.Y.: Overlook Press, 1979.

Longstreth, Richard. *City Center to Regional Mall: Architecture, the Automobile and Retailing in Los Angeles, 1920–1950*. Cambridge: MIT Press, 1997.

———. "The Diffusion of the Community Shopping Center Concept during the Interwar Decades." *Journal of the Society of Architectural Historians* 56 (September 1997), 268–93.

———. "J. C. Nichols, the Country Club Plaza, and Notions of Modernity." *Harvard Architecture Review* (1986), 121–35.

Love, John F. *McDonald's: Behind the Arches*. Rev. ed. New York: Bantam Books, 1995.

Lynch, Kevin. *The Image of the City*. Cambridge: Technology Press and Harvard University Press, 1960.

Lynes, Russell. *The Tastemakers*. New York: Grosset and Dunlap, 1954.

Mann, Dennis Alan, ed. *The Arts in a Democratic Society*. Bowling Green, Ohio: Bowling Green University Popular Press, 1977.

Margolies, John. *The End of the Road: Vanishing Highway Architecture in America*. New York: Penguin Books, 1981.

———. *Home Away from Home: Motels in America*. Boston: Little, Brown, 1995.

Marling, Karal Ann. *The Colossus of Roads: Myth and Symbol along the American Highway*. Minneapolis: University of Minnesota Press, 1984.

———, ed. *Designing Disney's Theme Parks: The Architecture of Reassurance*. Montreal: Canadian Center for Architecture; Paris: Flammarion, 1997.

Mayer, Harold M., and Richard C. Wade. *Chicago: Growth of a Metropolis*. Chicago: University of Chicago Press, 1969.

McMurry, Sally. *Families & Farmhouses in 19th Century America*. New York and Oxford: Oxford University Press, 1988.

Meikle, Jeffrey L. *Twentieth Century Limited: Industrial Design in America, 1925–1939*. Philadelphia: Temple University Press, 1979.

Minneapolis Institute of Art. *The World of Art Deco*. New York: E. P. Dutton, 1971.

Moore, Charles, Gerald Allen, and Donlyn Lyndon. *The Place of Houses*. New York: Holt, Rinehart, and Winston, 1974.

Moore, Charles W., Kathryn Smith, and Peter Becker. *Home Sweet Home: American Domestic Vernacular Architecture*. New York: Rizzoli; Los Angeles: Craft and Folk Art Museum, 1983.

Nairn, Ian. *The American Landscape: A Critical View*. New York: Random House, 1965.

National Trust for Historic Preservation, Tony P. Wren, and Elizabeth D. Mulloy. *America's Forgotten Architecture*. New York: Pantheon, 1976.

Naylor, David. *American Picture Palaces: The Architecture of Fantasy*. New York: Van Nostrand Reinhold, 1981.

Neil, J. Meredith. "What about Architecture?" *Journal of Popular Culture* 5 (1971), 280–88.

Norberg-Schulz, Christian. *Architecture: Meaning and Place*. New York: Rizzoli, 1988.

Oliver, Richard, and Nancy Ferguson. "Place, Product, Packaging." *Architectural Record* 163 (February 1978), 116–20.

Palliser, Palliser, and Co. *New Cottage Homes and Details*. 1887. Reprint. New York: Da Capo Press, 1975.

Patton, Phil. *Open Road: A Celebration of the American Highway*. New York: Simon and Schuster, 1986.

Pawley, Martin. *Architecture versus Housing*. New York: Praeger, 1971.

Placzek, Adolf, ed. *Macmillan Encyclopedia of Architects*. New York: Macmillan, 1982.

Poppeliers, John, et al. *What Style Is It? Guide to American Architectural Styles*. Washington, DC: National Trust for Historic Preservation, 1982.

Pulos, Arthur J. *American Design Ethic: A History of Industrial Design to 1940*. Cambridge: MIT Press, 1983.

———. *The American Design Adventure, 1940–1975*. Cambridge: MIT Press, 1988.

Rapoport, Amos. *House: Form and Culture*. Englewood Cliffs, N.J.: Prentice-Hall, 1969.

Renwick Gallery, National Collection of Fine Arts, Smithsonian Institution. *Signs of Life: Symbols in the American City*. New York: Aperture, 1976.

Reps, John W. *The Making of Urban America: A History of City Planning in the United States*. Princeton, N.J.: Princeton University Press, 1965.

Rudofsky, Bernard. *Architecture without Architects: A Short Introduction to Non-Pedigreed Architecture*. New York: Museum of Modern Art, 1965.

———. *The Prodigious Builders: Notes toward a Natural History of Architecture with Special Regard to Those Species That Are Traditionally Neglected or Downright Ignored*. New York: Harcourt Brace Jovanovich, 1977.

Sanders, Don, and Susan Sanders. *The American Drive-In Movie Theater*. Osceola, Wis.: Motorbooks International, 1997.

Schlereth, Thomas J. *Reading the Road: U.S. 40 and the American Landscape*. Knoxville: University of Tennessee Press, 1997.

———. *US 40: A Roadscape of the American Experience*. Indianapolis: Indiana Historical Society, 1985.

Sears, Roebuck and Company. *Sears, Roebuck Catalog of Houses, 1926*. Reprint. New York: Dover, 1991.

———. *Sears, Roebuck Home Builder's Catalog, 1910*. Reprint. New York: Dover, 1991.

Sharp, Dennis. *The Picture Palace and Other Buildings for the Movies*. New York: Praeger, 1969.

Sloan, Samuel. *The Model Architect*. Philadelphia: E. S. Jones, 1852.

Sommer, Robert. *Design Awareness*. San Francisco: Rinehart Press, 1972.

———. *Personal Space: The Behavioral Basis of Design*. Englewood Cliffs, N.J.: Prentice-Hall, 1969.

Stern, Robert A. M., Gregory Gilmartin, and John Montague Massengale. *New York 1900: Metropolitan Architecture and Urbanism, 1890–1915*. New York: Rizzoli, 1983.

Stern, Robert A. M., Gregory Gilmartin and Thomas Mellins. *New York 1930: Architecture and Urbanism between the Two World Wars*. New York: Rizzoli, 1987.

Stern, Robert A. M., Thomas Mellins and David Fishman. *New York 1960: Architecture and Urbanism between the Second World War and the Bicentennial*. New York: Monacelli Press, 1995.

Stevenson, Katherine Cole, and H. Ward Jande. *Houses by Mail: A Guide to Houses from Sears, Roebuck and Company*. Washington, D.C.: Preservation Press, 1986.

Stewart, Tabori, and Chang Stewart. *Roadside Food*. New York: Workman, 1986.

Stilgoe, John R. *Borderlands: Origins of the American Suburb, 1820–1939*. New Haven, Conn., and London: Yale University Press, 1988.

———. *Common Landscape of America, 1580 to 1845*. New Haven, Conn.: Yale University Press, 1981.

———. *Metropolitan Corridor: Railroads and the American Scene*. New Haven, Conn.: Yale University Press, 1983.

Strauss, Steve. *Moving Images: The Transportation Poster in America*. New York: Fullcourt Press, 1984.

Tate, Allen, and C. Ray Smith. *Interior Design in the Twentieth Century*. New York: Harper and Row, 1987.

Teague, Walter Dorwin. *Design This Day*. New York: Harcourt, Brace, 1940.

Tidworth, Simon. *Theatres: An Architectural and Cultural History*. New York: Praeger, 1973.

Upton, Del, ed. *America's Architectural Roots: Ethnic Groups That Built America*. Washington, D.C.: Preservation Press, 1986.

Valentine, Maggie. *The Show Starts on the Sidewalk: An Architectural History of the Movie Theatre*. New Haven, Conn.: Yale University Press, 1994.

Van Doren, Harold. *Industrial Design: A Practical Guide*. New York: McGraw-Hill, 1940.

Venturi, Robert. *Complexity and Contradiction in Architecture*. New York: Museum of Modern Art, 1966.

Venturi, Robert, Denise Scott Brown, and Steven Izenour. *Learning from Las Vegas*. 1972. Rev. ed. Cambridge: MIT, 1977.

Vernacular Architecture Forum. *Perspectives in Vernacular Architecture*. Semiannual. Annapolis, Md.: Vernacular Architecture Forum, 1982.

Veyra, Daniel I. *"Fill'er Up": An Architectural History of America's Gas Stations*. New York: Macmillan, 1979.

Weisberger, Bernard A., ed. *The WPA Guide to America: The Best of 1930s America As Seen by the Federal Writers' Project*. New York: Pantheon Books, 1985.

Wheeler, Gervase. *Rural Homes, or Sketches of Houses Suited to American Country Life, with Original Plans, Designs, etc.* New York: C. Scribner, 1851.

Whiffen, Marcus. *American Architecture since 1780: A Guide to the Styles*. Rev. ed. Cambridge: MIT Press, 1992.

Wilson, Richard Guy. "Abstraction versus Figuration, Utopia versus Context: The Place of Postmodernism in the Visual Arts." In *Critique of Modernity*, ed. R. Langbaum. Charlottesville: Center for Advanced Studies, University of Virginia, 1986, 87–95.

Wilson, Richard Guy, Dianne H. Pilgrim, and Dickran Tashjian. *The Machine Age in America, 1918–1941*. New York: Harry N. Abrams, 1986.

Wilson, Richard Guy and Jeff Vaughn. *The Old West Side*. Ann Arbor, Mich.: Old West Side Association, 1971.

Winter, Robert. *The California Bungalow*. Los Angeles: Hennessey and Ingalls, 1980.

Withey, Henry F., and Elsie R. Withey. *Biographical Dictionary of American Architects (Deceased)*. Los Angeles: New Age, 1956.

Witzel, Michael Karl. *The American Gas Station*. Osceola, Wis.: Motorbooks International, 1992.

Wolf, Gary Herbert. "The Gas Station: The Evolution of a Building Type Is Illustrated through a History of the Sun Oil Company Gasoline Station." M.Arch.H. thesis, University of Virginia, 1974.

Wolfe, Tom. *From Bauhaus to Our House*. New York: Farrar, Straus, and Giroux, 1981.

Woodward, George. *Woodward's National Architect*. 1868. Reprint. Watkins Glen, N.Y.: American Life Foundation and Study Institute, 1977.

Wright, Gwendolyn. *Building the Dream: A Social History of Housing in America*. New York: Pantheon Books, 1981.

Wurman, Richard Saul. *Making the City Observable*. Minneapolis: Walker Art Center; Cambridge: MIT Press, 1971.

Periodicals

American Architect and Building News. Boston and New York, 1876–1938.

American Builder. Chicago and New York, 1865–1895.

The American Home. New York, 1928– .

The Architectural Record. New York, 1891– .

Architectural Review and American Builder's Journal. Philadelphia, 1868–1870.

Better Homes and Gardens. Des Moines, Iowa, 1922– .

Bungalow Magazine. Los Angeles, 1909–1918.

Colonial Homes. New York, 1974– .

The Craftsman Magazine. New York, 1901–1916.

Early American Homes. Leesburg, Va., 1974– .

Early American Life. Harrisburg, Pa., 1970– .

Godey's Lady's Book and Lady's Magazine. Philadelphia, 1830–1898.

Historic Preservation (now *Preservation*). Washington, D.C., 1949– .

House and Garden. New York, 1901– .

House and Home: The Magazine of Housing. New York, 1952– .

The House Beautiful. Chicago and New York, 1896– .

Ladies Home Journal. New York, 1883– .

Landscape. Santa Fe, N. Mex., and Berkeley, Calif., 1851– .

Martha Stewart Living. New York, 1990– .

Nation's Restaurant News. New York, 1967– .

Old House Journal. Gloucester, Mass., 1973– .

Professional Builder and Apartment Business. Chicago, 1936– .

Progressive Architecture. Stamford, Conn., 1926–1995.

Qualified Remodeler. Chicago, 1975– .

Restaurant Business. New York, 1902– .

Roadside Magazine. Worcester, Mass., 1990– .

Society for Commercial Archeology Journal, Washington, D.C., 1978– .

Victorian Homes. Millers Falls, Mass., 1981– .

Web Sites

Avery Index to Architectural Periodicals. http://www.ahip.getty.edu/aka

HABS/HAER. http://www.cr.nps.gov/habshaer/

Movie Palace Resource Page. http://www.execpc.com/~hiawatha/mp

National Register of Historic Places. http://www.nr.nps.gov/nrishome.htm

Research Materials for Architecture and the Built Environment Located in Washington, DC. http://www.lib.umd.edu/Guest/DCARCHres

Roadside Magazine. http://www.roadsidemagazine.com

Society of Architectural Historians. http://www.sah.org

Society for Commercial Archeology. http://www.sca-roadside.org/

THE AUTOMOBILE

William R. Klink, Michael L. Berger, and Maurice Duke

The importance of the automobile in the everyday life of America in the twenty-first century cannot be overestimated. The automobile industry is the largest industry, according to some, in the United States. More than a mere means of transportation, the automobile has come to be recognized as an object of dreams, fantasy, and identity. The study of the automobile as a social and psychological force in society is a means to understanding national values and aspirations.

HISTORICAL OUTLINE

Although humans had dreamed of a self-propelled vehicle for centuries, not until the end of the nineteenth century did a practical road machine capable of sustained distances emerge for general use. Historians disagree on the actual inventor of the first American automobile. However, credit is usually given to Charles E. and J. Frank Duryea for the successful development (1893) and marketing of the gasoline motorcar that most resembles the one in use today. The Duryeas' success was abetted by their victory in the first American automobile race, held in 1895. This event was sponsored by the Chicago *Times-Herald* and thus resulted in considerable publicity for the new means of transportation in general and the Duryea car in particular.

When the automobile first appeared, it was treated as an object of curiosity, a plaything for the rich and a tinkering project for inventors or the hapless blacksmith who might be called upon to aid a motorist who by some mechanical malfunction had suddenly become a pedestrian. The automobile quickly took hold, however, capturing people's minds as well as their pocketbooks. Races, such as the Vanderbilt Cup road races of 1904–1916; reliability runs, like the Glidden Tours held between 1905 and 1913; and successful cross-country automobile trips, beginning in 1903 with that of Dr. H. Nelson Jackson all helped establish the

Ford assembly line, 1923. Courtesy of the Library of Congress

automobile as a viable means of transportation and a formidable challenger to the horse.

Although there was some early resistance to the motorcar, especially in rural areas, once its economic and social usefulness had been demonstrated, this hostility disappeared. "For the first time in world history," historian George E. Mowry has written, "mass man became the master of a complicated piece of power machinery by which he could annihilate distance."[1] Born into an America that had virtually no paved road system, the auto soon began to shrink the size of the continent, of whose vastness and inexhaustibility St. Jean de Crevecoeur had boasted just over a century before. Although still not completely trustworthy from a mechanical standpoint, automobiles became popular for cross-country expeditions—giving rise, incidentally, to a number of early automobile travel narratives and novels and for exploring places that mere decades before were out of range of the traveler or adventurer who had to rely on the horse, the ship, and/or the train.

When the automobile emerged from its novelty stage, its influence on American life became markedly greater. The mass production of cars like Henry Ford's Model T, which began in the first decade of the twentieth century, ushered in a new era of attitudes and convictions about the auto. Ford showed that a mechanically efficient motorcar could be produced, sold at a moderate price, and still be the source of significant profits for the manufacturer. Both the joys and woes of owning a self-propelled vehicle were now within the means of the average American.

While sudden death might lurk around the next curve, and the neighborhood horses might be terrified, not to mention the emerging noise and pollution problems, there was a new sense of freedom across the land. Urban dwellers could escape to the country for a day; isolated rural residents could visit each other and the nearby towns and cities more easily; and businesspeople could move more quickly in their daily routines. As several automotive historians have noted, there was a good match between the nature of motor travel and the American character. The individualism and personal mobility that Americans always had valued had found a new means of expression, and a new "escape valve" had been found for the stresses of modern society.

As the automobile became a way of life in America, so American life had to adjust to accommodate it. While the motorcar was shrinking the size of the continent, it was altering both its physical and social landscape as well. Service stations, garages, and parts warehouses popped up around the country at the same time that legislators and judges were pondering complex problems about how the use of the automobile should be governed. Also, culturally and socially, other changes were taking place. Clothing styles were altered to protect the motorist from the elements as he or she drove along in the open cars of the period. Hotels began giving way to auto camps, tourist cabins, and, eventually, the modern motel. The introduction of that word into our vocabulary showed that not even the language would remain unaffected by the cultural revolution brought forth by the automobile. City dwellers in increasing numbers found that they could live outside urban areas and motor to work, thus helping to create America's vast and sprawling suburbs.

The depression that began in 1929 brought the period of unbridled expansion to a close, but the car remained an important part of life during the 1930s. For athe rich, in a new era of American luxury, cars were introduced with the appearance of the Cord, Duesenberg, and sixteen-cylinder Cadillac. At the other end of the economic spectrum, the car was often the last refuge against the elements for the poor, the possession that was never sold, best exemplified by the Joad family's behavior in John Steinbeck's 1939 novel *The Grapes of Wrath*. The vast middle class of motorized Americans continued to set new records for motorized travel, though not new car purchases, even in these hard times.

The coming of World War II brought production of new cars to a standstill, as auto manufacturers retooled to produce the machinery of armed combat. Entering their first period of gasoline shortages, Americans now had to queue up to receive rationing stickers. "Is this trip necessary?" became the question of radio newscasters and politicians alike. The vehicles of the country began to turn more slowly, but the speed was destined to be regained and even vastly accelerated in the next decade.

Emerging victorious from World War II, the American, as Lewis Mumford has written in *The Highway and the City*, "sacrificed his life as a whole to the motorcar."[2] The pent-up demand for cars, combined with postwar prosperity, led to record sales in the late 1940s and 1950s. During the latter decade, often termed the "golden age" of the American automobile, cars became longer, more powerful, and more numerous, with two-car families no longer viewed as unusual. Design became more outlandish; witness the tail fin craze. Freeways and interstates took the place of the prewar highways, which now became relegated to secondary road status. Suburbs began the growth that was to allow them to surpass the cities in 1970 as the most populous residential areas.

More important from the sociocultural perspective, this decade saw the full flowering of outdoor drive-in movie theaters, dubbed "passion pits" by their critics; drive-in restaurants, where car-bound customers were often served by waitresses on roller skates; drive-in churches; and even drive-in funeral parlors. The popularity of automobile racing as a spectator sport grew enormously; new forms emerged, and greater commercialization occurred as it became a multimillion-dollar entertainment industry. The cars of yesteryear began reappearing on the nation's roads after having been reworked in various "customized" ways, "souped" up, and/or transformed into "hot rods," with their youthful creators maintaining that the cars reflected their innermost personalities.

Although there was some disenchantment with the automobile in the mid- and late 1960s, caused largely by questions of environmental pollution and safety, America's so-called love affair with the car continued relatively unabated in that decade, and a few new developments were added. Seemingly forever seeking vehicular freedom, many Americans yearned to leave the restricted confines of the highway for "off-road" adventures. Jeeps enjoyed a renaissance, specially produced recreational vehicles (RVs) made their appearance and were commercially successful, and motorized camping gained in popularity to the extent that national and state parks were no longer able to handle the demand effectively. The purchase and/or restoration of old cars gained in popularity as a hobby, with devotees apparently oblivious to the costs of a "pure" restoration. Finally, aspects of motoring that had long been considered exclusively European in nature, most notably, sports cars and grand prix motor racing, began to achieve a level of acceptance that would make them important circuits of the American automobile culture in the years to come.

By the early 1970s, cars were owned by 83 percent of American families, manufacturers could not keep up with demand, and the central place of the automobile in American life seemed assured for the foreseeable future. However, before the end of the decade, Americans were seriously questioning for the first time the role of the automobile (and its industry) in their lives and their dependency on it. The oil embargo of 1973 forced them to face the prospect that fossilized fuels might be depleted in the near future and the reality of gasoline prices that doubled before they leveled off. Americans witnessed the cost of new cars increasing two-fold and sometimes three-fold, and buyers experienced what was dubbed "sticker shock." Moreover, the motorcar, long suspected as a serious atmospheric pollutant, came under the study of scientists who proved such to be the case. Suddenly, the automobile and the industry that produced it became major problems for many Americans, and people began seriously to discuss controlling the sale and use of the automobile and even its total prohibition.

However, such stringent regulation never occurred. Oil shortages ceased, and gasoline prices actually went down. Inflation moderated, and the price of new cars stabilized. Federal and state emission control laws forced car manufacturers to produce less-polluting vehicles. But most important of all, for better or worse, the American public made it very clear that it wanted to keep the private automobile and the lifestyle that it had helped create, irrespective of the social, economic, and political costs involved.

Perhaps there is no better indication of the feelings in the 1990s that Americans had a right to the greatest cars no matter what the cost than the emergence of the best-selling so-called sport utility vehicles (SUVs). Costing 30 percent more than the traditional car, using 30 percent more fuel, and typically weighing 30 percent more, these vehicles were built on standard truck chassis and could be driven off-road. As the decade went on, these SUVs were increasingly outfitted with upscale creature comforts more commonly associated with luxury cars. These "automobiles" appealed to the independent spirit of their owners who, while rarely ever venturing off-road, nevertheless wanted power to do so. At the same time that such large vehicles became more popular, the popularity of small cars in general declined. To Americans in the 1990s, bigger was better, and more was better than less.

REFERENCE WORKS

There are many excellent one- or two-volume reference works that offer descriptions, technical data, and short summaries of the significance of the literally thousands of makes of cars that have been produced or planned since the 1890s. Unfortunately, they contain little or no information on the social or cultural significance of the vehicles.

The best available material for cultural historians is contained in four bibliographic reference volumes, from which one can cull automotive items of special interest. The broadest of these, *Technology and Values in American Civilization: A Guide to Information Sources* by Stephen H. Cutcliffe et al., is highly recommended. Composed of citations followed by brief annotations, this volume contains references to most of the significant books and articles up to 1980, all of which can be accessed through one of three indexes (author, title, or subject). A similar volume, *Motorsports: A Guide to Information Sources* by Susan Ebershoff-Coles and Charla Ann Leibenguth, ought to prove valuable to researchers in that area, although the items tend to be less scholarly (possibly by virtue of the subject) than the Cutcliffe volume. In addition, there is Bernard Mergen's *Recreational Vehicles and Travel: A Resource Guide*, which provides bibliographic essays on various aspects of the impact of RVs on American society. Finally, researchers interested in auto touring, or simply early motoring, should find Carey S. Bliss' *Autos Across America: A Bibliography of Transcontinental Automobile Travel, 1903–1940* to be particularly useful with its listing of personal accounts.

While space considerations limit the citations in this chapter to books, doctoral dissertations, and major articles, there is a wealth of scholarly material available in many other periodicals as well. An excellent reference source in this regard is *America: History and Life*, which is now available on-line for computer searches as well as in hard copy. The great advantage of this particular reference tool is that each bibliographic citation is followed by a full-paragraph description of its contents. Similar information for doctoral dissertations can be found in *Dissertation Abstracts*. In addition, *Writings on American History* and *Recently Published Articles*, both publications of the American Historical Association, can be useful sources of periodical citations. Furthermore, two scholarly journals, *Technology and Culture* and *Isis* (from the History of Science Society) publish yearly indexes of recently published books and articles, sometimes with brief annotations.

Finally, some mention should be made of the material that has been published in "auto buff" publications, those magazines and journals aimed at collectors and aficionados. Probably preeminent in this regard is *Automobile Quarterly*, a lavishly produced, beautifully illustrated, hardbound quarterly. Although the articles usually lack citations, and the space devoted to the photographs often exceeds that for the text, the narrative is clearly research-based and can be of assistance to researchers interested in the impact of a particular person, vehicle, motor race, and so on. *Automobile Quarterly* is indexed, and 1985 saw the publication of a cumulative index covering the first twenty volumes (1962–1982). Also in this genre is the bimonthly publication of the Antique Automobile Club of America, *Antique Automobile*, and the quarterly magazine of the Veteran Motor Car Club of America, *Bulb Horn*, both of which are also indexed. Access to these publications and to mass-circulation auto monthlies like *Road and Track* and *Car and Driver*, both of which regularly carry articles of popular cultural significance, can also be secured by using two privately printed periodical guides: *Automotive Literature Index*, compiled by A. Wallace, three volumes (1947–1976, 1977–1981, and 1982–1986) of which have appeared; and *Auto Index*, which has been published every other month since 1973 and in yearly compilations by volume. Care should be taken in using these indexes, since the placement of specific articles under the topical headings is sometimes questionable.

RESEARCH COLLECTIONS

By far the best collection of materials available for the study of the automobile in America is housed in the National Automotive History Collection of the Detroit Public Library. Its holdings number approximately 1 million items, including over 17,000 books, 8,000 bound periodicals, 300,000 photographs, and hundreds of thousands of one-of-a-kind pieces of ephemera. Fortunately for researchers, these holdings have been cataloged, and a description, by subject and author, of their contents is readily available in a two-volume work entitled *The Automotive History Collection of the Detroit Public Library: A Simplified Guide to Its Holdings*.

Another major collection is housed in the Free Library of Philadelphia. Although there is no published guide to its holdings, this collection contains a total of some 13,000 volumes and is concerned with all aspects of the automotive industry and its history. Of particular importance to social historians are the 17,000 photographs of automobiles, ranging from the late nineteenth century to the present. The Science and Technology Research Center of the New York Public Library also has extensive holdings on the automobile, as do the Cleveland, San Diego, and Flint, Michigan, public libraries.

Several major research universities also have amassed considerable collections. The DeGolyer Foundation Library of Southern Methodist University in Dallas holds over 90,000 volumes concerning the automobile, along with first editions by prominent authors, as well as manuscripts, photographs, and maps. At the Stuart A. Work Collection on automobile history at the University of California at Los Angeles, one can locate materials not only historical in nature but also centering on racing automobile shows and promotional events concerning the automobile. Not surprisingly, the University of Michigan is another good source of information, especially its Highway Safety Research Institute Library, which houses some 26,000 items centering on the automobile.

Finally, each of the Big Three automobile companies has libraries and archives that concern its own history and that of the industry in general. Such facilities are usually open to scholars upon application. The best of the three is the Archives and Research Library of the Henry Ford Museum and Greenfield Village in Dearborn, Michigan, which has over 20,000 volumes and extensive collections of periodicals, trade catalogs, photographs, and newspaper clippings.

HISTORY AND CRITICISM

Histories of the automobile began appearing as early as 1917 and continue down to the present. Listed alphabetically are some of the earlier ones that contain significant amounts of sociocultural information: Rudolph E. Anderson's *The Story of the American Automobile: Highlights and Sidelights*; Reginald M. Cleveland and S. T. Williamson's The *Road Is Yours: The Story of the Automobile and the Men behind It*; David L. Cohn's *Combustion on Wheels: An Informal History of the Automobile Age*; Frank Donovan's *Wheels for a Nation*; C. B. Glasscock's *The Gasoline Age: The Story of the Men Who Made It*; Frank E. Hill's *The Automobile: How It Came, Grew, and Has Changed Our Lives*; Hiram P. Maxim's *Horseless Carriage Days*; and M. M. Musselman's *Get a Horse!: The Story of the Automobile in America*. Of these books, the Cohn and Donovan volumes will probably prove most valuable to the social or cultural historian. In the 1990s, Walter J. Boyne's *Power behind the Wheel: Creativity and the Evolution of the Automobile* (1991) is probably the best volume dealing with the actual designers who have been the most influential on the technological and visual culture of the automobile. Also of value is *Car Wars*

President Theodore Roosevelt and Motorcade. Courtesy of the Denver Public Library

by Jonathan Mantle. This book looks at the marketing history of the automobile in the United States over the past fifty years, detailing how corporations gained and lost market share.

Despite the good intentions of these works, many might best be classified as "popular histories," aimed at a general audience and comparatively weak in analysis. Pioneering scholarly works of a sociological nature are best exemplified by John Mueller's 1928 dissertation entitled "The Automobile: A Sociological Study" and by Robert S. Lynd and Helen M. Lynd's *Middletown: A Study in Contemporary American Culture* (1929) and *Middletown in Transition: A Study in Cultural Conflicts* (1937), both of which analyze the automobile's impact on the community of Muncie, Indiana.

It was not until 1965, with the publication of John B. Rae's *The American Automobile: A Brief History* that one got the first book-length, scholarly treatment of this subject. Rae's work opened up the field to serious study, and the next fifteen years saw the publication of several important works of interest to the social historian, beginning with James J. Flink's *America Adopts the Automobile, 1895–1910*, which explores the sociocultural milieu within which the automobile came of age. Flink's book was followed by Rae's *The Road and the Car in American Life*, Reynold M. Wik's *Henry Ford and Grassroots America*, Warren J. Belasco's *Americans on the*

Road, Michael L. Berger's *The Devil Wagon in God's Country*, and Howard L. Preston's *Automobile Age Atlanta*, all of which are described later.

The scholarly movement that Rae set in motion in 1965 with his "brief history" reached a type of fruition with the publication of Flink's *The Automobile Age* in 1988. Hailed by reviewers as a definitive treatment of the subject, Professor Flink's book is a comprehensive history that masterfully combines analysis of both industrial developments and societal impacts. While Flink's emphasis is on the American experience, he does a fine job of placing that experience in worldwide perspective. *The Automobile Age* should be the starting point for most serious students of the subject. Peter Ling's *America and the Automobile* (1990) brings together the historiography of the Progressive and Populist movements, grounding them in cultural geography and urban sociology to show the role of the automobile in urban society in America. Ronald Primeau's *Romance of the Road: The Literature of the American Highway* examines how road narratives create community among writers and readers and the love of travel, speed, and open space.

Two collections of essays have helped identify potentially rich areas for future sociocultural research. These volumes are *The Automobile in American Life*, edited by Charles L. Sanford, and *The Automobile and American Culture*, edited by David L. Lewis and Laurence Goldstein. Both are wide-ranging books, with selections concerning a number of social issues ignored, or casually treated, by most popular histories. Of the two, Sanford's is the more traditional, with the primary emphasis on the human dimensions of economic issues. Nonetheless, most of the readings wrestle with the question of social costs and benefits, for topics as diverse as the assembly line, automotive design, and possible replacements for the car.

The more recent Lewis and Goldstein volume is a pioneering one in that it is the first to bring together scholarly research exploring the car's influence on the cultural mainstream. Thus, essays are included that analyze the car's influence on art, music, film, literature, and poetry. In addition, such social concerns as sex, the status of women and teenagers, and the symbolic dimensions of the automobile are treated. It is also one of the first collections to include fictional treatments of the motorcar as well. Popular histories continued to be published in the 1970s and 1980s, benefiting from the concurrent scholarly research and evidencing much more concern with sociocultural questions than their predecessors. Among the more notable works have been Raymond Flower and Michael W. Jones' *100 Years on the Road: A Social History of the Car*, which delivers what it promises, although with a heavily European focus; Leon Mandel's *Driven: The American Four-Wheeled Love Affair*, in which the author applies his version of social psychology to analyze what he sees as the multivariate impact of the car; Julian Pettifer and Nigel Turner's *Automania: Man and the Motor Car*, which provides an international overview of the auto's influence on several areas usually ignored in such volumes, for example, courtship, art, music, movies, death, and Third World nations; and Stephen W. Sears' *The American Heritage History of the Automobile in America*. The most recent contribution to this area is the work of two British psychologists, Peter Marsh and Peter Collett. Entitled *Driving Passion: The Psychology of the Car*, it is one of the first book-length works to concentrate on the psychological satisfactions associated with car ownership and driving.

Although Americans have not always acknowledged it, the social impact of the automobile as a vehicle is inseparable from the roads that it traverses. The first scholarly road conference held after World War II recognized this fact, as can be seen throughout its published proceedings, *Highways in Our National Life: A Symposium*, edited by Jean Labatut and Wheaton J. Lane. Lewis Mumford in *The Highway and the City* and John B. Rae in *The Road and the Car in American Life* start from the same premise but reach very different conclusions regarding the benefits/drawbacks of that pairing.

More recently, there has been renewed interest in this topic. Phil Patton's *Open Road: A Celebration of the American Highway* is a historical overview of the entire subject, with considerable attention to how the American lifestyle was changed by the growth of the interstate system. In a more popular vein, but useful nonetheless, is *Automerica: A Trip down U.S. Highways from World War II to the Future*, by the Ant Farm design group. Of the most recent popular histories, *Highways to Heaven: The Auto biography of America* (1992) by Christopher Finch tells about the rise of the automobile and how it transformed the landscape and lifestyle of the twentieth century, particularly in California. A nay-saying study is *Getting There: The Epic Struggle between Road and Rail in the American Century* by Stephen B. Goddard (1994). Goddard writes of how America is at risk because of its autocentric culture. Walter Russell Mead's article in *World Policy Journal*, "Trains, Planes and Automobiles: The End of the Postmodern Moment," discusses the social conditions and trends that involve the automobile at the end of the millennium.

The evolution of the roadside area adjacent to one major highway is portrayed and analyzed by George R. Stewart in *U.S. 40: Cross Section of the United States of America*, Thomas R. Vale and Geraldine R. Vale in *U.S. 40 Today: Thirty Years of Landscape Change in America*, and Thomas J. Schlereth's *U.S. 40: A Roadscape of the American Experience*. All three books treat the historic National Road (now U.S. 40) and its adjacent landscape and buildings as an "outdoor museum" whose study provides information regarding the changing nature of American society.

Two more special accounts offer further insight into the culture of the road. *Blue Highways: A Journey into America*, by William L. H. Moon, offers vignettes of people who live and/or work along the two-lanes-or-less "minor" highways that are usually portrayed in blue on road maps. In *L.A. Freeway: An Appreciative Essay*, David Brodsly explores the very nature of the freeway system and, as the *Los Angeles Times* notes, sees it "as the source of feelings, experiences and unique life patterns for the urban driver."[3]

Literary and Artistic Expression

The increased scholarly interest in the automobile has led to a number of books that treat specific cultural topics within the broader context of the car's impact on American life. One of these topics is the interaction between the car and literary and artistic expression. Preeminent in regard to the former is Cynthia Golomb Dettelbach's *In the Driver's Seat: The Automobile in American Literature and Popular Culture*, which analyzes the literary use to which many authors have put automobiles, especially in terms of formulating the American Dream. Another good analytical work, somewhat broader in focus, is Priscilla Lee Denby's doctoral dissertation, "The Self Discovered: The Car in American Folklore and Literature."

In *Man and Motor: The Twentieth Century Love Affair*, editor Derek Jewell collects and reprints myriad writings about the automobile from authors as distant in time as Rudyard Kipling and as contemporary as Henry Miller. In the same vein, but more restrictive in terms of the mode of expression, is *American Classic: Car Poems for Collectors*, edited by Mary Swope and Walter H. Kerr, which includes pieces by such well-known writers as e.e. cummings, Joyce Carol Oates, and Carl Sandburg. Finally, Henry Ford and the cars that he made were so important that they evoked short stories and essays by literary figures of the day. One interesting collection, entitled *The Best of Ford*, compiled and edited by Mary Moline, includes pieces by such authors as John Dos Passos, Walter Lippmann, H. L. Mencken, and Will Rogers.

Mention should be made of some highly praised novels that include motoring motifs. They include William Faulkner's *The Reivers*, F. Scott Fitzgerald's *The Great Gatsby*, Kenneth Grahame's *The Wind in the Willows*, Jack Kerouac's *On the Road*, Sinclair Lewis' *Babbitt* and *Main Street*, Robert M. Pirsig's *Zen and the Art of Motorcycle Maintenance*, and John Steinbeck's *The Grapes of Wrath*.

Although their designation as literature is questionable, advertisements do form a part of, and are influenced by, our culture, frequently telling us as much about the motoring public of yesteryear as the cars themselves. In this regard, *Auto Ads*, by Jane and Michael Stern, is clearly the best work. One hundred significant ads, spanning the history of the automobile, are reproduced and analyzed. Also good, but with a decidedly European emphasis, is Peter Roberts' *Any Colour So Long as It's Black: The First Fifty Years of Automobile Advertising*. Less satisfying from a scholarly perspective, but more extensive from the standpoint of reproducing specific American ads, are Q. David Bowers' *Early American Car Advertisements* and the more recent *The American Automobile: Advertising from the Antique and Classic Eras*, by Yasutoshi Ikuta. Finally, for a delightful look at a unique aspect of American advertising culture, see Frank J. Rowsome Jr.'s *The Verse by the Side of the Road: The Story of the Burma-Shave Signs*, those innovative roadside serial placards.

Mark Williams' *Road Movies: The Complete Guide to Cinema on Wheels* deals with the use to which automobiles have been put in popular films, as does Raymond Lee's *Fit for the Chase: Cars and the Movies*. The former contains an interesting introductory essay and good descriptions of films from the past four decades. The latter collates a large number of movie stills that contain automobiles in them but offers little discussion of the car's function in the scene in which it is pictured. Movies themselves are an important avenue of automobile lore. *Christine* portrays the car as scorned-lover nightmare, while in *Thelma and Louise* the car is a source of freedom, excitement, and ultimately doom. The popularity of NASCAR racing, the fastest growing sport in America in the 1990s, is a feature of *Days of Thunder*, a look at the life of the stock car driver and the pressures to win that come to bear in big-time auto racing. Don Graham's *Cowboys and Cadillacs: How Hollywood Looks at Texas* is an interesting account of the relationship between two cultural icons that have very much affected American society. George Barris, in *Cars of the Stars*, provides captioned photographs of the specialized vehicles that have been built for particular Hollywood celebrities, as does Floyd Clymer in the earlier *Cars of the Stars and Movie Memories*. Similarly, John A. Conde's *Cars with Personalities* provides photographs and captions of 573 celebrities with their cars, from 1896 to 1982. On the other hand, *The American Drive-In Movie Theatre* by Don and Susan Sanders deals with the rise and fall of the most popular venue to see these stars in the 1950s, the drive-in theater. *The Automobile and American Culture*, edited by David L. Lewis and Laurence Goldstein, contains two essays pertinent to this discussion. In "A Runaway Match: The Automobile and Film, 1900–1920," Julian Smith links the development of these two institutions, claiming a symbiotic relationship for the period under study. "Cars and Films in American Culture, 1929–1959," by Kenneth Hey, carries the story forward for another generation. Both essays begin to define and answer the scholarly questions that are essentially missing from the previously mentioned books.

The automobile also has influenced the fine and applied arts. In regard to the former, the best work is *Automobile and Culture*, by Gerald Silk et al., an oversized book that combines fine color and black-and-white illustrations with a superior text. The latter provides a historical survey of the image of the car in art from Leonardo da Vinci to the present and the factors that combine to influence automotive design. An earlier, less ambitious attempt at somewhat the same task was D. B. Tubbs' *Art and the Automobile*, which examines posters, paintings, sculpture, mascots, and car styling in general. Richard Martin's "Fashion and the Car in the 1950s" in the *Journal of American Culture* (Fall 1997) places fashion history, magazines, and automobiles in conjunction to examine the interplay among them.

In a more popular vein, Sally Henderson and Robert Landau in *Billboard Art* do a good job of presenting and analyzing the history of outdoor advertising art and the societal values that it represents. Warren H. Anderson's *Vanishing Roadside America* also concentrates on outdoor advertising, using fine color drawings by the author, rather than photographs, for illustrations to evoke nostalgia for the roadside of the 1930s and 1940s.

Architecture is well treated in a scholarly manner by Chester H. Liebs in *Main Street to Miracle Mile: American Roadside Architecture*, Karal Ann Marling in *The Colossus of Roads: Myth and Symbol along the American Highway*, and, in a more specific way, in *"Fill'er Up": An Architectural History of America's Gas Stations* by Daniel L. Vieyra. More in the nature of photographic essays exploring commercial archaeology are *The Well-Built Elephant and Other Roadside Attractions: A Tribute to American Eccentricity* by J.J.C. Andrews; *Souvenirs from the Roadside West* by Richard Ansaldi; *Highway as Habitat* by Ulrich Keller, with its emphasis on the road culture in the 1940s and 1950s; *The End of the Road: Vanishing Highway Architecture in America* by John Margolies, which concentrates on motels, gas stations, and "enchanted villages"; and Samuel R. Ogden's *America the Vanishing: Road Life and the Price of Progress*. James Howard Kunstler's *The Geography of Nowhere: The Rise and Decline of America's Man-Made Landscape* takes a look at the impact of highways in the land use planning of urban areas. A book specifically concerned with architecture and the automobile and the roads is Jim Heiman's *Car Hops and Curb Service: A History of American Drive-In Restaurants 1920–1960*. It features historical photographs, menus, and matchbook covers, among other things chronicling the roadside food experience prior to the era of McDonalds.

Clearly related to artistic expression are the design and styling of automobiles themselves. A good survey of this topic through the mid-1970s is Paul C. Wilson's *Chrome Dreams: Automobile Styling since 1893*, which includes sections regarding the influence of popular tastes on automotive design. A brief, popular overview of the same subject is available in *Fifty Years of American Automotive Design, 1930–1980*, by Dick Nesbitt, which attempts to explain the societal influences that inspired these changes. A more specialized work, *Fins and Chrome* by E. John

DeWaard, focuses on American automobiles of the 1950s. What distinguishes this picture book from others is the attention that the author pays to the interaction between vehicular design and human personality traits, particularly in terms of customizing. The first in-depth analysis of the car design profession in the United States done from the perspective of an art historian is *The Art of American Car Design* by C. Edson Armi, 1988. Here the car as an art object and its designer as an artist receive rigorous academic analysis. *A Century of Automotive Style: 100 Years of American Car Design* by Michael Lamm and Dave Holls gives a history from the Model T to 1995 of the interplay between styling, marketing, and sales.

The individualized "hot rod" or "custom car," which reached its apogee in the 1950s, has never completely disappeared. One of the earliest books on this phenomenon is Eugene Jaderquist and Griffith Borgeson's *Best Hot Rods*. Done in the early 1950s, it is useful today because it gives reference data about the beginning of hot-rodding. Such practices are entertainingly described in Tom Wolfe's *The Kandy-Kolored Tangerine-Flake Streamline Baby*, which scrutinizes the fad of automobile customizing and hot-rod building on the West Coast. A more traditional approach to the subject is *Showtime: The Story of the International Championship Auto Shows and the Hot Rod Custom Car World: A Twenty-Year History*, by Michael Sheridan and Sam Bushala, which provides both a factual catalog and an appreciation of these one-of-a-kind cars.

The Family and the Community

Of all the cultural dimensions of American life that the motorcar has influenced, one of the more neglected has been family life and the community. From such case studies we might learn how the motorcar has influenced schooling and other educational services, religious life, health care, and law and order. There are a few pioneering books in this regard, such as Reynold M. Wik's *Henry Ford and Grassroots America*, a study of the rural response to Ford's life and work. Similar in subject to the Wik volume is Michael L. Berger's *The Devil Wagon in God's Country: The Automobile and Social Change in Rural America, 1893–1929*, which is one of the few purely social histories of the automobile, with chapters on the farm family, the rural community, leisure, religion, education, and health and the environment. The impact of the car on small-town life is analyzed by Norman T. Moline in *Mobility and the Small Town, 1900–1930*, a study of Oregon, Illinois. A somewhat different perspective is provided by John A. Jakle in *The American Small Town: Twentieth Century Place Images*, which attempts to show how the transition from dependency on rail to motor transportation changed the stereotypic view of the small town as a place type.

Unfortunately, similar specialized studies for suburban America have yet to be written, a particularly ironic situation given the debt that such localities owe to the automobile for their existence. One possible explanation for this state of affairs is that the development of suburbia, particularly in the years following World War II, and that of the car are inseparably intertwined.

Thus, it could be argued that a separate book on the topic is probably unnecessary, since every study of suburbia must include a discussion of the automobile as one of the central themes. Two recent books do this in a prominent way. Kenneth T. Jackson's *Crabgrass Frontier: The Suburbanization of the United States*, easily the best study to date, does an excellent job of analyzing how the car and other means of transportation have influenced the development of residential areas. In *Contemporary Suburban America*, Peter O. Muller analyzes the socioeconomic functioning of such areas and concludes that the auto-centered suburb is unlikely to change in the foreseeable future. Finally, with its regional focus, Ashleigh E. Brilliant's doctoral dissertation, "Social Effects of the Automobile in Southern California during the Twenties," offers valuable insights into how the car changed family life and community institutions in both suburbia and Los Angeles.

Urban America has been somewhat better served, in that we have some studies that exclusively devote themselves to the multiple influences of the car. From a historical vantage point there are Howard L. Preston's *Automobile Age Atlanta: The Marketing of a Southern Metropolis, 1900–1935* and Joel A. Tarr's lengthy essay *Transportation Innovation and Changing Spatial Patterns in Pittsburgh, 1850–1934.* Additional investigations of this type are needed, especially since national studies tend to blur distinctions among geographic regions, socioeconomic classes, ethnic and religious groups, and so on. A more general treatment of the car's early influence on urban development is "American Cities and the Coming of the Automobile, 1870–1910," a doctoral dissertation by Clay McShane.

While most of the books mentioned in the previous three paragraphs pay some attention to the automobile's impact on family life, there has been surprisingly little scholarly analysis of how the car has specifically influenced the lives of women. Typical of what was available until recently were chapters like "Milady at the Wheel," in M. M. Musselman's 1950 popular history *Get a Horse!: The Story of the Automobile in America*; essays such as Charles L. Sanford's " 'Woman's Place' in American Car Culture," which is reprinted in the Lewis and Goldstein collection cited earlier; and personal accounts of feminine motor exploits, for example, Alice Huyler Ramsey's *Veil, Duster, and Tire Iron.* (In 1909, Ramsey became the first woman successfully to complete a transcontinental motor trip.) Fortunately, 1987 saw the completion of two doctoral dissertations in this area: Beth Kraig's "Woman at the Wheel: A History of Women and the Automobile in America" and Virginia J. Scharff's "Reinventing the Wheel: American Women and the Automobile, 1910–1930." Virginia Scharff, in *Taking the Wheel: Women and the Coming of Age of the Automobile* (1991), develops the perceptions about gender that have determined attitudes about the design, use, and mythology of cars in American social history to show the role that women have played and still play in the evolution of the automobile and its use in American culture. In the spring of 1995, the *Journal of Popular Culture* published Nancy Tillman Romalov's "Mobile Heroines: Early Twentieth Century Girls' Automotive Series." It places the reading habits of teenage girls into the discussion of automobiles, feminist studies, and American history.

A number of scholarly studies attempts to assess the influence of the automobile on the nature and availability of urban transportation and the impact of that, in turn, on human behavior. Some of the earliest work in this regard was done by Lewis Mumford, one of America's most respected urban historians. Two of his books, *The City in History: Its Origins, Its Transformations, and Its Prospects* and *The Highway and the City*, judge the automobile to be a devastatingly negative force on America's cities. More recently, K. H. Schaeffer and Elliott Sclar, in *Access for*

All: Transportation and Urban Growth, have maintained that the quality of human life depends on the amount of access that we have to one another and that the automobile has reached its limits in terms of enhancing such access.

The problem of balancing the advantages and disadvantages of the private automobile vis-à-vis the various forms of mass transit is an ongoing one. Its origins lie in governmental policies and regulations promulgated in the first third of the twentieth century, and this public policy issue has been the basis of several important works: Paul Barrett's *The Automobile and Urban Transit: The Formation of Public Policy in Chicago, 1900–1930*; Scott L. Bottles' *Los Angeles and the Automobile: The Making of the Modern City*; Mark S. Foster's *From Streetcar to Superhighway: American City Planners and Urban Transportation, 1900–1940*; David J. St. Clair's *The Motorization of American Cities*; Ronald A. Buel's *Dead End: The Automobile in Mass Transportation*; and John Meyer and Jose A. Gomez-Ibanez's *Autos, Transit, and Cities*, a comprehensive Twentieth Century Fund Report that explores the interaction between transportation and the quality of urban life. Finally, Helen Leavitt's *Superhighway—Superhoax*, a polemical attack on the motivations and actions of highway supporters, still makes interesting reading nearly two decades after its publication. Explaining ways in which the automobile can become less of an issue in anybody's life is Moshe Safdie's *The City after the Automobile*. It makes the argument that better and different urban planning and the automobile's becoming less of a necessity will result in less pollution and less wasted time and money. Safdie's prescription is less stringent than that offered in Jane Holtz Kay's *Asphalt Nation: How the Automobile Took over America*, which argues for various car-related fees to force pedestrianism back into American cities.

Recreation and Leisure

Almost from the beginning, Americans recognized the enormous potential of the car as a vehicle for recreational purposes. Easily the best introduction to this topic is *Americans on the Road: From Autocamp to Motel, 1910–1945* by Warren J. Belasco. The author does an excellent job of linking the emergence of the motel business to such social issues as class conflict, the growth of the consumer ethic, and the weakening of family ties. A broader perspective is offered by John A. Jakle in his *The Tourist: Travel in Twentieth Century North America*, which contains four chapters devoted exclusively to the automobile. Also useful in this regard is John Baeder's *Gas, Food, and Lodging*, which uses postcards as illustrations to portray the changing face of roadside culture (including both people and places) that travelers encountered between 1918 and 1939. In a humorous vein, Jack Barth et al. have written *Roadside America*, which describes some of the more bizarre tourist attractions that have appeared alongside our nation's highways. (See the earlier section on architecture for additional references in this realm.)

Americans interested in motorized travel soon realized the advantages that might accrue from being able to bring something akin to their house along with them. Such thinking led to the commercial development of the car trailer, the mobile lounge, and the van. Two good introductions to the multiple aspects of this phenomenon are provided by Margaret J. Drury's *Mobile Homes: The Unrecognized Revolution in American Housing* and Michael A. Rockland's *Homes on Wheels. Airstream*, by Robert Landau and James Phillippi, is an uncritical descrip-

Auto workers. © Painet

tion of the history and way of life associated with one of the most famous of these vehicles.

The car culture also has spawned a host of leisure-time hobbies that require little or no travel for participation. While probably the best-known one is the restoration of antique cars, there are others, such as the collection of automotive toys, mascots, ornaments, license plates, and even automotive art. A fine overview of the field can be found in *Automobile Quarterly's Complete Handbook of Automobile Hobbies*, edited by Beverly Rae Kimes. Also good are Jack Martells' *Antique Automobile Collectibles* and, with a more international flavor, Michael Worthington-Williams' *Automobilia: A Guided Tour for Collectors*.

In regard to automotive toys, the most recent and probably definitive work is Lillian Gottschalk's *American Toy Cars and Trucks, 1894–1942*. In addition to physically describing 475 different items, almost all American-made, Gottschalk does an excellent job of linking their histories to those of the real cars that they represent. The text also is accompanied by superior photographic work. Another good work, covering a later period in which Japanese and German toy makers excelled to an extent unequaled since, is Dale Kelley's *Collecting the Tiny Toy Car, 1950–1970*. Also worth examining is *The World of Model Cars*, edited by Vic Smeed, which discusses not only collecting and building such vehicles but also the racing of radio-controlled models. The latter is covered in more detail in Robert Schleicher's *Model Car Racing Tradition*.

Not everyone into collecting model cars purchases the work of others. There is another group of hobbyists who enjoy making their own. Some insight into this form of leisure can be gained by perusing *The Complete Book of Model Car Building* by Dennis Doty, *Scratchbuilding Model Cars* by Saul Santos, and *The Complete Car Modeller* by Gerald A. Wingrove.

In addition to full-size and model cars, many Americans have chosen to collect ornamental parts of automobiles. Representative of the literature in this regard are William C. Williams' *Motoring Mascots of the World*, a study of hood ornaments; Keith Marvin's *License Plates of the World*; Scott Anderson's *Check the Oil: Gas Station Collectibles with Prices*; and Jim Evans' *Collectors Guide to Automotive Literature*, the latter defined as sales brochures, stock certificates, and other ephemera.

Racing

So much has been written on motor racing, some of it excellent and unfortunately some of it of dubious quality, that it is difficult to know where to begin research on the topic. The intent of this section is to send those interested to the books that yield the most information on motor racing as a sport, as opposed to the drivers or their machines.

A comprehensive survey of the American scene, from its beginning in 1895 to 1973, can be found in Albert R. Bochroch's *American Automobile Racing*. For more in-depth examinations of two particular types of racing, see Lyle K. Engel's *Road Racing in America* and his *Stock Car Racing U.S.A.* The broader world of the latter is portrayed in *Grand National Stock Car Racing: The Other Side of the Fence* by W. Michael Lovern and Bob Jones Jr., and *Fast as White Lightning: The Story of Stock Car Racing* by Kim Chapin, both of which attempt to capture the emotions of those involved in such racing, including drivers, mechanics, owners, sponsors, families, and fans.

The flavor of contemporary racing on dirt tracks is presented in John Sawyer's *The Dusty Heroes*. *Grand Prix: The Cars, the Drivers, the Circuits* by David Hodges et al. provides a contemporary history of this type of racing and American participation in it.

A number of books focus on memorable automobile races. Many of the latter have had significant impact on American sports culture. *The Great Auto Races*, a handsome volume written and lavishly illustrated by Peter Helck, centers on the early years of competition. Broader in coverage are *Great Moments in Speed* by Ross Olney, *The Shell Book of Epic Motor Races* by Peter Roberts, and *Great Moments in Auto Racing* by Irwin Stambler. In a more specifically historical vein, there is Albert Bochroch's *Americans at LeMans: An Illustrated History of the Twenty-four Hour Race from 1923 to 1975* and the same author's *Trans-Am Racing, 1966–1985: Detroit's Battle for Pony Car Supremacy*; Peter Helck's *The Checkered Flag*, which reviews early racing up to 1916; Fred J. Wagner's *The Saga of the Roaring Road: A Story of Early Auto Racing in America*; *Dirt Tracks to Glory: The Early Days of Stock Car Racing as Told by the Participants* by Sylvia Wilkinson; and *The Illustrated History of Sprint Car Racing, 1896–1942* and *The Mighty Midgets*, which traces developments in that area from 1933 to 1976, both by Jack C. Fox.

The annual Indianapolis 500, often dubbed the greatest spectacle in racing, has been the subject of uncounted articles as well as hundreds of books. In the latter category, among the more useful are *500 Miles to Go: The Story of the Indianapolis*

Speedway by Al Bloemker; *Indy 500: More than a Race* by Tom Carnegie, which vividly describes the monthlong preparations for the race and offers behind-the-scenes vignettes; *The Indianapolis 500: A Complete Pictorial History* by John and Barbara Devaney, a remarkably complete and well-illustrated study; and Brock W. Yates' *The Indianapolis 500: The Story of the Motor Speedway*. Finally, *The Indy 500: An American Institution under Fire*, by Ron Dorson, describes the ill-fated 1973 race and its aftermath.

Four accounts of contemporary American racing by "outsiders" are worth the attention of those interested in an in-depth look at the sport. They are *Fast Lane Summer: North American Road Racing*, by Leon Mandel; *Fast Guys, Rich Guys and Idiots: A Racing Odyssey on the Border of Obsession*, by Sam Moses; *The Stainless Steel Carrot*, by Sylvia Wilkinson; and *Sunday Driver*, by Brock Yates. The Mandel volume offers some fine glimpses of what day-to-day life is like for those involved in road racing. Moses, the motor sports writer for *Sports Illustrated*, finds himself caught up, both physically and emotionally, in the world of professional motor racing as a result of a "typical" assignment and attempts to explain why. Wilkinson's book follows the ups and downs of a professional driver during an entire season. Automotive journalist Yates decided that in order to write well about racing, he needed the actual experience on the track, and *Sunday Driver* chronicles his year of racing in the Trans Am series. Observations similar to those found in these books, but from a very different perspective, are provided in *Race Drivers' Wives: Twenty-four Women Talk about Their Lives*, by Jean and John Berry.

The types of motor racing previously mentioned are spectator sports, run on tracks or marked road courses. However, one type of competition began on the streets, still remains there to some extent, and is largely participatory in nature—drag racing. A fair overview of this subject is provided in *Petersen's History of Drag Racing* by Dave Wallace, which chronicles the development of this sport over thirty years. *Street Was Fun in '51*, by Albert Drake, helps explain the factors that converged at that historical period to make drag racing so popular. These two works and others provide a nonscholarly background for the enthusiast. We still lack a serious sociological study of the phenomenon of drag racing.

Finally, some mention should be made of the spectacular increase in the use of off-road vehicles, the so-called SUVs, for recreational purposes. They have evolved from the surplus World War II jeep to become a major class of vehicles unto themselves, with models sold by all the major car manufacturers. Researchers interested in this topic should begin by consulting Bernard Mergen's *Recreational Vehicles and Travel: A Resource Guide*.

Socioeconomic Problems

Despite the generally positive attitude shown by Americans toward the automobile, both the number and variety of critical appraisals have been increasing in recent years. One of the first books to view motorcars as less than desirable was John Keats' 1958 *The Insolent Chariots*. Aimed at a general audience, Keats' book provides a strong indictment of the cars and management of the Detroit automotive industry. He also discusses that industry's failure to hear and heed the voice of the public in terms of production and safety. In a more recent and scholarly work, *The Car Culture*, James J. Flink turns away from his previously positive view of the automobile to attack the nature of the car industry and what it has done to American society and values. Although Flink's perspective is, by his own admission, a partisan one, this still is an important work of social history from one of our premier automotive historians.

Most criticism, however, has been of a more specific kind. One of the most controversial books in this regard was written by consumer advocate Ralph Nader in 1965. *Unsafe at Any Speed: The Designed-in Dangers of the American Automobile* accused General Motors of callous negligence in the design and manufacture of the rear-engine Corvair automobile and eventually led to GM's abandonment of that model.

Actually, the question of safety in the car and on the road has been an ongoing one since the early days of motoring, in both mechanical and human terms. One of the pioneering scholarly works in this regard was *Passenger Car Design and Highway Safety*, the proceedings of a 1961 conference on research. Similar in concept to Nader's book and appearing the same year was *Safety Last: An Indictment of the Automobile Industry*, by Jeffrey O'Connell and Arthur Myers. For a more historical view, see Joel W. Eastman's *Styling vs. Safety: The American Automobile Industry and the Development of Automotive Safety, 1900–1966*. Finally, insight into what highway carnage meant in one era of American history is provided in Anedith J. B. Nash's doctoral dissertation entitled "Death on the Highway: The Automobile Wreck in American Culture, 1920–1940."

Another major socioeconomic problem associated with the automobile is that of pollution, with its air, solid waste, and visual dimensions. In the early and mid-1970s, there appeared a number of excellent, broadly based studies on this topic, including John Robinson's *Highways and Our Environment*; Frank P. Grad et al., *The Automobile and the Regulation of Its Impact on the Environment*; and, for a world-wide view, *The Automobile and the Environment: An International Perspective*, prepared by the Organization for Economic Co-operation and Development and edited by Ralph Gakenheimer. More specifically, in *Yellowstone: A Wilderness Besieged*, Richard A. Bartlett assigns to the automobile a fair share of the blame for the ecological problems in what is probably our best-known national park.

These socioeconomic problems, in concert with threats to our gasoline supply, spiraling car prices, and increased sales of Japanese automobiles in the United States, led to a series of books in the 1970s challenging the place of the automobile in American society. For instance, Kenneth R. Schneider, in *Autokind vs. Mankind: An Analysis of Tyranny, a Proposal for Rebellion, a Plan for Reconstruction*, boldly asserts his thesis, which "challenges the automobile for what it does to life in the cities and the stranglehold it has on society" and concludes that the automobile must be removed from society. Automobile journalist John Jerome reaches the same conclusion in *The Death of the Automobile: The Fatal Effect of the Golden Era, 1955–1970*. Emma Rothschild attacks the corporate influence on consumers and autoworkers in a collection of essays entitled *Paradise Lost: The Decline of the Auto-Industrial Age*, which also foresees the time when the automobile will be gone, replaced by a number of viable alternatives. Finally, in *Beyond the Automobile: Reshaping the Transportation Environment*, Tabor R. Stone offers a plan for a transportation system that would obviate the need for most motorcars.

During this period, the two positive voices were John B. Rae and B. Bruce-Biggs. Rae continued to defend both the automotive industry and the car's influence on American society in all his writing, but most notably in *The Road and the Car in American Life*. Bruce-Biggs' *The War against the Automobile* is a direct counterattack against the antiautomobile forces, even including Ralph Nader.

NOTES

1. George E. Mowry, *The Urban Nation, 1920–1960*, vol. 6 of *The Making of America*, ed. David Donald, 6 vols. (New York: Hill and Wang, 1965–1968), 17.
2. Lewis Mumford, *The Highway and the City* (New York: Harcourt, Brace, and World, 1963), 235.
3. Edgardo Contini, "Passionate Ode to the Freeway," review of *L.A. Freeway: An Appreciative Essay* by David Brodsly, *Los Angeles Times*, January 14, 1982: 14.

BIBLIOGRAPHY

Books and Articles

Anderson, Rudolph E. *The Story of the American Automobile: Highlights and Sidelights*. Washington, D.C.: Public Affairs Press, 1950.

Anderson, Scott. *Check the Oil: Gas Station Collectibles with Prices*. Lombard, Ill.: Wallace-Homestead, 1987.

Anderson, Warren H. *Vanishing Roadside America*. Tucson: University of Arizona Press, 1981.

Andrews, J.J.C. *The Well-Built Elephant and Other Roadside Attractions: A Tribute to American Eccentricity*. New York: Congdon and Weed, 1984.

Ansaldi, Richard. *Souvenirs from the Roadside West*. New York: Harmony Books, 1978.

Ant Farm [Lord, Chip]. *Automerica: A Trip down U.S. Highways from World War II to the Future*. New York: E. P. Dutton, 1976.

Armi, C. Edson. *The Art of American Car Design*. University Park: Pennsylvania State University Press, 1988.

The Automotive History Collection of the Detroit Public Library: A Simplified Guide to Its Holdings. 2 vols. Boston: G. K. Hall, 1966.

Baeder, John. *Gas, Food, and Lodging*. New York: Abbeville Press, 1982.

Barrett, Paul. *The Automobile and Urban Transit: The Formation of Public Policy in Chicago, 1900–1930*. Philadelphia: Temple University Press, 1983.

Barris, George. *Cars of the Stars*. Middle Village, N.Y.: Jonathan David, 1974.

Barth, Jack, et al. *Roadside America*. New York: Simon and Schuster, 1986.

Bartlett, Richard A. *Yellowstone: A Wilderness Besieged*. Tucson: University of Arizona Press, 1985.

Belasco, Warren J. *Americans on the Road: From Autocamp to Motel, 1910–1945*. Cambridge: MIT Press, 1979.

Berger, Michael L. *The Devil Wagon in God's Country: The Automobile and Social Change in Rural America 1893–1929*. Hamden, Conn.: Archon Books, 1979.

Berry, Jean, and John Berry. *Race Drivers' Wives: Twenty-four Women Talk about Their Lives*. Hazel Crest, Ill.: Berry, 1982.

Bliss, Carey S. *Autos across America: A Biography of Transcontinental Automobile Travel, 1903–1940*. Los Angeles: Dawson's Book Shop, 1972.

Bloemker, Al. *500 Miles to Go: The Story of the Indianapolis Speedway*. New York: Coward-McCann, 1961.

Bochroch, Albert R. *American Automobile Racing*. New York: Viking, 1974.

————. *Americans at LeMans: An Illustrated History of the Twenty-four Hour Race from 1923 to 1975*. Tucson: Aztex, 1976.

————. *Trans-Am Racing, 1966–1985: Detroit's Battle for Pony Car Supremacy*. Osceola, Wis.: Motorbooks International, 1986.

Bottles, Scott L. *Los Angeles and the Automobile: The Making of the Modern City*. Berkeley: University of California Press, 1987.

Bowers, Q. David, ed. *Early American Car Advertisements*. New York: Crown, 1966.

Boyne, Walter J. *Power behind the Wheel: Creativity and the Evolution of the Automobile*. New York: Artabras, 1991.

Brilliant, Ashleigh E. "Social Effects of the Automobile in Southern California during the Twenties." Ph.D. diss., University of California, Berkeley, 1964.

Brodsly, David. *L.A. Freeway: An Appreciative Essay*. Berkeley: University of California Press, 1981.

Bruce-Biggs, B. *The War against the Automobile*. New York: E. P. Dutton, 1977.

Buel, Ronald A. *Dead End: The Automobile in Mass Transportation*. Englewood Cliffs, N.J.: Prentice-Hall, 1972.

Carnegie, Tom. *Indy 500: More Than a Race*. New York: McGraw-Hill, 1986.

Carpenter, John, dir. *Christine*. Columbia Pictures, 1983.

Chapin, Kim. *Fast as White Lighting: The Story of Stock Car Racing*. New York: Dial Press, 1981.

Cleveland, Reginald M., and S. T. Williamson. *The Road Is Yours: The Story of the Automobile and the Men behind It*. New York: Greystone Press, 1951.

Clymer, Floyd. *Cars of the Stars and Movie Memories*. Los Angeles: Floyd Clymer, 1954.

Cohn, David L. *Combustion on Wheels: An Informal History of the Automobile Age*. Boston: Houghton Mifflin, 1944.

Conde, John A. *Cars with Personalities*. Keego Harbor, Mich.: Arnold Porter, 1982.

Cutcliffe, Stephen H., et al. *Technology and Values in American Civilization: A Guide to Information Sources*. Detroit: Gale Research, 1980.

Days of Thunder. Tony Scott, dir. Paramount Pictures, 1990.

Denby, Priscilla Lee. "The Self Discovered: The Car in American Folklore and Literature." Ph.D. diss., Indiana University, 1981.

Dettelbach, Cynthia Golomb. *In the Driver's Seat: The Automobile in American Literature and Popular Culture*. Westport, Conn.: Greenwood Press, 1976.

Devaney, John, and Barbara Devaney. *The Indianapolis 500: A Complete Pictorial History*. Chicago: Rand McNally, 1976.

DeWaard, E. John. *Fins and Chrome*. Greenwich, Conn.: Crescent Books, 1982.

Donovan, Frank. *Wheels for a Nation*. New York: Crowell, 1965.

Dorson, Ron. *The Indy 500: An American Institution under Fire*. Newport Beach, Calif.: Bond/Parkhurst Books, 1974.

Doty, Dennis. *The Complete Book of Model Car Building*. Blue Ridge Summit, Pa.: TAB Books, 1981.

Drake, Albert. *Street Was Fun in '51*. Okemos, Mich.: Flat Out Press, 1982.

Drury, Margaret J. *Mobile Homes: The Unrecognized Revolution in American Housing*. New York: Praeger, 1972.

Eastman, Joel W. *Styling vs. Safety: The American Automobile Industry and the Development of Automotive Safety, 1900–1966*. Lanham, Md.: University Press of America, 1984.

Ebershoff-Coles, Susan, and Charla A. Leibenguth. *Motorsports: A Guide to Information Sources*. Detroit: Gale Research, 1979.

Engel, Lyle K. *Road Racing in America*. New York: Dodd, Mead, 1971.

———. *Stock Car Racing U.S.A.* New York: Dodd, Mead, 1973.

Evans, Jimmie R. H. *Collectors Guide to Automotive Literature*. Sioux City, Iowa: Larsen's Printing, n.d.

Faulkner, William. *The Reivers*. New York: Random House, 1962.

Finch, Christopher. *Highways to Heaven: The Auto biography of America*. New York: HarperCollins, 1992.

Fitzgerald, F. Scott. *The Great Gatsby*. New York: Scribner's, 1925.

Flink, James J. *America Adopts the Automobile, 1895–1910*. Cambridge: MIT Press, 1970.

———. *The Automobile Age*. Cambridge: MIT Press, 1988.

———. *The Car Culture*. Cambridge: MIT Press, 1975.

Flower, Raymond, and Michael W. Jones. *100 Years on the Road: A Social History of the Car*. New York: McGraw-Hill, 1981.

Foster, Mark S. *From Streetcar to Superhighway: American City Planners and Urban Transportation*, 1900–1940. Philadelphia: Temple University Press, 1981.

Fox, Jack C. *The Illustrated History of Sprint Car Racing, 1896–1942*. Speedway, Ind.: Carl Hungness, 1985.

———. *The Mighty Midgets: The Illustrated History of Midget Auto Racing*. Speedway, Ind.: Carl Hungness, 1985.

Gakenheimer, Ralph, ed. *The Automobile and the Environment: An International Perspective*. Cambridge: MIT Press, 1978.

Glasscock, C. B. *The Gasoline Age: The Story of the Men Who Made It*. Indianapolis: Bobbs-Merrill, 1937.

Goddard, Stephen B. *Getting There: The Epic Struggle between Road and Rail in the American Century*. Chicago: University of Chicago Press, 1996.

Gottschalk, Lillian. *American Toy Cars and Trucks, 1894–1942*. New York: Abbeville Press, 1986.

Grad, Frank P., et al. *The Automobile and the Regulation of Its Impact on the Environment*. Norman: University of Oklahoma Press, 1975.

Graham, Don. *Cowboys and Cadillacs: How Hollywood Looks at Texas*. Austin: Texas Monthly Press, 1984.

Grahame, Kenneth. *The Wind in the Willows*. New York: Scribner's, 1933.

Heiman, Jim. *Car Hops and Curb Service: A History of American Drive-in Restaurants 1920–1960*. San Francisco: Chronicle Books, 1996.

Helck, Peter. *The Checkered Flag*. New York: Scribner's, 1967.

———. *The Great Auto Races*. New York: Harry N. Abrams, 1975.

Henderson, Sally, and Robert Landau. *Billboard Art*. San Francisco: Chronicle Books, 1980.

Hill, Frank E. *The Automobile: How It Came, Grew, and Has Changed Our Lives*. New York: Dodd, Mead, 1967.

Hodges, David, et al. *Grand Prix: The Cars, the Drivers, the Circuits*. New York: St. Martin's Press, 1981.

Ikuta, Yasutoshi. *The American Automobile: Advertising from the Antique and Classic Eras*. San Francisco: Chronicle Books, 1988.

Jackson, Kenneth T. *Crabgrass Frontier: The Suburbanization of the United States*. New York: Oxford University Press, 1985.

Jaderquist, Eugene, and Griffith Borgeson. *Best Hot Rods*. New York: Arco, 1953.

Jakle, John A. *The American Small Town: Twentieth Century Place Images*. Hamden, Conn.: Archon Books, 1982.

———. *The Tourist: Travel in Twentieth Century North America*. Lincoln: University of Nebraska Press, 1985.

Jerome, John. *The Death of the Automobile: The Fatal Effect of the Golden Era, 1955–1970*. New York: W. W. Norton, 1972.

Jewell, Derek, ed. *Man and Motor: The Twentieth Century Love Affair*. New York: Walker, 1967.

Kay, Jane Holtz. *Asphalt Nation: How the Automobile Took over America*. Berkeley: University of California Press, 1998.

Keats, John. *The Insolent Chariots*. Philadelphia: J. B. Lippincott, 1958.

Keller, Ulrich. *Highway as Habitat: A Roy Stryker Documentation, 1943–1955*. Santa Barbara: University Art Museum, University of California, Santa Barbara, 1985.

Kelley, Dale. *Collecting the Tiny Toy Car, 1950–1970*. West Chester, Pa.: Schiffer, 1984.

Kerouac, Jack. *On the Road*. New York: Viking Press, 1958.

Kimes, Beverly Rae, ed. *Automobile Quarterly's Complete Handbook of Automobile Hobbies*. Princeton, N.J.: Princeton Publishing, 1981.

Kraig, Beth. "Woman at the Wheel: A History of Women and the Automobile in America." Ph.D. diss., University of Washington, 1987.

Kunstler, James Howard. *The Geography of Nowhere: The Rise and Decline of America's Man-Made Landscape*. New York: Simon and Schuster, 1994.

Labatut, Jean, and Wheaton J. Lane, eds. *Highways in Our National Life: A Symposium*. Princeton, N.J.: Princeton University Press, 1950.

Lamm, Michael, and Dave Holls. *A Century of Automotive Style: 100 Years of American Car Design*. Stockton, Calif.: Lamm-Morada, 1996.

Landau, Robert J., and James M. Phillippi. *Airstream*. Salt Lake City: Gibbs M. Smith, 1984.

Leavitt, Helen. *Superhighway—Superhoax*. New York: Doubleday, 1970.

Lee, Raymond. *Fit for the Chase: Cars and the Movies*. Cranbury, N.J.: A. S. Barnes, 1969.

Lewis, David L., and Laurence Goldstein, eds. *The Automobile and American Culture*. Ann Arbor: University of Michigan Press, 1983.

Lewis, Sinclair. *Babbitt*. New York: Harcourt, Brace, 1922.

———. *Main Street*. New York: Harcourt, Brace, 1920.

Liebs, Chester H. *Main Street to Miracle Mile: American Roadside Architecture*. Boston: New York Graphic Society/Little, Brown, 1985.

Ling, Peter. *America and the Automobile*. New York: St. Martin's Press, 1990.

Lovern, W. Michael, and Bob Jones Jr. *Grand National Stock Car Racing: The Other Side of the Fence*. Richmond: Fast Co. of Virginia, 1982.

Lynd, Robert S., and Helen M. Lynd. *Middletown: A Study in Contemporary American Culture*. New York: Harcourt, Brace, 1929.

————. *Middletown in Transition: A Study in Cultural Conflicts*. New York: Harcourt, Brace, 1937.

Mandel, Leon. *Driven: The American Four-Wheeled Love Affair*. New York: Stein and Day, 1977.

————. *Fast Lane Summer: North American Road Racing*. Mill Valley, Calif.: Square-Books, 1981.

Mantle, Jonathan. *Car Wars: Fifty Years of Greed, Treachery, and Skullduggery in the Global Marketplace*. New York: Arcade, 1995.

Margolies, John. *The End of the Road: Vanishing Highway Architecture in America*. New York: Viking Press, 1981.

Marling, Karal Ann. *The Colossus of Roads: Myth and Symbol along the American Highway*. Minneapolis: University of Minnesota Press, 1984.

Marsh, Peter, and Peter Collett. *Driving Passion: The Psychology of the Car*. Boston: Faber and Faber, 1987.

Martells, Jack. *Antique Automobile Collectibles*. Chicago: Contemporary Books, 1980.

Martin, Richard, "Fashion and the Car in the 1950s." *Journal of American Culture* (Fall 1997), 51–66.

Marvin, Keith. *License Plates of the World*. Troy, N.Y.: Privately printed, 1963.

Maxim, Hiram P. *Horseless Carriage Days*. New York: Harper and Brothers, 1937.

McShane, Clay. "American Cities and the Coming of the Automobile, 1870–1910." Ph.D. diss., University of Wisconsin, Madison, 1975.

Mead, Walter Russell. "Trains, Planes and Automobiles: The End of the Postmodern Moment." *World Policy Journal* (Winter 1995), 13–31.

Mergen, Bernard. *Recreational Vehicles and Travel: A Resource Guide*. Westport, Conn.: Greenwood Press, 1985.

Meyer, John R., and Jose A. Gomez-Ibanez. *Autos, Transit, and Cities*. Cambridge: Harvard University Press, 1981.

Moline, Mary, ed. *The Best of Ford*. Van Nuys, Calif.: Rumbleseat Press, 1973.

Moline, Norman T. *Mobility and the Small Town, 1900–1930: Transportation Change in Oregon, Illinois*. Research Paper No. 132. Chicago: Department of Geography, University of Chicago, 1971.

Moon, William L. H. *Blue Highways: A Journey into America*. Boston: Atlantic-Little, Brown, 1983.

Moses, Sam. *Fast Guys, Rich Guys and Idiots: A Racing Odyssey on the Border of Obsession*. Jamestown, R.I.: September Press, 1986.

Mueller, John H. "The Automobile: A Sociological Study." Ph.D. diss., University of Chicago, 1928.

Muller, Peter O. *Contemporary Suburban America*. Englewood Cliffs, N.J.: Prentice-Hall, 1981.

Mumford, Lewis. *The City in History: Its Origins, Its Transformations, and Its Prospects*. New York: Harcourt, Brace, and World, 1961.

————. *The Highway and the City*. New York: Harcourt, Brace, and World, 1963.

Musselman, M. M. *Get a Horse!: The Story of the Automobile in America*. Philadelphia: J. B. Lippincott, 1950.

Nader, Ralph. *Unsafe at Any Speed: The Designed-in Dangers of the American Automobile*. New York: Grossman, 1965.

Nash, Anedith J. B. "Death on the Highway: The Automobile Wreck in American Culture, 1920–1940." Ph.D. diss., University of Minnesota, 1983.

Nesbitt, Dick. *Fifty Years of American Automotive Design, 1930–1980*. New York: Beckman House, 1985.

O'Connell, Jeffrey, and Arthur Myers. *Safety Last: An Indictment of the Automobile Industry*. New York: Random House, 1965.

Ogden, Samuel R. *America the Vanishing: Road Life and the Price of Progress*. Brattleboro, Vt.: Stephen Greene Press, 1969.

Olney, Ross. *Great Moments in Speed*. Englewood Cliffs, N.J.: Prentice-Hall, 1970.

Passenger Car Design and Highway Safety: Proceedings of a Conference on Research. New York: Association for the Aid of Crippled Children and Consumers Union of U.S., 1962.

Patton, Phil. *Open Road: A Celebration of the American Highway*. New York: Simon and Schuster, 1986.

Pettifer, Julian, and Nigel Turner. *Automania: Man and the Motor Car*. Boston: Little, Brown, 1984.

Pirsig, Robert M. *Zen and the Art of Motorcycle Maintenance*. New York: William Morrow, 1974.

Preston, Howard L. *Automobile Age Atlanta: The Making of a Southern Metropolis, 1900–1935*. Athens: University of Georgia Press, 1979.

Primeau, Ronald. *Romance of the Road: The Literature of the American Highway*. Bowling Green, Ohio: Bowling Green State University Popular Press, 1999.

Rae, John B. *The American Automobile: A Brief History*. Chicago: University of Chicago Press, 1965.

———. *The Road and the Car in American Life*. Cambridge: MIT Press, 1971.

Ramsey, Alice Huyler. *Veil, Duster, and Tire Iron*. Covina, Calif.: Castle Press, 1961.

Roberts, Peter. *Any Colour So Long as It's Black: The First Fifty Years of Automobile Advertising*. Devon, England: David and Charles, 1976.

———. *The Shell Book of Epic Motor Races*. New York: Arco, 1965.

Robinson, John. *Highways and Our Environment*. New York: McGraw-Hill, 1971.

Rockland, Michael A. *Homes on Wheels*. New Brunswick, N.J.: Rutgers University Press, 1980.

Romalov, Nancy Tillman. "Mobile heroines: Early Twentieth Century Girls' Automotive Series." *Journal of Popular Culture* (Spring 1995), 231–43.

Rothschild, Emma. *Paradise Lost: The Decline of the Auto-Industrial Age*. New York: Random House, 1973.

Rowsome, Frank J., Jr. *The Verse by the Side of the Road: The Story of the Burma-Shave Signs*. Brattleboro, Vt.: Stephen Greene Press, 1965.

Safdie, Moshe. *The City after the Automobile: An Architect's Vision*. Boulder, Colo.: Westview Press, 1998.

Sanders, Don, and Susan Sanders. *The American Drive-In Movie Theatre*. Osceola, Wis.: Motorbooks International, 1997.

Sanford, Charles L., ed. *The Automobile in American Life*. Troy, N.Y.: Center for the Study of Human Dimensions of Science and Technology, Rensselaer Polytechic Institute, 1977.

Santos, Saul. *Scratchbuilding Model Cars*. Blue Ridge Summit, Pa.: TAB Books, 1982.

Sawyer, John. *The Dusty Heroes*. Speedway, Ind.: Carl Hungness, 1978.

Schaeffer, K. H., and Elliott Sclar. *Access for All: Transportation and Urban Growth*. New York: Columbia University Press, 1980.

Scharff, Virginia J. "Reinventing the Wheel: American Women and the Automobile, 1910–1930." Ph.D. diss., University of Arizona, 1987.

———. *Taking the Wheel: Women and the Coming of Age of the Automobile*. Albuquerque: University of New Mexico Press, 1991.

Schleicher, Robert H. *Model Car Racing Tradition*. Radnor, Pa.: Chilton, 1979.

Schlereth, Thomas J. *U.S. 40: A Roadscape of the American Experience*. Indianapolis: Indiana Historical Society, 1985.

Schneider, Kenneth R. *Autokind vs. Mankind: An Analysis of Tyranny, a Proposal for Rebellion, a Plan for Reconstruction*. New York: W. W. Norton, 1971.

Sears, Stephen W. *The American Heritage History of the Automobile in America*. New York: American Heritage, 1977.

Sheridan, Michael, and Sam Bushala. *Showtime: The Story of the International Championship Auto Shows and the Hot Rod Custom Car World: A Twenty-Year History*. Pontiac, Mich.: Promotional Displays, 1980.

Silk, Gerald, et al. *Automobile and Culture*. New York: Harry N. Abrams, 1984.

Smeed, Vic, ed. *The World of Model Cars*. Secaucus, N.J.: Chartwell Books, 1980.

St. Clair, David J. *The Motorization of American Cities*. New York: Praeger, 1986.

Stambler, Irwin. *Great Moments in Auto Racing*. New York: Scholastic Book Services, 1968.

Steinbeck, John. *The Grapes of Wrath*. New York: Viking Press, 1939.

Stern, Jane, and Michael Stern. *Auto Ads*. New York: Random House, 1979.

Stewart, George R. *U.S. 40: Cross Section of the United States of America*. Boston: Houghton Mifflin, 1953.

Stone, Tabor R. *Beyond the Automobile: Reshaping the Transportation Environment*. Englewood Cliffs, N.J.: Prentice-Hall, 1971.

Swope, Mary, and Walter H. Kerr, eds. *American Classic: Car Poems for Collectors*. College Park, Md.: SCOP, 1985.

Tarr, Joel A. *Transportation Innovation and Changing Spatial Patterns in Pittsburgh, 1850–1934*. Chicago: Public Works Historical Society, 1978.

Thelma and Louise. Tony Scott, dir. MGM-UA, 1991.

Tubbs, D. B. *Art and the Automobile*. London: Butterworth Press, 1978.

Vale, Thomas R., and Geraldine R. Vale. *U.S. 40 Today: Thirty Years of Landscape Change in America*. Madison: University of Wisconsin Press, 1983.

Vieyra, Daniel L. *"Fill 'er Up". An Architectural History of America's Gas Stations*. New York: Collier Books, 1979.

Wagner, Fred J. *The Saga of the Roaring Road: A Story of Early Auto Racing in America*. Los Angeles: Floyd Clymer, 1949.

Wallace, A. *Automotive Literature Index, 1947–1976*. Toledo: Privately printed, 1981.

———. *Automotive Literature Index, 1977–1981*. Toledo: Privately printed, 1983.

———. *Automotive Literature Index, 1982–1986*. Toledo: Privately printed, 1988.

Wallace, Dave. *Petersen's History of Drag Racing*. Los Angeles: Petersen, 1981.

Wik, Reynold M. *Henry Ford and Grassroots America*. Ann Arbor: University of Michigan Press, 1972.

Wilkinson, Sylvia. *Dirt Tracks to Glory: The Early Days of Stock Car Racing as Told by the Participants*. Chapel Hill, N.C.: Algonquin Books, 1983.

———. *The Stainless Steel Carrot: An Auto Racing Odyssey*. Boston: Houghton Mifflin, 1973.

Williams, Mark. *Road Movies: The Complete Guide to Cinema on Wheels*. New York: Proteus, 1982.

Williams, William C. *Motoring Mascots of the World*. Osceola, Wis.: Motorbooks International, 1979.

Wilson, Paul C. *Chrome Dreams: Automobile Styling since 1893*. Radnor, Pa.: Chilton, 1976.

Wingrove, Gerald A. *The Complete Car Modeller*. New York: Crown, 1978.

Wolfe, Tom. *The Kandy-Kolored Tangerine-Flake Streamline Baby*. New York: Farrar, Straus, and Giroux, 1965.

Worthington-Williams, Michael. *Automobilia: A Guided Tour for Collectors*. New York: Hastings House, 1979.

Yates, Brock W. *The Indianapolis 500: The Story of the Motor Speedway*. Rev. ed. New York: Harper and Row, 1961.

———. *Sunday Driver*. New York: Farrar, Straus, and Giroux, 1972.

Periodicals

America: History and Life. Santa Barbara, Calif., 1964— .

Antique Automobile. Hershey, Pa., 1935— .

Auto Index. Suffern, N.Y., 1973— .

Automobile Quarterly. Newport Beach, Calif., 1962– .

Bulb Horn. Brookline, Mass., 1939– .

Car and Driver. Ann Arbor, Mich., 1955– .

Dissertation Abstracts. Ann Arbor, Mich., 1938– .

Isis. Philadelphia, 1912– .

Recently Published Articles. Washington, D.C., 1976– .

Road and Track. Newport Beach., Calif., 1947– .

Technology and Culture. Chicago, 1959– .

Writings on American History. Washington, D.C., 1918– .

Glidden Tour Parade at Belle Isle, Detroit, Michigan, 1909. Courtesy of the Library of Congress

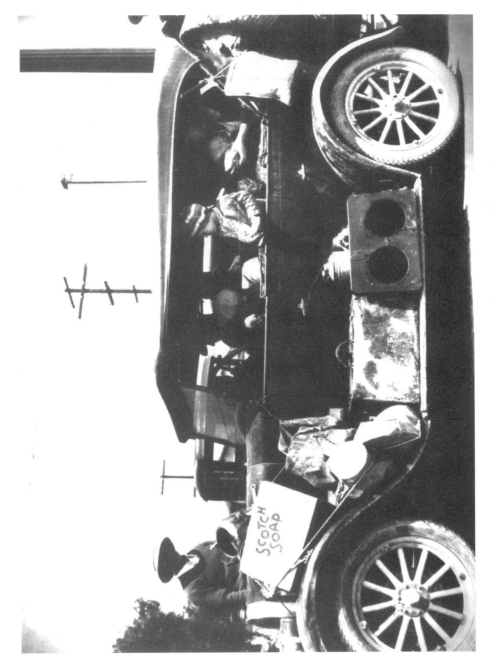

Oklahoma Dust Bowl refugees, San Fernando, California, 1935. Courtesy of the Library of Congress

Automobile race, Indianapolis, Indiana, 1938. Courtesy of the Library of Congress

A drive-in restaurant, 1942. Courtesy of the Library of Congress

Picnic, 1942. Courtesy of the Library of Congress

Mothers Against Drunk Driving billboard. © Skjold

Mother teaching daughter safe driving skills. © Skjold

Electric car. © Painet

Solar car. © Painet

Family vacation. © Painet

BIG LITTLE BOOKS

Ray Barfield

"Big Little Book" is a trademark that has become firmly lodged as a generic term encompassing parallel product lines of several publishers, primarily from the depression and World War II decades. Emerging from a finely tuned sense of the five-and-dime or variety store market, the Big Little Books, Better Little Books, New Better Little Books, Big Big Books, Little Big Books, Jumbo Books, Fast Action Books, and related series became prized possessions of children in a wide socioeconomic range of American homes, beginning with the first title in 1932 and tapering off with the advent of television at midcentury. Some recent attempts at reviving the Big Little Book format have been moderately successful, but the earlier series remains the best remembered. Copies of early titles, most of them originally priced at one dime, now bring $25 to more (sometimes much more) than $100 on the collectors' market. Many nostalgists are willing to pay such prices to reclaim artifacts of childhood memory, but Big Little Books have a broader value: they well represent the times that produced them.

Big Little Books were well proportioned for young hands. Most were an inch or so thick (thus, "big"), almost 4" wide and 4 ½" tall (thus compact or "little"). The pioneering Whitman Publishing Company Big Little Books were soon followed by closely similar volumes with similar series titles from Saalfield Publishing Company, the Five Star Library, and others. Most were hardbound or "board-covered," cased-in books with bright, four-color covers, the early volumes often showing deco touches in lettering and decoration. Generally, the left-hand text pages, set in ten or twelve lines of rather large type, faced black-and-white illustrations, sometimes drawn by the publishers' staff artists but more often adapted by them from comic strip panels or movie stills. Speech balloons were usually eliminated, and illustrations were extended or trimmed to fit the lined panel space. The initial Big Little Books were slightly larger than their successors, but even after the major publishers had settled on a standard shape for easy holding by six- to twelve-year-olds, they continued to experiment with format variations as a way of defining several subseries. Thus, the peak period of Big Little Book production also saw the development of penny and nickel versions as well as advertising give-away and premium lines. These were smaller or thinner than the ten- or fifteen-cent volumes (and sometimes directly condensed from them), but, like the full-length titles, they generally featured adaptations of comic strips and films, with a sprinkling of publisher-created protagonists and nursery tale, riddle, and joke books.

Usually printed in single editions numbering hundreds of thousands of copies per title, Big Little Books were often scorned by public school teachers and li-brarians, while children's book reviewers and the book-trade press had little in-terest in them. The absence of such "official" endorsement notwithstanding and despite the vulnerabilities of their highly acidic pulp pages and fragile spines (as well as sacrifices to World War II paper recycling drives and end-of-childhood house cleanings), tens of thousands of 1930s and 1940s Big Little Books survive. Many carry birthday or Christmas gift inscriptions from mothers, aunts, or grand-fathers who might never have dreamed of investing in "those ol' comic books." The bindings of Big Little Books gave them a kind of legitimacy, and they were equally fun to toss around or to pore over.

Sometimes seen as having finally "lost out to" comic books, to television, or simply to changing times, the early Big Little Books have achieved the status of memory-evoking, period-characterizing artifacts. They may be seen as props for the leading juvenile characters in such films as *Thieves like Us* (1974, directed by Robert Altman) and *A Christmas Story* (1983, based on an autobiographical story by Jean Shepherd). Several title and price guides have emerged from the collectors' community, but academic-scholarly interest has been limited chiefly to the illus-trative purposes of the social historian.

HISTORICAL OUTLINE

Obviously, the long and colorful tradition of children's illustrated books forms the broad background to the development of Big Little Books. Also, early news-paper comics reprint volumes from such publishers as the Frederick A. Stokes Company and Cupples and Leon stand as general predecessors to the comic book experiments of George Delacorte (1929), the Ledger Syndicate, and M. C. Gaines (1933) and equally to the first Big Little Book *The Adventures of Dick Tracy*, adapted by Whitman from Chester Gould's *Chicago Tribune* strip in 1932. More specifically, however, the Big Little Book emerged from the ironic outcome of one event—the near-collapse of the Western Printing and Lithographing Com-pany after a major creditor's default in 1916—and from the shaping skills of Sam-uel Lowe, who guided Western's Whitman division through more than twenty highly successful years.

In promotional brochures and in several drafts of an in-house company history, the story of Western Printing and Lithographing Company, which changed its name to Western Publishing Company in the summer of 1960, reads like a ro-mance of American capitalism. According to the unsigned brochure *Western Ways*, the company began to take shape in 1907, when Edward H. Wadewitz (1878–1955), part-time bookkeeper for the West Side Printing Company in Racine, Wis-consin, fell heir to that modestly equipped firm "partly in lieu of wages." He and

Roy A. Spencer (1880–1956), a veteran newspaper pressman, secured a $1,500 loan and, with three other employees, continued operating from the basement of a State Street hat store. A younger brother, William R. (Bill) Wadewitz, who would become company president in 1957, began his career by pushing a two-wheeled delivery cart through the streets of Racine. In 1910 the firm was incorporated as Western Printing and Lithographing Company, and by 1914 its job-printing orders had reached $100,000, a dramatic contrast to the first-year sales of $9,000 less than a decade earlier.

The year 1916 brought the crisis out of which the young firm found a new and major direction. Western found itself principal creditor of a Chicago book publisher, the Hamming-Whitman Company, which declared bankruptcy. As the anonymous promotional book *The Story of Western, 1907–1965* tells it, "Western had on its hands many thousands of completed books and works in process, for which it could never hope to collect from its customers." Making the best of its dilemma, "Western, on Feb. 9, 1916, acquired 'all the assets of said Hamming-Whitman Company of every nature and description, including office furniture, manufactured stock, work in process, unprinted stock, copyrights, plates, dies, drawings, contracts, orders for stock, material and all goodwill.' " Two weeks later Whitman Publishing Company was organized as a wholly owned subsidiary, and Western was launched toward its eventual long-term status as the world's largest producer of children's books, games, and so on.

Soon after World War I, Samuel Lowe (1884–1952) became Whitman's president and began the innovations that assured its success. Setting up an "activity room" in which to try out children's books and games, he took careful note of how the company's young guests responded to various mock-up items. In the early 1930s he tested dummy copies of the first few Big Little Books before taking them to a New York trade show, where they gained the approval of chain store buyers. In 1933, the year after the initial Big Little Book was published, Lowe led Whitman into an exclusive long-term contract to produce books featuring Walt Disney Studio characters, and *Mickey Mouse* became one of the earliest Big Little Book titles to reach the Woolworth, Kresge, Kress, and other chain store counters. Lowe's association with Whitman and his general direction of its line continued until 1940, when he set up the company that carried his name. At his death in 1952, *Publishers Weekly* credited Lowe with bringing Whitman to a production level of "more than 6,000,000 volumes a year," adding, "He had a genius for sensing the trends in the mass market for books and he had courage and ingenuity in trying out new ideas." The Big Little Book was one of the ideas on which he gambled and won hugely.

Whitman's format-establishing 700 series Big Little Books, published between 1932 and 1936, included titles suggesting a wide variety of appeal. The *Big Little Mother Goose Book* (at 576 pages, the longest Big Little Book ever published), *The Big Little Paint Book* (published in hardcover and softcover editions of slightly differing lengths), and *Once Upon a Time* were meant for very young children; adaptations of *Robinson Crusoe*, *Treasure Island*, and *The Spy* borrowed the high culture legitimacy of literary classics; *The World War in Photographs* served an educational purpose; *Buffalo Bill and the Pony Express*, *Cowboy Stories*, and *Billy the Kid*, among others, satisfied appetites for Wild West material. Mickey Mouse was featured in five 700-series titles, one of them offered in four length, size, and

Tom Beatty, Ace of the Service, 1934. Courtesy of the Library of Congress

cover variations. *Tom Beatty, Ace of the Service*, the first of many G-man titles from the 1930s, was offered in a "New Size Detective Series," while the 4 ½" × 5" "Movie Size" included Clyde Beatty in *Lions and Tigers* (sometimes thought to be the first Big Little Book because it bears an unusal number, 653), Lionel Barrymore in a much-altered film version of *Moby Dick*, Katharine Hepburn in *Little Women*, Charlotte Henry in *Alice in Wonderland*, and Ken Maynard in *Gun Justice*. Oddly, Robert Ripley's newspaper panel *Believe It or Not!* was assigned the movie size. The first two Dick Tracy, the first two Little Orphan Annie, and the first Mickey Mouse titles as well as *Houdini's Big Little Book of Magic* were among the ten books sharing the initial size (3 ⅞" × 4 ⅜" × 1 ½"), while many other of the 700-series comic strip adaptations, featuring Chester Gump, Buck Rogers, Smitty, Tarzan of the Apes, Moon Mullins and Kayo, Tailspin Tommy, Skippy, Alley Oop, and Tiny Tim, appeared in the slightly smaller dimensions that were to become standard. The 700 series, in addition to the experimental air suggested by its variety of subjects and book sizes, is characterized by a degree of disdain for bibliographic nicety: on some books the listed copyright date is that of the source material in its original form, while other books more conventionally list the Whitman publication date.

Succeeding and partly overlapping the 700 series were the two 1100 series published between 1934 and 1937. Of the 128 titles assigned 1100 numbers (with many numbers repeated from the first series to the second), three were offered in the standard size, fifteen appeared in the movie size, and two film adaptations were given unusually large dimensions (5 ¼" × 6 ¼"). New titles carried established characters into the 1100 series, and Flash Gordon, Don Winslow of the Navy, Skeezix from *Gasoline Alley*, Terry and the Pirates, Mandrake the Magician, Felix the Cat, Jungle Jim, Smilin' Jack, the Phantom, Popeye, and Donald Duck were added. Both Herman Brix and Johnny Weismuller were featured in adaptations of Tarzan films, and Tom Mix, Buck Jones, and Tim McCoy appeared in B-western novelizations. From animated cartoons came Betty Boop and Oswald the Lucky Rabbit, the latter of these being little more than a badly drawn promotional effort for Carl Laemmle Studios. *The Laughing Dragon of Oz*, the sole early Big Little Book version of an L. Frank Baum novel and today one of the rarest Whitman titles, appeared in the first 1100 series, and the second 1100 group saw emerging or growing emphases on characteristic 1930s themes and preoccupations: crime and police methodology (*G-Man on the Crime Trail*, *In the Name of the Law*, *G-Man vs. the Red X*, *Secret Agent X-9*, *Radio Patrol*, *Dan Dunn*, *Secret Operative 48*, *On the Trail of the Counterfeiters*), aviation (*Flying the Sky Clipper with Winsie Atkins*, *Tailspin Tommy and the Island in the Sky*, *Jimmie Allen in the Air Mail Robbery*, *Skyroads with Hurricane Hawk*, Capt. Eddie Rickenbacker's *Hall of Fame of the Air*, *Smilin' Jack and the Stratosphere Ascent*), and the ominous international picture (*Dr. Doom*, *International Spy*, *Faces Death at Dawn*). *Little Annie Rooney and the Orphan House* and *Apple Mary and Dennie Foil the Swindlers* (from the Martha Orr strip later reshaped into Mary Worth) portrayed depression-era poverty with Dickensian pathos, but *Perry Winkle and the Rinkeydinks*, *Kayo in the Land of Sunshine*, *Symphony Featuring Donald Duck*, *Mutt and Jeff*, and *Popeye Sees the Sea* were pure, cloudless fun. Although the source material of most 1930s titles depicted African Americans as subservient and perpetually astonished, the second 1100 series book *Joe Louis, the Brown Bomber*, illustrated with Wide World Press Service photographs, emphasized its subject's triumphs. Within the second 1100 series, the Joe Louis biography and *The Texas Ranger on the Trail of the Dog Town Rustlers* share the same number (1135), another sign of casualness in the publisher's numbering system.

Between 1937 and 1949 Whitman produced six 1400 series, most with distinctive innovations or format adjustments. During the first 1400 series (1937–1938) Whitman rechristened its line "Better Little Books" to minimize consumer confusion of its Big Little Books with Saalfield Publishing Company's Little Big Books, calculatedly similar in name and almost identical in format. Through overprinting, Whitman blacked out the circular logos carrying the "Big Little Book" designations on about a dozen already-prepared titles. These have been termed "transition books" by Larry Lowery, author of an especially useful collectors' guide, who also sees the first 1400 series as the dividing line between the golden age and the silver age in Big Little Book publication. Other noteworthy features of the first 1400 series include movement toward standardizing length (at 432 pages); adaptations of Blondie and Dagwood from the comic page, Gene Autry from Western movies, and Charlie McCarthy, the Gang Busters, and Jack Armstrong from radio; and the addition of Whitman-commissioned or staff-produced titles, several of which were meant for girl readers: *Mary Lee and the Mystery of the Indian Beads* (written and illustrated by Alice Andersen), *Kay Darcy and the Mystery Hideout* (written under the pen name Irene Ray by Margaret Sutton, well known for her Judy Bolton series), and *Peggy Brown and the Runaway Auto Trailer* (authored by Kathryn Heisenfelt and, like a number of other Whitman titles of the period, carrying the distinctive artwork of Henry E. Vallely, a veteran illustrator for Chicago newspapers).

While the second 1400 series (1937–1938) continued the innovations begun in the first, the third (1939–1941) pushed toward a slicker, more "commercial" appearance. The traditional back-cover illustrations, often panoramic extensions of the front covers, were replaced by promotional lists of Big Little Book characters or, on some volumes, by explanations of the new "See 'Em Move" or "Flip it" feature, simulating movie animation through small serial drawings added to the upper right corners of the right-side illustration pages. The third 1400 series also brought the first Big Little Book adaptations of Fred Harman's Red Ryder, done in a dashingly sketchy style, and when Whitman's negotiations for adding Superman to its line failed, the publisher created its own, *Maximo, the Amazing Superman*, with art by Henry E. Vallely and text by Big Little Book veteran Russell R. Winterbotham.

The fourth (1941–1943) and the fifth (1943–1946) 1400 series introduced All Pictures Comics, in which no typeset text was needed because the speech balloons of the adapted comic strips were retained. *Keep 'Em Flying, U.S.A., for America's Defense, Steve Hunter of the U.S. Coast Guard, Ray Land of the Tank Corps, U.S.A., Pilot Pete and His Dive Bomber*, and *Allen Pike of the Parachute Squad, U.S.A.*, all created by the Whitman staff, shared a cover-art style that approximated that of war comic books from the same period. Wartime paper shortages reduced book lengths from 432 pages in the fourth series to 352 in the fifth. In the fifth series the no-reissue policy was relaxed to permit shortened versions of earlier Blondie, Donald Duck, and Mickey Mouse titles. Popular characters introduced in the early to mid-1940s included Roy Rogers and Bugs Bunny.

In the late 1940s, signs of trouble were clear. The sixth 1400 series (1946–1949) saw another length squeeze (to 288 pages) and an increasing emphasis on only the most popular comic book characters. An altered format, projecting a new leanness at slightly more than 3" wide and 5" high, was called a New Better Little Book. In contrast to the exuberant variety seen in the fifty titles of the 1943–1946 fifth 1400 series, the new format, also designated the 700–10 series, yielded only fifteen books featuring Walt Disney, Walter Lantz, and Warner Brothers cartoon characters, the most popular western stars, and one each of Blondie and Tarzan. Single primary colors were added to interior illustrations in a belated attempt to counter the comic book's four-color appeal.

Through most of the 1950s, Big Little Book production was suspended, and Whitman promotional material of that period almost entirely ignored the fact that the company had manufactured and hugely profited from massive numbers of these books. A tentative revival came in 1958 with the release of six titles constituting the medium-sized Big Little Book TV Series: *Wyatt Earp*, Walt Disney's *Andy Burnett on Trial, The Buccaneers, Gunsmoke, The Adventures of Jim Bowie*, and *Sir Lancelot*.

The 2000 series, closer to the traditional Big Little Book dimensions and featuring comic strip as well as television characters, was issued from 1967 to 1969. Illustrations were printed in four colors, and some titles were twice reissued with reprint-distinguishing endpapers.

By the 1970s, the Woolworth stores that had temptingly displayed the original titles had been largely supplanted by suburban K-Mart outlets, and in 1973 the newer chain asked Whitman to produce yet another series, the 5700 group. Called "a BLB Classic," some of these "limpbound" or glued softcover titles were revisions of much earlier titles. The black-and-white books in the series revived the "Flip it" feature, while the remaining titles had four-color illustrations. These books were several times reprinted, their cover prices escalating from twenty-nine to seventy-nine cents. After completing its K-Mart contract, Whitman continued to develop modest numbers of titles, finally releasing a Superman book (in 1980) and mixing old and new favorites: Popeye, the Lone Ranger, Tom and Jerry, the Incredible Hulk, Spiderman, and the Pink Panther.

Always a flexible enterprise, Whitman Publishing Company issued a number of subsidiary series, especially in the mid- to late 1930s. Some were for direct sale in the same stores that stocked "regular" Big Little Books; others were "prizes" to be given away at shoe stores, movie theaters, and gasoline stations. For many of the mid-1930s softcover premiums, Whitman eliminated about one-third of the length of the basic-line originals, and the back covers held Cocomalt, Amoco Gas, or other sponsors' ads. On Tarzan Ice Cream and Buddy Book premiums, the back covers doubled as coupons to be collected to earn further premium books. Contemporary with these were boxed sets called Wee Little Books (1934–1935), published six titles to a set and featuring Mother Goose rhymes, biblical characters, Mickey Mouse, and Little Orphan Annie. Three-to-a-box Top Line Comics sets featured popular comic strip characters, and the fourteen Big Big Books of 1934 to 1938 were essentially enlarged (to 7 ¼" × 9 ½" × 1 ½") Big Little Books featuring Little Orphan Annie, Dick Tracy (two titles), Skippy, Tarzan, Buck Rogers, Mickey Mouse, Popeye, Tom Mix, Buck Jones, and Terry and the Pirates. The Famous "Funnies" Cartoon Books and the nickel-priced Famous Hardbound Cartoon Books of the same years were thinner (sixty-four to sixty-eight pages) variations on the same adapt a comic theme. In 1938 and 1939, Whitman introduced five series of thirty-two-page penny books measuring 2 ½" × 3 ½", ranging from the Famous Comic Strip Story series (Dick Tracy, Smokey Stover, the Texas Ranger, and others) to the Fun Book Series (*Dreams, Hobbies, Learn to Be a Ventriloquist*) and a ten-item Walt Disney Picture Book series. Three Tall Comic Books, more than 8" high, were devoted to Andy Panda, Bugs Bunny, and Mickey Mouse. In short, Whitman Publishing Company, developer of the Big Little Book, stretched the genre to include many types of subjects, lengths, and dimensions.

If Whitman Publishing Company had a dramatic beginning, its chief competitor in the inexpensive juveniles field evolved quietly in the years after Arthur Saalfield purchased the publishing interests of Akron's Werner Manufacturing Company, a major bookbinding firm, in 1899. Passing through three generations of its namesake family, the Saalfield Publishing Company was especially noted for its paper doll and coloring books. In 1934, two years after Whitman had defined the genre with its *The Adventures of Dick Tracy*, Saalfield challenged its Wisconsin competitor by issuing six oblong Little Big Books in both hardcover and softcover bindings. The Saalfield entries featured Popeye, Just Kids, Tim Tyler, Little Annie Rooney, the Katzenjammer Kids, and Krazy Kat, and these were followed in the same year by various-sized adaptations of other comic strips (*Brick Bradford, Polly and Her Pals*), literary classics (*Black Beauty, Tom Sawyer*), and motion pictures (Our Gang comedies, Jackie Cooper in *Peck's Bad Boy*, Laurel and Hardy, Shirley Temple).

The second year of Saalfield's Little Big Book production brought such diverse film adaptations as *The Story of Will Rogers*, Bela Lugosi in *Chandu the Magician*, and Claudette Colbert and Clark Gable in *It Happened One Night*. Boy Scout and sports subseries appeared in 1936 and 1937, yielding such titles as *Tommy of Troop Six*, *The Hockey Spare*, *The Winning Point*, and *Stan Kent, Freshman Fullback*.

By 1938, Saalfield Little Big Books had settled into a shape closely imitative of Whitman's Big Little Books. Although Whitman continued to emphasize licensed comic strip characters, Saalfield's 1938 list was chiefly made up of staff-produced (and often amateurishly drawn) cowboy titles. The same year saw the series title changed to Jumbo Books, but Saalfield continued to use its now established length (400 pages) and dimensions. During the 1938–1940 span of Jumbo Books production, Wild West titles continued to dominate, supplemented by a sprinkling of G-man titles and comic strip characters, including Li'l Abner, Major Hoople of *Our Boarding House*, Abbie an' Slats, and Napoleon and Uncle Elby. After 1940, Saalfied withdrew from the Big Little Book field but continued to produce handsome children's books of other kinds. Its *Peanuts* coloring books were highly successful in the mid-1960s, but the firm folded in the early 1970s.

The Saalfield Little Big Books are potentially confused with the Little Big Books and Little Big Classics published between 1934 and 1939 by McLoughlin Brothers of Springfield, Massachusetts, founded in 1828 and recognized by John Tebbel as the nation's first publisher of children's books. Most of these half dozen titles, however, are for very young children, and the format is more traditional than that of the Saalfield and Whitman books.

Dell Publishing Company and Fawcett Publishing Company are best known for comic books and other types of softbound publications—paperback novels, how-to-do-it books and periodicals, and similar mass market lines—but both firms made brief forays into the Big Little Book market. Recycling stories of Bulletman and Bulletgirl, Captain Marvel, Minute-Man, and Spy Smasher from its *Whiz Comics* and *Master Comics*, Fawcett produced only four of its Dime Action Books, all issued in 1941. The Dime Action title echoes that of Dell's Fast Action series of the late 1930s and early 1940s. Identified by a diamond-shaped cover logo containing the series name, Dell's Fast Action Books were produced by Whitman and featured that company's most popular Big Little Book characters. Fast Action Books, all softbound, were taller than the standard Whitman series. Particularly sought by contemporary collectors is the Fast Action version of Edgar Rice Burroughs' *John Carter of Mars*, with drawings by Alex Raymond, best remembered for his work on the Flash Gordon and Secret Agent X-9 comic strips.

Recalling Whitman's early movie series format, four books spotlighting radio comedians were published in 1934 and 1935 by the Goldsmith Publishing Company, the juveniles imprint of M. A. Donohue and Company. Each sixty-four-page book had a cover photograph of its subject, and the interior drawings preserve early work of Henry Vallely, whose thin, agile line would take on a more mature firmness in later Whitman and Dell Fast Action titles. The Goldsmith stories of Eddie Cantor, of Jack Pearl in his Baron Munchausen persona, of Ed Wynn as the Fire Chief, and of Joe Penner as proprietor of a vaudeville-inspired duck farm incorporated a large amount of fantasy and were aimed at a younger readership than most Whitman and Saalfield books. A foreword to each Goldsmith book proclaimed, "Our ideal—to publish good books for red blooded boys and girls, without any thing in the stories or illustrations which may cause fright, suggest fear, or glorify mischief."

In 1933 and 1934, using the dimensions of Whitman Big Little Books (but generally offering fewer pages), the World Syndicate Publishing Company issued five High Lights of History Series titles: *Buffalo Bill*, *Daniel Boone*, *Kit Carson*, *Pioneers of the Wild West*, and *The Winning of the West*. These were adapted from the 1920s newspaper educational feature of the same series title, written and illustrated by J. Carroll Mansfield. Three books were offered in alternative bindings, apparently on the assumption that cartoony board covers would attract Big Little Book-conditioned young buyers, while the simulated leather covers suggested a more traditional appeal to gift-buying elders.

Another New York-based early Whitman competitor was Engle-Van Wiseman Book Corporation's Five Star Library, published in 1934 and 1935, just as the Big Little Book format was becoming well established. The taller-than-wide Five Star Library books were principally adaptations of feature and B-western films from RKO, Columbia, Universal, Warner Brothers, Monogram, and other studios. Popular child star Jackie Cooper was featured in *Oliver Twist* and *Dinky*, and Mickey Rooney as Puck grinned from the cover of the volume based on Max Reinhardt's 1935 film of *A Midsummer Night's Dream*. Franklin Delano Roosevelt was featured in *The Fighting President*, from a Universal release, while Rex, King of the Wild Horses, dominated the book version of Columbia's *Stampede*. Cowboy star Tim McCoy (in both western and aviation stories), John Wayne, Buck Jones, and Ken Maynard appeared in Five Star Library books, while Katharine Hepburn in *The Little Minister* and Douglas Fairbanks Sr. in *Robin Hood* lent special star quality to the series.

Using a circular logo similar to Whitman's, the Lynn Publishing Company released a series of film and comic strip adaptations in 1935 and 1936. Among the feature films novelized were 20th Century Fox's *Les Miserables*, with Fredric March and Charles Laughton, and *Call of the Wild*, starring Loretta Young and Clark Gable; *Ceiling Zero*, with James Cagney and Pat O'Brien, from Warner Brothers; Paramount's *Trail of the Lonesome Pine*, with Henry Fonda and Fred MacMurray; and, from MGM, Ronald Coleman in *A Tale of Two Cities* and Wallace Beery and Jackie Cooper in *O'Shaughnessy's Boy*. Chic Young's *Blondie and Dagwood* was a four-color offering, unusual for the date, but most of Lynn's comic art titles were adapted from rather obscure strips. Young's brother Lyman was the artist for *Curley Harper at Lakespur*, and another Lynn book, *Donnie and the Pirates*, was Darrell McClure's imitative tribute to Milton Caniff's *Terry and the Pirates*.

If Saalfield, Lynn, the Five Star Library, and others were Whitman Publishing Company's competitors in the early years of Big Little Book-format production, still others have essayed the genre since Whitman returned to the field in the late 1950s. Ottenheimer's book versions of television cartoons, Waldman and Son's Moby Illustrated Classics, several limited-edition titles, and Chronicle Books' recent Mighty Chronicles continue to redefine the genre's scope.

Ottenheimer Publishers of Baltimore, incorporated in 1890, began issuing soft-cover Big Little Book-sized books in 1977. All are stories of the Flintstones, Yogi Bear, and Huckleberry Hound, licensed from Hanna-Barbera Productions. Ottenheimer's Flintstones title *The Mystery of Many Missing Things* is a reworking of *The Case of the Many Missing Things*, published by Whitman in 1968.

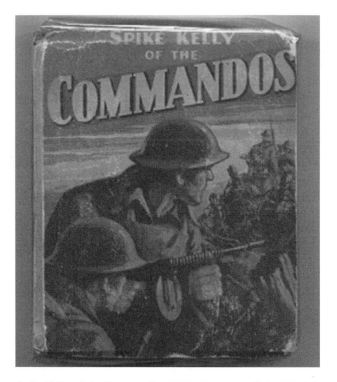

Spike Kelly of the Commandos, 1953. Courtesy of the Library of Congress

Waldman and Son, publisher of a mix of children's materials reminiscent of Saalfield's catalog in earlier years, came to the Big Little Book field in 1977 with its Moby Books, distinguished by a silhouette logo of an apparently cheerful whale. The initial set included condensations of *Heidi*, *A Connecticut Yankee in King Arthur's Court*, *Little Women*, and *Treasure Island*, while *The Merry Adventures of Robin Hood*, *The Count of Monte Cristo*, *Moby Dick*, and two titles each by Charles Dickens and Mark Twain were among the 1979 editions. In 1983 the series was further extended by twelve titles, including Kipling's *Captains Courageous*, Lew Wallace's *Ben-Hur*, Alexandre Dumas' *The Man in the Iron Mask*, H. G. Wells' *The Time Machine* and *The War of the Worlds*, and still more from Dickens and Twain. In contrast to the one-dime price of the 1930s Whitman and softcover Saalfield titles, Moby Books are marked for sale at $1.25.

Less sustained recent forays into the publishing of Big Little Books deserve mention. In 1977 the McDonald's fast-food chain issued *The Wizard of Oz*, *Tom Sawyer*, *Black Beauty*, and *A Christmas Carol* as premiums over a two-month period. Four years later, a Punxsutawney, Pennsylvania, science fiction illustrator, Joe Wehrle Jr., evoked the Big Little Book genre in his privately published *Cauliflower Catnip*, the adventures (with adult overtones) of a feline detective. Andrews and McMeel, a Universal Press Syndicate affiliate, gathered panels from Tom Wilson's newspaper cartoon into *Ziggy's BIG Little Book* in 1983 and *Alphabet Soup Isn't Supposed to Make Sense!—Ziggy's BIG Little Book 2* in 1984. The Big Little Book Collectors Club of America has issued limited-edition volumes celebrating the early Big Little incarnations of Dick Tracy (in forty-eight-page premium book format, 1994) and Tarzan (in the Fast Action format, 1996).

In 1996 San Francisco's lively Chronicle Books offered a set of *Star Wars* adaptations in connection with the theatrical rerelease of the already-classic Lucas film space trilogy. A fraction of an inch shorter and the same width as the standard Whitman Big Little Books of half a century ago, these books were called "Little Chronicles—a brand new series with a nostalgic twist." The series has since metamorphosed into Mighty Chronicles, "the little books with the big punch," 320-page volumes with 150 color-highlighted illustrations facing text pages of eight or fewer lines. Recent titles include *Raiders of the Lost Ark, The Lost World: Jurassic Park, The Mask of Zorro, Xena, Warrior Princess*, and *Terminator 2: Judgment Day*, and more are promised. While most of the early Whitman and Saalfield books in this genre originally sold for a depression dime, the Mighty Chronicles retail for $9.95.

REFERENCE WORKS

Mentioned only incidentally in film encyclopedias and in histories of comic art, Big Little Books are being given detailed consideration in nearly a dozen guides of varying scopes and ambitions. Meant primarily for latter-day collectors, all provide at least general information on the genre's development. Two create numbering systems for keeping track of the hundreds of titles published, and some suggest market values for copies surviving in rough to mint condition. Even the sketchiest of these guides will act as a starting point for the resourceful researcher, and the best of them contains a considerable amount of detail equally useful to the collector and the scholar.

In 1970, Dale Manesis published 300 copies of *Whitman: A Listing of Big Little Books and Related Publications Printed by the Whitman Publishing Company*, a twenty-four-page guide beginning with the caveat that a full list of Whitman titles might be a "near-impossible" achievement, since "it is unlikely that even Whitman has a complete record of all items it published." Manesis first lists Big Little and Better Little Books alphabetically by titles, followed by lists of premiums and their sponsors (if known), Dell Fast Action Books, Big Big Books, nickel and penny books, the Chubby Books for very young readers (omitted by most guides), Wee Little Book sets, Walt Disney Story Books, and partial listings of the Racine publisher's paint books, puzzles, playing cards, coloring sets, and games featuring Big Little Book characters. Having the tentative and apologetic tone of a pioneering effort, the Manesis guide is most useful in its listings, incomplete though they are, of the secondary publications that most later accountings have passed over.

Michael Resnick's 1973 *Official Guide to Comic Books and Big Little Books*, which achieved its second edition in 1977, devotes its last thirty pages to an alphabetical listing of various publishers' Big Little Book titles, preceded by a page-and-a-half overview. The listing comes within a respectable distance of being complete to the date of its publication, but it does not specify publishers, authors, artists, copyright dates, or publishers' numbers. Designation of penny books is inconsistent.

Also in 1973, James Ashton of Ashton Publications in Middleton, Indiana, issued the first of a projected annual series of price guides. The 131-page *Ashton's Big*

Little Book Catalog and Price Guide, 1973 was designed primarily to create "advertising savings" by suggesting a title-and-condition coding system as an alternative to the publishers' own sometimes confusing spine numbers. Identifying authors but not artists, the Ashton guide gives a reasonably full accounting of Whitman and Dell Fast Action, Saalfield, Engle-Van Wiseman Five Star Library, World Syndicate, and Lynn series through the 1960s and adds a brief definition of grading standards, an editorial defense of Big Little Books as the first reading matter of a generation of American children, and short sketches of Whitman's and Saalfield's roles in the field. Illustrated pages from 1930s Whitman and Saalfield wholesale catalogs are usefully reproduced.

Issued in 1981 and still available (from Educational Research Corporation, P.O. Box 1242, Danville, Calif. 94526) is *Lowery's The Collector's Guide to Big Little Books and Similar Books*, in many ways the best of the guides yet published. Larry Lowery's 380-page book divides Big Little Book publication into Golden, Silver, and Modern ages and then, publisher by publisher, gives details on each book cataloged within the publishers' numerical series. Lowery's own numbering system indicates the order of the books' publication, and each of the three major period divisions in his guide begins with a brief account of "The Setting," the historical and social milieu in which the books appeared. Lowery also summarizes each publisher's history and product range.

Each entry in the Lowery guide indicates the year of publication; author, artist, or movie studio providing the material; book size, specified to the fraction of an inch; length; type of binding; and details of cover or length variation. For some comic strip adaptations, the dates of original newspaper publication are given, and for books based on radio programs, the broadcast dates and networks are identified. Almost all entries include thumbnail-sized black-and-white photographs of the book covers, scaled to reflect the cover dimensions of the respective series. The Lowery guide omits only a few recently discovered titles or printing variations, but it has the advantage of being supplemented by a bimonthly newsletter and an Internet Web site, http://www.biglittlebooks.com. (See History and Criticism in this chapter.)

In 1983 James Stuart Thomas' *The Big Little Book Price Guide* appeared in Wallace-Homestead Book Company's collectibles guide series but was soon withdrawn by the publisher in settlement of a copyright infringement suit. Thomas' alphabetized title listings make no distinctions among the seven Whitman Big Little Book series, but he does account for some related series not detailed in other guides, such as the mid-1940s Mystery and Adventure series hardbacks, also known as the Authorized Editions (2300 series).

Robert M. Overstreet, well known for his periodically revised comic book price guides, provided a brief introduction to Big Little Books and an alphabetical titles list in the 1987 edition of his *The Official Overstreet Price Guide Companion*, a pocket-sized book of more than 500 pages, that also lists selected comic book titles and prices, to be updated annually.

Price Guide to Big Little Books and Better Little, Jumbo, Tiny Tales, A Fast-Action Story, etc. was issued by L-W Book Sales in 1995. Clearly meant as a book-spotting guide for visitors to flea markets, antique shops, and yard sales, this book offers half-sized color photographs of vintage Big Little Books from all publishers and a spotty representation of related younger children's books. An unsigned one-page history of the Big Little Book genre is the bulk of this guide's editorial matter.

In 1996 Larry Jacobs issued his *Big Little Books: A Collector's Reference and Value Guide*, intended to be "a thorough review of Whitman books" and saving other publishers' lists for "future writing." Brimming with enthusiasm, Jacobs gives succinct accounts of the publisher's history, the finding, care, and storage of the books, and his own collecting adventures. The alphabetical title listings blend the major 700 and 1100 series together, and the color illustrations are similar to those in the L-W Book Sales *Price Guide*. The Jacobs guide is especially useful for its presentation of Blue Ribbon Pop-Up and Waddle Books, devoted to nursery story, Disney, and comic strip characters.

An even more personal evocation of Big Little and related books (chiefly Whitman's) is film director Bill Borden's *The Big Book of Big Little Books*, written with Steve Posner and published in 1997 by Chronicle Books. Borden, who has had a hand in developing that publisher's Mighty Chronicles titles, makes no claims of scholarly completeness. Rather, through lavishly presented selective illustration and an exuberant text he shares his pleasure in his own collection of about 400 Whitman books in varying conditions. This book is a fine starting point for any latecomer who wonders why Big Little Books have had so strong a hold, then and now, on their enthusiasts.

RESEARCH COLLECTIONS

Since Big Little Books have never been anthologized and, with the exception of a few rewritten (often abbreviated) and redrawn titles in a late revival series, have not been reprinted, the researcher will necessarily seek the 1932–1950 titles in large collections, the fullest of which are generally in the hands of private collectors. However, the Library of Congress and several university and municipal libraries hold sizable numbers. Because of the relatively fragile nature of these books, most libraries forbid circulation and interlibrary borrowing, but some allow photocopying. Some libraries prefer—a few insist—that researchers traveling to their collections give prior notice of their needs.

As a copyright depository collection, the Library of Congress' Rare Books and Special Collections Division holds one of the largest publicly accessible concentrations of Big Little Books: 520 titles, including 328 Whitman, 104 Saalfield, twenty-six Dell, twelve McLoughlin Brothers, eleven Lynn, and thirty-nine others. Big Little Books might also be found in other divisions of the library but have not yet been systematically identified. As is true of many large collections, recent publications in this genre are not included in the Rare Book and Special Collections Division's holdings, inventory lists of which may be consulted in its reading room.

Two university libraries place Big Little Books in the context of children's outstanding literature collections. The Kerlan Collection in the Children's Literature Research Collections at the University of Minnesota's Walter Library, well known for its dime novel holdings, contains a substantial, cataloged Big Little Book inventory, despite the theft of about 200 books in 1997. The Department of Special Collections at the Kenneth Spencer Research Library, the University of Kansas, Lawrence, sees Big Little Books as components of its science fiction holdings and especially of its late eighteenth- to early twentieth-century children's books. The aim here is for "a representative sampling of the genre," not completeness. According to Spencer librarian Alexandra Mason, "Reasonable mail requests for information will be answered." Visitors may access Big Little Books by author and, for most Whitman Big Little Books and Better Little Books, by series. Whitman titles are dominant in the Spencer Library's selection of about 150 Big Little Books from the 1930s and 1940s.

The Popular Culture Library at Bowling Green State University, Bowling Green, Ohio, also holds about 150 Big Little Books, chiefly Whitman books from the 1932–1950 period, although a few later titles appear in the mimeographed inventory list. In recent years the Popular Culture Library has moved increasingly toward a closed-stacks situation to protect its vulnerable materials, but visitors will find that the library's operating hours during the academic year are generous. The interlibrary loan policy allows staff photocopying of chapters or articles only, but, at present, patron photocopying is unrestricted.

Other university libraries contain large to medium-sized collections. Nearly 900 volumes are held by the library of California State University at Fullerton, while the Department of Special Collections in the Shields Library at the University of California at Davis has 230 cataloged Big Little Books, and the Special Collections Department at the Northwestern University, Evanston, Illinois Library, counts 114 volumes: four Saalfield and the remainder Whitman. The latter collection will microfilm any of its volumes at the user's expense. An author-title listing is available in Northwestern's Special Collections Department; these books are not included in the Main Library's cataloging system.

About fifty leading-publisher Big Little Books have been placed, as a representative sampling of the genre, within the renowned Comic Art Collection at Michigan State University in East Lansing. Particularly noteworthy here is the availability of correspondence from Gaylord Du Bois about his career as a Big Little Book and comic book writer. The titles are fully cataloged, and *Comic Art Collection*, a quarterly limited-circulation newsletter from the Russel B. Nye Popular Culture collection, maintains a register of Big Little Book research libraries.

Smaller samplings of Big Little Books may be found in interesting juxtapositions with related material in still other collections. A bequest to the Special Collections/Rare Book Center of the Ft. Lauderdale Public Library in Broward County, Florida, has placed about 400 Big Little Books among other popular culture items. The Archive of Popular Culture at the University of Pittsburgh Library's Special Collections Department has only a handful of titles, but it also owns more than eighty 1920s and 1930s Whitman novels. The Library of Communication and Graphic Art at the Ohio State University in Columbus houses titles based on Milton Caniff's *Terry and the Pirates*, and the Special Collections division holds the Big Little Books related to another celebrated state son, Eddie Rickenbacker. Kent State University's libraries received much of the Saalfield Publishing Company archival material when that firm was dissolved.

Whitman Publishing Company's own file copies were sold to a collector-dealer some time ago, but researchers needing information on the Racine-based company that pioneered the genre will want to consult the library of the State Historical Society of Wisconsin, 816 State Street, Madison 53706. An assiduous gatherer of materials related to all kinds of Wisconsin interests, this institution has brought

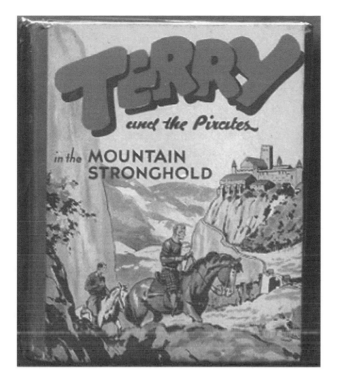

Terry and the Pirates, 1941. Courtesy of the Library of Congress

together (and made available in hard copy or on microfilm) numerous Whitman promotional brochures, catalogs, and several in-house company histories. The Big Little Times periodical has also been microfilmed by the State Historical Society of Wisconsin. All materials are carefully cataloged.

In Canada, Doug Kendig maintains the Comic Research Library at Tappen, B.C. V0E 2X0. Mainly a gathering of comic strips and related memorabilia, the Comic Research Library does hold 380 Big Little Books, which may be seen by appointment. Reference questions sent by mail are cheerfully handled.

HISTORY AND CRITICISM

Very little formal academic criticism on Big Little Books has been attempted. In two chapters of his *G-Men: Hoover's FBI in American Popular Culture*, Richard Gid Powers has shown how the crime titles illustrate a once-obscure Washington agency's expanding influence: "The Comic Strip G-Man" documents J. Edgar Hoover's negative reaction to *Secret Agent X-9*, which was adapted into two Big Little Books, while the later chapter "The Junior G-Men" draws illustrative details from the Whitman books *Junior G-Men and the Counterfeiters* and *G-Man on the Crime Trail*. A more general approach may be found in Francis J. Molson's *Journal of Popular Culture* article "Films, Funnies and Fighting the War: Whitman's Children's Books in the 1940s," which lists Big Little Books characters and titles but provides few details on the genre per se.

The *Big Little Times*, a bimonthly publication for members of the Big Little Book Collectors Club of America, was begun by John Stallknecht in 1982 as a continuing supplement to *Lowery's The Collector's Guide to Big Little Books and Similar Books*. Early issues were made up of quizzes, question-and-answer pages, collectors' letters, and lists of titles and characters. Larry Lowery, serving as editor since the beginning of volume 2, has brought an increasing variety of content and a degree of graphic polish to this newsletter. Each issue spotlights one or more characters adapted to, or created for, Big Little Books. The films, radio series, cereal premiums, and other media featuring these characters are detailed, background on artists and writers is given, and each such article ends with a full bibliographic description of all the titles and related series in which the character under consideration appears. The *Big Little Times* also reprints newspaper clippings and magazine articles, chiefly from hobbyists' periodicals, about Big Little Books and their collectors, and it has treated such subjects as Big Little Book editorial bloopers, printing and binding errors, trademarks, copyrights, newly discovered length and cover variations, foreign editions, intended reading levels, and the care and storage of these books. This bimonthly's ads give a good sense of the availability or rarity of particular titles in the collectors' market. Subscriptions ($12.00 per year) and back issues are available through the Big Little Book Collectors Club of America, P.O. Box 1242, Danville, Calif. 94526. The organization's Web site, maintained by editor Larry Lowery and providing links to other sites, may be found at http://www.biglittlebooks.com.

If the study of Big Little Books has been more fully a collector's preoccupation than an academic interest, writers of popular period histories and memorabilia "catalogs" have found them richly evocative, especially of depression-era childhood. In the 1930–1940 volume of the Time-Life series *This Fabulous Century*, the "Dream Factory" chapter recalls them as "squat, 400-page cubes of type and pictures," and one spread places five Flash Gordon Big Little Books beside an example of Alex Raymond's Sunday newspaper page and a Flash Gordon movie serial still. In *The Great American Depression Book of Fun*, John O'Dell puts these books in the context of the "toys, games, and high adventures" of the period, and five books jointly written by Robert Heide and John Gilman make much of Big Little Books as period artifacts. In their *Dime-Store Dream Parade: Popular Culture 1923–1955*, they boldly assert, "Few things represent the 'feel' of the 1930s more than a Big Little Book," and this statement is repeated in a later collaboration, *Starstruck: The Wonderful World of Movie Memorabilia*, which also contains a "Hollywood Big Little Books" subsection. In their *Cartoon Collectibles*, focused on every type of Disney item, Big Little Books are seen as "a child's first introduction to the novel form," while their *Cowboy Collectibles* and *Home Front America: Popular Culture of the World War II Era* include appropriate examples from the genre.

The Big Little Book has had its critics—and not necessarily published ones. For young readers the story illusion was sometimes shattered when the illustrations lost synchronization with the text, one racing pages ahead of the other. Sometimes the preordained page count ran out before the plotline did, creating a huddled or a very abrupt ending, as in *Chester Gump at Silver Creek Ranch*, where Chester and a friend are left "trying to get out of the cavern to safety," with only a vague suggestion of their escape, which is "another story." The original comic strip panels, too, were subjected to procrustean stretching and trimming, with speech balloons being replaced by crosshatching or architectural doodling.

Despite some compromises in handling their source material, Big Little Books served as agents of imagination and even as definers of experience, as relatively recent novels and autobiographies have shown. For instance, in *World's Fair*, his novel of late-1930s New York City boyhood, E. L. Doctorow uses the newsstand purchase of a Flash Gordon Big Little Book as a crystallizing detail in the young protagonist's perception of "New York and its excitements." In *Growing Up*, a Pulitzer Prize-winning evocation of small-town depression childhood, Russell Baker remembers his sources of delight: "My idea of a perfect afternoon was lying in front of the radio rereading my favorite Big Little Book, *Dick Tracy Meets Stooge Viller*." Baker also recalls with characteristic irony that the uncommitted profits of his *Saturday Evening Post* sales were "mine to squander on vices of my choice, which were movies, Big Little Books, and two-for-a-penny Mary Jane bars." Likewise, the illustrator Maurice Sendak, quoted in Selma G. Lanes' survey of his artwork, has remembered the vivid impression that a Big Little Book made on him: "I must have been five or six years old, and in the next apartment lived a girl my age who had marvelous books, like the Big Little Book of *David Copperfield*, with photographs of Freddie Bartholomew in it. That's who I thought David Copperfield was for a very long time."

BIBLIOGRAPHY

Books and Articles

Ashton, James F. *Ashton's Big Little Book Catalog and Price Guide, 1973*. Middleton, Ind.: Ashton, 1973.

Baker, Russell. *Growing Up*. New York: Congdon and Weed, 1982.

Borden, Bill, with Steve Posner. *The Big Book of Big Little Books*. San Francisco: Chronicle Books, 1997.

Doctorow, E. L. *World's Fair: A Novel*. New York: Random House, 1985.

"Fiftieth Anniversary Observed by Saalfield." *Publishers Weekly* 157 (March 11, 1950), 1350–51.

Heide, Robert, and John Gilman. *Cartoon Collectibles: Fifty Years of Dime-Store Memorabilia*. Garden City, N.Y.: Doubleday, 1983.

———. *Cowboy Collectibles*. New York: Harper and Row, 1982.

———. *Dime-Store Dream Parade: Popular Culture 1925–1955*. New York: E. P. Dutton, 1979.

———. *Home Front America: Popular Culture of the World War II Era*. San Francisco: Chronicle Books, 1995.

———. *Starstruck: The Wonderful World of Movie Memorabilia*. Garden City, N.Y.: Doubleday, 1986.

Jacobs, Larry. *Big Little Books: A Collector's Reference and Value Guide*. Paducah, Ky.: Collector Books, 1996.

Kaiser, John W. "The History of Big Little Books." *Big Little Times* 4 (September–October 1985), 9–10.

Knapp, Ed. "Big Little Books." *Rarities* 4 (May–June 1983), 50–57.

Lanes, Selma G. The *Art of Maurice Sendak*. New York: Harry N. Abrams, 1980.

Longest, David. *Character Toys and Collectibles*. Paducah, Ky.: Collector Books, 1984.

Lowery, Larry. *Lowery's The Collector's Guide to Big Little Books and Similar Books*. Danville, Calif.: Educational Research and Applications, 1981.

Madison, Charles Allen. *Book Publishing in America*. New York: McGraw-Hill, 1966.

Manesis, Dale. *Whitman: A Listing of Big Little Books and Related Publications Printed by the Whitman Publishing Company*. Milwaukee: Dale Manesis, 1970.

Molson, Francis J. "Films, Funnies and Fighting the War: Whitman's Children's Books in the 1940s." *Journal of Popular Culture* 17 (Spring 1984), 147–54.

Mussey, Virginia Howell. "Books—Five Cents, Ten Cents and Up." *Publishers Weekly* 134 (October 1, 1938), 1280–83.

Nuhn, Roy. "Big Little Books: Giant Action in Tiny Packages." *Collectors' Showcase* 2 (February 1983), 38–42.

"Obituary Notes: Samuel T. Lowe." *Publishers Weekly* 161 (February 23, 1952), 999.

O'Dell, John. The *Great American Depression Book of Fun*. New York: Harper and Row, 1981.

Overstreet, Robert M. *The Official Overstreet Price Guide Companion*. New York: Ballantine, 1987.

Powers, Richard Gid. *G-Men: Hoover's FBI in American Popular Culture*. Carbondale: Southern Illinois University Press, 1983.

Price Guide to Big Little Books and Better Little, Jumbo, Tiny Tales, A Fast-Action Story, etc. Gas City, Ind.: L-W Book Sales, 1995.

Resnick, Michael. *Official Guide to Comic Books and Big Little Books*. 2nd ed. Florence, Ala.: House of Collectibles, 1977.

"Samuel Lowe Organizes Firm to Issue Cheap Books." *Publishers Weekly* 138 (November 16, 1940), 1905.

The Story of Western, 1907–1965: Fifty-Eight Years of Progress in the Graphic Arts. Racine, Wis.: Western, [1965].

Tebbel, John William. *A History of Book Publishing in the United States*. 4 vols. New York: R. R. Bowker, 1978.

Thomas, James Stuart. *The Big Little Book Price Guide*. Des Moines, Iowa: Wallace-Homestead, 1983.

———. "Open Letter: Price Guide Claims Are Disputed." *Comics Buyer's Guide*, no. 647 (April 11, 1986), 48.

Time-Life editors. *This Fabulous Century*. 6 vols. New York: Time-Life Books, 1969.

Western Ways—Products and Practices of the Western Publishing Company. [Kenosha, Wis. (?)]: Western, [1962 (?)].

Periodicals

Big Little Times. Danville, Calif., 1982– .

Comics Buyer's Guide. Iola, Wis., 1970– .

BUSINESS

David A. Brat and Richard F. Welch

The relation between business and popular culture is something of a paradox. On the one hand, all of life is related to business. Business produces most every part and parcel of the popular culture that we study, from jazz bands, to vaudeville, to theater, to amusement parks, to modern film. Is it essential that we understand this productive aspect of business? Will it inform our understanding of society as seen through popular culture? M. Thomas Inge has noted that we should study popular culture because "there is no more revealing index to the total character and nature of a society than an examination of its popular arts and the way it spends its leisure time."[1] Business in large part provides the context and wherewithal for the leisure time that we enjoy.

On the other hand, business is not leisure and business is not play. Is it popular culture? This is the paradox. As Norman F. Cantor and Michael S. Werthman have put it, "The rules which regulate the games people play differ from those prescribed for most human activities inasmuch as a man may choose to play. . . . These choices are not open in the larger, more public game of life that depends on political and economic compulsion [i.e., business]. The quality of volition therefore informs the whole history of popular culture."[2]

It appears that this "quality of volition" is one criterion that helps in distinguishing between business proper and the business of popular culture. Thus, many topics in business may be considered popular culture.

The literature on business and popular culture reflects this same tension. The literature captures many aspects of business culture, concerning "the way" that we conduct business, "the way" that we choose to produce, "the way" that we choose to advertise and promote our work, "the way" that we choose to legitimize business itself through various ideas and systems of thought. The way that we choose to pursue these aspects of business is informed by the "quality of volition," which informs and is informed by popular culture.

At the same time, there is little in the current popular literature on business itself. This makes sense. The literature focuses on "the way" we conduct business, not the conduct of business itself. In addition, the literature to this date has not reflected on itself yet through literature reviews or summary statements concerning business and popular culture. In this sense, this chapter is unusual.

A decade has passed since the last entry on business and popular culture in this volume. The field has exploded. Every imaginable aspect of business has been covered in the popular culture literature. However, very few reference works exist at present to direct readers and researchers to this mass of work. Richard Welch provided a fine history and summary of the standard business literature in the 1989 entry, and it follows directly. The present entry complements this work by providing an instruction manual that points the reader to new avenues for investigating business and popular culture that did not exist at the last writing. This brief entry is not meant to be exhaustive in any sense, but we do believe that it will open the appropriate doors for the initial investigation of business and popular culture.

In the interest of efficiency, we begin this brief introduction with the immediate links of interest and then extend the chapter into a historic outline, reference works, research collections, history and criticism, and bibliography.

The easiest way to gain broad exposure to the field at minimal cost is to browse the Web. Two sites merit special mention as they provide launching pads for a vast amount of related information. This information includes libraries, bibliographies, and leading scholars in the field, as well as articles, books, and book reviews, all of which are related to business and popular culture and are at your immediate command through these links. As the Web links may change over the years, the formal links have been placed in footnotes. The institutions represented are found in the text.

The first is the combined Popular Culture Association (PCA) and American Culture Association (ACA) Web page.[3] Both of these organizations are interdisciplinary in nature and welcome all disciplines and scholars. When you join, you receive the *Journal of Popular Culture* or the *Journal of American Culture*. This page provides links to history sites, discussion groups, Web pages for other associations, book reviews, national meetings, and many other relevant resources.

Two examples of material available through the PCA/ACA Web page provides an idea of the scope of information available at such sites. The first is the Chorba/Lane Report for the *New York Times* book reviews on popular culture and American culture topics. The purpose of these reports is to broadcast basic information concerning books relevant to the study of popular culture and American culture, books that might be reviewed for H-PCAACA (http://www2.h-net.msu.edu/~pcaaca/), the home page of the PCA and ACA (and then published in the *Journal of Popular Culture* and the *Journal of American Culture*). The second example is the King Report, which includes books of interest to the PCA/ACA members in the *Chronicle of Higher Education*.

The second major Web page of interest to popular culture researchers is that of the Department of Popular Culture at Bowling Green State University.[4] This department has been a leader in the scholarly movement to investigate popular culture since its inception in 1973. Dr. Ray Browne's early efforts in the Department of English led in 1973 to the establishment of the Department of Popular Culture as an M.A. program, followed by the establishment of the undergraduate

Businessman working on laptop computer. © Skjold
Photographs

major a year later. Previously, in 1967, Browne had founded the *Journal of Popular Culture*; and in 1969 he founded the scholarly association for the study of popular culture, the PCA, which has been headquartered since its inception at Bowling Green State University. This Web site provides links to the Departmental Mission Statement, Faculty Biographies, the Center for Popular Culture Studies, Undergraduate Studies in Popular Culture, Graduate Studies in Popular Culture, and Research Resources.

While the explosion in electronic information sources since 1980 has drastically changed the research landscape, a historical sense of where this field comes from and the sources that have informed our modern perceptions of popular culture remain important. In that spirit, a short introduction is useful.

When you awoke this morning, you probably stumbled from bed, showered, rummaged through your closet looking for adequate clothes, wandered into the kitchen, and, glancing at the clock, decided if time allowed for a hearty breakfast or just a cup of coffee. All these activities and almost every other activity in our society are influenced by—and in many cases are dictated by—business. What we do first in the morning, what we wear, what we listen to and/or read, even what we plan to eat for lunch are controlled in large part by the business at which we labor. Of all the cultural institutions that affect our lives, none seems to be as all-pervasive, as all-encompassing as business.

Among its numerous accomplishments, business has established and controls our monetary system—our money is based on the needs of business to monitor the flow of goods. It has created our national obsession with time—our idea of "weekend" would not exist without the workweek; and our news organizations set their schedules to accommodate business' time clocks. Business dictates who is a productive member of society and who is not and sets the standards for what the culture expects of a "productive" lifestyle. Business influences fashion, mass media, food consumption, science, and even religion.

Business has provided popular artists with fodder for a variety of artifacts—literature like Sinclair Lewis' Zenith Trilogy, plays like *How to Succeed in Business without Really Trying* and *Stop the World, I Want to Get Off*, films like *Citizen Kane* and *Baby Boom*, songs like "Allentown" and "Sixteen Tons," and even sports teams like the Pittsburgh Steelers and the Green Bay Packers.

Nowhere has the influence of business been as pronounced as on our political and governmental institutions. One only needs to examine the federal executive branch to see the influence of business. We have a secretary of labor, a secretary of transportation, a Securities and Exchange Commission, a Federal Communication Commission, a Federal Trade Commission, an Internal Revenue Service, and countless other agencies—all directed at monitoring and controlling business.

In politics, we have reached an age when political divisions are influenced less by social, religious, or regional differences than by the type of work that one does. Obviously, this political concept is not new. What is new is that the class structure created by business is not defined by economics but by lifestyle. This development has reached its fulfillment in the young, upwardly mobile individuals who have flourished in the high-pressure worlds of finance, marketing, and high-tech industry. These Yuppies are not "capitalists" in a traditional Marxist sense of the word. Where traditional capitalists designed transgenerational empires, the new capitalists create businesses that are nothing more than commodities to be sold as soon as the price is right. This "get rich now" atmosphere prevalent in the business world has carried over into "Yuppie" politics. This lifestyle revolution has created a politically conservative, but dishearteningly disinterested, pool of future business leaders who look to political leaders equally attuned to the here and now.

Trying to focus on the concept "business" clearly and concisely has been an endeavor that has taxed many historians for many centuries. Samuel Johnson's 1755 *Dictionary of the English Language*, for instance, gives nine definitions for business—from "employment; multiplicity of affairs," to "To do one's business," "To kill, destroy or ruin him." By the time we arrive at the modern *Oxford English Dictionary*, we find several pages devoted to "business."

There are four ways that the popular culture researchers commonly view business: as a standardizing mechanism for society, as a formal context for personal interaction, as a cultural institution, and as a ritual. These last two have gained prominence in the last four decades, when "doing business" has come to mean more than buying and selling commodities; now it stands for a pattern of living and a cultural institution. Each view has its own lexicon and direction. Fortunately, a wealth of documentation offers access to the field in general no matter which view the researcher might care to address.

HISTORICAL OUTLINE

History suggests that America was founded not on religious, cultural, militaristic, or geocentric grounds but on the basic drive for unimpeded free enterprise. No one can deny the influence of business on the Puritan settlers, whose blend of Christianity and business ethic set a standard that continues in full force today.

Some of the earliest historical documents tell of business transactions: agrarian barter; stone, iron, and bronze manufacture; moneylending; and the buying and selling of the necessities and amenities of life. Modern American business institutions, however, are rooted most directly in the aggressive entrepreneurial fervor of seventeenth-century Europe and the Industrial Revolution of eighteenth-century England.

From the time of Columbus, those who braved the dangers of crossing the Atlantic in wooden ships had, somewhere in their motivation, the desire to make their fortune in the New World. Even the Puritans, escaping the religious persecution of seventeenth-century England, had pragmatism intermingled with their religious fervor. The Robert Keayne case of 1639 clearly demonstrated that Puritanism had as much stock in assuring that business progressed smoothly as it did in enforcing a stringent adherence to the Bible. Keayne was censured by the civil authorities in Boston for inappropriate pricing practices. But his case also prompted John Cotton, a Puritan clergyman, to lay down rules of good business practice from the pulpit. These rules included not selling above current market price and not overcharging to compensate for losses incurred in the course of business. Cotton also proposed that the good Christian kept the faith if he or she worked at some acceptable livelihood—a philosophy that has evolved over the last three centuries into our Protestant work ethic. This concept surfaced again in 1657 in England through the writing of Richard Baxter, a Puritan preacher who noted that the good Christian would attend to his or her business responsibilities diligently when not in the service of God.

Even as America suffered through its birth pains, commerce continued unabated. The colonists were now free, and the vast agricultural properties of the South and the mills of the North that processed southern cotton turned many of the former rebels into a moneyed upper class. The new Americans, however, did not take advantage of the unlimited resources, wide-open market, and growing workforce to create an indigenous industrial base. The flow of goods from England and Europe satisfied most of the needs of Americans, and local manufacturing was left to produce only those household items too marginal in profit to be imported.

As war loomed in Europe at the end of the eighteenth century, and the flow of imported goods began to dwindle, Americans sought alternatives to importation. In 1790, Samuel Slater, an English apprentice, defied strict laws against the export of English technology and arrived in America with the plans for steam-driven cloth machinery in his head. He put his knowledge to work in the northern mills and revolutionized cloth production. At the same time, Eli Whitney, whose cotton gin was facilitating higher yields from southern plantations, was setting up a mass-production plant in 1798 for the manufacture of muskets eventually used to arm the American army in 1812. His innovative production technique—making inter-

Chinese men at work on the Central Pacific Railroad, 1877. Courtesy of the Library of Congress

changeable parts en masse—was adapted to numerous other products and sparked American business' interest in greater manufacturing self-sufficiency.

In 1825, English inventors put Watt's steam engine on wheels, and the Industrial Revolution became mobilized. Railroads arrived in America just as the heavily populated eastern seaboard was struggling to support its masses. With the newfound mobility, businesses could expand as far as tracks could be laid. The federal government, which at this point had little to offer the state-dominated society, took the lead in the expansionist drive to open the West. It undertook the development of major transportation systems, interconnecting roads, canals, and rail lines that not only afforded access to the West but generated the need for a new form of management once the systems fell into private hands—one that could deal with a more technologically intensive industry spread over great distances.

Matching the physical expansion of American business, equally radical changes were taking place in the way that business was being conducted. William Mitchell wrote the first American text on accounting in 1796, revolutionizing the system that had been mired in ponderous English business practices. A trade boom between 1790 and 1808 caused by wars in Europe moved American merchants to the forefront of world trade, greatly expanding American shipping fleets and the attendant shipbuilding industries. With the infusion of working capital generated by this new trade, a sophisticated banking system quickly evolved that helped to pass this cash flow on to other sectors of the economy.

As industry and trade blossomed—and the western expansion opened new sources of raw materials and new population centers—the country became factionalized along lines of business specialization. The South, founded on its agricultural might, continued to develop its agrarian control; the North pushed ahead with its industrial specialization; and the West looked to mining and oil. The rapid expansion and overextension of the early 1800s, as well as the creation of large, diversified corporations consuming enormous amounts of capital, led to depressed markets and a stock market crash in 1857. This depression was just one of a series of financial crises that rocked the country from 1830 through the end of the century, causing bank closures and stock runs and leading to the passage of protectionist laws in many states, laws that worked to isolate the South and led to rebellion.

Just as the Civil War caused a major shift in the social structure of the country, it sparked increased industrialization and capitalization in the North. The fortunes made during the war were put to use extending the American frontier to California. By 1890 two-thirds of the American population lived outside the northeastern corridor and was growing at a rate twice as rapidly as Europe.

Although America was experiencing a population boom, there were still plenty of work and land that beckoned the impoverished peoples in Ireland, Italy, and Eastern Europe who flocked to the "promised land." Although their lot in America may have been better than the lives that many had left, the "promise" of America was not exactly as promised. As Thomas Griffin notes in his *Waist-High Culture*:

> [In contrast to] Emma Lazarus' moving welcome inscribed on the Statue of Liberty . . . [America] did not want Europe's aged and sick; it wanted Europe's strong and willing arms. Come and pitch in—the work won't be pleasant at first because ditches must be dug, railroad tracks laid, coal mined and steel molded; the hours will be long and the cities congested. You may know nothing better than this all your lives, because you started late and your tongue is incomprehensible and you stink of garlic, but everything will be open to your children.[5]

With the influx of European labor on the East Coast and Chinese labor on the West Coast, industry prospered, absorbing the new Americans as rapidly as they disembarked. Many of these new workers had been witness to the infant labor movements rocking Europe, and they soon began to stir up unrest over the deplorable conditions in which they were forced to work. As the country moved into the twentieth century, the federal government, which had remained silent during business' expansionist period, was forced to confront the social misdeeds being committed in the name of free enterprise. Not only did the government attempt to better the lot of the working class through a range of legislation from child labor laws to wage controls, but it took steps to ensure that the growing corporate institution did not develop into an oligarchy. In a major reversal of policy, the federal government passed the Sherman Anti-Trust Act in 1890, which limited the untethered growth of big business by outlawing price and market fixing. In

1914, the Federal Trade Commission was created to give greater regulatory powers to the central government.

World War I not only gave American business a much needed economic boost but demonstrated the power that could be unleashed by industry in a war effort. The war also generated greater concern for the needs of the individual, and by 1924, more than 1.5 million workers were represented by company-sanctioned worker organizations inside companies, although unions as such were still having difficulty making inroads because of strong industry resistance.

Although the future looked rosy for American business after World War I, there were storm clouds on the horizon. The single most devastating blow to American business was the Great Depression in the 1930s. Fomented by overextended banks, runaway speculation, and a tax structure that encouraged savings and discouraged investment, the depression demonstrated how fragile an economic structure had been created by a business institution left relatively unimpeded by government.

After that fateful day in October 1929 when the stock market collapsed—with the resultant crumbling market and industrial systems—the federal government finally finished the job begun in 1890. It took control of the economy and established a structure that would prevent such catastrophes in the future through a series of legislative moves that put a halt to untethered business. The Securities and Exchange Act of 1934 severely restricted the methods by which stock was traded and required businesses selling stock to publish annual financial statements for public scrutiny. The Banking Act of 1935 gave greater powers to the Federal Reserve Board in monitoring the national cash flow, including control over interest rates. The Social Security Act of 1935 set up a national system for unemployment insurance. The Wagner Act of 1935 established the National Labor Relations Board and opened industry to unimpeded unionization.

When the country entered World War II, the economy was well on its way to full recovery. Business and government had established a not-always-comfortable partnership in running the country's business. War once more showed how American industry could rise to the occasion as the nation's industrial might mobilized to meet the challenge of global warfare. During the war, technologies flourished, as did innovative manufacturing systems. When the war ended, America was well prepared to turn these new skills to peacetime production.

From World War II to the present, American business has once more become the nation's dominant institution. The relationship between business and government continues to be adversarial on a number of battlefields, but the regulators seem less strident and businesses more sophisticated in managing their relationship. Four major themes now dominate business: social consciousness, information orientation, merger motivation, and internationalism.

Companies today have come to realize that it is not enough to market a product; they must be good neighbors, caring as much about the environment, the growth of the nation, and the safety of their customers as they do about sales, quotas, and territories.

America has passed through the industrial age into the information age, with factories fully automated and all but the simplest jobs requiring some involvement with computers. In the next twenty years, half of all jobs in America will involve communication in some form as the need to control and disseminate information becomes a major function of business.

As the cost of doing business rises, many corporations have turned to the merger as a means of spreading the risks. At first, merger mania was confined to a few specialized industries such as steel and oil, usually involving major competitors buying out smaller companies. In today's world of mergers, however, there is greater emphasis on diversification—spreading the financial risks over a number of product lines to avoid a downturn in one market that could sink a specialized corporation.

Merger mania has helped develop the final trend of modern business—that of creating corporations that extend beyond the borders of their home country. The differences in international wage structures, particularly in the Third World, have made cheap labor readily available to foreign companies. This development, in turn, has lowered the cost of goods to a point where these same Third World countries have become viable markets for American goods. To accommodate this ever-expanding consumer world, corporations have extended themselves around the globe, and these corporations are quickly, but quietly, disrupting the age-old image of "nation." To whom does an American working for a Japanese construction company under the direction of a Swiss architect in the Egyptian desert owe his or her allegiance?

American business will likely lead the world into the future, but American business institutions will not be the same as those envisioned by the Puritans in seventeenth-century New England, the colonial traders of the eighteenth century, the railroad barons of the nineteenth century, or the predepression financial tycoons. The future business institutions in America will envelop many nations and many people doing many different things for many different purposes.

REFERENCE WORKS

With a topic as broad as business, identifying the pertinent reference sources can be problematic. However, certain key documents can give researchers entry points into the institutional structure of business. The obvious starting point is the dictionaries that provide us with the lingua franca of business. For a precise guide to businesses, Jerry Rosenberg's *Dictionary of Business and Management* offers short, concise definitions for more than 8,000 business terms. A more esoteric (and historical) view of business terms can be found in the 1804 edition of *A Commercial Dictionary Containing the Present State of Mercantile Law, Practice and Custom*, compiled by Joshua Montefiore. This book gives a fascinating insight into the business environment of the eighteenth century, including business geography. Other business dictionaries of note are Albert Giordano's *Concise Dictionary of Business Terminology*, J. Harold Janis's *Modern Business Language and Usage in Dictionary Form*, and Michael Rice's *Prentice-Hall Dictionary of Business, Finance and Law*. For more in-depth discussions of specific business terms, the three-volume *Encyclopedia of American Economic History: Studies of the Principal Movements and Ideas*, edited by Glenn Porter, offers detailed entries.

Although not exclusively American, another important primer for the business researcher is *The World of Business* by Edward C. Bursk and others from the Harvard Business School. It has synthesized the literature of business from Hammurabi to the twentieth century. Its introduction also provides an excellent overview of business in its broadest applications. Also of note is Michael Lavin's *Business*

Information: How to Find It, How to Use It. Not only does it provide sources for information about individual companies, statistical data, and special topics, but it explains how to read these sources and how to set up searches for specific information. A good companion work is *Business and Economics Books 1876–1983*, which indexes more than 143,000 titles by subject, author, and title.

For earlier works on business and economics, *The Economic History of the United States prior to 1860*, edited by Thomas Orsagh, and *Guide to Business History* by Henrietta Larson contain bibliographic data back to the 1600s. Both are divided by specific economic topics.

When seeking information concerning specific U.S. companies, the best sources are *Standard and Poor's Register of Corporations, Directors and Executives* and Dun and Bradstreet's *Million Dollar Directory*. Standard and Poor's, in three volumes, lists 45,000 corporations; each entry includes top management, gross revenue figures, number of employees, and a brief description of the company's business. The listing also notes if the company is a subsidiary and its board of directors if publicly held. Volume 2 focuses on individual business people, noting their corporate positions and any directorships that they might hold.

The *Million Dollar Directory* catalogs 160,000 businesses with net worth over $500,000. The alphabetical listings include sales and number of employees, Standard Industrial Classification codes, and top managers. A supplementary directory lists the "Top 50,000 Companies," whose net worth averages $1.8 million. Also included are cross-reference sections by geography and industrial classification.

Standard and Poor's also publishes its *Industry Surveys*, which provide statistical and marketing information for specific industries. The basic analysis sections are supplemented during the year with current analyses that provide more timely reports on activities within that industry. Any particular analysis begins with a narrative of activities for the past year that covers marketing, regulatory, and economic factors that have had an impact on the industry. Each section has numerous graphs and charts drawn from government and private sources.

Innumerable reference books focus on specific aspects of business institutions. Two that are particularly interesting are Gary M. Fink's *Labor Unions* and *Professional Dissent: An Annotated Bibliography and Resource Guide* by James S. Bowman and others. *Labor Unions* contains sketches of more than 200 unions, including where and when they were founded as well as significant events in their development. *Professional Dissent*, although not exclusively focused on business, cites articles and books drawn from what the authors call the "Age of the Whistle-Blower." Citations include works about dissent in business, government, science, and the professions, as well as citations on laws and court cases concerning internal dissent.

For information concerning individuals in business, one of the most complete sources is Marquis' *Who's Who in Finance and Industry*, which contains comprehensive biographical data on approximately 18,000 business executives. These leaders have been chosen more for their influence on the business community than for their income or position. The biographies include work résumé, family, club membership, and political affiliation.

Other reference works of note are *Business Periodicals Index, Predicast F & S Index, Where to Find Business Information: A Worldwide Guide for Everyone Who Needs Answers to Business Questions* by David M. Brownstone and Gordon Carruth, *Busi-*

ness Information Sources by Lorna M. Daniells, *The Encyclopedia of Business Information Sources, Ward's Directory of 51,000 Largest U.S. Corporations*, and *Who Owns Whom*.

Along with reference books, business is well represented in nationally accessible databases, many of which are now available on the World Wide Web. Though most of these are commercial, proprietary services, many government-sponsored databases are now freely accessible on the Web, including EDGAR, a database of Securities and Exchange Commission filings, and census and tax information hosted by the Census Bureau and the U.S. Treasury, respectively. STAT-USA Internet, a commercial service of the Department of Commerce, provides U.S. business and economic information, including access to the National Trade Database Bank (NTDB). Other commercial business databases include the Gale Group's (formerly, Information Access Corporation's) General Business File ASAP, for research on business and management topics as well as information on over 100,000 companies, and their Business Index ASAP, for articles on all aspects of business. Business Periodicals Index is now available on-line as Wilson Business Abstracts, and this and several other business databases are available through OLC's FirstSearch service. ABI/INFORM Global provides extensive coverage of business and management topics, and Lexis-Nexis's ACADEMIC UNIVERSE provides on-line access to full-text news, business, and legal information.

RESEARCH COLLECTIONS

Public, collegiate, and private business libraries around the country offer extensive collections of works exclusively on business. Stanford University's Graduate School of Business houses more than 430,515 volumes, 180,891 corporate reports, and 2,096 periodical subscriptions. Columbia University's Thomas J. Watson Library of Business and Economics houses 350,000 volumes with business documents and materials dating from 1821. Cleveland Public Library's Business, Economics, and Labor Department houses 111,440 volumes with extensive information concerning Cleveland-area businesses. The University of Pennsylvania's Lippincott Library of the Wharton School houses 231,772 volumes.

Pertinent business collections on microfilm (all from UMI Research Collections) include *American Association for Labor Legislation [AALL], 1905–1943*, which has collected the correspondence, organizational papers, and research materials of the AALL. *American Labor Unions: Constitutions and Proceedings 1836–1982* contains the constitutions, reports, and debates of 250 active and inactive U.S. labor unions; a companion collection is *American Labor Union: Officer Reports*. Also available are the collected correspondence and writings of Eugene V. Debs, labor activist and leader of the Socialist Party in America. At the opposite end of the spectrum are the collected papers of Collis P. Huntington (1856–1901), the founder of the Central Pacific Railroad Company, the Southern Pacific Railroad Company, and the California Republican Party. The writings of John Mitchell, an early force behind the United Mine Workers Union, have been collected and include correspondence, union minutes, and eighty-three photographs of Mitchell and the union.

HISTORY AND CRITICISM

American business, as has been pointed out, started slowly. Those interested in writing about the theories underlying economics in the seventeenth and eighteenth centuries were in Britain; consequently, there are few truly American sources of business writing prior to 1750. America formulated its economic structure on the works of John Mill and Adam Smith, and Smith's *Wealth of Nations* was, during our early history, the primary guide for our economic development.

Some early works that bear mention, however, include two pamphlets, written in 1767 and 1786, that address the state of America's economy. The first, *The Commercial Conduct of the Province of New York Considered and the True Interest of That Colony Attempted to Be Shewn*, its author identified only as "A Linen Draper," was circulated among the members of the Society of Arts, Agriculture, and Economy, and its twenty pages lamented the poor economic conditions found in New York despite what appeared to be thriving trade.

The second pamphlet, *The Commercial Conduct of the United States of America Considered*, follows the same theme as the earlier piece; the author is identified as "A Citizen." It was written for public consumption but was aimed explicitly at legislators. It begins, "The profession of a merchant is trade; they consult their own interest; but it is the Legislature only which can check and prohibit an intemperate, inpolitic, and luxurious commerce." The piece goes on to suggest that government needed to take greater control of commerce to put a stop to ruthless businesspeople.

One of the first works to examine American commerce closely was written by a Frenchman, Jacques Pierre Brissot de Warville, in 1795. The work, *The Commerce of America with Europe*, attempts to examine in some detail the exact commercial relationship established between the infant United States and its European trading partners. In his preface, Brissot de Warville reprints Lord Sheffield's comment that "England would always be the storehouse of the United States."

In 1806, Samuel Blodget compiled *Economica: A Statistical Manual for the United States of America*, which summarized trade and commercial activity in the country. He produced a similar manual in 1810.

From a historical standpoint, little was done by American economic scholars before 1860. This may have been a result of the nation's dependence on foreign trade as well as a need to establish business institutions before writing about them. Ezra Seaman's *Essays on the Progress of Nations, in Productive Industry, Civilization, Population, and Wealth*, published in 1846, was one of the first retrospective looks at American economic development.

Around the turn of the century, a proliferation of works attempt to review the short history of American business. William Babcock Weeden's *Economic and Social History of New England, 1620–1789* concentrates primarily on the agrarian nature of commerce. A. M. Simon's *Class Struggle in America* (1906) is unique for its application of Marxist theory to American business. Guy Stevens Callender's *Selections from the Economic History of the United States, 1765–1860* (1909) excerpts letters and pamphlets that deal with early American business. More comprehensive reviews of business history were Harold Underwood Faulkner's *American Economic History* (1924) and Clive Day's *History of the Commerce of the United States* (1925).

Two more recent works that present a definitive business history are *200 Years*

Orson Welles in *Citizen Kane*, 1941. Kobol Collection/RKO

of American Business and *The Evolution of the American Economy*. In *200 Years*, Thomas C. Cochran condenses the diverse development of the American business community into a descriptive narrative of the four major areas in business development: "The Business Revolution, 1776–1840"; "A National Market, 1840–90"; "Adjusting to Bigness, 1890–1930"; and "The Age of Demand, 1930–Present." In each era, he describes the technological advances that fomented expanding industry as well as the economic, political, and social trends in the nation that changed how business is conducted. *The Evolution of the American Economy* by Sidney Ratner, James Soltow, and Richard Sylla takes a more analytical view of American business, focusing on trends and statistical evidence to support the changes that our economy has experienced. Although not a history of business, another important work is W. Jett Lauck's *Political and Industrial Democracy*, which traces the employer–worker relationship from 1776 to 1926. Its major thesis is that the spirit of cooperation created by World War I led to the democratization of business, specifically in the development of workers' councils that, by 1926, represented more than 1.5 million workers nationwide.

For an in-depth historical view of the individual in business, Miriam Beard has compiled a two-volume work, *A History of Business*, that analyzes the people who control business and how those people have changed in style and motivation. Volume 2 starts with the eighteenth century and covers both American and international business. Courtney Robert Hall, in his *History of American Industrial Science*, does a similar analysis for the development of technologies that fostered our present industrial complex. Along with a general overview of industry, Hall includes detailed accounts of particular industries, from mining and rubber to paper and electronics.

Several authors have compiled historical anthologies that trace the development of American economic theory through the writings of America's premier economists. Henry William Spiegel's *The Rise of American Economic Thought* brings together the theories most influential in the early formation of the American system of business, including those of Benjamin Franklin, Mathew Carey, Thomas Cooper, and Simon Newcomb. Robert Heilbroner's *The Worldly Philosophers* also reviews the economic philosophies of European and American theorists and applies their thinking to modern American business. In a more pragmatic vein, John Brooks has compiled first-person accounts of the evolution of corporate America in *The Autobiography of American Business*. Among the accounts are those of Andrew Carnegie, Henry Ford, Helena Rubenstein, and Bernard Baruch.

Although innumerable histories of business exist, there is an equally large body of nonhistorical works that deal with business that could be of interest to researchers. These can be divided into two categories: theory and practice. The former works tend to explore the impact of capitalism on our society and the impact of society on capitalism. One of our most prolific writers in this area is John Kenneth Galbraith, who had produced, among other works, *American Capitalism* (1952, 1956), *The Affluent Society* (1958), and *The New Industrial State* (1967). In *American Capitalism*, he attempts to explain how a system that seems in total violation of sound economic practice has managed to succeed. He also confronts the ambiguities created by our rogue economy and the insecurities generated by those ambiguities. As he explains in his opening chapter, "Man cannot live without an economic theology—without some rationalization of the abstract and seemingly inchoate arrangements which provide him with his livelihood."

In *The Affluent Society*, he takes a critical view of the American passion for the acquisition of wealth and the apparent apathy toward advancing American economic thought caused by this passion. In *The New Industrial State*, which Galbraith saw as a continuation of his earlier work, he postulates that the forces inducing human behavior are directed more by the market than by the individual. A counterpoint to this Galbraithian theory is that proposed by George Lodge in *The New American Ideology*, which suggests that, through our industrialization, we have passed beyond John Locke's sense of individualism into an ideology of communitarianism. This ideology exhibits itself in greater involvement of workers in management and in a shift in focus by corporations from consumers to community.

A writer as prolific as Galbraith is Milton Friedman, who has taken a long look at the tempestuous relationship between business and government and has concluded that much of what is wrong in business today is a result of an overwatchful federal government. In *Capitalism and Freedom*, written with his wife Rose, Friedman takes exception to the admonition offered by John Kennedy in his inaugural—"Ask not what your country can do for you, but what you can do for your country." Friedman sees this call as establishing an imbalance between the governed and the government. He suggests that what Kennedy should have said was, "What can the country offer me in my quest to accomplish my personal goals?" The body of the work attempts to outline how competitive capitalism can work only in a free enterprise system. In *Free to Choose: A Personal Statement*, written eighteen years after *Capitalism*, Milton and Rose Friedman continue to expand on Adam Smith's basic premise of economics—that successful enterprise is based on voluntary cooperation. They see this premise violated by the federal government's restrictive involvement in American business practices. In addition to these works, Friedman has written *The Great Contraction 1929–1933* (with Anna J. Schwartz), *Essays in Positive Economics*, and *An Economist's Protest: Columns in Political Economy*.

A work that appeared soon after the publication of *American Capitalism* and that takes up the theme of economic change is Adolf Berle's *The Twentieth Century Capitalist Revolution*. His primary thesis is that institutionalized American industry is at a crossroads, one path leading toward the assumption of a guiding role in our society, and the other to destruction. He sees American business particularized in the modern corporation and suggests that dramatic changes in corporate life are needed to ensure that industry makes the right choice. An equally dire harbinger of dramatic business change is Robert L. Heilbroner's *Business Civilization in Decline*, published in 1976. Despite its negative title, the work explicates how business in America will have to undergo both a structural and philosophic evolution to keep pace with societal and governmental shifts.

Another aspect of business that has received considerable attention is the concept of work. A seminal work in this area is Studs Terkel's *Working*. This book is a collection of personal accounts of day-to-day life in the work setting told through the experiences of a diverse assemblage of workers—from miners to models, to telephone operators, to executives. Terkel points out in his introduction that "this book, being about work, is, by its very nature, about violence—to the spirit as well as the body." At the other end of the spectrum is Bernard Lefkowitz's

Breaktime, which collects the impressions of people who have dropped out and what the payoff is for not working.

A more theoretical approach to working is offered by Gale Miller in *It's a Living: Work in Modern Society*, which posits a typology ranging from peasant work through industrial, professional, and countercultural work. Miller discusses the applicable historical precedents that have influenced work as well as the social reality attendant on the type of work that one does. An equally detailed examination of work is presented in Carl Kaufmann's *Man Incorporate: The Individual and His Work in an Organized Society*. The author focuses on how work has restructured our view of ourselves and our place in society from a historical perspective.

An area of particular interest in the modern business setting is the impact of corporate climate on the institution. Terrence Deal and Allan Kennedy investigate this aspect of business in *Corporate Cultures: The Rites and Rituals of Corporate Life*. Through case studies of specific corporations, the authors explore how culture, defined as an overriding value system, is fostered and maintained through corporate rituals.

Business writers also are fascinated with predicting the future. One of the most notable of these works is John Naisbitt's *Megatrends*, which isolates ten trends that portend radical changes in American society. Among these are the shift from an industrial- to an information-based society, greater emphasis on innovation and self-reliance, the migration of workers from the North, and the obsolescence of representative democracy. A more specialized view of these changes is Max Ways' *The Future of Business: Global Issues in the Eighties and Nineties*.

As with any institution as volatile and ever-changing as business, there is a plethora of how-to books that attempt to arm the prospective businessperson with the knowledge, skills, and defenses needed to survive. Some take a lighter tone in discussing the subject, such as the "Peter" trilogy by Laurence J. Peter. Starting with *The Peter Principle*, written with Raymond Hull in 1969, the authors set forth his philosophy that business tends to promote individuals to the highest level of their incompetence. Within his less-than-serious message is the recommendation—to both employers and individuals—that people should avoid the ever-upward drive endemic to business. In *The Peter Prescription* (1972), he offers specific remedies to the "Peter Principle," and in *The Peter Pyramid*, published in 1986, he applies his theory on a larger scale to government, businesses, and institutions. Along the same line, Robert Townsend attempts to show "how to stop the Corporation from stifling people and strangling profits" in *Up the Organization*.

A more earnest approach to self-help is offered by *In Search of Excellence* by Thomas Peters and Robert Waterman, which explains those elements of modern business practice that guarantee success. Other works offering a more pragmatic approach to self-help include *How to Do Business and Succeed in It* by A. W. Astor, *Always Live Better than Your Clients* by Isadore Barmash, *The Corporate Prince: Machiavelli Reviewed for Today* by Richard D. Funk, *Business Wargames* by G. James Barrie, *Funny Business: A Senile Executive's Guide to Power and Success* by E. Alfred Osborne, *Game Plans: Sports Strategies for Business* by Robert Keidel, and *The Invisible War: Pursuing Self-Interest at Work* by Samuel A. Culbert and John J. McDonough.

On the darker side of business, a number of authors have dealt with the crimes, legal and ethical, committed in the name of higher profits. Addressing the ills of the corporate world has long been of interest to authors. Perhaps the earliest such antagonists were the "muckrakers" of the turn of the century. Named by Teddy Roosevelt for the character in *Pilgrim's Progress* who could not see the beauty of the world around him because he was too busy raking through the muck below his feet, the modern American muckraker relished exposing the foibles and follies of business and government. John Harrison and Harry Stein have collected a series of articles that explore the goals and motivations of these pioneers in *Muckraking: Past, Present and Future*. A new gang of muckrakers has taken the corporate world to task for its excesses in recent years. Vance Packard has carried the muckrakers' banner into the second half of the twentieth century. Among his numerous scathing exposés is *The Pyramid Climbers*, which strips away the veil of mystery surrounding the modern corporate executive to expose hustlers, trained, packaged, and programmed to succeed at any cost.

In *Up against the Corporate Wall*, Prakash Sethi reviews a number of infamous business cases that, he suggests, have altered our view of corporate ethics. Included among these are Dow Chemical's reaction to nationwide protests over its production of napalm, the 1969 California farmworkers' strike and subsequent grape boycott, and the battle between President Kennedy (and later President Johnson) and the American steel giants over price controls. Robert L. Heilbroner's *In the Name of Profit* puts the men running the supercorporations under the microscope to explore their values and why they act the way they do. In the same vein, Roger D'Aprix notes, in the introduction to *In Search of a Corporate Soul*, "A truism about American society in the final third of a century is that almost every speck of it has been assigned to one organization or another." His book, following this premise, asks if the modern corporation has acted as a responsible steward for what the society has placed in its hands. In *The Gamesman*, Michael Maccoby creates a typology of the modern business manager, whom he sees as the beneficiary of the modern corporate system. Through an analysis of detailed interviews with 250 top executives, Maccoby identifies four basic managerial types: the craftsman, who enjoys the process of making something; the jungle fighter, whose motivation is the acquisition and defense of power; the company man, whose interest is maintaining organizational integrity; and the gamesman, who is a team player but out to win for his employer and himself. Similarly, *The Naked Manager* by Robert Heller deals with the games that managers play and how these games have led to mismanagement.

In addition to the numerous books available on business, one source of interest to the researcher is the range of business magazines. America's desire to keep abreast of the happenings in business has a long history. Business magazines have been a part of the American corporate world since the turn of the century. One of the earliest is *Forbes*, founded in 1917, which continues today as a prestigious business magazine. Created by Bertie Forbes, a Scot who had cut his journalistic teeth at the *New York Journal of Commerce* and the *Commercial and Financial Chronicle*, *Forbes* created a family publishing dynasty that still holds the reins of the magazine today. Although focused primarily on economic activity within the business community, *Forbes* also offers a forum for commentary, personality profiles, and lifestyle articles.

Forbes dominated the business community for eleven years before two serious

Interior of a cotton gin. Courtesy of the Library of Congress

contenders appeared. Both arrived on the eve of the Great Depression but survived the ensuing panic to take their place beside *Forbes* as the leaders in the business magazine field. *Business Week* hit the streets in 1929 with a no-nonsense approach to business that gave it a "workhorse" image in contrast to *Forbes'* executive style. *Fortune*, published by Time, Inc., came out in 1929 and challenged *Forbes* in style and content; it differentiated itself from its competition by instituting the single-company profile, later adopted by its two major competitors. Today, the three magazines vary little in content, although *Forbes* and *Fortune* still maintain the slick style that they established at their inception.

Among the more recent entries into the general business magazine field are *Nation's Business* (1911), the house organ of the U.S. Chamber of Commerce; *Money* (1972) which, true to its name, focuses on the control and use of money by companies and corporate executives; *Inc.* (1979), written in a high-gloss style for the entrepreneur or middle manager with sights set on the executive board-room; and *Venture* (1979), an all-out entrepreneurial guide for success. These general business magazines are joined by more than 10,000 other general and specialized magazines for every aspect of business. These are both horizontal (dealing with a particular business function, such as accounting, across industries) and vertical (dealing with a particular industry, such as advertising or steel production).

The academic community has been equally prolific in creating journals that monitor the activities of business. Perhaps the most famous of these is *Harvard*

Business Review, which began publication in 1922. Although structured, as are most academic journals, with contributing scholars, it has avoided limiting readership only to academe. Other academic journals of note are *American Economic Review*, from the American Economic Association; *Business History Review*, from the Harvard Business School; *Journal of Business*, from the University of Chicago; *Journal of Economics and Business*, from Temple University; *Journal of Education for Business*, from the Helen Dwight Reid Educational Foundation; and *Quarterly Journal of Economics*, from Harvard University. Of equal importance for the popular culture researcher are the numerous state-based business reviews, usually published by state universities. Some of these, like *Indiana Business Review*, *Arkansas Business and Economic Review*, *Georgia Business and Economic Conditions*, and *Oklahoma Business Bulletin*, began before 1933.

In concluding this chapter, it may be helpful to list and summarize a few of the most popular business titles that have appeared in the last decade. Because this list is potentially endless, it emphasizes some of the books that have made the *New York Times* best-sellers list very recently, and even these selections have been chosen with the usual bias of the authors. One will quickly notice that most of these books provide quick and thematic worldviews concerning the workplace and ways to conquer, rise, excel, succeed, and get extremely rich, all while having fun. For other books of interest, it is always helpful to remember that companies such as Amazon.com provide titles, authors, and book reviews from a variety of sources at the touch of a button and can be a valuable tool in your initial research. Here are a few examples of what is available.

In *The Joy of Work: Dilbert's Guide to Finding Happiness at the Expense of Your Co-Workers*, Scott Adams has provided a dialogue between the man and his fans disguised as a tongue-in-cheek guide to surviving the corporate life. Chapters on "Office Pranks" and "Surviving Meetings" reveal how in office blocks across America, life is imitating art imitating life, creating a pleasantly postmodern working environment.

Harry Beckwith takes on the challenge of depicting the tremendous transformation from the manufacturing-based economy to the service economy in *Selling the Invisible: A Field Guide to Modern Marketing*. The invisible aspect that he has in mind refers not to particular features of services provided but to the "relationships" and the ways in which companies do business in the service economy. The Saturn automobile is contrasted with the Saturn way of doing business.

In a more serious work, *Against the Gods: The Remarkable Story of Risk*, Peter Bernstein has written a comprehensive history of people's efforts to understand risk and probability, beginning with early gamblers in Greece and running through modern chaos theory. Bernstein's thesis states that "this book tells the story of a group of thinkers whose remarkable vision revealed how to put the future at the service of the present. By showing the world how to understand risk, measure it, and weigh its consequences, they converted risk-taking into one of the prime catalysts that drives modern Western society."

Another book that reveals the lighter side of risk-taking, Richard Branson's autobiography, *Losing My Virginity: How I've Survived, Had Fun, and Made a Fortune Doing Business My Way*, provides a business thriller that documents the rise of a European business empire. Branson's airline, retailing, and cola businesses all emerged as Branson took outrageous personal and professional chances against the advice of the mainstream. It is an enjoyable story of entrepreneurial survival. If Branson's piece pushes one over the edge, Richard Carlson has shown readers how to interact more peaceably and joyfully with colleagues, clients, and bosses and reveals tips to minimize stress and bring out the best in themselves and others. *Don't Sweat the Small Stuff* is an inspirational and practical read, one of a series by Carlson.

Captains of Consciousness: Advertising and the Social Roots of the Consumer Culture remains a classic in the field. Stuart Ewen provides a fascinating look at the rise of American consumer culture and illustrates the context of social developments that shaped the life and mind of twentieth-century America. Jeffrey Fox presents seventy-five commonsense rules about successfully conducting your career in *How to Become a CEO: The Rules to the Top of Any Organization*. Rules like "Don't Have a Drink with the Gang" are accompanied by a page or two of succinct and thought-provoking explanation. Michael Gerber's *The E-Myth Revisited* argues that entrepreneurs—typically brimming with good, but distracting, ideas—make poor businesspeople. He establishes an incredibly organized and regimented plan freeing the entrepreneur's mind to build the long-term success of the business.

The following six books are all about potential. *The Goal: A Process of Ongoing Improvement/Cassettes* by Eliyahu Goldratt is a fully dramatized version of a practical guide to business in fictional form. The goal of the book is to enhance productivity and provide personal fulfillment. *The 48 Laws of Power* suggests that learning the game of power requires a certain way of looking at the world, a shifting of perspective, writes Robert Greene. The laws share a simple premise: certain actions always increase one's power, while others decrease it and even ruin us. The laws cull their principles from many great schemers throughout history. Lou Holtz, the master motivator of Notre Dame football fame, devises a game plan for all types of success in *Winning Every Day*. Suze Orman adds another wrinkle to success in *The 9 Steps to Financial Freedom*. After becoming a wealthy broker with a huge investment firm, Orman was profoundly unhappy. She had not yet achieved "financial freedom," a concept that transcends simple money management and enters into the psychological and even spiritual power that money has in our lives. How can you enter the ranks of America's wealthy? Read *The Millionaire Next Door: The Surprising Secrets of America's Wealthy* by Thomas Stanley and William Danko. This book has made the rounds and is becoming part of the business lexicon as it represents the virtues of sacrifice, discipline, and hard work, qualities that are discouraged in our high-consumption society. Finally, at a higher level of abstraction, David Morris Potter provides one of the seminal books on understanding what it means to be an American and on what makes our character distinctive, if not unique. Potter was a remarkable professor of American history at Stanford, and his book, *People of Plenty: Economic Abundance and the American Character*, reflects his ability to communicate a vast body of knowledge to a wide audience.

The final set of books are all related by their attention to business laws and the gathering of business information. *Guts: The Seven Laws of Business That Made Chrysler the World's Hottest Car Company* is written by Robert Lutz, the hard-driving former Chrysler president. Lutz tells how he helped engineer a second comeback at Chrysler with "hard work, hard thinking and, yes, guts." Michael Lavin notes in the preface to *Business Information: How to Find It, How to Use It* that the business environment of the twenty-first century may be defined by three phrases: "emerging global economy, transnational corporations, and world marketplace." The book promises skills and access to these new dimensions of the business world. *The Wall Street Journal Guide to Planning Your Financial Future: The Easy-to-Read Guide to Planning for Retirement* by Kenneth Morris provides just what it says from a source that has gained the respect of the business community. Similarly, *Investing for Dummies* by Eric Tyson continues the "for Dummies" series, whether you are dumb about golf or investing. This is for those who need a step away from anxiety and complexity.

On a more serious and focused note, *The 22 Immutable Laws of Marketing: Violate Them at Your Own Risk*, has been called the bible of marketing. The world-renowned marketing consultants and best-selling authors Al Ries and Jack Trout distill everything that they have learned in over forty years of marketing into the laws. Finally, since this chapter has focused to a certain extent on the virtues and efficiency of the Internet, we include *Customers.Com: How to Create a Profitable Business Strategy for the Internet and Beyond* by Patricia Seybold. Drawing on sixteen case studies of companies as diverse as Boeing, Babson College, and Hertz, Seybold identifies the factors that make e-commerce work successfully.

NOTES

1. M. Thomas Inge, *Handbook of American Popular Culture* (Westport, Conn.: Greenwood Press, 1990), xxiii.
2. Ibid.
3. http://h-net2.msu.edu/~pcaaca/popindex.html; http://h-net2.msu.edu/~pcaaca/
4. http://www.bgsu.edu/departments/popc/mission.html
5. Thomas Griffith, *The Waist-High Culture* (New York: Grosset and Dunlap, 1959), 1.

BIBLIOGRAPHY

Adams, Scott. *The Joy of Work: Dilbert's Guide to Finding Happiness at the Expense of Your Co-Workers*. New York: HarperCollins, 1998.

Advertising Age, ed. *How It Was in Advertising: 1776–1976*. Chicago: Crain Books, 1976.

Allen, James Sloan. *The Romance of Commerce and Culture: Capitalism, Modernism, and the Chicago-Aspen Crusade for Cultural Reform*. Chicago: University of Chicago Press, 1983.

Astor, A.W. *How to Do Business and Succeed in It*. New York: Street and Smith, 1890.

Atwan, Robert, Barry Orton, and William Vesterman. *American Mass Media: Industries and Issues*. 3rd ed. New York: Random House, 1986.

Baran, Paul, and Paul Sweezy. *Monopoly Capital: An Essay on the American Economic and Social Order*. New York: Monthly Review Press, 1966.

Barmash, Isadore. *Always Live Better than Your Clients*. New York: Dodd, Mead, 1983.

Barrie, G. James. *Business Wargames*. New York: Penguin Books, 1986.

Beard, Miriam. *A History of Business*. 2 vols. Ann Arbor: University of Michigan Press, 1938.

Beckwith, Harry. *Selling the Invisible: A Field Guide to Modern Marketing*. Chicago.: Audio-Tech Business Book Summaries.

Berle, Adolf A., Jr. *The Twentieth Century Capitalist Revolution*. New York: Harcourt, Brace, 1954.

Bernstein, Peter L. *Against the Gods: The Remarkable Story of Risk*. New York: John Wiley Sons, 1998.

Best, Fred, comp. *The Future of Work*. Englewood Cliffs, N.J.: Prentice-Hall, 1973.

Bining, Arthur. *The Rise of American Economic Life*. New York: Scribner's, 1943.

Blodget, Samuel. *Economica: A Statistical Manual for the United States of America*. 1806. Reprint. New York: A. M. Kelly, 1964.

Borden, Neil H. *The Economic Effects of Advertising*. Chicago: R. D. Irwin, 1942. Reprint. New York: Arno Press, 1976.

Bowden, Witt. *The Industrial History of the United States*. New York: Adelphi, 1930.

Bowman, James S., Frederick A. Elliston, and Paula Lockhart. *Professional Dissent: An Annotated Bibliography and Resource Guide*. New York: Garland, 1984.

Branson, Richard. *Losing My Virginity: How I've Survived, Had Fun, and Made a Fortune Doing Business My Way*. London: Virgin, 1998.

Brissot de Warville, Jacques Pierre. *The Commerce of America with Europe, Particularly with France and Great Britain*. 1795.

Brooks, John. *The Autobiography of American Business*. Garden City, N.Y.: Doubleday, 1974.

Brown, Richard D., and George J. Petrello. *Introduction to Business*. New York: Macmillan, 1979.

Brownstone, David M., and Gordon Carruth. *Where to Find Business Information: A Worldwide Guide for Everyone Who Needs Answers to Business Questions*. New York: Wiley, 1982.

Bryant, Keith L., Jr., and Henry C. Dethloff. *A History of American Business*. Englewood Cliffs, N.J.: Prentice-Hall, 1983.

Bursk, Edward, Donald T. Clark, and Ralph W. Hidy. *The World of Business*. New York: Simon and Schuster, 1962.

Business and Economics Books 1876–1983. 4 vols. New York: R. R. Bowker, 1983.

Business, Economics Books and Serials in Print. New York: R. R. Bowker, 1973– . Annual.

Business Periodicals Index. New York: H. W. Wilson, 1958– .

Callender, Guy Stevens. *Selections from the Economic History of the United States, 1765–1860*. Boston: Ginn, 1909.

Carlson, Richard. *Don't Sweat the Small Stuff at Work: Simple Ways to Minimize Stress and Conflict While Bringing Out the Best in Yourself and Others*. Sydney: Bantam, 1999.

Caves, Richard. *American Industry: Structure, Conduct, Performance*. Englewood Cliffs, N.J.: Prentice-Hall, 1964.

Cawelti, John G. "America on Display: The World's Fairs of 1876, 1893, 1933." In *The Age of Industrialism in America*, ed. Frederic Jaher. New York: Free Press, 1968.

Clapp, Jane. *Professional Ethics and Insignia*. Metuchen, N.J.: Scarecrow Press, 1974.

Cochran, Thomas C. *200 Years of American Business*. New York: Basic Books, 1977.

Corey, Lewis. *The Decline of American Capitalism*. New York: Covici Friede, 1934.

Costello, Patricia. *Stories from American Business*. Englewood Cliffs, N.J.: Prentice-Hall, 1987.

Covey, Stephen R. *The 7 Habits of Highly Effective People*. Provo, Utah: Franklin Covey, 1989.

Culbert, Samuel A., and John J. McDonough. *The Invisible War: Pursuing Self-Interest at Work*. New York: Wiley, 1980.

Cunningham, William H. *Introduction to Business*. Cincinnati: SW, 1984.

Daniells, Lorna M. *Business Information Sources*. Berkeley: University of California Press, 1985.

D'Aprix, Roger M. *In Search of a Corporate Soul*. New York: AMACOM, 1976.

Day, Clive. *History of the Commerce of the United States*. New York: Longmans, 1925.

Deal, Terrence E., and Allan A. Kennedy. *Corporate Cultures: The Rites and Rituals of Corporate Life*. Reading, Mass.: Addison-Wesley, 1982.

Dent, Harry S. *The Roaring 2000s*. New York: Simon and Schuster Trade, 1999.

Encyclopedia of Business Information Sources. Detroit: Gale Research, 1983.

Ewen, Stuart. *Captains of Consciousness: Advertising and the Social Roots of the Consumer Culture*. New York: McGraw-Hill, 1977.

Faulkner, Harold Underwood. *American Economic History*. 1924. New York: Harper and Row, 1976.

Fink, Gary M. *Labor Unions*. Westport, Conn.: Greenwood Press, 1977.

Fletcher, Gordon A. *The Keynesian Revolution and Its Critics*. New York: St. Martin's Press, 1987.

Fox, Jeffrey J. *How to Become a CEO: The Rules to the Top of Any Organization*. Los Angeles: Audio Renaissance, 1998.

Fox, Richard Wightman, and Jackson T. Lears, eds. *The Culture of Consumption: Critical Essays in American History, 1860–1960*. New York: Pantheon, 1983.

Frederick, John H. *The Development of American Commerce*. New York: Appleton, 1932.

Friedman, Milton. *An Economist's Protest: Columns in Political Economy*. Glen Ridge, N.J.: Thomas Horton, 1972.

———. *Essays in Positive Economics*. Chicago: University of Chicago Press, 1953.

Friedman, Milton, and Rose Friedman. *Capitalism and Freedom*. Chicago: University of Chicago Press, 1962.

———. *Free to Choose: A Personal Statement*. New York: Harcourt Brace Jovanovich, 1980.

Friedman, Milton, and Anna Jacobson Schwartz. *The Great Contraction 1929–1933*. Princeton, N.J.: Princeton University Press, 1965.

Funk, Richard D. *The Corporate Prince: Machiavelli Reviewed for Today*. New York: Vantage Press, 1986.

Galbraith, John K. *The Affluent Society*. Boston: Houghton Mifflin, 1958.

———. *American Capitalism: The Concept of Countervailing Power*. Boston: Houghton Mifflin, 1956.

———. *Economic Development*. Cambridge: Harvard University Press, 1964.

———. *The New Industrial State*. Boston: Houghton Mifflin, 1967.

Gerber, Michael E. *The E-Myth Revisited: Why Most Small Businesses Don't Work and What to Do about It*. New York: HarperBusiness, 1995.

Gilliland, Charles E., Jr., ed. *Readings in Business Responsibility*. Braintree, Mass.: D. H. Mark, 1969.

Giordano, Albert G. *Concise Dictionary of Business Terminology*. Englewood Cliffs, N.J.: Prentice-Hall, 1981.

Goldratt, Eliyahu M. *The Goal: A Process of Ongoing Improvement/Cassettes*. St. Paul, Minn.: Penguin-HighBridge Audio, 1993.

Goleman, Daniel. *Working with Emotional Intelligence*. Newport Beach, Calif.: Books on Tape, 1998.

Goodall, Francis. *Bibliography of Business History*. Brookfield, Vt.: Gower, 1987.

Gras, Norman S. *Business and Capitalism: An Introduction to Business History*. New York: A. M. Kelly, 1939.

Greene, Robert. *The 48 Laws of Power*. Sydney: Hodder Headline, 1998.

Hall, Courtney Robert. *History of American Industrial Science*. New York: Library, 1954.

Harrison, John M., and Harry Stein. *Muckraking: Past, Present and Future*. University Park: Pennsylvania State University Press, 1973.

Hay, Robert D., and Edmund R. Gray. *Business and Society: Cases and Text*. Cincinnati: South-Western, 1981.

Hayck, F. A., ed. *Capitalism and the Historians*. Chicago: University of Chicago Press, 1954.

Heilbroner, Robert L. *Business Civilization in Decline*. New York: W. W. Norton, 1976.

———. *The Worldly Philosophers*. New York: Simon and Schuster, 1980.

———, ed. *In the Name of Profit*. Garden City, N.Y.: Doubleday, 1972.

Heller, Robert. *The Naked Manager: Games Executives Play*. New York: E. P. Dutton, 1985.

Hickman, Craig R., and Michael Silva. *Creating Excellence*. New York: NAL Books, 1984.

Holtz, Lou. *Winning Every Day: The Game Plan for Success*. New York: HarperBusiness, 1998.

Horowitz, Daniel. *The Morality of Spending: Attitudes toward the Consumer Society in America, 1875–1940*. Baltimore: Johns Hopkins University Press, 1985.

Howey, Richard S. *A Bibliography of General Histories of Economics 1692–1975*. Lawrence: Regents Press of Kansas, 1982.

Humphrey, Edward. *An Economic History of the United States*. New York: Century Historical Series, 1931.

Janis, J. Harold. *Modern Business Language and Usage in Dictionary Form*. Garden City, N.Y.: Doubleday, 1984.

Johnson, Harold L. *Business in Contemporary Society: Framework and Issues*. Belmont, Calif.: Wadsworth, 1971.

Jones, Donald G. *Business Ethics Bibliography, 1971–1975*. Charlottesville: University Press of Virginia, 1977.

Kaufmann, Carl. *Man Incorporate: The Individual and His Work in an Organized Society*. Garden City, N.Y.: Doubleday, 1967.

Keidel, Robert. *Game Plans: Sports Strategies for Business*. New York: E. P. Dutton, 1985.

Kirkland, Edward C. *A History of American Economic Life*. New York: Crofts, 1932.

Larson, Henrietta M. *Guide to Business History*. Cambridge: Harvard University Press, 1948.

Lauck, W. Jett. *Political and Industrial Democracy 1776–1926*. New York: Funk and Wagnalls, 1926.

Lavin, Michael R. *Business Information: How to Find It, How to Use It*. Phoenix: Oryx Press, 1987.

Lefkowitz, Bernard. *Breaktime*. New York: Hawthorn Books, 1979.

Levine, Lawrence. *Highbrow/Lowbrow: The Emergence of Cultural Hierarchy in America*. Cambridge: Harvard University Press, 1986.

Linden, Eugene. *Affluence and Discontent: The Anatomy of Consumer Societies*. New York: Viking Press, 1979.

Lodge, George C. *The New American Ideology*. New York: Hawthorn Books, 1979.

Lovett, Robert W. *American Economic and Business History: A Guide to Information Sources*. Detroit: Gale Research, 1971.

Lutz, Robert A. *Guts: The Seven Laws of Business That Made Chrysler the World's Hottest Car Company*. New York: Wiley, 1998.

Maccoby, Michael J. *The Gamesman*. New York: Simon and Schuster, 1976.

Mayros, Van. *Business Information: Applications and Sources*. Radnor, Pa.: Chilton, 1983.

Miller, Gale. *It's a Living: Work in Modern Society*. New York: St. Martin's Press, 1981.

Million Dollar Directory. Annual. Parsippany, N.J.: Dun and Bradstreet, 1979–   .

Montefiore, Joshua. *A Commercial Dictionary Containing the Present State of Mercantile Law, Practice and Custom*. Philadelphia: James Humphreys, 1804.

Morris, Kenneth M. *The Wall Street Journal Guide to Planning Your Financial Future: The Easy-to-Read Guide to Planning for Retirement*. New York: Lightbulb Press, 1998.

Moskowitz, Milton, Michael Katz, and Robert Levering. *Everybody's Business: An Almanac*. San Francisco: Harper and Row, 1980.

MOW International Research Team. *The Meaning of Work*. London: Harcourt Brace Jovanovich, 1987.

Naisbitt, John. *Megatrends*. New York: Warner Books, 1982.

Orman, Suze. *The 9 Steps to Financial Freedom*. New York: Crown, 1999.

Orsagh, Thomas, ed. *The Economic History of the United States prior to 1860*. Santa Barbara, Calif.: ABC-CLIO, 1975.

Osborne, E. Alfred. *Funny Business: A Senile Executive's Guide to Power and Success*. New York: AMACOM, 1979.

Packard, Vance. *The Pyramid Climbers*. New York: McGraw-Hill, 1962.

Parkinson, C. Northcote. *Big Business*. Boston: Little, Brown, 1974.

Pascarella, Perry. *The New Achievers*. New York: Free Press, 1984.

Peter, Laurence J., and Raymond Hull. *The Peter Prescription*. New York: William Morrow, 1972.

———. *The Peter Principle*. New York: William Morrow, 1969.

———. *The Peter Pyramid or Will We Ever Get the Point?* New York: William Morrow, 1986.

Peters, Thomas J., and Nancy K. Austin. *A Passion for Excellence: The Leadership Difference*. New York: Random House, 1985.

Peters, Thomas J., and Robert H. Waterman Jr. *In Search of Excellence*. New York: Harper and Row, 1982.

Plooan, Stephen M., and Mark Levine. *Die Broke: A Radical, Four-Part Financial Plan*. New York: HarperBusiness, 1998.

Porter, Glenn, ed. *Encyclopedia of American Economic History: Studies of the Principal Movements and Ideas*. 3 vols. New York: Scribner's, 1980.

Potter, David Morris. *People of Plenty: Economic Abundance and the American Character*. Chicago: University of Chicago Press, 1954.

Predicast F & S Index. Published monthly with quarterly and annual cumulations. Cleveland: Predicast, 1968– .

Pusateri, C. Joseph. *A History of American Business*. Arlington Heights, Ill.: Harlan Davidson, 1984.

Ratner, Sidney, James H. Soltow, and Richard Sylla. *The Evolution of the American Economy*. New York: Basic Books, 1979.

Rice, Michael Downey. *Prentice-Hall Dictionary of Business, Finance and Law*. Englewood Cliffs, N.J.: Prentice-Hall, 1983.

Ries, Al, and Jack Trout. *The 22 Immutable Laws of Marketing: Violate them at Your Own Risk*. Hinsdale, IL.: Audio-Tech Business Book Summaries, 1998.

Rosenberg, Jerry M. *Dictionary of Business and Management*. New York: Wiley, 1978.

Saunders, Alta. *The Literature of Business: Contemporary*. Westport, Conn.: Greenwood Press, 1946.

Schlessinger, Bernard. *The Basic Business Library: Core Resources*. Phoenix: Oryx Press, 1983.

Seaman, Ezra C. *Essays on the Progress of Nations, in Productive Industry, Civilization, Population, and Wealth*. 1846.

Sethi, S. Prakash. *Up against the Corporate Wall*. Englewood Cliffs, N.J.: Prentice-Hall, 1972.

Seybold, Patricia. *Customers.com: How to Create a Profitable Business Strategy for the Internet and Beyond*. New York: New York Times Business, 1998.

Simons, A. M. *Class Struggle in America*. Chicago: Kerr, 1906.

Singewald, Frank D. *To Succeed in Business, Get There, Honestly If You Can, but Get There*. Pompano Beach, Fla.: Exposition Press, 1982.

Smith, Adam. *The Wealth of Nations*. Edited by Edwin Cannan. Chicago: University of Chicago Press, 1976.

Spiegel, Henry William. *The Rise of American Economic Thought*. Philadelphia: Chilton, 1960.

Standard and Poor's Industry Surveys. Annual. New York: Standard and Poor's, 1973– .

Standard and Poor's Register of Corporations, Directors and Executives. Annual. New York: Standard and Poor's, 1928– .

Stanley, Thomas J., and William Dank. *The Millionaire Next Door: The Surprising Secrets of America's Wealthy*. Thorndike, Maine: G. K. Hall, 1999.

Sturdivant, Frederick D. *Business and Society: A Managerial Approach*. Homewood, Ill: Richard D. Irwin, 1977.

Terkel, Studs. *Working*. New York: Random House, 1974.

Townsend, Robert. *Up the Organization*. New York: Alfred A. Knopf, 1970.

Tucker, Kenneth A., ed. *Business History: Selected Readings*. Totowa, N.J.: Biblio Distribution Center, 1977.

Tyson, Eric. *Investing for Dummies*. Foster City, Calif.: IDG Books Worldwide, 1997.

U.S. Department of Commerce Library Catalog. List of Publications from the U.S. Government Printing Office from 1790 through 1950.

Vlahos, Olivia. *Doing Business: The Anthropology of Striving, Thriving, and Beating Out the Competition*. New York: Franklin Watts, 1985.

Voos, Henry. *Organizational Communication: A Bibliography*. Rutgers, N.J.: Rutgers University Press, 1967.

Ward's Directory of 51,000 Largest U.S. Corporations. Annual. Petaluma, Calif: B. H. Ward, 1980– .

Ways, Max, ed. *The Future of Business: Global Issues in the Eighties and Nineties*. New York: Pergamon Press, 1978.

Weeden, William Babcock. *Economic and Social History of New England, 1620–1789*. 2 vols. Boston: Houghton Mifflin, 1890.

Who Owns Whom. London: Roskill, 1973– . (North American edition published annually.)

Who's Who in Finance and Industry. Annual. Chicago: Marquis Who's Who, 1936– .

Williamson, Harold, ed. *The Growth of the American Economy: An Introduction to the Economic History of the United States*. New York: Prentice-Hall, 1944.

Winch, Donald. *James Mill: Selected Economic Writings*. Chicago: University of Chicago Press, 1966.

Wright, Chester W. *Economic History of the United States*. New York: McGraw-Hill, 1941.

Periodicals

American Economic Review. Nashville, 1911– .

Arkansas Business and Economic Review. Fayetteville, Ark., 1933– .

Business History Review. Boston, 1926– .

Business Marketing. Chicago, 1983– .

Business Periodicals Index. New York, 1958– .

Business Week. New York, 1929– .

Du Pont Magazine. Wilmington, Del., 1913– .

Forbes. New York, 1917– .

Fortune. New York, 1929– .

Georgia Business and Economic Conditions. Athens, Ga., 1929– .

Harvard Business Review. Boston, 1922– .

Inc. Magazine. Boston, 1979– .

Indiana Business Review. Bloomington, 1926– .

Journal of Business. Chicago, 1928– .

Journal of Economics and Business. Philadelphia, 1949– .

Journal of Education for Business. Washington, D.C., 1928– .

Mississippi Business Review. Mississippi State, 1939– .

Money. New York, 1972– .

Nation's Business. Washington, D.C., 1911– .

Oklahoma Business Bulletin. Norman, Okla., 1928– .
Pennsylvania Business Survey. University Park, Pa., 1938– .
Quarterly Journal of Economics. New York, 1886– .
Venture, the Magazine for Entrepreneurs. New York, 1979– .

CATALOGS

Evelyn Beck

As Kurt Vonnegut envisions the end of the world in his novel *Cat's Cradle*, it is made more bearable for the survivors by a bomb shelter equipped with all of life's necessities—a chemical toilet, a short-wave radio, twin beds, and a Sears, Roebuck catalog.

Catalogs—those elaborate advertising books—have inspired a peculiar kind of worship in the past century. In 1972, on the centennial of the Montgomery Ward catalog, Richard Nixon called catalogs "an American tradition."[1] They are important, especially as an anthropological tool in discovering the desires of middle-class Americans. By showing us what men and women of the past century have wanted, needed, and done without to purchase, the catalog gives us an intimate, extraordinarily detailed glimpse into the American home.

There has not, however, been much scholarly writing on catalogs. The main attention has been business-oriented (with many articles appearing on the growing number and variety of catalogs) and nostalgic (with a flurry of reprints of old Sears catalogs). The publication of one reprint was initiated by an American history teacher who wanted to include an 1890s catalog in his college course in order to give his students an accurate sense of the period.

Most of the useful analysis of catalogs is, appropriately, historical, but very little has appeared in the past few decades. A number of books were published in the 1940s, when Sears, Roebuck and Co. was the number one retail business in America. Since then, much of what has been written about catalogs is brief and scattered through a variety of news, business, and advertising magazines.

HISTORICAL OUTLINE

The history of the catalog is actually a history of mail order, for the catalog served as the primary tool by which ambitious businessmen changed the buying habits of Americans. Because colonial America was not an industrial nation, merchandise ordered through the mail came from abroad. George Washington and Thomas Jefferson were among those who purchased goods from England before the American Revolution; after 1776, most mail-order items came from France. In 1744 Benjamin Franklin sold scientific and academic books in America's first catalog, which he also printed. The first native American mail-order business began around 1830 on a very small scale in New England. Credit for the earliest known effort to sell exclusively by mail on a major scale goes to E. C. Allen of Augusta, Maine, who offered such merchandise as recipes for washing powder beginning in 1870. But it was not until 1872, when Montgomery Ward rented a small shipping room and distributed one-page price lists to farmers in a cooperative organization called the National Grange of the Patrons of Husbandry, that American mail order really got under way.

For years, farmers had bought all they required from the general store, which had become, even more than a source of goods, a local gathering place where people could catch up on the local gossip and engage in informal political debates. Perhaps more important, it was run by a townsman—often a leading citizen—who understood the insecurities of farm life and who thus extended annual credit to all. But farmers were growing increasingly dissatisfied with the abuses of middlemen, who raised the prices on merchandise as much as 100 percent, and with the limited selection from which to buy. Also a concern for busy farmers was having to travel to the general store, often many miles away, whenever they needed something. Tired of the lack of alternatives, farmers banded together in what became known as "the Grange" to eliminate the middleman and exercise more control over how and where they spent their money.

Montgomery Ward, a shrewd entrepreneur, made himself their man and even labeled his mail-order operation "the Original Grange Supply House." Because he worked out of Chicago, with its easy access to manufacturers and wholesalers, he boasted a large inventory and a much greater selection than the general store, and because the farmers bought in large quantities, Ward could offer them lower prices. But, most important, Ward offered his merchandise by mail. As farmers prospered, they had more money but less time to spend making their own clothes and tools. As farming became more mechanized, the need for machinery increased. From the one-page price list grew "the Farmer's Bible," a mail-order catalog designed to meet these needs.

Ward's success in the new mail-order field soon led to competition. Richard Sears, also operating out of Chicago, began selling watches by mail in 1886 and then went into business with A. C. Roebuck, offering an increasingly varied catalog of merchandise that eventually established him as the mail-order giant. In 1882, the Spiegel, May, Stern Company had begun offering goods by mail, followed by the Larkin Company in 1885 and the National Cloak and Suit Company in 1888. Montgomery Ward and Sears, the biggest firms, became fierce competitors, but the main threat to their enterprises came from outside their organizations.

Small-town merchants felt threatened by the mail-order companies, whose lower prices were draining away their customers. Even more humiliating, the general-store owner was also the town postmaster, and he found himself delivering catalogs and sending off orders and then distributing the merchandise as it arrived. The tensions erupted into open warfare. Local merchants enlisted the country press, lecturers on the Chautauqua and Lyceum circuits, preachers, public officials, and banks to voice their opposition. Customers were denounced for "sending money off to the Chicago millionaires,"[2] and Sears and Montgomery Ward resorted to sending catalogs and goods in unmarked packages to protect their customers from harassment. Country merchants organized Saturday evening bonfires in the public square, offering prizes to those who brought the most catalogs to burn and even giving a free moving picture ticket to every child who contributed a catalog to the blaze. Contests encouraged the writing of poetry denouncing mail-order houses, and into the vocabulary came such euphemisms as "Monkey Ward," "Shears and Rawbuck," and "Rears and Soreback." In perhaps a greater, if less original, insult, catalog houses were also tagged "cat houses" in contempt.

Attempts to discredit the men behind the mail-order houses flourished, too. Rumors that Richard Sears was a Negro were so widespread that the company published a photograph of a very white-faced Sears in several catalogs to end the gossip. Sears' merchandise, too, was smeared. The most popular story insisted that a sewing machine offered by the catalog actually turned out to be a needle and thread. Of course, some of the bad publicity was justified; none of the companies were above deceitful advertising to increase profits. Sears once sold miniature furniture in an ad that seemed to imply that it was life-size, and as late as 1937, Spiegel introduced a line of clothing called "the famous Saindon Models," never mentioning that Saindon was not a famous designer but simply the company secretary.

People who bought from Sears and Montgomery Ward also had to be careful, as they were the object of many desperate threats. In one case, a man running for mayor of Warsaw, Iowa, threatened to fire any city employee caught buying through mail order. However, these attacks did little to discourage doing business with catalogs and in fact served as free advertising, for the critics of mail order were often more hurt by public opinion than were the targets of their criticism.

Furthermore, mail-order merchants won the biggest battle. Rural free delivery, which brought mail to the farms and which had been strongly opposed by local store owners, was approved in 1893 and begun in 1896, making it easier for farmers to shop by mail and even less likely that they would shop in town. The adoption of parcel post in 1913 was an added bonus; postal rates fell, and packages, which previously could not exceed four pounds, now could weigh as much as eleven pounds, eliminating such practices as shipping an eight-pound overcoat in halves, in separate parcels, along with a needle and thread for assembly. The greatest advantage of local stores ceased to exist when mail-order companies began to offer their customers credit.

As the mail-order companies grew, so did their catalogs. An early price list from Montgomery Ward listed 163 items, most of them for one dollar, including hoop skirts, paper collars, and a backgammon set. Soon the catalogs were issued biannually and, except for a few financially difficult years, included progressively more pages. By 1874, Ward's catalog had 32 pages; by 1899, it numbered 1,036 pages. Today, the biggest catalogs are several thousand pages thick—a situation good for laughs on the 1980s television sitcom *Cheers* when mail carrier Cliff Claven once stumbled into the bar, exhausted, explaining, "The new Sears catalog just came out." Except for a few unsuccessful years when Sears and Ward charged customers for the catalogs, they have been offered free or, more recently, for a fee that is refunded with the first purchase.

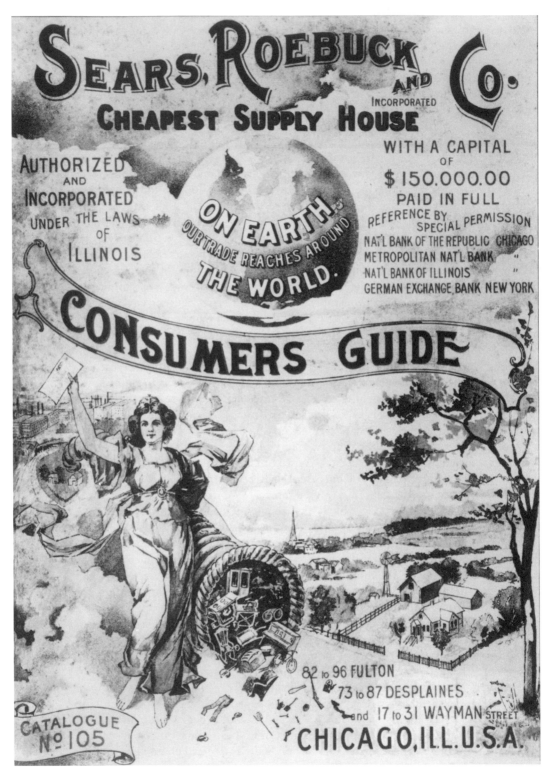

Sears, Roebuck and Co. catalog. Courtesy of the Library of Congress

The design of the catalogs has also undergone tremendous change. Originally, detailed drawings and written descriptions along with editorial comments and customer testimonials crammed each page, leaving very little white space; eventually, merchandise was more liberally spaced throughout. The artwork progressed from illustrations (which often used the heads of celebrities, such as Theodore Roosevelt), to halftones, to black and white, and then to the predominant use of color photographs using live models. Early catalogs did not include an index, since the merchants expected customers to read their tomes carefully from cover to cover. Also interesting is the overall conservatism of the catalogs. Ward and Sears emphasized good taste, respectability, and wholesomeness. Sears' taboos have included "too full" brassieres, "sexy" legs in stocking ads, and illustrations of women (and later men) smoking and drinking. But times change, and by 1972, a Ward's cover featuring a young woman wearing only a bikini drew many complaints but also a noticeable increase in orders placed.

Both the design and the merchandise offered in the catalogs in many ways reflect American popular culture. One writer calls them "an invaluable record of American life . . . a diary of the times created by the people."[3] According to another writer, "Its pages marked life's passages—the baseball glove youngsters played with behind the barn, the pocket watch wives gave their husbands for Christmas, the one-hundred-piece set of real English china that homemakers bought for $11.75, the talcum powder mothers sprinkled on their firstborn child. The Sears catalog epitomized home and America."[4]

Through the additions and omissions, one can see many changes in American life. Liquor, for example, appeared in the 1874 Ward's catalog but disappeared the following year after Prohibitionists objected. The obstacles faced by the struggling suffrage movement are suggested in the 1905 Sears catalog by a "(Bathing) Suit Worn by Man Who Opposed Votes for Women." Three decades later, however, women have evidently made strides, for birth control devices such as contraceptive jellies and vaginal sprays appear, though they are listed covertly as "feminine hygiene needs." As for blacks in the early twentieth century, we can sense their tenuous position by their labeling as "coons" and "darkies" in a 1905 catalog offering a group of records called "Negro Shouts," a chorus of "happy" blacks singing about their freedom.

The presence of American soldiers in two world wars becomes clear in the Sears catalogs published from the beginning of one conflict to the end of another. In 1918, "Dresses for Mourning and General War" are one sign of the U.S. entry into World War I. The higher prices in the 1920 catalog reflect the rapid inflation that followed American military involvement, and the crash of commodity prices caused by the depression of 1920–1921 rendered 1920 catalogs useless. Indicative of the mood preceding World War II is a particularly sentimental page of the 1937 catalog headed "America looks forward," featuring a young man and woman holding hands as they prepare to venture down a road, presumably life's path.

But the newest war soon invades the pages, and the toy section of the 1941 catalog features an unusually large number of tanks, machine guns, and dive-bombers. By 1942, the catalog reflects wartime shortages, as it has 196 fewer pages and 103 omitted items (mostly hardware such as electrical appliances), which manufacturers could not supply. But the editors stoically admonish, "To make sure that the men who are fighting our battles have the guns and planes and tanks and ships they need, we at home must do without."[5] By 1944, the further reductions of the Sears and Ward's catalogs are partly explainable by the government's wartime paper-saving program.

Technological advancements emerge as the scope of merchandise offered changes. The popularity of the sewing machine in the 1890s is one sign of a major revolution taking place on the farm. Signs of mechanical progress and the increasing use of electricity in rural areas are the many electrical gadgets offered, such as lamps and irons. Another major step forward is indoor plumbing; in the 1930s Sears recommends the Deluxe Handee Indoor Toilet because "much of the stomach disorders and intestinal ill-health suffered by our adult rural population can often be traced to lack of convenient toilet facilities and the resultant development of the 'deferring habit.' "[6] Another sign of the growing concern for health care is the amount of space that Sears devoted to drugs and patent medicines. The 1905 catalog offers such wonder drugs as "Sears' Cure for the Opium and Morphine Habit" and "Injection No. 7" for treatment of gonorrhea. Other offerings over the years included "Dr. Rose's Obesity Powder," "French Arsenic Complexion Wafers," and "Dr. Worden's Female Pills for All Female Diseases." Doctors in this era were few and were not available in many areas, even to those who could afford treatment. Besides, many doctors were illiterate, and their methods not entirely trusted. But as the medical profession evolved and as the government stepped in to outlaw quack cures with the Pure Food and Drug Act of 1906 and the creation of the Federal Drug Administration in 1927, patent medicines faded from the catalog pages. Sears once sold handguns and rifles through its catalog pages, too. Automobiles appeared in the 1909 catalog, and though they were dropped after three years because they did not prove profitable through mail order, the number of automobile accessories that occupied more and more pages is a sure sign of the increasing importance of cars in America.

As technology advanced, people found themselves with more leisure time. A few of the most popular items were bicycles and musical instruments, both of which proved early big sellers for Sears. Like most Americans, mail-order customers adored moving pictures, and the influence of Hollywood is suggested by the appearance of celebrity names and faces in the catalog. The 1935 edition features a photograph of "Max Factor Supervising Claudette Colbert's Make-up" and includes endorsements of such items as lace panties by Ginger Rogers and Loretta Young.

One of the most obvious ways that the catalog reflects change is in fashion. Men's suits become tighter (and then looser), women's skirts shorter (and then longer and then shorter), and corsets give way to girdles. Hairstyles change, too; in 1925, illustrations of bobbed hair accompany offers for the necessary accessories. Cosmetics become increasingly important, and the 1909 catalog instructs women, "There are very few who are hopelessly homely. Because You Are Married Is No Excuse for Neglecting Your Personal Appearance."[7]

Also revealing are the lines of unsuccessful merchandise, those items that tried and failed to entice customers. The rise of grocery store chains saw the discontinuance of groceries in the Ward's catalog, and prefabricated homes bowed out when too many customers could not pay. More recently, the department store catalogs' turn almost entirely to clothing suggests the changing retail marketplace and the rise of specialty catalogs.

The affection felt by so many for mail-order catalogs manifested itself in a kind of worshipful folklore. Stories about the importance of Sears, Roebuck and Company to its customers gave the firm and its founder godlike qualities. While campaigning, former Georgia governor Eugene Talmadge told voters that their only three friends were "God Almighty, Sears, Roebuck, and Eugene Talmadge."[8] The most popular story, told in a variety of ways, involves a small boy who, when asked by his Sunday school teacher the origin of the Ten Commandments, confidently replied, "Sears, Roebuck." Other tales involved Richard Sears' integrity and honesty, which assumed legendary proportions. The most notorious of these describes an incident on a streetcar when the conductor dropped and broke his watch. When Sears, a passenger, discovered that the watch had been purchased from his company, he told the man, "We guarantee our watches not to fall out of people's pockets and break," and promptly sent him a new one.[9]

What quickly became known as "the Farmer's Bible" and "the Great Wish Book" has enjoyed tremendous popularity for many years. During World War I, the book most often requested by hospitalized soldiers was a Sears catalog. As Sears' partner, Julius Rosenwald, explained, "[T]he catalog helps our soldier boys to escape the miseries of war and live happily again, if only for a little while, amid the scenes of their childhood at home."[10] More recently, when Sears sponsored a contest for snapshots of children (the winners to be used as models in the 1981 spring catalog), 50,000 entries flooded the central office.

Today, over one-third of adults in the United States make at least one mail-order purchase per year out of the millions of catalogs that go out in the mail. Each household received an average of 88 catalogs in 1997, according to one estimate; others have put the number at well over 100. Without mail order and direct mail advertising and selling, the U.S. Post Office would be without a full third of its revenues. Mail order accounts for 18 percent of all U.S. retail sales, and in their heyday three of the biggest catalog houses (Sears, Montgomery Ward, and Spiegel) used about 118,000 tons of paper annually. According to the Direct Marketing Association, consumer catalog sales totaled $38.6 billion in 1995, a rise of 5.5 percent since 1990. Mail orders account for over 7 percent of all general, apparel, and furniture sales.

A variety of organizations have recognized the significant niche that mail order has carved for itself in American history. In 1946, a New York group of book lovers included the Montgomery Ward catalog in its collection of 100 American books with the greatest influence on American life. In 1972, the U.S. Postal Service issued a commemorative stamp honoring the "100th Anniversary of Mail Order." Many history books use catalog illustrations and photographs to show how Americans lived, and an American Heritage picture history of America from 1872 to 1972 uses many Montgomery Ward illustrations to show how the mail-order industry has affected lifestyles.

Thus, the catalog not only reflects change but influences it as well. Montgomery Ward and Sears catalogs have been credited with encouraging consumers to purchase newfangled "necessities" that they might previously have done without, as in the case of indoor plumbing. The way that catalog houses conduct their business—offering goods for a single set price—helped to bring an end to the bargaining system. The catalogs are even credited with helping to standardize the language, for items were named in the Chicago dialect and also ordered that way.

The habit of ordering clothes instead of making them helped set age-size standards very much in use today. Catalogs also helped advance advertising techniques, as they pioneered in the use of accurate, detailed illustrations of merchandise. Americans got used to increasingly higher qualities of goods and came to expect a policy that initially shocked local merchants: satisfaction guaranteed or your money back. The use of catalogs in country schools to identify objects unfamiliar to the students was recognized by the U.S. Post Office, which classified mail-order publications as aids in the dissemination of knowledge (and thus entitled them to lower second-class rates).

The mail-order industry itself has undergone innovations; many orders are now made by phone and charged to credit cards, and more and more items can be ordered via home shopping networks on cable television, through CD-ROMs, and, most significantly, via the Internet. Compiling the catalog has also become easier as computers reveal not only which items don't sell well and should be removed but also the preferences of individual customers. Even though Americans are less dependent on mail order due to the growing number of discount retail stores and the ease of travel on highways, mail order and the catalog continue to thrive, for their advantages—great variety, quality, ease, and credit—still appeal to shoppers. In 1995, more than 13 billion catalogs were mailed out.

Today there are three kinds of mail order: big mail-order houses, which offer great variety; novelty houses, which sell gadgets, food gift packs, and arts and crafts; and small company catalogs, which supply hard-to-find items. J. C. Penney now reigns as the mail-order leader, but hundreds of other firms have entered the market. One can now buy camping gear from L.L. Bean, tarantulas from a small Arizona firm, and very exclusive merchandise such as a 300-gallon elephant aquarium for $120,000 from the famous Neiman-Marcus Christmas catalog. A company called Spytech hawks two-way mirrors, telephone encryption devices, and wristwatch video cameras but assumes no responsibility for the use to which its merchandise is put. Perhaps the catalog of catalogs is the *Whole Earth Catalog*, the bible of the hippie movement in the 1960s and the winner of a National Book Award in 1971 for one of its later versions. From this mail-order manual, one is directed where to find such items as solar-powered beanies and artificial insemination for lesbians. The *Millenium Whole Earth Catalog* was published in 1995. However, despite the increasing fragmentation of the catalog market, more people continue to order women's apparel and accessories through the books than anything else, with home products a close second.

Catalogs are also increasingly targeted to specific population groups. J. C. Penney's produces a Fashion Influences catalog geared to African Americans, with such merchandise as black Santa figurines and tablecloths imprinted with African designs. Catalogs mailed to gay men and women include *Shocking Gray*, *Olivia*, *Proud Enterprises*, and *Made in Gay America*. Some of these publications donate a portion of profits from selected items to agencies and groups supporting the gay community, such as a Texas AIDS foundation. In the future, companies hope to be able to create an individual catalog for each customer.

One of the newest innovations is the "magalog," a hybrid catalog/magazine. Neiman Marcus' *The Book* is sold eight times a year at newsstands for ten dollars. Woven into pages of merchandise are articles about fashion trends and interviews with designers. In the premier issue of *A&F Quarterly*, Abercrombie & Fitch gave

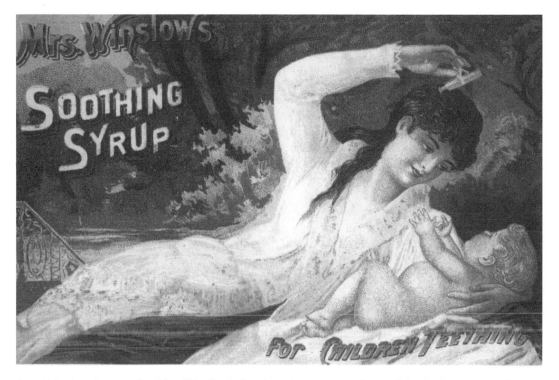

An 1887 advertisement for Mrs. Winslow's Soothing Syrup, a popular medicine in the 1880s and 1890s. Courtesy of the Library of Congress

tips on job hunting and buying a dog in between pages selling blue jeans and sweaters. Barneys New York offered *The Love Book*, a short story in which love blooms when a girl appears for a date wearing the company's $1,415 black velvet dress.

The melding of fiction and advertising copy has produced a peculiar brand of writing. Sometimes the catalogs include serious fiction, like Land's End's David Mamet story, its three-part fiction series, and its stories about shorts from short story writers. (It also planted a nonfiction article on cotton harvesting near catalog ads for cotton sheets and sweaters.) But consider the Nat Sherman Catalog's "Nat Stories" about Nat and New York cigars. In one,

> there was an explosion "like Joe Louis's one-two," and Nat saw this dark blue Packard screech off down Broadway and in its wake not ten feet away saw "my first real live stiff." . . . The dearly departed was one Vincent D'Aquino, or Queer Vinnie. What got him on the wrong side of his play-mates was anyone's guess, but the dicks were most interested in where he was going when he got whacked. Nat would tell you, "It was no mystery to me, because Mr. Vincent (as he was called in the store) had been one of my best customers."[11]

The epitome of catalogese is the much-parodied J. Peterman catalog, which was itself satirized in a Doonesbury comic strip (on January 23, 1994) and on television's hippest sitcom of the 1990s, *Seinfeld*, with Peterman himself a recurring character. A sample of the Peterman catalog's emotive advertising copy is a description of a sleeveless shift that "would be the Zen of summer dressing. . . . Except. Except for the 20-inch slit in the back through which your caramel or ivory calves show."[12]

Whether or not the ardent devotion for these books that exist almost exclusively to sell merchandise is justified, catalogs are historical documents of popular culture. One writer sees in the Montgomery Ward and Sears catalogs "the unrefined ore of much of current regionalism. Here is what Faulkner hopes to startle, and what Lewis once tried to awaken . . . Eden before the fall."[13] Another lauds the catalog's influence on our culture as "comparable to that of the cotton gin, the six-shooter, the model-T flivver, and the million-dollar movie."[14] Sears itself called its catalog "a modern convenience to be classed with electric power, the telephone and the telegraph."[15] Or perhaps there is more truth in the assertion that "mail order catalogs . . . are the greatest invention in the interest of pure fantasy since the discovery of hard-core pornography."[16] Whatever their proper place in our collective consciousness, they contain much of American life worth reviewing.

RESEARCH COLLECTIONS

The major sources of catalog collections are the catalog publishers themselves.

Montgomery Ward and Company's Corporate Research Library in Chicago has the only complete set of Montgomery Ward catalogs available for public use. A partial set (1916–1968) is housed at Radcliffe College's Schlesinger Library on the History of Women.

Sears, Roebuck and Company has a complete set of catalogs from 1886 to 1993 at its Merchandise Development and Testing Laboratory Library and also at its Archives, Business History and Information Center, both in Chicago. There are over 6,000 volumes. The Library of Congress has on microfilm every Sears catalog from 1892 to 1956. Sixty-nine rolls of microfilm containing more than 160 catalogs from 1888 to 1967 have been placed in over 100 libraries throughout the United States. The Carnegie Library of Pittsburgh has a complete set of Sears catalogs from 1888, classified and indexed.

Another source of Sears catalogs is the Disney Productions Library in Burbank, California. Walt Disney was known for having one of the largest Sears catalog collections on the coast; he used them as a reference tool for period costumes and frequently loaned them to other studios.

A source of both Sears and Ward catalogs is the Chicago Historical Society Library. It contains catalogs of major mail-order houses and many special industries and stores, primarily in Chicago, since the late nineteenth century.

Windmill Press has issued a number of books featuring toys from Sears and Montgomery Ward catalogs from the 1950s and 1960s, aimed at nostalgic baby boomers who want to remember Lionel Trains, Betsy Wetsy, and Chatty Cathy. Dover Books has a series of catalog reprints featuring fashions, houses, antiques, and furniture.

A number of specialty catalogs have also been reprinted recently and serve as useful historical references on various subjects. These include *The Great Catalog of the C. H. Stoelting Company, 1930–1937*, which presents a collection of psychological apparatus used until the 1930s, and *The Griswold Mfg. Co., 1918 Catalog Reprint*, which focuses on cast iron history.

What may be the largest collection of catalogs open to the public can be found at the National Museum of American History in Washington, D.C. In 1997 the Smithsonian Institution Libraries purchased the Franklin Institute's trade-catalog collection of 56,500 catalogs. Of the 235,000 items, 45,000 can be accessed by computer.

A specialized collection that might be of interest to catalog researchers is a vertical file of mail-order ads and pamphlets at the Alfred C. Kinsey Institute for Sex Research at Indiana University.

Collections related to mail order are available at the Dartnell Corporation Publishing-Research Library in Chicago and at the Direct Mail/Marketing Association Information Center in New York.

Finally, anyone interested in starting his or her own catalog collection can select preferences from twenty-four categories by writing to the Direct Mail/Marketing Association, Mail Preference Service, 6 East 43 Street, New York, New York 10017. Ask for the "More Mail" form. The *Great Catalog Guide*, a directory of over 250 catalogs, is available from the same address for three dollars.

HISTORY AND CRITICISM

Most of the information about the history of catalogs is included in histories of the founders of the mail-order firms. By far, the best material can be found on Richard Sears and Sears, Roebuck and Company. The best is Borris Emmet and John E. Jeuck's hefty *Catalogues and Counters: A History of Sears, Roebuck and Company*. It provides a thorough, detailed history of mail order, including Montgomery Ward, and also gives a detailed analysis of merchandise in the Sears catalogs and how it reflects historical and social change. It is especially revealing regarding the initial hatred of mail-order houses, the influence that the world wars had on catalog content and design, and the folklore that sprang up around Richard Sears. It also contains an extensive bibliography of related books and articles up to 1948.

Also good, though far less detailed, is Louis E. Asher and Edith Heal's *Send No Money*. Though the book is in some ways a defense of Sears, it offers some interesting behind-the-scenes information, for Louis Asher was the manager of Sears' advertising and catalog department. For example, Asher warns against reading too much social history into the choice of catalog merchandise; he cites the fact that books offered were often those out of copyright and thus cheaper, rather than apt indicators of popular taste.

David L. Cohn's 1940 *The Good Old Days: A History of American Morals and Manners as Seen through the Sears, Roebuck Catalogs 1905 to the Present* is the only book written solely to gauge the influence of catalogs. It requires some weeding through to get to the useful information, but it is revealing on how the catalogs reflect the evolving stature of women and blacks, for example.

Several books about Richard Sears and his company have appeared recently. These include Donald R. Katz's *The Big Store: Inside the Crisis and Revolution at Sears*, Arthur C. Martinez's *Hard Road to the Softer Side: Lessons from the Transformation of Sears*, Frederick Asher's *Richard Warren Sears: Icon of Inspiration*, and

Gordon Lee Weil's *Sears, Roebuck, U.S.A.: The Great American Catalog Store and How It Grew.*

Fewer books have been written about Montgomery Ward, but an excellent—and relatively recent—one is Frank B. Latham's *1872–1972: A Century of Serving Consumers. The Story of Montgomery Ward.* A useful history of mail order, it is especially good in its analysis of the effects that current events—especially postal changes—had on mail order and on the intense advertising war between Ward and Sears. It also provides detailed descriptions of the changes in the Ward catalogs over the years concerning size and design and Montgomery Ward promotional campaigns.

Montgomery Ward is also the focus of Booton Herndon's *Satisfaction Guaranteed: An Unconventional Report to Today's Consumers.* A chapter on "The Wonderful, Wonderful Catalog" is somewhat helpful, but overall the book is too general, and the tone is trite.

A book that focuses on the relationship between Sears and Montgomery Ward is Cecil C. Hoge's *First Hundred Years Are the Toughest: What We Can Learn from the Century of Competition between Sears and Ward's.*

A well-done history of Spiegel is *The Credit Merchants: A History of Spiegel, Inc.* by Orange A. Smalley and Frederick D. Sturdivant. It offers a great deal of minor information about the Spiegel catalog and mail order in general. It also includes an index with many listings under "Catalogs."

There are other useful histories. Mark Stevens' 1979 *"Like No Other Store in the World": The Inside Story of Bloomingdale's* offers some interesting catalog trivia. Ralph M. Hower's *History of Macy's of New York 1858–1919: Chapters in the Evolution of the Department Store* shows the influence of Montgomery Ward on Macy's use of catalogs but also shows how the catalog was a flop for a big city store with large operating costs.

J. C. Penney wrote a number of books, but they are very general and written mainly to promote his Christian beliefs. Somewhat more useful is Norman Beasley's *Main Street Merchant: The Story of the J. C. Penney Company.* It discusses how potential mergers with Montgomery Ward and then with Sears led Penney's into mail order. A more recent biography is Mary Elizabeth Curry's *Creating an American Institution: The Merchandising Genius of J. C. Penney*, which focuses on Penney's entrepreneurial skills.

There are also many articles available on L.L. Bean, a highly successful catalog pioneer, and the unusual *Whole Earth Catalog*. These include "Using the Old Bean" by John Skow in *Sports Illustrated*, "The L.L. Bean Sublime" by Benjamin DeMott in *Harper's*, and *Newsweek*'s "Whole Earth Revisited" by Lynn Langway and Pamela Abramson. As new mail-order empires are built, articles and books appear on their founders. Lillian Vernon explains her success with eccentric low-cost merchandise in *An Eye for Winners*.

Among the more inclusive books on the mail-order houses is Maxwell Sroge's *Inside the Leading Mail Order Houses*, which gives sales statistics on the top 250 mail-order houses (which, amazingly, represent only 2 percent of all mail-order firms). Godfrey M. Lebhar's *Chain Stores in America 1859–1962* includes a history of Sears and sales figures for Sears and Montgomery Ward. A useful article is *Time*'s 1982 cover story, "Catalogue Cornucopia," which focuses on the business boom of the growing catalog market. A more recent analysis of mail order and catalogs is a 1994 *Consumer Reports* article called "Mail-Order Shopping: Which Catalogs Are Best?"

An increasing number of books are available about mail order, but almost all are how-tos for the entrepreneur, and few devote much attention to catalogs. The most relevant is Richard S. Hodgson's *The Dartnell Direct Mail and Mail Order Handbook*, which has a chapter entitled "Catalogs and Price Lists," which focuses on technical considerations, especially catalog layout, and offers reasons behind the success of some of the biggest catalog companies.

A number of books on advertising include some discussion of catalogs. Frank Spencer Presbrey's *The History and Development of Advertising* offers a concise history of mail order and describes the influence that catalogs have had on advertising technique. Daniel Pope's *The Making of Modern Advertising* discusses E. C. Allen and mail-order papers. In *The Story of Advertising*, James Playsted Wood focuses on Sears, Roebuck and Company and how magazine ads lured people to examine the catalogs. Allan Marin's *Fifty Years of Advertising as Seen through the Eyes of Advertising Age 1930–1980* includes partial reprints of some articles on Richard Sears that give a sense of his importance in the first half of the twentieth century.

Many history books use catalog covers or pages as illustrations. A sampling includes the National Geographic Society's *We Americans*, Alistair Cooke's *America*, Gilman M. Ostrander's *American Civilization in the First Machine Age: 1890–1940*, and Mary Cable and American Heritage's *American Manners and Morals: A Picture History of How We Behaved and Misbehaved*.

There have been few really good articles analyzing the influence of catalogs on American culture. One of the best is Arthur G. Kimball's "Sears Roebuck and Regional Terms" in a 1963 issue of *American Speech*, which analyzes how the Sears catalog has influenced linguistic changes, especially in rural areas. The author examines catalog indexes over several decades to show changes in speech patterns.

Language is one of the catalog influences discussed in Fred E. H. Schroeder's "Semi-Annual Installment on the American Dream: The Wish Book as Popular Icon" in *Icons of Popular Culture*. Also discussed are the catalog's influence on age-size standards and how the catalog represents a dream of material success for any American, regardless of status. William Safire credits mail-order catalogs with the dubious distinction of coining new word combinations to describe colors and notes abundant grammatical errors in a brief satirical essay on "Cataloguese" for *The New York Times Magazine*.

Also useful are Fred Powledge's "1652 Pages of the American Dream" in *Esquire*, which analyzes lifestyle changes through the Sears catalog; George Milburn's "Catalogues and Culture" in *Good Housekeeping*, which discusses how catalogs have helped raise the standard of living by raising expectations; and Lovell Thompson's "Eden in Easy Payments" in a 1937 issue of the *Saturday Review of Literature*, which reviews the contents of that year's Sears catalog. John Garvey's "Dream Books" in *Commonweal* discusses how reprints of Sears catalogs, as well as the L.L. Bean and Whole Earth catalogs, are great for remembering the good old days. Other articles from the *Saturday Review of Literature* include Louis Greenfield's "Trade Winds," which shows the importance of catalogs in bringing literature to rural populations, and Jo Hubbard Chamberlin's "The Big Book," which describes how catalog items have changed over the years (to 1939). Michael Alcorn discusses the houses designed from nineteenth-century architectural catalogs in "Catalog Castles" in the *Journal of American Culture*; the focus on facades left interiors unremarkable.

A brief, though fascinating, article is Michael Kernan's "The Object at Hand" from *Smithsonian Magazine*. He discusses how an 1887 catalog conjures a world before refrigerators: items related to iceboxes were ice tongs, ice ponds, gang saws, and "leather shoulder pads for the ice man to rest the 80-pound chunk on as he lugged it into your house."[17] He also explains how an old trade catalog was used to settle a recent lawsuit about the explosion of an old water heater.

Sears's decision to stop producing its big catalog in 1993 (it continues to publish smaller specialty catalogs) inspired a number of tributes. (Montgomery Ward shut down its catalog operation in 1985 but resuscitated it in 1992 through a partnership with Fingerhut.) In "An Ode to the Big Book" in *Time*, Paul Gray, who calls the Sears catalog "a moral force in American life,"[18] is best at discussing the catalog's influence on rural dwellers, who once made up 70 percent of Americans. The catalog, he says, "provided a view of the world beyond the village green, the town intersection, the empty horizon. . . . So *this* is what people who work in offices are wearing. *That* is what an up-to-date kitchen is supposed to contain. And *this* is what ladies look like in their underwear."[19] Joseph Gustaitis' article for *American History Illustrated*, "Closing the Book," gives many examples of Sears' changing merchandise and how it reflects changes in American culture. Of particular interest is his list of items that Sears sold at "loss-leader" prices and his analysis of Americans' waning interest in home musical entertainment and reliance on patent medicine.

The best sources, however, remain the great "wish books" themselves.

NOTES

1. Frank B. Latham, *1872–1972: A Century of Serving Consumers. The Story of Montgomery Ward*, 2nd ed. (Chicago: Montgomery Ward, 1972), 96.

2. Ibid., 40.

3. David L. Cohn, *The Good Old Days: A History of American Morals and Manners as Seen through the Sears, Roebuck Catalogs 1905 to the Present* (New York: Simon and Schuster, 1940), xxiii.

4. Joseph Gustaitis, "Closing the Book," *American History Illustrated* 28 (July/August 1993), 38.

5. Boris Emmet and John E. Jeuck, *Catalogues and Counters: A History of Sears, Roebuck and Company* (Chicago: University of Chicago Press, 1950), 473.

6. Mary Cable and the Editors of American Heritage, *American Manners and Morals: A Picture History of How We Behaved and Misbehaved* (New York: American Heritage, 1969), 354.

7. Ibid., 339.

8. Emmet and Jeuck, 254.

9. Ibid., 84.

10. Gustaitis, 38.

11. James R. Rosenfield, "Targeting Pet Owners and Smokers," *Direct Marketing* 58 (April 1996), 26.

12. "Mail-Order Shopping: Which Catalogs Are Best?" *Consumer Reports* 59 (October 1994), 624.

13. Lovell Thompson, "Eden in Easy Payments," *Saturday Review of Literature* 15 (April 3, 1937), 15.

14. George Milburn, "Catalogues and Culture," *Good Housekeeping* 122 (April 1946), 181.

15. Gustaitis, 37.

16. Fred Powledge, "1652 Pages of the American Dream," *Esquire* 74 (December 1970), 190.

17. Michael Kernan, "The Object at Hand," *Smithsonian Magazine* 22 (April 1991), 32.

18. Paul Gray, "An Ode to the Big Book," *Time* 141 (February 8, 1993), 67.

19. Ibid.

BIBLIOGRAPHY

Books and Articles

Adams, Margaret, ed. *Collectible Dolls and Accessories of the Twenties and Thirties from Sears, Roebuck and Co. Catalogs*. Mineola, N.Y.: Dover, 1986.

Alcorn, Michael. "Catalog Castles." *Journal of American Culture* 20 (Fall 1997), 1–11.

American Mail Order Fashions, 1880–1900. A Long Ago Book. N.p.: n.p., 2000.

"America's Wish Book." *Time* 124 (August 20, 1984), 89.

Ash, Lee. *Subject Collections: A Guide to Book Collections and Subject Emphases as Reported by University, College, Public, and Special Libraries and Museums in the United States and Canada*. 6th ed. New York: R. R. Bowker, 1985.

Asher, Frederick. *Richard Warren Sears: Icon of Inspiration*. New York: Vantage Press, 1997.

Asher, Louis E., and Edith Heal. *Send No Money*. Chicago: Argus Books, 1942.

Associated Press. "Mail-Order Catalog Aids World's Needy." *Greenville News*, May 18, 1983: 3B.

"At Least There Are No Columns—Yet." *U.S. News & World Report* 123 (October 13, 1997), 10.

Barlow, Ronald S. *The Great American Antique Toy Bazaar, 1879–1945: 5,000 Old Engravings from Original Trade Catalogs, the Evolution of Dolls & Toys*. Sherman Oaks, Calif.: Windmill Press, 1998.

Beasley, Norman. *Main Street Merchant: The Story of the J. C. Penney Company*. New York: Whittlesey House, 1948.

The Best of Sears Collectibles 1905–1910. N.p.: n.p., 1976.

Bjorncrantz, C. E. "Sears' Big Book: Dinosaur or Phoenix?" *Direct Marketing* 49 (July 1986), 71.

Blum, Stella, ed. *Everyday Fashions of the Thirties as Pictured in Sears Catalogs*. Mineola, N.Y.: Dover, 1986.

"Bosom Boards and Buggies." *Time* 67 (April 16, 1956), 98.

Brann, W. L. *The Romance of Montgomery Ward and Company*. New York: Campbell, Starring, 1929.

Brubach, Holly. "Mail-order America." *New York Times Magazine* 143 (November 21, 1993), 54–64.

"Building the Catalog That Brings in $150,000,000 a Year by Mail." *Printer's Ink* 100 (July 19, 1917), 3.

Cable, Mary, and the Editors of American Heritage. *American Manners and Morals: A Picture History of How We Behaved and Misbehaved*. New York: American Heritage, 1969.

"Catalog Innovations: Montgomery Ward, Sears, Roebuck, and Chicago Mail Order Company." *Printer's Ink* 190 (February 2, 1940), 45–46.

"Catalogue Cornucopia." *Time* 120 (November 8, 1982), 72–73, 75–76, 78–79.

Chamberlin, Jo Hubbard. "The Big Book." *Saturday Review of Literature* 20 (May 13, 1939), 10–12.

Cohn, David L. *The Good Old Days: A History of American Morals and Manners as Seen through the Sears, Roebuck Catalogs 1905 to the Present.* New York: Simon and Schuster, 1940.

Colonna, Phyllis. *The Power of Integrity, Featuring the Story of J. C. Penney.* N.p.: n.p., 1984.

"A Computerized Catalog of Catalogs." *Newsweek* 99 (March 8, 1982), 82.

Cooke, Alistair. *Alistair Cooke's America.* New York: Alfred A. Knopf, 1973.

Curry, Mary Elizabeth. *Creating an American Institution: The Merchandising Genius of J. C. Penney.* Garland Studies in Entrepreneurship. New York: Garland, 1997.

Darnay, Brigitte T., ed. *Directory of Special Libraries and Information Centers.* 8th ed. Detroit: Gale Research, 1981.

De La Iglesia, Maria Elena. *The New Catalogue of Catalogues: The Complete Guide to World-Wide Shopping by Mail.* New York: Random House, 1975.

DeMott, Benjamin. "The L.L. Bean Sublime." *Harper's* 269 (September 1984), 27.

De Vries, Leonard, and Ilonka van Amstel. *The Wonderful World of American Advertising 1865–1900.* London: John Murray, 1973.

Emmet, Boris, and John E. Jeuck. *Catalogues and Counters: A History of Sears, Roebuck and Company.* Chicago: University of Chicago Press, 1950.

Erbes, P. J., Jr. "Catalog Comeback: Alleged to Have Been on Its Deathbed Ten Years Ago, Mail Order Thrives Today as Never Before." *Printer's Ink* 191 (April 5, 1940), 11–13.

———. "Catalog No. 126: Ward's 55th Anniversary Book." *Printer's Ink* 178 (January 28, 1937), 121–22.

———. "Catalog Progress: Study of Current Sears and Ward Books." *Printer's Ink* 176 (August 6, 1936), 37.

———. "Newest New Catalog: Sears, Roebuck's Latest Offering Drastically Modernized." *Printer's Ink* 186 (January 26, 1939), 149–53.

Flower, Sidney. *The Mail Order Business.* Chicago: S. Flower, 1902.

Garvey, John. "Dream Books." *Commonweal* 103 (February 27, 1976), 150–51.

Goldstein, Sue. *The Underground Shopper: A Guide to Discount Mail-Order Shopping.* New York: Andrews and McMeel, 1983.

"Goodbye, Great Wish Book." *Time* 126 (August 12, 1985), 38.

Gottschalk, Mary. "Gay Cachet." *San Jose* (California) *Mercury News,* September 19, 1993: 1H.

Gray, Paul. "An Ode to the Big Book." *Time* 141 (February 8, 1993), 66–67.

Greenfield, Louis. "Trade Winds." *Saturday Review of Literature* 24 (October 18, 1941), 40.

Gustaitis, Joseph. "Closing the Book." *American History Illustrated* 28 (July/August 1993), 36–39, 70.

Herndon, Booton. *Satisfaction Guaranteed: An Unconventional Report to Today's Consumers.* New York: McGraw-Hill, 1972.

Hetrick, R. *Guitar History: Gibson Catalog of the Sixties.* Vol. 3. Westport, Conn.: Bold Strummer, 1991.

The History and Progress of Montgomery Ward and Co. . . . the Romance of the Golden Rule and Some Interesting Facts About the Mail Order Business. Chicago: Montgomery Ward, 1925.

"History of Sears and Roebuck." *American History Illustrated* (June 1986), 34–39.

Hodgson, Richard S. *The Dartnell Direct Mail and Mail Order Handbook.* 2nd ed. Chicago: Dartnell, 1974.

Hoge, Cecil C. *First Hundred Years Are the Toughest: What We Can Learn from the Century of Competition between Sears and Ward's.* N.p.: n.p., 1988.

Hoke, Henry. "Two Winners with Help from a Friend." *Direct Marketing* 58 (February 1996), 34–39.

Holland, Thomas, ed. *Boys' Toys of the Fifties and Sixties: Memorable Catalog Pages from the Legendary Sears Christmas Wishbooks 1950–1969.* Sherman Oaks, Calif.: Windmill Press, 1997.

———. *The Doll & Teddy Bear Department: Memorable Catalog Pages from the Legendary Sears Christmas Wishbooks of the 1950s and 1960s.* Vol. 1. Sherman Oaks, Calif.: Windmill Press, 1997.

———. *Girls' Toys of the Fifties and Sixties: Memorable Catalog Pages from the Legendary Sears Christmas Wishbooks 1950–1969.* Sherman Oaks, Calif.: Windmill Press, 1997.

———. *More Boys' Toys of the Fifties and Sixties: Memorable Catalog Pages from the Legendary Sears Christmas Wishbooks 1950–1969.* Sherman Oaks, Calif.: Windmill Press, 1998.

———. *The Toy Train Department: Electric Train Pages from the Great Montgomery Ward Christmas Catalogs of the 1950's and 1960's.* Sherman Oaks, Calif.: Windmill Press, 1998.

Holmes, Steven. "In Chicago: A Sears Catalogue of Kids." *Time* 116 (July 7, 1980), 6.

Homes in a Box: Modern Homes from Sears. Schiffer Design Book. Atglen, Pa.: Schiffer, 1997.

Hower, Ralph M. *History of Macy's of New York 1858–1919: Chapters in the Evolution of the Department Store.* Cambridge: Harvard University Press, 1943.

Hudson, Wilma J. *J. C. Penney: Golden Rule Boy.* N.p.: n.p., 1972.

"Is the Store Becoming Obsolete?" *Time* 112 (November 27, 1978), 94.

Katz, Donald R. *The Big Store: Inside the Crisis and Revolution at Sears.* N.p.: n.p., 1989.

Kent, Rosemary. "King of the Catalogs." *Texas Monthly* 5 (December 1977), 118–43.

Kernan, Michael. "The Object at Hand." *Smithsonian Magazine* 22 (April 1991), 32–33.

Kerwin, Ann Marie. "Magalog Invades Magazine Territory." *Folio: The Magazine for Magazine Management* 25 (November 15, 1996), 25.

Kimball, Arthur G. "Sears-Roebuck and Regional Terms." *American Speech* 38 (October 1963), 209–13.

Kurath, Hans. *A Word Geography of the Eastern United States.* Ann Arbor: University of Michigan Press, 1949.

Langway, Lynn, and Pamela Abramson. "Whole Earth Revisited." *Newsweek* 96 (November 17, 1980), 100, 103.

Latham, Frank B. *1872–1972: A Century of Serving Consumers. The Story of Montgomery Ward*. 2nd ed. Chicago: Montgomery Ward, 1972.

Lebhar, Godfrey M. *Chain Stores in America 1859–1962*. 3rd ed. New York: Chain Store, 1963.

Lee, James. *Twenty-five Years in the Mail Order Business*. Chicago: A. E. Swett, 1902.

Leypoldt, F., Lynds E. Jones, and R. R. Bowker. *The American Catalogue. 1880–1911*. Reprint. New York: Peter Smith, 1941.

Mack, R. N. "Catalog of Woes." *Natural History* (March 1990), 44–53.

Mahoney, Tom. *The Great Merchants: The Stories of Twenty Famous Retail Operations and the People Who Made Them Great*. New York: Harper and Brothers, 1955.

"Mail-Order Books." *Business Week* 152 (June 26, 1943), 86–87.

"Mail-Order Shopping: Which Catalogs Are Best?" *Consumer Reports* 59 (October 1994), 621–27.

Mann, E. B. "The Good Old Days." *Field & Stream* 92 (June 1987), 66–67, 101–3.

Marin, Allan, ed. *Fifty Years of Advertising as Seen through the Eyes of Advertising Age 1930–1980*. Chicago: Crain Communications, 1980.

Martinez, Arthur C. *Hard Road to the Softer Side: Lessons from the Transformation of Sears*. New York: Times Books, 1998.

Maynard, Roberta. "Selling by the Book." *Nation's Business* 84 (September 1996), 58–61.

Milburn, George. "Catalogues and Culture." *Good Housekeeping* 122 (April 1946), 181–84.

"Millions by Mail." *Forbe*, 117 (March 15, 1976), 82.

Montgomery, M. R. *In Search of L.L. Bean*. N.p.: n.p., 1987.

Morris, Nomi. "Welcome to Spics R Us." *Maclean's* 109 (September 2, 1996), 30.

Nash, Kim S. " 'Net Shopping Not So Merry." *Computerworld* 31 (December 8, 1997), 37–38.

Olian, Joanne, ed. *Everyday Fashions 1909–1920 As Pictured in Sears Catalogs*. Mineola, N.Y.: Dover, 1995.

117 House Designs of the Twenties. Mineola, N.Y.: Dover, 1992.

"One 33J3663F and a 7J4202F: The Buying-by-Catalogue Boom." *Newsweek* 63 (May 25, 1964), 88–90.

Ostrander, Gilman M. *American Civilizations in the First Machine Age: 1890–1940*. New York: Harper and Row, 1970.

Packard, Vance. *The Hidden Persuaders*. New York: David McKay, 1957.

Palder, Edward L. *The Catalog of Catalogs VI: The Complete Mail-Order Directory*. 6th ed. Bethesda, Md.: Woodbine House, 1999.

Penney, James Cash. *Fifty Years with the Golden Rule*. New York: Harper, 1950.

———. *View from the Ninth Decade: Jottings from a Merchant's Daybook*. New York: T. Nelson, 1961.

Pope, Daniel. *The Making of Modern Advertising*. New York: Basic Books, 1983.

Powledge, Fred. "1652 Pages of the American Dream." *Esquire* 74 (December 1970), 190–93, 251–52.

Presbrey, Frank Spencer. *The History and Development of Advertising.* New York: Greenwood Press, 1968.

Quinn, Judy. "A&M's Pretensions to Parody." *Publishers Weekly* 244 (June 9, 1997), 17.

Ray, Debra, and George Reis. "Catalog Sales Projected to Reach $74.6 Billion by Year End." *Direct Marketing* 59 (August 1996), 20–25.

Reed, J. D. "Magalogs in the Mailbox." *Time* 126 (September 2, 1985), 73.

Rheingold, Howard. "On the Millenium Road." *Whole Earth Review* 85 (Spring 1995), 96–99.

Rips, Rae Elizabeth. "An Introductory Study of the Role of the Mail-Order Business in American History, 1872–1914." Master's thesis, University of Chicago, 1938.

Riviere, William A. *The L.L. Bean Guide to the Outdoors.* New York: Random House, 1981.

Roebuck, Alvah C. "Early and Some Later History of Sears, Roebuck and Co." 2 vols. Manuscript. Chicago, 1940.

Rosenfield, James. R. "Deconstructing L.L. Bean's New Holiday Catalog—A Masterpiece of Its Genre." *Direct Marketing* 59 (November 1996), 42–45.

———. "In the Mail." *Direct Marketing* 57 (January 1995), 34–37.

———. "Targeting Pet Owners and Smokers." *Direct Marketing* 58 (April 1996), 24–28.

Safire, William. "Cataloguese." *The New York Times Magazine* (November 26, 1995), 26.

Schell, Frank J. *The Catalog: Yesterday, Today, Tomorrow.* (Pamphlet distributed by Sears, Roebuck and Co., Chicago, n.d.)

Schmid, Jack. "Catalog Creative Breakthroughs." *Target Marketing* 21 (May 1998), 44–47.

Schroeder, Fred E. H. "Semi-Annual Installment on the American Dream: The Wish Book as Popular Icon." In *Icons of Popular Culture*, ed. Marshall Fishwick and Ray B. Browne. Bowling Green, Ohio: Bowling Green University Press, 1970, 73–86.

"Sears Catalog: Right at Home." *Design Quarterly* 167 (Winter 1996), 10.

Skow, John. "Using the Old Bean." *Sports Illustrated* 63 (December 2, 1985), 84.

Smalley, Orange A., and Frederick D. Sturdivant. *The Credit Merchants: A History of Spiegel, Inc.* Carbondale: Southern Illinois University Press, 1973.

Spero, James, ed. *Collectible Toys and Games of the Twenties and Thirties from Sears, Roebuck and Co. Catalogs.* Mineola, N.Y.: Dover, 1989.

Sroge, Maxwell, with Bradley Highum. *Inside the Leading Mail Order Houses.* 2nd ed. Colorado Springs: M. Sroge, 1984.

Stevens, Mark. *"Like No Other Store in the World": The Inside Story of Bloomingdale's.* New York: Crowell, 1979.

Stevenson, Katherine Cole. *Houses by Mail: A Guide to Houses from Sears, Roebuck and Company.* Washington, D.C.: Preservation Press, 1986.

"The Stores and the Catalogue." *Fortune* 11 (January 1935), 69–74.

"Taking on Content." *Target Marketing* 21 (May 1998), 34–37.

Thompson, Lovell. "Eden in Easy Payments." *Saturday Review of Literature* 15 (April 3, 1937), 15–16.

Tyler, Poyntz, ed. *Advertising in America.* New York: H. W. Wilson, 1959.

Ulanoff, Stanley M. *Advertising in America: An Introduction to Persuasive Communication*. New York: Hastings House, 1977.

Vernon, Lillian. *An Eye for Winners: How I Built One of America's Greatest Direct-Mail Businesses*. New York: HarperCollins, 1997.

Wagner, Mitch. "Net Returns Come Slowly for Catalog Firms." *Computerworld* 31 (May 26, 1997), 12.

Wathey, Patricia Wogen. *The International Mail-Order Shopping Guide*. Englewood Cliffs, N.J.: Prentice-Hall, 1984.

We Americans. Washington, D.C.: National Geographic Society, 1975.

Weil, Gordon Lee. *Sears, Roebuck, U.S.A.: The Great American Catalog Store and How It Grew*. N.p.: Stein and Day, 1977.

Wickware, Francis Sill. "Into the Towns and across the Border: Concluding the Life and Times of Sears, Roebuck." *Collier's* 124 (December 24, 1949), 30–32, 66–67.

———. "The Life and Times of Sears, Roebuck." *Collier's* 124 (December 3, 1949), 18–19, 42–43.

———. " 'Please Rush the Gal in the Pink Corset': Continuing the Life and Times of Sears, Roebuck." *Collier's* 124 (December 17, 1949), 20–21, 73–74.

———. " 'We Like Corn, on or off the Cob': Continuing the Life and Times of Sears, Roebuck." *Collier's* 124 (December 10, 1949), 20–21, 73–74.

Wiggins, Oveta. "Black Is Bountiful." *(Hackensack, N.J.) The Record*, February 12, 1995: B1.

Wilkinson, Deborah M. "Mail Order Madness." *Black Enterprise* 26 (July 1996), 123–25.

Wood, James Playsted. *The Story of Advertising*. New York: Donald Press, 1958.

Wood, Robert Elkington. *Mail Order Retailing Pioneered in Chicago*. New York: Newcomen Society of England, American Branch, 1948.

Worthy, James. *Shaping an American Institution: Robert E. Wood and Sears, Roebuck*. Urbana: University of Illinois Press, 1984.

Catalogs and Reprints

Aladdin "Built in a Day" House Catalog, 1917. Dover Books on Architecture. Mineola, N.Y.: Dover, 1995.

Bloomingdale's Illustrated 1886 Catalog: Fashions, Dry Goods and Housewares. Mineola, N.Y.: Dover, 1988.

1897 Sears Roebuck Catalogue. Introduction by S. J. Perelman. Edited by Fred L. Israel. New York: Chelsea House, 1993.

Gimbel's Illustrated 1915 Fashion Catalog. Reprint. Mineola, N.Y.: Dover, 1994.

Fashions of the Early Twenties: The 1921 Philipsborn Catalog. Dover Books on Fashion. Mineola, N.Y.: Dover, 1996.

Franklin Simon Fashion Catalog for 1923. Dover Books on Costume. Mineola, N.Y.: Dover, 1994.

Griswold Mfg. Co., 1918 Catalog Reprint. Marion, Ind.: L-W Publishing and Book Sales, 1996.

The Herman Miller Collection: The 1955/1956 Catalog. Schiffer Book for Collectors and Designers. Atlgen, Pa.: Schiffer, 1998.

Illustrated Jewelry Catalog, 1892. Mineola, N.Y.: Dover, 1998.

The Last Whole Earth Catalog: Access to Tools. Menlo Park, Calif.: Portola Institute, 1971.

Limbert Arts and Crafts Furniture: The Complete 1903 Catalog. Dover Books on Antiques and Furniture. Mineola, N.Y.: Dover, 1992.

Montgomery Ward & Co. Catalogue and Buyer's Guide No. 57. Spring and Summer 1895. Mineola, N.Y.: Dover, 1969.

The 1902 Edition of the Sears, Roebuck Catalogue. New York: Bounty Books, 1993.

1927 Edition of the Sears, Roebuck Catalogue. Edited by Alan Mirken. New York: Bounty Books, 1970.

Popplestone, John, and Ryan Tweney, eds. *The Great Catalog of the C.H. Stoelting Company, 1930–1937: A Facsimile Reproduction.* Scholars' Facsimiles & Reprints. N.p.: Stoelting, 1997.

Sears, Roebuck and Company Catalogs 1888/89–1993. Chicago: Sears, Roebuck (microfilm).

Sears, Roebuck and Co. Consumers Guide: Fall 1900. Northfield, Ill.: DBI Books, 1970.

Sears, Roebuck and Co. 1908 Catalogue No. 117: The Great Price Maker. Ed. Joseph J. Schroeder Jr. Chicago: Gun Digest, 1987.

Sears, Roebuck and Co. 1908 Solid Comfort Vehicles: Runabouts, Buggies, Phaetons, Surreys, Spring and Delivery Wagons, Pony Rigs, Cutters and Sleighs, Road Carts. Princeton, N.J.: Pyne Press, 1971.

Sears, Roebuck Catalog of Houses, 1926: An Unabridged Reprint. Mineola, N.Y.: Dover, 1991.

Sears, Roebuck Home Builder's Catalog. Mineola, N.Y.: Dover, 1990.

Whole Earth Epilog. Baltimore: Penguin Books, 1974.

Women's and Children's Fashions of 1917: The Complete Perry, Dame & Co. Catalog. Reprint. Mineola, N.Y.: Dover, 1992.

CHILDREN'S LITERATURE

R. Gordon Kelly and Lucy Rollin

The relationship between children's literature and the mainstream of the nation's literary and intellectual life was particularly close in the late nineteenth century, when, for example, three successive editors of the *Atlantic Monthly*, Thomas Bailey Aldrich, Horace Scudder, and William Dean Howells, all, at one time or another, wrote expressly for children. In this century, however, there has been significantly less overlap. Few major twentieth-century American authors have written for children, and in the development of higher education, the study of children's books was relegated to the intellectual periphery of schools of education and library science. Until recently, writing about children's books, as well as the books themselves, issued with a few notable exceptions from a cozy enclave cut off in large measure from modern literary and intellectual trends. As a consequence, "children's literature" all too often designates a narrowly belletristic tradition that excludes much that is of interest in the history of books for children, including works of great popularity. From the ubiquitous primers of the seventeenth and eighteenth centuries, the phenomenally popular stories of Horatio Alger in the nineteenth century, the adventures of Nancy Drew and the Hardy boys in the early twentieth century, to R. L. Stine's Goosebumps series in the 1990s, some children's books, however undistinguished in literary quality, have reached very large numbers of readers. Moreover, much of the literature directed to children is "popular" literature in the sense that it is highly conventional and intended to appeal to the largest possible audience. This is as true of the moral tale, the principal form of antebellum fiction for children, as it is of the works of Alger and the numerous series books produced both early and late in the twentieth century. Thus, there is ample justification for including a chapter on children's books in a handbook on popular culture.

Although there has been an increasing interest in the history and criticism of children's literature in the last thirty years, much of the work that has appeared reflects a conventional and unimaginative belletristic orientation, lacking scope and theoretical sophistication. Fortunately, the most interesting and promising work in the field deals with the cultural significance of popular books for children, such as the antebellum moral tale, the fairy tale, the novels of Alger, the Oz fantasies of L. Frank Baum, and the products of Walt Disney's studio. Children's books are especially deserving of a contextualist approach because they give form and specificity in ways considered appropriate for impressionable minds to matters of crucial importance: cultural definitions of what is; what is good, true, and beautiful; and what things go together. Children's books are an accessible, readily available feature in an elusive enterprise—the creation, maintenance, and modification of meaning in society. We have finally begun to examine children's books in America from this perspective and to locate them in the cultural contexts in which they were written, read, and selectively preserved and made available to successive generations of American children.

HISTORICAL OUTLINE

The following summary of the history of books for children in the United States departs in two important ways from the capsule histories to be found, for example, in most textbooks on children's literature. First, it emphasizes changes in the social and intellectual factors shaping the creation of children's books. One does not have to be a philosophical idealist to admit that concepts of the child and his or her needs constitute crucial aspects of an author's intention, nor need one be a Marxist to accept that changes in technology can significantly affect the production of books, including books for children. Second, we have not assumed that the development of literature for children can easily or unambiguously be interpreted as an increasingly faithful delineation of social reality appropriate to the child's needs and interests, for the very concept of these needs and interests has undergone significant change in the last two centuries and is changing even now.

Histories of children's literature have often been written as if fidelity to life and a due regard for the true nature of the child are asymptotic with the present— that as we approach the present, books for children, with numerous exceptions duly noted, are, on balance, both truer to life and truer to what we take to be the essence of childhood than books published decades or centuries ago. The view is understandable, though scarcely pardonable. The children's books of colonial America especially lie on the far side of a cultural divide that few would-be historians of children's literature have endeavored to cross, being content to dismiss books written before the first quarter of the nineteenth century as narrowly sectarian, gloomy, and morbid, to note a few of the charges leveled at them by modern commentators. What is being condemned is not the literature so much as the view of human nature, including child nature, that pervades the primers and catechisms, those most popular of children's books produced in the seventeenth and eighteenth centuries. However, literature for children was more diverse than that, for in addition to the religious manuals and conduct books, there were biography, fiction, animal stories, riddles, fables, nursery rhymes, fairy tales, and picture books. A leading historian of early books for children only slightly overstates the situation when he observes that "speaking broadly, I know of no kinds of children's books published today which were not also published in the seventeenth century."[1] Moreover, it is clear that writers for children sought in a variety

Jack and the Beanstalk. Courtesy of the Library of Congress

of ways to appeal to, and influence the mind of, the child reader—as they understood it—since a major aim was to arouse in the child the desire for saving knowledge.

The emergence of modern children's literature is conventionally dated from the middle of the eighteenth century and credited, rather too narrowly, to the entrepreneurial genius of John Newbery, whose first venture in colorfully printed books written to amuse as well as edify children was *A Little Pretty Pocket Book* (1744), by which time books for children had been highly vendible for several decades. From the 1750s, Newbery's little books were imported or pirated by American printers and booksellers, most notably, Isaiah Thomas in Worcester, Massachusetts.

Americans remained heavily dependent on British books for children until well into the nineteenth century, but in the 1820s, the spirit of literary nationalism began to stir interest in the creation of a truly American literature for children. Much of the literature was religious, though not narrowly sectarian. Interdenominational tract societies, such as the American Sunday School Union, established in 1818, and the American Tract Society, founded the following year, produced vast quantities of books and pamphlets for the religious and moral edification of American youth, most of it presented in the attractive format that derived from Newbery and his American imitators. Around 1825, Edmund Munroe and David Francis, two of the most active pirates of British books, printed the first modern compilation of Mother Goose rhymes; their 1833 revised edition set the tone for these rhymes in America and engendered a kind of ownership among Americans for this popular genre.

The future of American children's literature, however, did not lie in the efforts of the tract societies but in the work of such popular and prolific antebellum moralists as Jacob Abbott and Samuel Griswold Goodrich, better remembered as the genial, avuncular Peter Parley. Goodrich eventually wrote over 100 books designed to introduce his young readers to the facts of geography, history, and natural science in an informal and entertaining way—often by employing a travelogue format. Abbott, trained as a Unitarian minister, was even more prolific than Goodrich. In a series of books devoted to the educational and moral development of a good boy, Rollo, Abbott managed to hint at how an individualized child character might be created, and in a later series, the *Franconia* stories, he drew on his childhood memories of Maine in describing a group of children growing up in a rural village.

Until the 1850s, the moral tale, designed primarily to instruct the young in the civic virtues of obedience, piety, self-reliance, and self-discipline, was the principal form of secular fiction addressed to American children, but in the decade before the Civil War, there was a perceptible broadening of children's literature. William Taylor Adams, writing as Oliver Optic, introduced more adventure into boys' books while still adhering, in an early book like *The Boat Club* (1855), to the moral values of the day. Like the adventure tale, stories of family life, later a staple of girls' fiction, also have their origins in the 1850s in such popular works as *The Wide, Wide World* (1850) by Elizabeth Wetherell (Susan Bogart Warner) and Maria Cummins' *The Lamplighter* (1854), both of which illustrate the rewards accruing to faith, fortitude, and patience. Even fantasy, a form generally uncongenial to the New England temperament, can be traced to the 1850s in the work of the minor transcendentalist Christopher Pearse Cranch, *The Last of the Huggermuggers* (1855).

After the Civil War, American children's literature flowered in a manner that surprised even the most hopeful critics of children's books a decade before. Most of the differences that set off early nineteenth-century books for children from their counterparts in the 1870s and 1880s can be traced in large measure to the altered views about the nature and needs of children typically held by children's authors, publishers, and, later, librarians. By 1850, the concept of infant depravity ceased to be a major factor in shaping books for children and was replaced by a conception of the child as innocent and good.

Childhood came to be acknowledged as a separate stage of life valuable in itself, a time during which the child's capacity for wonder and imagination could be freely and safely indulged. This view of childhood affected virtually every aspect of child nurture from discipline to clothing and diet and had a profound effect on books for children. The extraordinary achievements in children's literature from 1865 to the turn of the century are owed directly and decisively to widespread acceptance of this altered view of the child.

Other factors of a more mundane sort also contributed to the expansion, diversification, and specialization of publishing for children that occurred after the Civil War. Population increases and comparatively high levels both of income and of literacy in the United States contributed to a rapid expansion of audiences for books of all kinds. Developments in printing technology speeded up the process of publication, making possible more attractive books at lower prices. Improvements in transportation, especially the creation of a continental rail system, meant that the market for children's books could be organized on a national basis. The growth of public education and the founding of public libraries also stimulated the demand for children's books.

To these demographic and technological factors, which in isolation merely describe a capacity for growth, must be added factors of belief and value. The development of literature for children after the Civil War was owed not only to the new views of childhood described earlier but also to the profound faith in the social and individual benefits of education—a faith deeply rooted in democratic thought—and to a conception of art, which, in its more exalted formulations, promised a kind of secular salvation through works of imaginative genius.

As a consequence of these views, writers for children, as well as editors and publishers, rejected the overt didacticism that had characterized the antebellum moral tale and sought to shift the emphasis in children's books from instruction to entertainment and pleasure. Nevertheless, this shift in emphasis can be overstated. The rejection of a particular form of moralizing after 1860 did not entail rejecting the moral values espoused by earlier writers, such as Goodrich and Abbott. Self-reliance, courage, and independence, if not religious faith, composed a core of values that underwent little change in the course of the century, although the literary forms in which they were expressed changed markedly. An astute student of the change correctly observes: "The assertion of freedom from moral didacticism, far from being a move toward aesthetic autonomy, was made within a definite and circumscribed moral framework."[2]

Much of the history of children's literature in the last third of the nineteenth century is foreshadowed in books and periodicals that appeared in the five years following the Civil War. The most notable single work is Louisa May Alcott's *Little Women* (1867), which provided a model for much subsequent fiction centered on family life. Earlier practitioners of the boys' adventure story, such as Oliver Optic, were joined by Harry Castlemon (Charles Austin Fosdick) and Horatio Alger Jr., whose *Ragged Dick* (1868) was the first of more than 100 novels depicting the rise (or, often, the restoration) to respectability of impoverished, often homeless boys. A popular sentimental girls' series began in 1868 with the publication of *Elsie Dinsmore* by Martha Farquharson Finley.

The works of Castlemon, Alger, and Finley defined a gray area of literary and moral respectability—not as objectionable as the dime novels and story papers, a rank undergrowth of cheap, sensational fiction that flourished despite the contempt heaped upon it by custodians of the nation's cultural life—but certainly not as praiseworthy as the work of Harriet Beecher Stowe, John Townsend Trowbridge, Louisa May Alcott, and a host of other, mainly New England writers who dominated the quality juvenile periodicals of the period: *Our Young Folks*, *Riverside Magazine*, *Wide Awake*, *Youth's Companion*, and, preeminently, *St. Nicholas*. In the thirty years following its establishment in 1873, *St. Nicholas*, under the able editorship of Mary Mapes Dodge, made available to American children the work of the best-regarded juvenile authors in Britain and the United States.

With the turn of the century, new types of children's books appeared, but there was little change in the social and intellectual factors underlying the creation of children's literature. Interest in folk tales and fairy tales, formerly limited almost exclusively to British materials and the work of the Brothers Grimm and Hans Christian Andersen, broadened to include the traditional tales of other countries. Animal stories became popular after the turn of the century, with the publication of Alfred Ollivant's *Bob, Son of Battle* (1898), Jack London's *The Call of the Wild* (1903), and the work of Ernest Thompson Seton. An even more popular new form was the school sports story, which reflected the increasing prominence of athletics in national life in the 1880s and 1890s. The Frank Merriwell stories of Burt L. Standish (Gilbert Patten), derived in large measure from the dime-novel tradition, and the work of more ambitious juvenile novelists, such as Ralph Henry Barbour, owed much to Thomas Hughes' widely read story of life at Rugby, *Tom Brown's School Days* (1857).

Such books as Kate Douglas Wiggin's *Rebecca of Sunnybrook Farm* (1903) and Dorothy Canfield Fisher's *Understood Betsy* (1917) were notable contributions in the early twentieth century to the well-established domestic story tradition inaugurated by *Little Women*, while L. Frank Baum enriched the rather thin tradition of American fantasy with *The Wonderful Wizard of Oz* (1900) and more than a dozen sequels. Another staple of juvenile publishing, the series adventure for boys, underwent development at the turn of the century at the hands of Edward Stratemeyer, who followed up his success with the Rover Boys by creating the Motor Boys and Tom Swift, among others. Retaining control of each series' concept, Stratemeyer hired writers willing to work to his formula and published their work under a series of pseudonyms. Between 1910 and 1920 a number of series books for girls appeared: the Motor Girls, Girl Aviator, and the popular Ruth Fielding series. In 1929 and 1930 Stratemeyer's most popular series first appeared: the Hardy Boys and Nancy Drew. Following his death in 1930, Stratemeyer's production-line methods of quality control were successfully continued by his daughter, Harriet Stratemeyer Adams, who took credit for the Nancy Drew books until Mildred Wirt Benson, in the 1990s and several years after Adams' death, sued for, and won, recognition of her essential work on the series.

Stratemeyer's rationalization of series book production has an analogue in the world of quality publishing for children. The growth of children's libraries and the professionalization of children's librarianship in the late nineteenth and early twentieth centuries, together with the establishment of National Book Week in 1919, the appointment in the same year of Louise Seaman Bechtel as children's book editor at Macmillan, and the concentration of children's book reviewing in the hands of librarians and educationists—all influenced the creation of children's literature, especially after 1920, in ways that are not yet well understood. Part of the effect, however, has been to maintain critical standards that appear to have changed little since the 1870s.

The decade of the 1930s saw the publication of some notable examples of the family story and the juvenile historical novel as well as some excellent retellings of traditional folktales. The picture book, however, is the principal form of children's book in which there has been dramatic improvement, owing largely to new color printing processes. The achievements of writers in the 1930s notwithstanding, the history of American children's literature in the century following the Civil War is marked by a proliferation of types but a singular continuity of underlying cultural values and assumptions.

The mid-1960s witnessed dramatic changes in the world of children's books, changes that had their proximate origins in the civil rights movement, the sexual revolution, and the emergence of the youth culture. Increased sensitivity to racial, ethnic, and gender discrimination combined with a less protective (or more honest) attitude toward children to permit franker treatment of a range of social themes—divorce, drug abuse, mental illness—than had been earlier permitted in books for children. Writers like S. E. Hinton, Judy Blume, Norma Klein, and Robert Cormier, aided by publishers who sensed the potential of the newly affluent youth market, subsequently colonized the world made familiar by J. D. Salinger's *The Catcher in the Rye* (1951). Young Adult literature, known in the trade as "YA," resulted from publishers' encouragement of writers like Hinton, Blume, Klein, and Cormier to treat teenage concerns from a teen point of view.

Coincident with the introduction of new themes and conventions of realism, federal support for public and school libraries sustained a boom in children's book publishing in the late 1960s. The reduction of that support in the 1970s translated directly into less institutional buying, still the major support for the industry, and the subsequent recession of the early Reagan years was particularly hard on children's book publishing. Several companies stopped publishing children's books altogether (McGraw-Hill, Follett, Coward-McCann), while others cut back substantially (e.g., Doubleday and Scribner's). Reduced institutional buying was offset to a point by increased space given over to children's books in bookstore chains, but the rising cost of publishing, together with reduced institutional buying and a markedly more conservative political and social climate in the early 1980s, put pressure on publishers to come up with books designed for the largest possible audience. The most significant new trend in the early 1980s was the commercial success of preteen and teenage romance series, following the introduction of Scholastic's Wildfire imprint. With print orders averaging 150,000 per title, other publishers were quick to follow Scholastic's lead. Condemned by their critics as trashy, sexist, and socially conservative, the romance series created the large audiences demanded by the new economics of publishing, which also included in the 1990s the decline of separate children's bookstores as huge conglomerates like Barnes and Noble and Borders bookstores increasingly controlled the book-buying public.

Greater parental concern with early childhood development may be responsible in part for the 1980s proliferation of books for very young children. At the other end of the spectrum, Young Adult literature is widely considered to have peaked in the 1970s and early 1980s, when the genre was defined by the "problem novel." Such books dealt generally, in teen language, with the insufficiencies of parents and home and the lack of communication between adults and their children. Teenage suicide and child abuse, both widely publicized in the early 1980s, were prominent themes realistically treated in such books. The 1980s also saw an increase in series fiction for preteen girls, especially those by Francine Pascal, a trend that reflects the overall conservatism of the decade.

Although romance fiction continues to thrive, it was overtaken in popularity in the 1990s by horror fiction for both children and young adults, a genre also considered trashy but also perhaps actively dangerous to young minds. R. L. Stine's Goosebumps series and Christopher Pike's YA novels about teens menaced by murder continue to top best-seller lists. Teachers and librarians, however, in response to the needs of their ethnically diverse classrooms, are requesting more books about other cultures. While publishers such as Scholastic attempt to satisfy this need, they continue to pour out popular literature that young people are likely to buy themselves.

REFERENCE WORKS

As it has in all fields of research, the Internet now provides instant access to a variety of informational sources, some more reliable than others. The most varied and reliable Web site is the Children's Literature Web Guide, maintained at the University of Calgary, which offers many links to other sites covering authors, award-winning books, research guides and indexes, book selections, reviews, and organizations. Other useful Web sites on children's and young adult literature are maintained through the Rutgers University School of Communication: Vandergrift's Children's Literature Page and Vandergrift's Young Adult Literature Page. The Children's Book Council maintains its own page, as does the Society of Children's Book Writers and Illustrators. Among listservs, Child-lit tends to be academic in its discussions, while Kitlit-L includes librarians, authors, and parents among its members. But when seeking information on or about the Web, one must keep in mind the frequency and rapidity with which Internet sites change.

Electronic addresses (URLs) for these sites and listservers may be found in Mark West's *Everyone's Guide to Children's Literature*, one of the most accessible print guides to the entire field. What this guide lacks in comprehensiveness it makes up for in clarity and ease of use. Among older, more distinctly academic print guides, *Children's Literature: A Guide to Reference Sources*, by Virginia Haviland, former head of the children's division, Library of Congress, and *The World of Children's Literature*, by Anne Pellowski, are both most useful for works published before 1965. Haviland's *Guide* is a selective annotated bibliography of books, articles, and pamphlets on the history, selection and evaluation, illustration, authorship, and principal genres of books for children. The scope of the volume is limited largely to the professional literature of librarianship and education; however, there are a few references to the substantial body of writing about children's literature by historians, literary scholars, and the occasional psychologist or sociologist who ventured into the field. Pellowski's *The World of Children's Literature* is especially useful for its multicultural materials, containing an international bibliography of monographs, series, and multivolume works, organized by country, relating to various aspects of writing for children, including the history and criticism of children's books, library work with children, criteria and techniques of writing for children, lists of recommended books, and children's reading interests. An elaborate index permits the reader to locate items about a given author, type of children's book, or theme. The brief historical introduction to children's literature in the United States is unusual for its account of social factors shaping the production of books for children in this country.

Journals tend to identify with one of three approaches to children's literature: academic, pedagogical, and marketing for either libraries or bookshops. Among academic journals, *Children's Literature* is the most scholarly. Issued annually by the Children's Literature Association, it emphasizes critical approaches to books for children. The association's *Quarterly*, while sharing the critical focus of *Children's Literature*, is a livelier forum for the membership, drawn principally from the ranks of English departments. The *Lion and the Unicorn*, published three times yearly, is a theme- and genre-centered journal with aesthetic preoccupations similar to those that inform *Children's Literature*. More interested in pedagogy is *Children's Literature in Education*, a joint venture of British and American professors, which grew out of a 1969 British conference on the role of children's fiction in education. With its roots in the problems in schools, *Children's Literature in Education* has always had a broader mandate than the critical journals founded in the 1970s in this country. The *Horn Book Magazine*, long the only American periodical devoted exclusively to children's literature, addresses the needs of booksellers and librarians for selective capsule reviewing and advertisements for new books. It also publishes critical articles, speeches by authors, and occasional historical studies, though most are not written by historians. Articles on children's literature also appear regularly in the *Journal of Youth Services in Libraries* (until 1987 known as *Top of the News*), the quarterly journal of the Children's Services Division and Young Adult Services Division of the American Library Association.

Biographical information on children's authors and illustrators is almost an industry of its own. The most comprehensive reference guide is Joyce Nakamura's *Children's Authors and Illustrators*, now in its fifth edition, which lists over 20,000 writers and artists whose work is available in English. The work also serves as an individual guide to the principal sources of biographical information such as the *Book of Junior Authors and Illustrators*, the first of which appeared in 1934. Its most recent edition is the *Seventh Book of Junior Authors and Illustrators*, edited in 1996 by Sally Holmes Holtze. Anne Commire's series *Something about the Author*, now in its ninety-eighth volume, remains an indispensable source of biographical information. In the mid-1990s a subset was made available in CD-ROM format. Edited by Gerard J. Senick and Joanna Brod, *Something about the Author Autobiography Series*, in its twenty-fourth volume in 1997, does not generally include full biographical information, and many authors and illustrators of interest have been omitted from it. *Twentieth-Century Children's Writers*, now edited by Laura Standley Berger, collects entries consisting of a short biography, complete bibliography, and a brief critical essay on English-language authors of fiction, poetry, and drama for children. Young adults now have their own biography series, *Authors and Artists for Young Adults*. From Gale, in twenty-one volumes as of 1997 and now edited by Thomas McMahon, its subjects include painters, cartoonists, songwriters, and film directors as well as writers. Ted Hipple's three-volume *Writers for Young Adults* is more compact, with an excellent foreword by Robert Cormier. Very usable is Bernard Drew, *The 100 Most Popular Young Adult Authors: Biographical Sketches and Bibliographies*, though it seems to rely on the Gale series *Authors and Artists for Young Adults* for much of its information. Two articles by David L. Greene describe limited circulation, special interest periodicals devoted to children's authors, such as *Newsboy*, the journal of the Horatio Alger Society, and the *Baum Bugle*, published by the International Wizard of Oz Club: "Children's Literature Journals: Author Society Journals and Fanzines" and "Children's Literature Periodicals on Individual Authors, Dime Novels, Fantasy."

For biographical information on illustrators, the standard source is *Illustrators of Children's Books, 1744–1945*, by Bertha E. Mahoney Miller, Louise P. Latimer, and Beulah Folmsbee, which provides information on 500 illustrators whose work has appeared in picture books in this country. Supplements appeared in 1958 and 1968. Martha E. Ward and Dorothy A. Marquardt's *Illustrators of Books for Young People*, with 750 entries, is also valuable. Limited in scope but providing many valuable insights into the golden age of children's illustration is Susan E. Meyer's *A Treasury of the Great Children's Book Illustrators*, which covers thirteen major illustrators of the late nineteenth and early twentieth centuries.

The most complete listing of contemporary books for children is *Children's Books in Print*, an annual trade bibliography published by R. R. Bowker since 1970. Its companion volume, *Subject Guide to Children's Books in Print*, lists books under 7,000 categories. Other indexes include Norma O. Ireland's *Index to Fairy Tales, 1949–1972, including Folklore, Legends, and Myths in Collections*, which has been updated in three companion volumes. *Children's Catalogue*, first published in 1909, is a selection aid for librarians. The seventeenth edition, edited by Anne Price and Juliette Yaakov, appeared in 1996.

An invaluable historical bibliography of books for children is D'Alte A. Welch's "A Bibliography of American Children's Books Printed prior to 1821," originally published serially in the *Proceedings of the American Antiquarian Society* and then reprinted as a single volume in which, unfortunately, the valuable notes on the British originals of American books were eliminated. Primarily interested in books intended for leisure reading, Welch excluded from his bibliography school books, catechisms, conduct manuals, and other popular materials that were intended solely or primarily for instruction. The usefulness of the bibliography is enhanced by Welch's survey of private and institutional collections of early American juveniles as well as by notes indicating libraries that own copies of the books listed.

Specialized bibliographies for children's literature are numerous. For the vast literature of the dime novel, Charles Bragin's *Bibliography of Dime Novels, 1860–1964* provides valuable guidance. Deidre Johnson's *Stratemeyer Pseudonyms and Series Books* is an equally valuable guide to the Stratemeyer syndicate's numerous

Little Red Riding Hood. Courtesy of the Library of Congress

popular series. Dorothy Blythe Jones, *An "Oliver Optic" Checklist*, catalogs the series, nonseries stories, and magazine publications of the prolific William Taylor Adams, who also wrote under the pseudonyms Gayle Winterton, Warren T. Ashton, and Brooks McCormick.

Genre bibliographies include Barbara K. Harrah's *Sports Books for Children*, which lists 3,500 titles that were in print in January 1977. Ruth Nadelman Lynn's *Fantasy for Children*, now in its fourth edition, is indispensable for works written in the past 100 years and offers both bibliogaphical data and biocritical information, including books, book chapters, articles, and dissertations. *Children's Fiction Series* by Philip H. Young lists 1,234 titles of series for children and young adults and includes an introductory overview of the development of this genre. For researchers interested in teen reading, Diana Tixier Herald's *Teen Genreflecting* offers genre groupings of works popular with young adults.

The increasing demand for multicultural materials has resulted in a growing number of useful reference works. The following is only a small suggestion of the available reference guides. In addition to older works such as Augusta Baker's pioneering *The Black Experience in Children's Books* and Arlene B. Hirschfelder's *American Indian Stereotypes in the World of Children*, Barbara Rollock has edited *Black Authors and Illustrators of Children's Books*, and Helen E. Williams has assembled *Books by African-American Authors and Illustrators for Children and Young Adults*.

Vicki Anderson's *Native Americans in Fiction* is a guide to 765 books dealing with 116 tribes. Isabel Schon's *A Hispanic Heritage* is a guide to juvenile books treating Hispanic culture, and Meena Khorana assembled more than 900 annotated entries of English-language books for *The Indian Subcontinent in Literature for Children and Young Adults*. More general guides are Alethea K. Helbig and Agnes Regan Perkins' *This Land Is Our Land* and Rudine Sims Bishop's *Kaleidoscope: A Multicultural Booklist for Grades K–8*.

Over 400 children's periodicals are listed in R. Gordon Kelly's *Children's Periodicals of the United States*, the most extensive compilation to date. Lavinia G. Dobler's *The Dobler World Directory of Youth Periodicals* provides selective international coverage through 1970. The preeminent American children's magazine, *St. Nicholas* (1873–1944), is indexed by Anna Lorraine Guthrie (through 1920) and more selectively by John Mackay Shaw, *The Poems, Poets and Illustrators of St. Nicholas Magazine, 1873–1943*.

Some students of children's literature have argued that the serious reviewing of children's books did not really begin until just after World War I with the work of Anne Carroll Moore in the *New York Herald Tribune*. This view is rendered indefensible by Richard L. Darling's excellent monograph *The Rise of Children's Book Reviewing in America, 1865–1881*. Darling demonstrates beyond cavil that children's books were widely reviewed in periodicals of all kinds and frequently judged by critical standards not significantly different from those in use during the last seventy years.

In recent years the reviewing of children's books has been increasingly restricted to a handful of specialized professional periodicals, of which the most important in terms of affecting a book's commercial success are *School Library Journal* and *Booklist*, the latter published by the American Library Association as a selection guide for small and medium-sized public libraries, as well as schools and junior colleges. The *New York Times Book Review*, the *Horn Book Magazine*, *Language Arts*, *English Journal*, and the *Bulletin of the Center for Children's Books* also do extensive reviewing of children's books. Much of this reviewing activity is superficial, however, with few reviews in excess of 300 words. Reviews since 1975 are listed in *Children's Book Review Index*. *Children's Literature Review*, now in its fiftieth volume and edited chiefly by Ann Bloch and Carolyn Riley, excerpts reviews of children's books.

Lists of selected children's books are legion. Only a representational few are mentioned here. Among the most current and influential are those published annually by the National Council of Teachers of English. *Books for You*, edited in 1992 principally by Shirley Wurth, annotates teen reading, while *Your Reading*, edited in 1996 by Barbara G. Samuels and G. Kylene Beers, selects books for junior high and middle school readers. The American Library Association and the University of Chicago publish "best of the best" lists, and Bowker also publishes *Best Books for Children*, *Best Books for Senior High Readers*, and *Best Books for Junior High Readers*, all edited by John T. Gillespie. The needs of preschool children are addressed in Lois Winkel and Sue Kimmel's *Mother Goose Comes First*, which annotates books and sound recordings. John Gordon Burke's *Choices for Young Readers: A Comprehensive Selection of the Best Children's Books* is available in both book and CD-ROM format. An example of a selection made by young readers themselves (a rarity) is *Teens' Favorite Books: Young Adult Choices 1987–1992*, published by the International Reading Association in cooperation with a committee of the Children's Book Council. The historical development of approved lists of books has not received the systematic attention that the subject deserves, but Esther Jane Carrier's *Fiction in Public Libraries, 1876–1900*, especially the chapter "Fiction for Young People," reveals the terms of the debate over appropriate principles of selection that concerned late-nineteenth-century librarians.

As the number of awards given for children's books has proliferated, so have books about them. The Children's Book Council regularly compiles a list of such awards: *Children's Books: Awards & Prizes*. The tenth edition in 1996 lists 213 awards and prizes, including new awards for nonfiction, poetry, and books treating the gay and lesbian experience. The Newbery and Caldecott awards, given annually by the American Library Association to the best work of fiction for children and best-illustrated book, respectively, still dominate the field in America. Recent information about them is available in the association's *Newbery and Caldecott Awards: A Guide to the Medal and Honor Books*, which augments its lists with an essay on the origin and terms of the award. Jim Roginski's *Newbery and Caldecott Medalists and Honor Book Winners* is now in its second edition. Older works that include still useful information are those by Bertha E. Mahoney Miller and Elinor W. Field, *Newbery Medal Books, 1922–1955* and *Caldecott Medal Books, 1938–1957*; and Lee Kingman, *Newbery and Caldecott Medal Books, 1956–1965*. These volumes are especially valuable for the authors' acceptance papers reproduced in them. Kingman produced two more volumes, for 1966–1975 and for 1976–1985, also published by Horn Book.

The presence of sexism in children's literature has been an issue for three decades. Compilations of materials deemed nonsexist are *A Guide to Non-Sexist Children's Books*. Volume 1 was edited by Judith Adell, Hilary D. Klein, and Jordan Miller, and volume 2 by Denise Wilms and Ilene Cooper.

Two textbooks have long been preeminent in the field of children's literature; both are designed for college-level children's literature courses in education departments and rely heavily on capsule summaries and prescriptions for what constitutes "good" literature. May Hill Arbuthnot's *Children and Books* was first published in 1947. An eighth edition, edited by Zena Sutherland, appeared in 1991. *Children's Literature in the Elementary School*, by Charlotte Huck, first published in 1961 and most recently revised with Susan Hepler in 1996, aims to introduce prospective elementary teachers to the various types of literature for children and offers an outline for a classroom literary program. These two textbooks are now joined by Donna E. Norton's *Through the Eyes of a Child*, in its fifth edition in 1999. Like some other recent textbooks, Norton's comes with a CD-ROM supplement. A particularly lively and unusual textbook is Perry Nodelman's *The Pleasures of Children's Literature*, which emphasizes that literature is first of all a pleasure, while encouraging students to think about their own attitudes toward childhood. Rebecca J. Lukens' *A Critical Handbook of Children's Literature*, in its sixth edition in 1998, approaches the teaching of children's literature by defining and illustrating fundamental literary concepts such as plot, character, and setting and then attempting to establish prescriptive norms for what constitutes a good plot, effective characters, and so on in an abstract and absolute sense.

In the 1970s, some textbooks began emphasizing social relevance over literary merit. One such was *Now upon a Time*, by Myra P. Sadker and David M. Sadker, which, though out of print, is still valuable for sections on sexism and violence in children's books. A similar textbook, *Children's Literature: An Issues Approach*, by Masha K. Rudman, entered a third edition in 1995.

Several collections of essays on children's literature are valuable. Virginia Haviland's *Children and Literature: Views and Reviews* contain over seventy essays concerning the history, major genres, and the development in several foreign countries of children's literature. *Only Connect*, now in its third edition and compiled by Sheila Egoff, collects articles that deal with children's literature as part of all literature. Emphasized are the relationship between children and books, fantasy in children's literature, the relationship of children's authors to their work, and the characteristics of the contemporary literary situation. In the companion volume to their anthology *Classics of Children's Literature*, now entering its fifth edition, Charles Frey and John Griffith offer original insights along with historical and biographical information on those classics in the essays contained in *The Literary Heritage of Childhood: An Appraisal of Children's Classics in the Western Tradition*. *The Hewins Lectures, 1947–1962*, edited by Siri Andrews, is a collection of addresses given annually in commemoration of the pioneer children's librarian Caroline M. Hewins. Most are devoted to historical topics, especially the work of New England authors of the last century such as A.D.T. Whitney, Eliza White, Laura Richards, and Lucretia Hale. Nicholas Tucker's *Suitable for Children? Controversies in Children's Literature* draws heavily on British writing but brings together a fine set of essays on fairy stories, comics, and children's classics. Articles on the value of children's literature round out the collection. Especially useful for the student of popular culture is Mark West's *Children, Culture, and Controversy*, which focuses exclusively on American children's issues and includes essays on horror comics and the so-called New Realism. Some fifty articles on all phases of children's literature that appeared originally in the *Horn Book Magazine* between 1949 and 1966 are collected in *Horn Book Reflections on Children's Books and Reading*, edited by Elinor Whitney Field.

A particularly lively collection of personal essays is Selma G. Lanes' *Down the Rabbit Hole*. Concerned with the quality of children's books but not given to repeating pious inanities, Lanes is a sensitive, informed, and incisive commentator on topics ranging from the demise of *St. Nicholas Magazine*, to the recent proliferation of picture books and the value of Dr. Seuss. Lanes also has some acute and useful things to say about the constraints imposed by the economics of the children's book trade. Anne Scott MacLeod in *American Childhood* offers useful insights and historical contexts about popular American literature such as the Nancy Drew series, Alger's books, and YA literature. Louise Seaman Bechtel's *Books in Search of Children* consists of speeches and essays by Macmillan's pioneer children's editor. Another editor, Jean Karl, in *From Childhood to Childhood*, reflects upon the making of children's books from the vantage point of twenty years' experience. Two books by influential children's librarians are Frances Clarke Sayers' *Summoned by Books* and Lillian H. Smith's *The Unreluctant Years*. Smith's, first published in 1953 and reprinted in 1991, is arguably the most influential statement of the standards and goals for criticism of children's books that has appeared since World War II.

RESEARCH COLLECTIONS

A full listing of children's literature research materials in American libraries, with annotations, is contained in Vol. 1 of Lee Ash and William G. Miller, *Subject Collections*. Dolores Blythe Jones identified 300 collections in *Special Collections in Children's Literature: An International Directory*. A small, but unusually well-annotated, list is contained in Mark West's *Everyone's Guide to Children's Literature*, which includes Web site and electronic mail addresses. It is now possible to browse listings in some collections via the Internet.

Brief overviews of the history and diversity of collections of children's literature are provided in two useful articles: James H. Fraser, "Children's Literature Collections and Research Libraries," and Frances Henne, "Toward a National Plan to Nourish Research in Children's Literature." "Research Collections in New England," by Ruth Hayes, Priscilla Moulton, and Sarah Reuter, describes nearly fifty collections of children's books held by New England colleges, universities, historic societies, public libraries, and religious associations.

The rich holdings of the Library of Congress are summarized by Virginia Haviland in "Serving Those Who Serve Children: A National Reference Library of Children's Books." The two-volume *Children's Books in the Rare Book Division of the Library of Congress* reproduces the card catalog of the collection. The origins and development of the outstanding collection of the colonial and antebellum books for children housed at the American Antiquarian Society are described by Frederick E. Bauer Jr., "Children's Literature and the American Antiquarian Society." A similar survey of the Pierpont Morgan Library collection is Gerald Gottlieb's "Keeping Company with the Gutenbergs." *Early Children's Books and Their Illustration*, with text by Gerald Gottlieb and a fine introductory essay by the noted British social historian J. II. Plumb, includes descriptions of a few American books, but this sumptuously produced catalog of an exhibit at the Pierpont Morgan Library is essential to any serious student of American children's literature. Another of the outstanding collections of children's books in the country is at the Free Library of Philadelphia. *Early American Children's Books*, by A.S.W. Rosenbach, catalogs some 680 items printed before 1836 that form the nucleus for this collection. A *Checklist of Children's Books, 1837–1876*, by Barbara Maxwell, extends Rosenbach's coverage of this important collection.

Unlike Rosenbach and other notable collectors of children's books, Irvin Kerlan, who gave his collection to the University of Minnesota, concentrated his efforts primarily on twentieth-century materials (initially, award-winning books), but in addition to books, he collected correspondence, original illustrations, manuscripts, book dummies, and press proofs, thus permitting the study of a work from its inception to its final form. *The May Massee Collection*, by George V. Hodowanec, describes a research collection at the William Allen White Library, Emporia State University. Massee, the second children's book editor, worked first at Doubleday (1922–1932) before going to Viking, where she remained until 1960. The collection consists of books for which she served as editor as well as manuscripts, correspondence, and original artwork. A collection especially useful for students of popular culture is that of Ruth Baldwin, now held at the Smathers Libraries at the University of Florida. Baldwin was interested in books that chil-

227

dren actually read, so the collection contains popular works, many printed before 1820.

HISTORY AND CRITICISM

The most comprehensive new history of children's literature has been assembled by Peter Hunt. *Children's Literature: An Illustrated History* is a lavishly illustrated and produced volume, stronger on English children's books but containing two excellent chapters on American children's literature. John Rowe Townsend's *Written for Children*, in its sixth American edition in 1997, still provides a useful overview, and *The Oxford Companion to Children's Literature*, edited by Humphrey Carpenter and Mari Prichard, is especially strong on material from the eighteenth and nineteenth centuries, though, like Hunt's book, it concentrates its efforts mostly on British children's literature and contains some errors in its information about American children's literature. An unusual history is John Goldthwaite's intriguing and well-written *The Natural History of Make-Believe*, tracing the organic links among works of fantasy for children. Still useful as a starting point for a consideration of critical trends is *Crosscurrents of Criticism*, edited by Paul Heins of *Horn Book Magazine*, which reprints essays from that journal from the period 1968–1977. A major new overview of American children's and YA authors, devoted mostly to the twentieth century but containing some nineteenth-century authors, is Anita Silvey's *Children's Books and Their Creators*, which includes commentary by the authors themselves.

In an earlier article, "American Children's Literature: An Historiographical Review," R. Gordon Kelly described and evaluated the development of historical writing on children's literature in America. The most authoritative brief account of the development of literature for children in this country is Fred Erisman's essay "Children's Literature in the United States, 1800–1940," but some older discussions of children's books in America are still useful: Charles Welsh, "The Early History of Children's Books in New England"; Elva S. Smith, *A History of Children's Literature: A Syllabus with Selected Bibliographies*; and Rosalie V. Halsey, *Forgotten Books of the American Nursery*. Smith's *History* was reissued in a revised and enlarged edition in 1980 under the joint editorship of Margaret Hodges and Susan Steinfirst. William Sloane's *Children's Books in England and America in the Seventeenth Century* convincingly argues that seventeenth-century books for children were varied both in subject matter and in the means chosen to appeal to youthful minds. Still valuable as an account of the popular primers of the eighteenth century, Paul Leicester Ford's *The New England Primer* includes a reprint of a 1727 edition, the oldest copy extant.

Anne Scott MacLeod's *A Moral Tale: Children's Fiction and American Culture, 1820–1860* is the best study to date of the didactic fiction of the antebellum period. Particularly valuable are her efforts to relate the moral tales to the social dislocation of the period. "Values Expressed in American Children's Readers, 1800–1850," by Richard DeCharms and Gerald H. Moeller, is still useful, in part for the method of content analysis employed in the study.

The thirty-five years between the end of the Civil War and the turn of the century saw an expansion and diversification of children's literature as well as a shift in emphasis from instruction to entertainment. Many of the changes can be

Cinderella. Courtesy of the Library of Congress

traced in the children's periodicals of the period. John Morton Blum's *Yesterday's Children* is both an excellent anthology compiled from *Our Young Folks*, the prototypical New England literary magazine for children, and a cogent analysis of the social values expressed in its pages. Lovell Thompson's *Youth's Companion* is a rewarding anthology of articles and stories from the pages of the most popular and longest-lived of American juvenile periodicals. R. Gordon Kelly's *Mother Was a Lady* analyzes the structure of values exemplified in the major children's periodicals of the post–Civil War period, including *St. Nicholas, Youth's Companion,* and *Young Folks. Children's Periodicals of the United States,* edited by Kelly, profiles 100 American periodicals for children and, as noted earlier, lists over 400 periodicals with their dates and places of publication. Still helpful is Frank Luther Mott's standard work, *A History of American Magazines.*

The business of publishing books for children is a relatively neglected area of study, but three monographs on important nineteenth-century publishers by Raymond Kilgour deserve mention: *Estes and Lauriat; Messrs. Roberts Brothers, Publishers;* and *Lee and Shepard.* The latter, a year-by-year account of books published and moneys paid to authors, includes material on the public reception of the firm's books as well as biographical information on house authors and brief descriptions of selected books brought out by the firm. Later trends can be explored through

Robin Gottlieb's *Publishing Children's Books in America, 1919–1976*, an annotated bibliography of articles appearing in trade journals such as *Publishers Weekly* and in the principal journals used by librarians. George V. Hodowanec's guide to the May Massee collection, cited earlier, is also relevant. Children's book publishers are listed in *Children's Books in Print*. Supplementing that list is the third edition of *Alternative Press Publishers of Children's Books*, edited by Kathleen T. Horning. In *Getting Books to Children*, Joseph Turow takes a sharply focused, case-study approach to publisher–market relations.

A reliable overview of changes in children's literature at the end of the nineteenth century is Russel B. Nye's "The Juvenile Approach to American Culture, 1870–1930." Arthur Prager, in *Rascals at Large; or, the Clue in the Old Nostalgia*, writes affectionately but incisively about the popular heroes of his childhood reading: the Hardy boys, Tom Swift, Don Sturdy, Bomba the Jungle Boy, and a host of other series characters whose exploits go unsung in the standard histories. Interesting perspectives on the writing and publishing of the Nancy Drew series, especially the discovery of Mildred Wirt Benson as the author of most of the books, are contained in *Rediscovering Nancy Drew*, edited by Carolyn Stewart Dyer and Nancy Tillman Romalov.

Substantial interpretive and critical studies of children's authors have advanced in number and quality in recent years. The Children's Literature Association *Quarterly* now devotes an occasional issue to extensive bibliographies; the majority of the entries concern authors and illustrators. Among monographs, *A Sense of Story* by the British critic and children's author John Rowe Townsend remains a thoughtful assessment of nineteen contemporary British, American, and Australian writers.

Alcott, Alger, and Baum, the major popular figures of the late nineteenth century, have attracted some of the best criticism. One of the most notable students of Louisa May Alcott's writing is Madeleine B. Stern. *Louisa's Wonder Book* reprints a heretofore unknown Alcott juvenile and provides a revised bibliography of Alcott's writings. More recently, Stern and Daniel Shealy edited a collection of Alcott's periodical stories, *From Jo March's Attic: Stories of Intrigue and Suspense*. Shealy, with the help of Stern and Joel Myerson, has also edited *Freaks of Genius: Unknown Thrillers by Louisa May Alcott*. On Horatio Alger, the work of Gary Scharnhorst and Jack Bales, *The Lost Life of Horatio Alger, Jr.*, is indispensable. Still valuable are John Seelye, "Who Was Horatio?"; Robert Falk, "Notes on the 'Higher Criticism' of Horatio Alger, Jr."; and Frank Gruber, *Horatio Alger, Jr.: A Biography and Bibliography*. Still the best single essay on Alger, R. Richard Wohl's "The Rags to Riches Story: An Episode in Secular Idealism," can be supplemented by John G. Cawelti's discussion of Alger in *Apostles of the Self-Made Man*, which places Alger in the context of earlier fiction about street children, and Michael Zuckerman's "The Nursery Tales of Horatio Alger, Jr." Dee Garrison, "Custodians of Culture in the Gilded Age: The Public Librarian and Horatio Alger," describes librarians' efforts to counter Alger's popularity in the late nineteenth century. Madonne M. Miner's psychoanalytic essay on *Ragged Dick* explores, among other issues, its complex attitudes toward money.

The popular Oz books by L. Frank Baum have also attracted the interest of cultural historians. Baum's life and work are ably described in *The Wizard of Oz and Who He Was*, by Martin Gardner and Russel B. Nye. Fred Erisman, "L. Frank

Baum and the Progressive Dilemma," analyzes the differences between the Oz books and Baum's more realistic series, Aunt Jane's Nieces. Henry Littlefield, "The Wizard of Oz: Parable on Populism," argues for a coherent pattern of political reference in *The Wonderful Wizard of Oz*, Baum's first Oz book. S. J. Sackett, "The Utopia of Oz," reconstructs the Utopian vision allegedly informing the Oz series. In 1996, Nancy Tystad Koupal edited a collection of Baum's newspaper columns from 1890 to 1891 that he titled *Our Landlady*.

Daniel Roselle's *Samuel Griswold Goodrich* is the best account of the life and work of the prolific and influential antebellum children's author who created the appealing persona of Peter Parley. John L. Cutler's *Gilbert Patten and His Frank Merriwell Saga* is a sympathetic biographical and literary analysis of a popular author generally ignored in the standard histories of children's literature. The work of Frank R. Stockton, a frequent contributor to *St. Nicholas* and one of the few American fantasy writers for children in the nineteenth century, is competently examined by Martin I. J. Griffin in *Frank R. Stockton: A Critical Biography*. An excellent critical and cultural study of classic American children's books of the late nineteenth and early twentieth centuries is Jerry Griswold's *Audacious Kids: Coming of Age in America's Classic Children's Books*. Griswold sees a mythic pattern in these books that reflects the efforts of America to find its own identity.

Several studies have dealt with various genres of children's literature. A particularly fine example is *The Uses of Enchantment*, a Freudian inquiry into the significance of fairy tales for the psychological development of young children, by the gifted psychotherapist Bruno Bettelheim. First published in 1976, it was reissued in 1989. An earlier, neglected study on the same topic is Julius E. Heuscher, *A Psychiatric Study of Fairy Tales*. More wide-ranging psychoanalytic critique of various works of popular children's fiction may be found in Lucy Rollin and Mark I. West, *Psychoanalytic Responses to Children's Literature*, which offers analyses based on object relations as well as depth psychology. Jack Zipes and Maria Tatar have emerged as the preeminent commentators on fairy tales in recent years. Zipes, who has also translated and collected the work of the Grimms and others, is especially useful as cultural commentary and as an example of the application of Marxist critique to children's literature. His latest book is *Happily Ever After: Fairy Tales, Children, and the Culture Industry*. In addition to her essays and criticism, Tatar has edited *The Classic Fairy Tales*, containing a comparative presentation of the texts of several tales and a selection of foundational essays about them. Another area of children's folklore, the Mother Goose rhymes, receives a cultural and psychological analysis in *Cradle and All*, by Lucy Rollin.

Renewed appreciation of the picture book in the last twenty-five years has stimulated an interest in the historical development of this form of children's book. Barbara Bader, *American Picturebooks from Noah's Ark to the Beast Within*, is still a useful survey; Joyce Irene Whalley's *Cobwebs to Catch Flies* is limited to illustrated books of the eighteenth and nineteenth centuries. *Myth, Magic, and Mystery: 100 Years of American Children's Picture Book Illustration*, compiled by Trinkett Clark and H. Nichols B. Clark, is based on a exhibition from the Chrysler Museum of Art. Lois Kuznets' *When Toys Come Alive* offers a wide-ranging and insightful study of toy characters in children's fiction, while Ruth B. Bottigheimer explores a neglected area of popular children's literature in *The Bible for Children, from the Age of Gutenberg to the Present*. Teen romance fiction is addressed from a sociological perspective in *Becoming a Woman through Romance* by Linda K. Christian-Smith, who spent time in high schools interviewing and interacting with girls who read romances.

Gender and ethnicity have occupied many critics in recent years. Bobbie Ann Mason offers a feminist reading of the Nancy Drew and other series in *The Girl Sleuth*, while Roberta Trites addresses the fairy tale in *Waking Sleeping Beauty*. Beverly Lyon Clark has studied the contradictions of gender in school stories in *Regendering the School Story: Sassy Sissies and Tattling Tomboys*, and Shirley Foster and Judy Simons reread girls' classic books from a feminist perspective in *What Katy Read*. Among treatments of ethnic or racial groups in books for children, one of the earliest and most influential analyses, Nancy Larrick's "The All-White World of Children's Books," reported that fewer than 10 percent of the 5,000 trade books for children published in the period 1962–1964 included black characters. Among the most comprehensive studies of the image of blacks in literature is Dorothy M. Broderick's *Image of the Black in Children's Fiction*, which treats books published from 1827 to 1967. Rudine Sims, *Shadow and Substance*, examines the Afro-American experience in books published between 1965 and 1979. Black stereotypes in series fiction are described by Paul C. Deane, "The Persistence of Uncle Tom." *The Black American in Books for Children*, edited by Donnarae MacCann and Gloria Woodard, is a useful collection of readings on the topic. The two editors also produced another collection of readings on racism, *Cultural Conformity in Books for Children*. Jane Bingham's "The Pictorial Treatment of Afro-Americans in Books for Children, 1930–1968" summarizes her doctoral research. Michelle Martin offers an interesting discussion of the racial ideology of Little Black Sambo in "Hey, Who's the Kid with the Green Umbrella?"

The increased attention to theory in academic discussions of adult literature has finally made itself felt in critical material on children's literature as well. Roderick McGillis ably demonstrates the application of contemporary theory to several major children's books in *The Nimble Reader*, while Peter Hunt advocates "childist" criticism in *Criticism, Theory, and Children's Literature*. Perry Nodelman's brilliant *Words about Pictures* applies mostly semiotic theory to a selection of picture books, but his conclusions will have a major impact on how children's literature scholars view all picture books. John Cech's gracefully written *Angels and Wild Things* explores the work of Maurice Sendak from an archetypal viewpoint. John Noell Moore reveals the complexity of several YA books by applying several contemporary theories to them in *Interpreting Young Adult Literature*.

Various theories of culture have recently found an especially fertile field in the study of film and of Walt Disney and his work. Douglas Street's *Children's Novels and the Movies* contains essays on a varied selection of film adaptations of famous children's books. Eric Smoodin has edited two collections of essays on all aspects of Walt Disney: *Animating Culture: Hollywood Cartoons from the Sound Era* and *Disney Discourse: Producing the Magic Kingdom*. Feminist critique dominates *From Mouse to Mermaid: The Politics of Film, Gender, and Culture* edited by Elizabeth Bell, Lynda Haas, and Laura Sells, which examines Disney's adaptations of *The Jungle Book*, *The Little Mermaid*, *Mary Poppins*, and other children's books. Bell's and Smoodin's books are written mostly for film scholars, but the impact of film on children's books today makes them important to researchers in children's literature.

NOTES

Jessica L. Vaughan provided research assistance for this chapter.

1. William Sloane, *Children's Books in England and America in the Seventeenth Century* (New York: King's Crown Press, 1955), 4–5.

2. E. Geller, "Somewhat Free: Post Civil War Writing for Children," *Wilson Library Bulletin* 51 (1976), 175.

BIBLIOGRAPHY

Books and Articles

Adell, Judith, Hilary D. Klein, and Jordan Miller, eds. *A Guide to Non-Sexist Children's Books, Vol. I: To 1976*. Chicago: Academy Press, 1987.

Anderson, Vicki. *Native Americans in Fiction: A Guide to 765 Books for Librarians and Teachers, K–9*. Jefferson, N.C.: McFarland, 1994.

Andrews, Siri, ed. *The Hewins Lectures, 1947–1962*. Boston: Horn Book, 1963.

Arbuthnot, May Hill. *Children and Books*. Chicago: Scott, Foresman, 1947.

Ash, Lee, and William G. Miller, eds. *Subject Collections*. Vol. 1. 7th ed. New York: R. R. Bowker, 1993.

Bader, Barbara. *American Picturebooks from Noah's Ark to the Beast Within*. New York: Macmillan, 1976.

Baker, Augusta. *The Black Experience in Children's Books*. New York: New York Public Library, 1971. New edition by Barbara Rollock, 1989.

Bauer, Frederick E., Jr. "Children's Literature and the American Antiquarian Society." *Phaedrus* 3 (Spring 1976), 5–8.

Bechtel, Louise Seaman. *Books in Search of Children*. New York: Macmillan, 1969.

Bell, Elizabeth, Lynda Haas, and Laura Sells, eds. *From Mouse to Mermaid: The Politics of Film, Gender, and Culture*. Bloomington: Indiana University Press, 1995.

Berger, Laura Standley, ed. *Twentieth Century Children's Writers*. 4th ed. Detroit: St. James Press, 1995.

Bettelheim, Bruno. *The Uses of Enchantment: The Meaning and Importance of Fairy Tales* (1976). New York: Random House, 1989.

Bingham, Jane. "The Pictorial Treatment of Afro-Americans in Books for Children, 1930–1968." *Elementary English* 48 (November 1971), 880–85.

Bishop, Rudine Sims. *Kaleidoscope: A Multicultural Booklist for Grades K–8*. Urbana, Ill.: National Council of Teachers of English, 1994.

Bloch, Ann, Carolyn Riley, et al., eds. *Children's Literature Review*. Detroit: Gale Research, 1999.

Blum, John Morton, ed. *Yesterday's Children: An Anthology Compiled from the Pages of "Our Young Folks," 1865–1873*. Boston: Houghton Mifflin, 1959.

Bottigheimer, Ruth B. *The Bible for Children, from the Age of Gutenberg to the Present*. New Haven, Conn.: Yale University Press, 1996.

Bragin, Charles. *Bibliography of Dime Novels, 1860–1964*. Rev. ed. Brooklyn, N.Y.: Dime Novel Club, 1964.

Broderick, Dorothy M. *Images of the Black in Children's Fiction*. New York: R. R. Bowker, 1973.

Brown, Sterling. *The Negro in American Fiction*. Washington, D.C.: Associates in Negro Folk Education, 1937. Reprint. Ayer, 1972.

Burke, John Gordon. *Choices for Young Readers: A Comprehensive Selection of the Best Children's Books*. CD-ROM. Evanston, Ill.: John Gordon Burke, 1997.

Carpenter, Humphrey, and Mari Prichard. *The Oxford Companion to Children's Literature*. New York: Oxford University Press, 1984.

Carrier, Esther Jane. *Fiction in Public Libraries, 1876–1900*. New York: Scarecrow Press, 1965.

Cawelti, John G. *Apostles of the Self-Made Man*. Chicago: University of Chicago Press, 1965. Reprint. 1988.

Cech, John. *Angels and Wild Things: The Archetypal Poetics of Maurice Sendak*. University Park: University of Pennsylvania Press, 1995.

Children's Book Review Index. Detroit: Gale Research, 1975– .

Children's Books: Awards and Prizes. New York: Children's Book Council, 1996.

Children's Books in Print. New York: R. R. Bowker, 1970– .

Children's Books in the Rare Book Division of the Library of Congress. 2 vols. Totowa, N.J.: Rowman and Littlefield, 1976.

Christian-Smith, Linda K. *Becoming a Woman through Romance*. New York: Routledge, 1990.

Clark, Beverly Lyon. *Regendering the School Story: Sassy Sissies and Tattling Tomboys*. New York: Garland, 1996.

Clark, Trinkett, and H. Nichols B. Clark. *Myth, Magic, and Mystery: 100 Years of American Children's Book Illustration*. New York: Robert Rinehart, Chrysler Museum of Art, 1996.

Commire, Anne, ed. *Something about the Author*. Detroit: Gale Research, 1971– .

Cutler, John L. *Gilbert Patten and His Frank Merriwell Saga: A Study in Sub-Literary Fiction, 1896–1913*. Orono: University of Maine, 1934.

Darling, Richard L. *The Rise of Children's Book Reviewing in America, 1865–1881*. New York: R. R. Bowker, 1968.

Deane, Paul C. "The Persistence of Uncle Tom: An Examination of the Image of the Negro in Children's Fiction Series." *Journal of Negro Education* 37 (Spring 1968), 140–45.

DeCharms, Richard, and Gerald H. Moeller. "Values Expressed in American Children's Readers, 1800–1850." *Journal of Abnormal and Social Psychology* 64 (February 1962), 136–42.

DeMontreville, Doris, and Donna Hill, eds. *The Third Book of Junior Authors*. New York: H. W. Wilson, 1972.

DeMontreville, Doris, Donna Hill, and Elizabeth Crawford, eds. *The Fourth Book of Junior Authors and Illustrators*. New York: H. W. Wilson, 1978.

Dobler, Lavinia G. *The Dobler World Directory of Youth Periodicals*. 3d ed. New York: Citation Press, 1970.

Drew, Bernard A. *The 100 Most Popular Young Adult Authors: Biographical Sketches and Bibliographies*. Englewood, Colo.: Libraries Unlimited, 1996.

Dyer, Carolyn Stewart, and Nancy Tillman Romalov, eds. *Rediscovering Nancy Drew*. Iowa City: University of Iowa Press, 1995.

Egoff, Sheila, ed. *Only Connect*. Toronto: Oxford University Press, 1969. 3rd ed. 1996.

Erisman, Fred. "Children's Literature in the United States, 1800–1940." In *Lexicon Zur Kinder- und Jugendliteratur*, ed. Klaus Doderer. Vol. 2. Weinheim and Basel/Pullachbei. Munich: Beltz Verlag and Verlag Dokumentation, 1988.

———. "L. Frank Baum and the Progressive Dilemma." *American Quarterly* 20 (Fall 1968), 616–23.

Falk, Robert. "Notes on the 'Higher Criticism' of Horatio Alger, Jr." *Arizona Quarterly* 19 (Summer 1963), 151–67.

Field, Elinor Whitney, ed. *Horn Book Reflections on Children's Books and Reading*. Boston: Horn Book, 1969.

Ford, Paul Leicester, ed. *The New England Primer*. New York: Teachers College Press, 1962.

Foster, Shirley, and Judy Simons. *What Katy Read: Feminist Re-Readings of "Classic" Stories for Girls*. Iowa City: University of Iowa Press, 1995.

Fraser, James H. "Children's Literature Collections and Research Libraries." *Wilson Library Bulletin* 50 (October 1975), 128–30.

———, ed. *Society and Children's Literature*. Boston: Godine, 1978.

Frey, Charles, and John Griffith, eds. *Classics of Children's Literature*. 5th ed. New York: Prentice-Hall, 1999.

———. *The Literary Heritage of Childhood: An Appraisal of Children's Classics in the Western Tradition*. Westport, Conn.: Greenwood Press, 1987.

Fuller, Muriel, ed. *More Junior Authors*. New York: H. W. Wilson, 1963.

Gardner, Martin, and Russel B. Nye. *The Wizard of Oz and Who He Was*. East Lansing: Michigan State University Press, 1957.

Garrison, Dee. "Custodians of Culture in the Gilded Age: The Public Librarian and Horatio Alger." *Journal of Library History* 6 (October 1971), 327–36.

Gillespie, John T., ed. *Best Books for Children*. New York: R. R. Bowker, *1990*.

———. *Best Books for Junior High Readers*. New York: R. R. Bowker, 1991.

———. *Best Books for Senior High Readers*. New York: R. R. Bowker, 1991.

Goldthwaite, John. *The Natural History of Make-Believe: A Guide to the Principal Works of Britain, Europe, and North America*. New York: Oxford University Press, 1996.

Gottlieb, Gerald. *Early Children's Books and Their Illustration*. New York: Pierpont Morgan Library, 1975.

———. "Keeping Company with the Gutenbergs." *Wilson Library Bulletin* 50 (October 1975), 154–56.

Gottlieb, Robin. *Publishing Children's Books in America, 1919–1976: An Annotated Bibliography*. New York: Children's Book Council, 1978.

Greene, David L. "Children's Literature Journals: Author Society Journals and Fanzines." *Phaedrus* 2 (Spring 1975), 16–20.

———. "Children's Literature Periodicals on Individual Authors, Dime Novels, Fantasy." *Phaedrus* 3 (Spring 1976), 22–24.

Griffin, Martin I. J. *Frank R. Stockton: A Critical Biography*. Philadelphia: University of Pennsylvania Press, 1939.

Griswold, Jerry. *Audacious Kids: Coming of Age in America's Classic Children's Books*. New York: Oxford University Press, 1992.

Gruber, Frank. *Horatio Alger, Jr.: A Biography and a Bibliography*. West Los Angeles, Calif.: Grover Jones, 1961.

Guthrie, Anna Lorraine, comp. *Index to St. Nicholas, Volumes 1–45*. New York: H. W. Wilson, 1920.

Halsey, Rosalie V. *Forgotten Books of the American Nursery*. Boston: Goodspeed, 1911. Reprint. Gordon, 1972.

Harrah, Barbara K. *Sports Books for Children: An Annotated Bibliography*. Metuchen, N.J.: Scarecrow Press, 1978.

Haviland, Virginia. "Serving Those Who Serve Children: A National Reference Library of Children's Books." *Quarterly Journal of the Library of Congress* 22 (1965), 300–316.

———, ed. *Children and Literature: Views and Reviews*. Glenview, Ill.: Scott, Foresman, 1973.

———. *Children's Literature: A Guide to Reference Sources*. Washington, D.C.: Library of Congress, 1966.

Hayes, Ruth, Priscilla Moulton, and Sarah Reuter. "Research Collections in New England." *Phaedrus* 3 (Spring 1976), 13–21.

Heins, Paul, ed. *Crosscurrents of Criticism: Horn Book Essays, 1968–1977*. Boston: Horn Book, 1977.

Helbig, Alethea K., and Agnes Regan Perkins. *This Land Is Our Land: A Guide to Multicultural Literature for Children and Young Adults*. Westport, Conn.: Greenwood Press, 1994.

Henne, Frances. "Toward a National Plan to Nourish Research in Children's Literature." *Wilson Library Bulletin* 50 (October 1975), 131–37.

Herald, Diana Tixier. *Teen Genreflecting*. Englewood, Colo.: Libraries Unlimited, 1997.

Heuscher, Julius E. *A Psychiatric Study of Fairy Tales: Their Origin, Meaning and Usefulness*. 2d rev. ed. Springfield, Ill.: Charles C. Thomas, 1974.

Hipple, Ted, ed. *Writers for Young Adults*. 3 vols. New York: Scribner's/Simon and Schuster Macmillan, 1997.

Hirschfelder, Arlene B. *American Indian Stereotypes in the World of Children: A Reader and Bibliography*. Metuchen, N.J.: Scarecrow Press, 1982.

Hodowanec, George V., ed. *The May Massee Collection: Creative Publishing for Children, 1923–1963, A Checklist*. Emporia, Kans.: William Allen White Library, Emporia State University, 1979.

Holtze, Sally Holmes. *Seventh Book of Junior Authors and Illustrators*. New York: H. W. Wilson, 1996.

Horning, Kathleen T., ed. *Alternative Press Publishers of Children's Books: A Directory*. 3rd ed. Madison, Wis.: Cooperative Book Center, 1988.

Huck, Charlotte S., and Susan Hepler. *Children's Literature in the Elementary School*. 6th ed. Madison, Wis.: Brown and Benchmark, 1996.

Human- and Anti-Human Values in Children's Books: A Content Rating Instrument for Educators and Concerned Parents. New York: Council on Interracial Books for Children, 1976.

Hunt, Peter, ed. *Children's Literature: An Illustrated History*. New York: Oxford University Press, 1995.

———. *Criticism, Theory, and Children's Literature*. Cambridge, Mass.: Basil Blackwell, 1991.

Ireland, Norma O., ed. *Index to Fairy Tales, 1949–1972, including Folklore, Legends, and Myths in Collections*. Metuchen, N.J.: Scarecrow Press, 1973.

———. *Index to Fairy Tales, 1973–1977: Including Folklore, Legends and Myths in Collections*. Metuchen, N.J.: Scarecrow Press, 1985.

———. *Index to Fairy Tales, 1978–1986: Including Folklore, Legends, and Myths in Collections*. Metuchen, N.J.: Scarecrow Press, 1989.

Johnson, Deidre. *Stratemeyer Pseudonyms and Series Books: An Annotated Checklist of Stratemeyer and Stratemeyer Syndicate Publications*. Westport, Conn.: Greenwood Press, 1982.

Jones, Dolores Blythe, comp. *An "Oliver Optic" Checklist: An Annotated Catalog Index to the Series, Nonseries Stories, and Magazine Publications of William Taylor Adams*. Westport, Conn.: Greenwood Press, 1985.

———. *Special Collections in Children's Literature: An International Directory*. Chicago: American Library Association, 1995.

Jordan, Alice M. *From Rollo to Tom Sawyer*. Boston: Horn Book, 1948.

Karl, Jean. *From Childhood to Childhood*. New York: John Day, 1970.

Kelly, R. Gordon. "American Children's Literature: An Historiographical Review." *American Literary Realism* 6 (Spring 1973), 89–108.

———. *Mother Was a Lady: Self and Society in Selected American Children's Periodicals, 1865–1890*. Westport, Conn.: Greenwood Press, 1974.

———, ed. *Children's Periodicals of the United States*. Westport, Conn.: Greenwood Press, 1984.

Khorana, Meena. *The Indian Subcontinent in Literature for Children and Young Adults: An Annotated Bibliography of English-Language Books*. Westport, Conn.: Greenwood Press, 1991.

Kilgour, Raymond. *Estes and Lauriat: A History, 1872–1898*. Ann Arbor: University of Michigan Press, 1957.

———. *Lee and Shepard: Publishers for the People*. Hamden, Conn.: Shoe String Press, 1965.

———. *Messrs. Roberts Brothers, Publishers*. Ann Arbor: University of Michigan Press, 1952.

Kingman, Lee, ed. *Newbery and Caldecott Medal Books, 1956–1965*. Boston: Horn Book, 1965.

———. *Newbery and Caldecott Medal Books, 1966–1975*. Boston: Horn Book, 1976.

———. *Newbery and Caldecott Medal Books, 1976–1985*. Boston: Horn Book, 1986.

Koupal, Nancy Tystad, ed. *Our Landlady: L. Frank Baum*. Lincoln: University of Nebraska Press, 1996.

Kuznets, Lois Rostow. *When Toys Come Alive: Narratives of Animation, Metamorphosis, and Development*. New Haven, Conn.: Yale University Press, 1994.

Lanes, Selma G. *Down the Rabbit Hole: Adventures and Misadventures in the Realm of Children's Literature*. New York: Atheneum, 1971.

Larrick, Nancy. "The All-White World of Children's Books." *Saturday Review of Literature* 48 (September 11, 1965), 63–65.

Littlefield, Henry. "The Wizard of Oz: Parable on Populism." *American Quarterly* 16 (Spring 1964), 47–58.

Lukens, Rebecca J. *A Critical Handbook of Children's Literature*. 6th ed. Reading, Mass.: Addison-Wesley, 1998.

Lynn, Ruth Nadelman. *Fantasy for Children and Young Adults: An Annotated Bibliography*. 4th ed. New Providence, N.J.: R. R. Bowker, 1995.

Lyon, Betty Longeneker. "A History of Children's Secular Magazines Published in the United States from 1789 to 1899." Ed.D. diss., Johns Hopkins University, 1942.

MacCann, Donnarae, and Gloria Woodard, eds. *The Black American in Books for Children: Readings in Racism.* 2nd ed. Metuchen, N.J.: Scarecrow Press, 1985.

———. *Cultural Conformity in Books for Children: Further Readings in Racism.* Metuchen, N.J.: Scarecrow Press, 1977.

MacLeod, Anne Scott. *American Childhood: Essays on Children's Literature of the Nineteenth and Twentieth Centuries.* Athens: University of Georgia Press, 1994.

———. *A Moral Tale: Children's Fiction and American Culture, 1820–1860.* Hamden, Conn.: Archon, 1975.

Martin, Michelle. "Hey, Who's the Kid with the Green Umbrella? Re-evaluating the Black-a-Moor and Little Black Sambo." *Lion and Unicorn* 22:2 (1998), 147–162.

Mason, Bobbie Ann. *The Girl Sleuth: A Feminist Guide.* Old Westbury, N.Y.: Feminist Press, 1975. Reprint. University of Georgia Press, 1995.

Matthews, Harriet L. "Children's Magazines." *Bulletin of Bibliography* 1 (April 1899), 133–36.

Maxwell, Barbara, comp. *Checklist of Children's Books, 1837–1876.* Philadelphia: Free Library of Philadelphia, 1975 (mimeo).

McGillis, Roderick. *The Nimble Reader: Literary Theory and Children's Literature.* New York: Twayne, 1996.

McMahon, Thomas, ed. *Authors and Artists for Young Adults.* Vol. 21. Detroit: Gale, 1997.

Meyer, Susan E. *A Treasury of the Great Children's Book Illustrators.* New York: Harry N. Abrams, 1987.

Miller, Bertha E. Mahoney, and Elinor W. Field, eds. *Newbery Medal Books, 1922–1955.* Boston: Horn Book, 1955.

———. *Caldecott Medal Books, 1938–1957.* Boston: Horn Book, 1957.

Miller, Bertha E. Mahoney, Louise P. Latimer, and Beulah Folmsbee. *Illustrators of Children's Books, 1744–1945.* Boston: Horn Book, 1947.

Miller, Bertha E. Mahoney, Ruth Hill Viguers, and Marcia Dalphin. *Illustrators of Children's Books, 1946–1956.* Boston: Horn Book, 1958.

Miner, Madonne. "Horatio Alger's *Ragged Dick*: Projection, Denial, and Double-Dealing." *American Imago* 47 (1990), 233–48.

Moore, John Noell. *Interpreting Young Adult Literature: Literary Theory in the Secondary Classroom.* Portsmouth, N.H.: Boynton Cook, 1997.

Mott, Frank Luther. *A History of American Magazines.* 5 vols. Cambridge: Harvard University Press, 1938–1968.

Nakamura, Joyce, ed. *Children's Authors and Illustrators: An Index to Biographical Dictionaries.* 5th ed. Detroit: Gale Research, 1994.

Newbery and Caldecott Awards: A Guide to the Medal and Honor Books. Chicago: American Library Association, 1992.

Nodelman, Perry. *The Pleasures of Children's Literature.* 2nd ed. White Plains, N.Y.: Longman, 1996.

———. *Words about Pictures: The Narrative Art of the Children's Picture Books*. Athens: University of Georgia Press, 1988.

Norton, Donna E. *Through the Eyes of a Child: An Introduction to Children's Literature*. 5th ed. New York: Prentice-Hall, 1999.

Nye, Russel B. "The Juvenile Approach to American Culture, 1870–1930." In *New Voices in American Studies*, ed. Ray B. Browne. West Lafayette, Ind.: Purdue University Press, 1966.

Pellowski, Anne. *The World of Children's Literature*. New York: R. R. Bowker, 1968.

Pflieger, Pat. *A Reference Guide to Modern Fantasy for Children*. Westport, Conn.: Greenwood Press, 1984.

Prager, Arthur. *Rascals at Large; or, the Clue in the Old Nostalgia*. Garden City, N.Y.: Doubleday, 1971.

Price, Anne, and Juliette Yaakov, eds. *Children's Catalogue*. 17th ed. New York: H. W. Wilson, 1996.

Rahn, Suzanne. *Children's Literature: An Annotated Bibliography of the History and Criticism*. New York: Garland, 1981.

Roginski, Jim, comp. *Newbery and Caldecott Medalists and Honor Book Winners: Bibliographies and Resource Material through 1991*. 2nd ed. New York: Neal Schuman, 1992.

Rollin, Lucy. *Cradle and All: A Cultural and Psychoanalytic Study of Nursery Rhymes*. Jackson: University Press of Mississippi, 1992.

Rollin, Lucy, and Mark I. West. *Psychoanalytic Responses to Children's Literature*. Jefferson, N.C.: McFarland, 1999.

Rollock, Barbara, ed. *Black Authors and Illustrators of Children's Books: A Biographical Dictionary*. 2nd ed. Hamden, Conn.: Garland, 1992.

Roselle, Daniel. *Samuel Griswold Goodrich, Creator of Peter Parley: A Study of His Life and Work*. Albany: State University of New York Press, 1968.

Rosenbach, A.S.W. *Early American Children's Books*. Portland, Maine: Southworth, 1933. Reprint: Martino, 1995.

Rosenberg, Judith K. *Young People's Books in Series: Fiction and Non-fiction, 1975–1991*. Englewood, Colo.: Libraries Unlimited, 1992.

Rudman, Masha Kabakow. *Children's Literature: An Issues Approach*. 3rd ed. White Plains, N.Y.: Longman, 1995.

Sackett, S.J. "The Utopia of Oz." *Georgia Review* 14 (Fall 1960), 275–91.

Sadker, Myra P., and David M. Sadker. *Now upon a Time: A Contemporary View of Children's Literature*. New York: Harper and Row, 1977.

Samuels, Barbara G., G. Kylene Beers, et al., eds. *Your Reading: An Annotated Booklist for Middle School and Junior High*. Urbana, Ill.: National Council of Teachers of English, 1996.

Sayers, Frances Clarke. *Summoned by Books*. New York: Viking, 1965.

Scharnhorst, Gary, and Jack Bales. *The Lost Life of Horatio Alger, Jr*. Bloomington: Indiana University Press, 1985.

Schon, Isabel. *A Hispanic Heritage, Series III: A Guide to Juvenile Books about Hispanic People and Cultures*. Metuchen, N.J.: Scarecrow Press, 1988.

Seelye, John. "Who Was Horatio?" *American Quarterly* 17 (Winter 1965), 749–56.

Senick, Gerard J., and Joanna Brod, eds. *Something about the Author Autobiography Series, Vol. 24.* Detroit: Gale, 1997.

Shaw, John McKay, comp. *The Poems, Poets and Illustrators of St. Nicholas Magazine, 1873–1943: An Index.* Tallahassee: Florida State University Press, 1965.

Shealy, Daniel, ed. *Freaks of Genius: Unknown Thrillers by Louisa May Alcott.* Assoc. eds. Madeleine B. Stern and Joel Myerson. Westport, Conn: Greenwood Press, 1991.

Silvey, Anita, ed. *Children's Books and Their Creators.* New York: Houghton Mifflin, 1995.

Sims, Rudine. *Shadow and Substance: Afro-American Experience in Contemporary Children's Fiction.* Urbana, Ill.: National Council of Teachers of English, 1982.

Sloane, William. *Children's Books in England and America in the Seventeenth Century.* New York: King's Crown Press, 1955.

Smith, Elva S. *A History of Children's Literature: A Syllabus with Selected Bibliographies.* Chicago: American Library Association, 1937. Rev. and enlarged by Margaret Hodges and Susan Steinfirst. Chicago: American Library Association, 1980.

Smith, Lillian H. *The Unreluctant Years: A Critical Approach to Children's Literature.* Chicago: American Library Association, 1953. Reprint. 1991.

Smoodin, Eric, ed. *Animating Culture: Hollywood Cartoons from the Sound Era.* New Brunswick, N.J.: Rutgers University Press, 1993.

———. *Disney Discourse: Producing the Magic Kingdom.* New York: Routledge, 1994.

Sprug, Joseph W., ed. *Index to Fairy Tales, 1987–1992: Including 310 Collections of Fairy Tales, Folktales, Myths and Legends with Significant pre-1987 Titles Not Previously Indexed.* Metuchen, N.J.: Scarecrow Press, 1994.

Stern, Madeleine B. *Louisa's Wonder Book: An Unknown Alcott Juvenile.* Mt. Pleasant, Mich.: Clarke Historical Library, Central Michigan University, 1975.

Stern, Madeleine B., and Daniel Shealy, eds. *From Jo March's Attic: Stories of Intrigue and Suspense.* Boston: Northeastern University Press, 1993.

Street, Douglas, ed. *Children's Novels and the Movies.* New York: F. Ungar, 1983.

Subject Guide to Children's Books in Print. New York: R. R. Bowker, 1970.

Sutherland, Zena, and May Hill Arbuthnot. *Children's Books.* 8th ed. New York: HarperCollins, 1991.

Tatar, Maria, ed. *The Classic Fairy Tales.* Norton Critical Edition. New York: W. W. Norton, 1999.

Teens' Favorite Books: Young Adults' Choices 1987–1992. Newark, Del.: International Reading Association, 1992.

Thompson, Lovell, ed. *Youth's Companion.* Boston: Houghton Mifflin, 1954.

Townsend, John Rowe. *A Sense of Story: Essays on Contemporary Writers for Children.* Boston: Horn Book, 1973.

———. *Written for Children: An Outline of English-Language Children's Literature.* 6th American ed. Lanham, Md.: Scarecrow Press, 1997.

Trites, Roberta. *Waking Sleeping Beauty: Feminist Voices in Children's Novels.* Iowa City: University of Iowa Press, 1997.

Tucker, Nicholas. *Suitable for Children? Controversies in Children's Literature.* Berkeley: University of California Press, 1976.

Turow, Joseph. *Getting Books to Children: An Exploration of Publisher–Market Relations.* Chicago: American Library Association, 1979.

Viguers, Ruth Hill. *Margin for Surprise: About Books, Children and Librarians.* Boston: Little, Brown, 1964.

Ward, Martha E., and Dorothy A. Marquardt. *Illustrators of Books for Young People.* 2nd ed. Metuchen, N.J.: Scarecrow Press, 1975.

Welch, D'Alte A. "A Bibliography of American Children's Books Printed prior to 1821," *Proceedings of the American Antiquarian Society* 73 (1963), pt. 1: 121–324, pt. 2: 465–596; 74 (1964), pt. 2: 260–382; 75 (1965), pt. 2: 271–476; 77 (1967), pt. 1:44–120, pt. 2: 281–535.

Welsh, Charles. "The Early History of Children's Books in New England." *New England Magazine,* n.s. 20 (April 1899), 147–60.

West, Mark I. *Children, Culture, and Controversy.* Hamden, Conn.: Shoe String Press, 1988.

———. *Everyone's Guide to Children's Literature.* Fort Atkinson, Wis.: Highsmith Press, 1997.

Whalley, Joyce Irene. *Cobwebs to Catch Flies: Illustrated Books for the Nursery and Schoolroom.* Berkeley: University of California Press, 1975.

Williams, Helen E. *Books by African-American Authors and Illustrators for Children and Young Adults.* Chicago: American Library Association, 1991

Wilms, Denise, and Ilene Cooper. *A Guide to Non-Sexist Children's Books, Vol. II: 1976–1985.* Chicago: Academy Press, 1987.

Winkel, Lois, and Sue Kimmel. *Mother Goose Comes First: An Annotated Guide to the Best Books and Recordings for Your Pre-School Child.* New York: Henry Holt, 1990.

Wohl, R. Richard. "The Rags to Riches Story: An Episode in Secular Idealism." In *Class, Status and Power,* ed. Reinhard Bendix and Seymour M. Lipset. 2nd ed. Glencoe, Ill.: Free Press, 1966.

Wurth, Shirley, ed. *Books for You: A Booklist for Senior High Students.* Urbana, Ill.: National Council of Teachers of English, 1992.

Young, Philip H. *Children's Fiction Series: A Bibliography, 1850–1950.* Jefferson, N.C.: McFarland, 1997.

Zipes, Jack. *Happily Ever After: Fairy Tales, Children, and the Culture Industry.* New York: Routledge, 1997.

Zukerman, Michael. "The Nursery Tales of Horatio Alger, Jr." *American Quarterly* 24 (May 1972), 191–209.

Periodicals

Advocate. Athens, Ga., 1981–1986.

Bibliographic Index. New York, 1937– .

Booklist. Chicago, 1905– .

Bulletin of the Center for Children's Books. Chicago, 1948– .

Children's Literature. New Haven, Conn., 1972– .

Children's Literature in Education. New York, 1970– .

English Journal. Urbana, Ill., 1912– .

Horn Book Magazine. Boston, 1924– .

Journal of Youth Services in Libraries (formerly *Top of the News*). Chicago, 1946– .

Language Arts (formerly, *Elementary English*). Urbana, Ill., 1924– .
Lion and the Unicorn. Brooklyn, 1977– .
The New Advocate. Boston, 1987– .
New York Times Book Review. New York, 1896– .
Phaedrus: An International Annual of Children's Literature Research. New York, 1973–1988.
Publishers Weekly. New York, 1872– .
School Library Journal. New York, 1954– .

Selected Web Sites

The Children's Literature Web Guide. http://www.ucalgary.ca/dkbrown/index.html
Vandergrift's Children's Literature Page. http://www.scils.rutgers.edu/special/kay/childlit.html
Young Adult Literature. http://www.ct.net~patem/yalit

CIRCUS AND WILD WEST EXHIBITION

Judith A. Adams-Volpe

Mid- to late-nineteenth-century America spawned many forms of popular entertainment that responded to a burgeoning desire for unpretentious, easily accessible amusements. This cultural period coincided with mass immigration, the emergence of a "new middle class" as the dominant population group, the rise of technology in industry and everyday life, the concentration of populations in cities, the expansion of the frontier, and decreasing standard work hours. Two forms of popular entertainment—the circus and the Wild West exhibition—emerged as appealing alternatives to theater. The comparatively passive nature of their audiences makes these two types of shows distinct from the other major growing entertainments of the period, amusement parks and fairs. These latter two types of entertainment are considered in a separate chapter. The circus and the Wild West exhibition share a blending of performance, animals, and exotic curiosities. They both display what Kenneth Tynan calls "high definition performance," a quality shared by authentic stars "to communicate the essence of one's talent to an audience with economy, grace, no apparent effort, and absolute, hard-edged clarity of outline" (*Sound of Two Hands Clapping* [London: Cape, 1975]). The Wild West exhibition was engendered within the circus, its gestation being in the "specs" or spectacular pageant segments of the Big Top.

The circus has survived to the present day through its ability to evolve in size and format in response to cultural trends, effective business practices, variable thematic focus, and audience desires. In contrast, the Wild West exhibition relatively quickly fell victim to the popularity of motion pictures and the silver screen's ability to portray the rapidly disappearing frontier. It also suffered from the limited spectrum of its acts and displays, the aging of its authentic western heroes and performers, and inept business management. But despite its brief run, the Wild West exhibition indelibly influenced American consciousness and images of western life—the frontier, cowboys, and Indians. Both entertainments were created to appeal to a broad spectrum of the public; they were affordable, very fast-paced, and immediately understood. They presented spectacle, action, suspense, and the exotic to audiences seeking diversion from dreary and habitual living and work environments. Like other forms of popular entertainment, they also provided the appearance of danger and the impression of education. The pleasure of the live circus performance remains appealing and vibrant today even as we get more and more of our entertainment from technological gadgets within our personal living space.

HISTORICAL OUTLINE

The Circus

Marcello Truzzi's (1973) widely referenced definition of the circus articulates the elements of its genesis: "a traveling and organized display of animals and skilled performances within one or more circular stages known as 'rings' before an audience encircling these activities." While the word "circus" is a direct borrowing from the Latin word for "ring" or "circle," the modern circus is not derivative of such antiquities as Rome's Circus Maximus. Its origins reside in England with exhibitions presented by riding masters displaying acrobatic and equestrian skills. Between 1768 and 1773 in London, Philip Astley developed entertainments presented in a ring featuring horsemanship acts that he expanded with jugglers, acrobats, trapeze artists, additional trained animals, and clowns. As such, he is considered the father of the modern circus. In 1772 he took his show to France and later traveled throughout Europe as far as Belgrade. When England and France went to war, he leased his Paris circus to the Franconi family, which is credited with standardizing the circus ring at forty-two feet in diameter. Circus entertainments spread relatively quickly throughout Europe and to America.

Although there is documentation of troupes of itinerant performers in the colonies as early as 1716, Thomas Pool presented public entertainments in Philadelphia in 1785 featuring his equestrian skills, trained horses, and a burlesque entitled "The Taylor Humourously Riding to New York." By adding this comedy feature, "between the parts a Clown to amuse the spectators," Pool expanded the equestrian exhibition with clowns, an essential element of the circus. The first performance in America to be billed as a circus was presented by John Bill Ricketts in 1793 in Philadelphia. A Scotsman, Ricketts was an apprentice of Charles Hughes, Philip Astley's chief rival in London. Ricketts added an acrobat and a rope walker to the equestrian feats and clowns. His circus became an established entertainment as a result of visits by President George Washington, a superb horseman. Washington and Ricketts became friends who rode together, and in 1797 Washington presented the white horse that he rode during the Revolutionary War, named Jack, to Ricketts for display as the first sideshow attraction of the American circus. Throughout the mid- and late-1790s, Ricketts took his show on the road to New York, Boston, Albany, and other cities in America and Canada. His chief clown, John Durang, created an extensive memoir of the first thirty years of life in an American circus, *The Memoirs of John Durang (American Actor, 1785–1816)*. He graphically documents what the early traveling circus was like:

> I rode the foxhunter, leaping over the bar with the mounting and dismounting while in full speed, taking a flying leap on horseback through a paper

P. T. Barnum & Co. circus poster. © CORBIS

sun, in character of a drunken man on horseback, tied in a sack standing on two horses while I changed to woman's clothes; rode in full speed standing on two horses, Mr. Ricketts . . . standing on my shoulders, with Master Hutchins . . . standing in the attitude of Mercury on Mr. Ricketts shoulders.

But it was not all daredevil feats and applause:

I ventured thro' the storm as I knew my presence was necessary to be at the circus. . . . The roof of the circus leaked, and was very wet. In riding the Tailor, the horse's legs slipt from under him and he fell flat on his side with my leg under him. I escaped the misfortune of breaking it, but my knee swelled very much, after which I danced a hornpipe to show the people I was not hurt—yet . . . I was layed up and for three days. An old French doctor cured me—she also cured a woman of cancer in the breast by applying a live toad to the part affected. (Quoted in John Culhane, *The American Circus; An Illustrated History*, New York: Henry Holt, 1990, 6)

Ricketts and his circus soon experienced calamities similar to those that many of its successors would face. His circus buildings in both New York and Philadelphia were destroyed by fire in 1799, and Ricketts was left bankrupt and homeless. He decided to take his circus to the West Indies, but pirates attacked and seized the ship, all the horses, and the lumber that Ricketts brought to erect a circus building. One of his star performers, a young boy, became ill and died. Discouraged, Ricketts set sail for England in late 1800, but he was lost at sea. However, he had launched the saga of the American circus.

The area around Somers, in eastern upstate New York, became an active "cradle" for the circus with a number of menagerie and circus entrepreneurs and companies residing there. Hackaliah Bailey partnered with other menagerie owners to show Old Bet, an elephant brought to America from Africa around 1808. Old Bet was a sensation, and many traveling menageries were spawned by her success. Bailey built the Elephant Hotel in Somers with his profits. Old Bet was shot to death by a ruffian in 1816, and, like many promoters after him, Bailey displayed her skeleton for an admission fee. He buried her in Somers complete with a tall granite monument topped by a gold-lacquered wooden elephant. Old Bet established the appeal of the elephant as an attraction, and pachyderms have been standard features of the circus ever since. A merger of a number of enterprises in the Somers area occurred in 1835 with joint management of all properties, the allocation of animals to various shows, and the designation of nonconflicting show routes. Isaac A. Van Amburgh became the syndicate's first famous lion tamer, known for putting his head in a lion's mouth. He was so highly paid as a superstar that he started his own circus.

The opening of the Erie Canal in 1825 facilitated travel by the growing number of circuses, and in the same year a tent was first used for itinerant performances. In the first half of the nineteenth century, the distinctive nature of the American circus took shape. Water and some rail travel was supplemented by horse-drawn conveyance, leading to circus parades in towns where shows were presented. First appearing in 1837 in Albany, New York, the free circus parade became a standard feature leading to magnificently carved and decorated circus wagons, bands, and calliopes creating an exotic spectacle in many towns throughout the East and Midwest. The circus moved west following the 1849 gold rush to California. In the period 1840–1870, numerous prominent enterprises were performing with success, such as the George F. Bailey Circus, several circuses of Seth B. Howes, the Mabie Brothers Circus, the John Robinson Circus, Spalding and Roberts Circus, Dan Costello Circus, Dan Rice Circus, and W. W. Cole Circus.

The real circus barons emerged after 1870, including Adam Forepaugh, James A. Bailey, P. T. Barnum, and the Ringling Brothers. In 1873 multiple circus rings were introduced by Andrew Haight and his Great Eastern Circus and Menagerie. The "Big Top" was rising in towns across America, and the golden age of the American circus was poised to emerge. The cultural concept of "superlative" is linked to P. T Barnum, America's first extraordinary promoter and showman. Barnum worked on America's sense of wonder through the presentation of the unique, whether it be the largest or the smallest, the strangest or absolute humbug.

Phineas Taylor Barnum was born in Bethel, Connecticut, in 1810, only about twenty miles from the Somers, New York, area. Thrown into jail for libel while a newspaper publisher, Barnum staged a spectacular parade upon his release with forty horsemen, sixty carriages of citizens, himself, and a band in a carriage drawn by six horses. In 1836 he associated himself and a juggler with a small traveling circus, but within the year he created his own show called "Barnum's Grand Scientific and Musical Theatre," comprising a clown, acrobat, magician, four horses, and two wagons. Unsuccessful, Barnum was in New York City in 1841 making a noncash "sucker's deal" to purchase Scutter's American Museum, a collection of curiosities. Many of Barnum's early "curiosities" or freaks were fakes or humbugs, such as a 161-year-old nurse and the "Feejee Mermaid." He thus introduced the element of illusion as reality to the circus and to popular culture, a trend away from reality to image that has continued to accelerate in our technological age. Barnum's most famous attractions, however, were real and legitimate. In 1842 Barnum engaged five-year-old Charles Stratton, a perfectly proportioned midget at twenty-five inches in height, the victim of a pituitary disorder. The little boy soon became Tom Thumb, circus curiosity. As an adult, Tom Thumb was only ten inches taller, and Barnum promoted him into a worldwide sensation during most of the small man's life. He was adored by Queen Victoria, and his wedding to Lavinia Warren was a sensation in Europe and America, with a reception given in the couple's honor by President Lincoln.

In 1871 Barnum joined with traveling circus owners W. C. Coup and Dan Costello to create "the great show enterprise" under the largest tent in history with the greatest number of performers and horses to date, not to mention several well-publicized "freaks." Due to the size of the enterprise, Coup conceived of a specially designed circus train. As of 1872, Barnum's huge show traveled by its own railroad train and offered two-ring productions. From an artistic point of view, the two- and eventually three-ring circuses sacrificed artistry and intimacy for spectacle. Audience attentions became scattered, but people felt that they were getting more than they paid for. The public began to refer to Barnum's circus as "the Greatest Show on Earth," a designation that Barnum would soon copyright as the name of his show.

In 1880, Barnum reached an agreement with his major rival, James Bailey, to combine the two circuses and to present in three rings. Bigger was better, especially with the newest attraction, Jumbo, the largest elephant ever displayed. Coming from the London Zoo, Jumbo grossed $336,000 for Barnum and Bailey in just six weeks. Twelve feet tall at the shoulders and weighing six and a half tons, Jumbo is considered the greatest circus attraction in American history. But his glory would last less than four seasons because Jumbo was tragically and horribly killed by a freight train while the circus was being loaded on its own train in St. Thomas, Ontario. Millions mourned Jumbo. Barnum, of course, turned the disaster into a publicity extravaganza, claiming that Jumbo saved a tiny elephant by throwing it off the tracks just as the train collided with the behemoth. Barnum and Bailey split in 1885, but following several setbacks, including losing the Madison Square Garden contract, Barnum was forced to give Bailey full control of the circus in 1887 under the new name Barnum & Bailey's Greatest Show on Earth.

The individuals most clearly associated with the contemporary American circus, the Ringling Brothers, were from Baraboo, Wisconsin, and came to the circus scene in the mid-1880s. By 1890 the five brothers, Al, Otto, Alfred, Charles, and John (two other brothers did not join them), had a large traveling circus moving by rail. In 1892 the twenty-two railroad cars carrying the circus had the worst train crash in its history as it hurled headlong into a lake from a collapsed bridge, killing forty horses. Only four circus personnel were seriously hurt, however, and the show missed only one engagement. By 1895, nearly doubled in size, the Ringlings invaded eastern states, moving into Barnum's territory. At the end of the 1897 season, Bailey took the Barnum & Bailey enterprise on a successful five-year European tour, but he had left America to the Ringlings. After the deaths of both Barnum and Bailey, the Ringlings bought their rivals' circus outright, eventually creating the "Ringling Brothers and Barnum and Bailey Combined Shows" in 1919 at the end of World War I. That season's Madison Square Garden show marked the highest point for the circus in America.

In the years from 1870 to 1920, the circus was the vehicle bringing spectacle, grandeur, exotic animals, remarkable and dangerous performance, and simple fun and laughter as well as cultures and traditions of foreign lands to the American public, not just in large cities but throughout the nation. The predominant European circus performers were readily welcomed by the waves of immigrants flock-

Circus parade, Salida, Colorado, 1880. Courtesy of the Denver Public Library

ing to America. During this peak period, there were approximately 100 circuses in America. The circus during the jazz age and depression featured "star" performers such as Alfredo Codona, the first trapeze artist consistently to complete a triple somersault. Lillian Leitzel, a superb aerialist and beauty, married Codona, resulting in a tumultuous relationship. She was killed as the result of a fall when her brass swivel ring heated and cooled so much from the friction of her turns that it snapped. Clyde Beatty, the superstar animal trainer of the period, used primarily fear and threats to control his lions and tigers. The legendary clowns were Otto Griebling, Emmett Kelly as "Weary Willy," and Lou Jacobs. Delicate Bird Millman danced on a tightwire performing intricate steps as if she were on a ballet stage. May Worth was the quintessence of bareback riders, living her whole life in the circus. She completed with ease tricks that few men and no other women could do, including the back-backward somersault beginning with her back toward the horse's head, throwing herself contrary to the forward motion of the steed, and simultaneously somersaulting and twisting to land facing forward.

During the 1940s and 1950s the circus declined, as did other forms of popular amusement due to competition from motion pictures and television. Also during this time, the larger circuses suffered fires, train wrecks, poor management, union troubles, and escalating moving costs. The worst catastrophe in circus history occurred on July 6, 1944, in Hartford, Connecticut when a fire erupted during a Ringling show being held under an immense tent. Within ten minutes the entire Big Top was consumed, and 168 people, including at least eighty-four children, lost their lives. The deaths were due largely to panic as people tried to exit via the entranceway instead of getting out under the tent flaps all around the enclosure. Most were trampled and suffocated. People did not regain confidence in attending the circus under canvas until General George C. Marshall brought his grandson to the Ringling circus in Washington, D.C., in the spring of 1945. One notable exception to this period of decline occurred during World War II, when John Ringling North organized a ballet for fifty elephants choreographed by George Balanchine, with original music by Igor Stravinsky and costumes designed by Norman Bel Geddes. The idea was inspired by Disney's film *Fantasia* (1940). On opening night, bella ballerina Vera Zorina, married to Balanchine, joined the ensemble. Stravinsky's music is titled "Circus Polka." But by the 1950s, the days of the itinerant tent circus where nearly over. On July 16, 1956, in Pittsburgh, John Ringling North folded the Big Top for the last time, returned to winter quarters, and the Greatest Show on Earth never again performed in a tent.

Ringling Brothers and Barnum and Bailey Circus was purchased in 1967 by Irving Feld for $8 million. With two circuses performing simultaneously during each season in permanent stadiums or auditoriums in larger cities, Feld created a format that was both profitable and popular. He brought Las Vegas glitz to the circus and incredible talent, led by the premier animal trainer of all time, Gunther Gebel-Williams. Gebel-Williams used trust, affection, and constant attention to train his animals, including lions, tigers, leopards, horses, dogs, elephants, and even goats. The Flying Wallenda family persists as the greatest high-wire artists despite the deaths during performances of several family members. Miguel Vazquez completed the long-quested quadruple somersault on the flying trapeze in performance on July 10, 1982, in Tucson, Arizona. Feld established a Clown College that trains nearly all the circus clowns performing today. He also racially integrated the circus, presenting many black performers for the first time in America. Black performers had been limited to freaks or curiosities in American circuses until Feld began to feature them starting with the Bronx's King Charles Troupe of unicyclists in 1968. Feld sold the circus to Mattel in 1971, but his son, Kenneth, still manages the enterprise.

The small, intimate, one ring circus was the growing trend in the late 1980s and 1990s. Artistry and intimacy replaced overwhelming spectacle, allowing the audience to fully appreciate skill and creativity. These circuses started to appear in the 1970s and continue to have growing success with their strong feeling of ensemble, evocation of mood, and return to the pure traditions of circus as performance. The high-level skills of the performers are augmented by sophisticated theatricality and technical expertise. These impressive one-ring circuses have strong ties to a particular city, being much less nomadic than their extravagant predecessors. The most long-standing and best-known one-ring circuses are Paul Binder's Big Apple Circus (New York), Guy Laliberte and Guy Caron's Cirque du Soleil (Montreal), Ivor David Balding's Circus Flora (St. Louis), Valentin Gneushev's Moscow Circus (New York), and Larry Pisoni and Peggy Snider's Pickle Family Circus (San Francisco). Cedric Walker runs UniverSoul Circus (Atlanta), the only touring circus owned and operated by an African American. Opening in 1994, its performers include the King Charles Unicycle Troupe, the first black trapeze artist, a female clown, and a female lion tamer. Music is hot and pulsating, and performances are augmented by laser light shows. In the new millennium, about seventy circuses are performing in the United States.

Any account of the American circus would be incomplete without attention to words and concepts that the circus brought into our cultural consciousness and language. Among these are the following:

"Jumbo": the colossally big, larger than expected.

"White Elephant": Barnum's touted sacred white elephant turned out to be gray; thus, the term refers to something dubious, of limited value, or a venture that proves to be a conspicuous failure.

"Ballyhoo": sensational advertisement, exaggerated publicity, noisy shouting.

"Grease Joint": hot dog and burger stands on the midway.

"Roustabout": a laborer employed for transient jobs.

"Big Top": large circus tent.

"Throwing his hat in the ring": Woodrow Wilson began his bid for reelection by throwing his hat in the center ring of the circus.

"Get this show on the road": the call of the circus manager to get the wagons rolling toward the next venue.

"Rain or Shine": phrase originated in circus advertising.

"Hold your horses": a warning to protect onlookers on horseback when the elephants enter the circus parade.

As we become more and more immured in the electronic isolation created by the technology of the personal entertainment centers in our homes, the circus will continue to be one of the few events where we come together as audience and community to enjoy the immediacy of daring, skill, and theatricality, as well as to celebrate the human spirit. From Old Bet and Jumbo, to Gunther Gebel-Williams with his leopard serenely draped around his shoulders, we transcend the ordinary with performers who excel and surpass our expectations, giving us wonder and delight. Perhaps the current revival of the circus signals that we are tiring of the shallowness and impersonality of illusion and technology-enhanced "virtual" experience and that we desire to be immersed in the real—people and animals performing genuinely challenging, amazing, and daring feats. Circus lover Ernest Hemingway, in the 1953 program for the Ringling Brothers and Barnum and Bailey Circus, exclaimed that "the circus is good for you. It is the only spectacle I know that, while you watch it, gives the quality of a happy dream."

The Wild West Exhibition

William Frederick "Buffalo Bill" Cody and the Wild West Exhibition are totally associated. One did not exist without the other. Cody originated the formula for success beginning in 1882, and there were no extant shows by the year after his death in 1917. While the run of these exhibitions was quite brief, they significantly influenced American culture in terms of our images of the cowboy, the American Indian, and our consciousness about the process of winning the American West, as well as the promise and lure of the frontier. Rodeo emerged during the same period, but it is a distinct enterprise with its emphasis on competitive sport and prize money. As created by Cody, the Wild West show is defined simply as an exhibition illustrating scenes and events characteristic of the American Far West frontier.

Buffalo Bill Cody was born in Iowa in 1846, the son of a farmer and sawmill operator. When he was just six years old, he reportedly witnessed the death of his older brother when the horse that his brother was riding suddenly reared and

Buffalo Bill. Courtesy of the Library of Congress

flung herself on her back, crushing the boy to death. Cody vowed to be an accomplished rider impervious to such accidents. His life actually coincides with the settlement of the western territories. At age eleven he worked as a messenger between wagon trains for the freight company of Majors and Russell; then he became a Pony Express rider. He joined the Union army, serving as a dispatch rider. After the war, he was a stagecoach driver, and he worked for the U.S. Cavalry participating in several major battles with the Indians of the northern plains. Then he hunted buffalo to feed construction crews of the Union Pacific Railroad. His claims of slaughtering thousands of buffalo led to his famous moniker. During the period when the United States was engaged in putting down Indian resistance to settlement of lands west of the Mississippi, Cody was in demand as a scout and guide who combined extensive knowledge of the western terrain with excellent marksmanship, endurance, and familiarity with Indian ways. He was awarded the Congressional Medal of Honor in 1872, but it was revoked in 1916 because it was not earned through military combat. Also in 1872, he was elected to the Nebraska legislature, but he soon resigned this office.

Buffalo Bill was a western hero known to Americans through the press and more importantly via many dime novels so popular in the 1870s and 1880s. These novels depicted his exploits as a horseman, hunter, and Indian fighter who killed and scalped the Cheyenne warrior Yellow Hair. Cody began his show business career in New York in the early 1870s, starring in *The Scouts of the Prairie*, written by dime novelist Ned Buntline. In 1882 Cody returned to his then-hometown, North Platte, Nebraska, where he owned a ranch, and planned a Fourth of July extravaganza, "the Old Glory Blowout." This spectacle featured over 1000 cowboys competing in exhibitions of riding, roping, and shooting and also featured the legendary Deadwood Stagecoach.

Exhibitions of western animals and skills were evident in the circus around the mid-nineteenth century. P. T. Barnum displayed a herd of buffalo in New York in 1843. Native Americans were exhibited as curiosities as early as 1827, and George Catlin operated an Indian gallery in Philadelphia in the 1830s. Tyler's Indian Exhibition toured with Isaac Van Amburgh's menagerie/circus in 1855, and James Capen "Grizzly" Adams presented an exhibit of western animals in 1860. Cody, however, is credited with consolidating the elements, adding dramatic tableaus, and popularizing the Wild West outdoor entertainment.

In partnership with Dr. William F. Carver, dentist, sharpshooter, and buffalo hunter, Cody created the "Rocky Mountain and Prairie Exhibition" in 1883. The traveling show played under the open skies due to space requirements for spectacular displays of buffalo hunting and rescues of stagecoaches and settlers from Indian attacks. While his cast of cowboys and plainsmen could put on a tremendous show, they liked booze more than showmanship. Carver and Cody had a falling out, and Carver may have won the whole show on a flip of a coin. By 1884, Cody teamed up with promoter/manager Nate Salsbury in New York City, putting Salsbury in charge of his traveling show. The new show was titled "Buffalo Bill's Wild West, America's National Entertainment." After hiring the incomparable shootist Annie Oakley in 1884, the show became a major success. Oakley's marksmanship skills were phenomenal. Using a mirror, she could shoot backwards to hit little glass balls tossed by her husband; she could shoot from a galloping pony, always hitting her targets; and she could hit the thin edge of a playing card at thirty paces. Sitting Bull joined the exhibition for five months in 1885. In future years, Cody always featured a famous Indian chief. The show's first long stand was at Staten Island in the summer of 1886, where Cody enjoyed unprecedented success.

During the late 1880s, Cody and Salsbury's show became one of the most popular entertainments ever known. It quickly became less itinerant, transitioning to long engagements on permanent sites, becoming a grand spectacle in Madison Square Garden, and then moving to Europe. Cody and Salsbury rented Madison Square Garden for a winter engagement in 1886–1887. Steele MacKaye was hired to convert the Wild West into a grand pageant of American pioneer life titled "The Drama of Civilization." Massive cyclorama scenery, huge fans producing wind for a cyclone, wild animals leased from Adam Forepaugh's circus, and hundreds of authentic cowboys and Indians all contributed to the spectacular scenarios that depicted the four epochs: the Primeval Forest, the Prairie, the Cattle Ranch, and the Mining Camp. Later, an attack on an emigrant wagon train and a reenactment of a major military battle were added, first the Battle of Little Big Horn and later the Battle of San Juan Hill.

Buffalo Bill's Wild West crossed the ocean to England in 1887, Queen Victoria's Jubilee year. Cody's show dominated the American Exposition there. The queen, the Prince of Wales, and the English public were entranced by the exotic presentation of a romanticized American West. The show played to 30,000–40,000 people a day on the grounds of Earl's Court; then they took the show on to Birmingham and Manchester. Cody's Wild West Exposition was an international success for the rest of the century. The Wild West went to Paris for the Exposition Universale in 1889 and continued to tour Europe until 1893. The American western frontier became a cultural fad throughout Europe, due not only to Cody's exhibitions but also to the extreme popularity of the American dime novel in translated versions. In fact, the two forces spurred large numbers of Europeans to immigrate to America, lured by the promise and opportunity of the frontier.

Cody's Wild West achieved its greatest success at the World's Columbian Exposition of 1893. Salsbury could not get space on the grounds, so he rented a lot directly across from the exhibition entrance. With its new name, "Buffalo Bill's Wild West and Congress of Rough Riders of the World," the show played to packed houses the entire summer, and profits reached nearly $1 million.

The formula of the show remained essentially the same, whether divided into "epochs" for the grand Madison Square Garden shows or in the smaller-scale touring shows. The exhibition contained eighteen to twenty acts, including a grand review of international riders and horses, Annie Oakley's shooting, a horse race with international entrants, Pony Express rider, Indian attacks on trains and the Deadwood stagecoach, Arabian/Cossack/Mexican horsemen, cowboy feats such as lassoing and riding unbroken broncos, musical bands, Cody's sharpshooting, a buffalo hunt, and a grand finale, similar to the circus spectaculars, depicting a legendary event such as the Battle of Little Big Horn. By including buffalo in his show, Cody turned from hunter to environmentalist, drawing attention to the danger of extinction of the American bison.

As early as 1913, the cultural impact of Buffalo Bill's Wild West was widely understood. Nebraska Ned, in his *Buffalo Bill and His Daring Adventures in the Romantic Wild West*, articulates the show's popular appeal in a simple manner:

> He learned that it was not fine acting, in the accepted meaning of the phrase, that was most popular with the people. It was the appearance of real Indians, real guides, real scouts, real cowboys, real Buffaloes, real bucking horses, and last but not least, real Buffalo Bill, who had already become in the minds of the American people the Ideal American Plainsman. (174–75)

There were many entrepreneurs eager to copy Buffalo Bill's success. Gordon W. Lillie created his "Pawnee Bill's Historical Wild West Exhibition and Indian Encampment" in 1887; circus man Adam Forepaugh developed "The Forepaugh and Wild West Combination" in 1888. Doc Carver, Buffalo Bill's first partner, started his own "Wild America." Even former outlaws Cole Younger and Frank James, Jesse's brother, launched a show in 1903. George Miller's "101 Ranch Real Wild West" opened in 1908. In the course of a thirty-five-year history, there were over 100 Wild West enterprises. Especially after the turn of the century, the shows expanded the focus from the American West, adding exotic performers and animals from all over the world, including the Far East. Blending with the cowboys were Hindu magicians, Singahalese dancers, Australian bushmen, and many more. Notorious or famous western personalities appeared in the exhibitions, such as Chief Joseph, Red Cloud, Geronimo, and Calamity Jane.

Annie Oakley. Courtesy of the Library of Congress

But expansion and the limited repertoire led to shabby enterprises. By 1909 even Buffalo Bill had to merge operations with Pawnee Bill. Cody's enterprise began its degeneration as early as 1894, when Nate Salsbury became a semi-invalid. Salsbury died in 1902. His managerial and organizational skills were critical to Cody, who did not have the business sense to be able to plan itineraries or move the traveling show. Pawnee Bill came to the rescue for a while, but Cody could not keep ahead of his creditors. His excessive drinking added to his decline. By 1914 Cody was forced to join the rival "101 Ranch" show. He began having fainting spells and confided to a friend that he "lived in mortal fear of dying in the saddle in front of an audience." His last appearance was in 1916 in Portsmouth, Virginia. He set out for his mountain home in his namesake town, Cody, Wyoming. He died in bed at the Denver home of his sister on January 10, 1917.

Mourning Cody, Theodore Roosevelt wrote that "his name, like that of Kit Carson, will always be associated with old adventure and pioneer days of hazard and hardship. . . . He embodied those traits of courage, strength and self-reliant hardihood which are vital to the well-being of our nation" (*New York Times*, February 11, 1917). Roosevelt's words express the essence of the western frontier that Buffalo Bill instilled in the American consciousness. During the years 1883–1917, when he concentrated his energies on his popular Wild West entertainment, he also established the town of Cody, Wyoming, founded a stage line between Cody and Yellowstone Park, bought and managed a ranch near Cody, started an irrigation company in the Big Horn Basin, and started a company making western films. These and other enterprises were all aimed at bringing more people to the western frontier.

Like Buffalo Bill, many of his countrymen fail to grow up and settle down. He gave us the pioneer sense of unlimited possibilities and adventure. His depiction of Native Americans, of course, was detrimental and inaccurate. It took over half a century to address a revision and accurate understanding of Native American culture and history. But he established a cultural myth of the American West with two distinct images, the West as barbaric, dangerous, and hostile, with a flip side of promise, opportunity, personal bravery, and accomplishment. Each three-hour performance of his show neatly reinforced both views of the West for audiences in America as well as in Europe.

REFERENCE WORKS: CIRCUS

The major research collections for the American circus are the Circus World Museum Library in Baraboo, Wisconsin, with a collection especially rich in advertising materials (Robert L. Parkinson has prepared the guide *Circus World Museum Library: A Guide to Its Holdings and Services*); the Illinois State University Circus and Related Arts Collection in Normal, Illinois, perhaps the most balanced research collection (Robert Sokan's bibliographic guide is mentioned later); the Joseph T. McCaddon Collection in the Firestone Library of Princeton University, which holds the working papers of the Barnum and Bailey Circus 1890–1910; the Hertzberg Circus Collection in the San Antonio Public Library, with emphasis on nineteenth-century materials; and the McCord Theatre Collection in Fondren Library at Southern Methodist University. Specialized collections include the Joe E. Ward Collection of circus memorabilia in the Hoblitzelle Theatre Arts Library at the University of Texas at Austin; the Westervelt Collection of Barnum material at the New York Historical Society; the Ringling Museum of the Circus in Sarasota, Florida; and the Somers (New York) Historical Society with materials on the early American circus from the area called the "cradle of the American circus." Researchers may also wish to contact the Circus Historical Society in Jackson, Michigan; the Barnum Museum in Bridgeport, Connecticut; the Clown Hall of Fame and Research Center in Delavan, Wisconsin; and the International Circus Hall of Fame in Peru, Indiana.

The most comprehensive guide to literature related to the circus is Raymond Toole-Stott's four-volume *Circus and Allied Arts, a World Bibliography*, and his selective list, *A Bibliography of the Books on the Circus in English from 1773 to 1964*. These volumes contain over 15,000 entries in thirteen languages; however, they are much more valuable for research on foreign antecedents than on the circus in America. Volume 1 includes sections on Philip Astley, P. T. Barnum, and William F. Cody; volume 2 includes pantomime and equestrian exhibitions; volume 3 provides a listing of periodicals and the compiler's choice of 100 best circus books.

Robert Sokan's *A Descriptive and Bibliographic Catalog of the Circus and Related Arts Collection at Illinios State University, Normal, Illinois*, lists 1,373 items and is a guide to this research collection. The most useful research guides for those interested in the American circus and Wild West exhibition are "The American

Circus" and "The Wild West Exhibition" chapters in Don Wilmeth's *Variety Entertainment and Outdoor Amusements; A Reference Guide*. These guides are somewhat abbreviated and updated in Wilmeth's chapter "Circus and Outdoor Entertainment" in the 1989 edition of the *Handbook of American Popular Culture*. For popular entertainment in general, Wilmeth's *American and English Popular Entertainment* is invaluable. Wilmeth's two monographs cover most major sources, including dissertations, through 1981. Richard Flint provides a brief review of circusiana in "A Selected Guide to Source Material on the American Circus," in the *Journal of Popular Culture* (Winter 1972).

Anthony D. Hippisley Coxe provides a history of most circus acts through the first half of the twentieth century in *A Seat at the Circus*. Nelle Neafie's *A P.T. Barnum Bibliography* is the only substantial, focused bibliographic treatment of a major circus personage. The language of the circus is covered by Don Wilmeth in his *The Language of American Popular Entertainment: A Glossary of Argot, Slang, and Terminology*. Specifically circus words are discussed by Joe McKennon in *Circus Lingo*. Fiction, especially novels, dealing with the circus or its famous figures can be accessed through Donald K. Hartman and Gregg Sapp's *Historical Figures in Fiction* and Hartman and Jerome Drost's *Themes and Settings in Fiction*. The index *America: History and Life* provides the best access to scholarly journal literature on the circus in America. To date there is no encyclopedia devoted to the circus.

HISTORY AND CRITICISM: CIRCUS

There are several substantive general histories of the circus in America. George L. Chindahl's *History of the Circus in America* is especially strong on the nineteenth century, and it is the most fully documented source. An appendix provides a listing of American circuses and menageries existing between 1771 and 1956. Earl Chapin May's *The Circus from Rome to Ringling* is a fine single-volume historical survey, as is Joe McKennon's *Horse Dung Trail: Saga of American Circus*, covering the years 1856 through 1940, when circuses traveled in horse-drawn wagons. Charles P. Fox and Tom Parkinson's *Circus in America* provides good coverage of the circus in its golden age or heyday from approximately 1870 through the 1920s. For generalist interest, Mildred and Wolcott Fenner's *The Circus: Lure and Legend* is an impressionistic collection of essays and articles with fine illustrative treatment. To bring the history of the circus in America more up-to-date, John Culhane's *The American Circus; An Illustrated History* provides detailed, yet entertaining, coverage to 1990. It has excellent documentation, illustrations, and an extensive chronology, making it the best one-volume history. *The American Circus* by Wilton Eckley is a factual chronicle useful for undergraduate students, but it lacks documentation, and illustrations are meager. It covers the period from the birth of the railroad circus in the later nineteenth century to the demise of the tent circus in 1956. Works providing broader international coverage are Rupert Croft-Cooke and Peter Cotes' *Circus: A World History*; Peter Verney's *Here Comes the Circus*; and David Jamieson and Sandy Davidson's *The Colorful World of the Circus*. These three volumes do not give the American circus much attention, and they are lean on documentation. George Speaight's *A History of the Circus* provides more coverage and documentation of the American circus in its concentration on great performers and their acts. Performers are also the focus of

LaVahn G. Hoh and William H. Rough's *Step Right Up! The Adventure of Circus in America*, which looks at the evolution of the circus as an art form. It spans from the introduction of the circus, through its era as big business, to its decline, and to its revival in recent decades. A good source for illustrative materials on the early circus is Charles Philip Fox's *Old Time Circus Cuts: A Pictorial Archive of 202 Illustrations*. Some notable non-English language works are Henry Thetard's *La Merveilleuse Histoire du cirque*; Rolf Lehman's *Circus: Magie der Manege*; and Dominique Jando's *Histoire mondiale du cirque*.

The most scholarly accounts of the English antecedents and model for the early American circus are A. H. Saxon's two books *Enter Foot and Horse: A History of Hippodrama in England and France* and *The Life and Art of Andrew Ducrow and the Romantic Age of the English Circus*. Ducrow (1793–1842) is considered by many to be the most creative trick rider in circus history. He performed in, and was director of, Astley's Circus in London. Also useful are the nineteenth-century work by Thomas Frost, *Circus Life and Circus Celebrities*; and M. Willson Disher's 1937 volume, *Greatest Show on Earth; Astley's—Afterwards Sanger's—Royal Amphitheatre of the Arts, Westminster Bridge Road*.

The early period of the American circus is quite well documented. One of the major research sources is Stuart Thayer's *Annals of the American Circus 1793–1829* and its sequel, *Annals of the American Circus, Vol. II: 1830–1847*. These volumes present thorough research based largely on old newspaper files. An invaluable primary source dealing with the first four decades of the American circus is *The Memoirs of John Durang (American Actor, 1785–1816)*, edited by Alan S. Downer. Durang was an important member of John Ricketts' circus, and his memoirs provide vibrant and dramatic documentation of life as an itinerant circus performer. James A. Moy's dissertation, "John B. Ricketts's Circus 1793–1800," is the fullest account of America's first substantial circus. Two early works of interest are Joseph Cowell's 1844 book *Thirty Years Passed among the Players in England and America* and William W. Clapp Jr.'s 1853 volume *A Record of the Boston Stage*.

It becomes immediately evident that the largest proportion of book-length publications on the American circus focus on specific enterprises, performers, or owners or certain aspects of the circus such as clowns, poster art, and parades. The literature is immense, thus, this listing must be quite selective. Turning first to studies of particular circus enterprises and the circus in a specific time period or area, the following are useful and informative, generally combining facts and anecdotal material. The nineteenth-century circus in America is covered in W. C. Coup's *Sawdust and Spangles: Stories and Secrets of the Circus*; Al G. Field's *Watch Yourself Go By*; Esse F. O'Brien's *Circus: Cinders to Sawdust*; and John C. Kunzog's *Tanbark and Tinsel*. Richard E. Conover chronicles three major circuses of the late nineteenth century in his three short books *The Affairs of James A. Bailey*; *The Great Forepaugh Show*; and *Give 'Em a John Robinson*. The Robinson circus is also the topic of Gil Robinson's *Old Wagon Show Days*. Bob Barton looks at the Cole Brothers circus during the 1890s in *Old Covered Wagon Show Days*. Rowe's California circus, born in the gold rush days, is the subject of *California's Pioneer Circus, Joseph Rowe, Founder*, edited by Albert Dressler. This volume combines memoirs and personal correspondence. Circuses on the American frontier are covered more broadly in Chang Reynold's *Pioneer Circuses of the West*.

Moving into the twentieth century, Gene Fowler looks at the Sells-Floto circus in *Timber Line: A Story of Bonfils and Tammen*. The circus in the 1920s is given an inside view in Courtney Ryley Cooper's *Under the Big Top*. Jill Freedman's *Circus Days* is a pictorial essay on the Beatty-Cole circus. An excellent book that opens new lines of inquiry on the Ringling Brothers circuses is Gene Plowden's *Those Amazing Ringlings and Their Circus*. Also of interest is Charles Philip Fox's *A Ticket to the Circus: A Pictorial History of the Incredible Ringlings*. Itineraries of the Ringling circus are available in O. H. Kurtz's *Official Route Book of Ringling Brothers' World's Greatest Railroad Shows, Season of 1892* and in *Beneath White Tents: Official Route Book of the Ringling Brothers' World's Greatest Shows, Season of 1894*. American Heritage Magazine published the pictorial *Great Days of the Circus*. Warren A. Reeder, in *No Performance Today*, thoroughly covers the Hagenbeck-Wallace circus train wreck in 1918. Wisconsin's circus history, largely related to the Ringlings, is covered in Richard E. Conover's *The Circus: Wisconsin's Unique Heritage* and in Dean Jensen's beautifully produced *The Biggest, the Smallest, the Longest, the Shortest*. Circuses and menageries appearing in Manhattan and environs through 1948 are documented in George C. Odell's *Annals of the New York Stage, Vol. IV*. Marcello Truzzi has edited a special in-depth section in the *Journal of Popular Culture* titled, "Circuses, Carnivals and Fairs." Topics of focus are the carnival social system, legitimate and illegitimate games and gambling, wild animal displays, and the circus in transition.

The more contemporary circus scene is investigated by Edwin Martin and Don Wilmeth in their *Mud Show: American Tent Circus Life*, which provides photographic studies of seven traveling tent circuses. A fascinating glimpse of the third-rate Hoxie Brothers traveling circus during the 1974 season is provided in the similarly titled *Mud Show: A Circus Season*, by Fred Powledge. The revival of the one-ring circus as artistry and sophisticated theatricality in the last two decades has received scholarly treatment by Ernest Albrecht in *The New American Circus*. Two of these new circuses have book-length treatments in Terry Lorant and Jon Carroll's *The Pickle Family Circus*, Peter Angelo Simon's *Big Apple Circus*, and Hana Machotka's *The Magic Ring: A Year with the Big Apple Circus*. "The Circus: An International Art" is the theme of a special issue of *UNESCO Courier* (January 1988), containing articles on the modern circus, the art of the circus spectacular, circus in film, the clown profession, and the circus in China.

Biographies, autobiographies, and reminiscences by and about circus owners and performers also abound. P. T. Barnum's life is the subject of much literature. The best documented study of Barnum's career in its social, economic, and entertainment contexts is *Humbug: The Art of P. T. Barnum* by Neil Harris. Irving Wallace's biography, *The Fabulous Showman: The Life and Times of P. T. Barnum*, is popularized but reliable. Barnum's autobiography is titled *Barnum's Own Story*; and he also wrote *Struggles and Triumphs: Or, The Life of P. T. Barnum, Written by Himself*. Both are filled with self-congratulatory puffery but remain interesting. Morris R. Werner's *Barnum* was considered the standard biography until superseded by the works of Harris and Wallace. Other useful sources are Joel Benton's *Life of Hon. Phineas T. Barnum*, largely based on Barnum's autobiography; Barnum and Helen Ferris collaborated on *Here Comes Barnum*, a collection from Barnum's own writings; Raymund Fitzsimons' authoritative *Barnum in London*; Harvey W. Root's *The Unknown Barnum*, a discussion of the traits that made Barnum unique; Constance Rourke's *Trumpets of Jubilee*, which includes treatment of the myths surrounding Barnum; and Helen Wells' *Barnum: Showman of America*.

The literature on Barnum's circus performers is also abundant. Charles S. Stratton, known worldwide as Tom Thumb, is given solid treatment in Alice Curtis Desmond's *Barnum Presents General Tom Thumb*. He and his wife, Lavinia Magri, are both covered in Mertie E. Romaine's *General Tom Thumb and His Lady*. Sylvester Bleeker and A. H. Saxon assisted Lavinia to write *The Autobiography of Mrs. Tom Thumb*. Chang and Eng, the Siamese twins, are the subjects of Irving and Amy Wallace's *The Two: A Biography*; and Kay Hunter's *Duet for a Lifetime: The Story of the Original Siamese Twins*. Equestrian and manager Fred Bradna details his years with the Barnum and Bailey Circus along with those of his wife, who was also a famous equestrian performer, in *The Big Top: My Forty Years with the Greatest Show on Earth*, written with Hartzell Spence.

The Ringlings have extensive biographical treatment. Henry Ringling North (with Alden Hatch) covers the Ringling family in *The Circus Kings*, which is biased but informative, as does Alvin F. Harlow in *The Ringlings*. Two press agents have written memoirs of their work with the Ringling circus: Dexter W. Fellows' *This Way to the Big Top Show: The Life of Dexter Fellows* (with Andrew A. Freeman), and F. Beverly Kelley's *It Was Better than Work*. Respected popular culture scholar Otis Ferguson wrote of the Ringling Brothers circus in a 1940 article originally in the *New Republic*, "The Circus On the Road." It is reprinted in *The Otis Ferguson Reader*, edited by Dorothy Chamberlain and Robert Wilson. Michael Burke, in *Outrageous Good Fortune*, chronicles his experience as the general manager of the Ringling circus during its last years as a tent show. The disastrous fire at the Ringling circus during its tent performance in Hartford, Connecticut, on July 6, 1944, is investigated in two recent volumes: Don Massy and Rick Davey's *A Matter of Degree: The Hartford Circus Fire and the Mystery of Little Miss 1565*, and Stewart O'Nan's *The Circus Fire: A True Story*. Featured performers in the Ringling shows are treated in book-length works. Tito Gaona's life as a premier trapeze artist with the Ringlings in the 1960s and 1970s is presented in *Born to Fly: The Story of Tito Gaona*, written by Gaona with Harry L. Graham. The legendary Wallenda family of high wire artists is covered in *Wallenda*, Ron Morris' biography of the family patriarch Karl Wallenda. Gargantua, the Ringling's gorilla star during the depression years, is the subject of two popularized biographies, James A. Ware's *Gargantua the Great* and Gene Plowden's more popularized *Gargantua: Circus Star of the Century*.

Wild animal trainers have written an unusual number of autobiographies or memoirs. America's first famous lion tamer was Isaac Van Amburgh, who performed in the early half of the nineteenth century in menageries and circuses. In his time, he was the only trainer to put his head into a lion's mouth. His life is chronicled by O. J. Ferguson in *A Brief Biographical Sketch of I. A. Van Amburgh*. Surprisingly, there were several quite early women animal trainers and performers. Lucia Zora rebelled from a conservative American upbringing in Cazenovia, New York, to become the first featured female trainer of wild animals, mostly lions, in America. She tells her story in her *Sawdust and Solitude*. Mabel Stark performed with her tigers in the Ringling Brothers circus in the 1920s and 1930s and was the greatest woman cat trainer of her time. She has written *Hold That Tiger*, her autobiography. More recently, the career of tiger trainer Pat Derby is covered in her book *The Lady and Her Tiger*, written with Peter S. Beagle.

The two most famous American circus animal trainers were Clyde Beatty, who performed with the Ringlings and in his own enterprise during the 1920s and 1930s, and the contemporary trainer who has outclassed all of his predecessors, Gunther Gebel-Williams, performing throughout the 1980s with Irvin and Kenneth Feld's Ringling Brothers and Barnum and Bailey Circus. Beatty coauthored with Edward Anthony a chronicle of his career, *Facing the Big Cats: My World of Lions and Tigers*, which incorporates most of Beatty's earlier work, *The Big Cage*. Gebel-Williams' career is documented by Susan Rosenkranz in *Lord of the Rings: Gunther Gebel-Williams*. Memoir volumes related to the careers of other animal trainers are *Ways of the Circus; Being the Memoirs and Adventures of George Conklin, Tamer of Lions*, written with Harvey W. Root; Lorenz Hagenbeck's *Animals Are My Life*; Alfred Court's *My Life with the Big Cats*; and Charly Baumann's *Tiger, Tiger: My 25 Years with the Big Cats* (with Leonard A. Stevens). Early methods of animal training are presented in Frank Bostock's *The Training of Wild Animals*. Joanne Carol Joys' *The Wild Animal Trainer in America* provides a full history and an investigation of training methods. A wide-ranging, scholarly study is Heinrich Hediger's *Studies of the Psychology and Behaviour of Captive Animals in Zoos and Circuses*. Bill Ballantine presents a comprehensive analysis of animal training in *Wild Tigers and Tame Fleas*. The career of the chief veterinarian of the Ringling Brothers and Barnum and Bailey Circus is detailed by J. Y. Henderson in *Circus Doctor*, as told to Richard Taplinger.

Other famous performers, performing families, or owners are the subjects of many useful and interesting books. Wide-ranging, behind-the-scenes stories about circus performers, owners and others are found in David Lewis Hammarstrom's *Behind the Big Top*. Annals of the Hunt circus are provided in Charles T. Hunt's memoir, *The Story of Mr. Circus*. One of the great families of the circus, the Cristiani family of circus owners, acrobats, and equestrian performers, is followed in *The Christianis*, by Richard Hubler. The life of an acrobat is related by Ernest Schlee Millette, as told to Robert Wyndham, in *The Circus That Was*. High-wire artist Philippe Petit chronicles his career in *On the High Wire*. Petit became famous when he danced and juggled on a wire strung between the twin towers of the World Trade Center in 1974. Essayist, photographer, and cultural commentator Jill Krementz created *A Very Young Circus Flyer*, a documentary on then nine-year-old Tato Farfan, training as a trapeze artist with the Flying Farfans. By the age of twelve, Tato could perform the triple somersault from the trapeze.

A few additional memoirs or anecdotal volumes of a more general nature are bareback rider John H. Glenroy's nineteenth-century *Ins and Outs of Circus Life*; W. C. Thompson's *On the Road with a Circus*, the author's experiences with the Forepaugh-Sells Circus around 1900; Dixie Willson's inside view of the circus and its people in the early part of this century, *Where the World Folds Up at Night*; Robert Lewis Taylor's collection of essays from the *New Yorker, Center Ring: The People of the Circus*, which provides excellent information on various performers around midcentury; and Edwin P. Norwood's two books *The Other Side of the Circus* and *The Circus Menagerie*. Courntey Ryley Cooper has produced four volumes about circus life: *Circus Day, Lions 'N' Tigers 'N' Everything, Under the Big Top*, and *With the Circus*.

Trained circus horses. © Painet

The circus clown is treated most comprehensively and with excellent documentation in John H. Towsen's *Clowns*. This is an authoritative history of the clown throughout history, written by a graduate of Irvin Feld's Clown College. George Speaight's survey, *The Book of Clowns*, is also a comprehensive account. Other valuable works are Beryl Hugill's *Bring On the Clowns*; Lowell Swortzell's *Here Come the Clowns: A Cavalcade of Comedy from Antiquity to the Present*; George Bishop's *The World of Clowns*; and Douglas Newton's *Clowns*. Phyllis A. Roger's dissertation, "The American Circus Clown," delineates the process of becoming a clown and gives an ethnographic description of the world from a clown's point of view. The story of Clown College, established by Irvin Feld, is provided in *Clown Alley* by Bill Ballantine. The best explanation of the broad range of clown skills is presented by master teacher Hovey Burgess in *Circus Techniques*. Burgess taught the arts of juggling, stilt walking, and unicycle riding at Clown College. Two of America's famous clowns are remembered in biographies. Dan Rice, one of the earliest circus clowns in America, is the subject of Don Carle Gillette's *He Made Lincoln Laugh: The Story of Dan Rice*. Emmett Kelly, known to the world as Weary Willie, wrote his autobiography, *Clown: My Life in Tatters and Smiles*. It includes much information on the art of clowning.

Other specific aspects of the circus have received critical attention. The circus parade is covered in three well-documented and lavishly illustrated volumes, *The Great Circus Street Parade in Pictures*, by Charles Philip Fox and F. Beverly Kelley;

Circus Parades: A Pictorial History of America's Pageant by Charles Philip Fox; and *The Great Circus Parade* by Herbert Clement and Dominique Jando. Other useful works are Gene Plowden's *Singing Wheels and Circus Wagons* and his *Merle Evans, Maestro of the Circus*, the career of Ringling's bandleader. Fox also provides a comprehensive history of circus horses in *A Pictorial History of Performing Horses*. Circus posters are covered in Jack Rennert's *100 Years of Circus Posters* and Charles Philip Fox's *American Circus Posters in Full Color*. Sideshow banners in the nineteenth century are studied as instruments of allure and seduction in *Freak Show: Sideshow Banner Art* by Carl Hammer and Gideon Bosker. The history and nature of circus advertising, with extensive illustrations, are found in *Billers, Banners, and Bombast: The Story of Circus Advertising*, by Charles Philip Fox and Tom Parkinson. The career of a press agent is provided in Gene Plowden's *Circus Press Agent: The Life and Times of Roland Butler*.

The movement of circuses by trains is comprehensively covered by Tom Parkinson and Charles Philip Fox in *The Circus Moves by Rail*, which includes many illustrations and informative commentary. Fox earlier wrote *Circus Trains*. Joe McKennon provides a detailed account of the mechanics of moving a large circus by railroad in *Logistics of the American Circus*.

The "freaks" displayed in circus sideshows and amusement midways have received much critical attention. The most scholarly and provocative account is Leslie Fiedler's *Freaks: Myths and Images of the Secret Self*. More directly focused on sideshow curiosities is Ricky Jay's *Learned Pigs & Fireproof Women: Unique, Eccentric and Amazing Entertainers: Stone Eaters, Mind Readers, Poison Resisters, Daredevils, Singing Mice, etc. etc. etc.* Also comprehensive are Colin Clair's *Human Curiosities* and Frederick Drimmer's *Very Special People: The Struggles, Loves and Triumphs of Human Oddities*. *Freak Show Man* chronicles the career of performer Harry Lewiston, as told to Jerry Holtman. Also of interest are Daniel Mannix's *We Who Are Not as Others*, Albert Parry's *Tattoo: Secrets of a Strange Art*, and Jan T. Gregor's look at the Jim Rose Circus Sideshow, *Circus of the Scars: The True Inside Odyssey of a Modern Circus Sideshow*.

Some scholarly studies that see aspects of the circus in a wider sociological context should also be mentioned. Paul Bouissac's *Circus and Culture: A Semiotic Approach* creates a unique method to examine the circus from the view of a linguist. He studies circus acts as multimedia language. Marion Faber looks at circus performers in terms of literary and philosophical influence in *Angels of Daring: Tightrope Walker and Acrobat in Nietzsche, Kafka, Rilke and Thomas Mann*. Aspects of the impact of the circus on American theater are analyzed in Ron Jenkins' *Acrobats of the Soul: Comedy and Virtuosity in Contemporary American Theatre*. Circus performers are covered in Henry T. Sampson's *The Ghost Walks: A Chronological History of Blacks in Show Business, 1865–1910*.

A number of periodicals focus on the circus or feature detailed coverage of circus enterprises in the contexts of scholarly study, business research, or general interest. *Billboard* is the major source for business and performance information in this century. The *New York Clipper* (1853–1924) covered the American circus well in the nineteenth century. *Bandwagon*, published by the Circus Historical Society, provides articles on specific circuses and particular time periods. Quality and depth of contributions vary, but this journal is always informative and establishes a needed chronicle since 1959. *White Tops* is the publication of the Circus

Fans of America. *Amusement Business* gives minimal coverage of the circus along with all other amusement enterprises, as does *Variety*, covering show business in general. *Circus Report* provides news on contemporary circus enterprises. *World's Fair*, first appearing in the early 1980s, presented occasional historical articles relative to the circus. *Le Cirque dans l'Univers* is a superb international journal published since 1949 for the Club de Cirque in France.

REFERENCE WORKS: WILD WEST EXHIBITION

Major collections of Wild West exhibition materials are held in the Western History Department of the Denver Public Library in Denver, Colorado; the Circus World Museum in Baraboo, Wisconsin; and the Buffalo Bill Historical Center in Cody, Wyoming. The University of Oklahoma archives in Norman, Oklahoma, holds materials on the 101 Wild West and Pawnee Bill's Wild West shows. Other significant collections are held by the Nebraska State Historical Society and the Arizona Pioneers Historical Society. Don Wilmeth provides a useful selective bibliography of sources published through 1980 in the chapter "The Wild West Exhibition" in his *Variety Entertainment and Outdoor Amusements: A Reference Guide*.

HISTORY AND CRITICISM: WILD WEST EXHIBITION

Most of the histories of the circus in America cited in the previous section provide some attention to the Wild West exhibition, but there is a growing literature devoted more specifically to this form of entertainment. The most comprehensive study is Don Russell's *The Wild West; Or, A History of the Wild West Shows*, which also includes many exceptional photographs. These shows are connected to rodeo in Kristine Frederiksson's *American Rodeo, from Buffalo Bill to Big Business*. She notes that by 1885 there were more than fifty Wild West shows touring the country. William Brasmer provides a negative analysis of "The Wild West Exhibition and the Drama of Civilization" as theater in a chapter in *Western Popular Theatre*, edited by David Mayer and Kenneth Richards. To place the Wild West show in the context of other forces creating the myth of the American frontier, Ray Billington's *Land of Savagery, Land of Promise* is an exceptionally useful study. William W. Savage Jr.'s *The Cowboy Hero: His Image in American History and Culture* documents the impact of the Wild West show, most specifically, Cody's enterprises, on the image of the cowboy.

Most of the published studies and other material focus on Buffalo Bill Cody and his exhibitions. The best biography of Cody is Don Russell's *The Lives and Legends of Buffalo Bill*, which contains an extensive bibliography. Sarah J. Blackstone presents a detailed history of the shows in *Buckskins, Bullets and Business: A History of Buffalo Bill's Wild West*. Walter Havinghurst's *Buffalo Bill's Great Wild West Show* is written for younger readers. In *Buffalo Bill and the Wild West*, Henry Blackman Sell and Victor Weybright combine biography with an analysis of the Wild West presentations and Cody's legend. Richard J. Walsh and Milton Salsbury provide an extensive study of the process by which Cody became a legend through the skillful use of publicity in *The Making of Buffalo Bill: A Study in Heroics*. The show's advertisements themselves are presented by Jack Rennert in *100 Posters* of *Buffalo Bill's Wild West*. Excellent illustrative material is also available in *The West of Buffalo Bill*, with an introduction by Harold McCracken. Other useful biographies are Nellie Snyder Yost's *Buffalo Bill: His Family, Friends, Fame, Failures, and Fortunes*; John Burke's *Buffalo Bill, the Noblest Whiteskin* is a popularized account that focuses on both Cody's life and the individuals associated with the show; and Rupert Croft-Cooke and W. S. Meadmore's sympathetic *Buffalo Bill: The Legend, the Man of Action, the Showman*. Alice J. Hall's "Buffalo Bill and the Enduring West" is a perceptive and lengthy article appearing in *National Geographic*. Cody's autobiography, *Life and Adventures of Buffalo Bill*, is not particularly readable or trustworthy. The 1917 edition includes a final chapter on Cody's death by Col. William Lightfoot Visscher. His sister, Julia Cody Goodman, presents an accurate account in her *Buffalo Bill, King of the Old West*, written with Elizabeth Jane Leonard. This volume offers corrections to another sister's book, Helen Cody Wetmore's *Last of the Great Scouts*. Cody's unhappy wife, Louisa, left the record of a failed marriage in her *Memories of Buffalo Bill*, written with Courtney Ryley Cooper. Other sources worth consultation include Stella Adelyne Foote's *Letters from Buffalo Bill*; Henry Inman and William F. Cody's *The Great Salt Lake Trail*; Dan Muller's *My Life with Buffalo Bill*; and Frank Winch's sentimental, but informative, account of Cody's show and his greatest rival, *Thrilling Lives of Buffalo Bill and Pawnee Bill*.

The 1903–1907 European tour of Cody's show is covered in Charles Eldridge Griffin's *Four Years in Europe with Buffalo Bill*. The role of the dime novel in Cody's fame and popularity is extensively discussed in Albert Johannsen's three-volume work *The House of Beadle and Adams*, a thorough source on the major publisher of dime novels. Another collateral study concerns the travels of Native Americans abroad, including with the Wild West shows, Carolyn Thomas Foreman's *Indians Abroad*. Dee Brown documents the association of Buffalo Bill and Sitting Bull in *Bury My Heart at Wounded Knee*. Another account of Cody's interaction with Native Americans is *Buffalo Bill and the Indians or Sitting Bull's History Lesson*, a motion picture script by Alan Rudolph and Robert Altman. Some primary materials about the shows are provided in *Buffalo Bill's Wild West and Congress of Rough Riders of the World: Historical Sketches and Programme, Greater New York*.

Cody's associates and featured performers have received attention, especially Annie Oakley. Isabelle S. Sayers presents a factual account and over 100 illustrations in *Annie Oakley and Buffalo Bill's Wild West*. A popularized biography is Walter Havinghurst's *Annie Oakley of the Wild West*. There is no definitive biography of Oakley to date, but also helpful are Edmund Collier's *The Story of Annie Oakley* for younger readers; Courtney Ryley Cooper's *Annie Oakley, Woman at Arms*; and Steward H. Holbrook's *Little Annie Oakley and Other Rugged People*. Her niece, Annie Fern Swartwout, provides *Missie: An Historical Biography of Annie Oakley*. Doc Carver, Cody's early partner, receives definitive biographical treatment in Raymond W. Thorp's *Spirit Gun of the West: The Story of Doc W. F. Carver*. Wild Bill Hickok, who toured with one of Cody's shows in 1873 and had his own exhibitions, is covered in Mildred Fiedler's *Wild Bill and Deadwood* and in Joseph G. Rosa's *They Called Him Wild Bill*. Dime novelist Ned Buntline (Edward Zane Carroll Judson), who popularized Buffalo Bill, his exploits, and his associations with Cody, is the subject of Jay Monaghan's *The Great Rascal: The Life and Adventures of Ned Buntline*.

Other Wild West entertainments in competition with Cody's are documented. Cody's greatest rival, Pawnee Bill, and his shows are covered in Glenn Shirley's informative history *Pawnee Bill: A Biography of Major Gordon W. Lillie*, which also provides much information on the Wild West shows in general. The 101 Ranch is the subject of Michael Wallis' recent book *The Real Wild West: The 101 Ranch and the Creation of the American West*. Ellsworth Collings and Alma Miller England's *The 101 Ranch* also provides a comprehensive account of the Miller Brothers' enterprise. Less reliable is Fred Gipson's *Fabulous Empire: Colonel Zack Miller's Story*. Tom Mix, Wild West performer who became a western movie star, is the subject of two biographies by family members, Paul E. Mix's *The Life and Legend of Tom Mix*, and Olive Stokes Mix's *The Fabulous Tom Mix*. Harry Tammen and Fred Bonfils' Floto Dog and Pony Show, a later enterprise, is treated in Gene Fowler's *Timberline: A Story of Bonfils and Tammen*. A later enterprise is the subject of Fred D. Pfening Jr.'s *Col. Tim McCoy's Real Wild West and Rough Riders of the World*. Will Rogers, who worked in Wild West shows in his early career and was greatly influenced by them, has received scholarly biographical analysis in William R. Brown's *Imagemaker: Will Rogers and the American Dream*.

The circus periodicals listed in the previous section, *New York Clipper*, *Bandwagon*, and early issues of *Billboard*, contain extensive material on the Wild West exhibitions. Journals and magazines devoted largely to the West that occasionally provide articles on the shows are *American West*, *Nebraska History*, *Old West*, and *True West*.

BIBLIOGRAPHY

General Sources

Hartman, Donald K., and Jerome Drost. *Themes and Settings in Fiction: A Bibliography of Bibliographies*. New York: Greenwood Press, 1988.

Hartman, Donald K., and Gregg Sapp. *Historical Figures in Fiction*. Phoenix, Ariz.: Oryx Press, 1994.

Toole-Stott, Raymond. *A Bibliography of the Books on the Circus in English from 1773–1964*. Derby, England: Harpur, 1964.

———. *Circus and Allied Arts, a World Bibliography*. 4 vols. Derby, England: Harpur and Sons, 1958–1971.

———. *Circus and Allied Arts, a World Bibliography, Vol. 5: 1500–1982*. London: Circus Friends Association of Great Britain, 1992.

Wilmeth, Don B. "Circus and Outdoor Entertainment." In *Handbook of American Popular Culture*, ed. M. Thomas Inge. New York: Greenwood Press, 1979, 173–203.

———. *The Language of American Popular Entertainment: A Glossary of Argot, Slang, and Terminology*. Westport, Conn.: Greenwood Press, 1981.

———. *Variety Entertainment and Outdoor Amusements: A Reference Guide*. Westport, Conn.: Greenwood Press, 1982.

———, ed. *American and English Popular Entertainment: A Guide to Information Sources*. Detroit: Gale Research, 1980.

Circus

Albrecht, Ernest. *The New American Circus*. Gainesville: University Press of Florida, 1995.

American Heritage Magazine. *Great Days of the Circus*. New York: American Heritage, 1962.

Ballantine, Bill. *Clown Alley*. Boston: Little, Brown, 1982.

————. *Wild Tigers and Tame Fleas*. New York: Rinehart, 1958.

Barnum, Phineas Taylor. *Barnum's Own Story; The Autobiography of P. T. Barnum, Combined and Condensed from the Various Editions Published during His Lifetime*. Ed. Waldo R. Browne. New York: Viking, 1927.

————. *Here Comes Barnum*. Written with Helen Josephine Ferris. New York: Harcourt, Brace, 1932.

————. *Struggles and Triumphs; or The Life of P. T. Barnum, Written by Himself*. 1869. Reprint. New York: Arno Press, 1970.

Barton, Bob. *Old Covered Wagon Show Days, as Told to G. Ernest Thomas*. New York: E. P. Dutton, 1939.

Baumann, Charly, with Leonard A. Stevens. *Tiger, Tiger: My 25 Years with the Big Cats*. Chicago: Playboy Press, 1975.

Beatty, Clyde, with Edward Anthony. *Facing the Big Cats: My World of Lions and Tigers*. Garden City, N.Y.: Doubleday, 1965.

Beneath White Tents: Official Route Book of the Ringling Brothers' World's Greatest Shows, Season of 1894. Buffalo, N.Y.: Courier, 1894.

Benton, Joel. *Life of Hon. Phineas T. Barnum*. Chicago: M. A. Donohue, 1891.

Bishop, George Victor. *The World of Clowns*. Los Angeles: Brooke House, 1976.

Bostock, Frank. *The Training of Wild Animals*. New York: Century, 1903.

Bouissac, Paul. *Circus and Culture: A Semiotic Approach*. Bloomington: Indiana University Press, 1976.

Bradna, Fred, as told to Hartzell Spence. *The Big Top: My Forty Years with the Greatest Show on Earth*. New York: Simon and Schuster, 1952.

Burgess, Hovey. *Circus Techniques: Juggling, Equilibristics, & Vaulting*. New York: Drama Book Specialists, 1976.

Burke, Michael. *Outrageous Good Fortune*. Boston: Little, Brown, 1984.

Chindahl, George L. *History of the Circus in America*. Caldwell, Idaho: Caxton Printers, 1959.

"The Circus, an International Art." Special issue, *UNESCO Courier* 41 (January 1988).

Clair, Colin. *Human Curiosities*. New York: Abelard-Schuman, 1968.

Clapp, William W., Jr. *A Record of the Boston Stage*. 1853. Reprint. New York: Benjamin Blom, 1968.

Clement, Herbert, and Dominique Jando. *The Great Circus Parade*. Photography by Tom Nebbia. Milwaukee: Gareth Stevens, 1989.

Conklin, George, with Harvey W. Root. *Ways of the Circus; Being the Memoirs and Adventures of George Conklin, Tamer of Lions*. New York: Harper, 1921.

Conover, Richard E. *The Affairs of James A. Bailey: New Revelations on the Career of the World's Most Successful Showman*. Xenia, Ohio: Richard E. Conover, 1957.

————. *The Circus: Wisconsin's Unique Heritage*. Baraboo, Wis.: Circus World Museum, 1967.

————. *Give 'Em a John Robinson: A Documentary on the Old John Robinson Circus*. Xenia, Ohio: Richard E. Conover, 1965.

————. *The Great Forepaugh Show*. Xenia, Ohio: Richard E. Conover, 1959.

Cooke, Charles. *Big Show*. New York: Harper and Brothers, 1938.

Cooper, Courtney Ryley. *Circus Day*. New York: Farrar and Rinehart, 1931.

————. *Lions 'N' Tigers 'N' Everything*. Boston: Little, Brown, 1924.

————. *Under the Big Top*. Boston: Little, Brown, 1923.

————. *With the Circus*. Boston: Little, Brown, 1928.

Coup, W. C. *Sawdust and Spangles: Stories and Secrets of the Circus*. 1901. Reprint. Washington, D.C.: Paul A. Ruddell, 1961.

Court, Alfred. *My Life with the Big Cats*. New York: Simon and Schuster, 1955.

Cowell, Joseph. *Thirty Years Passed among the Players in England and America*. New York: Harper, 1844.

Coxe, Antony D. Hippisley. *A Seat at the Circus*. London: Evans Brothers, 1951.

Croft-Cooke, Rupert, and Peter Cotes. *Circus: A World History*. New York: Macmillan, 1976.

Culhane, John. *The American Circus; An Illustrated History*. New York: Holt, 1990.

Derby, Pat, with Peter S. Beagle. *The Lady and Her Tiger*. New York: Dutton, 1976.

Desmond, Alice Curtis. *Barnum Presents General Tom Thumb*. New York: Macmillan, 1954.

Disher, M. Willson. *Greatest Show on Earth. Astley's—Afterwards Sanger's—Royal Amphitheatre of the Arts, Westminster Bridge Road*. 1937. Reprint. New York: Benjamin Blom, 1969.

Dressler, Albert, ed. *California's Pioneer Circus, Joseph Rowe, Founder; Memoirs and Personal Correspondence Relative to the Circus Business through the Gold Country in the Fifties*. San Francisco: H. S. Crocker, 1926.

Drimmer, Frederick. *Very Special People: The Struggles, Loves and Triumphs of Human Oddities*. New York: Amjon, 1973.

Durang, John. *The Memoirs of John Durang (American Actor, 1785–1816)*. Ed. Alan S. Downer. Pittsburgh: University of Pittsburgh Press, 1966.

Durant, John, and Alice Durant. *Pictorial History of the American Circus*. New York: A. S. Barnes, 1957.

Eckley, Wilton. *The American Circus*. Boston: Twayne, 1984.

Faber, Marion. *Angels of Daring: Tightrope Walker and Acrobat in Nietzsche, Kafka, Rilke and Thomas Mann*. Stuttgart: Akademischer Verlag Hans-Dieter Heinz, 1979.

Fellows, Dexter W., and Andrew A. Freeman. *This Way to the Big Top: The Life of Dexter Fellows*. New York: Viking Press, 1936.

Fenner, Mildred S., and Wolcott Fenner, eds. *The Circus: Lure and Legend*. Englewood Cliffs, N.J.: Prentice-Hall, 1970.

Ferguson, O. J. *A Brief Biographical Sketch of I. A. Van Amburgh*. New York: Samuel Booth, 1861.

Ferguson, Otis. "The Circus on the Road." In *The Otis Ferguson Reader*, ed. Dorothy Chamberlain and Robert Wilson. Highland Park, Ill.: December Press, 1982.

Fiedler, Leslie. *Freaks: Myths and Images of the Secret Self*. New York: Simon and Schuster, 1978.

Field, Al G. *Watch Yourself Go By*. Columbus, Ohio: Spaar and Glenn, 1912.

Fitzsimons, Raymund. *Barnum in London*. New York: St. Martin's Press, 1970.

Flint, Richard W. "A Selected Guide to Source Material on the American Circus." *Journal of Popular Culture* 6 (Winter 1972), 615–19.

Fowler, Gene. *Timber Line: A Story of Bonfils and Tammen*. New York: P. F. Collier and Son, 1933.

Fox, Charles Philip. *Circus Parades: A Pictorial History of America's Pageant*. Watkins Glen, N.Y.: Century House, 1953.

———. *Circus Trains*. Milwaukee: Kalmbach, 1947.

———. *A Pictorial History of Performing Horses*. New York: Bramhall House, 1960.

———. *A Ticket to the Circus: A Pictorial History of the Incredible Ringlings*. New York: Bramhall House, 1959.

———, ed. *American Circus Posters in Full Color*. New York: Dover, 1978.

———. *Old Time Circus Cuts: A Pictorial Archive of 202 Illustrations*. New York: Dover, 1979.

Fox, Charles Philip, and F. Beverly Kelley. *The Great Circus Street Parade in Pictures*. New York: Dover, 1978.

Fox, Charles Philip, and Tom Parkinson. *Billers, Banners and Bombast: The Story of Circus Advertising*. Boulder, Colo.: Pruett, 1985.

———. *Circus in America*. Waukesha, Wis.: Country Beautiful, 1969.

Freedman, Jill. *Circus Days*. New York: Crown, 1975.

Frost, Thomas. *Circus Life and Circus Celebrities*. 1895. Reprint. Detroit: Singing Tree Press, 1970.

Gaona, Tito, with Harry L. Graham. *Born to Fly: The Story of Tito Gaona*. Los Angeles: Wild Rose, 1984.

Gillette, Don Carle. *He Made Lincoln Laugh: The Story of Dan Rice*. New York: Exposition Press, 1967.

Glenroy, John H. *Ins and Outs of Circus Life, or Forty-Two Years Travel of John H. Glenroy Bareback Rider, through United States, Canada, South America, and Cuba*. Boston: M. M. Wing, 1885.

Gregor, Jan T. *Circus of the Scars: The True Inside Odyssey of a Modern Circus Sideshow*. Seattle: Brennan Dalsgard, 1998.

Hagenbeck, Lorenz. *Animals Are My Life*. Translated by Alec Brown. London: Bodley Head, 1956.

Hammarstrom, David Lewis. *Behind the Big Top*. New York: A. S. Barnes, 1980.

Hammer, Carl, and Gideon Bosker. *Freak Show: Sideshow Banner Art*. San Francisco: Chronicle Books, 1996.

Harlow, Alvin F. *The Ringlings*. New York: Julian Messner, 1951.

Harris, Neil. *Humbug: The Art of P. T. Barnum*. Boston: Little, Brown, 1973.

Hediger, Heinrich. *Studies of the Psychology and Behaviour of Captive Animals in Zoos and Circuses*. New York: Criterion Books, 1955.

Henderson, J. Y., as told to Richard Taplinger. *Circus Doctor*. Boston: Little, Brown, 1952.

Hoh, LaVahn G., and William H. Rough. *Step Right Up! The Adventure of Circus in America*. White Hall, Va.: Betterway, 1990.

Hubler, Richard Gibson. *The Cristianis*. Boston: Little, Brown, 1966.

Hugill, Beryl. *Bring On the Clowns*. Secaucus, N.J.: Chartwell Books, 1980.

Hunt, Charles T. *The Story of Mr. Circus*. Rochester, N.H.: Record Press, 1954.

Hunter, Kay. *Duet for a Lifetime: The Story of the Original Siamese Twins*. New York: Coward-McCann, 1964.

Jamieson, David, and Sandy Davidson. *The Colorful World of the Circus*. London: Octopus Books, 1980.

Jando, Dominique. *Histoire mondaile du cirque*. Paris: Jean-Pierre Delange, 1977.

Jay, Ricky. *Learned Pigs & Fireproof Women: Unique, Eccentric and Amazing Entertainers: Stone Eaters, Mind Readers, Poison Resisters, Daredevils, Singing Mice, etc. etc. etc*. New York: Villard Books, 1986.

Jenkins, Ron. *Acrobats of the Soul: Comedy and Virtuosity in Contemporary American Theatre*. New York: Theatre Communication Group, 1988.

Jensen, Dean. *The Biggest, the Smallest, the Longest, the Shortest*. Madison: Wisconsin House, 1975.

Joys, Joanne Carol. *The Wild Animal Trainer in America*. Boulder, Colo.: Pruett, 1983.

Kelley, F. Beverly. *It Was Better than Work*. Gerald, Mo.: Patrice Press, 1982.

Kelly, Emmett. *Clown: My Life in Tatters and Smiles*. New York: Prentice-Hall, 1954.

Krementz, Jill. *A Very Young Circus Flyer*. New York: Alfred A. Knopf, 1979.

Kunzog, John C. *Tanbark and Tinsel*. Jamestown, N.Y.: Privately printed, 1970.

Kurtz, O. H., comp. *Official Route Book of Ringling Brothers' World's Greatest Railroad Shows, Season of 1892*. Buffalo, N.Y.: Courier, 1892.

Lehman, Rolf. *Circus: Magie der Manege*. 2 vols. Hamburg: Hoffman und Campe, 1979.

Lewiston, Harry, as told to Jerry Holtman. *Freak Show Man*. Los Angeles: Holloway House, 1968.

Lorant, Terry, and Jon Carroll. *The Pickle Family Circus*. San Francisco: Chronicle Books, 1986.

Machotka, Hana. *The Magic Ring: A Year with the Big Apple Circus*. Intro. Paul Binder. New York: Morrow, 1988.

Magri, M. Lavinia, with Sylvester Bleeker and A. H. Saxon. *The Autobiography of Mrs. Tom Thumb: (Some of My Life Experiences)*. Hamden, Conn.: Archon Books, 1979.

Mannix, Daniel. *We Who Are Not as Others*. New York: Pocket Books, 1976.

Martin, Edwin, and Don B. Wilmeth. *Mud Show: American Tent Circus Life*. Albuquerque: University of New Mexico Press, 1988.

Massy, Dan, and Rick Davey. *A Matter of Degree: The Hartford Circus Fire and the Mystery of Little Miss 1565*. Hartford, Conn.: Willow Brook Press, 2000.

May, Earl Chapin. *The Circus from Rome to Ringling*. 1932. Reprint. New York: Dover, 1963.

McKennon, Joe. *Circus Lingo*. Sarasota, Fla.: Carnival, 1980.

———. *Horse Dung Trail: Saga of American Circus*. Sarasota, Fla.: Carnival, 1975.

———. *Horse Dung Trail: Saga of American Circus, Index*. Sarasota, Fla.: Carnival, 1979.

———. *Logistics of the American Circus*. Sarasota, Fla.: Carnival, 1977.

Millette, Ernest Schlee, as told to Robert Wyndham. *The Circus That Was*. Philadelphia: Dorrance, 1971.

Morris, Ron. *Wallenda, a Biography of Karl Wallenda*. Chatham, N.Y.: Sagarin Press, 1976.

Moy, James S. "John B. Ricketts's Circus 1793–1800." Ph.D. diss., University of Illinois, 1977.

Neafie, Nelle. *A P. T. Barnum Bibliography*. Lexington: University of Kentucky Press, 1965.

Nebraska Ned, pseud. *Buffalo Bill and His Daring Adventures in the Romantic Wild West*. Baltimore: I. and M. Ottenheimer, 1913.

Newton, Douglas. *Clowns*. New York: Franklin Watts, 1957.

North, Henry Ringling, and Alden Hatch. *The Circus Kings: Our Ringling Family Story*. Garden City, N.Y.: Doubleday, 1960.

Norwood, Edwin P. *The Circus Menagerie*. Garden City, N.Y.: Doubleday and Page, 1929.

————. *The Other Side of the Circus*. Garden City, N.Y.: Doubleday and Page, 1926.

O'Brien, Esse F. *Circus: Cinders to Sawdust*. San Antonio: Naylor, 1959.

Odell, George C. *Annals of the New York Stage, Vol. IV*. New York: Columbia University Press, 1928.

O'Nan, Stewart. *The Circus Fire: A True Story*. New York: Doubleday, 2000.

Parkinson, Robert L. *Circus World Museum Library: A Guide to Its Holdings and Services*. Baraboo, Wis.: The Museum, 1973.

Parkinson, Tom, and Charles Philip Fox. *The Circus Moves by Rail*. Boulder, Colo.: Pruett, 1978.

Parry, Albert. *Tattoo: Secrets of a Strange Art*. 1933. Reprint. New York: Macmillan, 1971.

Petit, Philippe. *On the High Wire*. New York: Random House, 1985.

Plowden, Gene. *Circus Press Agent: The Life and Times of Roland Butler*. Caldwell, Idaho: Caxton Printers, 1984.

————. *Gargantua: Circus Star of the Century*. New York: Bonanza Books, 1972.

————. *Merle Evans, Maestro of the Circus*. Miami, Fla.: E. A. Seemann, 1971.

————. *Singing Wheels and Circus Wagons*. Caldwell, Idaho: Caxton Printers, 1977.

————. *Those Amazing Ringlings and Their Circus*. New York: Bonanza Books, 1967.

Powledge, Fred. *Mud Show: A Circus Season*. New York: Harcourt Brace Jovanovich, 1975.

Reeder, Warren A. *No Performances Today; June 22, 1918, Ivanhoe, Indiana*. Hammond, Ind.: North State Press, 1972.

Rennert, Jack. *100 Years of Circus Posters*. New York: Darien House, 1974.

Reynolds, Chang. *Pioneer Circuses of the West*. Los Angeles: Westernlore Press, 1966.

Robinson, Gil. *Old Wagon Show Days*. Cincinnati: Brockwell, 1925.

Rogers, Phyllis A. "The American Circus Clown." Ph.D. diss., Princeton University, 1979.

Romaine, Mertie E. *General Tom Thumb and His Lady*. Taunton, Mass.: W. S. Sullwold, 1976.

Root, Harvey Woods. *The Unknown Barnum*. New York: Harper and Brothers, 1927.

Rosenkranz, Susan. *Lord of the Rings: Gunther Gebel-Williams*. Washington, D.C.: Ringling Brothers and Barnum and Bailey Combined Shows, 1988.

Rourke, Constance. *Trumpets of Jubilee, Henry Ward Beecher, Harriet Beecher Stowe, Lyman Beecher, Horace Greeley, P. T. Barnum*. New York: Harcourt, Brace, 1927.

Sampson, Henry T. *The Ghost Walks: A Chronological History of Blacks in Show Business, 1865–1910*. Metuchen, N.J.: Scarecrow Press, 1988.

Saxon, A. H. *Enter Foot and Horse: A History of Hippodrama in England and France*. New Haven, Conn.: Yale University Press, 1968.

———. *The Life and Art of Andrew Ducrow and the Romantic Age of the English Circus*. Hamden, Conn.: Shoe String Press, 1978.

Simon, Peter Angelo. *Big Apple Circus*. New York: Penguin Books, 1978.

Sokan, Robert. *A Descriptive and Bibliographic Catalog of the Circus and Related Arts Collection at Illinois State University, Normal, Illinois*. Bloomington, Ill.: Scarlet Ibis Press, 1975.

Speaight, George. *The Book of Clowns*. New York: Macmillan, 1980.

———. *A History of the Circus*. New York: A. S. Barnes, 1980.

Stark, Mabel. *Hold That Tiger*. Caldwell, Idaho: Caxton Printers, 1938.

Swortzell, Lowell. *Here Comes the Clowns: A Cavalcade of Comedy from Antiquity to the Present*. New York: Viking Press, 1978.

Taylor, Robert Lewis. *Center Ring: The People of the Circus*. New York: Doubleday, 1956.

Thayer, Stuart. *Annals of the American Circus 1793–1829*. Manchester, Mich.: Rymack Printing, 1976.

———. *Annals of the American Circus, Vol II: 1830–1847*. Seattle: Peanut Butter, 1976.

Thetard, Henry. *La Merveilleuse Histoire du cirque*. 2 vols. Paris: Prisma, 1947.

Thompson, William Carter. *On the Road with a Circus*. New York: New Amsterdam Book, 1905.

Towsen, John H. *Clowns*. New York: Hawthorn Books, 1976.

Truzzi, Marcello, ed. "Circuses, Carnivals and Fairs." In-Depth Section. *Journal of Popular Culture* 6 (Spring 1973), 529–619.

Verney, Peter. *Here Comes the Circus*. New York and London: Paddington Press (Distributed in United States by Grosset and Dunlap), 1978.

Wallace, Irving. *The Fabulous Showman: The Life and Times of P. T. Barnum*. New York: Knopf, 1959.

Wallace, Irving, and Amy Wallace. *The Two: A Biography*. London: Cassell, 1978.

Ware, James A. *Gargantua the Great*. New York: William Morrow, 1959.

Wells, Helen. *Barnum: Showman of America*. New York: McKay, 1957.

Werner, Morris Robert. *Barnum*. New York: Harcourt, Brace, 1924.

Willson, Dixie. *Where the World Folds Up at Night*. New York: D. Appleton, 1932.

Zora, Lucia. *Sawdust and Solitude*. Boston: Little, Brown, 1928.

The Wild West Exhibition

Billington, Ray. *Land of Savagery, Land of Promise: The European Image of the American Frontier in the Nineteenth Century*. New York: Norton, 1980.

Blackstone, Sarah J. *Buckskins, Bullets, and Business: A History of Buffalo Bill's Wild West*. Westport, Conn.: Greenwood Press, 1986.

Brasmer, William. "The Wild West Exhibition and the Drama of Civilization." In *Western Popular Theatre*, ed. David Mayer and Kenneth Richards. London: Methuen, 1977, pp. 133–56.

Brown, Dee Alexander. *Bury My Heart at Wounded Knee: An Indian History of the American West*. New York: Holt, Rinehart, and Winston, 1971.

Brown, William R. *Imagemaker: Will Rogers and the American Dream*. Columbia: University of Missouri Press, 1970.

Buffalo Bill's Wild West and Congress of Rough Riders of the World: Historical Sketches and Programme, Greater New York. New York: Fless and Ridge Printing, 1897.

Burke, John. *Buffalo Bill, the Noblest Whiteskin*. New York: G. P. Putnam, 1973.

Cody, Louisa F., and Courtney Ryley Cooper. *Memories of Buffalo Bill*. New York: D. Appleton, 1919.

Cody, William F. *Life and Adventures of Buffalo Bill*. Chicago: Stanton and Van Vliet, 1917.

Collier, Edmund. *The Story of Annie Oakley*. New York: Grosset and Dunlap, 1956.

Collings, Ellsworth, and Alma Miller England. *The 101 Ranch*. 1937. Reprint. Norman: University of Oklahoma Press, 1987.

Cooper, Courtney Ryley. *Annie Oakley, Woman at Arms*. New York: Duffield, 1927.

Croft-Cooke, Rupert, and W. S. Meadmore. *Buffalo Bill: The Legend, the Man of Action, the Showman*. London: Sidgwick and Jackson, 1952.

Fiedler, Mildred. *Wild Bill and Deadwood*. New York: Bonanza Books, 1965.

Foote, Stella Adelyne, ed. *Letters from Buffalo Bill, Taken from the Originals Now on Exhibit at the Wonderland Museum, Billings, Montana*. Billings, Mont.: Foote, 1954.

Foreman, Carolyn Thomas. *Indians Abroad*. Norman: University of Oklahoma Press, 1943.

Fowler, Gene. *Timber Line: A Story of Bonfils and Tammen*. New York: P. F. Collier and Son, 1933.

Fredricksson, Kristine. *American Rodeo, from Buffalo Bill to Big Business*. College Station: Texas A&M University Press, 1985.

Gipson, Fred. *Fabulous Empire: Colonel Zack Miller's Story*. Boston: Houghton Mifflin, 1946.

Goodman, Julia Cody, with Elizabeth Jane Leonard. *Buffalo Bill, King of the Old West*. New York: Library, 1955.

Griffin, Charles Eldridge. *Four Years in Europe with Buffalo Bill*. Albia, Iowa: State, 1908.

Hall, Alice J. "Buffalo Bill and the Enduring West." *National Geographic* 160 (July 1981), 76–103.

Havinghurst, Walter. *Annie Oakley of the Wild West*. New York: Macmillan, 1954.

———. *Buffalo Bill's Great Wild West Show*. New York: Random House, 1945.

Holbrook, Stewart Hall. *Little Annie Oakley and Other Rugged People*. New York: Macmillan, 1948.

Inman, Henry, and William F. Cody. *The Great Salt Lake Trail*. New York: Macmillan, 1898.

Johannsen, Albert. *The House of Beadle and Adams*. 3 vols. Norman: University of Oklahoma Press, 1950–1962.

Leonard, Elizabeth Jane, and Julia Cody Goodman. *Buffalo Bill, King of the Old West*. Ed. James William Hoffman. New York: Library, 1955.

Mix, Olive Stokes. *The Fabulous Tom Mix*. Englewood Cliffs, N.J.: Prentice-Hall, 1957.

Mix, Paul E. *The Life and Legend of Tom Mix*. New York: A. S. Barnes, 1972.

Monaghan, Jay. *The Great Rascal: The Life and Adventures of Ned Buntline*. New York: Bonanza Books, 1951.

Muller, Dan. *My Life with Buffalo Bill*. Chicago: Reilly and Lee, 1948.

Pfening, Fred D., Jr. *Col. Tim McCoy's Real Wild West and Rough Riders of the World*. Columbus, Ohio: Pfening and Snyder, 1955.

Rennert, Jack. *100 Posters of Buffalo Bill's Wild West*. New York: Darien House, 1976.

Rosa, Joseph G. *They Called Him Wild Bill*. Norman: University of Oklahoma Press, 1964.

Rudolph, Alan, and Robert Altman. *Buffalo Bill and the Indians or Sitting Bull's History Lesson*. New York: Bantam Books, 1976.

Russell, Don. *The Lives and Legends of Buffalo Bill*. Norman: University of Oklahoma Press, 1960.

——. *The Wild West; Or, A History of the Wild West Shows*. Fort Worth: Amon Carter Museum of Western Art, 1970.

Savage, William W., Jr. *The Cowboy Hero: His Image in American History and Culture*. Norman: University of Oklahoma Press, 1979.

Sayers, Isabelle S. *Annie Oakley and Buffalo Bill's Wild West*. New York: Dover, 1981.

Sell, Henry Blackman, and Victor Weybright. *Buffalo Bill and the Wild West*. New York: Oxford University Press, 1955.

Shirley, Glenn. *Pawnee Bill: A Biography of Major Gordon W. Lillie*. Lincoln: University of Nebraska Press, 1958.

Swartwout, Annie Fern. *Missie; An Historical Biography of Annie Oakley*. Blanchester, Ohio: Brown, 1947.

Thorp, Raymond W. *Spirit Gun of the West: The Story of Doc W. F. Carver*. Glendale, Calif.: Arthur H. Clark, 1957.

Wallis, Michael. *The Real Wild West: The 101 Ranch and the Creation of the American West*. New York: St. Martin's Press, 1999.

Walsh, Richard J., and Milton S. Salsbury. *The Making of Buffalo Bill: A Study in Heroics*. New York: A. L. Burt, 1928.

The West of Buffalo Bill; Frontier Art, Indian Crafts, Memorabilia from the Buffalo Bill Historical Center. Intro. Harold McCracken. New York: Harry N. Abrams, 1974.

Wetmore, Helen Cody. *Last of the Great Scouts*. Duluth, Minn.: Duluth Press, 1899.

Winch, Frank. *Thrilling Lives of Buffalo Bill and Pawnee Bill*. New York: S. L. Parsons, 1911.

Yost, Nellie Snyder. *Buffalo Bill: His Family, Friends, Fame, Failures, and Fortunes*. Chicago: Swallow Press, 1979.

Periodicals

America: History and Life. Santa Barbara, Calif.: 1964– .
American West. Tucson, 1964–1990.
Amusement Business. Nashville, 1961– .
Bandwagon. Columbus, Ohio, 1959– .
Billboard. New York, 1894– .
Circus Report. El Cerrito, Calif., 1927– .
Le Cirque dans l'Univers. Vincennes, France, 1949– .
Nebraska History. Lincoln, Nebr., 1918– .
New York Clipper. New York, 1853–1924.
Old West. Stillwater, Okla., 1964– .
True West. Stillwater, Okla., 1953– .
Variety. Los Angeles, 1905– .
White Tops. White Stone, Va., 1927– .
World's Fair. Corte Madera, Calif., 1981–1995.

Circus parade. Courtesy of the Denver Public Library

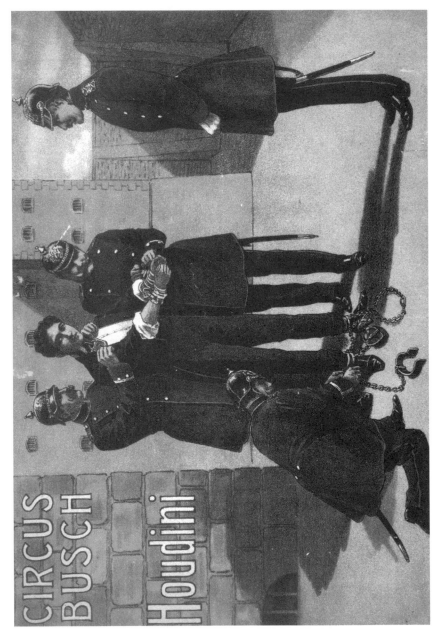

Houdini and the circus. Courtesy of the Library of Congress

The circus ring, Luna Park, Coney Island, New York. Courtesy of the Library of Congress

Pickle Family Circus tightrope walker. © Painet

Toddler with clown at the Shrine Circus, St. Paul, Minnesota. © Skjold Photographs

Acrobat. © Painet

Circus clowns with trained poodles. © Painet

COMIC BOOKS

M. Thomas Inge

The comic book has been one of the most popular and widely read of the mass literary media in this century by both children and adults, with as many as 200 million copies a year published in the United States alone. Originated in 1933 as a vehicle for reprinting newspaper strips, the comic book soon went its separate way as a distinctive narrative art form that related the adventures of characters and superheroes whose roots and inspiration are found in popular detective and science fiction, American folklore, and European mythology. Although the superhero dominated the form at the start, titles were also devoted to adventure, romance, war, crime, horror, western stories, fantasy, fairy tales, and funny animal stories (the last a direct descendant of the ancient form of the animal fable).

The peak year of 1941 saw over 160 titles in print, and while economic problems plague current publishers, the comic book has remained a significant part of America's reading matter. The characters have such a hold on the American imagination that the movie industry has turned out a seemingly endless series of motion pictures about them, such as the Superman and Batman films, Flash Gordon, Buck Rogers, the Swamp Thing, Conan the Barbarian, and the X-Men, or for the television screen, Wonder Woman, the Hulk, Spider-Man, and Captain Marvel.

What accounts for the popularity and staying power of comic book art? In the first place, it appeals to the senses; the brightly colored pages and heavily outlined figures grip the attention of the reader and, like all art, satisfy the urge of the eye to place the riotous colors of life into a balanced perspective. Second, it appeals to the imagination in its role as narration, and, like all literature, it satisfies the thirst for vicarious adventure into worlds and experiences outside daily reality. Finally, it appeals to the mind in its effort to create rational order out of the chaos of existence by reducing conflict and complexity into a simplified and therefore less threatening moral battle between the forces of good and evil. Not all comic book art successfully achieves these three aesthetic appeals, but at its best, the comic book can simultaneously satisfy the visual, imaginative, and moral sensibilities.

HISTORICAL OUTLINE

Depending upon where one begins historically, the comic book is only about seventy years old. While the first comic books arguably may have been the hardcover reprint collections of popular newspaper comic strips, such as *The Yellow Kid*, *Mutt and Jeff*, *Buster Brown*, and *Bringing up Father*, published between 1897 and the late 1920s, the first comic magazine in the familiar 7 ½" × 10" size printed in full color with a glossy paper cover was *Funnies on Parade*, issued in 1933.

Funnies on Parade also contained Sunday newspaper reprints, but it was designed to be given away as a premium with Procter and Gamble products. The 10,000 copies went so rapidly that after several more premium products, the publisher issued the first number of *Famous Funnies* in 1934. Designed to be sold in chain stores for ten cents, the 35,000 copies printed were promptly sold, and *Famous Funnies* became the first monthly comic magazine and continued publication for more than twenty years, reaching a maximum circulation of nearly 1 million copies. Imitations of this successful format followed, but the comic magazine did not achieve distinction until the publishers began to commission original material for its pages, as happened with *More Fun*, *Detective Comics*, and *Action Comics* from National Periodical Publications.

The first issue of *Action Comics* in 1938 guaranteed the success of the comic book and contributed to American mythology its first original superhero since the days of Davy Crockett and Paul Bunyan—Superman. The creation of two childhood friends from Cleveland, Ohio, Jerry Siegel and Joe Shuster, and partly inspired by the protagonist of Philip Wylie's novel *Gladiator* (1930), Superman leaped into the American imagination faster than a speeding bullet. His presence as an alien from another planet, sent here by his parents from the doomed Krypton; his unlimited strength, ability to fly, and X-ray vision; and his dual identity, which called for his assumption of the appearance of a mild-mannered newspaper reporter—these qualities intrigued readers like those of few other figures in American literature. Many a mild-mannered reader enjoyed imaginatively setting aside his or her glasses to leap into the sky with Superman as he fought for Truth, Justice, and the American way (never mind the incongruity of an interplanetary alien, without citizenship papers, fighting for our nation's principles). In *American Folklore*, Richard Dorson cited Superman as an example of how "American life glorifies brawn and muscle in contrast to mind and intellect." However, when under disguise as Clark Kent, Superman does assume the role of an intellectual, with even the stereotyped attributes of clumsiness, ineptitude, and meekness. Perhaps this combination of qualities—the brawn with the brain, the perfect balance of a sound body with a sound mind that was the Greek ideal—constitutes his special appeal.

The enormous success of Superman soon spawned a multitude of imitators, literally hundreds of superheroes who populated the pages of competing comic books, the more popular and originally conceived being Batman and Robin the Boy Wonder, the Human Torch, Sub-Mariner, Wonder Woman, Captain America, Plastic Man, Blackhawk, Daredevil, the Flash, Green Lantern, Hawkman,

Green Arrow, Sandman, the Atom, Doll Man, and Blue Beetle, each characterized by a particular strength or ability, some odd physical characteristic, or a mystical secret origin.

Only one truly rivaled Superman—C. C. Beck's Captain Marvel, a satirically drawn spoof of superheroes modeled after film actor Fred MacMurray and lovingly called by his admirers "the Big Red Cheese." When Captain Marvel from Fawcett Publications began to outsell Superman, National Periodical Publications began a lawsuit to claim copyright infringement, an odd allegation since among the multitude of superheroes, Captain Marvel was the least like Superman. The case was pursued so relentlessly, however, that in 1953 Fawcett Publications canceled its entire comic book line and relinquished the rights to the character rather than fight further in court. Ironically, twenty years later National Periodical Publications itself revived the character under the name Shazam in an effort to capitalize on the fond memories held by many older readers.

All comic books during these formative years were not devoted to flying, leaping, and fighting superheroes. There were adventure stories about Sheena, Queen of the Jungle; the Shadow; Doc Savage; and the Spirit as beautifully rendered and carefully plotted by master artist/writer Will Eisner. There were romance and teenage comic books, best exemplified by Archie, who has remained a student at Riverdale High for sixty years, surely the longest retention on record. There were funny animal and kiddie comic books, such as *Looney Tunes and Merrie Melodies*, featuring Porky Pig, Bugs Bunny, and Elmer Fudd; *Walt Disney's Comics and Stories*, featuring Mickey Mouse and the whole Disney gang, especially Donald Duck and Scrooge McDuck as strikingly developed by author/artist Carl Barks; *Animal Comics*, featuring Walt Kelly's original version of Albert Alligator and Pogo Possum; and *Little Lulu*, as charmingly re-created by John Stanley after Marjorie Henderson Buell's *Saturday Evening Post* feature.

Most significantly, there were the crime comic books, largely modeled after the remarkable series of gangster films produced during the 1930s and prominently represented in 1942 by Charles Biro and Lev Gleason's *Crime Does Not Pay*. In spite of explicit morals best summarized in the title, alarmed parents were disturbed by its realistic depiction of murder and mayhem and factual accounts of how crimes were committed. This tradition was continued eight years later by William M. Gaines under the EC (Entertaining Comics) imprint and expanded to include horror, science fiction, and war in a series of the best-written and most imaginatively drawn comic books in the history of the medium—*Tales from the Crypt*, *The Vault of Horror*, *The Haunt of Fear*, *Weird Science*, *Weird Fantasy*, *Crime SuspenStories*, *Two-Fisted Tales*, and *Frontline Combat* among them. While young readers were stirred by the stunning artwork and the carefully crafted stories with their philosophical, social, and moral messages, adults could see only the violence, the gothic plots, and the sensually drawn women. Thus, these splendid products of the imagination were soon under the scrutiny of a U.S. Senate Subcommittee on Juvenile Delinquency.

Before the Senate got to them, however, a psychiatrist named Dr. Fredric Wertham was already condemning comic books. As senior psychiatrist for the Department of Hospitals in New York City from 1932 to 1952, Dr. Wertham had interviewed hundreds of juvenile delinquents and inevitably found that they were eager readers of comic books. Even though he admitted that not a single child ever told him "as an excuse for a delinquency or for misbehavior that comic books were to blame," Wertham spun out an elaborate argument that they were a prime stimulus for destructive and criminal behavior in his 1954 book *Seduction of the Innocent*. While his intentions were good, his proofs were ill-conceived and simplistic. One example will suffice, an argument offered by Dr. Wertham to a young girl for not reading *Wonder Woman*, an argument that not only is illogical but at the same time contains an unconscious ethnic slur against Latins and their eating habits and discredits the ability of a child to distinguish between fantasy and reality:

> "Supposing," I told her, "you get used to eating sandwiches made with very strong seasonings, with onions and peppers and highly spiced mustard. You will lose your taste for simple bread and butter and for finer food. The same is true of reading comic books. If later on you want to read a good novel it may describe how a young boy and girl sit together and watch the rain falling. They talk about themselves and the pages of the book describe what their innermost little thoughts are. This is what is called literature. But you will never be able to appreciate that if in comic-book fashion you expect that any minute someone will appear and pitch both of them out of the window." (64–65)

However unsound his theories, the public response to his book and the attention of the Senate Subcommittee generated so much political and economic pressure that the comic book publishers joined forces to organize a self-policing system known as the Comics Code Authority, to which all material was to be submitted prior to publication. Guidelines of the authority prohibit displays of corrupt authority, successful crimes, happy criminals, the triumph of evil over good, violence, concealed weapons, the death of a policeman, sensual females, divorce, illicit sexual relations, narcotics or drug addiction, physical afflictions, poor grammar, and the use of the words "crime," "horror," and "terror" in the title of a magazine or a story. In the strangest passage of all, it appears that something called "the classic tradition" permits the portrayal of certain kinds of evil:

> Vampires, ghouls and werewolves shall be permitted to be used when handled in the classic tradition such as Frankenstein, Dracula and other high callibre literary works written by Edgar Allen [*sic*] Poe, Saki, Conan Doyle and other respected authors whose works are read in schools throughout the world.

Since neither Poe, Saki [H. H. Munro], nor Doyle wrote about vampires and werewolves, one wonders how their works can be used as a source of the "classic tradition."

These guidelines, the most severe form of censorship applied to any mass medium, prevented comic book artists and writers after 1954 from dealing with the real world in any kind of truthful fashion and from addressing themselves to any of the significant social and political problems of the modern world. The result of the code was effectively to stifle the art of the comic book from reaching the aesthetic standards toward which the EC publishing firm was moving. William

Gaines quietly closed down the EC operation, took the idea behind one of his comic book titles called *Mad*, and developed it into this country's most popular satiric magazine.

The establishment of the code marked the conclusion of what historians call the golden age in comic book history. The only type that could thrive was the superhero books, which depicted a world where good and evil were clearly distinguishable, and justice always prevailed. In the late 1950s, under the editorship of Julius Schwartz, new artists and writers at National Periodical Publications gradually revived their stable of characters—Superman, Batman, Wonder Woman, and others—and moved from a dozen surviving titles to become once again the major comic book publisher, that is, until Stan Lee came on the scene.

Beginning as an editorial assistant and copywriter at age seventeen with the Timely Comics Group, Lee worked with the firm through the 1940s as it changed names to Atlas and finally to Marvel, serving as chief editor from 1942 to 1972, when he became publisher. In 1961 Lee teamed up with comic book veteran Jack Kirby to produce the first of a new breed of superheroes more attuned to the 1960s and 1970s in *Fantastic Four*, featuring a team of characters invested with human failings. The concept of the "superhero with problems" was given its most successful formulation in 1962, when Lee collaborated with artist Steve Ditko to create Spider-Man, a figure who ultimately would rival Superman's popularity and become a symbol for the youthful insecurities of the 1960s. Beset with personality problems, rejection, allergy attacks, failures, an overprotective aunt, and an unsuccessful love life, Peter Parker is accidentally bitten by a radioactive spider to become Spider-Man, an antihero among the superpowered whose successes are undermined by a series of antagonists who rob him of the respect that he deserves. Their new series of titles would eventually lead Marvel into the sales arena as the only contender to National Periodical Publications in volume and readership.

While both Marvel and National Periodical Publications, now simply known as DC (after the initials of one of their most successful titles, *Detective Comics*), continued to work within the guidelines of the Comics Code Authority, some adjustments to changes in the social and political climate have been possible. In 1971, for example, the guidelines were changed to allow for stories about drug addiction, as long as it was presented as a "vicious habit" in no way pleasurable, justifiable, or easily cured. At the request of the Office of Health, Education, and Welfare in Washington, Stan Lee published a three-part story called "And Now the Goblin," beginning in the May 1971 *Amazing Spider-Man*, and the subject was handled with great tact and no misunderstanding about the harmful effects of drugs. More recently DC, in cooperation with President Reagan's drug awareness campaign, published two special issues of the then-popular title *The New Teen Titans* on the drug problem in public schools for distribution to elementary school children throughout the nation.

The newly expanded and changed marketplace for comic books has influenced the effectiveness of the Comics Code Authority. The original purpose of the code's seal of approval was to alert the newsdealer to the suitability of what was being sold to children, and the parental pressure in the dealer's own neighborhood guaranteed that no book without the seal would go on sale at the newsstand. Now many dealers do not want to sell comic books at all because of the small profit margin, and a great many comic books are sold at comic specialty shops with a

A boy enjoying a "Superman" comic book. Courtesy of the Library of Congress

large adult and teenage clientele. Stories rejected by the authority office have been known to appear in special editions without the seal at such comic shops, and numerous independent publishers have appeared who submit none of their material for approval and sell only to the shops.

In 1986 public criticism of adult-oriented material in comic books reached a new pitch on television shows, in newspaper editorials, and from fundamentalist religious groups. In response, DC Comics decided in December to inaugurate its own rating system for comic books so as to alert parents and purchasers to those titles meant for mature readers and those meant for all age groups. Many of the artists and writers for DC resigned because they had not been consulted or because they objected to what they saw as "in-house-censorship." What few commentators have noted, however, is that the entire controversy is simply a sign of growth and maturation, that the artists and writers are finally addressing some of those controversial issues with which the comic book must deal if it is to realize its full potential as an art form in the twenty-first century.

A major problem in the comic book industry has always been the fact that sales figures, rather than quality, all too often determine whether a title will be kept in print, which is, of course, only a sound business practice. Another problem has been the fact that until recently most comic book work was hired out on a freelance basis, and the artists and writers maintained no reprint rights or future control of the material. The creators of Superman sold their rights to the character for $130 and, after leaving the publisher, received no royalties or income until late in their lives when public pressure led to the awarding of a retirement pension and credit for the creation. Also the pay has not been high, and most artists and writers stay with comic book work only until more lucrative employment develops, but it serves as an excellent showcase for their talent—the popular fantasy artist Frank Frazetta worked in comics before he became the rage of paperback and poster art. Rates of pay are now higher than they have ever been, and the publishers offer contracts that determine ownership of the original art and provide royalties on future reprint rights.

One promising development for the future of the comic book is the effort to produce more adult-oriented and lengthier works in that format. James Warren began the trend in 1965, when he published a series of magazine-sized, black-and-white comic books called *Creepy* and *Eerie*, to be joined in 1969 by *Vampirella*. Sold as adult magazines and thus outside the control of the Comics Code Authority, Warren returned to gothic and horror themes of the 1950s and produced a volume of stories that at their best rival the work in the EC line (sometimes utilizing the same artists from that firm). Paralleling this development was the publication of limited-circulation underground comic books, which intentionally set out to violate every guideline of the code and many of the mores of the larger society. Although much self-indulgence and bad art ensued, the undergrounds served as a proving ground and nurtured the talents of some of the most promising and original artists of the 1970s, such as Robert Crumb, Gilbert Shelton, S. Clay Wilson, Richard Corben, Art Spiegelman, Trina Robbins, Ted Richards, Victor Moscoso, Dennis Kitchen, Justin Green, and Rand Holmes, all brilliant in their individual ways and holding promise of finer work to come.

Although the adaptation of the comic book form to the novel and lengthy works of fiction has been under way for many years, we have witnessed the publication of several notable examples in this line, such as Richard Corben's *Bloodstar* (1976), Jack Katz's *The First Kingdom* (1978), *The Silver Surfer* by Stan Lee and Jack Kirby (1978), and Will Eisner's *A Contract with God and Other Tenement Stories* (1978), the last an especially impressive application of comic art to urban ethnic experiences of the 1940s. Both DC and Marvel Comics regularly publish "graphic novels" featuring their main characters, the most notable and controversial example being a futuristic version of Batman in *The Dark Knight Returns* (1986) by Frank Miller and the postmodern *Arkham Asylum* (1989) by Grant Morrison and Dave McKean. The most serious experiment in this area, certainly in terms of subject matter, is Art Spiegelman's book-length treatment of the Holocaust in animal fable form, based on his brief, but startling, 1972 story "Maus." Published initially as chapters in Spiegelman's experimental magazine *Raw* and partially supported by a Guggenheim grant, *Maus* was issued in two volumes in 1986 and 1991 to wide critical acclaim and was awarded a Pulitzer Prize in 1992. The innovative *Watchmen* (1987) by Alan Moore and Dave Gibbons was a self-reflexive meditation on the history of the comic book and Western civilization in general. By the turn of the century, such graphic novels as *Jimmy Corrigan: The Smartest Kid on Earth* (2000) by Chris Ware and *David Boring* (2000) by Daniel Clowes were routinely reviewed in the *New York Times Book Review* and other mainstream media.

Perhaps the most challenging, but promising, development ahead lies in the direction of educational uses of the comic book. Teachers no longer fear that comic books will take students away from literature—rather, we know now many children first learn to read them and then go on to more sophisticated levels of reading. Recent experiments with the use of comics in the classroom demonstrate that slow readers and children with learning disabilities can be helped through their use. Although both National Periodical Publications, especially under the leadership of publisher Jenette Kahn, and Marvel Comics have experimented with educational materials based on their properties, no one has turned out a package that successfully combines the automatic appeal of comic art with clearly articulated educational goals. Either the lesson gets lost in the art, or the message subdues the entertainment value, perhaps because these materials are usually produced by teams of artists, writers, and educational consultants rather than by a single creative mind who can combine educational theory with a full grasp of the aesthetics of comic art. Publishers have also realized the value of comic art in creating appealing textbooks. All sorts of text, from freshman English rhetorics and readers to mathematics, political science, and history books, incorporate cartoons and comic characters in order to elucidate major points and teach through humor.

It may be true that the comic book has not fully reached its aesthetic potential as narrative and visual art, but the numerous bright spots and accomplishments are sufficient to suggest its genuine potential as an art form of the future. Given the fact that we have become a society in which the majority of information is conveyed by visual means, and if the Gutenberg revolution is indeed over, as some would have us believe, the comic book of the future may remain one of our last links with the printed word.

REFERENCE WORKS

A good many of the reference works and encyclopedias discussed in the chapter on "Comic Strips" elsewhere in this volume contain material on both comic strip and comic book artists and characters. A number of artists and writers have worked in both fields at one time or another, and several characters have appeared in both forms, so the reader should consult nearly all the reference works considered there. The works discussed in this chapter focus only on the world of comic books.

While *The Comic Book Price Guide* by Robert M. Overstreet began in 1970 as a selling-price reference for dealers and collectors, it has grown through annual revisions and expansions into the single most important source of information about the history of the comic book. A comprehensive listing of comic book titles from 1933 to the present, dates of first and last issues, publishing companies, and important artists has been supplemented with updated information on comic book collecting, fan publications, comic book conventions, a history of the development of comic books, and other special features. The text is copiously illustrated with comic book covers. Overstreet's *Guide* has also served to stabilize the vigorous market that has grown up around collectors and fandom. A useful adjunct to Overstreet is the annual *Comic Book Checklist & Price Guide*, edited since 1994 by Maggie Thompson and Brent Frankenhoff, in that it focuses entirely on titles published since 1961, or what is called the silver age of comic books. There are several Overstreet imitations available, such as Alex Malloy's *Comics Values Annual* since 1992, but except for a second opinion on market values of rare titles, they offer little competition. All of them, however, provide additional features, such as interviews and special articles on artists, titles, publishers, and trends, which have research value, so older editions should never be abandoned for the new ones. The underground comic book publishing phenomenon was thoroughly documented by Jay Kennedy in *The Official Underground and Newave Comix Price Guide*. A beginning effort to index some 50,000 issues of titles by artist, writer, and character was made by Johnny Lauck and John R. G. Barrett Jr. in their 1996 *Comic Book Index*.

A standard source of biographical data on comic book artists and writers is *The Who's Who of American Comic Books* in four volumes, edited by Jerry Bails and Hames Ware. This work has been greatly expanded by a revised version available only on computer disk from the compiler Jerry Bails, 21101 East 11 Mile, St. Clair Shores, Mich. 48081 (JerryBails@aol.com). Conscientiously compiled and edited, each entry provides birth and death dates, pen names, art schools attended, major influences, and career data, including major publishers and comic book credits. Most of the information was obtained directly from the artists and writers themselves. At least two comic artists have been given comprehensive bibliographic treatment. Glenn Bray's *The Illustrated Harvey Kurtzman Index: 1939–1975* catalogs Kurtzman's innovative work for comic books (he created *Mad*), magazines, newspapers, and films, with some 200 examples of his art reprinted in an attractive, usefully arranged format. Donald M. Fiene's *R. Crumb Checklist of Work and Criticism* is a comprehensive and detailed annotated listing of practically everything that underground cartoonist Robert Crumb has drawn (comic books, book illustrations, greeting cards, record covers, etc.) and everything written or drawn about him. There are a variety of indexes (titles, characters, autobiographical pieces, collaborations, etc.), a chronology of Crumb's life and career from 1943 to 1980, and numerous illustrations. Fiene's book is a model bibliographic effort for a diverse, productive, and elusive artist, probably one of the most influential of the last two decades. Fiene's work is helpfully supplemented by Carl Richter's *Crumb-ology: The Works of R. Crumb, 1981–1994*. Biographical data on several hundred artists, writers, inkers, letterers, and other creative professionals, submitted by the subjects themselves, have been gathered in *Comic-Book Superstars* by Don and Maggie Thompson. Similar information on over 150 artists, along with full bibliographies of their published work, can be found in Alex G. Malloy's convenient *Comic Book Artists*.

The first volume of *The Encyclopedia of Comic Book Heroes* by Michael L. Fleisher contains over 1,000 entries on every major and minor character to appear in the Batman stories, with 100 pages entirely devoted to the life and adventures of Batman himself. The second and third volumes provide similar coverage for Wonder Woman and Superman, respectively. Although eight volumes were announced, only three were published. *The Encyclopedia of Superheroes* by Jeff Rovin is an alphabetically arranged catalog of information on more than 1,300 heroic figures and crime fighters from the comics, film, folklore, television, popular literature, radio, and computer games, with the great majority drawn from comic books. Each entry includes the hero's alter ego, first appearance, occupation when not fighting opponents, costume, weapons, biography, a characteristic quotation, and a commentary by Rovin, descriptive but often critical as well. While Rovin notes that superbeings and gods are as old as known history and found in all cultures, only those heroes are included in the encyclopedia who possess an extraordinary power, work for the common good rather than selfish reasons, are never vindictive, operate on earth, and assume an alter ego and a distinctive costume. Appendixes provide data on superhero teams, obscure and minor figures, and foreign superheroes. There are illustrations and an index.

The Comic Book Reader's Companion by Ron Goulart provides informative entries, arranged alphabetically, on hundreds of comic books characters, titles, and terminology, and *The Slings & Arrows Comic Guide*, edited by Frank Plowright, includes similar summaries and appreciative analyses of almost 3,000 comic book titles published mainly since the 1950s. Most of the major and some of the minor characters who have been adapted to film are surveyed by William Schoell in *Comic Book Heroes of the Screen*. Roy Thomas' *The All-Star Companion* is a comprehensive and well-illustrated guide to anything and everything having to do with the Justice Society of America, a league of DC superheroes. The book is so rich in information by such a variety of hands that an index would have made it even more valuable.

Also useful is Jerry Bails' *The Collector's Guide: The First Heroic Age*, an extensive effort "to list all costumed and super-heroes strips appearing from 1934 through 1947 in comic books, including reprints of newspaper strips and adaptations of heroes from pulps to radio." Publishers and artists are also listed. Complementing this volume is Howard Keltner's *Index to Golden Age Comic Books*, an alphabetically arranged index to approximately 98 percent of the golden age comic books of the 1940s and 1950s, with notes on publication dates, front cover and interior features, and other useful bibliographic data on over 8,000 issues of 300 titles in the superhero line. It was revised and expanded in 1998.

The Full Edition of the Complete E.C. Checklist (*Revised*), by Fred von Bernewitz and Joe Vucenic, focuses on the life of one publisher, Entertaining Comics, generally regarded as the producers of the best-drawn and best written comic books published in America during the early 1950s. The contents of all issues are listed with biographical sketches of the main artists and writers who collaborated on the series. The checklist was generously and handsomely expanded in 2000 into *Tales of Terror! The EC Companion* by Fred von Bernewitz and Grant Geissman with additional interviews, articles, bibliographies, and archival material essential to an understanding of the history of the EC firm. *The Photo-Journal Guide to Comic Books* by Ernst and Mary Gerber duplicates in full color the covers of over 22,000 issues, and Gerber's *The Photo-Journal Guide to Marvel Comics* exhaustively does the same for the Marvel titles. Both are fascinating archives of influential popular art. George Olshevsky's *Marvel Comics Index* is an extensive computerized project that in fourteen projected volumes was to catalog all of the superhero stories published in Marvel comic books since November 1961 (when the first issue of the *Fantastic Four* appeared). The first ten of the volumes are devoted to the Amazing Spider-Man, Conan the Barbarian, the Avengers and Captain Marvel, the Fantastic Four (including the Silver Surfer and the Human Torch), Doctor Strange, Thor, the Incredible Hulk, Sub-Mariner, Captain America, and Iron Man. A synopsis of each character's history, information on artists and writers, and several cross-indexes are included. A number of artist, title, and publisher checklists have been published in full and fragmentary form in scattered fan magazines and separate pamphlets, but no one has undertaken to assemble a guide to this material.

Both Marvel and DC have published valuable illustrated guides to all the characters that populate their comic book stories: *The Official Handbook of the Marvel Universe* in eight squarebound, paperback volumes, and *Who's Who: The Definitive Directory of the DC Universe* as a twenty-six-issue comic book series. In an effort to place their characters in a larger chronological perspective, DC has also published a two-volume *History of the DC Universe* by Marv Wolfman and George Pérez.

Although it is designed as a game book, there is a lot of information buried in *The Pow! Zap! Wham! Comic Book Trivia Quiz* by Michael Uslan and Bruce Solomon, with almost 100 comic book covers reproduced. Other specialized reference items are *The Comic Book Custer* by Brian W. Dippie and Paul A. Hutton, an annotated checklist of the appearances of General George A. Custer in comic books and strips; and George Thomas Fisher's *The Classic Comics Index*, which indexes all authors, subjects, and topics covered in the 169-issue run of *Classics Illustrated* and related Gilberton publications. A thoroughly researched and invaluable guide to all the Classics series is *The Complete Guide to Classics Collectibles* by Dan Malan. While there is much misinformation in *Cartoons and Comics in the Classroom*, edited by James L. Thomas, the book does reprint a few useful suggestions for using comic books in the teaching of reading, English, history, and languages.

In *Graphic Novels: A Bibliographic Guide to Book-Length Comics*, D. Aviva Rothschild documents and describes, often in full detail, the contents of over 400 titles, although she uses a very broad definition of what constitutes a graphic novel. Briefer, but more sharply focused are Steven Weiner's *100 Graphic Novels for Public Libraries* and *The 101 Best Graphic Novels*. Chapters on *Mad, Humbug, Help!, National Lampoon*, and other comics-related humor magazines are included in David E. E. Sloane's excellent *American Humor Magazines and Comic Periodicals*. The constantly expanding world of Internet Web sites related to comics is recorded in *The Incredible Internet Guide to Comic Books and Superheroes* by James R. Flowers Jr., with over 1,900 listed and providing an amazing array of information. A major project operating since 1994 is *The Grand Comic-Book Data Base Project* (http://www.comics.org).

The publication of fan magazines and amateur press publications about comic art began in the 1950s and reemerged in the 1960s as a significant development in the history of American magazines. Much of the pioneer scholarship about the comics first appeared in these pages, and extremely useful biographical and bibliographical information can be found there. The history and development of this phenomenon has been traced in fond detail by participant Bill Schelly in both an original and an expanded edition of *The Golden Age of Comic Fandom*. The origins and legal history of an organization to protect fans from money lost to unscrupulous mail-order dealers are described in *Fandom: Confidential* by Ron Frantz, a former administrator of the program. The annual editions of *Fandom Directory* by Harry and Mariane Hopkins have provided since 1979 easy access to thousands of collectors, fans, dealers, clubs, publications, conventions, and research libraries of interest to fandom.

The most widely circulated and read publication for collectors who wish to buy and sell comic books and related material is a tabloid, the *Comics Buyer's Guide*, originated in 1971 by Alan L. Light (under the title the *Buyer's Guide for Comics Fandom*). Krause Publications assumed ownership in 1983 and appointed Don and Maggie Thompson as editors. In addition to advertisements, the weekly includes feature articles, news stories, columns, reviews, cartoons, and a letter column in which readers vigorously debate issues and controversies with the editors and each other. Another popular publication is the *Comics Journal*, edited by Gary Groth, a monthly magazine with lengthy essays, in-depth interviews, review columns by leading commentators on the comics, and an aggressive editorial policy that often places the magazine in the center of controversy. Both the *Guide* and the *Journal* make for lively reading.

Other publications with valuable professional and historic data include *Comic Book Marketplace*, a general-interest magazine for collectors, and several periodicals issued by TwoMorrows Publishing, *Comic Book Artist*, *Alter Ego*, and *Comicology*, which offer conversations with, and articles about, artists, writers, publishers, and other creative people. A good research collection should have complete runs of all these publications at a minimum.

RESEARCH COLLECTIONS

Most American libraries—public, private, and academic—never subscribed to, or made any efforts to preserve, comic books. They were viewed as ephemeral publications that catered to illiteracy and had little cultural or historic value. Only recently has this opinion changed; thus, there are relatively few substantial collections to consult for research, and these have been built through the efforts of individuals who had the foresight to recognize their worth—not simply as investment items but as documents that relate to the cultural and social patterns of the twentieth century.

A leader in this development has been Randall W. Scott, who single-handedly has built the invaluable Russel B. Nye Popular Culture Collection in the Library at Michigan State University, East Lansing, Mich. 48824–1048, and assembled the largest collection of comic books easily available to researchers in the United States. Scott has also acquired a collection of reference books and extensive files of fan publications, journals, and materials related to the history and development of the comic book. Through his efforts, the Michigan State University Library has become the major research center for the comic book anywhere in the world, and it is likely to remain so. A guide to its extensive holdings through 1993 has been published by Scott as *The Comic Art Collection Catalog*. The most recent descriptive listing of other libraries with significant collections is found in Scott's *Comics Librarianship: A Handbook*. What should be a major resource—the Library of Congress—has lost a large part of its copyright deposit collection over the years through either neglect or lax security.

HISTORY AND CRITICISM

The first full-length volume on the comic book was neither a history nor an appreciation. The purpose of *Seduction of the Innocent* by psychologist Fredric Wertham, published in 1954, was to prove that comic books, especially of the crime and horror variety, were a major contributor to juvenile delinquency. Although his data were scientifically invalid, Wertham's book upset many parent and teacher groups and added to the general hysteria of the McCarthy era, resulting in a congressional investigation chaired by Estes Kefauver. Anticipating the investigation, in October 1954, the Comics Magazine Association of America moved to adopt a self-regulating Comics Code Authority with the most stringent code ever applied to any of the mass media. Wertham's book, therefore, remains of significant cultural and historic interest.

A summary and chronology of the institutional attacks on juvenile delinquency and its reputed causes in American popular culture on the part of governmental agencies, political groups, sociologists, intellectuals, and parents during the 1950s are found in James Gilbert's *A Cycle of Outrage*. Gilbert focuses in particular on the crusades against films and comic books, and he analyzes the arguments of Wertham and the Kefauver Senate Subcommittee. Gilbert finds their evidence inconclusive and contradictory. So, too, does Amy Kiste Nyberg in her thorough and thoughtful study *Seal of Approval: The History of the Comics Code*, a necessary starting point for further research. The report *Juvenile Delinquency*, issued by the U.S. Congress, Senate Committee on the judiciary, has been made available in a reprint from Greenwood Press. Martin Barker's *A Haunt of Fears* is a study of the British campaign against comic books in the 1950s. Barker discovers that the campaign was originated and covertly sponsored by the Communist Party, that the comic books under question were primarily American imports, and that a large part of the campaign was inspired by nationalistic and anti-American sentiments. Comic books, along with American film and mass media, were viewed as seductive, corrupting influences on British culture during World War II. Barker provides thorough analyses of selected stories to demonstrate that the meanings were exactly opposite to the claims of the detractors but that they did seriously question the assumptions of American and British society about the nature of life, the reality of childhood, and the roots of human behavior. Another positive British perspective on the power and appeal of horror comics is the testimony of Stephen Sennitt in *Ghastly Terror! The Horrible Story of the Horror Comics*. John A. Lent demonstrates how the campaign became a worldwide phenomenon in *Pulp Demons: International Dimensions of the Postwar Anti-Comics Campaign*.

Before Wertham, Gershon Legman had issued early warnings about the baneful effect of violence in the comics in *Love & Death: A Study in Censorship* in 1949. Also in tune with Wertham are the comments of Gillian Freeman in *The Undergrowth of Literature*. Freeman fears that costumed superheroes will inspire fantasies of fetishism and sadomasochism. A chapter of Ron Goulart's *The Assault on Childhood* traces how he feels that the comic book industry "ignored its potential and became preoccupied with murder, torture, sadism and storm-trooper violence."

John Fulce's *Seduction of the Innocent Revisited* is a shrill, pretentious, and inaccurate account from the Christian right of obscenity, the occult, and violence in comic books of the 1980s, while John Springhall demonstrates in *Youth, Popular Culture and Moral Panics* that such attacks have been cyclic in British and American culture for almost two centuries, from the days of the penny dreadfuls to contemporary comics, film, and television. It seems that any sort of juvenile working-class literature or entertainment has always become the easy scapegoat to blame for all kinds of criminal behavior and social ills. Wertham and all his alarmist colleagues are given a gentle and good-humored debunking from the Canadian perspective of novelist Mordecai Richler in a short essay that gives its title to the book, *The Great Comic Book Heroes and Other Essays*.

The first writer to inaugurate what he claimed would be a full-scale history of the comic book was James Steranko, himself a talented comic book artist. Volume 1 of *The Steranko History of Comics* finds that pulp fiction of the 1930s was the single most important source of inspiration to the development of the comic book and then traces the histories of Superman, Batman, Captain America, Captain Marvel, and the DC comic books. Volume 2 continues the coverage of Captain Marvel and related Fawcett superheroes, the Blackhawks and other airborne characters, Plastic Man and the Quality Comic Books titles, and Will Eisner's Spirit. Encyclopedic in detail, there is more information in these two volumes than most readers can easily assimilate, but Steranko's staff of contributors have a high regard for the distinctive qualities of comic book art and view it as a part and reflection of the total context of popular culture. Unfortunately, none of the promised following four volumes have appeared. Though primarily an anthology of selected stories, Jules Feiffer's *The Great Comic Book Heroes* has a lengthy introduction in which artist/author Feiffer reminisces about his days in the comic book industry and provides his personal commentary on the meaning of the superhero. Another genius of the comics, Harvey Kurtzman, produced his own personal, but lively, historical commentary with Michael Barrier in *From Aargh! To Zap: Harvey Kurtzman's Visual History of the Comics*. Published as a catalog for an exhibition held at Ohio State University, M. Thomas Inge's *The American Comic Book* contains a brief history, an analysis of selected stories from the EC science fiction comic books, interviews with publishers Stan Lee and Jenette Kahn, and additional essays by Stan Lee, Will Eisner, and Ray Bradbury.

A single-volume history is *Comix: A History of Comic Books in America* by Les Daniels. Daniels provides a sensible outline of the major developments and reprints over twenty stories, four of them in color. His final chapter deals with the development of underground comic books, generally called "comix" to distinguish them from the traditional publications. Partly a radical rejection of the Comics Code Authority and partly a natural development of the counterculture underground press, comix provided artists with unrestricted freedom to write and draw to the limits of their imagination, something that has seldom been possible in comic art. While shameless obscenity and bad taste abound, several striking talents emerged from the movement—Robert Crumb remains the best known—and much highly original work was accomplished. Mark James Estren attempted to produce *A History of the Underground Comics*, which is difficult to accomplish because the publishing centers have ranged from California to the Midwest to New York, and the artists have never been eager to cooperate with researchers and critics. While much of his commentary is debatable, Estren has assembled an excellent cross-section of representative art by the major figures, many of whom are allowed to speak for themselves through interviews and letters, and a useful checklist of underground titles by comix scholar Clay Geerdes concludes the volume. It is an engaging grab bag of reading matter about an important cultural development.

Ron Goulart's *Great History of Comic Books* in 1986 was a richly detailed overview of the main trends and developments, with attention to many often overlooked titles, characters, and artists. He went on to prove himself the champion of comic book historians with such follow-ups as *Over 50 Years of American Comic Books*, *Great American Comic Books*, and *Comic Book Culture: An Illustrated History*. These are lush, heavily illustrated volumes that combine text and picture in stimulating surveys based on a lifetime of experience with, and love for, the medium. Another highly productive writer on the subject has been Mike Benton. *The Comic Book in America: An Illustrated History* by Benton in 1989 was followed over the next few years by five more specialized histories: *Horror Comics*, *Superhero Comics of the Silver Age*, *Science Fiction Comics*, *Superhero Comics of the Golden Age*, and *Crime Comics*. These, too, are thoroughly illustrated and handsome surveys with essays on major characters and artists and extensive checklists of titles.

This tradition of high production values has been continued in works by two British authors, Paul Sassiene's *The Comic Book*, which combines a history of both U.S. and British comics with extensive checklists of titles published in both countries, and Roger Sabin's *Comics, Comix & Graphic Novels: A History of Comic Art*, which is rich in cultural and aesthetic insights. This is also true of Sabin's more focused study of *Adult Comics: An Introduction*, again examining both British and American material. Sabin's objective, European perspective allows him insights less nationalistic than those of American writers. It is useful, as well, to see American comics as part of an international cultural phenomenon. Nicky Wright's *The Classic Era of American Comics* appears largely derivative from entirely unacknowledged sources. Its 230 heavily illustrated pages have neither footnotes nor bibliography.

Drawing on her own personal experience and extensive research, Trina Robbins has written two feminist-oriented histories, *The Great Women Super Hereos* and *From Girls to Grrrlz: A History of Women's Comics from Teens to Zines*. She displays a remarkable breadth of knowledge in these little-explored areas of a largely male-oriented medium. Another seldom explored topic, pornographic comics, is addressed for the first time with authority in a book by Bob Adelman, *Tijuana Bibles: Art and Wit in America's Forbidden Funnies, 1930s–1950s*. Although largely an anthology of the eight-page comic booklets, the commentaries by Art Speigelman, Richard Merkin, and Madeline Kripke demonstrate just how closely these true underground comics were related in parodic and sociological ways to mainstream American life and culture. Focusing on the early pre-Superman years of the comic book, Charles Wooley's *History of the Comic Book 1899–1936* traces with meticulous and careful research the development of the precursors to the modern comic book, its earliest form as a reprint publication for comic strips, and the beginning efforts to produce original material for comic book publication.

In *The Comic Book Heroes*, Will Jacobs and Gerard Jones undertake an analysis of the contents and style of the comic book from 1956, the silver age, to the present, with a major focus on the dominant publishers DC and Marvel. In chronologically arranged chapters, they examine the trends in superheroes and the artists and writers who have made the comic book into a creative medium of increasing breadth and sophistication. Although marketing problems and conservative editorial practices are causes for concern, they feel that comic books remain a significant force in mainstream entertainment. The first edition of this valuable work was greatly expanded, updated, and largely rewritten in the 1997 second edition. Richard Reynolds attempts to define and characterize the evolving mythology of the comic book heroes, from Superman and Batman to the X-Men and the Watchmen, in his useful study *Super Heroes: A Modern Mythology*.

Most of the major comic book publishers have been the subjects of company histories in the last decade. Les Daniels has written two lush and richly illustrated authorized histories, *Marvel: Five Fabulous Decades of the World's Greatest Comics* and *DC Comics: Sixty Years of the World's Favorite Comic Book Heroes*. Both reflect the advantages and disadvantages of being company-approved projects, but Daniels is meticulous in his research and captures the characters of the two dominant forces in the field. The EC firm and its most enduring product, *Mad*, has been explored more frequently than any other, as in *Tales from the Crypt: The Official Archives* by Digby Diehl (covering both the EC comic books and the television series based on them), *Completely Mad: A History of the Comic Book and Magazine* by Maria Reidelbach, and *Good Days and Mad*, a memoir by *Mad* writer Dick DeBartolo. Another staff writer, Frank Jacobs, has provided commentary on the covers of 400 issues of the comic-book-turned-magazine in *Mad: Cover to Cover*. An incredibly rich resource for the study of *Mad* is found in the CD-ROM collection *Totally Mad* from the Broderbund Company. It includes the complete contents of more than 500 issues of *Mad* through December 1998, along with search engines keyed to artists, writers, features, and subject matter, all available on seven disks. Histories of smaller firms include Michael Vance's *Forbidden Adventures: The History of the American Comics Group* and Dave Schreiner's *Kitchen Sink Press: The First 25 Years. The Iger Comics Kingdom* by Jay Edward Disbrow is a brief overview of the way that one comic book production shop worked.

Most serious study of comic art seems to have focused on how it reflects or relates to society and the culture out of which it has grown. Only now are we witnessing the development of a body of writing that attempts to assess the comics on their own terms, by measuring their worth against their own developed standards and aesthetic principles rather than by the irrelevant yardsticks of other related arts. A collection of essays mainly on comic book superheroes helped initiate this development, *All in Color for a Dime*, edited by Dick Lupoff and Don Thompson. Many of the essays originated in a series of fan magazine articles and still bear the stylistic and judgmental marks of their origin. A second volume, also edited by Thompson and Lupoff, *The Comic-Book Book*, is a marked improvement in this regard. In style and judgment, many of these essays are distinguished. The purpose of *Moviemaking Illustrated: The Comicbook Filmbook*, by James Morrow and Murray Suid, is to teach the technical principles of filmmaking, but the textbook utilizes nothing but frames from Marvel comic books and thereby makes many valuable points about the complex sound and visual techniques of comic art.

Will Eisner, a creator of the comic book and one of the most influential masters of comic art, discusses his ideas and theories on the practice of telling stories in graphic form in *Comics & Sequential Art*. Separate chapters, thoroughly illustrated by examples of his own work, treat imagery, timing, framing, and anatomy, and he discusses comics as a form of reading, learning, and teaching. Eisner views comics as a distinct artistic discipline and a literary/visual form, the development of which was accelerated by advances in graphic technology and visual communication in the twentieth century. This is one of the best books ever written on the aesthetics of comic art, and it will remain an essential work in the field for artists and readers alike. Eisner expanded upon these ideas in a useful follow-up volume, *Graphic Storytelling*. *The Comic-Stripped American* by Arthur Asa Berger is a collection of his pieces (including discussions of Superman, Batman, and Marvel comics) on the ways that comics reflect our culture, many of them stimulating and provocative but also debatable.

Several books published in the last decade of the twentieth century helped to establish a solid critical footing on which sound commentary and criticism can proceed. The first of these is Joseph Witek's *Comic Books as History*. After establishing a set of principles through which the reader can understand how the portrayal of history can be invested with meaning in selected comic book stories, Witek devotes full chapters to three artists noted for their attempts to deal with historical and autobiographical material: Jack Jackson, Art Spiegelman, and Harvey Pekar. The result is a classic statement on the power and importance of comic art in the serious pursuit of understanding and truth. The second major work is *Understanding Comics* by Scott McCloud, a challenging, imaginative, and complex explication of the main features and functions of comic art and related entirely in the form of a comic book. Medium and message coalesce in a critical tour de force that continues to spark debate and upset long-held assumptions about the comics as an art form. McCloud expands on his views of the potential of comic art not only to survive but to adapt to new computer technology and digital developments in *Reinventing Comics*, also cast as a comic book. McCloud's theories have inspired much disagreement and humorous criticism, as in Dylan Sisson's clever parody, *Filibusting Comics*.

Robert C. Harvey elucidates all the major artists and works in *The Art of the Comic Book: An Aesthetic History* by bringing to bear his theories about verbal-visual blending expressed in his earlier book, *The Art of the Funnies*. His evaluations are sensibly and sensitively attuned to the special properties of the comics as a new narrative art form. In the tradition of British cultural studies, with an emphasis on politics and economics, Martin Barker addresses the ideological influence of comic books in *Comics: Ideology, Power and the Critics*. His focus is mainly on British comics with glances at American examples, but his theories are equally applicable in the United States, even if they invite serious debate. Barker collaborated with another cultural studies expert, Roger Sabin, in an extended and enlightening study of the ways that one classic work of American literature has been adapted to film, television specials, and comic books in *The Lasting of the Mohicans: History of an American Myth*. Also employing the British cultural studies model in a survey of the language, forms, and structural principles of comics is *Reading Comics: Language, Culture, and the Concept of the Superhero in Comic Books* by Mila Bongco.

A comprehensive and useful survey of the place of comic books in the nation's history and culture is found in Bradford W. Wright's *Comic Book Nation: The*

Transformation of Youth Culture in America, with specific emphasis on the ways political and economic issues have shaped their development. Two collections of articles that contain stimulating assessments of the cultural significance of comic books, especially the contributions of Gene Kannenberg, are *The Graphic Novel*, edited by Jan Baetens, and *Illuminating Letters: Typography and Literary Interpretations*, edited by Paul C. Gutjahr and Megan L. Benton. Valuable studies and compilations of material about specific publishers include William B. Jones' *Classics Illustrated: A Cultural History, with Illustrations*, P. C. Hamerlinck's *Fawcett Companion*, David A. Roach and Jon B. Cooke's *The Warren Companion*, and Robert B. Fowler's *The World of Jack T. Chick*. The last documents the hundreds of Christian comic booklets commonly distributed free in truck stop restrooms.

Although reader-response criticism is fairly new to comics scholarship, two excellent examples have already been published. *Comic Book Culture: Fanboys and True Believers* by Matthew J. Pustz assesses what readers look for in their reading through extensive interviews with customers of one comic book shop in Iowa, as well as letters and comments in fan publications. *Black Superheroes, Milestone Comics, and Their Fans* by Jeffrey A. Brown examines the products of one company devoted to African American superheroes and summarizes what black and other minority and white readers find engaging in them. Both pursue data difficult to obtain through traditional methodology but essential to continuing research.

The thirteen essays in *Comics & Culture: Analytical and Theoretical Approaches to Comics*, edited by Anne Magnussen and Hans-Christian Christiansen, are mainly by European hands and represent the work of a new generation of comics scholars abroad. Attuned to current critical theory and well grounded in research, they suggest that a good deal of excellent work is forthcoming from Europe. Basically historical in his approach, William W. Savage Jr. reads a selection of comic book stories published in the decade after World War II for their reflection of Cold War attitudes and national insecurities in *Comic Books and America, 1945–1954*. Steve Baker's *Picturing the Beast: Animals, Identity and Representation*, about the role images that animals play in contemporary popular culture, includes discussions of Art Spiegelman's *Maus*, Walt Disney's Mickey Mouse, and other cartoon portrayals of animals. Baker studies the meaning of such representations. M. Thomas Inge's *Perspectives on American Culture* includes essays on comic books; the adaptation of works by Melville to film, television, radio, and comic books; and comics based on the works of Mark Twain. Paul Davies' *Exactly 12¢ and Other Convictions* is a brief personal statement on how comic books have influenced his life for the better, written in the form of letters addressed to Stan Lee and Jack Kirby.

The intriguing figure of Batman has attracted the attention of numerous critical theorists with an interest in cultural studies, gender issues, and reader response. Lively examples are found in *The Many Lives of the Batman*, edited by Roberta E. Pearson and William Uricchio, and *Batman Unmasked: Analyzing a Cultural Icon* by Will Brooker. Because homosexuality and other provocative issues are raised in both books, when the publishers asked permission of DC to reprint illustrations, they were denied. Chip Kidd documents every conceivable form of collectible in *Batman Collected*, with engaging photographs. Several DC-sponsored volumes by Les Daniels provide unprovocative, but sound, historic surveys of major figures: *Superman: The Complete History*, *Superman: The Golden Age*, *Batman: The Golden Age*, and *Wonder Woman: The Complete History*. All are attractive and well-illustrated volumes. *Superman at Fifty: The Persistence of a Legend*, edited by Dennis Dooley and Gary Engle, gathers over two dozen appreciations of the Man of Steel on the occasion of the fiftieth anniversary of his first appearance in *Action Comics*. The history of a different kind of comic book hero is surveyed, with frequent reprinting of stories, in Charles Phillips' *Archie: His First 50 Years*, about the nation's favorite eternal high school student.

Ron Goulart's *The Great Comic Book Artists* showcases the work of sixty accomplished artists with a single-page biographical and appreciative essay devoted to each. Fewer artists are treated but with fuller commentary and more extensive illustration in *Masters of Comic Book Art* by P. R. Garrick. In addition to his several histories of the comics mentioned earlier, Mike Benton has written *Masters of Imagination: The Comic Book Artists Hall of Fame*, a collection of biographical and appreciative essays on thirteen major figures: Will Eisner, Joe Shuster, Jack Kirby, C. C. Beck, Jack Cole, Carl Barks, Walt Kelly, Basil Wolverton, Harvey Kurtzman, Wally Wood, Bernard Krigstein, Alex Toth, and Steve Ditko. Among the figures highlighted in *Dream Makers: Six Fantasy Artists at Work*, by Martyn Dean and Chris Evans, are comic book artists Michael Kaluta, Berni Wrightson, and Charles Vess. A great deal of information about numerous comic book artists, along with full-color reproductions of forty classic covers, has been gathered in Richard O'Brien's *The Golden Age of Comic Books: 1937–1945*.

The New Comics, edited by Gary Groth and Robert Fiore, reprints interviews with more than twenty-seven artists and writers from the pages of *The Comics Journal*. Because they have been abbreviated here, the original lengthier versions in the journal remain essential resource material. In *Comic Book Rebels: Conversations with the Creators of the New Comics*, Stanley Wiater and Stephen R. Bissette gather their original interviews with over twenty practicing contemporary artists and writers. A valuable addition to the book is an annotated checklist of books about the comics. Other collections include Mark Salisbury's *Artists on Comic Art* and Will Eisner's *Will Eisner's Shop Talk*. *Streetwise*, edited by Jon B. Cooke and John Morrow, with a perceptive introduction by Charles Hatfield, is a collection of over thirty autobiographical comic book stories that provide informative insights into the lives and attitudes of the artists. Some forty professionals are interviewed about entering the field in one of the best guides for aspiring creators, *The Business of Comics* by Lurene Haines.

Frank Jacobs' *The Mad World of William M. Gaines* is partly a biography and partly a personal memoir about the publisher responsible for the distinguished EC line of comic books and, later, *Mad* magazine. One-half of Michael Barrier's *Carl Barks and the Art of the Comic Book* is biography, and the remainder is an annotated bibliography of Barks' fine work, especially on the Donald Duck and Scrooge McDuck stories in the Disney comic books. Barks has emerged as a true master of visual narrative and satire. One of Barks' more notable creations was given his own biographical treatment in *An Informal Biography of Scrooge McDuck* by Jack Chalker. A related item is *How to Read Donald Duck: Imperialist Ideology in the Disney Comic* by Ariel Dorfman and Armand Mattelart. Originally published in South America and translated into English in 1975, this tract attempts to demonstrate how Disney comic books were used in Chile before Salvador Allende to promote capitalistic ideology, but the research was faulty, and the book has been largely discredited.

Only a few comic book artists have undertaken to write their own autobiographies and usually with the help of others. Such efforts include *Batman and Me: An Autobiography* by Bob Kane with Tom Andrae, *My Life as a Cartoonist* by Harvey Kurtzman with Howard Zimmerman, and *The Amazing World of Carmine Infantino* by Carmine Infantino with J. David Spurlock. Boody Gordon Rogers tells his own story unaided in *Homeless Bound*, but he tells little about his career as a comic book artist. The comics scholar and sometime cartoonist Robert C. Harvey confesses his love for, and amply demonstrates his ability to draw, beautiful, buxom women in *Not Just Another Pretty Face*, along with some ruminations about his life and career. A good deal about Robert Crumb's reflections on his own life can be gleaned from *Your Vigor for Life Appalls Me: Robert Crumb Letters, 1958–1977*, a fascinating collection of correspondence with two friends, Marty Pahls and Mike Britt. Over forty of Crumb's friends, fellow artists, and contemporaries celebrate the man and his work in Monte Beauchamp's *The Life and Times of R. Crumb*. A generous selection of examples of his work from his entire career are interlaced with hand-lettered autobiographical essays in the handsome *R. Crumb Coffee Table Art Book*, edited by Peter Poplaski. An important project in progress is *The Complete Crumb Comics*, which will eventually reprint nearly everything that he has drawn.

A number of books largely designed to reprint selections from their work contain significant biographical material on the artists as well. These include *The Art of Jack Kirby* by Ray Wyman Jr., *Jack Davis: Some of My Good Stuff* complied by Hank Harrison, *Dan DeCarlo* by Mary Smith, *Joe Kubert: The War Years* by Al Dellinges, *Wolvertoons: The Art of Basil Wolverton* by Dick Voll, *Jack Cole and Plastic Man* by Art Spiegelman and Chip Kidd and *Gil Kane: The Art of the Comic Book* by Daniel Herman.

ANTHOLOGIES AND REPRINTS

The reprinting of comic book material has occurred with much less frequency than of comic strips, possibly because of the expense of color reproduction, which is necessary to do it properly. The first hardcover anthology of selected comic book stories was Jules Feiffer's *The Great Comic Book Heroes* in 1965, a best-selling volume that partly spurred the commercial nostalgia market development.

Michael Barrier and Martin Williams surveyed thousands of comic book stories to make their selection for *A Smithsonian Book of Comic-Book Comics*, and the result is an excellent sampler of thirty-two stories that they feel show the comic book at its very best. Brief introductions helpfully place the stories in their historic and cultural contexts.

One of the major comic book publishers, National Periodical Publications, or DC Comics, devoted a special publication, *Famous First Edition*, to oversized, full-color, facsimile reproductions of valuable first issues: *Action* No. 1, *Detective* No. 27, *Sensation* No. 1, and *Whiz Comics* No. 2, which introduced Superman, Batman, Wonder Woman, and Captain Marvel, respectively, as well as *Batman* No. 1, *Superman* No. 1, *Wonder Woman* No. 1, *Flash Comics* No. 1, and *All Star Comics* No. 3. The first five of these were issued in hardcover editions by Lyle Stuart. In 1989, the same publisher began to issue a high-quality series of anthologies devoted to important characters and titles called the DC Archive Editions. The first to be published were *Superman Archives Volume I* and *Batman Archives Volume I*, and the series has continued with additional volumes devoted to these characters as well as the Flash, Green Lantern, Starman, Hawkman, Plastic Man, Captain Marvel, Wonder Woman, Black Canary, the Justice League of America, the League of Super-Heroes, and the New Teen Titans. While he was not a DC character, the series also includes Will Eisner's *The Spirit*. Within a decade, over fifty volumes appeared, with more to come. Each has a historical introduction and biographical notes. The comic strip versions of the two most influential DC characters have been collected in four boxed volumes: *Superman: The Dailies, 1939–1942*, *Superman: The Sunday Classics, 1939–1943*, *Batman: The Dailies, 1943–1946*, and *Batman: The Sunday Classics, 1943–1946*. All were subsequently issued in paperback editions. The hardcover versions, as well as the DC Archive Editions, are expensive because of the high production values, but they are indispensable for reading and research.

Under the editorship of Stan Lee, Marvel Comics has released a series of popular, squarebound, paperback anthologies drawing together some of the best stories about selected superhero figures in full color. Among these are *Origins of Marvel Comics*, *Son of Origins of Marvel Comics*, *Grandson of Origins of Marvel Comics*, *Bring on the Bad Guys*, *The Superhero Women*, *The Incredible Hulk*, *Marvel's Greatest Superhero Battles*, *The Amazing Spider-Man*, *Dr. Strange*, *The Fantastic Four*, *Captain America*, *The Invincible Iron Man*, *The Uncanny X-Men*, and *Mighty Marvel Team-Up Thrillers*. Beginning in 1996, Marvel also began to issue a series of "Essential" volumes beginning with *The Essential Spider-Man*, *The Essential X-Men*, and *The Essential Wolverine*, followed by more than twenty titles devoted to these characters as well as the Fantastic Four, Avengers, Silver Surfer, Hulk, Conan, and Captain America. These are thick, paperbound editions, printed in black and white on inexpensive paper, each with more that 500 pages of over twenty issues of continuity, modeled after the Japanese manga. The lack of color and pagination renders them less useful for research, but they are a bargain for readers who want a quick survey of years of continuity about one character. Marvel occasionally releases one-shot reprint collections in color, like *Captain America: The Classic Years* by Joe Simon and Jack Kirby.

DC has released a series focusing on genres, such as *Heart Throbs* edited by Naomi Scott, *America at War* and *Mysteries in Space*, both edited by Michael Uslan, as well as several hardcover volumes devoted to major figures, such as *Secret Origins of the DC Super Heroes*, edited by Dennis O'Neil; *Batman from the 30s to the 70s*; *Wonder Woman*; *Shazam! from the Forties to the Seventies*; and *Superman from the Thirties to the Seventies*, updated subsequently through the 1980s. In 1971 a selection from the EC titles was published in an oversized volume as *Horror Comics of the 1950s*, edited by Ron Barlow and Bob Stewart. A selection of *The Best of Archie* by John Goldwater is also available. A substantial number of collections from the underground comic books have been issued, and they are listed in the checklist at the end of this chapter under anthologies.

Three major publication projects have been completed to bring into print in oversized, hardcover volumes some of the classic works of comic book art. A complete set of all published titles in the EC comic book series was issued by Russ Cochran Publisher, as well as the complete works by Carl Barks for the Walt Disney comic book titles and John Stanley for the *Little Lulu* series by Another

Rainbow Publishing. These are deluxe, slipcased volumes, printed on high-quality paper, and shot in black and white from the original art. They also contain excellent historical and critical introductions and essays. All the sets are indispensable for research libraries.

Many of the major paperback publishers issue from time to time collections of comic book stories, as do the smaller alternative presses supplying collectors and comic book shops. The easiest way to find out about these is to obtain the catalogs of a major distributor, such as Bud Plant, P.O. Box 1689, Grass Valley, Calif. 95945.

BIBLIOGRAPHY

Books and Articles

Adelman, Bob. *Tijuana Bibles: Art and Wit in America's Forbidden Funnies, 1930s–1950s*. New York: Simon and Schuster, 1997.

Baetens, Jan, ed. *The Graphic Novel*. Leuven, Belgium: Leuven University Press, 2001.

Bails, Jerry. *The Collector's Guide: The First Heroic Age*. Detroit: Jerry Bails, 1969.

Bails, Jerry, and Hames Ware, eds. *The Who's Who's of American Comic Books*. 4 vols. Detroit: Jerry Bails, 1973–1976. Rev. and expanded on computer disk.

Baker, Steve. *Picturing the Beast: Animals, Identity, and Representation*. Urbana: University of Illinois Press, 2001.

Barker, Martin. *Comics: Ideology, Power, and the Critics*. Manchester, U.K.: Manchester University Press, 1989.

———. *A Haunt of Fears: The Strange History of the British Horror Comics Campaign*. London: Pluto Press, 1984. Reprint. Jackson: University of Mississippi, 1992.

Barker, Martin, and Roger Sabin. *The Lasting of the Mohicans: History of an American Myth*. Jackson: University Press of Mississippi, 1995.

Barrier, Michael. *Carl Barks and the Art of the Comic Book*. New York: M. Lilien, 1981.

Beatty, Scott. *Batman: The Ultimate Guide to the Dark Knight*. New York: Dorling Kindersley, 2001.

Beauchamp, Monte, ed. *The Life and Times of R. Crumb: Comments from Contemporaries*. Northampton, Mass.: Kitchen Sink Press, 1998.

Benton, Mike. *Comic Book Collecting for Fun and Profit*. New York: Crown, 1985.

———. *The Comic Book in America: An Illustrated History*. Dallas: Taylor, 1989. Rev. ed., 1993.

———. *Crime Comics: The Illustrated History*. Dallas: Taylor, 1993.

———. *Horror Comics: The Illustrated History*. Dallas: Taylor, 1991.

———. *Masters of Imagination: The Comic Book Artists Hall of Fame*. Dallas: Taylor, 1994.

———. *Science Fiction Comics: The Illustrated History*. Dallas: Taylor, 1992.

———. *Superhero Comics of the Golden Age: The Illustrated History*. Dallas: Taylor, 1992.

———. *Superhero Comics of the Silver Age: The Illustrated History*. Dallas: Taylor, 1991.

Berger, Arthur Asa. *The Comic-Stripped American*. New York: Walker, 1973.

Bernewitz, Fred von, and Grant Geissman. *Tales of Terror! The EC Companion*. Seattle: Fantagraphics Books/Gemstone, 2000.

Bernewitz, Fred von, and Joe Vucenic. *The Full Edition of the Complete E.C. Checklist (Revised)*. Los Alamos, N. Mex.: Wade M. Brothers, 1974.

Bongco, Mila. *Reading Comics: Language, Culture, and the Concept of the Superhero in Comic Books*. New York: Garland, 2000.

Bray, Glenn. *The Illustrated Harvey Kurtzman Index: 1939–1975*. Sylmar, Calif.: Glenn Bray, 1976.

Brooker, Will. *Batman Unmasked: Analyzing a Cultural Icon*. London: Continuum, 2000.

Brown, Jeffrey A. *Black Superheroes, Milestone Comics, and Their Fans*. Jackson: University Press of Mississippi, 2001.

Carlson, Raymond. *A Guide to Collecting and Selling Comic Books*. New York: Pilot Books, 1976.

Chalker, Jack. *An Informal Biography of Scrooge McDuck*. Baltimore: Mirage Press, 1974.

Cooke, Jon B., and John Morrow, eds. *Streetwise: Autobiographical Stories by Comic Book Professionals*. Raleigh, N.C.: TwoMorrows, 2000.

Crumb, Robert. *Your Vigor for Life Appalls Me: Robert Crumb Letters, 1958–1977*. Seattle: Fantagraphics, 1998.

Daniels, Les. *Batman: The Golden Age*. San Francisco: Chronicle Books, 2000.

———. *Comix: A History of Comic Books in America*. New York: Outerbridge and Dienstfrey, 1971.

———. *DC Comics: Sixty Years of the World's Favorite Comic Book Heroes*. Boston: Little, Brown, 1995.

———. *Marvel: Five Fabulous Decades of the World's Greatest Comics*. New York: Harry M. Abrams, 1991.

———. *Superman: The Complete History*. San Francisco: Chronicle Books, 1998.

———. *Superman: The Golden Age*. San Francisco: Chronicle Books, 1999.

———. *Wonder Woman: The Complete History*. San Francisco: Chronicle Books, 2000.

Davies, Paul. *Exactly 12¢ and Other Convictions*. Toronto: ECW Press, 1994.

"DC Comics Releases Comic-Book Editorial Standards." *The Comics Buyer's Guide*, no. 684 (December 26, 1986), 16–17.

Dean, Martyn, and Chris Evans. *Dream Makers: Six Fantasy Artists at Work*. Surrey, U.K.: Paper Tiger Books, 1988.

DeBartolo, Dick. *Good Days and Mad*. New York: Thunder's Mouth Press, 1994.

DeFalco, Tom. *Spider-Man: The Ultimate Guide*. New York: Dorling Kindersley, 2001.

Dellinges, Al. *Joe Kubert: The War Years*. San Francisco: Al Dellinges, 1991.

Diehl, Digby. *Tales from the Crypt: The Official Archives*. New York: St. Martin's Press, 1996.

Dippie, Brian W., and Paul A. Hutton. *The Comic Book Custer: A Bibliography of Custeriana in Comic Books and Comic Strips*. Bryan, Tex.: Publication No. 4 Brazos Corral of the Westerners, 1983.

Disbrow, Jay Edward. *The Iger Comics Kingdom*. El Cajon, Calif.: Blackthorne, 1985.

Dooley, Dennis, and Gary Engle, eds. *Superman at Fifty: The Persistence of a Legend*. Cleveland, Ohio: Octavia Press, 1987.

Dorfman, Ariel, and Armand Mattelart. *How to Read Donald Duck: Imperialist Ideology in the Disney Comic*. Trans. by David Kunzle. New York: International General, 1975.

Dorson, Richard. *American Folklore*. Chicago: University of Chicago Press, 1959.

Eisner, Will. *Comics & Sequential Art*. Tamarac, Fla.: Poorhouse Press, 1985.

———. *Graphic Storytelling*. Tamarac, Fla.: Poorhouse Press, 1995.

———. *Will Eisner's Shop Talk*. Milwaukie, Oreg.: Dark Horse Comics, 2001.

Estren, Mark James. *A History of Underground Comics*. San Francisco: Straight Arrow Books, 1974.

Feiffer, Jules. *The Great Comic Book Heroes*. New York: Dial Press, 1965.

Fiene, Donald M. *R. Crumb Checklist of Work and Criticism*. Cambridge, Mass.: Boatner Norton Press, 1981.

Fisher, George Thomas. *The Classic Comics Index*. Nottingham, N.H.: Thomas Fisher, 1986.

Fleisher, Michael L. *The Encyclopedia of Comic Book Heroes*. Vol. 1, *Batman*. Vol. 2, *Wonder Woman*, Vol. 3, *Superman*. New York: Macmillan, 1976– .

Flowers, James R., Jr. *The Incredible Internet Guide to Comic Books and Superheroes*. Tempe, Ariz.: Facts on Demand Press, 2000.

Fowler, Robert B. *The World of Jack T. Chick*. San Francisco: Last Gasp, 2001.

Frantz, Ron. *Fandom: Confidential*. Mena, Ark.: Midguard, 2000.

Freeman, Gillian. *The Undergrowth of Literature*. London: Thomas Nelson, 1967.

Fulce, John. *Seduction of the Innocent Revisited*. Lafayette, La.: Huntington House, 1990.

Garrick, P. R. *Masters of Comic Book Art*. New York: Images Graphiques, 1978.

Gerber, Ernst. *The Photo-Journal Guide to Marvel Comics*. 2 vols. Minden, Nev.: Gerber, 1991.

Gerber, Ernst, and Mary Gerber. *The Photo-Journal Guide to Comic Books*. 2 vols. Minden, Nev.: Gerber, 1989–1990.

Gifford, Denis. *The International Book of Comics*. New York: Crescent Books, 1984.

Gilbert, James. *A Cycle of Outrage: America's Reaction to the Juvenile Delinquent in the 1950s*. New York: Oxford University Press, 1986.

Goulart, Ron. *The Assault on Childhood*. Los Angeles: Sherbourne Press, 1969.

———. *Comic Book Culture: An Illustrated History*. Portland, Oreg.: Collectors Press, 2000.

———. *The Comic Book Reader's Companion*. New York: HarperCollins, 1993.

———. *Great American Comic Books*. Lincolnwood, Ill.: Publications International, 2001.

———. *The Great Comic Book Artists*. New York: St. Martin's Press, 1986.

———. *Great History of Comic Books*. Chicago: Contemporary Books, 1986.

———. *Over 50 Years of American Comic Books*. Chicago: Mallard Press, 1991.

Groth, Gary, and Robert Fiore, eds. *The New Comics*. New York: Berkley Books, 1988.

Gutjahr, Paul C., and Megan L. Benton, eds. *Illuminating Letters: Typography and Literary Interpretation*. Amherst: University of Massachusetts Press, 2001.

Haines, Lurene. *The Business of Comics*. New York: Watson-Guptill, 1998.

Hamerlinck, P. C. *Fawcett Companion*. Raleigh, N.C.: TwoMorrows Publishing, 2001.

Harrison, Hank. *Jack Davis: Some of My Good Stuff*. Livonia, Mich.: Stabor Press, 1990.

Harvey, Robert C. *The Art of the Comic Book: An Aesthetic History*. Jackson: University Press of Mississippi, 1996.

———. *Not Just Another Pretty Face: The Confessions and Confections of a Girlie Cartoonist*. Seattle: Aeon, 1996.

Heffelfinger, Charles. *The Classics Handbook*. 3rd ed. Tampa, Fla.: Charles Heffelfinger, 1986.

Herman, Daniel. *Gil Kane: The Art of the Comic Book*. Neshannock, Penn.: Hermes Press, 2001.

Hopkins, Harry A., and Mariane S. Hopkins. *Fandom Directory*. Springfield, Va.: Fandata, 1979 (and subsequent annual editions).

Huxley, David. *Nasty Tales: Sex, Drugs, Rock 'n' Roll, and Violence in the British Underground*. Manchester, England: Critical Vision, 2001.

Infantino, Carmine, and J. David Spurlock. *The Amazing World of Carmine Infantino: An Autobiography*. Lebanon, N.J.: Vanguard Productions, 2000.

Inge, M. Thomas. *The American Comic Book*. Columbus: Ohio State University Libraries, 1985.

———. *Perspectives on American Culture: Essays on Humor, Literature, and the Popular Arts*. West Cornwall, Conn.: Locust Hill Press, 1994.

Jacobs, Frank. *Mad: Cover to Cover*. New York: Watson-Guptill, 2000.

———. *The Mad World of William M. Gaines*. New York: Lyle Stuart, 1972.

Jacobs, Will, and Gerard Jones. *The Comic Book Heroes: From the Silver Age to the Present*. New York: Crown, 1985. Rev. ed. Rocklin, Calif.: Prima, 1997.

Jones, William B., Jr. *Classics Illustrated: A Cultural History, with Illustrations*. Jefferson, N.C.: McFarland, 2001.

Kane, Bob, and Tom Andrae. *Batman and Me: An Autobiography*. Forestville, Calif.: Eclipse Books, 1989.

Keltner, Howard. *Index to Golden Age Comic Books*. Detroit: Jerry Bails, 1976. Rev. ed., 1998.

Kennedy, Jay. *The Official Underground and Newave Comix Price Guide*. Cambridge, Mass.: Boatner Norton Press, 1982.

Kidd, Chip. *Batman Collected*. Boston: Little, Brown, 1996.

Kurtzman, Harvey, and Michael Barrier. *From Aargh! To Zap! Harvey Kurtzman's Visual History of the Comics*. New York: Prentice-Hall, 1991.

Kurtzman, Harvey, and Howard Zimmerman. *My Life as a Cartoonist*. New York: Pocket Books, 1988.

Lauck, Johnny, and John R. G. Barrett Jr. *Comic Book Index*. Battle Creek, Mich.: Alternate Concepts, 1996.

Legman, Gershon. *Love & Death: A Study in Censorship*. New York: Breaking Point, 1949. Reprint. New York: Hacker Art Books, 1963.

Leiter, Marcia. *Collecting Comic Books*. Boston: Little, Brown, 1983.

Lent, John A., ed. *Pulp Demons: International Dimensions of the Postwar Anti-Comics Campaign*. Cranbury, N.J.: Associated University Presses, 1999.

Lupoff, Dick, and Don Thompson, eds. *All in Color for a Dime*. New Rochelle, N.Y.: Arlington House, 1970. Reprint. Iola, Wis.: Krause, 1997.

Magnussen, Anne, and Hans-Christian Christiansen, eds. *Comics & Culture: Analytical and Theoretical Approaches to Comics*. Copenhagen, Denmark: Museum Tusculanum Press, University of Copenhagen, 2000.

Malan, Dan. *The Complete Guide to Classics Collectibles*. St. Louis, Mo.: Malan Classical Enterprises, 1992.

Mallory, Michael. *Marvel: The Characters and Their Universe*. New York: Hugh Lauter Levin Associates, 2001.

Malloy, Alex. *Comics Values Annual: The Comic Books Price Guide*. Radnor, Pa.: Wallace-Homestead Book, 1992.

———, ed. *Comic Book Artists*. Radnor, Pa.: Wallace-Homestead, 1993.

McCloud, Scott. *Reinventing Comics*. New York: Paradox Press, 2000.

———. *Understanding Comics*. Northampton, Mass.: Tundra, 1993.

Morrow, James, and Murray Suid. *Moviemaking Illustrated: The Comicbook Filmbook*. New York: Hayden, 1973.

Nyberg, Amy Kiste. *Seal of Approval: The History of the Comics Code*. Jackson: University Press of Mississippi, 1998.

O'Brien, Richard. *The Golden Age of Comic Books: 1937–1945*. New York: Ballantine Books, 1977.

The Official Handbook of the Marvel Universe. 8 vols. New York: Marvel Comics Group, 1986–1987.

Olshevsky, George. *Marvel Comics Index*. Vol. 1, *The Amazing Spider-Man*. Vol. 2, *Conan and the Barbarians*. Vol. 3, *Avengers and Captain Marvel*. Vol. 4, *Fantastic Four*. Vol. 5, *The Mighty Thor*. Vol. 6, *Heroes from Strange Tales*. Vol. 7A, *Heroes from Tales to Astonish, The Incredible Hulk*. Vol. 7B, *Heroes from Tales to Astonish, The Sub-Mariner*. Vol. 8A, *Heroes from Tales of Suspense, Captain America*. Vol. 8B, *Heroes from Tales of Suspense, Iron Man and Others*. Toronto, Canada: G and T Enterprises, 1975–   .

Overstreet, Robert M. *The Comic Book Price Guide*. Cleveland, Tenn.: Overstreet, 1970 (and subsequent annual editions).

Pearson, Roberta E., and William Uricchio, eds. *The Many Lives of the Batman: Critical Approaches to a Superhero and His Media*. New York: Routledge, 1991.

Phillips, Charles. *Archie: His First 50 Years*. New York: Abbeville, 1991.

Plowright, Frank, ed. *The Slings & Arrows Comic Guide*. London: Aurum Press, 1997.

Poplaski, Peter, ed. *R. Crumb Coffee Table Art Book*. Northampton, Mass.: Kitchen Sink Press, 1997.

Pustz, Matthew J. *Comic Book Culture: Fanboys and True Believers*. Jackson: University Press of Mississippi, 1999.

Reidelbach, Maria. *Completely Mad: A History of the Comic Book and Magazine*. Boston: Little, Brown, 1991.

Reitberger, Reinhold, and Wolfgang Fuchs. *Comics: Anatomy of a Mass Medium*. Trans. Nadia Fowler. Boston: Little, Brown, 1972.

Reynolds, Richard. *Super Heroes: A Modern Mythology*. Jackson: University Press of Mississippi, 1994.

Richler, Mordecai. *The Great Comic Book Heroes and Other Essays*. Toronto, Canada: McClelland and Stewart, 1978.

Richter, Carl. *Crumb-ology: The Works of R. Crumb, 1981–1994*. Sudbury, Mass.: Water Row Press, 1995.

Roach, David A., and Jon B. Cooke, eds. *The Warren Companion*. Raleigh, N.C.: TwoMorrows Publishing, 2001.

Robbins, Trina. *From Girls to Grrlz: A History of Women's Comics from Teens to Zines*. San Francisco: Chronicle Books, 1999.

———. *The Great Women Super Heroes*. Northampton, Mass.: Kitchen Sink Press, 1996.

Rogers, Boody Gordon. *Homeless Bound*. Seagraves, Tex.: Pioneer Book, 1984.

Rothschild, D. Aviva. *Graphic Novels: A Bibliographic Guide to Book-Length Comics*. Englewood, Colo.: Libraries Unlimited, 1995.

Rovin, Jeff. *The Encyclopedia of Superheroes*. New York: Facts on File, 1985.

Sabin, Roger. *Adult Comics: An Introduction*. London: Routledge, 1993.

———. *Comics, Comix & Graphic Novels: A History of Comic Art*. London: Phaidon Press, 1996.

Salisbury, Mark. *Artists on Comic Art*. London: Titan Books, 2000.

Sanderson, Peter. *The Marvel Universe*. New York: Abrams, 2000.

———. *The Ultimate X-Men*. New York: Dorling Kindersley, 2001.

Sassiene, Paul. *The Comic Book*. Edsion, N.J.: Chartwell Books, 1994.

Savage, William W., Jr. *Comic Books and America, 1945–1954*. Norman: University of Oklahoma Press, 1990.

Schelly, Bill. *The Golden Age of Comic Fandom*. Seattle: Hamster Press, 1995. Rev. ed., 1999.

Schoell, William. *Comic Book Heroes of the Screen*. New York: Citadel Press, 1991.

Schreiner, Dave. *Kitchen Sink Press: The First 25 Years*. Northampton, Mass.: Kitchen Sink Press, 1994.

Scott, Randall W. *The Comic Art Collection Catalog: An Author, Artist, Title and Subject Catalog of the Comic Art Collection, Special Collections Division, Michigan State University Libraries*. Westport, Conn.: Greenwood Press, 1993.

———. *Comics Librarianship: A Handbook*. Jefferson, N.C.: McFarland, 1990.

———. *European Comics in English: A Bio-Bibliography*. Jefferson, N.C.: McFarland, 2001.

Sennitt, Stephen. *Ghastly Terror! The Horrible Story of the Horror Comics*. Manchester, U.K.: Critical Vision/Headpress, 1999.

Simon, Joe, and Jim Simon. *The Comic Book Makers*. New York: Crestwood/II, 1990.

Sisson, Dylan. *Filibusting Comics*. Seattle: Fantagraphics Books, 1995.

Sloane, Davie E. E., ed. *American Humor Magazines and Comic Periodicals*. Westport, Conn.: Greenwood Press, 1987.

Smith, Mary. *Dan DeCarlo*. Holliston, Mass.: Mary Smith, 1992.

Spiegelman, Art, and Chip Kidd. *Jack Cole and Plastic Man*. San Francisco: Chronicle Books, 2001.

Springhall, John. *Youth, Popular Culture and Moral Panics*. New York: St. Martin's Press, 1998.

Steranko, James. *The Steranko History of Comics*. 2 vols. Wyomissing, Pa.: Supergraphics, 1970–1972.

Thomas, James L., ed. *Cartoons and Comics in the Classroom: A Reference for Teachers and Librarians*. Littleton, Colo.: Libraries Unlimited, 1983.

Thomas, Roy, ed. *The All-Star Companion*. Raleigh, N.C.: TwoMorrows, 2000.

Thompson, Don, and Dick Lupoff, eds. *The Comic-Book Book*. New Rochelle, N.Y.: Arlington House, 1973. Reprint. Iola, Wis.: Krause, 1998.

Thompson, Don, and Maggie Thompson, eds. *Comic-Book Superstars*. Iola, Wis.: Krause, 1993.

Thompson, Maggie, and Brent Frankenhoff. *Comic Book Checklist & Price Guide*. Iola, Wis.: Krause, 1994– .

Totally Mad. CD-ROM. Novato, Calif.: Broderbund, 1999.

Twichell, James B. *Preposterous Violence: Fables of Aggression in Modern Culture*. New York: Oxford University Press, 1989.

Umphlett, Wiley Lee. *Mythmakers of the American Dream: The Nostalgic Vision in Popular Culture*. Lewisburg, Pa.: Bucknell University Press, 1983.

U.S. Congress. Senate Committee on the Judiciary. *Juvenile Delinquency: Comic Books, Motion Pictures, Obscene and Pornographic Materials, Television Programs*. Westport, Conn.: Greenwood Press, 1969.

Uslan, Michael, and Bruce Solomon. *The Pow! Zap! Wham! Comic Book Trivia Quiz*. New York: William Morrow, 1977.

Vance, Michael. *Forbidden Adventures: The History of the American Comics Group*. Westport, Conn.: Greenwood Press, 1996.

Voll, Dick, ed. *Wolvertoons: The Art of Basil Wolverton*. Seattle: Fantagraphics, 1989.

Weiner, Steven. *100 Graphic Novels for Public Libraries*. Northampton, Mass.: Kitchen Sink Press, 1996.

———. *The 101 Best Graphic Novels*. New York: NBM Publishing, 2001.

Weist, Jerry. *The Comic Art Price Guide*. Gloucester, Mass.: Arcturian Books, 2000.

Wertham, Fredric. *Seduction of the Innocent*. New York: Holt, Rinehart, and Winston, 1954. Reprint. Port Washington, N.Y.: Kennikat Press, 1972.

Who's Who: The Definitive Directory of the DC Universe. 26 issues. New York: DC Comics, March 1985–April 1987.

Wiater, Stanley, and Stephen R. Bissette. *Comic Book Rebels: Conversations with the Creators of the New Comics*. New York: Donald I. Fine, 1993.

Witek, Joseph. *Comic Books as History: The Narrative Art of Jack Jackson, Art Spiegelman, and Harvey Pekar*. Jackson: University Press of Mississippi, 1989.

Wolfman, Marv, and George Pérez. *History of the DC Universe*. 2 vols. New York: DC Comics, 1986.

Wooley, Charles. *History of the Comic Book 1899–1936*. Lake Buena Vista, Fla.: Charles Wooley, 1986.

Wright, Bradford W. *Comic Book Nation: The Transformation of Youth Culture in America*. Baltimore: Johns Hopkins University Press, 2001.

Wright, Nicky. *The Classic Era of American Comics*. Chicago: Contemporary Books, 2000.

Wyman, Ray, Jr. *The Art of Jack Kirby*. Orange, Calif.: Blue Rose Press, 1992.

Anthologies and Reprints

Barlow, Ron, and Bob Stewart, eds. *Horror Comics of the 1950s*. Franklin Square, N.Y.: Nostalgia Press, 1971.

Barrier, Michael, and Martin Williams, eds. *A Smithsonian Book of Comic-Book Comics*. Washington, D.C.: Smithsonian Institution Press, 1981.

Batman from the 30s to the 70s. New York: Crown, 1971.

The Best of the Rip Off Press. 2 vols. San Francisco: Rip Off Press, 1973–1974.

Boxell, Tim. *Commies from Mars—The Red Planet, The Collected Works*. San Francisco: Last Gasp, 1985.

The Carl Barks Library. 30 vols. Scottsdale, Ariz.: Another Rainbow, 1983–1990.

The Complete EC Library. 58 vols. West Plains, Mo.: Russ Cochran/Gemstone, 1979–1996.

Crumb, Robert. *The Complete Crumb Comics*. Seattle: Fantagraphics Books, 1987– .

———. *Fritz the Cat*. New York: Ballantine Books, 1969.

———. *Head Comix*. New York: Ballantine Books, 1970.

———. *Robert Crumb's Carload o' Comics: An Anthology of Choice Strips and Stories—1968 to 1976*. New York: Bélier Press, 1976.

DC Comics. The DC Archive Editions. *All Star Comics Archives*, vols. 1–7; *Atom Archives*; *Batman Archives*, vols. 1–5; *Batman, The Dark Knight Archives*, vols. 1–3; *Black Canary Archives*; *Black Hawk Archives*; *The Flash Archives*, vols. 1–3; *Golden Age Flash Archives*; *Golden Age Green Lantern Archives*; *Golden Age Starman Archives*; *The Green Lantern Archives*, vols. 1–3; *Hawkman Archives*; *Justice League of America Archives*, vols. 1–7; *Legion of Super-Heroes Archives*, vols. 1–11; *New Teen Titans Archives*; *Plastic Man Archives*, vols. 1–3; *Shazam Archives*, vols. 1–2; *The Spirit Archives*, vols. 1–6; *Supergirl Archives*; *Superman Archives*, vols. 1–5; *Superman: The Action Comics Archives*, vols. 1–3; *Wonder Woman Archives*, vols. 1–2; *World's Finest Comics Archives*, vols. 1–2. New York: DC Comics, 1989– .

Donahue, Don, and Susan Goodrick, eds. *The Apex Treasury of Underground Comics*. New York: Quick Fox, 1974.

Feiffer, Jules, ed. *The Great Comic Book Heroes*. New York: Dial Press, 1965.

Goldwater, John. *The Best of Archie*. New York: G. P. Putnam, 1980.

Griffith, Bill, and Jay Kinney. *The Young Lust Reader*. Berkeley, Calif.: And/Or Press, 1974.

Kane, Bob. *Batman: The Dailies, 1943–1946*. New York: DC Comics/Kitchen Sink Press, 1990.

———. *Batman: The Sunday Classics, 1943–1946*. New York: DC Comics/Kitchen Sink Press, 1991.

Kurtzman, Harvey, and Will Elder. *Playboy's Little Annie Fanny*. 2 vols. Chicago: Playboy Press, 1966, 1972. Expanded ed. 2 vols. Milwaukie, Oreg.: Dark Horse Comics, 2000.

Lee, Stan. *The Amazing Spider-Man*. New York: Simon and Schuster, 1979.

———. *Bring on the Bad Guys*. New York: Simon and Schuster, 1976.

———. *Captain America*. New York: Simon and Schuster, 1979.

———. *Dr. Strange*. New York: Simon and Schuster, 1979.

———. *The Fantastic Four*. New York: Simon and Schuster, 1979.

———. *Grandson of Origins of Marvel Comics*. New York: Marvel Comics, 1998.

———. *The Incredible Hulk*. New York: Simon and Schuster, 1978.

———. *The Invincible Iron Man*. New York: Marvel Comics, 1984.

———. *Marvel's Greatest Superhero Battles*. New York: Simon and Schuster, 1978.

———. *Mighty Marvel Team-Up Thrillers*. New York: Marvel Comics, 1985.

———. *Origins of Marvel Comics*. New York: Simon and Schuster, 1974.

———. *Son of Origins of Marvel Comics*. New York: Simon and Schuster, 1975.

———. *The Superhero Women*. New York: Simon and Schuster, 1977.

———. *The Uncanny X-Men*. New York: Marvel Comics, 1984.

The Little Lulu Library. 18 vols. Scottsdale, Ariz.: Another Rainbow, 1985–1992.

Lynch, Jay, ed. *The Best of Bijou Funnies*. New York: Links Books, 1975.

Marvel Comics. *The Essential Ant-Man*; *The Essential Avengers*, vols. 1–3; *The Essential Captain America*; *The Essential Conan*; *The Essential Fantastic Four*, vols. 1–2; *The Essential Hulk*, vols. 1–2; *The Essential Silver Surfer*; *The Essential Spider-Man*, vols. 1–4; *The Essential Thor*, *The Essential Uncanny X-Men*, vols. 1–4; *The Essential Wolverine*, vols. 1–3; *The Essential X-Men*, vols. 1–3. New York: Marvel Comics, 1996– .

O'Neil, Dennis, ed. *Secret Origins of the DC Super Heroes*. New York: Crown Harmony Books, 1976.

Pekar, Harvey. *American Splendor*. Garden City, N.Y.: Doubleday, 1986.

———. *More American Splendor*. Garden City, N.Y.: Doubleday, 1987.

Scott, Naomi, ed. *Heart Throbs: The Best of DC Romance Comics*. New York: Simon and Schuster, 1979.

Shazam! from the Forties to the Seventies. New York: Harmony Books, 1977.

Shelton, Gilbert. *The Complete Fabulous Furry Freak Brothers*. Auburn, Calif.: Rip Off Press, 2001.

Siegel, Jerry, and Joe Shuster. *Superman: The Dailies, 1939–1942*. New York: DC Comics/Kitchen Sink Press, 1998.

———. *Superman: The Sunday Classics, 1939–1943*. New York: DC Comics/Kitchen Sink Press, 1998.

Simon, Joe, and Jack Kirby. *Captain America: The Classic Years*. New York: Marvel Comics, 1998.

Superman from the Thirties to the Eighties. New York: Crown, 1983.

Superman from the Thirties to the Seventies. New York: Crown, 1971.

Sutton, Laurie S., ed. *The Great Superman Comic Book Collection*. New York: DC Comics, 1981.

Toth, Alex. *The Complete Classic Adventures of Zorro*. Orange, Calif.: Image Comics, 2001.

Uslan, Michael, ed. *America at War: The Best of DC War Comics*. New York: Simon and Schuster, 1979.

———. *Mysteries in Space: The Best of DC Science Fiction Comics*. New York: Simon and Schuster, 1980.

Wonder Woman. New York: Holt, Rinehart, and Winston, 1972.

Periodicals

Alter Ego. Raleigh, N.C., 1999–   .
Comic Book Artist. Raleigh, N.C., 1998–   .
Comic Book Marketplace. Coronado, Calif., 1991–   .
Comicology. Raleigh, N.C., 2000–   .
Comics Buyer's Guide. Iola, Wis., 1970–   .
Comics Journal. Seattle, 1977–   .
Famous First Editions. New York, 1975–1979.
International Journal of Comic Art. Drexel Hill, Pa., 1999–   .

COMIC STRIPS

M. Thomas Inge

Except for the attention of a few psychologists, sociologists, educationists, and media specialists, American comic art has been the most generally neglected area of popular culture until very recently. What has been written in the past has usually been of a disparaging and condescending nature by critics who at least recognized the broad popular appeal of the comics but who also often viewed them as subversive threats to highbrow culture and social stability. Very few writers found more than ephemeral value in the funnies and comic books, and even fewer recognized the unique aesthetics of this hybrid form of narrative art.

The daily and Sunday comic strips are part of the reading habits of more than 100 million people at all educational and social levels in the United States. Any mass medium that plays so heavily on the sensibilities of the populace deserves study purely for sociological reasons, but comic art is important for other reasons as well. While the roots of comic art may be heavily European, the comics as we know them today are arguably a distinctively American art form that has contributed significantly to the culture of the world, from Picasso, to the pop art movement. They derive from popular patterns, themes, and concepts of world culture—just as Dick Tracy was inspired by Sherlock Holmes (notice the similarity in noses) and as Flash Gordon and Superman draw on the heroic tradition to which Samson, Beowulf, Davy Crockett, and Paul Bunyan belong. The comics also serve as revealing reflectors of popular attitudes, tastes, and mores, and they speak directly to human desires, needs, and emotions.

Historical studies, biographies, anthologies, and periodicals have begun to proliferate rapidly in this subject area in the past few decades, partly because some publishers have wished to tap the lucrative nostalgia market, but in many cases because others have begun to recognize the importance of documenting this part of our national heritage. Much of the best work has originated in amateur and limited press-run publications authored by collectors and devotees of the art form. The study of comics has become a part of high school, college, and university curricula throughout this country and abroad, and annual conventions are held on a national and regional scale for collectors, artists, and fans. This chapter provides a brief historic summary of the development of the comic strip in particular and a guide to the most useful reference works and resources for those who wish to study the subject. The editorial cartoon and comic book are treated in separate chapters.

HISTORICAL OUTLINE

While some historians would trace the comic strip to prehistoric cave drawings, the medieval Bayeux tapestry, the eighteenth-century print series of such artists as William Hogarth, the illustrated European broadsheet, the nineteenth-century illustrated novels and children's books, or European and American humorous periodicals, the American comic strip as we know it may have been influenced by all of these antecedents, yet it remains a distinct form of expression unto itself and has been viewed primarily as an American phenomenon. It may be defined as an open-ended dramatic narrative about a recurring set of characters, told with a balance between narrative text and visual action, often including dialogue in balloons, and published serially in newspapers. The comic strip shares with drama the use of such conventions as dialogue, scene, stage devices, gesture, and compressed time, and it anticipated such film techniques as montage (before Eisenstein), angle shots, panning, close-ups, cutting, and framing. Unlike the play or the film, however, the comic strip is usually the product of one artist (or an artist and a writer) who must be a combined producer-scriptwriter-director-scene designer at once and bring his or her characters to life on the flat space of a printed page, with respect for the requirements of a daily episode that takes less than a minute's reading time. These challenges make fine comic art difficult to achieve and contribute to its distinctive qualities.

Identifying the first comic strip is not easy. Some would suggest James Swinnerton's 1895 feature for the *San Francisco Examiner*, *Little Bears and Tykes* (often incorrectly identified as *Little Bears and Tigers*), in which bear cubs, who had been used in spot illustrations for the newspaper since 1893, adopted the human postures of small children. Others more commonly suggest Richard Outcault's *The Yellow Kid*, who first appeared in the May 5, 1895, issue of the *New York World*, a street urchin in the middle of riotous activities set in the low-class immigrant sections of the city and identified by the title "Hogan's Alley." Unlike Swinnerton, Outcault developed a central character in his use of the Kid, eventually clad in a yellow shift on which his dialogue was printed, and by 1896 he had moved from a single-panel cartoon to the format of a progressive series of panels with balloon dialogue, which would become the definitive form of the comic strip.

Outcault's use of contemporary urban reality in his backgrounds, which had counterparts in the naturalistic novels of Stephen Crane, Frank Norris, and Theodore Dreiser, would not reappear in the comics for over two decades and even then in the safe midwestern environment of Sidney Smith's *The Gumps* of 1917, which emphasized the pathos of lower-middle-class life, and Frank King's *Gasoline Alley*, a year later, where the use of chronological time first entered the comics in following the growth of a typical American family. Most of the popular strips that came on the heels of the Kid in the following three decades used humor and

George Herriman, creator of *Krazy Kat*, self-portrait, 1922. Courtesy of M. Thomas Inge

fantasy as their major modes, such as Rudolph Dirk's *The Katzenjammer Kids*, one of the longest running comic strips in existence; Fredrick Burr Opper's several wacky creations, *Happy Hooligan, Maude the Mule,* and *Alphonse and Gaston*; Richard Outcault's penance for his illiterate outlandish Kid, *Buster Brown*; Winsor McCay's *Little Nemo in Slumberland*, the most technically accomplished and aesthetically beautiful Sunday page ever drawn; Bud Fisher's *Mutt and Jeff*, the first continuous daily comic strip and the first successful comic team in the funnies; George Herriman's classic absurdist fantasy and lyrical love poem *Krazy Kat*; Cliff Sterret's abstractly written and drawn family situation comedy *Polly and Her Pals*; George McManus' *Bringing Up Father*, whose central characters, Maggie and Jiggs, became a part of American marital folklore; Billy De Beck's tribute to the sporting life, *Barney Google*; Elzie Segar's *Thimble Theater*, which in 1929, after a ten-year run, introduced Popeye to the world; and Frank Willard's boardinghouse farce *Moon Mullins*. These were the years when the terms *comics* and *funnies* became inseparably identified with this new form of creative expression, even though comedy and humor were not to remain its primary content.

Although some adventurous continuity and suspense had been used in C. W. Kahles' burlesque of melodrama, *Hairbreath Harry*, in 1906, Roy Crane's *Wash Tubbs* of 1924 and George Storm's *Phil Hardy* and *Bobby Thatcher* of 1925–1927 established the adventure comic strip, and Harold Gray's *Little Orphan Annie*, also of 1924, drew on the picaresque tradition in a successful combination of exotic adventure and homespun, right-wing philosophy. The adventure strip would not become a fully developed genre, however, until 1929 and the appearance of the first science fiction strip, *Buck Rogers*, by Richard W. Calkins and Phil Nowlan, and the successful tradition of the classic primitive hero from the novels of Edgar Rice Burroughs, *Tarzan* (most beautifully drawn in those years first by Harold Foster and later by Burne Hogarth). The 1930s and 1940s were to be dominated by adventure titles, such as Chester Gould's *Dick Tracy*, Vincent Hamlin's *Alley Oop*, Milton Caniff's *Terry and the Pirates* and his postwar *Steve Canyon*, Alex Raymond's *Flash Gordon*, Lee Falk's *Mandrake the Magician* (drawn by Phil Davis) and *The Phantom* (drawn by Ray Moore), Harold Foster's *Prince Valiant*, Fred Harman's *Red Ryder*, Fran Striker's *The Lone Ranger* (drawn primarily by Charles Flanders), Alfred Andriola's *Charlie Chan* and *Kerry Drake*, Will Eisner's *The Spirit*, and Roy Crane's second contribution to the tradition, *Buzz Sawyer*. Related by the use of the same devices of mystery and suspense and also developed during these years were the soap opera strips, among the best known of which were *Mary Worth*, by Allen Saunders and Dale Connor (a reincarnation of Martha Orr's 1932 antidote for the depression, *Apple Mary*); writer Nicholas Dallis' *Rex Morgan, M.D.* (drawn by Marvin Bradley and Frank Edgington), followed in 1952 by *Judge Parker* (drawn by Dan Heilman and later by Harold LeDoux) and in 1961 by *Apartment 3-G* (drawn by Alex Kotzky); and Stanley Drake's 1953 collaboration with writer Elliott Caplin, *The Heart of Juliet Jones*.

During the 1950s and 1960s satire flourished and dominated comic strips, although it was consistently present at least from 1930, when Chic Young's *Blondie* satirized at first flappers and playboys of the jazz age and subsequently the institution of marriage in what would prove to be for decades the most popular comic strip in the world. Al Capp's hillbilly comedy of 1934, *Li'l Abner* (with little of the authentic southern humor that Billy De Beck had used in *Snuffy Smith*), evolved into an influential forum for ridiculing the hypocrisies and absurdities of the larger social and political trends of the nation. Just as Capp used the denizens of Dogpatch as vehicles for his satire, other artists of postwar America would follow his example and use even more imaginative vehicles, such as the fantasy world of children in *Peanuts* by Charles Schulz, the ancient form of the animal fable by the master of comic mimicry, Walt Kelly, in *Pogo*, an anachronistic military life in the durable *Beetle Bailey* by Mort Walker, an imagined world of prehistoric man by Johnny Hart in *B.C.*, and the absurd world of a medieval kingdom in *The Wizard of Id* by Johnny Hart and Brant Parker. During the 1970s, this trend would continue in such strips as Dik Browne's *Hagar the Horrible*, which relies on a farcical re-creation of life among Viking plunderers, but it would also move in interesting new directions. Russel Myer's *Broom Hilda*, a wacky ancient witch, lives in a totally abstract world in the imaginative tradition of Herriman's *Krazy Kat*, while Garry Trudeau's *Doonesbury* moved into the realistic world of the radical student generation of the 1970s (but updated to follow his characters into their postgraduate lives).

One of the most popular and controversial strips of the 1980s was *Bloom County* by Berke Breathed. Like *Doonesbury*, the satire was often keyed to immediate political and social events, and, like *Pogo*, the cast of characters included several anthropomorphic creatures, including the endearing penguin Opus. Breathed's strip, however, maintained an identity and sense of humor quite its own and unlike any other. Because of their astute commentary on contemporary affairs, both Trudeau and Breathed have been awarded Pulitzer Prizes for editorial cartooning, as has Jules Feiffer, whose weekly cartoon essay was closer to the comic strip than the political cartoon. Crossing over in the other direction are several political cartoonists who have turned to the comic strip as a more subtle and entertaining way to provide commentary on modern life and mores, such as Doug Marlette's southern-based *Kudzu*; Jeff MacNelly's contribution to the animal fable tradition, *Shoe*; Mike Peter's combination of cultural satire and nursery rhyme lore, *Mother Goose and Grimm*; and Aaron Magruder's send-up of Afrocentric ethnic attitudes, *Boondocks*. Each of these strips in its individual way marks a distinct advance in the form and content of modern satiric comic strips.

The travails of the modern woman, caught between the demands of a profession and traditional female roles, were treated by several strips in the 1980s, including *Cathy* by Cathy Guisewite, *Sally Forth* by Greg Howard, *On the Fastrack* by Bill Holbrook, and *For Better or for Worse* by Lynn Johnston. The fantasy worlds of animals and children and combinations thereof have continued to supply a basis of humor for a number of popular strips, such as *Garfield* by Jim Davis, *Marvin* by Tom Armstrong, and *Calvin and Hobbes* by Bill Watterson, the last one of the most psychologically astute treatments of childhood and the imagination ever to grace the pages of newspapers. A new direction in comics humor was charted by Gary Larson's *The Far Side* and James Unger's *Herman*, both actually single-panel cartoons rather than comic strips and both bringing a sense of the absurd and the bizarre to the funny papers that perhaps is a sign of things to come. The introduction of Bill Griffith's underground Dada fantasy strip, *Zippy the Pinhead*, to mainstream newspapers is an indication of such a trend, as well as Bud Grace's acerbic *Ernie* (later called *The Piranha Club*).

American comic art faces an uncertain future. The space allotted to single comic strips by newspapers has grown increasingly smaller, while syndicate and editorial preference often deters the most creative and therefore possibly unsettling strips, even though such formerly forbidden topics as homosexuality, premarital sex, and abortion have been allowed to enter the funnies. Yet the comic strips remain one of the most singularly attractive features of the newspaper, and even though over a century old, they have not yet reached their full potential as a powerful form of humanistic expression.

REFERENCE WORKS

The sound bibliographical and reference work that must precede historical and critical research has not been entirely accomplished yet for the comics, but a few noteworthy efforts have been made, and much good work is in progress. What should have been a comprehensive and useful checklist of secondary data—the *International Bibliography of Comics Literature*, by Wolfgang Kempkes—was marred by inaccuracies, incomplete data, and inconvenience. It has been fully replaced by a four-volume set completed by John A. Lent: *Comic Books and Comic Strips in the United States*; *Comic Art of Europe*; *Comic Art in Africa, Asia, Australia, and Latin America*; and *Animation, Caricature, and Gag and Political Cartoons in the United States and Canada*. Obviously international in scope and comprehensive in coverage (over 28,900 items are listed), the material is helpfully arranged in topical categories moving from general to specialized studies. One caution should be noted, however. Lent's reach is so exhaustive that he has swept up a few bibliographic ghosts. Occasionally, too, one could ask for fuller information on place and source of publication, and the title of an article is not always sufficient indication of the contents. In any case, any research on comic strips and comic books must begin here. The second place to turn is Randall W. Scott's *The Comic Art Collection Catalog: An Author, Artist, Title, and Subject Catalog of the Comic Art Collection, Special Collections Division, Michigan State University Libraries*. While complete only through 1990, it indexes one of the largest collections of comics-related material in the United States. The perils, problems, and their solutions in building such a collection are engagingly discussed in Scott's *Comics Librarianship: A Handbook*. Additional advice can be found in essays in *Popular Culture and Acquisitions*, edited by Allen Ellis. Also still invaluable is Scott's *Comic Books and Strips: An Information Sourcebook*, which lists and describes more than 1,000 publications about the comics, including popular anthologies, periodicals, collection catalogs, fan publications, and commentary. A list of forty-three libraries with special collections of comics and original art is also provided, along with author, title, and subject indexes.

The main body of the *The World Encyclopedia of Comics*, edited by Maurice Horn, consists of more than 1,400 cross-referenced entries, arranged alphabetically devoted to either an artist, a writer, a comic strip title, or a comic book character, and prepared by an international group of contributors. Additional materials include a short history of the development of comic art, a chronology, an original analytic inquiry into the aesthetics of the comics by the editor, a history of newspaper syndication, a glossary, a selected bibliography, and several appendixes and indexes. The first edition contained a number of typographical errors, and the critical comments were often biased. Unfortunately, the revised edition mainly added new material rather than addressed the problems of the original text. Relevant information also will be found in Horn's *The World Encyclopedia of Cartoons*, similar in structure to the preceding, except that here the almost 1,400 entries deal with the cartoonists, animators, editors, and producers and the works that they create in the fields of animation, gag cartoons, syndicated comic panels, editorial cartoons, caricature, and sports cartoons. The entries are supplemented with an overview of caricature and cartoons, a brief history of humor magazines, a world summary of animated cartoons, a chronology, a glossary, and a history of the periodicals *Puck*, *Life*, and *Judge*.

Another reference project initiated by Maurice Horn was the valuable *Contemporary Graphic Artists* series, of which only three volumes were issued by Gale Research Company. Each volume contained biographic, bibliographic, and critical assessments of present and past illustrators, animators, cartoonists, designers, and other graphic artists, but with an emphasis on comic artists. Much of the information was obtained directly from the artists, many of whom provided comments on their own work. The first volume in 1986 contained an essay, "The Graphic Arts: An Overview," that defined the areas covered by the series. Horn's *100 Years of American Newspaper Comics: An Illustrated Encyclopedia* brings together in a convenient volume 420 entries on the more important comic strip titles.

Ron Goulart's *The Encyclopedia of American Comics* collects over 600 entries on comic strips, comic books, characters, and their creators. They provide a useful balance to the Horn volumes in opinion and judgment. *Comics between the Panels* by Steve Duin and Mike Richardson is an intentionally "irreverent and idiosyncratic" collection of hundreds of entries on creators, artists, writers, companies, fans, conventions, publishers, and related topics. What it lacks in documentation and reliability may be made up for by its rich use of anecdotes and lively style, also true for the 150 some entries in *100 Years of Comics*, issued by the Starlog Group, which are engaging but not always accurate. Dave Strickler's *Syndicated Comic Strips and Artists, 1924–1995* is an index of 4,700 comics and 3,300 artists and creators listed in the annual *Editor & Publisher Syndicate Directory* for over seventy years. This has been superseded, however, by Allan Holtz's work-in-progress, *Stripper's Guide to U.S. Comic Strips and Cartoon Panels*, a comprehensive listing based on an examination of American newspapers and documentary evidence. It is being issued in both printed and computerized forms at regular intervals and when completed will constitute an essential research tool.

Two checklists of characters adapted to film have been published, with synopses and filmographies: *Hollywood and the Comics* by David Hofstede with fifty-five entries and *The Comics Come Alive: A Guide to Comic-Strip Characters in Live-Action Productions* by Roy Kinnard with eighty-six entries. Carl Horak has produced both *A Steve Canyon Companion* and *A Terry and the Pirates Companion*, providing authoritative plot summaries for the complete runs of Milton Caniff's two classic strips. Victor E. Wichert has produced a helpful index to *Names Used in the Dick Tracy Comic Strip 1931–1977*. Even more impressive is Wichert's thorough and comprehensive guide to Dick Tracy characters, *The Dick Tracy Encyclopedia, Oct. 4, 1931–Dec. 25, 1977*, a model of its kind which will hopefully inspire similar efforts on other major strips. Another worthy effort is *The Pogopedia: A Codex of the Walt Kelly Pogo Works* by Nik Lauer, Leo Taflin, and Christopher M. Lauer. All sorts of unusual and bizarre facts are gathered in Craig Yoe's remarkable *Weird but True Toon Factoids.* The best guide for collectors of original art is *Collecting Original Comic Strip Art!* by Jeffrey M. Ellinport. A thorough listing of early efforts to reprint comic strips in compilations and, later, comic books was completed by Denis Gifford, *American Comic Strip Collections, 1884–1939: The Evolutionary Era.*

In *Women and the Comics*, Trina Robbins and Catherine Yronwode, a comic book artist and editor, respectively, provide a comprehensive catalog with brief commentary on the work of over 500 women cartoonists and writers in America from 1901 to 1984. In a field thought to have been dominated by men, the authors find that almost from the start comic strips and, later, comic books have employed feminine talent extensively, although their names were concealed or lost to history. *Great Cartoonists and Their Art* is a collection of personal and biographical essays on comic strip and editorial artists whose work was collected over the years by editorial cartoonist Art Wood. Wood includes quotations from the artists, background on the business, and the technical details of producing cartoons and comics for publication. Similar biographical and professional data can be gleaned from *"To Cartooning": 60 Years of Magic* by Jud Hurd, founder and editor of the invaluable interview journal *Cartoonist Profiles.*

Will Eisner, a creator of the comic book and one of the most influential masters of comic art, discusses his ideas and theories on the practice of telling stories in graphic form in *Comics & Sequential Art.* Separate chapters, thoroughly illustrated by examples of his own work, treat imagery, timing, framing, and anatomy, and he discusses comics as a form of reading, learning, and teaching. Eisner views comics as a distinct artistic discipline and a literary/visual form, the development of which has been accelerated by advances in graphic technology and visual communication in this century. This is one of the best books ever written on the aesthetics of comic art. An engaging and witty overview of the various symbolic devices and shorthand visual images used by cartoonists is *The Lexicon of Comicana* by Mort Walker. While written tongue-in-cheek, the book is a valuable guide to the devices that make comic art distinctive.

Denis Gifford's *Encyclopedia of Comic Characters* contains entries on over 1,200 characters with notes on their creators, place of publication, beginning and ending dates, and description. Most of the characters are British, but quite a few American ones are included. *A Doonesbury Index* by Allan D. Satin is a comprehensive index to the characters, real people, topics, and themes that appeared in G. B. Trudeau's comic strip from 1970 through 1983. Future historians of politics and popular culture in the 1970s will find this extremely valuable. A complete guide to the appearances of one character in all the possible media is found in Fred M. Grandinetti's *Popeye: An Illustrated History of E. C. Segar's Character in Print, Radio, Television and Film Appearances, 1929–1993.*

Teachers wishing to use comics in an educational context will find some useful suggestions in *Cartoons and Comics in the Classroom*, edited by James L. Thomas. It must be used with caution as a reference, however, since it contains some inaccurate information about the history of comics and since many of the articles are written with a degree of condescension for the art form. A briefer set of practical exercises is found in the pamphlet *Comics in the Classroom* by M. Thomas Inge. *The Art of the Comic Strip* by Shirley Glubok and *Funny Papers: Behind the Scenes of the Comics* by Elaine Scott were both written for children, the first a history of the medium and the second a more practical survey of how comics are created, drawn, and published. Both are beautifully illustrated. Anyone interested in entering the profession will find more advice than can easily be digested in Lee Nordling's comprehensive *Your Career in the Comics*.

RESEARCH COLLECTIONS

Except for isolated instances, most public and university libraries have made no effort to collect or preserve comic strips, comic books, or related materials. Even the Library of Congress files of comic books were carelessly maintained, and much of the material has disappeared over the years. Some of the best collections are in the hands of private collectors and not generally open to the public.

The major research center for the comic strip is the Cartoon Research Library, 27 West 17th Avenue Mall, Ohio State University, Columbus, Ohio 43210–1393 (E-mail cartoons@osu.edu). Begun with a gift from Milton Caniff of his entire library, papers, and research files, under the expert direction of Lucy Caswell, the collection has grown rapidly with extensive gifts of papers, publications, and art from cartoonists and their professional associations. It has also absorbed the major part of the collection of the San Francisco Academy of Comic Art established by Bill Blackbeard. The library hosts major exhibitions and conferences on the comic arts on a regular basis. The International Museum of Cartoon Art in Boca Raton, Florida, and the Cartoon Art Museum in San Francisco both emphasize original art and provide important exhibitions and seminars open to the public.

Over forty research institutions with strong collections in the comic arts are identified in Randall W. Scott's *Comic Books and Strips: An Information Sourcebook* and *Comics Librarianship: A Handbook*, as well as the *Directory of Popular Culture Collections* by Christopher D. Geist and others. These collections grow stronger as society and donors begin to recognize the importance of preserving popular culture artifacts.

HISTORY AND CRITICISM

It must be noted that because so little of the basic bibliographic and reference work had been completed, early books discussed in the following pages abound to one degree or another in errors and mistaken assumptions. Many authors assumed that the beginning date for a daily or Sunday strip was the first appearance in their local newspapers or the first date on which it was syndicated, whereas it may have begun months earlier. The syndicates themselves have kept very few records and even incomplete files of proof sheets for the strips that they distributed. Omitted from discussion here are the many important historical and appreciative studies of American comics published abroad in Europe or South America.

A History of American Graphic Humor, by William Murrell, was the first authoritative history of the development of pictorial satire and cartooning in America to include the comics. While he devotes only a few appreciative pages to the comic strip, the work is still valuable as a panorama of the forms of visual art that have influenced the comics. The earliest full-length book entirely devoted to American comic art was Martin Sheridan's *Comics and Their Creators* in 1942. Not actually an organized history, it consisted primarily of biographical sketches and interviews with the artists and writers of over seventy-five of the most popular newspaper comics, copiously illustrated with portraits and reproductions of the strips. It remains a useful resource for some of the primary data on the views and working habits of the cartoonists. The earliest full-scale history was *The Comics*, by Coulton Waugh, a practicing comic artist and devoted scholar of the subject. While many of his facts were faulty, Waugh attempted a comprehensive survey of the important movements and types of comic strips from *The Yellow Kid* through the first decade of the modern comic book. His insights into the reasons for the popularity of certain strips, his comments on the aesthetic principles behind them, and his early effort to define the medium make Waugh's pioneer effort of lasting interest, although he had little appreciation for the comic book as it had developed, and he appeared to accept without question some of the highbrow standards often applied to popular art by the self-appointed guardians of high culture.

The next effort on the part of a single author to chart the history of the medium was Stephen Becker's *Comic Art in America*, although his interests were broader than Waugh's in that he envisioned his book, according to its pretentious subtitle, as "a social history of the funnies, the political cartoons, magazine humor, sporting cartoons, and animated cartoons." Casting his net so broadly led to much superficiality, and his commentary is often derivative, but the volume is a useful storehouse of over 390 illustrations and sample sketches. The text is kept to an absolute minimum, and the illustrations are at a maximum in *The Penguin Book of Comics*, by George Perry and Alan Aldridge, aptly described in its subtitle as "a slight history." Originally published in French in conjunction with an exhibition of comic art at the Louvre and the joint product of six contributors headed by Pierre Couperie, *A History of the Comic Strip* is understandably uneven, yet it contains some of the most provocative comments yet ventured on the aesthetics, structure, symbolism, and themes in comic art. A general survey was undertaken by comic artist Jerry Robinson, *The Comics: An Illustrated History of Comic Strip Art*. Robinson provided a readable and interesting text complemented by thirteen original essays by eminent artists about the theories behind their work.

Assembled as a catalog for an exhibition at the University of Maryland, Judith O'Sullivan's *The Art of the Comic Strip* contains a brief history with emphases on Winsor McCay, George McManus, George Herriman, and Burne Hogarth, a compilation of short biographies and bibliographic references on 120 comic artists, a chronology of important dates, and a bibliography. *Comics: Anatomy of a Mass Medium*, by Reinhold Reitberger and Wolfgang Fuchs, is a broad effort by two German scholars to relate the comics to their social context and developments in other mass media, but faulty secondary sources and inaccessible primary material led to an inordinate number of factual and other errors, which no one corrected in the process of translation. What was promised to be the most ambitious effort yet undertaken to describe *The History of the Comic Strip* yielded two volumes by David Kunzle: *The Early Comic Strip* in 1973 and, seventeen years later, *The Nineteenth Century*. The first traces to 1825 the development of narrative art in the European broadsheet, which Kunzle sees as a form of the comic strip as he defines it in the introduction. Volume 2 continues the survey by examining comic cartoon narratives in prints, books, and satiric journals in England, France, and Germany mainly, with special emphases on the work of Rodolphe Töpffer, Honoré Daumier, Gustave Doré, Leoncé Petit, and Wilhelm Busch, among others. The result is an impressive, carefully documented, and detailed account of the antecedents to, and influences on, the comic strip, but he stops short of applying any of it to the appearance of the actual comic strip itself at the end of the nineteenth century. Kunzle sees those who choose to believe the modern comic strip is mainly an American development as wrongheaded and chauvinistic.

While we still lack a thorough and authoritative history of the comic strip in America, a number of efforts in the last decade can be consulted with profit. One of the best is Robert C. Harvey's *Children of the Yellow Kid: The Evolution of the American Comic Strip*, a fully illustrated survey sensitive to both the aesthetic and cultural forces that have shaped the medium. Other useful historical studies include *America's Great Comic-Strip Artists* by Richard Marschall, focused on sixteen master cartoonists; *The Great American Comic Strip: One Hundred Years of Cartoon Art* by Judith O'Sullivan, who brings to the subject the perceptions of an art historian; and *The Funnies: 100 Years of American Comic Strips* by Ron Goulart, enriched by an acquaintance with many of the cartoonists discussed and their professional world. The primary purpose of *Comics as Culture* by M. Thomas Inge is to trace connections between the comics and the larger cultural trends in the United States. Also of interest are *A Century of Women Cartoonists* by Trina Robbins; *Calvin & Hobbes, Garfield, Bloom County, Doonesbury and All That Funny Stuff* by James Van Hise; and *Great American Comics: 100 Years of Cartoon Art* by M. Thomas Inge. Nowhere are the connections between "high" art and the comics explored with greater authority and definitiveness than in the essential *High & Low: Modern Art and Popular Culture* by Kirk Vanedoe and Adam Gopnik.

The bookshelf of biographies of major comic artists is gradually expanding. Most early efforts took the form of brief personal memoirs or picture books in which the text was incidental to the illustrations. Examples of such promotional books are *Milton Caniff: Rembrandt of the Comic Strip* by John Paul Adams and *Charlie Brown, Snoopy and Me* by Charles M. Schulz and R. Smith Kiliper. As each anniversary of *Peanuts* passed, Schulz published volumes interlaced with autobiographical memoirs, such as *Charlie Brown & Charlie Schulz* by Lee Mendelson and Schulz (twentieth anniversary), *Peanuts Jubilee: My Life and Art with Charlie Brown and Others* by Schulz (twenty-fifth), *Happy Birthday, Charlie Brown* by Mendelson and Schulz (thirtieth), *You Don't Look 35, Charlie Brown* by Schulz (thirty-fifth), *Charles M. Schulz: 40 Years, Life and Art* (fortieth) by Giovanni Trimboli, *Around the World in 45 Years: Charlie Brown's Anniversary Celebration* (forty-fifth) by Schulz and R. Smith Kiliper, and *Peanuts: A Golden Celebration* (fiftieth) by Schulz, with a selection of strips made by Patrick McDonnell and Karen O'Connell. *Good Grief: The Story of Charles M. Schulz* is an anecdotal biography prepared with the cooperation of Schulz by Rheta Grimsley Johnson. Engaging insights into Schulz's life and career can be found in the interviews collected in M. Thomas Inge's *Charles M. Schulz: Conversations*. David Michaelis is writing a full-scale authorized biography. Walt Kelly's anthology *Ten Ever-lovin' Blue-eyed Years with Pogo* is another anniversary volume with significant autobiographical content.

Peter Marzio's *Rube Goldberg: His Life and Work* is a full-scale biographical account of Goldberg's versatile career and an interpretation of his art. Marzio achieves a sense of Goldberg's personality and character and provides the kind of treatment that other artists deserve. Goldberg's autobiography has been incorporated in Clark Kinnaird's *Rube Goldberg vs. the Machine Age*. *Rube Goldberg: Inventions* by Maynard Frank Wolfe includes a brief biography. Harold Davidson's

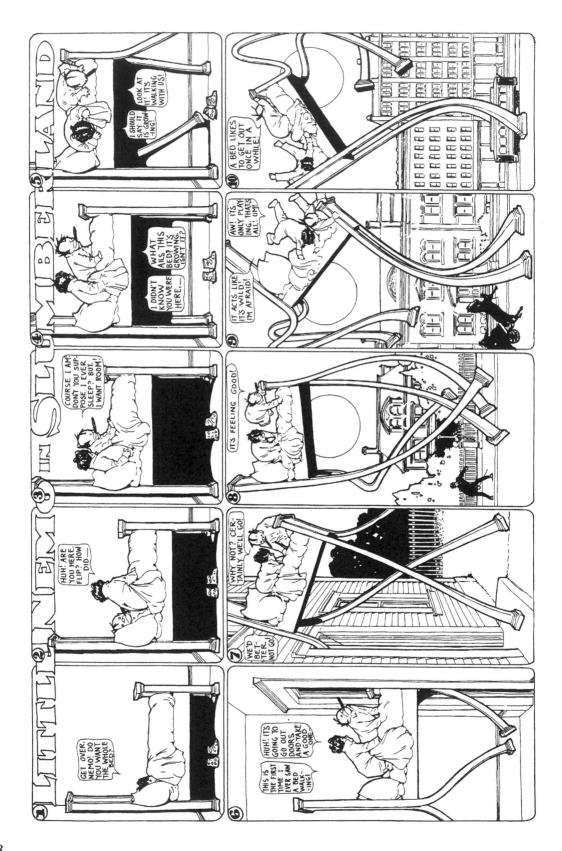

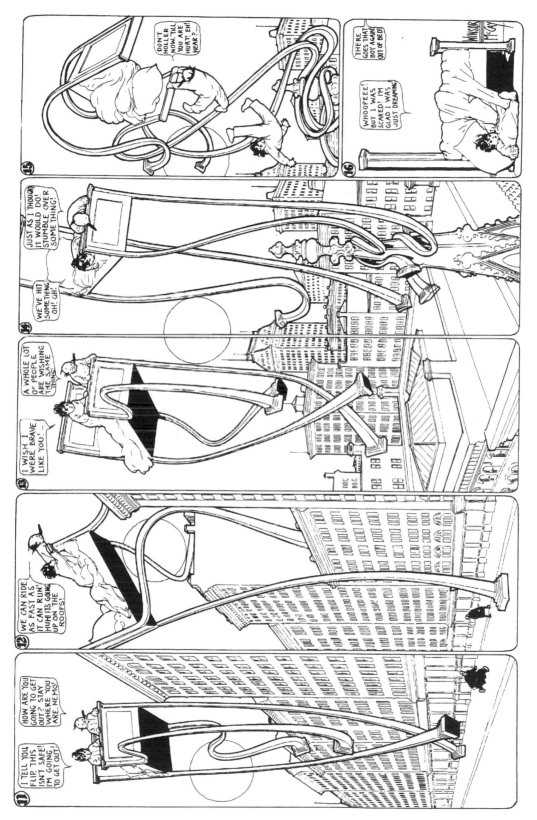

Winsor McCay's *Little Nemo in Slumberland*, 1908. Courtesy of M. Thomas Inge

Jimmy Swinnerton: The Artist and His Work is a beautifully designed and printed survey of the career of a major early cartoonist.

In *Krazy Kat: The Comic Art of George Herriman*, Patrick McDonnell, Karen O'Connell, and Georgia Riley de Havenon provide an overview of Herriman's life and career through an assemblage of unpublished letters, documents, photographs, and artwork for friends, as well as an extensive selection of *Krazy Kat* comic strips. Joseph M. Cahn's *The Teenie Weenies Book: The Life and Art of William Donahey* reports on a little-discussed artist. For more than sixty-five years, Donahey wrote and illustrated a color newspaper feature for the funny pages about a group of Lilliputian characters called *The Teenie Weenies*. The most lavishly produced biographical account that we have is John Canemaker's *Winsor McCay: His Life and Art*. In the text, Canemaker emphasizes McCay's importance in American cultural history through his creation of *Little Nemo in Slumberland*, the most beautiful comic strip in the history of the form, and the production of *Gertie the Dinosaur*, which established the potential of the animated film long before Disney. The illustrations are stunning.

Models of the way that the works and lives of comic artists should be treated are found in two biographies by Shelley Armitage, *John Held, Jr.: Illustrator of the Jazz Age* and *Kewpies and Beyond: The World of Rose O'Neill*. She combines scrupulous research with a balanced critical appreciation for the way that the cartoons and comic strips of Held and O'Neill both reflected and influenced the fads, fashions, and movements of their times. Aspects of the life of Al Capp can be gleaned from his memoirs, *My Well-Balanced Life on a Wooden Leg*, and those of his brother Elliott Caplin, *Al Capp Remembered*. Alexander Theroux's monograph *The Enigma of Al Capp* adds little that is new. A full-scale biography is needed. African American comic artist Oliver W. Harrington, creator of the character Bootsie for black newspapers and exiled political cartoonist, tells much of his own life story in *Why I Left America and Other Essays*, and his powerful art is showcased along with a brief biography by M. Thomas Inge in *Dark Laughter: The Satiric Art of Oliver W. Harrington*. Hank Ketcham fully describes his life and adventures as creator of the world's favorite mischievous child in *The Merchant of Dennis the Menace*. In a similar, thoroughly illustrated fashion, Mort Walker surveys his life and career before and after Beetle Bailey in *Mort Walker's Private Scrapbook: A Celebration of 50 Years of Comic Excellence*. Robert C. Harvey has written an impressive and well-designed biography of a highly talented, but often overlooked, cartoonist in *Accidental Ambassador Gordo: The Comic Strip Art of Gus Arriola*. Harvey has also written brief sketches of over 150 cartoonists who are represented by the revealing self-portraits in *A Gallery of Rogues: Cartoonists' Self-Caricatures*, based on the remarkable Mark Cohen collection of originals housed at the Ohio State University Cartoon Research Library.

Several anthologies contain significant information about the lives and times of the artists represented. For example, Bill Blackbeard's handsome edition of *R. F. Outcault's The Yellow Kid* contains not only a complete reprint of that comics feature but a 120-page introduction to its biographical and cultural backgrounds. This is required reading for anyone interested in Outcault and the origins of the comic strip. Biographical data can be gathered, too, from *Hal Foster: Prince of Illustrators* by Brian M. Kane, *The Lives behind the Lines . . . 20 Years of for Better or for Worse* by Lynn Johnston, *20 Years and Still Kicking! Garfield's Twentieth*

Anniversary Collection by Jim Davis, *Nell Brinkley and the New Woman in the Early 20th Century* by Trina Robbins, *The World of Andy Capp* by Reg Smythe and Les Lilley, *In Your Face: A Cartoonist at Work* by Doug Marlette, *Barney Google and Snuffy Smith: 75 Years of an American Legend* by Brian Walker, and *Dick Tracy: America's Most Famous Detective*, edited by Bill Crouch Jr. This last strip by Chester Gould is comprehensively surveyed and given a thorough cultural analysis in Garyn G. Roberts' *Dick Tracy and American Culture: Morality and Mythology, Text and Context*.

Maurice Horn has published several thematic studies of the comics. His *Comics of the American West* is a heavily illustrated survey of the major western strips and books and their basic symbolic themes, and his *Women in the Comics* surveys in a similar fashion the images and roles of women as reflected in the comics. A third book, *Sex in the Comics*, is an informal discussion of the presence of sexual behavior in comic strips and books of the mainstream and underground varieties. *Ethnic Images in the Comics*, edited by Charles Hardy and Gail F. Stern, is an exhibition catalog, but it contains more information than is available anywhere else in its seven essays on blacks, Jews, Asians, and other ethnic groups as portrayed in the comics. Another valuable exhibition catalog is *The Comic Art Show*, edited by John Carlin and Sheena Wagstaff, which is a comprehensive look at the influence of cartoons and comics on painting and the fine arts. It contains information not found elsewhere.

The History of Little Orphan Annie by Bruce Smith surveys the history of Harold Gray's famous orphan and her various permutations into a radio show, motion pictures, and the musical stage. Gray's political attitudes and the problems that these caused are also discussed. Smith also assembled *The World according to Daddy Warbucks*, appropriately subtitled *Capitalist Quotations from the Richest Man in the World*. Most of the quotations supporting free enterprise are culled from others, but occasionally Warbucks is quoted. *The Popeye Story* by Bridget Terry contains some background information on E. C. Segar's comic strip, but its primary concern is the making of the motion picture. Charles Schulz's *Peanuts* is examined from a variety of theoretical perspectives—artistic, cultural, psychological, and political—in *The Graphic Art of Charles Schulz*, edited by Joan Roebuck, with essays by Roebuck, M. Thomas Inge, Elliott Oring, and Umberto Eco and a memoir by Bill Mauldin. This was the catalog for an exhibition organized to celebrate the strip's thirty-fifth anniversary. The chronology and bibliography are especially useful. Mort Walker speaks out against his critics in *Miss Buxley: Sexism in Beetle Bailey?* with a good deal of disarming humor.

In *Backstage at the Strips*, Mort Walker provides an engaging insider's tour of the world of comic strip artists, how the strips are created, and who the people are who draw and read them. Ron Goulart's *The Adventurous Decade* is an informal and subjective history of the adventure comic strips during the 1930s, when the American funnies came of age. The interviews that Goulart conducted with living veterans of the period enrich the volume, which tends to adopt a studied controversial view in its critical judgments of the work of classic artists. In the catalog for the Smithsonian Institution's bicentennial exhibition, *A Nation of Nations*, edited by Peter Marzio, there is an essay by M. Thomas Inge and Bill Blackbeard on the influences of Europe on the development of the comic strip and the later influences of the fully developed American comic strip and book on the culture of the world at large. An offshoot of interest in comics is the large market for toys and merchandise based on the more popular characters, such as Mickey Mouse, Buck Rogers, Superman, or Little Orphan Annie. An extensive number of these mass-produced artifacts have been photographed and cataloged in Robert Lesser's *A Celebration of Comic Art and Memorabilia*.

Throughout the years the popular magazines, newspapers, and journals of commentary have published hundreds of articles and essays on the comics, many worthwhile, others superficial, and still others steeped in disdain for the subject. Most of this material is listed in the Lent bibliographies. A useful anthology of some of the better essays is *The Funnies: An American Idiom*, edited by David Manning White and Robert H. Abel.

Several critics who have undertaken general assessments of popular culture have devoted portions of their studies to comic art. One of the earliest was Gilbert Seldes in his 1924 pioneer survey of the mass media, *The 7 Lively Arts*. Though somewhat apologetically, Seldes found some virtues in "the 'vulgar' comic strip" in one chapter of that title, but his essay on George Herriman and *Krazy Kat* was one of the first partly to define Herriman's unique genius. In *The Astonished Muse*, Reuel Denney finds the comics deeply rooted in the larger conventions and traditions of art and literature, especially naturalism, and Leo Lowenthal calls for more serious study of the comics in *Literature, Popular Culture, and Society*. One chapter of Charles Beaumont's *Remember? Remember?* praises the daily funnies for their beauty, imagination, communication, and general good to the world. Perhaps some of the most fruitful, provocative, and rational comments are found in Alan Gowans' *The Unchanging Arts*. Gowans recognizes the extent to which the popular visual arts play a functional part in the total context of society and finds the comics one of the century's major art forms. A social scientist who has specialized in writing about the subject is Arthur Asa Berger, whose books include *Li'l Abner: A Study in American Satire*, the first book-length study of a single comic strip; *The Comic-Stripped American*, a series of pieces on the way that comics reflect our culture; and *Pop Culture*, a collection of essays, with three on the comics.

A special category of interpretive books are the "gospel" studies. Robert L. Short began the trend with *The Gospel according to Peanuts* and followed the phenomenal success of that book with *The Parables of Peanuts*. Then came *The Gospel according to Superman* by John T. Galloway Jr., *The Gospel according to Andy Capp* by D. P. McGeachy III, and *Good News for Grimy Gulch* by Del Carter (based on Tom K. Ryan's comic strip *Tumbleweeds*). These books basically are sermons or theological disquisitions illustrated by the comics in question and make little commentary of a significant sort on their meaning or value, except insofar as they are all concerned with the problems of human existence. Jeffrey H. Loria's *What's It All About, Charlie Brown?* is a similar kind of book that describes with frequent illustrations the philosophical and psychological meaning of *Peanuts*.

Most serious study of comic art seems to have focused on how it reflects or relates to society and the culture out of which it has grown. Only now are we witnessing the development of a body of writing that attempts to assess the comics on their own terms, by measuring their worth against their own developed standards and aesthetic principles rather than by the irrelevant yardsticks of other related arts. A collection of essays mainly on comic book superheroes helped initiate this development: *All in Color for a Dime*, edited by Dick Lupoff and Don

Thompson. Many of the essays originated in a series of fan magazine articles and still bear the stylistic and judgmental marks of their origin. A second volume, also edited by Thompson and Lupoff, *The Comic-Book Book*, is a marked improvement in this regard. In style and judgment, many of these essays are distinguished. Although most of Maurice Horn's *75 Years of the Comics* is devoted to reprinting sample pages from an exhibition at the New York Cultural Center, his excellent ten-page introduction was one of the best efforts at the time to define comic art as it relates to the other narrative arts and on its own internal principles. In *The Art of Humorous Illustration*, Nick Meglin has assembled appreciative, fully illustrated tributes to twelve illustrators, including comic artists Sergio Aragones, Jack Davis, Mort Drucker, Johnny Hart, and Arnold Roth. The purpose of *Moviemaking Illustrated: The Comicbook Filmbook*, by James Morrow and Murray Suid, is to teach the technical principles of filmmaking, but the textbook utilizes nothing but frames from Marvel comic books and thereby makes many valuable points about the complex sound and visual techniques of comic art. *The Art of the Comic Strip*, edited by Walter Herderg and David Pascal, is noteworthy for its excellent choice of illustrations and the perceptive quality of the brief notes and commentary (originally a special issue of *Graphis* magazine). Also of interest is *The Very Large Book of Comical Funnies*, compiled by the staff of the *National Lampoon* as a good-natured satire on the plethora of historic and appreciative books about the comics but which in its own way displays an appreciative sense of what makes the comics special. In a similar category is *Mad Magazine*'s send-up "The Comics" in *Mad Super Special* (Fall 1981), which includes a feature in which several cartoonists— Charles Schulz, Wait Kelly, Ken Ernst and Allen Saunders, Mort Walker, and Mell Lazarus—draw the strip that they would really like to do instead of the one that they do every day.

Academic criticism of a theoretical kind on the comics has only recently begun. Some of the earliest and most culturally sensitive criticism of major consequence was written in a series of essays for little magazines in the 1960s by Donald Phelps, the first critic to receive a Guggenheim Grant to write about comic strips. These have been collected in *Reading the Funnies: Looking at Great Cartoonists*. "The Comics as Culture," edited by M. Thomas Inge in 1979, is a special issue of the *Journal of Popular Culture* that includes essays on Walt Kelly, Milton Caniff, and the Tarzan comic strip and an especially valuable article entitled "The Aesthetics of the Comic Strip," by Robert C. Harvey. Two other articles on the aesthetics of comic art to be recommended, also from the *Journal of Popular Culture*, are "The Funnies, the Movies and Aesthetics" by Earle J. Coleman (1985) and "Comic Art: Characteristics and Potentialities of a Narrative Medium" by Lawrence L. Abbott (1986).

Robert C. Harvey revised his essay just mentioned as the first chapter of his 1994 study *The Art of the Funnies: An Aesthetic History*. His basic premise is that in effective comic strips, the visual and the verbal are both essential to communication. If the strip can be understood on the basis of the pictures or the words alone, then the artist is not fulfilling the potential of the medium. The remainder of his book is an appreciation of what he considers the best examples of American comics viewed in their artistic contexts. Many of Harvey's essays on classic comic strips are essential reading. David Carrier claims that his book, *The Aesthetics of Comics*, "is the first by an analytic philosopher to identify and solve the aesthetic problems posed by comic strips and to explain the relationship of this artistic genre to other forms of visual art." Whether or not Carrier definitively "solves" anything is open to discussion; nevertheless, he offers a carefully articulated, thorough, and complex argument on behalf of taking the comics seriously. With George Herriman's *Krazy Kat* and Gary Larson's *The Far Side* as his main exhibits, Carrier's theories, based on the work of Arthur Danto, Ernst Gombrich, and other aesthetic and critical theorists, are provocative.

The European contributors of essays to *Forging a New Medium: The Comic Strip in the Nineteenth Century*, edited by Charles Dierick and Pascal Lefévre, basically expand upon the work and ideas of David Kunzle about European precursors to the comic strip. In the last chapter, Kunzle himself at last turns his gaze to America to look for prescient examples in the comic weeklies, but he still stops short of the comic strip itself. The narrative cartoons that he cites from *Judge* and *Puck* are well known, although he believes that such scholars as O'Sullivan, Inge, Goulart, and Marschall are "ignorant" of them. Ian Gordon's *Comic Strips and Consumer Culture, 1890–1945* fully documents how comic strip characters and conventions contributed to the expansion of mass consumer culture in America and promoted consumerist values and materialism. Norman Solomon believes that he has found a more recent example of corporate buyout and betrayal in his literal-minded exposé of Scott Adams, *The Trouble with Dilbert: How Corporate Culture Gets the Last Laugh*. Solomon was inspired by the Marxist study of comic books *How to Read Donald Duck* by Ariel Dorfman and Armand Mattelart, and like those two passionate revolutionaries, Solomon's political ideology obscures his vision and sense of humor. *Understanding the Funnies: Critical Interpretations of Comic Strips*, edited by Gail W. Pieper, is an uneven collection, but several of the essays offer useful insights and information.

The presence of self-referentiality in the comics is discussed in a chapter of Michael Dunne's perceptive *Metapop: Self-Referentiality in Contemporary American Popular Culture*, and the concept is given fuller exploration in a study of what M. Thomas Inge calls "metacomics" in his *Anything Can Happen in a Comic Strip: Centennial Reflections on an American Art Form*. While Nicholas Rookes takes in all of modern art in his study of *Humor in Art: A Celebration of Visual Wit*, he frequently turns to comic strips, comic books, and cartoons to support his points. *When Toys Come Alive: Narratives of Animation, Metamorphosis, and Development* by Lois Rostow Kuznets has a chapter on Bill Watterson's *Calvin and Hobbes; Daddy's Girl: Young Girls and Popular Culture* by Valerie Walkerdine discusses Harold Gray's *Little Orphan Annie* and several British girls' comic books; and *New Perspectives on Women and Comedy*, edited by Regina Barreca, includes two essays on women cartoonists.

The publication of fan magazines and amateur press publications about comic art began in the 1950s and reemerged in the 1960s as a significant development in the history of American magazines. Much of the pioneer scholarship about the comics first appeared in those pages, and extremely useful biographical and bibliographical information can be found there. A history of their development and a listing of titles would require more space than is available for this entire chapter, and it would be almost impossible to assemble a file of back issues of most of them. The comments here are restricted to only a few of the most professional, informative, and regularly published periodicals to which subscriptions are available. The most widely circulated and read publication about the world of comic art is *Comics Buyer's Guide*, originated in 1971 by Alan L. Light (under the title *Buyer's Guide for Comics Fandom*). Krause Publications assumed ownership in 1983, and Don and Maggie Thompson became editors. In addition to advertisements for collectors, the weekly includes feature articles, news stories, columns, reviews, and a letters column in which readers vigorously debate issues and controversies with the editors and each other. The second most popular is the *Comics Journal*, a monthly magazine edited by Gary Groth with lengthy essays, in-depth interviews, review columns by leading commentators on the comics, and an aggressive editorial policy that often places the magazine in the center of controversy. Both the *Guide* and the *Journal* make for lively reading, but both contain a good deal more material about comic books than about comic strips. This is not the case with the quarterly *Cartoonist Profiles*, which specializes in interviews with living comic strip artists and profiles on classic artists of the past. A wealth of professional and historic data is found in each issue. A source of reprints of classic strips of the past and groundbreaking essays on major artists was the magazine *Nemo: The Classic Comics Library*. Nemo has been replaced by *Hogan's Alley: The Magazine of the Cartoon Arts*, with its emphasis on invaluable biographical and historical material. For four bright years, comics scholarship was blessed with the impressive journal *Inks: Cartoon and Comic Art Studies*, edited by Lucy Caswell at Ohio State University. A complete file of the four volumes belongs in any research collection devoted to comic art. In 1999, after *Inks* had ceased publication, John A. Lent began the *International Journal of Comic Art*, which takes as its scholarly purview all forms of comic art in the world at large and documents the latest trends in critical thought about the field of study.

ANTHOLOGIES AND REPRINTS

From the very beginning of the American comic strip in the 1890s, paperback collections of the most widely read titles were popular publications. Thus, *The Yellow Kid*, *Foxy Grandpa*, *Buster Brown*, and *Mutt and Jeff* appeared in series of reprints, and in 1933 the first comic book, *Funnies on Parade*, was composed of reprints of Sunday and daily strips in color. Over the years various comics would find their way into paperback anthologies and less often into hardcover collections. Usually considered of ephemeral value, few copies survive and are considered collector's items. One of the first substantial anthologies of American cartoons, complete with historical introductions and annotations, was Thomas Craven's *Cartoon Cavalcade* in 1943. Interspersed among the chronologically arranged examples of political and gag cartoons filling over 400 pages were selections from all the popular newspaper comic strips.

The publisher who initiated a program of reprinting classic comic strips in the most responsible format, in selected complete runs with authoritative introductions, was the late Woody Gelman of Nostalgia Press. Beginning with Alex Raymond's *Flash Gordon* in 1967, Gelman published one or more volumes a year in his series the Golden Age of Comics. He also issued a series of anthologies of selected daily strips entitled *Nostalgia Comics*. The ultimate result of his program is an extensive bookshelf of handsomely produced collections of the classic comic strips, preserved for convenient reading and future research.

The most ambitious reprint operation undertaken was the Classic American Comic Strips series by Hyperion Press of Westport, Connecticut, under the editorship of Bill Blackbeard. Series I contained twenty-two volumes in large format and in hardcover or paperback editions. Drawing on the archives of the San Francisco Academy of Comic Art, each volume contained complete sequential reprints from the first or peak years of selected daily and Sunday strips and an introduction by an authority on the subject of that volume. Unfortunately, the project was discontinued. Blackbeard, in collaboration with Martin Williams, also produced the most lavish general anthology to appear, *The Smithsonian Collection of Newspaper Comics*. This is an essential volume in any library for the general reader and researcher alike, as is the second Blackbeard compilation with Dale Crain, *The Comic Strip Century*, a handsome, two-volume selection from 100 years of newspaper offerings.

Over the years several trade and paperback publishers have issued collections of the most popular strips. Among them are Avon Books, Ballantine, Bantam, Dell, Fawcett, Grosset and Dunlap, Holt, Rinehart, and Winston, New American Library, Pyramid Books, and Simon and Schuster. Andrews and McMeel specializes in reprint volumes. For a list of available titles, one should consult their catalogs, as the books go in and out of print with unpredictable frequency. Also a number of specialty publishers now frequently issue reprint series and volumes, such as Fantagraphics Books and NBM (Nantier-Beall-Minoustchine Publishing Company). The last firm has successfully seen into print a reproduction in twelve hardcover volumes of the complete run of Milton Caniff's *Terry and the Pirates*, the first such reprint project of a major, long-run comic strip to reach completion. The series editor, Bill Blackbeard, has managed a complete reprinting of Roy Crane's *Wash Tubbs and Captain Easy* in a similar format. Other comic strips that are to be reprinted in complete uniform sets, if the publishers succeed, include E. C. Segar's *Popeye* (Fantagraphics Books), Milton Caniff's *Steve Canyon* (Kitchen Sink Press), Harold Gray's *Little Orphan Annie* (Fantagraphics), Al Capp's *Li'l Abner* (Kitchen Sink), George Herriman's *Krazy Kat* (Eclipse Books), Hal Foster's *Prince Valiant* (Fantagraphics), and the complete comic book works of Charles Crumb (Fantagraphics).

Three reprints of historically important comic strips should receive special note. Since 1926, schoolchildren in Texas have been taught their state history through *Texas History Movies*, a comic strip by Jack Patton and John Rosenfield Jr., first published in the *Dallas Morning News* and later reprinted in numerous collections and textbooks, despite its use of ethnic stereotypes and racial slurs. Even today, *Texas History Movies* is available in a complete oversized reprint volume and in two abbreviated and edited editions (with the racism and offensive language removed). *Han Ola og han Per* was a Norwegian American comic strip drawn by Peter Julius Rosendahl from 1918 to 1935 for the *Decorah-Posten*, a Norwegian-language newspaper in Iowa. It has continuously been reprinted ever since in various newspapers. The first 223 of the 599 published are collected in a volume available from the Norwegian-American Historical Association with historical and biographical introductions by the editors, Joan N. Buckley and Einar Haugen. The entire anthology is in both Norwegian and English and provides a most unusual source for studying the assimilation of a major ethnic group in the American Midwest. Asian American immigrant life was treated in a fascinating comic strip collected in *The Four Immigrants Manga: A Japanese Experience in San Francisco, 1904–1924* by Henry (Yoshitaka) Kiyama.

The number of anthologies of reprinted comic strips is so extensive that they cannot easily be discussed here. Instead the reader will find a list of some of these in the Anthologies and Reprints section of the bibliography at the end of this chapter. In most cases those I have selected include introductory appreciations, background essays, biographical notes, or other additional material that will be of interest to the reader and researcher.

BIBLIOGRAPHY

Books and Articles

Abbott, Lawrence L. "Comic Art: Characteristics and Potentialities of a Narrative Medium." *Journal of Popular Culture* 19 (Spring 1986), 155–76.

Adams, John Paul. *Milton Caniff: Rembrandt of the Comic Strip*. New York: David McKay, 1946.

Armitage, Shelley. *John Held, Jr.: Illustrator of the Jazz Age*. Syracuse, N.Y.: Syracuse University Press, 1987.

———. *Kewpies and Beyond: The World of Rose O'Neill*. Jackson: University Press of Mississippi, 1994.

Baker, Steve. *Picturing the Beast: Animals, Identity and Representation*. Manchester, U.K.: Manchester University Press, 1993.

Barreca, Regina, ed. *New Perspectives on Women and Comedy*. Philadelphia: Gordon and Breach, 1992.

Beaumont, Charles. *Remember? Remember?* New York: Macmillan, 1963.

Becker, Stephen. *Comic Art in America*. New York: Simon and Schuster, 1959.

Berger, Arthur Asa. *The Comic-Stripped American*. New York: Walker, 1973.

———. *Li'l Abner: A Study in American Satire*. New York: Twayne, 1970. Reprint. Jackson: University Press of Mississippi, 1994.

———. *Pop Culture*. New York: Pflaum/Standard, 1973.

Blackbeard, Bill, ed. *R. F. Outcault's The Yellow Kid*. Northampton, Mass.: Kitchen Sink Press, 1995.

Cahn, Joseph M. *The Teenie Weenies Book: The Life and Art of William Donahey*. La Jolla, Calif.: Green Tiger Press, 1986.

Canemaker, John. *Winsor McCay: His Life and Art*. New York: Abbeville Press, 1987.

Caplin, Elliott. *Al Capp Remembered*. Bowling Green, Ohio: Bowling Green State University Popular Press, 1994.

Capp, Al. *My Well-Balanced Life on a Wooden Leg*. Santa Barbara, Calif.: John Daniel, 1991.

Carlin, John, and Sheena Wagstaff, eds. *The Comic Art Show: Cartoons in Painting and Popular Culture*. New York: Fantagraphics Books, 1983.

Carrier, David. *The Aesthetics of Comics*. University Park: Pennsylvania State University Press, 2000.

Carter, Del. *Good News for Grimey Gulch*. Valley Forge, Pa.: Judson Press, 1977.

Coleman, Earle J. "The Funnies, the Movies and Aesthetics." *Journal of Popular Culture* 18 (Spring 1985), 89–100.

Couperie, Pierre et al. *A History of the Comic Strip.* Trans. by Eileen B. Hennessey. New York: Crown, 1968.

Crouch, Bill, Jr. *Dick Tracy: America's Most Famous Detective.* New York: Citadel, 1987.

Davidson, Harold. *Jimmy Swinnerton: The Artist and His Work.* New York: Hearst Books, 1985.

Davis, Jim. *20 Years and Still Kicking! Garfield's Twentieth Anniversary Collection.* New York: Ballantine Books, 1998.

Denney, Reuel. *The Astonished Muse.* Chicago: University of Chicago Press, 1958.

Dierick, Charles, and Pascal Lefévre, eds. *Forging a New Medium: The Comic Strip in the Nineteenth Century.* Brussels, Belgium: VUB University Press, 1998.

Duin, Steve, and Mike Richardson. *Comics between the Panels.* Milwaukie, Oregon: Dark House Comics, 1998.

Dunne, Michael. *Metapop: Self-Referentiality in Contemporary American Popular Culture.* Jackson: University Press of Mississippi, 1992.

Eisner, Will. *Comics & Sequential Art.* Tamarac, Fla.: Poorhouse Press, 1985.

Ellinport, Jeffrey M. *Collecting Original Comic Strip Art!* Norfolk, Va.: Antique Trader Books, 1999.

Ellis, Allen, ed. *Popular Culture and Acquisitions.* New York: Haworth Press, 1992.

Foster, Harold, and Burne Hogarth. *Tarzan in Color.* 20 vols. New York: Nantier-Beall-Minoustchine, 1987–1997.

Galloway, John T., Jr. *The Gospel according to Superman.* Philadelphia: Lippincott and A. J. Holman, 1973.

Geist, Christopher D., Ray B. Browne, Michael T. Marsden, and Carole Palmer. *Directory of Popular Culture Collections.* Phoenix, Ariz.: Oryx Press, 1989.

Gifford, Denis. *American Comic Strip Collections, 1884–1939: The Evolutionary Era.* Boston: G. K. Hall, 1990.

———. *Encyclopedia of Comic Characters.* Essex, England: Longman, 1987.

Glubok, Shirley. *The Art of the Comic Strip.* New York: Macmillan, 1979.

Goldberg, Todd, and Carl Horak. *A Prince Valiant Companion.* Mountain Home, Tenn.: Manuscript Press, 1992.

Gordon, Ian. *Comic Strips and Consumer Culture, 1890–1945.* Washington, D.C.: Smithsonian Institution Press, 1998.

Goulart, Ron. *The Adventurous Decade.* New Rochelle, N.Y.: Arlington House, 1975.

———. *The Funnies: 100 Years of American Comic Strips.* Holbrook, Mass.: Adams, 1995.

———, ed. *The Encyclopedia of American Comics.* New York: Facts on File, 1990.

Gowans, Alan. *The Unchanging Arts.* Philadelphia: J. B. Lippincott, 1971.

Grandinetti, Fred M. *Popeye: An Illustrated History of E. C. Segar's Character in Print, Radio, Television and Film Appearances 1929–1993.* Jefferson, N.C.: McFarland, 1994.

Hardy, Charles, and Gail F. Stern, eds. *Ethnic Images in the Comics.* Philadelphia: Balch Institute for Ethnic Studies, 1986.

Harrington, Oliver W. *Why I Left America and Other Essays.* Ed. M. Thomas Inge. Jackson: University Press of Mississippi, 1993.

Harvey, Robert C. *Accidental Ambassador: The Comic Strip Art of Gus Arriola.* Jackson: University Press of Mississippi, 2000.

———. "The Aesthetics of the Comic Strip." *Journal of Popular Culture* 12 (Spring 1979), 640–52.

———. *The Art of the Funnies: An Aesthetic History.* Jackson: University Press of Mississippi, 1994.

———. *Children of the Yellow Kid: The Evolution of the American Comic Strip.* Northampton, Mass.: Kitchen Sink Press, 1996.

———. *A Gallery of Rogues: Cartoonists' Self-Caricatures.* Columbus: Ohio State University Cartoon Research Library, 1998.

Hayward, Jennifer. *Consuming Pleasures: Active Audiences and Serial Fictions from Dickens to Soap Opera.* Lexington: University Press of Kentucky, 1997.

Herderg, Walter, and David Pascal, eds. *The Art of the Comic Strip.* Zurich: Graphis Press, 1972.

Hofstede, David. *Hollywood and the Comics.* N.p.: Zanne-3, 1991.

Holtz, Allan. *Stripper's Guide to U.S. Comic Strips and Cartoon Panels.* Tavares, Fla.: Round Table Software, 1995–   .

Horak, Carl. *A Steve Canyon Companion.* Mountain View, Tenn.: Manuscript Press, 1996.

———. *A Terry and the Pirates Companion.* Manitou Springs, Colo.: SPFC Productions, 2000.

Horn, Maurice. *Comics of the American West.* New York: Winchester Press, 1977.

———. *75 Years of the Comics.* Boston: Boston Book and Art, 1971.

———. *Sex in the Comics.* New York: Chelsea House, 1985.

———. *Women in the Comics.* New York: Chelsea House, 1977.

———. *Contemporary Graphic Artists.* 3 vols. Detroit: Gale Research, 1986–1988.

———, ed. *100 Years of American Newspaper Comics.* New York: Gramercy Books, 1996.

———. *The World Encyclopedia of Cartoons.* Revised ed. New York: Chelsea House 1999.

———. *The World Encyclopedia of Comics.* Revised ed. New York: Chelsea House, 1999.

Hurd, Jud. *"To Cartooning": 60 Years of Magic.* Fairfield, Conn.: Profiles Press, 1993.

Inge, M. Thomas. *Anything Can Happen in a Comic Strip: Centennial Reflections on an American Art Form.* Columbus: Ohio State University Libraries and University Press of Mississippi, 1995.

———. *Comics as Culture.* Jackson: University Press of Mississippi, 1990.

———. *Comics in the Classroom.* Washington, D.C.: Smithsonian Institution Traveling Exhibition Service, 1989.

———. "Faulkner Reads the Funny Papers." In *Faulkner & Humor*, ed. Doreen Fowler and Ann J. Abadie. Jackson: University Press of Mississippi, 1986, 153–90.

———. *Great American Comics: 100 Years of Cartoon Art.* Washington, D.C.: Smithsonian Institution Traveling Exhibition Service, 1990.

———, ed. *Charles M. Schulz: Conversations.* Jackson: University Press of Mississippi, 2000.

———. "The Comics as Culture." *Journal of Popular Culture* 12 (Spring 1979), 630–754. Special issue.

———. *Dark Laughter: The Satiric Art of Oliver W. Harrington*. Jackson: University Press of Mississippi, 1993.

Inge, M. Thomas, and Bill Blackbeard. "American Comic Art." In *A Nation of Nations*, ed. by Peter Marzio. New York: Harper and Row, 1976, 600–609.

Johnson, Rheta Grimsley. *Good Grief: The Story of Charles M. Schulz*. New York: Pharos Books, 1989.

Johnston, Lynn. *The Lives behind the Lines . . . 20 Years of for Better or for Worse*. Kansas City, Mo.: Andrews McMeel, 1999.

Kelly, Walt. *Ten Ever-lovin' Blue-eyed Years with Pogo*. New York: Simon and Schuster, 1959.

Kempkes, Wolfgang. *International Bibliography of Comics Literature*. Detroit: Gale Research, 1971. Rev. ed. New York: R. R. Bowker/Verlag Dokumentation, 1974.

Ketcham, Hank. *The Merchant of Dennis the Menace*. New York: Abbeville Press, 1990.

Kidd, Chip, ed. *Peanuts: The Art of Charles M. Schulz*. New York: Pantheon, 2001.

Kinnaird, Clark, ed. *Rube Goldberg vs. the Machine Age*. New York: Hastings House, 1968.

Kinnard, Roy. *The Comics Come Alive: A Guide to Comic-Strip Characters in Live-Action Productions*. Metuchen, N.J.: Scarecrow Press, 1991.

Kiyama, Henry (Yoshitaka). *The Four Immigrants Manga: A Japanese Experience in San Francisco, 1904–1924*. Trans. by Frederick L. Schodt. Berkeley, Calif.: Stone Bridge Press, 1999.

Kunzle, David. *The History of the Comic Strip*. Vol. 1: *The Early Comic Strip*. Vol. 2: *The Nineteenth Century*. Berkeley: University of California Press, 1973, 1990.

Kuznets, Lois Rostow. *When Toys Come Alive: Narratives of Animation, Metamorphosis, and Development*. New Haven, Conn.: Yale University Press, 1994.

Lauer, Nik, Leo Taflin, and Christopher M. Lauer. *The Pogopedia: A Codex of the Walt Kelly Pogo Works*. Richfield, Minn.: Spring Hollow Books, 2001.

Lent, John A. *Animation, Caricature, and Gag and Political Cartoons in the United States and Canada: An International Bibliography*. Westport, Conn.: Greenwood Press, 1994.

———. *Comic Art in Africa, Asia, Australia, and Latin America: A Comprehensive International Bibliography*. Westport, Conn.: Greenwood Press, 1996.

———. *Comic Art of Europe: An International Comprehensive Bibliography*. Westport, Conn.: Greenwood Press, 1994.

———. *Comic Books and Comic Strips in the United States: An International Bibliography*. Westport, Conn.: Greenwood Press, 1994.

Lesser, Robert. *A Celebration of Comic Art and Memorabilia*. New York: Hawthorn Books, 1975.

Loria, Jeffrey H. *What's It All About, Charlie Brown?* New York: Holt, Rinehart, and Winston, 1968.

Lowenthal, Leo. *Literature, Popular Culture, and Society*. Englewood Cliffs, N.J.: Prentice-Hall, 1961.

Lupoff, Dick, and Don Thompson, eds. *All in Color for a Dime*. New Rochelle, N.Y.: Arlington House, 1970.

Ma, Sheng-Mei. *The Deathly Embrace: Orientalism and Asian American Identity.* Minneapolis: University of Minnesota Press, 2000.

Mad Magazine. "The Comics." *Mad Super Special,* no. 36 (Fall 1981). New York: E. C., 1981.

Marlette, Doug. *In Your Face: A Cartoonist at Work.* Boston: Houghton Mifflin, 1991.

Marschall, Richard. *America's Great Comic-Strip Artists.* New York: Abbeville Press, 1989.

Marzio, Peter. *Rube Goldberg: His Life and Work.* New York: Harper and Row, 1973.

McDonnell, Patrick, Karen O'Connell, and Georgia Riley de Havenon. *Krazy Kat: The Comic Art of George Herriman.* New York: Harry N. Abrams, 1986.

McGeachy, D. P., III. *The Gospel according to Andy Capp.* Richmond, Va.: John Knox Press, 1973.

Meglin, Nick. *The Art of Humorous Illustration.* New York: Watson-Guptill, 1973.

Mendelson, Lee, and Charles Schulz. *Charlie Brown & Charlie Schulz.* New York: World, 1970.

———. *Happy Birthday, Charlie Brown.* New York: Ballantine Books, 1979.

Morrow, James, and Murray Suid. *Moviemaking Illustrated: The Comicbook Filmbook.* New York: Hayden Book, 1973.

Murrell, William. *A History of American Graphic Humor.* 2 vols. New York: Whitney Museum of American Art and Macmillan, 1933, 1938.

National Lampoon. *The Very Large Book of Comical Funnies.* New York: National Lampoon, 1975.

Nordling, Lee. *Your Career in Comics.* Kansas City, Mo.: Andrews and McMeel, 1995.

O'Sullivan, Judith. *The Art of the Comic Strip.* College Park: University of Maryland, Department of Art, 1971.

———. *The Great American Comic Strip: One Hundred Years of Cartoon Art.* Boston: Little, Brown, 1990.

Perry, George, and Alan Aldridge. *The Penguin Book of Comics.* New York: Penguin Books, 1969. Rev. ed. 1971.

Phelps, Donald. *Reading the Funnies: Looking at Great Cartoonists.* Seattle: Fantagraphic Books, 2001.

Pieper, Gail W. *Understanding the Funnies: Critical Interpretations of Comic Strips.* Lisle, Ill.: Procopian Press, 1997.

Reitberger, Reinhold, and Wolfgang Fuchs. *Comics: Anatomy of a Mass Medium.* Trans. Nadia Fowler. Boston: Little, Brown, 1972.

Robbins, Trina. *A Century of Women Cartoonists.* Northampton, Mass.: Kitchen Sink Press, 1993.

———. *Nell Brinkley and the New Woman in the Early 20th Century.* Jefferson, N.C.: McFarland, 2001.

Robbins, Trina, and Catherine Yronwode. *Women and the Comics.* Guerneville, Calif.: Eclipse Books, 1985.

Roberts, Garyn G. *Dick Tracy and American Culture: Morality and Mythology, Text and Context.* Jefferson, N.C.: McFarland, 1993.

Robinson, Jerry. *The Comics: An Illustrated History of Comic Strip Art.* New York: Putnam's, 1974.

Roebuck, Joan, ed. *The Graphic Art of Charles Schulz*. Oakland, Calif.: Oakland Museum, 1985.

Rookes, Nicholas. *Humor in Art: A Celebration of Visual Wit*. Worcester, Mass.: Davis, 1997.

Satin, Allan D. *A Doonesbury Index: An Index to the Syndicated Daily Newspaper Strip "Doonesbury" by G. B. Trudeau, 1970–1983*. Metuchen, N.J.: Scarecrow Press, 1985.

Schulz, Charles. *Peanuts: A Golden Celebration*. New York: HarperCollins, 1999.

———. *Peanuts Jubilee: My Life and Art with Charlie Brown and Others*. New York: Holt, Rinehart, and Winston, 1975.

———. *You Don't Look 35, Charlie Brown*. New York: Holt, Rinehart, and Winston, 1985.

Schulz, Charles, and R. Smith Kiliper. *Around the World in 45 Years: Charlie Brown's Anniversary Celebration*. Kansas City, Mo.: Andrews and McMeel, 1994.

———. *Charlie Brown, Snoopy and Me*. Garden City, N.Y.: Doubleday, 1980.

Scott, Elaine. *Funny Papers: Behind the Scenes of the Comics*. New York: Morrow Junior Books, 1993.

Scott, Randall W. *Comic Books and Strips: An Information Sourcebook*. Phoenix, Ariz.: Oryx Press, 1989.

———. *Comics Librarianship: A Handbook*. Jefferson, N.C.: McFarland, 1990.

———, ed. *The Comic Art Collection Catalog: An Author, Artist, Title, and Subject Catalog of the Comic Art Collection, Special Collections Division, Michigan State University Libraries*. Westport, Conn.: Greenwood Press, 1993.

Seldes, Gilbert. *The 7 Lively Arts*. New York: Harper and Brothers, 1924. Rev. ed. Layton, Utah: Peregrine Smith and Sagamore Press, 1957.

Sheridan, Martin. *Comics and Their Creators*. Boston: Hale, Cushman, and Flint, 1942.

Short, Robert L. *The Gospel according to Peanuts*. Richmond, Va.: John Knox Press, 1964.

———. *The Parables of Peanuts*. New York: Harper and Row, 1968.

Smith, Bruce. *The History of Little Orphan Annie*. New York: Ballantine Books, 1982.

———. *The World according to Daddy Warbucks: Capitalist Quotations from the Richest Man in the World*. Piscataway, N.J.: New Century, 1982.

Smythe, Reg, and Les Lilley. *The World of Andy Capp*. London: Titan Books, 1990.

Solomon, Norman. *The Trouble with Dilbert: How Corporate Culture Gets the Last Laugh*. Monroe, Maine: Common Courage Press, 1997.

Starlog Group. *100 Years of Comics*. New York: Starlog Group, 1999.

Strickler, Dave. *Syndicated Comic Strips and Artists, 1924–1995: The Complete Index*. Cambria, Calif.: Comics Access, 1995.

Terry, Bridget. *The Popeye Story*. New York: Tom Doherty Associates, 1980.

Theroux, Alexander. *The Enigma of Al Capp*. Seattle: Fantagraphics, 1999.

Thomas, James L., ed. *Cartoons and Comics in the Classroom*. Littleton, Colo.: Libraries Unlimited, 1983.

Thompson, Don, and Dick Lupoff, eds. *The Comic-Book Book*. New Rochelle, N.Y.: Arlington House, 1973.

Trimboli, Giovanni. *Charles M. Schulz: 40 Years, Life and Art*. New York: Pharos Books, 1990.

Vanedoe, Kirk, and Adam Gopnik. *High & Low: Modern Art and Popular Culture*. New York: Museum of Modern Art, 1990.

Van Hise, James. *Calvin & Hobbes, Garfield, Bloom County, Doonesbury and All That Funny Stuff*. Las Vegas: Pioneer Books, 1991.

Walker, Brian. *Barney Google and Snuffy Smith: 75 Years of an American Legend*. Wilton, Conn.: Comicana Books and Ohio State University Libraries, 1994.

Walker, Mort. *Backstage at the Strips*. New York: Mason/Charter, 1975.

———. *The Lexicon of Comicana*. Port Chester, N.Y.: Museum of Cartoon Art, 1980.

———. *Miss Buxley: Sexism in Beetle Bailey?* Bedford, N.Y.: Comicana Books, 1982.

———. *Mort Walker's Private Scrapbook: A Celebration of 50 Years of Comic Excellence*. Kansas City, Mo.: Andrews McMeel, 2001.

Walkerdine, Valerie. *Daddy's Girl: Young Girls and Popular Culture*. Cambridge: Harvard University Press, 1997.

Waugh, Coulton. *The Comics*. New York: Macmillan, 1947. Reprint. Jackson: University Press of Mississippi, 1994.

White, David Manning, and Robert H. Abel, eds. *The Funnies: An American Idiom*. New York: Free Press, 1963.

Wichert, Victor E. *The Dick Tracy Encyclopedia, Oct. 4, 1931–Dec. 25, 1977*. Hopewell, N.J.: Wichert Gallery, 2001.

———. *Names Used in the Dick Tracy Comic Strip*. Hopewell, N.J.: Wichert Gallery, 2000.

Wolfe, Maynard Frank. *Rube Goldberg: Inventions*. New York: Simon and Schuster, 2000.

Wood, Art. *Great Cartoonists and Their Art*. Gretna, La.: Pelican, 1987.

Yoe, Craig. *Weird but True Toon Factoids*. New York: Gramercy Books, 1999.

Anthologies and Reprints

Blackbeard, Bill, ed. *Classic American Comic Strips*. 22 vols. Westport, Conn.: Hyperion Press, 1977. (Includes the following titles: Percy Crosby, *Skippy*; Billy De Beck, *Barney Google*; Clare Dwiggins, *School Days*; Harry Fisher, *A. Mutt*; Frank Godwin, *Connie*; Rube Goldberg, *Bobo Baxter*; George Herriman, *Baron Bean*; George Herriman, *The Family Upstairs*; Harry Hershfield, *Abie the Agent*; Harry Hershfield, *Dauntless Durham of the U.S.A*; Clifford McBride, *Napoleon*; Winsor McCay, *Winsor McCay's Dream Days*; George McManus, *Bringing Up Father*; Gus Mager, *Sherlocko the Monk*; Dick Moores, *Jim Hardy*; Frederick Opper, *Happy Hooligan*; Richard Outcault, *Buster Brown*; Elzie C. Segar, *Thimble Theater, Introducing Popeye*; Cliff Sterrett, *Polly and Her Pals*; George Storm, *Bobby Thatcher*; Harry Tuthill, *The Bungle Family*; and Edgar S. Wheelan, *Minute Movies*.)

Blackbeard, Bill, and Dale Crain, eds. *The Comic Strip Century*. 2 vols. Northampton, Mass.: Kitchen Sink Press, 1995.

Blackbeard, Bill, and Malcolm Whyte, eds. *Great Comic Cats*. San Francisco: Troubedor Press, 1981.

Blackbeard, Bill, and Martin Williams, eds. *The Smithsonian Collection of Newspaper Comics*. Washington, D.C.: Smithsonian Institution Press, 1977.

Breathed, Berke. *Billy and the Boingers Bootleg*. Boston: Little, Brown, 1987.

———. *Bloom County*. Boston: Little, Brown, 1983.

———. *Bloom County Babylon*. Boston: Little, Brown, 1986.

———. *Penguin Dreams and Stranger Things*. Boston: Little, Brown, 1985.

———. *Tales Too Ticklish to Tell*. Boston: Little, Brown, 1988.

———. *Toons for Our Times*. Boston: Little, Brown, 1984.

Briggs, Clare. *When a Feller Needs a Friend and Other Favorite Cartoons*. New York: Dover, 1975.

Browne, Dik. *The Best of Hagar*. Bedford, N.Y.: Comicana Books, 1986.

Bushmiller, Emie. *The Best of Emie Bushmiller's Nancy*. Ed. Brian Walker. Bedford, N.Y.: Comicana Books, 1988.

Caniff, Milton. *The Complete Dickie Dare*. Agoura, Calif.: Fantagraphics Books, 1986.

———. *Male Call*. Princeton, Wis.: Kitchen Sink Press, 1987.

———. *Milton Caniff's Steve Canyon*. Princeton, Wis.: Kitchen Sink Press, 1983– .

———. *Terry and the Pirates*. Franklin Square, N.Y.: Nostalgia Press, 1970.

———. *Terry and the Pirates*. 12 vols. New York: Nantier-Beall-Minoustchine, 1984–1987.

———. *Terry and the Pirates Color Sundays*. 12 vols. New York: Nantier-Beall-Minoustchine, 1990–1993.

Capp, Al. *The Best of Li'l Abner*. New York: Holt, Rinehart, and Winston, 1978.

———. *Li'l Abner*. 27 vols. Princeton, Wis.: Kitchen Sink Press, 1988–1998.

Crane, Roy. *Wash Tubbs and Captain Easy*. 18 vols. New York: Nantier-Beall-Minoustchine, 1987–1991.

Craven, Thomas, ed. *Cartoon Cavalcade*. New York: Simon and Schuster, 1943.

Crouch, Bill, ed. *Dick Tracy: America's Most Famous Detective*. Secaucus, N.J.: Citadel Press, 1987.

Crumb, Robert. *The Complete Crumb Comics*. Agoura, Calif.: Fantagraphics Books, 1987– .

———. *Fritz the Cat*. New York: Ballantine Books, 1969.

Davis, Jim. *Garfield Treasury*. New York: Ballantine Books, 1982.

———. *The Second Garfield Treasury*. New York: Ballantine Books, 1983.

Dille, Robert C., ed. *The Collected Works of Buck Rogers in the 25th Century*. New York: Chelsea House, 1969. Rev. ed., 1977.

Dirks, Rudolph. *The Katzenjammer Kids*. New York: Dover, 1974.

Falk, Lee, and Phil Davis. *Mandrake the Magician*. Franklin Square, N.Y.: Nostalgia Press, 1970.

Falk, Lee, and Ray Moore. *The Phantom*. Franklin Square, N.Y.: Nostalgia Press, 1969.

Feininger, Lyonel. *The Comic Strip Art of Lyonel Feininger*. Ed. Bill Blackbeard. Northampton, Mass.: Kitchen Sink Press, 1994.

Fleischer, Max. *Betty Boop*. New York: Avon Books, 1975.

Foster, Harold. *Prince Valiant*. 2 vols. Wayne, N.J.: Manuscript Press, 1982–1984.

———. *Prince Valiant*. 40 vols. Seattle: Fantagraphics Books, 1985–2000.

―――. *Prince Valiant Companions in Adventure*. Franklin Square, N.Y.: Nostalgia Press, 1974.

―――. *Prince Valiant in the Days of King Arthur*. Franklin Square, N.Y.: Nostalgia Press, 1974.

Fox, Fontaine. *Toonerville Trolley*. New York: Scribner's, 1972.

Galewitz, Herb, ed. *Great Comics Syndicated by the New York Daily News and Chicago Tribune*. New York: Crown, 1972.

Garner, Philip, ed. *Rube Goldberg: A Retrospective*. New York: Delilah Books, 1983.

Gilmore, Donald H. [pseud.]. *Sex in Comics*. 4 vols. San Diego: Greenleaf Classics, 1971.

Gould, Chester. *The Celebrated Cases of Dick Tracy, 1931–1951*. New York: Chelsea House, 1970.

―――. *Dick Tracy, the Thirties, Tommy Guns, and Hard Times*. New York: Chelsea House, 1978.

Gray, Harold. *Arf! The Life and Hard Times of Little Orphan Annie*. New Rochelle, N.Y.: Arlington House, 1970.

―――. *Little Orphan Annie*. Agoura, Calif.: Fantagraphic Books, 1987–   .

Guisewite, Cathy. *The Cathy Chronicles*. Kansas City, Mo.: Sheed, Andrews, and McMeel, 1978.

Herriman, George. *Krazy and Ignatz: The Complete Kat Comics*. Forestville, Calif.: Eclipse Books, 1988–   .

―――. *Krazy Kat*. New York: Henry Holt, 1946.

―――. *Krazy Kat*. New York: Grosset and Dunlap-Madison Square Press, 1969.

Hogarth, Burn. *Jungle Tales of Tarzan*. New York: Watson-Guptill, 1976.

―――. *Tarzan of the Apes*. New York: Watson-Guptill, 1972.

Holbrook, Bill. *On the Fastrack*. New York: Putnam's, 1985.

Howard, Greg. *Sally Forth*. New York: Fawcett Columbine-Ballantine Books, 1987.

Johnson, Crockett [David Johnson Leisk]. *Barnaby*. New York: Henry Holt, 1943.

―――. *Barnaby*. 6 vols. New York: Ballantine Books, 1985–1986.

Kane, Brian M. *Hal Foster: Prince of Illustrators*. Lebanon, N.J.: Vanguard Productions, 2001.

Keller, Charles. *The Best of Rube Goldberg*. Englewood Cliffs, N.J.: Prentice-Hall, 1979.

Kelly, Walt. *The Best of Pogo*. Ed. Mrs. Walt Kelly and Bill Crouch. New York: Simon and Schuster, 1982.

―――. *Outrageously Pogo*. New York: Simon and Schuster, 1985.

―――. *Pluperfect Pogo*. New York: Simon and Schuster, 1987.

―――. *Pogo Even Better*. New York: Simon and Schuster, 1984.

Kirkman, Rick, and Jerry Scott. *Butt-Naked Baby Blues*. Kansas City, Mo.: Andrews McMeel, 2001.

Lardner, Ring. *Ring Lardner's You Know Me Al*. New York: Harcourt Brace Jovanovich, 1979.

Larson, Gary. *The Far Side Gallery*. Kansas City, Mo.: Andrews, McMeel, and Parker, 1984.

―――. *The Far Side Gallery 2*. Kansas City, Mo.: Andrews, McMeel, and Parker, 1986.

―――. *The Far Side Gallery 3*. Kansas City, Mo.: Andrews and McMeel, 1988.

————. *The Far Side Gallery 4*. Kansas City, Mo.: Andrews and McMeel, 1993.

————. *The Far Side Gallery 5*. Kansas City, Mo.: Andrews and McMeel, 1995.

————. *Prehistory at the Far Side: A Tenth Anniversary Exhibit*. Kansas City, Mo.: Andrews McMeel, 1989.

Lee, Stan. *The Best of Spider-Man*. New York: Ballantine Books, 1986.

MacNelly, Jeff. *The Very First Shoe Book*. New York: Avon Books, 1978 and subsequent anthologies.

Marlette, Doug. *Even White Boys Get the Blues: Kudzu's First Ten Years*. New York: Crown, 1992.

————. *Kudzu*. New York: Ballantine Books, 1982. And subsequent anthologies.

McCay, Winsor. *The Best of Little Nemo in Slumberland*. Ed. Richard Marschall. New York: Stewart, Tabori, and Chang, 1997.

————. *Daydreams and Nightmares: The Fantastic Visions of Winsor McCay*. Ed. Richard Marschall. Westlake Village, Calif.: Fantagraphics Books, 1988.

————. *Dreams of the Rarebit Fiend*. New York: Dover, 1973.

————. *Little Nemo*. Franklin Square, N.Y.: Nostalgia Press, 1972, Dover, 1976.

————. *Little Nemo—1905–1906*. Franklin Square, N.Y.: Nostalgia Press, 1972.

————. *Little Nemo, 1905–1914*. Ed. Bill Blackbeard. New York: Evergreen and Benedict Taschen Verlag GmbH, 2000.

————. *Little Nemo in the Palace of Ice and Further Adventures*. New York: Dover, 1976.

McDonnell, Patrick. *Mutts*. Kansas City, Mo.: Andrews McMeel, 1996. And subsequent anthologies.

McManus, George. *Bringing Up Father*. New York: Scribner's, 1973.

————. *Jiggs Is Back*. Berkeley, Calif.: Celtic Book, 1986.

Messner, Otto. *Nine Lives to Live: A Classic Felix Celebration*. Ed. David Gerstein. Seattle: Fantagraphics Books, 1996.

Moores, Dick. *Gasoline Alley*. New York: Avon Books, 1976.

Nostalgia Comics. 6 vols. Franklin Square, N.Y.: Nostalgia Press, 1971–1974.

Outcault, Richard F. *Buster Brown*. New York: Dover, 1974.

Patton, Jack, and John Rosenfield Jr. *Texas History Movies*. Collector's Limited Ed. Dallas: Pepper Jones Martinez, 1970.

————. *Texas History Movies*. Abridged and rev. Dallas: Pepper Jones Martinez, 1985.

————. *Texas History Movies*. Abridged and rev. Austin: Texas Historical Association, 1986.

Raymond, Alex. *Flash Gordon*. Franklin Square, N.Y.: Nostalgia Press, 1967.

————. *Flash Gordon in the Planet Mongo*. Franklin Square, N.Y.: Nostalgia Press, 1974.

————. *Flash Gordon in the Underwater World of Mongo*. Franklin Square, N.Y.: Nostalgia Press, 1974.

————. *Flash Gordon into the Water of Mongo*. Franklin Square, N.Y.: Nostalgia Press, 1971.

Ripley, Robert L. *Ripley's Giant Believe It or Not!* New York: Warren Books, 1976.

Rosendahl, Peter J. *Han Ola og han Per*. Ed. Joan N. Buckley and Einar Haugen. Oslo: Universitetsforlaget, 1984.

Schulz, Charles. *Peanuts Treasury*. New York: Holt, Rinehart, and Winston, 1968.

————. *The Snoopy Festival*. New York: Holt, Rinehart, and Winston, 1974.

Scott, Jerry, and Jim Borgman. *Big Honkin' Zits*. Kansas City, Mo.: Andrews McMeel, 2001.

Segar, Elzie C. *The Complete E. C. Segar Popeye*. Agoura, Calif.: Fantagraphics Books, 1984–   .

Smith, Sidney. *The Gumps*. New York: Scribner's, 1974.

Trudeau, G. B. *The Bundled Doonesbury: A Pre-Millenial Anthology*. Kansas City, Mo.: Andrews McMeel, 1998.

———. *Doonesbury*. New York: McGraw-Hill, 1971. And subsequent anthologies.

———. *The Doonesbury Chronicles*. New York: Holt, Rinehart, and Winston, 1975.

———. *Doonesbury Deluxe*. New York: Holt, Rinehart, and Winston, 1987.

———. *Doonesbury Dossier*. New York: Holt, Rinehart, and Winston, 1984.

———. *Doonesbury's Greatest Hits*. New York: Holt, Rinehart, and Winston, 1978.

———. *Flashbacks: Twenty-Five Years of Doonesbury*. Kansas City, Mo.: Andrews McMeel, 1995.

———. *The People's Doonesbury*. New York: Holt, Rinehart, and Winston, 1981.

Unger, Jim. *The 1st Treasury of Herman*. Kansas City, Mo.: Andrews and McMeel, 1979. And subsequent anthologies.

Walker, Mort. *Beetle Bailey: Still Lazy after All These Years*. New York: Nautier-Beall-Minoustchine, 1999.

———. *The Best of Beetle Bailey*. Bedford, N.Y.: Comicana Books, 1984.

———. *The Best of Hi and Lois*. Bedford, N.Y.: Comicana Books, 1986.

———. *50 Years of Beetle Bailey*. New York: Nautier-Beaull-Minoustchine, 2000.

Watterson, Bill. *The Authoritative Calvin and Hobbes*. Kansas City, Mo.: Andrews and McMeel, 1990.

———. *Calvin and Hobbes*. Kansas City, Mo.: Andrews, McMeel, and Parker, 1985.

———. *The Calvin and Hobbes Tenth Anniversary Book*. Kansas City, Mo.: Andrews and McMeel, 1995.

———. *The Essential Calvin and Hobbes*. Kansas City, Mo.: Andrews and McMeel, 1988.

———. *Indispensable Calvin and Hobbes*. Kansas City, Mo.: Andrews and McMeel, 1992.

———. *Something under the Bed Is Drooling*. Kansas City, Mo.: Andrews and McMeel, 1988.

Willard, Frank. *Moon Mullins: Two Adventures*. New York: Dover, 1976.

Young, Dean, and Rick Marschall. *Blondie and Dagwood's America*. New York: Harper and Row, 1981.

Ziehm, Howard. *Golf in the Comic Strips*. Santa Monica, Calif.: General Publishing Group, 1997.

Periodicals

Cartoonist Profiles. Fairfield, Conn.: 1969–   .

Comics Buyer's Guide. Iola, Wis.: 1971–   .

Comics Journal. Seattle, 1977–   .

Hogan's Alley: The Magazine of the Cartoon Arts. Atlanta, Ga., 1995–   .

Inks: Cartoon and Comic Art Studies. Columbus, Ohio, 1994–1997.

International Journal of Comic Art. Drexel Hill, Pa., 1999–   .

Nemo: The Classic Comics Library. Seattle, 1983–1993.

COMPUTERS AND THE DIGITAL AGE

Ray Helton

"Mainframes," "workstations," "PCs," "desktops," "portables"—these terms describe types of computers. They come in a variety of sizes from mainframes that fill large rooms to devices small enough to fit in the palm of a hand. They have changed the way that society lives, learns, works, and plays. Traditional activities such as reading, exercising, and hobbies are taking on new dimensions because of computers and the Internet, a global network connecting millions of computers. Many people would prefer to spend Saturday nights in on-line chat rooms rather than talking to family and friends. While this behavior may sound cold and impersonal to some, Internet communication can offer companionship to the elderly or the lonely. Opportunity abounds for those who wish to debate the advantages and disadvantages of this phenomenon. The fact remains that technology creates new and different ways to do things. For example, within an average family, the digital technology exists to plan meals, use music tutorials to practice piano scales, plan activities using scheduling software, and capture family moments using digital cameras to share the pictures with relatives worldwide on the family Web site. As a stand-alone device, the computer is merely a tool. However, when looking beyond its technical structure, one may see how computers and the Internet are reshaping society's basic structure.

The Internet is a composite of computers, telecommunication networks, and electronic information. It is a worldwide broadcasting mechanism, a way to disseminate information, and a medium for collaboration and interaction among people and their computers without regard for geographic location. The culmination of its impact on popular culture has yet to be measured because it is so far-reaching. Digital cyberspace can be described as every place yet no place, because it has no geographic limitations. It is a virtual space that has been described as the new frontier. Phrases like "virtual reality," "cyberspace," "information superhighway," "information age," and "digital age" are often used in an attempt to categorize what is happening. Manuel Castells, a University of California (UC)-

Berkeley sociologist, offers one explanation of the significance of this period. In the digital new world, Castells sees the basic structure of society as far-flung networks—not the individual companies, governments, and institutions that defined the nineteenth-century power grid.

Technology historians have placed the societal changes brought on by computers and the Internet on the same scale as those that led to the Industrial Revolution, when machines replaced hand tools and society's basic structure was transformed. Digital is a process by which information is supplied and stored in the form of a series of binary digits. Digital information can include pictures, sound, and animation and can be accessed using computers and networks. Nicholas Negroponte, Massachusetts Institute of Technology (MIT) professor and author of *Being Digital*, describes the digital age as a force that cannot be denied or stopped. He outlines four powerful qualities of the digital age that he believes will result in its ultimate triumph: decentralizing, globalizing, harmonizing, and empowering.

In addition to offering new and different ways of doing things, the digital age also raises issues and poses challenges. Privacy, ethics, literacy, and economics are not new societal issues, but they have added dimension in the digital age. How will individuals who lack the economic means or access to telecommunications infrastructure fare in the digital age? Who owns the Internet? Are on-line conversations private? There is also a host of challenges in coping with the abundance of information that is created and distributed as a result of digital technologies. Experience with the year 2000—the problem of the millennium bug also known as Y2K—demonstrated the extent to which computer technology has penetrated the social fabric and our vulnerability. Many computers, appliances, and devices that use computer technology were not designed to recognize the year 2000 as a date. The Y2K challenge was and still is more than a technical issue; it has the potential to affect the lives of millions of people worldwide. On a large scale, programs and databases on mainframe computers at banks, hospitals, utility companies, airlines, credit agencies, and governmental agencies faced the possibility of not being able to distinguish between January 1, 2000, and January 1, 1900, with potentially serious, even disastrous repercussions. On a smaller scale some household appliances needed replacing because internal chips that control timers could not recognize the year 2000. Concerns over Y2K created a new industry. Millennium clocks, jewelry, clothing, and novelty items were sold in most retail stores. Computer programmers with COBOL and FORTRAN experience came out of retirement and commanded high salaries as consultants to help find solutions. Nightly newscasts and newspaper stories heightened public concern with survival suggestions.

This chapter provides an overview of the evolution of computing and the resulting digital age events that have influenced popular culture. Tremendous developments in this topic area make it nearly impossible to discuss it at length within the limited space of this chapter. A decision was made to review the digital age within the areas of virtual reality, education, commerce, democracy, and ethics. Many of the sources in this chapter are available on the Internet. Although electronic addresses have been provided, it is possible, given the changing nature of the Internet, that some of the addresses will change or soon may no longer exist.

Sponsoring organizations have been provided to assist readers seeking to locate the information at a future time.

HISTORICAL OUTLINE

Popular consciousness of computers began with science fiction. For example, the handheld communicators first introduced on the popular 1970s television series *Star Trek* may be compared to cellular phones and palm-sized computers of the 1990s. Laser ray guns were featured in science fiction long before lasers were used for surgery and industry in the 1990s. Computers once portrayed as futuristic in literature and films of the 1940s and 1950s became common realities present in homes and offices. Arthur C. Clarke and Stanley Kubrick shared an Oscar nomination in 1968 for the movie *2001: A Space Odyssey*. HAL, the film's starring computer, provided an intelligent, yet eerie, vision of human–computer interaction. Computers became increasingly visible in television programs and films. Later films such as *Blade Runner*, *RoboCop*, *The Terminator*, and *Terminator II* enticed the public. In the 1990s film plots became less futuristic by focusing more on the characters and less on the technology. For example, *The Net*, a 1997 film, featured a female programmer who solves a computer espionage case against an evil hacker. The 1998 release of *You've Got Mail* is an E-mail love story. Science fiction continued to evolve, with a new form called cyberpunk becoming popular in the 1980s. In 1975 John Brunner wrote *Shockwave Rider*, which inspired a new generation of computer enthusiasts, known as hackers.

To gain an in-depth understanding of the evolution of computers into popular culture, it is necessary to look beyond science fiction. Several comprehensive reference sources chronicle events and profile individual contributions. The *Encyclopedia of Computer Science and Engineering*, edited by Anthony Ralston, is one such source. Ralston provides the following account of the earliest events in computer history. Early computers have been traced to the abacus, which emerged over 5,000 years ago. However, the beginnings of modern computers can be attributed to the work of English mathematics professor Charles Babbage (1791–1871). Babbage first designed a machine to perform differential equations called the difference engine. Later, Babbage began work on the first general-purpose computer, called the analytical engine. Babbage's assistant, Augusta Ada King, countess of Lovelace (1815–1842) and daughter of English poet Lord Byron, was instrumental in the machine's design. She revised plans for the machine, secured funding from the British government, and promoted it to the public. Lady Lovelace's understanding of the machine allowed her to create instruction routines to be fed into the computer, making her the first female computer programmer. The U.S. Defense Department named a programming language ADA in her honor in the 1980s.

The Jacquard loom is thought to be the source of American inventor Herman Hollerith's idea of using punched cards to represent logical and numerical data. Developed for use in the 1890 U.S. National Census, his system, incorporating hand-operated tabulating machines and sorters, was highly successful and spread quickly to other countries. After a dispute with Hollerith, the Census Bureau developed a new tabulating system for the 1910 census involving mechanical sensing of card perforations. James Powers, lead engineer for the project, eventually

Students working on computer at an after-school program. © Skjold Photographs

left the Census Bureau to form his own company, which later became a part of Remington Rand. Hollerith's company merged with two others to become the Computing-Tabulating-Recording Company, which changed its name in 1924 to International Business Machines Corporation, better known as IBM. Punch cards were used for data processing until the 1960s.

Computers didn't play a prominent role in society until the 1940s. World War II hastened the development of computers. Howard Aiken, a Harvard engineer, approached IBM with a proposal for a large-scale calculator built from the mechanical and electromechanical devices that were used for punched card machines. The machine was called the Mark I and was described as being half the size of a football field and containing 500 miles of wiring. Historians believe that the most influential line of development during this time occurred at the University of Pennsylvania in the work of John Mauchly, J. Pepper Eckert, and their colleagues in 1943. This collaboration resulted in the development of the electronic numerical integrator and computer (ENIAC). ENIAC was initially intended for ballistics calculations but ended up being more general-purpose. ENIAC was 1,000 times faster than Mark I. In the mid-1940s John von Neumann joined the University of Pennsylvania team and designed the electronic discrete variable automatic computer (EDVAC). EDVAC was more economical to operate and had a larger internal memory than ENIAC. These computers were known as first-generation computers and can be characterized by the fact that each computer had a different machine language that told it how to operate.

By 1948, the invention of the transistor greatly changed the computer's development. The transistor replaced the large, cumbersome vacuum tube in televisions, radios, and computers. As a result, the size of electronic machinery began to shrink. The transistor was at work in the computer by 1956. Coupled with early advances in magnetic-core memory, transistors led to second-generation computers that were smaller, faster, more reliable, and more energy-efficient than their predecessors. The first large-scale machines to take advantage of this transistor technology were early supercomputers, Stretch by IBM and LARC by Sperry-Rand. These computers, both developed for atomic energy laboratories, could handle an enormous amount of data, a capability much in demand by atomic scientists. The machines were expensive and thought by many to be too powerful for the business sector.

From the early 1960s to the middle 1970s there were a number of commercially successful second-generation computers produced by Burroughs, Control Data, Honeywell, IBM, and Sperry-Rand. They were used in businesses, universities, and government agencies. These computers remained too expensive for mass purchase. However, the ability to store programs and programming languages made them relatively more affordable and paved the way for the development of computers for small business and personal use. The Intel 4004 chip, developed in 1971, placed all of the components of a computer (central processing unit, memory, and input and output controls) on a minuscule chip. Soon everyday household appliances such as microwave ovens, television sets, videocassette recorders, and automobiles with electronic fuel injection incorporated microprocessor technology.

The age of personal computing had arrived. Computers were no longer developed exclusively for large business or government contracts. The January 1975 cover of *Popular Electronics* featured an Altair computer kit on its cover. There was great demand for the Altair, and thousands were sold. Because early computer kits like the Altair were difficult to build, maintain, and operate, owners joined forces to form clubs or "users groups." The first users group, the Homebrew Club, was founded in March 1975. Located in the Santa Clara Valley south of San Francisco, now known as "Silicon Valley," the Homebrew Club produced several famous computer manufacturers. Steve Jobs and Steve Wozniak, members of the Homebrew Club, designed and produced the Apple I electronic circuit board, which served as a foundation for Apple Computers. Network computers or "dumb terminals" were being used in banks, insurance companies, schools, and libraries. Many of the first commercial databases were introduced in the early 1970s. Large repositories of information were stored on mainframe computers and accessed using dumb terminals and modems. The information industry emerged with online services from companies like Lockheed-Dialog and the Bibliographic Retrieval Service. The databases provided by these companies provided researchers with the ability to search for information on-line.

By the mid-1970s, computer manufacturers sought to bring computers to general consumers. These minicomputers came complete with "user-friendly" software packages that offered nontechnical users a variety of applications like word processing and spreadsheet programs. Pioneers in this field were Commodore, Radio Shack, and Apple Computers. The Boston Computer Society, founded in 1977 by Jonathan Rotenberg when he was thirteen years old, is described as the oldest and largest computer group in the world. Computer conferences and trade shows also became more prevalent.

One of the most prominent computer companies to emerge from the mid-1970s is Microsoft. Created in 1975 by Bill Gates and Paul Allen, Microsoft grew to become the world's largest designer of operating systems and software applications for personal computers. Gates and Allen, Harvard students and programming geniuses, designed the first programming language for the Altair. Microsoft BASIC was introduced and was followed up quickly with a disk management program called DiskBASIC. Many of Microsoft's first customers were Fortune 500 companies. By the end of 1976, Gates dropped out of Harvard and devoted his full attention to Microsoft. As new microprocessors entered the market, business grew for Microsoft. FORTRAN and COBOL programming languages were released in 1977 and 1978. The strategic release of these languages made Microsoft the leading distributor for microcomputer languages. The next new development was the creation of the Microsoft disk operating system, or MS-DOS. MS-DOS is thought to be one of the most important products in computer history. The release of the Windows operating system, which uses a graphical interface instead of text commands, and the release of Microsoft Word have made Microsoft the most prominent software company in the world. Microsoft's meteoric rise in the computing industry has not been without criticism. Microsoft's aggressive marketing strategy combined with its strong market dominance has resulted in concerns by market analysts and lawsuits by competitors. The *U.S. v. Microsoft* case raised serious issues. The federal government and nineteen states charged Microsoft with a range of abuses, including the alleged monopolization of the market for operating systems (OS) for personal computers by Windows, anticompetitive bundling of Internet Explorer with Windows, and various other exclusionary and anticompetitive acts against competitors and buyers. In December 1999, U.S. District Court judge Thomas Penfield Jackson issued his far-reaching "findings of fact" that found for the plaintiffs in almost all the allegations. Though a settlement has not been reached, the outcome of this case is likely to have implications on the entire computer industry because of the risk of government-mandated antitrust intervention.

In addition to Microsoft, there were other hardware and software giants. IBM introduced its microcomputer, also known as the personal computer, or PC, in 1981. In direct competition with IBM's PC was Apple's Macintosh line, introduced in 1984. Notable for its user-friendly design, the Macintosh offered an operating system that allowed users to move screen icons instead of typing instructions. Users controlled the screen cursor using a mouse, a device that mimicked the movement of one's hand on the computer screen.

In addition to strong computer sales, the early 1980s brought arcade video games to personal computers in the form of *Pacman*, *Donkey Kong*, *Space Invaders*, and *Asteroids*. Home video game systems such as the Atari 2600 created consumer interest in sophisticated, programmable home computers. Books, magazines, and software publication sales emerged as new and viable industries as the result of the popularity of computers. Books on microcomputers and related subjects grew into the largest single nonfiction area in publishing. Computer terminology became widely used as words like "chip," known as a snack food, also became known as a storage device; and "mouse," known as a small rodent, also became known as a device for moving around the computer screen.

As computers became smaller and more powerful, they were linked together, or networked. Networked computers allowed single computers to form electronic co-ops. Using direct wiring, called a local area network (LAN), these networks could reach enormous proportions called wide area networks (WAN). Early networks formed the foundation for the Internet. The Internet, a global web of computer circuitry, links computers worldwide into a single network. The U.S. Defense Advanced Research Projects Agency (DARPA) initiated a communications research project that resulted in the Internet. Primary support for the Internet has come from the U.S. government through federally funded research. During the late 1980s Internet use increased and expanded to include international and commercial organizations. In 1989 researchers at the European Organization for Nuclear Research (CERN, the acronym for the organization in French) created a worldwide network linking several supercomputers to facilitate access to data by physicists and other scientists via the Internet. This network evolved into the World Wide Web, created by Tim Berners-Lee, a physicist at CERN. Detailed historical information on the Internet and the Web can be found on the *World Wide Web Consortia* (W3C) Web site. W3C is led by Berners-Lee and provides standards for the Web. Unlike other information on the Internet, the Web contains hypermedia, that is, sound, text, graphics, animation, and video. It contains documents and pages that are linked together by a computer language called hypertext markup language. The global nature of the Web presents a "one world" concept. In 1938 H. G. Wells wrote *World Brain*, a book that in many ways anticipated the Internet and the Web. Wells predicted microscopic libraries in which a photograph of every important book and document in the world would be stored and made available to students. He also was an advocate for a "permanent world encyclopaedia" that would serve as a world brain by providing a means for storing and distributing information.

Newspapers and magazines helped create more public awareness of the Internet and the Web during the 1992 U.S. presidential election. Vice presidential candidate Al Gore made networks an administrative priority of the campaign and helped make the phrase "information superhighway" a metaphor for the Internet. During the first year of the Clinton–Gore administration, a task force was created, and funds were allocated to create the National Information Infrastructure (NII).

Describing the Web is a daunting task because in a sense it is a chameleon. Its constant changes allow it to reflect the good and the bad about society. The Web can be labeled a new type of information system, but its influence on society and popular culture makes it a new form of human communication. The World Wide Web is the fastest growing part of the Internet. It has redefined and transformed communication, research, entertainment, and commerce. It is always changing, growing, and reinventing itself. It is difficult to judge the size of the Internet. Monthly growth statistics can be found on the Internic Web site. The Internic is an organization that registers Web domain names. However, no one organization or agency governs the Internet or the Web. It provides a platform for free speech. Anyone can publish or discuss anything on the Internet at anytime. Young children and senior citizens are creating Web sites based on hobbies and special interests. Social organizations as well as racist and hate organizations are using the

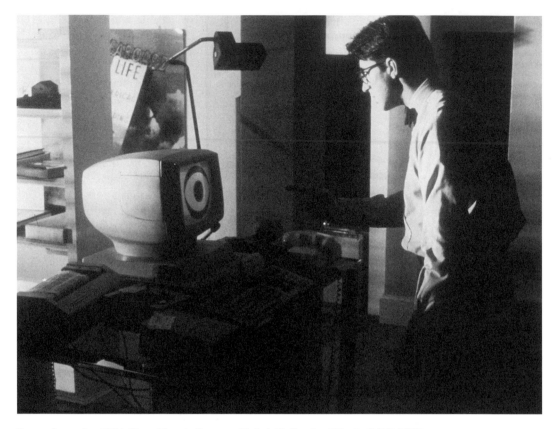

Scene from the 1984 film, *Electric Dreams*. Kobal Collection/Virgin/MGM/UA

Web to recruit members and to share information on their mission. Sexually explicit information is available in the form of magazines and Web sites created by individuals. It is used for teaching, learning, recreation, communication, business, and publishing. All of the information is available twenty-four hours a day and is increasing at a rate that is difficult to measure. Much of the information on the Web becomes obsolete or is removed by the individual who created the site, making the Web a dynamic and ever-changing environment.

Connectivity on such a broad scale has significant implications for popular culture. In the last few years there have been tens of thousands of news stories about the Web and the Internet. Scores of books, newsletters, conferences, workshops, and several television shows have been devoted to the topic. Many newspapers contain regular columns that feature tips, techniques, and favorite Web sites, all aimed at creating more awareness within the general public. Television commercials promote Internet services and its applications. A popular series of AT&T commercials features family scenarios that depict how the Internet can bring families together. Rural and remote communities as well as urban neighborhoods are receiving funding to pay for the telecommunications infrastructure needed to access the Internet. They are using it to inform and to reform. Connectivity can also have a less than positive side. Research studies on the social impact of the Web have shown that the more time people spend on-line, the more isolated they become. There is also concern over the number of minorities that are not using the Internet. A discussion on the social impact of computers and the Internet is presented in the History and Criticism section of this chapter.

REFERENCE WORKS

Traditionally, the term "reference work" has referred to printed materials designed to find specific items of information, rather than read cover to cover. While very few printed reference works focus solely on computers in popular culture, there are resources that provide general information on computers and the Internet. Printed dictionaries, encyclopedias, and directories are being produced in electronic format and distributed on CD-ROM, and the Internet has created virtual libraries. The Internet has expanded the definition of a reference source to include electronic guides, technical documentation, search engines, and research databases. A continually growing number of Internet guides and Web "how-to" books are being published. Most of these books follow a similar format and aim to instruct those who are new users in the best ways of accessing and using the Web. Of special note in this category is the _____ for Dummies series of self-help books written by Levine and Young (DOS for Dummies, Internet for Dummies, Windows for Dummies, and the like). There has also been a proliferation of Internet publications that target certain industries, occupations, and populations. The U.S. government is now distributing the majority of its information in electronic format. New reference guides have been written that point to government information on the Web. A number of printed reference works direct researchers to specific areas of information on the Web. It should be noted, however, that print Internet reference works become dated quickly because of the dynamic nature of the Web. The following print and electronic resources have been found to be useful when searching for information on computers and the Internet.

Print Resources

No single book addresses computers or the digital age in popular culture. However, the following books provide information on the history, people, and technologies that have had the most impact on the digital age:

Historical Dictionary of Data Processing by James Cortada.

Second Bibliographic Guide to the History of Computing, Computers, and the Information Processing Industry, comp. James W. Cortada.

Encyclopedia of Computer Science and Technology, ed. Jack Belzer, Albert G. Holzman, and Allen Kent.

Macmillan Encyclopedia of Computers.

Dictionary of Computer Terms by Douglas Downing.

The Software Encyclopedia.

A History of Computing Technology by Michael R. Williams.

Government Information on the Internet (2nd ed.) by Greg R. Notess.

Government Online by Max Lent.

American Computer Pioneers by Mary Northrup.

A History of Modern Computing by Paul E. Ceruzzi.

ELECTRONIC INFORMATION RESOURCES

Printed reference materials, such as dictionaries, indexes, and encyclopedias, can now be accessed on the Web using personal computers. Access to electronic information, especially reference materials, has had a great impact on teaching and learning. Among the key benefits of electronic information are broader access to information, individualized learning, and the fact that education can occur at any time and any place. The following Web sites contain information that may be valuable to anyone seeking to learn more about computers and the digital age. Due to the dynamic nature of the Web, users should consider accuracy, authority, and currency when using electronic information.

Computer Science Bibliographies. Collected bibliographies of scientific literature on computer science from a variety of sources. Compiled by subject experts worldwide, the collection is updated monthly and contains more than 930,000 references to journal articles, conference papers, and technical reports: http://liinwww.ira.uka.de/bibliography/index.html

HCI Bibliography: Human-Computer Interaction Publications and Resources. An on-line bibliography of human-computer interaction resources sponsored by the Association for Computing Machinery (ACM): http://www.acm.org/hcibib/

Electronic Directories

eBLAST: Encyclopædia Britannica's Internet Guide. Sponsored by Encyclopedia Britannica: http://www.eblast.com

Internet Service Providers Catalog. Sponsored by Net USA: http://www.netusa.net/ISP/

Microcomputer Abstracts. Available on CD-ROM and commercial database. Produced by Learned Information

Usenet Addresses Services. Provides addresses for electronic discussion lists. Sponsored by MIT: http://usenet-addresses.mit.edu/

Electronic Dictionaries and Encyclopedias

Dictionary of Hardware and Computing Terms. Published in 1996 by O'Reilly Publishing: http://www.ora.com/reference/dictionary/

Tech Encyclopedia. Provides definitions for more than 11,000 computer terms and concepts. Sponsored by CMPnet: http://www.techweb.com/encyclopedia/

Webopedia. An on-line dictionary and index for computer technology: http://www.webopedia.com/

Search Engines

The Web may appear to be a visual medium, but it is indexed textually. A search engine is a program that searches Web pages or documents for specified keywords and returns a list of the documents where the keywords were found. The following resources are a sampling of the types of search engines available for use.

All-in-One Search Page. Allows users to enter a keyword and simultaneously search it in a number of search engines: http://www.AllOneSearch.com/

Search Engine Showdown. A collection of summaries, reviews, statistics, and comparisons about the top Internet search engines: http://www.notess.com/search/

Search Engine Watch. Provides comparative summaries of Web search engines: http://www.searchenginewatch.com/

Yahoo! Search Engine. Software that searches the Web for information based on some criteria provided by the user: http://www.yahoo.com

Alta Vista Search Engine. Software that searches the Web for information based on some criteria provided by the user:http://www.altavista.com

Electronic Indexes

Indexes are another way to organize and access information on the Web. There are indexes on the Web on virtually any topic. The following sites guide users to information on the Web and the Internet.

Cyberstacks. An integrated collection of significant Web and other Internet resources categorized using the Library of Congress classification scheme. Sponsored by Iowa State University: http://www.public.iastate.edu/~CYBERSTACKS/

Librarians' Guide to the Internet. A searchable, annotated subject directory of more than 4,600 Internet resources selected and evaluated by librarians for their usefulness. Created in 1990 by reference librarian Carole Leita: http://sunsite.berkeley.edu/InternetIndex/

Electronic Magazines

Many magazines and journals related to the Internet and computers are available in electronic form. Some are available in both print and electronic formats. While many of the trade publications contain numerous advertisements, they also contain useful product reviews, industry news, and announcements. The following sites represent a small segment of available computer industry electronic magazines.

Netsurfer Digest: http://www.netsurf.com/nsd/index.html

Online, Inc.: http://www.onlineinc.com/

The Scout Report: http://scout.cs.wisc.edu/scout/report/

RESEARCH COLLECTIONS

No research collections are specifically devoted to computers and the Internet in popular culture. However, libraries at many universities have significant research collections related to computing and technology. Major collections are available at the Massachusetts Institute of Technology, Harvard University, Carnegie-Mellon University, and Stanford University. Private organizations, businesses, and individuals are creating physical museums and Web sites devoted to the history of computing and technology. A summary of these resources is listed:

Artificial Intelligence Center (AIC). Sponsored by SRI International. Founded in 1966, the AIC is one of the world's major centers of research in artificial intelligence: http://www.ai.sri.com/

Charles Babbage Institute of Computer History. Sponsored by the Charles Babbage Institute of Computer History (CBI), a research center at the University of Minnesota dedicated to promoting the study and preservation of the history of computing and information processing through historical research and archival activity: http://www.cbi.umn.edu/

The Computer Museum. A public, nonprofit institution that was founded in 1982. The History Center was created in 1996. The museum contains a comprehensive collection of computer artifacts as well as large multimedia and documentation archives: http://www.net.org/html/history/index.html

Computer Museum of America. Established in 1983 by Jim and Marie Petroff. The museum's mission is to preserve milestones in the computer industry and to chronicle those milestones for the enrichment and education of all. The museum is located on the campus of Coleman College in La Mesa, California: http://www.computer-museum.org/

History of Computing. Materials relating to the history of computing sponsored by the Department of Computer Science at Virginia Tech and in part by a grant from the National Science Foundation: http://ei.cs.vt.edu/~history/index.html

History of Computing. A collection of Web resources related to the history of computing and on-line, computer-based exhibits available worldwide. The Web site is hosted at Stanford University: http://palimpsest.stanford.edu/icom/vlmp/computing.html

Library of Congress. Provides access to digital collections, archives, catalogs, research services, and legislative information: http://www.lcweb.loc.gov/

Smithsonian Computer History. Selected materials from the Division of Computers, Information & Society, National Museum of American History: http://www.si.edu/resource/tours/comphist/computer.htm

HISTORY AND CRITICISM

"Paradigm shift" and "postmodern" are terms often used to describe the digital age or computers and the Internet. Futurists, business leaders, academics, and journalists often use these terms to describe the digital world that we are entering and how the changes are unlike anything that has ever been experienced before.

In *Monster or Messiah: The Computer's Impact on Society* by Walter Matthews, contributing writer Frederick E. Laurenzo provides an interesting summary of computers and progress. Laurenzo compares the impact of computers to the impact that railroads had in the nineteenth century. He believes that computers will fill a similar role in the postindustrial age. Amazing developments in computers, telecommunications, the Internet, and the Web have resulted in a digital revolution. The last ten years have shown an increase in the amount of information being published on the social implications of the digital age. A recent on-line search of the Library of Congress revealed that over 10,000 books had been assigned to the Internet subject headings category. This is due to the converging of computer and telecommunications technologies and the growing use by a broader percentage of the population.

The Internet has entered mainstream culture through Web sites devoted to popular music, celebrities, television series, and movies. Web addresses have replaced toll-free phone numbers in print, radio, and television advertisements. Magazines and journal articles appear on-line before they are available in print. One measure of celebrity is the number of Web sites and on-line discussion groups. For example, following the death of Princess Diana, thousands of new Web sites were created as a tribute. Free expression on the Internet is also part of its popular appeal. It is a forum for sexually explicit discussion groups and pornographic Web sites. Hate groups and gangs may use E-mail and Web sites to distribute propaganda and recruit new members. While the free flow of information on the Internet is a positive, it is also creates a concern for parents and public institutions who seek to filter access to explicit information. Policymakers took note of this concern in 1996, when the U.S. Congress drafted the Communications Decency Act (CDA). The provision sought to subject to criminal prosecution anyone displaying indecent or patently offensive material on the Internet that could be accessed by anyone under the age of eighteen. After widespread debate, the U.S. Supreme Court struck down the provision in 1997. The effects of digital technologies are far-reaching. This section provides an overview of resources that explore the social impact of computers and the Internet.

Virtual Reality

The level of interactivity between the individual and the computer creates a virtual reality, a place where it is difficult to determine where imagination begins and reality ends. Arthur and Marilouise Kroker's book entitled *Digital Delirium* provides an overview of the electronic culture. The volume is a compilation of writings from futurists who were rethinking technoculture in the 1990s. An interview with Paul Veriolio, a French technology theorist, states that virtual reality already has the upper hand. He states that the high level of technologies used during the Gulf War combined with live broadcasts and the ability for some families to communicate with troops via E-mail turned the war into the first "live" and virtual war. In cases like the Gulf War, Veriolio believes that virtual reality leads to de-realization. In *Computer Power and Human Reason*, Joseph Weinzenbaum explores the humanist role of computers. Published in 1976, Weinzenbaum expands on his beliefs that people have made the world too much into a computer and that the remaking of the world in the image of the computer started long before there were electronic computers. The mid-1970s may be considered to be the early days of personal computing. In her 1984 book *The Second Self*, Sherry Turkle, MIT psychologist/social scientist, paints cultural images of computing and contrasts the personal computer with personal meanings. The mid-1970s image of a person feeding an IBM batch card into a mainframe computer may be compared to cultural images in the 1990s of an individual in an airport using a laptop computer with an interactive display screen. Turkle found that the most common computer threat in the 1970s was an impersonal system that classified people like numbers. In the 1990s the threat became more personal as individuals became addicted to virtual relationships and environments through a machine. Eleven years later, Turkle continues to explore virtual relationships in *Life on the Screen: Identity in the Age of the Internet*. Turkle shares insights on how the Internet is causing individuals to reevaluate identities. She noted that many people who go on-line assume various names and personas and may even get involved in "virtual cross-dressing." Turkle explores the idea of men's going on-line as women to have relationships with women, but some of the women in these relationships are actually men. Numerous accounts have appeared on newscasts and in newspapers of how children, teens, and some adults have become victims after agreeing to meet their on-line mate. Other such relationships have resulted in marriages. In *The War of Desire & Technology at the Close of the Mechanical Age*, Allucquere R. Stone, an assistant professor at the University of Texas at Austin and director of the school's Advanced Communication Technologies Laboratory, provides an understanding of behavior patterns in on-line chat rooms and of electronic culture. In this text she asks why the Internet has emerged as more of a free-form social playground than a structured work space.

Some authors are taking a less than serious view of the digital age. For a humorous look at the impact that computers and networks are having on society, *Dave Barry in Cyberspace* is a must read. Barry, a journalist, provides a lighthearted look at the anxieties, situations, and absurdities created by cyberspace. Barry does more than define terminology; he traces the roots of "computerese" and discusses its influence on society and the English language. Bob Rankin, author and co-creator of the popular *Tourbus* Web site (http://www.tourbus.com/), takes the pain out of using the Internet with his book *Dr. Bob's Painless Guide to the Internet*. Aimed at new Internet users, this book provides a friendly overview of what's hot, what's cool, and just plain fun in cyberspace. Dinty W. Moore offers a humorous tour of the Internet in his book *The Emperor's Virtual Clothes: The Naked Truth about Internet Culture*. Moore's book targets individuals seeking to understand Internet culture and who are not sure that they really need to. John A. Barry's *Technobabble* provides definitions for the growing vocabulary of terms associated with hardware, software, and networks. Computer humor began appearing in comic strips in the 1980s. Computer gags, pranks, jokes, and teases are being distributed via E-mail and the Web. Some employers have implemented policies that discourage the use of employer-provided E-mail for such purposes. Editorial cartoons and comic strips often feature the problems that people have understanding and using computers. They also parody common situations such as purchasing computers and deciphering error messages. *Cathy*, *Ziggy*, *Doonesbury*, and *Dilbert* are a few popular comic strips that often contain computer and Internet humor. Ironically, these comic strips are also available on the Web. As long as computers continue to evolve, comics will have plenty of material.

Education

Computers and the Internet have changed the educational needs of society. Labor Department statistics predict that a high percentage of twenty-first-century jobs will be computer-related. The need by older adults for retraining has created a market for distance education. Educational literature supports the concept that lifelong learning is changing due to shifting demographics, globalization, and an emphasis on technology. The idea of lifelong employment is not applicable in the digital age. Cultural issues related to distance education lie in imbalances due to access and income. Minorities and low-income individuals, especially those in urban and rural areas, are less likely to have access to computers in schools and homes. Social, political, and government organizations have created computer literacy initiatives to help provide funding for hardware, software, infrastructure, and training to help close the gap. While technology has created the gap, it is also being used as a means for closing it. In *The Road Ahead*, Bill Gates emphasizes the fact that information created, stored, and distributed in digital formats necessitates new ways to impart knowledge. Gates uses as examples printed books, photographs, films, and videos, all currently being converted to digital information. The ability to access, use, and understand information from a variety of sources has created a new type of literacy. Paul A. Gilster provides an overview of the factors redefining literacy in his book *Digital Literacy*. Gilster addresses the human factors impacted by the consequences of technology and offers solutions for coping. After conversion to digital bits and bytes, information distribution and access raise many cultural issues. Trevor Haywood discusses these issues in *Info-Rich/Info-Poor: Access and Exchange in the Global Information Society*. Haywood provides an analysis of the inequities and controversies with the globalization and digitization of information. In this text, he provides a view of the world as an information system and discusses the values assigned and the uneven way that they are distributed.

Disconnected: Haves and Have-nots in the Information Age provides a moving and persuasive account of the social, moral, and ethical impact of information technology on society. William Wresch, the author, began writing this book as a Fulbright scholar in Africa. While teaching at the University of Namibia, he encountered the harsh social and economic realities of life without information. Through vivid personal accounts, data, and current events, he illustrates the inequities between the information-rich and the information-poor. The author presents readers with the hope that information technology can be used as a "means" to improve the quality of life.

Interactive CD-ROM and hypermedia technologies are used in conjunction with electronic access to libraries, the Web, and cable television/satellites for building virtual universities and schools. In higher education, students may select colleges and review programs via the Web, enroll on-line, and complete degree programs remotely. Once enrolled in distance education programs, they communicate with professors and peers electronically. In distance education, instruction and learning occur in different locations. What began as correspondence courses and for-credit television classes has evolved into virtual universities using the Web. Journals, magazines, and newspaper advertisements offer readers the chance to enroll and earn degrees at home. Using training technology, a single instructor or presentation can be simultaneously received in more than one location hundreds or thousands of miles away from the instructor or sender of the presentation. The exchange may be a one-way transmission of voice, data, and/or video, or it may involve a two-way communication process. Classes can take field trips, conduct lab experiments, and communicate with peers and scholars by videoconferencing on the Web. Readers interested in a general summary of literature related to distance education may use *Distance Education: An Annotated Bibliography* by Terry Ann Moody. For a more detailed understanding of distance education, Barry Willis provides a compilation of writings that discuss planning and implementation of a variety of technologies in *Distance Education: Strategies and Tools*.

The Web is one way to distribute distance education courses. As more universities and schools adopt this mode of instructional delivery, there is a growing need for teacher preparation and technology training for instructors. Much of the distance education literature addresses the instruction and delivery issues. In *Web-Based Instruction*, author Badrul Khan has assembled a collection of papers that provide a broad spectrum of information related to the design, development, delivery, management, and evaluation of Web-based instruction. Discussions on distance education, collaborative learning, active learning, and critical thinking are common areas of interest for training managers, librarians, professors, and K–12 teachers. They provide an extensive approach of how educators in any organization can use the Web to its fullest to improve teaching and learning. Vicki M. Hobbs and J. Scott Christianson examine the concept of virtual classrooms in *Virtual Classrooms: Educational Opportunity through Two-Way Interactive Television*. This text provides an overview of the various technology options, administration, and policy issues. It uniquely includes a discussion on investment and returns and considerations for cost-benefit analysis. While most texts reviewed for this section were found to focus on those who implement distance education, this guide was found to provide a clear, yet sometimes simplistic, overview of distance education from the learner's perspective. The guide is intended for first-time college students.

The perception of computers and the Internet varies among the young and the old. Older adults may view the computer as the authority and think that it is never wrong. Boys, girls, and adults of both sexes often think of computers as an area of interest for boys. As a result, a variety of video games have been created for girls. Justine Cassell and Henry Jenkins, editors of *From Barbie to Mortal Kombat*, discuss the aggressive, male-dominated world of video games. Teens and children born in the 1970s have a different image of computers because they have always been a part of their lives. Don Tapscott, author of *Growing Up Digital*, addresses the future of young Internet users in this text. Interviews provide insights into the unabashed ways that the young are grasping and using the Internet.

Electronic Commerce

Electronic commerce is not a new concept; however, the Internet has provided new possibilities and opportunities. For example, there is heightened interest in stock trading due to Internet services that offer real-time trading. This type of trading is fast, relatively easy, and addictive. Digital technologies are also transforming the way that business is conducted. Hundreds of thousands of companies large and small are conducting business on the Internet. Global competition and the ability to reach new markets are fueling electronic commerce, also referred to as e-business. Distribution, inventory control, purchasing, marketing, customer service, and banking can all be done electronically. Concerns about electronic commerce include the cost of access, security, taxes, and intellectual property rights. Soon-Yong Choi, Dale O. Stahl, and Andrew B. Whinston provide business models for the Internet in *The Economics of Electronic Commerce*. This text provides the reader with detailed coverage of digital versus physical products, copyright, quality control, and policy considerations. It provides traditional microeconomic standards to a new medium. In *Creating Value in the Digital Era*, Alf Chattell describes principles of the digital economy that define its value. Chattell considers human capital and human participation and vision to be of vital importance. Robert E. Littan and William A. Niskanen take a broader view of the effects of electronic commerce in *Going Digital: A Guide to Policy in the Digital Age*. Of special interest is the chapter entitled "Digital Skeptics and Pessimists," in which they take an objective look at the electronic commerce and acknowledge issues and concerns that do not make everyone a true believer in digital commerce.

Once a company has decided to conduct business on the Internet, there are many other considerations. Mary J. Cronin, author of *Doing More Business on the Internet*, offers guidelines to business on Web page creation, marketing, and an overview of commercial applications of the Internet. Cronin targets nontechnical managers and business owners with this book. *The Internet Marketing Plan* by Kim M. Bayne is a comprehensive guide for creating and implementing an integrated Internet marketing plan. Bayne, a marketing communications veteran, provides detailed instructions for managing an on-line presence. While some of the strategies apply to traditional marketing media, Bayne emphasizes the commitment that is critical to maintaining an on-line presence.

There are many considerations for employees and would-be employees of wired organizations. Job seekers will find that the literature available in *Using the Internet & the World-Wide Web in Your Job Search* by Fred E. Jandt and Mary B. Nemnich provides a step-by-step guide to finding a job using the Internet. Topics covered range from getting access to the Internet, finding job listings, applying for jobs, interviewing, and finally, either accepting or declining job offers. The most useful information is contained in the chapters that cover "Preparing Your Electronic Resume," "Submitting Your Electronic Resume," "Internet Job Hunting Netiquette," and the "Internet Interview." It also includes sections for college students seeking positions and offers advice for recruiters. Stephen Dahoney-Farina addresses the topic of telecommuting in his book entitled, *The Wired Neighborhood*. Doheny-Farina examines the seductiveness of the Internet in terms of its potential to allow more quality time with families and maintain closer contact with communities. He addresses telecommuting not in terms of feasibility but in terms of the quality of life that it creates.

Consumers of electronic commerce use electronic shopping carts to purchase merchandise via the Internet. On-line shoppers can browse the virtual aisles of bookstores, clothing stores, department stores, malls, auction sites, computer hardware retailers, florists, and sporting goods stores. They can also listen to samples from their favorite artists before purchasing music CDs. Entrepreneur Shawn Fanning was eighteen years old when he wrote the programming code for Napster. Napster is a music file-sharing system that allows anyone to download music to computers. The impact of Napster on popular culture has been phenomenal. Composers, artists, and music industry executives have waged legal battles claiming that Napster challenges their intellectual property rights. The Napster Web site has been ranked by some as one of the greatest Internet applications ever created.

Another popular e-commerce application is the ability to purchase airline tickets online. In *Doing More Business on the Internet*, Mary J. Cronin outlines the issues facing consumers and retailers and emphasizes that the model for buying and selling on the Internet is still evolving. Authentication, privacy, integrity, delivery and certification are the key issues discussed. Several large on-line retailers are listed here. Electronic marketing continues to grow, and most traditional retailers are opening storefronts on the Web; see for example, Amazon.com, a large book, music, and video retailer (http://www.amazon.com); e-bay, an on-line auction site (http://www.ebay.com/); and Napster, a large on-line community for music lovers that allows the downloading of music (http://www.napster.com/).

Social, Ethical, and Political Issues

The literature just discussed examines computers and digital information in technical, economic, and social terms. When these factors are considered together, they raise political and ethical questions that affect society. These questions include access, privacy, and ownership. The issue of equitable access and service are key components of democracy and will become increasingly important as more people depend on electronic information for news, information, and advocacy.

M. David Ermann, Mary B. Williams, and Michele S. Shauf provide a collection of essays in *Computers, Ethics, and Society*. The essays are thought-provoking and provide insights into the moral, social, and ethical dilemmas created when good people do things with computers that disturb others. The authors believe that our ethical and social standards have not yet adapted to the digital age. Bernard Carl Rosen discusses social order and the elitists of the technoservice economy in *Winners and Losers of the Information Revolution*. Rosen describes the elitists as highly educated specialists and manipulators of symbols who control and operate the financial, news, entertainment, publishing, health, and education industries. A critique of the politics and culture of the digital information age is presented in *Resisting the Virtual Life* by James Brook and Ian A. Boal. The authors view technologies as both tools for accomplishing specific goals and a new type of social structure. Brook and Boal provide the reader with a collection of essays that illustrate how technologies define and regulate social life. They also propose design criteria for democratic technologies.

Computers can also have a physical impact on users. The desire to have the newest and fastest computer gadgets and information overload are two areas that are creating stress. Authors Larry D. Rosen and Michelle M. Weil provide a diagnosis for a new ailment in their book entitled *TechnoStress: Coping with Technology @Work @Home @Play*. The authors define "technostress" as a reaction to technology and how people are changing due to its influence. It is a term that denotes the feeling of being overwhelmed and immobilized by the computerization that is transforming work, organizations, lifestyles, and personal relationships. Rosen and Weil provide the reader with insights into the struggles and the resulting physical outcomes of dealing with technology.

Privacy is a concern not unique to the digital age; however, when information travels across networks in digital form, privacy becomes a big issue. The ability to collect, assemble, and distribute data is enhanced over the Web. An electronic trail is left each time a Web site is visited. Personal privacy versus the public right to know is discussed at length in *Release 2.0: A Design for Living in the Digital Age* by Ester Dyson. Related issues such as information filtering, anonymity, governance, and security are also addressed. Through the use of scenarios, essays, opinions, anecdotes, and forecasts, Dyson provides a stimulating outline of coping in the digital age. The author achieved her goal of providing a framework for the new rights and rules of cyberspace. She is an advocate of making the digital age a better place to live.

The study of computers and the Internet in popular culture is a work in progress. New advances in technology have the potential to impact popular culture. So far, computers and the Internet offer opportunities to communicate with new people and new cultures, expand research using electronic books and journals, explore virtual museums, build new business enterprises, and provide a forum for free speech and artistic expression. As the Internet continues to grow and evolve, it will continue to affect society in new and different ways. There is still much to be explored and written.

BIBLIOGRAPHY

Books and Articles

Abshire, Gary M., ed. *The Impact of Computers on Society and Ethics: A Bibliography*. Morristown, N.J.: Creative Computing, 1980.

Albrecht, B. *What to Do After You Hit Return*. Menlo Park, Calif.: People's Press, 1975.

Albrecht, R. L. *BASIC: A Self Teaching Guide*. 2nd ed. New York: Wiley, 1978.

Arbib, Michael A. *Computers and the Cybernetic Society*. 2nd ed. New York: Academic Press, 1984.

Ashley, Michael, ed. *Souls in Metal*. New York: St. Martin's Press, 1977.

Asimov, Isaac. *I Robot*. New York: Gnome Press, 1950.

———. "Robbie." In *Science Fiction Thinking Machines*, ed. Groff Conklin. New York: Vanguard, 1954.

———. *Thinking Machines*. Milwaukee: Raintree Steck-Vaughn, 1981.

Austrian, Geoffrey. *Herman Hollerith*. New York: Columbia University Press, 1982.

Banks, M. *The Internet Unplugged*. Wilton, Conn.: Pemberton Press, 1997.

Barnaby, Frank. *The Automated Battlefield*. New York: Free Press, 1986.

Barron, Neil, ed. *Anatomy of Wonder: A Critical Guide to Science Fiction*. 2nd ed. New York: R. R. Bowker, 1981.

Barry, D. *Dave Barry in Cyberspace*. New York: Crown, 1996.

Barry, J. *Technobabble*. Cambridge: MIT Press, 1991.

Bayne, Kim M. *The Internet Marketing Plan*. New York: John Wiley, 2000.

Bell, Daniel. *The Coming of Post-Industrial Society*. New York: Basic Books, 1973.

Bellin, David, and Gary Chapman, eds. *Computers in Battle: Will They Work?* New York: Harcourt Brace Jovanovich, 1987.

Bellman, Richard. *An Introduction to Artificial Intelligence: Can Computers Think?* San Francisco: Boyd and Fraser, 1978.

Belzer, Jack, Albert G. Holzman, and Allen Kent, eds. *Encyclopedia of Computer Science and Technology*. 16 vols. New York: Mercel Dekker, 1975–1981.

Benton, Mike. *The Complete Guide to Computer Camps and Workshops*. Indianapolis: Bobbs-Merrill, 1984.

The Blue Book for the Atari Computer. Chicago: WIDL Video, 1983.

The Blue Book for the Commodore Computer. Chicago: WIDL Video, 1983.

Boden, Margaret. *Artificial Intelligence and Natural Man*. New York: Basic Books, 1977.

Bolter, J. David. *Turing's Matt: Western Culture in the Computer Age*. Chapel Hill: University of North Carolina Press, 1984.

Bork, Alfred. *Personal Computers for Education*. New York: Harper and Row, 1984.

Brand, Stewart, ed. *Whole Earth Software Catalog for 1986*. Garden City, N.Y.: Doubleday, 1985.

Brod, Craig. *TechnoStress: The Human Cost of the Computer Revolution*. Reading, Mass.: Addison-Wesley, 1984.

Brook, J., and I Boal, eds. *Resisting the Virtual Life: The Culture and Politics of Information*. San Francisco: City Lights; Monroe, Oreg.: Subterranean, 1995.

Brooks, Frederick P. The *Mythical Man—Month*. Reading, Mass.: Addison-Wesley, 1975.

Browning, Graeme, ed. *Electronic Democracy: Using the Internet to Influence American Politics*. Wilton, Conn.: Pemberton Press, 1996.

Brunner, J. *The Shockwave Rider*. New York: Harper and Row, 1975.

Burnham, David. *The Rise of the Computer State: The Threat to Our Freedoms, Our Ethics and Our Democratic Process*. New York: Random House, 1980.

Burns, Alan. *New Information Technology*. New York: Wiley, 1984.

Capck, Karcl. *R.U.R.* New York: Doubleday, 1923.

Carter, Ciel Michele. *Guide to Reference Sources in the Computer Sciences*. New York: Macmillan, 1974.

Cassell, Justine, and Henry Jenkins. *From Barbie to Mortal Kombat: Gender and Computer Games*. Cambridge: MIT Press, 1998.

Ceruzzi, Paul E. *A History of Modern Computing*. Cambridge: MIT Press, 1998.

Chattell, A. *Creating Value in the Digital Era: Achieving Success through Insight, Imagination, and Innovation*. Washington Square, N.Y.: New York University Press, 1998.

Choi, Soon-Yong, Dale O. Stahl, and Andrew B. Whinston. *The Economics of Electronic Commerce*. New York: Sams, 1997.

Churchland, Paul M. *Matter and Consciousness*. Cambridge: MIT Press, 1984.

Clarke, Arthur C. *2001: A Space Odyssey*. New York: New American Library, 1968.

Cohen, John. *Human Robots in Myth and Science*. Cranbury, N.J.: A. S. Barnes, 1967.

Computer Books and Serials in Print. New York: R. R. Bowker, 1985.

Conklin, Groff, ed. *Science Fiction Thinking Machines*. New York: Vanguard, 1954.

Connick, George. ed. *The Distance Learner's Guide*. Upper Saddle River, N.J.: Prentice-Hall, 1999.

Contento, W. *Index to Science Fiction Anthologies and Collections*. Boston: G. K. Hall, 1978.

Cooley, Mike. *Architect or Bee? The Human/Technology Relationship*. Boston: South End Press, 1980.

Cortada, James W., comp. *An Annotated Bibliography of the History of Data Processing*. Westport, Conn.: Greenwood Press, 1983.

———. *Historical Dictionary of Data Processing*. Westport, Conn.: Greenwood Press, 1987.

———. *Second Bibliographic Guide to the History of Computing, Computers, and the Information Processing Industry*. Westport, Conn.: Greenwood Press, 1996.

Covington, Michael A. *Dictionary of Computer Terms*. Hauppauge, N.Y.: Barron's, 1992.

Cronin, Mary J. *Doing More Business on the Internet: How the Electronic Highway Is Transforming American Companies*. New York: Van Nostrand Reinhold, 1995.

Current Index of Computer Literature. Bala-Cynwyd, Pa.: Information Research Institute, 1985.

Danziger, J. *People and Computers: The Impact of Computing on End Users in Organizations*. New York: Columbia University Press, 1986.

Darcy, Laura, and Louise Boston. *Webster's New World Dictionary of Computer Terms*. New York: Simon and Schuster, 1983.

Datapro Directory of Microcomputer Software. 3 vols. Delran, N.J.: Datapro Research Corporation, 1987.

Davies, Owen, and Mike Edelhart. *Omni Online Database Directory 1985*. New York: Macmillan, 1984.

Day, Donald B. *Index to the Science Fiction Magazines, 1926–1950*. Portland, Oreg.: Perri Press, 1952.

Deitel, Harvey M., and Barbara Deitel. *Computers and Data Processing*. New York: Academic Press, 1985.

Deken, J. *The Electronic Collage*. New York: William Morrow, 1981.

Dennett, Daniel C. *Brainstorms: Philosophical Essays on Mind and Psychology*. Montgomery, Vt.: Bradford, 1981.

Dertouzos, M. L., and J. Moses, eds. *The Computer Age: A Twenty-Year View*. Cambridge: MIT Press, 1980.

Desmonde, William H. *Computers and Their Uses*. Englewood Cliffs, N.J.: Prentice-Hall, 1964.

Didday, Richard L. *Computers—Caricatures and Cartoons*. Champaign, Ill.: Matrix, 1976.

Dietrich, E., ed. *Thinking Computers and Virtual Persons: Essays on the Intentionality of Machines*. San Diego: Academic Press, 1994.

Dizard, Wilson P., Jr. *The Coming Information Age: An Overview of Technology, Economics and Politics*. New York: Longman, 1982.

Doheny-Farina, S. *The Wired Neighborhood*. New Haven, Conn.: Yale University Press, 1996.

Downing, Douglas D. *Dictionary of Computer Terms*. New York: Barron's, 1995.

Dreyfus, Hubert L. *What Computers Can't Do*. New York: Harper and Row, 1972.

Dreyfus, Hubert L., and Stuart E. Dreyfus. *Mind over Machine: The Power of Human Intuition and Expertise in the Era of the Computer*. New York: Free Press, 1986.

Dyson, E. *Release 2.0: A Design for Living in the Digital Age*. New York: Broadway Books, 1997.

Edmunds, Robert A., ed. *The Prentice-Hall Encyclopedia of Information Technology*. Englewood Cliffs, N.J.: Prentice-Hall, 1987.

Ellul, Jacques. *The Technological Society*. Trans. by John Wilkinson. New York: Alfred A. Knopf, 1964.

Elwood, Roger, ed. *Invasion of the Robots*. New York: Paper Back Library, 1968.

Ermann, M. D., M. B. Williams, and Michele S. Shauf. *Computers, Ethics, and Society*. New York: Oxford University Press, 1990.

Evans, Christopher. *The Micro Millennium*. New York: Viking Press, 1979.

Feigenbaum, Edward A., and Pamela A. McCorduck. *The Fifth Generation Artificial Intelligence and Japan's Challenge to Life World*. Reading, Mass.: Addison-Wesley, 1983.

Fishman, Katherine Davis. *The Computer Establishment*. New York: Harper and Row, 1981.

Flaherty, Douglas. *Humanizing the Computer: A Cure for the Deadly Embrace*. Belmont, Calif.: Wadsworth, 1986.

Forester, Tom. *High-Tech Society: The Story of the Information Technology Revolution*. Cambridge: MIT Press, 1987.

———, ed. *The Information Technology Revolution*. Cambridge: MIT Press, 1985.

———. *The Microelectronics Revolution: The Complete Guide to New Technology and Its Impact on Society*. Cambridge: MIT Press, 1980.

Forsyth, Richard, ed. *Expert Systems: Principles and Case Studies*. New York: Chapman and Hall, 1984.

Frates, Jeffrey, and William Moldrup. *Computers and Life*. Englewood Cliffs, N.J.: Prentice-Hall, 1983.

Freedman, Alan. *The Computer Glossary*. New York: Computer Language, 1983.

Freedman, Warren. *The Right to Privacy in the Computer Age*. New York: Quorum Books, 1987.

Freiberger, Paul, and Michael Swaine. *Fire in the Valley: The Making of the Personal Computer*. Berkeley, Calif.: Osborne/McGraw-Hill, 1984.

Friedrichs, Guenter, and Adam Schaff, eds. *Microelectronics and Society: A Report to the Club of Rome*. New York: New American Library, 1982.

Froelich, Robert A. *The IBM PC (and Compatibles) Free Software Catalog and Directory*. New York: Dilithium, 1986.

Frude, Neil. *The Intimate Machine: Close Encounters with the New Computers*. London: Century, 1983.

Gale Directory of Databases, 1998. Detroit: Gale Research, 1998.

Gardner, Howard. *Frames of Mind: The Theory of Multiple Intelligences.* New York: Basic Books, 1983.

Gardner, M. "The Internet: A World Brain? H. G. Wells' World Brain." *The Skeptical Inquirer* 23:1 (Jan/Feb 1999): 12–14.

Garfinkel, Simson. *Database Nation: The Death of Privacy in the 21st Century.* Cambridge, Mass.: O'Reilly, 2000.

Garson, G. D. *Computer Technology and Social Issues.* Harrisburg, Pa.: Idea Group, 1995.

Gates, Bill. *Business at the Speed of Thought Using a Digital Nervous System.* New York: Time Warner, 1999.

———. *The Road Ahead.* New York: Viking, 1999.

Gelernter, D. *Machine Beauty: Elegance and the Heart of Computing.* New York: Basic Books, 1998.

Gill, Karamjit S., ed. *Artificial Intelligence for Society.* New York: Wiley, 1986.

Gilster, Paul A. *Digital Literacy.* New York: John Wiley, 1997.

Glossbrenner, Alfred. *The Complete Handbook of Personal Computer Communications.* New York: St. Martin's Press, 1983.

Goldstein, Herman H. *The Computer from Pascal to von Neumann.* Princeton, N.J.: Princeton University Press, 1972.

Gordon, M., A. Singleton, and C. Rickards. *Dictionary of New Information Technology Acronyms.* 2nd ed. London: Kogan Page, 1986.

Gottlieb, C. C., and A. Borodin, eds. *Social Issues in Computing.* New York: Academic Press, 1974.

Graham, Neill. *The Mind Tool.* 3rd ed. St. Paul: West, 1983.

Greenfield, Karl Taro. "Meet the Napster." *Time* 156 (October 2, 2000), 60–66.

Hamilton, T. "Bridging Humans and Technology." *Computing Canada*, December 19, 1996.

Han, H., and R. Stout. *The Internet Yellow Pages.* 2nd ed. Berkeley, Calif.: Osborne McGraw-Hill, 1995.

Harris, D. "The Electronic Funeral Mourning Versace." *Antioch Review* 56:2 (Spring 1998), 154.

Harris, S. *What's So Funny about Computers?* Los Altos, Calif.: Kaufmann, 1982.

Harrison, Harry, ed. *War with the Robots.* New York: Pyramid Books, 1962.

Haugeland, J. *Artificial Intelligence: The Very Idea.* Cambridge: MIT Press, 1985.

Haugeland, John C., ed. *Mind Design: Philosophy, Psychology, Artificial Intelligence.* Cambridge: MIT Press, 1981.

Haywood, T. *Info Rich/Info Poor: Access and Exchange in the Global Information Society.* London: Bowker-Saur, 1995.

Hildebrandt, Darlene Myers, ed. *Computer Information Directory.* 4th ed. Federal Way, Wash.: Pedaro, 1987.

Hobbs, V., and S. J. Christianson. *Virtual Classrooms: Educational Opportunity through Two-Way Interactive Television.* Lancaster, Pa.: Technomic, 1997.

Hodges, Andrew. *Alan Turing: The Enigma.* London: Burnett Books, 1983.

Hofstadter, Douglas R. *Godel, Escher, Bach: An Eternal Golden Braid.* New York: Basic Books, 1978.

Hofstadter, Douglas R., and Daniel C. Dennet. *The Mind's I: Fantasies and Reflections of Self and Soul.* New York: Basic Books, 1981.

Holtzman, Charles P. *What to Do When You Get Your Hands on a Microcomputer*. Blue Ridge Summit, Pa.: TAB Books, 1982.

Hopper, Grace, and Steven L. Mandell. *Understanding Computers*. St. Paul: West, 1984.

Index to the Science Fiction Magazines, 1966–1970. Cambridge, Mass.: New England Science Fiction Association, 1971.

Isaacs, Alan, ed. *The Multilingual Computer Dictionary*. New York: Facts on File, 1981.

Jandt, Fred E., and Mary B. Nemnich. *Using the Internet & the World-Wide Web in Your Job Search*. New York: JIST Publishing, 1996.

Jastrow, Robert. *The Enchanted Loom: The Mind in the Universe*. New York: Simon and Schuster, 1981.

Johnson, Deborah G., and John W. Snapper, eds. *Ethical Issues in the Use of Computers*. Belmont, Calif.: Wadsworth, 1985.

Katz, Leslie, ed. *Fairy Tales for Computers*. Boston: Nonpareil Books, 1969.

Khan, B. *Web-Based Instruction*. Englewood Cliffs, N.J.: Educational Technology, 1997.

Kidder, Tracy. *Soul of a New Machine*. Boston: Little, Brown, 1981.

Koch, T. *The Message Is the Medium: Online All the Time for Everyone*. Westport, Conn.: Praeger, 1996.

Kosslyn, Stephen Michael. *Ghosts in the Mind's Machine: Creating and Using Images in the Brain*. New York: W. W. Norton, 1983.

Kroker, A., and M. Kroker. *Digital Delirium*. New York: St. Martin's Press, 1997.

LAMP: Literature Analysis of Microcomputer Publications. Mahwah, N.J.: Soft Images, 1986.

Laudon, Kenneth C. *Dossier Society: Value Choices in the Design of National Information Systems*. New York: Columbia University Press, 1986.

Lechner, H. D. *The Computer Chronicles*. Belmont, Calif.: Wadsworth, 1984.

Lent, Max. *Government Online*. New York: HarperPerennial, 1995.

Levine, John R., Arnold Reinhold, and Margaret Levine-Young. *The Internet for Dummies*. 6th ed. Foster City, Calif.: IDG Books Worldwide, 2002.

Levy, Steven. *Hackers: Heroes of the Computer Revolution*. New York: Dell, 1984.

Lewis, Anthony O., ed. *Of Men and Machines*. London: E. P. Dutton, 1963.

Littan, R., and W. Niskanen. *Going Digital: A Guide to Policy in the Digital Age*. Washington, D.C.: Brookings Institution Press, 1998.

Lloyd, L. *Technology and Teaching*. Medford, N.J.: Information Today, 1997.

Logsdon, Tom. *Computers & Social Controversy*. Rockville, Md.: Computer Science Press, 1980.

———. *Computers Today and Tomorrow: The Microcomputer Explosion*. Rockville, Md.: Computer Science Press, 1985.

———. *How to Cope with Computers*. Rochelle Park, N.J.: Hayden, 1982.

Lovington, S. H. *Early British Computers: The Story of Vintage Computers and the People Who Built Them*. Bedford, Mass.: Digital, 1980.

Luckmans World Wide Web Yellow Pages. New York: Barnes and Noble Books, 1997.

Macmillan Encyclopedia of Computers. Ed. James G. Bitter. New York: Maxwell Macmillan International, 1992.

Mathews, W. *Monster or Messiah? : The Computer's Impact on Society*. Jackson: University Press of Mississippi, 1980.

Maxwell, B. *Washington Online: How to Access the Federal Government on the Internet*. Washington, D.C.: Congressional Quarterly, 1997.

McCorduck, Pamela. *Machines Who Think*. San Francisco: Freeman, 1979.

McGraw-Hill Encyclopedia of Science and Technology. 4th ed. 14 vols. New York: McGraw-Hill, 1977.

McKeown, Patrick G. *Living with Computers*. New York: Harcourt Brace Jovanovich, 1987.

Meadows, A. J., M. Gordon, A. Singleton, and M. Feeney. *Dictionary of Computing and Information Technology*. 3rd ed. New York: Nichols, 1987.

Metropolis, N., ed. *A History of Computing in the Twentieth Century*. New York: Academic Press, 1980.

Minsky, Marvin. *The Society of Mind*. New York: Simon and Schuster, 1985.

Moody, Terry Ann. *Distance Education: An Annotated Bibliography*. Englewood, Colo.: Libraries Unlimited, 1995.

Moore, Dinty W. *The Emperor's Virtual Clothes: The Naked Truth about Internet Culture*. Chapel Hill, N.C.: Algonquin Books, 1995.

Moritz, Michael. *The Little Kingdom: The Private Story of Apple Computer*. New York: William Morrow, 1984.

Morrison, P., and E. Morrison, eds. *Charles Babbage and His Calculating Engines: Selected Writings by Charles Babbage and Others*. New York: Dover, 1961.

Moscowitz, Sam, ed. *The Coming of the Robots*. New York: Collier, 1963.

Moshowitz, Abbe, ed. *Inside Information: Computers in Fiction*. Reading, Mass.: Addison-Wesley, 1977.

Mumford, Lewis. *The Myth of the Machine: The Pentagon of Power*. New York: Harcourt Brace Jovanovich, 1964.

Murphy, Brian. *Sorcerers and Soldiers: Computer War Games, Fantasies and Adventures*. Morris Plains, N.J.: Creative Computing Press, 1984.

Myers, Darlene. *Computer Science Resources: A Guide to Professional Literature*. White Plains, N.Y.: Knowledge Industry, 1981.

Naisbitt, John. *Megatrends: Ten New Directions Transforming Our Lives*. New York: Warner, 1982.

Negroponte, N. *Being Digital*. New York: Knopf, 1995.

———. "The Digital Revolution: Reason for Optimism." *The Futurist* (November 1995).

Newman, J. *The Computer: How It Is Changing Our Lives*. Washington, D.C.: U.S. News and World Report, 1972.

Nicita, Michael, and Ronald Petrusha. *The Reader's Guide to Microcomputer Books*. New York: Golden-Lee, 1984.

Nickerson, Raymond S. *Using Computers: Human Factors in Information Systems*. Cambridge.: MIT Press, 1986.

Nora, Simon, and Alan Minc. *The Computerization of Society: A Report to the President of France*. Cambridge: MIT Press, 1980.

Northrop, Mary. *American Computer Pioneers*. Springfield, N.J.: Enslow, 1998.

Notess, G. *Government Information on the Internet*. 2nd ed. Lanham, Md.: Bernan Press, 1998.

Papert, Seymour. *Mindstorms: Children, Computers, and Powerful Ideas*. New York: Basic Books, 1980.

Parker, D. *Crime by Computer*. New York: Scribner's, 1976.

Peat, F. David. *Artificial Intelligence: How Machines Think*. New York: Simon and Schuster, 1985.

Phillips, Gary. *IBM PC Public Domain Software*. Culver City, Calif.: Ashton-Tate, 1984.

Prenis, John. *The Computer Dictionary*. Philadelphia: Running Press, 1983.

Provenzo, Eugene F., Jr. *Beyond the Gutenberg Galaxy: Microcomputers and the Emergence of Post-Typographic Culture*. New York: Teachers College Press, 1986.

Pylyshyn, Z., ed. *Perspectives on the Computer Revolution*. Englewood Cliffs, N.J.: Prentice-Hall, 1970.

Ragland, B. *The Year 2000 Problem Solver: A Five-Step Disaster Prevention Plan*. New York: McGraw-Hill, 1997.

Ralston, Anthony, ed. *Encyclopedia of Computer Science and Engineering*. 2nd ed. New York: Van Nostrand Reinhold, 1983.

Randall, Brian. "An Annotated Bibliography on the Origins of Computers." *Annals of the History of Computing* 1 (October 1979), 1–73.

Rankin, Bob. *Dr. Bob's Painless Guide to the Internet*. New York: No Starch Press, 1996.

Raphael, Bertram. *The Thinking Computer: Mind Inside Matter*. San Francisco: Freeman, 1976.

Reimecke, Ian. *Electronic Illusions: A Skeptic's View of Our High-Tech Future*. New York: Penguin Books, 1984.

Rosen, B. *Winners and Losers of the Information Revolution: Psychosocial Change and Its Discontents*. Westport, Conn.: Praeger, 1998.

Rosen, Larry D., and Michelle M. Weil. *TechnoStress: Coping with Technology @Work @Home @Play*. New York: John Wiley, 1997.

Roszak, Theodore. *The Cult of Information: The Folklore of Computers and the True Art of Thinking*. New York: Pantheon, 1986.

Russell, Eric Frank, ed. *Men, Mountains and Machines*. New York: Dobson, 1955.

Saffo, P. *Desperately Seeking Cyberspace*. Hasbrouck Heights, N.J.: Hayden, 1989.

Schneiderman, Ben. *Software Psychology: Human Factors in Computer and Information Systems*. Cambridge, Mass.: Whithrop, 1980.

Schoeman, Ferdinand D., ed. *Philosophical Dimensions of Privacy: An Anthology*. Cambridge.: Cambridge University Press, 1984.

Scortia, T. N., and G. Zebrowski, eds. *Human Machines: An Anthology of Stories about Cyborgs*. New York: Vintage, 1975.

Shaiken, Harley. *Work Transformed: Automation and Labor in the Computer Age*. New York: Holt, Rinehart, and Winston, 1984.

Shallis, Michael. *The Silicon Idol: The Micro Revolution and Its Social Implications*. New York: Schocken Books, 1984.

Silverberg, Robert, ed. *Men and Machines*. New York: Meredith Press, 1968.

Simon, Herbert A. *The New Science of Management Decision*. New York: Harper and Row, 1960.

———. *The Sciences of the Artificial*. 2nd ed. Cambridge: MIT Press, 1969.

Sloan, Douglas, ed. *The Computer in Education: A Critical Perspective*. New York: Teachers College Press, 1984.

Slotnick, Daniel L., Evan M. Butterfield, Ernest S. Colantonio, Daniel Kopetzky, and Joan K. Slotnick. *Computers and Applications: An Introduction to Data Processing*. Lexington, Mass.: D. C. Heath, 1986.

Smith, Curtis C., ed. *Twentieth Century Science-Fiction Writers*. 2nd ed. Chicago: St. James Press, 1986.

Sobel, Robert. *IBM: Colossus in Transition*. New York: Time Books, 1981.

The Software Catalogue. 3 vols. New York: Elsevier, 1987.

The Software Encyclopedia. 2 vols. New York: R. R. Bowker, 1985.

Solomonides, Tony, and Les Levidow, eds. *Compulsive Technology: Computers as Culture*. London: Free Association Books, 1985.

Stern, Nancy. *From ENIAC to UNIVAC*. Bedford, Mass.: Digital Press, 1981.

Stern, Robert A., and Nancy Stern. *An Introduction to Computers and Information Processing*. 2nd ed. New York: Wiley, 1985.

Stevens, Lawrence. *Artificial Intelligence: The Search for the Perfect Machine*. Hasbrouck Heights, N.J.: Hayden, 1985.

Stone, Allucquere R. *The War of Desire & Technology at the Close of the Mechanical Age*. Cambridge, Mass.: MIT Press, 1995.

Strauss, Erwin S., ed. *The MIT Science Fiction Society Index to the S-F Magazine, 1951–1965*. Cambridge: MIT Press, 1966.

Tapscott, D. *Growing Up Digital: The Rise of the Net Generation*. New York: McGraw-Hill, 1998.

Thurber, K. T. "Buried Bytes: A History of the Personal Computer." *Popular Electronics* 12:4 (1999) 36.

Toffler, Alvin. *The Third Wave*. New York: William Morrow, 1980.

Tuck, Donald H. *The Encyclopedia of Science Fiction and Fantasy*. 3 vols. Chicago: Advent, 1974–1987.

Turkle, S. *Life on the Screen : Identity in the Age of the Internet*. New York: Simon and Schuster, 1995.

———. *The Second Self—Computers and the Human Spirit*. New York: Simon and Schuster, 1984.

Tymn, Marshall B., and M. Ashley, eds. *Science Fiction, Fantasy, and Weird Fiction Magazines*. Westport, Conn.: Greenwood Press, 1985.

Van Tassel, Dennie L., ed. *Computers, Computers, Computers: In Fiction and in Verse*. New York: Thomas Nelson, 1977.

Van Young, Sayre. *Microsource: Where to Find Answers to Questions about Microcomputers*. Littleton, Colo.: Libraries Unlimited, 1986.

Warrick, Patricia S. *The Cybernetic Imagination in Science Fiction*. Cambridge: MIT Press, 1980.

Weinzenbaum, Joseph. *Computer Power and Human Reason: From Judgement to Calculation*. San Francisco: Freeman, 1976.

Wells, H. G. *World Brain*. Garden City, N.Y.: Doubleday, 1938.

Wessel, Milton. *Freedom's Edge: The Computer Threat to Society*. Reading, Mass.: Addison-Wesley, 1974.

Wessells, Michael G. "Computers." In *Handbook of American Popular Culture*, ed. M. Thomas Inge, vol. 1, 2nd ed. Westport, Conn.: Greenwood Press, 1989, 229–57.

Westin, A. F. *Privacy and Freedom*. New York: Atheneum, 1967.

Wexelblatt, Richard, ed. *History of Programming Languages*. New York: Academic Press, 1982.

White, Lynn. *Medieval Technology and Social Change*. New York: Oxford University Press, 1966.

White, P. T. "Behold the Computer Revolution." *National Geographic* 138 (November 1970), 593–633.

Wiener, N. *The Human Use of Human Beings*. New York: Avon, 1950.

Williams, F., and J. Pavlik. *The People's Right to Know: Media, Democracy, and the Information Highway*. Hillsdale, N.J.: L. Erlbaum Associates, 1994.

Williams, Michael R. *A History of Computing Technology*. New York: IEEE Computer Society Press, 1997.

Willis, B., ed. *Distance Education: Strategies and Tools*. Englewood Cliffs, N.J.: Educational Technology, 1994.

Winner, Langdon. *Autonomous Technology: Technics-out-of-Control as a Theme in Political Thought*. Cambridge: MIT Press, 1977.

Wresch, W. *Disconnected: Haves and Have-nots in the Information Age*. New Brunswick, N.J.: Rutgers University Press, 1996.

Yazdani, M., and A. Narayanan, eds. *Artificial Intelligence: Human Effects*. New York: Wiley, 1984.

Journals

Abacus. New York, 1983– .

ACM Guide to Computing Literature. New York, 1973– .

Acorn User. London, 1982– .

AI and Society. New York, 1987– .

Annals of the History of Computing. Arlington, Va., 1979– .

Apple User. Stockport, England, 1981– .

Australian Personal Computer. Sydney, Australia, 1980.

Bits and Bytes. Christchurch, New Zealand, 1982– .

Business Computer Digest and Software Review. Washington, D.C., 1983– .

Business Week. New York, 1929– .

Byte. Peterborough, N.H., 1975– .

Calico. Provo, Utah, 1983– .

CALL A.P.P.L.E. Renton, Wash., 1978– .

Commodore Computer Club. Vancouver, B.C., 1979– .

Communications of the ACAL. New York, 1958– .

Compute! Greensboro, N.C., 1979– .

Computer and Video Games. London, 1981.

Computer Bookbase. Cerritas, Calif., 1982– .

Computer Entertainer. North Hollywood, Calif., 1982– .

Computers and People. Newtonville, Mass., 1967– .

Computers and Society. New York, 1973– .

Computers and the Humanities. Sarasota, Fla., 1966– .

Computers in Human Behavior. New York, 1985– .

Computerworld. Framingham, Mass., 1967– .

Computing Reviews. New York, 1960– .

Creative Computing. Morristown, N.J., 1974–1985.
Datamation. New York, 1957–   .

Organizations

Cyberspace Law Institute. The Cyberspace Law Institute studies, and helps to develop, the new forms of law and lawmaking required by the growth of global communications networks and on-line communities. http://www.cli.org/

Electronic Frontier Foundation (EFF). Founded in 1990 by Mitchell D. Kapor, founder of Lotus Development Corporation, EFF is a nonprofit, nonpartisan organization working in the public interest to protect fundamental civil liberties, including privacy and freedom of expression, in the arena of computers and the Internet. http://eff.bilkent.edu.tr/index.html

Electronic Privacy Information Center (EPIC). A public interest research center that advocates national attention on emerging civil liberties issues and protection of privacy, the First Amendment, and constitutional values. http://epic.org/

The Internet Society. A professional membership society that provides leadership in addressing issues that confront the future of the Internet and the organization home for groups responsible for Internet infrastructure standards, including the Internet Engineering Task Force (IETF) and the Internet Architecture Board (IAB). http://www.isoc.org/

National Institute of Standards and Technology. A governmental institute created to respond to industry and user needs for objective, neutral tests of information technology. http://www.itl.nist.gov/

The World Wide Web Consortium (W3C). Founded in 1994, the W3C is dedicated to leading the Web to its full potential by developing common protocols that promote its evolution and ensure its interoperability. The international industry consortium is jointly hosted by the Massachusetts Institute of Technology Laboratory for Computer Science (MIT/LCS) in the United States; the Institut National de Recherche en Informatique et en Automatique (INRIA) in Europe; and the Keio University Shonan Fujisawa Campus in Japan. The consortium is led by Tim Berners-Lee, director and creator of the World Wide Web. http://www.w3.org/

Consumer Periodicals

The following publications below are available in print and electronic form.

Boardwatch Magazine. Littleton, Colo., 1987–   . http://www.boardwatch.com
Byte: The Magazine of Technology Integration. Peterborough, N.H., 1975–   . http://www.byte.com
Computer Shopper. New York, 1979–   . http://www.5.zdnet.com/cshopper
Computerworld. Framingham, Mass. 1967–   . http://www.computerworld.com
Cybernautics Digest. Seattle, 1994–   . http://pscu.com/cyber
Datamation. Newton, Mass., 1957–   . http://www.datamation.com
FamilyPC. New York, 1994–   . http://www.zdnet.com/familypc

Home PC. Jericho, N.Y., 1994– . http://www.homepc.com

Infobahn Magazine. Foster City, Calif. 1995– . http://www.postmodern.com

Information Today. Medford, N.J., 1983– . http://www.infotoday.com

InfoWorld. San Mateo, Calif., 1979– . http://www.infoworld.com

Inside the Internet. Louisville, Ky., 1984– . http://www.cobb.zd.com

Interactive Age. Manhasset, N.Y., 1994– . http://techweb.cmp.com/ia

Internet Magazine. Torrance, Calif., 1997– . http://www.emap.com/internet

Internet Shopper. Westport, Conn., 1997– . http://www.internet-shopper.com

Internet Underground. Lombard, Iowa, 1995– . http://www.underground-online.com

Internet User. Westport, Conn., 1996– . http://www.pcmag.com/iu

LAN. San Francisco, 1986– . http://www.lanmag.com

MacUser. Foster City, Calif., 1985– . http://www.zdnet.com/macuser

Macworld: The Macintosh Magazine. San Francisco, 1984– . http://www.macworld.com

Online Magazine. Wilton, Conn., 1977– . http://www.onlineinc.com

PC/Computing. Foster City, Calif., 1988– . http://www.zdnet.com/pccomp/

PC Magazine. New York, 1982– . http://www.pcmag.com

PC Novice. Lincoln, Nebr. 1990– . http://www.pcnovice.com

PC Week. New York, 1984– . http://www.pcweek.com

PC World. Boston, 1982– . http://www.pcworld.com/

Web Week. Westport, Conn., 1995– . http://www.webweek.com

WebMaster. Framingham, Mass., 1996– . http://www.webmaster.com

Wired. San Francisco, 1992– . http://www.hotwired.com

Yahoo! Internet Life. New York, 1995– . http://www.yil.com

A hospital computer. © Painet

Uranium mine computer operator. © Painet

Government mainframe computer operator. © Painet

Fifth grade computer class. © Painet

Inventor J. W. Mauchly with electronic computer, 1948. © Bettmann/CORBIS

Computer used at the Los Alamos Scientific Laboratory in New Mexico. © CORBIS

Microsoft CEO Bill Gates. American Foreign Press
photo by Frederic J. Brown. © AFP/CORBIS

DANCE

Loretta Carrillo

Dance at its most popular level in America has served as a form of social, participatory recreation. Country or folk dancing and city or social dancing together
describe the major patterns. The history of recreational dance in this country,
moreover, parallels the development of dance as a form of popular stage entertainment and testifies to the great influence that each form has had upon the other.
Nineteenth-century minstrels borrowed jigs and clog dances from white and black
folk dancers who performed at city and plantation festivities, much as the spectacular Broadway musicals of the 1920s and 1930s borrowed from social dance of
the time. What the history of dance in America clearly shows is that Americans
have not only enjoyed watching dance but also nurtured a rich and varied tradition
of dance as a form of popular social recreation.

HISTORICAL OUTLINE

In early America, as in all lands, dance initially played a purely ceremonial role
as part of religious observances. Ritualistic Indian circle dances, replete with complex formations and incantations, constituted the only form of dance that European settlers in the New World encountered. The Puritans were strongly
discouraged from engaging in couple dancing. Increase Mather preferred "un-
mixed" dancing, and his condemnation of "promiscuous" couple dances dates from
the 1680s in the pamphlet *An Arrow against Profane and Promiscuous Dancing Drawn
Out of the Quiver of Scriptures*. Dance historian Nancy Chalfa Ruyter, however,
has corrected the popular misconception that the Puritans disapproved of all dancing; rather, she asserts that, by and large, dancing not only was considered pleasant
recreation but was an important element of a cultivated lifestyle. Couple dancing
along with Maypole and other festival dancing was certainly frowned upon, but
formation dances were the popularly accepted form of Puritan dance activity. A
later, more tolerant religious sect living in Albany, New York, the Shakers or

"Shaking Quakers" of Revolutionary days, actually incorporated step and round dances into their religious ceremonies. The Shakers believed that dancing was an angelic activity that helped rid them of sin and bring them closer to an ecstatic, ideal communion with God.

Other English, French, and Spanish colonists brought rich native traditions of folk dancing that included hornpipes and jigs in addition to stately court dances such as the minuet and gavotte. In England, John Playford's *The English Dancing Master, or Plaine and Easie Rules for the Dancing of Country Dances, with the Tune to Each Dance*, published in the 1650s, became a standard country dancing manual for English and European dancing masters. The publication of *The English Dancing Master* began the standardization of country dances, which made their way into society circles and challenged for the first time, according to historian Richard Nevell, the popularity of fancy drawing room dances of the wealthy.

Despite the railings of Puritan ecclesiastics such as Mather, a good number of New England Puritans and other colonists continued to dance. By 1716 Boston claimed two dancing masters, one of whom was forced to move to New York when the rivalry for authority and for students became too keen. John Griffith, the most famous of the colonial dancing masters, is said to have traveled along the eastern seaboard from Rhode Island as far south as Charleston, South Carolina, renting space, advertising in newspapers, and giving instructions in the popular dances of the day. By the mid-1700s, Virginians were dancing the court gavotte as well as the country reels outlined in Playford's manual. George Washington was reported to have especially enjoyed dancing the Sir Roger de Coverly, later known as the Virginia reel. In Philadelphia, the first "assembly" or ball was held in 1748, establishing a tradition of a yearly social gathering with dancing as the main activity. By the days of the American Revolution, city people and country folk in all the colonies were performing traditional contra dances as well as new occasional ones with names such as Jefferson and liberty and the Washington quickstep. Moreover, the wealthy classes in all regions of the country continued the tradition of court dances.

In the late eighteenth century, French entertainers and dancing masters such as the Alexander Placide family, who came to America to escape the terrors of the French Revolution, greatly influenced the course of theater as well as social dancing in America. Having the greatest influence in high society circles of Newport, New Hampshire, New York, and Philadelphia, the French dancing masters brought sophisticated versions of country dances, which they renamed *les contredanses*. So widespread was the French influence that the French quadrille, a slowed-down version of the minuet, became the forerunner of the American square dance. Also quite important was the effect that French and all dancing masters in America had well into the late nineteenth century upon improvising and complicating the country dance steps and upon standardizing their execution as well as developing dance rules of etiquette.

Anti-British sentiment in America in the late eighteenth and nineteenth centuries fostered general preference for the French quadrille over English contra dances, although rural areas of New England kept alive the English folk dancing tradition. In the southern Appalachian Mountains of Kentucky, West Virginia, North Carolina, and Tennessee, the Scottish and Irish settlers and their descendants continued to jig and clog, which eventually became the trademark of south-

Dance floor at the Hurricane Ballroom, New York. Courtesy of the Library of Congress

ern country dancing. Using native African rhythms and dances such as the "Giouba," which used figures of the court dances with hip movements of the Congo, the black slaves on southern plantations during this period incorporated the jig footwork rhythms into their own peculiar dance styles. This early black dance tradition was later perfected by the nineteenth-century jig and clog dancers or "buckdancers," such as William Henry Lane, known as Master Juba (derived from the "Giouba" dance), who gained wide popularity in America and Europe. Southern regional black dance in America, in addition, eventually blossomed in the early twentieth century into the tap and jazz forms perfected by black professional dancers. In another region of the country, western settlers and cowboy dancers of the period favored the cotillion with the "caller" who shouted out the dance formations. Western square dancers of the day danced the wagon wheel and the Texas star.

In the city, social dancing became increasingly refined and adapted rules of etiquette under the guidance of the dancing masters. Hundreds of manuals such as *Dick's Quadrille Book* (1878) were published during the 1800s dictating correct placement and deportment. Couple dancing had been popularized in the first half of the nineteenth century by the waltz and the polka, European country dances that were integrated into the quadrilles of the day. Initially considered scandalous because of the close contact of the couple, the waltz grew so popular that the dancing masters were forced to accept a refined version of it. However, the extent to which social dance in America was breaking away from the control of dancing masters was seen when, in 1883, fearful that dance would become vulgar without proper instruction, they formed the American National Association of Masters of Dancing to preserve the genteel way of dancing.

In a further attempt to exert control over social dance of the day, Allen Dodworth, New York's leading dancing master, published a manual in 1885 designed to show the proper, refined way to execute ballroom dancing. The manual, *Dancing and Its Relation to Education and Social Life*, placed importance on dancing as a form of cultivated behavior and contained a system of teaching with diagrams and musical scores. Also contributing to the effort to keep social dancing refined were regular articles in popular periodicals such as *Godey's Lady's Book*, which contained rules on proper dance deportment.

By the early 1900s, the waltz, the polka, and the schottische were the favorite social dances. Mrs. Cornelius Vanderbilt II was staging balls as the most important social events of the season, and "correct" dancing was fully accepted as a cultivated activity for high society. Social dancing was also established as a fixed feature of American social life at all levels. Around that time, however, the rich musical and dance traditions of southern blacks, which had been nurtured in New Orleans, were being seen and heard more frequently and were to change permanently the face of social dance in America by introducing a new sense of rhythm. New Orleans saloon music known as "ragtime," with its "ragged" or syncopated rhythm, gave rise to the turkey trot, grizzly bear, bunny hug, and the kangaroo dip. So popular did these dances become that they set off a dance craze that lasted well into the late 1920s. Far more daring than the tame waltz had been, these new dances allowed couples to hang on to each other and dance cheek to cheek.

Society matrons now thundered that deportment and etiquette had been completely lost in the new dances. Irene and Vernon Castle came to society's rescue, however, when between 1912 and 1919 they did much to popularize a refined way of performing the popular social dances of the period. The Castles performed the turkey trot, the tango, and the hesitation waltz with equal grace and elegance. Performing at afternoon *thes dansants* (tea dances) held at ballrooms and cabarets, the Castles gave rise to a new emphasis on refined social dancing. The Castles even created new dances such as the castle walk and gained wide popularity touring the United States and Europe giving demonstrations. Other dance demonstrators quickly followed the Castles' lead and performed in halls and ball-dining rooms in major cities all across America. Joan Sawyer and Jack Jarret, and Arthur Murray and Irene Hammond were all dance demonstrators during the period 1910–1920.

Given the immense popularity of social dancing during this period, popular music began to concentrate on music to dance by. Irving Berlin's "Alexander's Ragtime Band" was extremely popular, as was the "jazz" music of black musicians, which was now a more familiar sound to the white American public. The black bottom, the shimmy, and the varsity drag, dances adapted from the black tradition, were all summarily denounced as immoral. Paying no attention to pulpit preachers, however, the enthusiastic dancers of the 1920s continued to perform all of the new dances in public halls all over the country. The Charleston, appearing in the 1923 black performers' review *Running Wild*, along with Harry Fox's improvised routine in the Ziegfeld Follies, the fox-trot, quickly became the dances of the 1920s.

The public dance arena gained wide popularity during the 1920s, when hundreds of dance halls sprang up in San Francisco's Barbary Coast, New Orleans' French Quarter, Chicago's South Side, and New York's Bowery and Tenderloin District. Several types of halls catering to different clienteles and social classes developed. Municipal districts and civic groups such as clubs and lodges sponsored dances at public halls. Another type of public dance arena, the "taxi-dance" ballrooms, was for men only and offered dance partners for the price of a ticket. More elaborate dance palaces, complete with chandeliers and gilt drapes, could be found in major cities. The Roseland and the Savoy in New York, the Trianon and Aragon in Chicago, the Hollywood Paladium in Los Angeles, and similar arenas in Detroit, Cleveland, Cincinnati, and Denver entertained millions of dancers throughout the 1920s and 1930s.

The decade of the 1930s is perhaps best known as the classic period of the Broadway musical and the Hollywood musical film, both of which featured dancing. Musicians such as George Gershwin, Irving Berlin, and Cole Porter were composing music for Broadway shows, and Fred Astaire and Ginger Rogers reigned as the dance couple of Hollywood dance film. James Cagney, Shirley Temple, Bill "Bojangles" Robinson, George Raft, and Buddy Ebsen all performed routines and also contributed toward making dance the center of stage and film entertainment during the decade. In the social dance arena, Arthur Murray's mailorder dance instruction business was flourishing, and the lindy hop, created on the occasion of Charles Lindbergh's 1927 cross-Atlantic flight, became a very popular dance that incorporated the energetic movements of the Charleston and the black bottom. Young people were increasingly becoming the biggest followers of dance fads, particularly when the big dance bands and swing music along with jitterbugging became popular during the closing years of the decade.

Benny Goodman, Tommy Dorsey, Duke Ellington, Glenn Miller, and swing music became the rage in the 1940s. Jitterbugging quickly became the favorite dance of American servicemen and their dance partners in entertainment centers and canteens. The jitterbug was unquestionably perfected at Harlem's Savoy Ballroom, where dancers incorporated gymnastic feats such as airborne turns and tosses into the dance, and the best performers became dance demonstrators in their own right. The second feature of social dance during this period was the rage for Latin music and dances. Cesar Romero and Carmen Miranda performed the samba, rumba, conga, and mambo to music by Xavier Cugat, Tito Puente, and Perez Prado for an American dance public that diligently tried to learn the syncopated rhythm and hip movements. Generally, they settled for less complicated versions of Latin dances; however, the interest in the Latin rhythm never died. The resurgence of interest in social dance in the 1970s, in fact, was due, to a great extent, to the popularity of the hustle, a New York City Hispanic youth dance that required complex timing and an acute sense of rhythm.

With the decade of the 1950s came Elvis Presley and rock-and-roll music and dancing. In 1956 *American Bandstand*, a television program developed in Philadelphia and hosted by Dick Clark, provided an arena for teenagers to dance to the new music. Adults still preferred the fox-trot and the cha-cha and vocal hits by Frank Sinatra and Rosemary Clooney. The younger generation, on the other hand, danced the stroll and listened to music by Jerry Lee Lewis, Bill Haley and the Comets, the Everley Brothers, and the Platters.

Chubby Checker and the twist, a dance that both adults and teenagers found easy to perform, dominated the rock-and-roll dance scene in the early 1960s. The period also produced such fad dances as the mashed potatoes and the jerk, which, like the twist, separated the dancing couple and stressed the ingenuity of individual styles and movements. The French discotheque became popular in America during this time and developed as the nightspot where one could dance amid strobe lights and glittering decor. Black music and dance of the period came to be called the "Motown Sound" (the record label under which much of the music was produced). Such stars as Diana Ross and the Supremes, the Temptations, and Smokey Robinson and the Miracles were Motown celebrities. Social dancing in the mid- and late 1960s waned, however, as the Beatles began to revolutionize rock music. The rock concert replaced dancing as the popular social entertainment pastime when young people preferred listening to popular singers Jimi Hendrix, Janis Joplin, and Jefferson Airplane sing at rock festivals such as Woodstock and the Monterey Pop Festival. By the late 1960s, the drug culture had inspired and produced "acid rock," the ultimate in undanceable music.

In the 1970s, a return to dancing brought back the discos and a new, updated version of *American Bandstand*. The 1971 show *Soul Train* featured African American dances such as the breakdown and the scooby doo, which incorporated variations of the "lockstep" and showed once again black dance's emphasis on complicated rhythm and timing. The hustle, a dance originating in Hispanic barrios of New York City, was at the center of the dance craze of the 1970s and is credited with bringing back technique to social dancing. The New York City disco Studio 54 became the fashionable dancing spot for such celebrities as Liza Minelli and ballet superstar Mikhail Baryshnikov. In addition, the 1977 movie *Saturday Night Fever* gave the dance craze of the 1970s new life. Studios and instructors once again became popular, and television came up with programs such as *Dance Fever*, where dancing couples from across the country competed for prize money. The period also witnessed a nostalgic yearning for the good old days of dancing, and afternoon tea dances, held at hotels and clubs, featured programs of music from the 1930s and 1940s while couples glided across dance floors.

In more recent times, the popularity of new wave and punk rock music of the late 1970s and early 1980s attests to a new breed of dancers. Sporting Mohawk hairdos dyed pink, purple, or blue and wearing leather clothing, these dancers reject recent stylized movement. Their dancing is characterized by ritualistic-like jumping up and down while shivering and shaking the body. Break dancing was the most recent influence upon American social dance in the mid-1980s. Performed on the sidewalks and street corners of New York City and other large urban centers, break dancing, with its emphasis on athletic improvisation in the break dance idiom, has been perfected by African American and Latino ghetto youth, who have earned the status of exhibition performance dancers. The contemporary cult of punk rock and new wave music and the influence of break dancing provide the latest evidence that popular music and dancing are so closely connected that one inevitably influences and shapes the other.

While social dance developed in the late nineteenth and early twentieth centuries as the most popular form of recreational dance in America, country dancing

Line dancing. © Painet

remained popular in isolated regions and changed much less drastically than did social dance, particularly in the twentieth century. City dancing, as has been shown, responded to the innovations in popular music. Country dance, on the other hand, retained the patterns and innovations developed prior to the Civil War. Although such movement innovations as the "swing" and "waltz" steps were integrated, for example, into the square dances of the 1880s and 1890s, country dancing in America remained essentially unchanged through the nineteenth century. Country dancing and folk culture, however, experienced a revival with the 1918 publication of Elizabeth Burchenal's *Twenty-eight Contra Dances, Largely from the New England States*. Country dances from Maine to Massachusetts were rediscovered, and a sense of their historical value and that of folk lifestyles as well inspired the founding of centers committed to preserving and studying American folk cultures. In addition, western country dance was kept alive by Dorothy and Lloyd Shaw in Denver. Lloyd Shaw's *Cowboy Dances*, first published in 1939, renewed interest in western square dance, as did his troupe of demonstration dancers who toured the United States and Europe.

The last category of dance developed in America as a form of popular culture is defined as "national" or "ethnic" folk dance. While the English, Irish, and Scottish country dance traditions have had the greatest influence on the development of American country dance, other ethnic groups have kept alive national dances that reflect the mother country's culture. Defined more as demonstration rather than participational dances, ethnic folk dances such as the Israeli *hora* dance, the Mexican *el jarabe* courtship dance, the Scottish Highland fling, and the Italian *tarantella* have symbolic value in and of themselves. Though they can be, and very often are, performed by untrained dancers, their fullest expression is usually given by trained dancers in demonstrations at celebrations, festivities, or especially staged performances. An example can be seen in the Spanish flamenco dancers who not only have mastered the intricate footwork but can also execute the stylized body movements that suggest the sensuality at the heart of flamenco dance. Moreover, national or ethnic folk dances usually express a facet of the culture's history or are meant to show themes, like love, death, and war, common to all ethnic folk dances. Lastly, American ethnic folk dances express this country's heterogeneous cultural makeup and the influence that all folk cultures have had upon shaping a popular American dance tradition.

Dancing as a favorite American pastime has continued well into the last days of this century and has seen some new developments. The decade of the 1990s saw a crescendo of interest in numerous dance styles from the tango and the swing to new developments in hip-hop styles and West Coast *la quebradita* dancing among Chicano youth in Los Angeles. Fad dances such as the *lambada* and the *macarena* have had their fifteen minutes of fame. But country line dancing has become a regular Saturday night event in many a rural community center as well as in local cable television studios across the country. There has also been a keen interest in reviving and performing ethnic social dances that reflect the particular cultural traditions of American Indians, African Americans, and Latinos, among others.

While ballroom dancing has remained a vibrant exhibition event over the decades, it has attracted a recent popular level of interest, evidenced by lifestyle sections of major newspapers such as the *New York Times*, the *Washington Post*, the *Denver Post*, and the *Pittsburgh Post-Gazette*. Since 1990, all of these newspapers have reported on the popularity of ballroom dancing, of dance centers offering classes, and of social clubs featuring tango soirees or nights devoted to big band music and swing dancing. In the Washington, D.C. area, the 1990s revival in jitterbug or swing dancing was known as "hand dancing," which involves partners' holding hands and performing quick, six-step footwork. In different regions of the country the dance is known as "West Coast swing" or "Chicago stepping." Regardless of the region of the country or the style of swing dance in vogue, ballroom dancing has retained a hold on the American popular dance scene.

Recent developments in social dance among American youth attest to their ingenuity, their physical abilities, and their daring to challenge traditional boundaries of dance movement. African American and Latino hip-hop and step groups dominate the youth dance scene and deliver the routines that become the idiom of dance clubs and cabarets across the country. These exhibition dancers, often dressed in halter tops, tight-fitting pants, and army boots, perform precision step combinations together with freestyle movements that combine basic hip-hop steps such as the Roger rabbit, reebok and running man. On the West Coast, Chicano youth have donned jeans and cowboy boots and hats and developed a dance known as *la quebradita*, described clearly by Anne Marie Welsh, writing in the *San Diego Union-Tribune* (April 26, 1994): "Mixing elements of the polka, the Lindy and Western stomp dancing, couples perform the dance to *banda* music, which itself mixes the tinny blare of *mariachis* with the rhythms of the waltz and polka, played very fast." Although the fad is said to have had its start in San Diego, the musicians who play the music are from Guadalajara and Jalisco and thus represent a crossover movement that involves Mexican popular music being reinvented and popularized in the United States.

In the area of ethnic social dance, a 1998 exhibition sponsored by the National Museum of the American Indian staged performances and workshops devoted to social dances such as the rabbit dance and the snake dance in an effort to reveal a tradition of dancing not associated with ceremonies and war. In the same year, the Conjunto Folklorico Nacional de Cuba performed at Wolf Trap and the Spoleto Festival, revealing social dances not known outside Cuba. On the program were such dances as the tumba Francesa, a Haitian immigrant dance that begins in the manner of courtly French dancing but then switches to hip-swaying rhythms and steps. The Danza de los Apalencados, inspired by the Santeria religion, revealed the passion and dynamic interplay of spirituality and emotion. Critic Sarah Kaufman judged that the troupe's "raw spirit and crisp execution lent it an authentic feel often missing in other touring folk dance groups" (*Washington Post*, June 4, 1998).

The revival and huge success of tap dance have accounted for an interesting crossover phenomenon from social dance to performance dance, particularly in musical theater. Irish step dancing virtually took the country by storm in the popular review *Riverdance*. The virtuoso tap dancing revealed in the show complemented the general revival of tap dancing that was already under way in American stage dancing. Savion Glover has emerged as the young tap virtuoso credited with taking contemporary tap dancing to new intricacies of rhythm and accomplishment. Glover's talents have been showcased in such hits as *Jelly's Last Jam* in 1992 and the 1996 *Bring in da Noise, Bring in da Funk*. The interesting development of crossover, of one style of dance influencing the other, seems alive and well in performance dance, whether ballet, modern, jazz, or tap dance. Dance critics have noted, for instance, that the *Riverdance* choreography incorporates elements of the moon walk, while ethnic dance troupes freely borrow hip-hop movements. The trend appears to be a fusion of styles and of choreographers, as noted in modern dance's Mark Morris choreographing of *The Office* for the Zivili folk dance group, which specializes in dances of the former Yugoslavia. Morris has attempted to continue work in musical theater in his collaboration with Paul Simon in the short-lived Broadway production of *The Capeman*.

These crossover movements, especially in the incorporation of social dance styles and movements into performance dance idioms, whether modern or tap dance, attest to the powerful presence that social dance continues to exert upon performance dance in America today.

REFERENCE WORKS

Reference materials devoted solely to social, folk, and ethnic dance are almost nonexistent. The researcher must make use of general dance reference materials, searching for sections within general reference works. The major reference work for all dance studies is the ten-volume *Dictionary Catalogue of the Dance Collection*, housed at Lincoln Center, which catalogs all materials in the collection up to 1973. Entries on social, folk, and ethnic dance are included in the over 300,000 entries. The annual *Bibliographic Guide to Dance* continues where the *Dictionary*

Catalogue leaves off and lists materials for the Lincoln Center collection since 1973.

Another, older, standard dance reference tool that lists works on American dance forms is Paul D. Magriel's *A Bibliography of Dancing: A List of Books and Articles on the Dance and Related Subjects*, with its supplement covering 1936–1940. Mary H. Kaprelian's *Aesthetics for Dancers: A Selected Annotated Bibliography*, published by the American Alliance for Health, Physical Education and Recreation, lists books and journal articles arranged by topic. Useful general dance dictionaries include Barbara Naomi Cohen-Stratyner's *Biographical Dictionary of Dance*, which profiles dance figures spanning the last four centuries of dance history in Europe and America. Walter G. Raffe's *Dictionary of the Dance* is another general reference work, providing historical, critical, and technical information on dance through the ages. Among useful encyclopedias and handbooks are Anatole Chujoy's *The Dance Encyclopedia* and Agnes de Mille's *The Book of the Dance*. While mainly a ballet encyclopedia, Chujoy's book contains lengthy, authoritative articles on various forms of dance and is a standard reference work in the area. Much more pertinent to the American dance scene and, more precisely, to the development of social dance, de Mille's book offers a well-illustrated treatment of American dance history by a major American dance pioneer. The *Guide to Dance Periodicals* indexes articles devoted to dance alphabetically by author and subject. Other general indexes and abstracts that dance researchers find as helpful tools include the *Arts and Humanities Citation Index*, the *Humanities Index*, and the *Reader's Guide to Periodical Literature*. Two other quite useful indexes are the *Music Index* and the *Art Index*. Specific compilations of dance research, notably dissertations, published by the American Association for Health, Physical Education, Recreation and Dance include Esther Pease's *Compilation of Dance Research, 1901–1964*; *Research in Dance I*, a 1968 supplement to the previous volume; *Research in Dance II*, which covers research completed and in progress from 1967 through 1972; *Research in Dance III*, a listing of theses and dissertations for advanced degrees from 1971 to 1982; and *Completed Research in Health, Physical Education, Recreation and Dance*, an annual listing of research since 1959. Lastly, a major project, *The International Encyclopedia of Dance*, edited by Selma Jeanne Cohen, was finally published in 1998 by Oxford University Press and, as promised, covers the entire field of dance. It is an indispensable tool for all dance researchers.

RESEARCH COLLECTIONS

The Dance Collection of the New York Public Library at Lincoln Center is the most comprehensive dance library in the United States and probably in the world. The collection covers all aspects of dance and features all manner of manuscripts, films, playbills, and special collections. The Harvard Theatre Collection has extensive rare materials on early American dance, as do the Hoblitzelle Theatre Arts and Perry Castaneda Libraries at the University of Texas at Austin. Major university libraries, including the University of California at Los Angeles, Yale, Cornell, the University of Chicago, the Indiana University School of Music, and the University of Michigan, all have quite respectable general collections of dance materials adequate for the researcher interested in topics in dance as a form of popular culture.

HISTORY AND CRITICISM

General Books and Articles

A good place to begin researching the history of popular dance in America is, in general, histories that attempt to place the development of America's popular dance forms in a broad context of dance as a performance art. A newcomer to the field would find Curt Sachs' classic 1937 *World History of Dance* a comprehensive and scholarly history of the dance through the ages. Evelyn Porter's *Music through Dance* is still a valuable early general history; it devotes the last two chapters to the development of nineteenth- and twentieth-century social dances and, in addition, includes a valuable treatment of the jazz age and the close relationship between the music and dance of the ragtime era. An invaluable general introductory text is Paul D. Magriel's *Chronicles of the American Dance*. Although the collection's main focus is on dance as a performance art, it has three very important articles: "Juba and American Minstrelsy," "The Dodworth Family and Ballroom Dance in New York," and "Dance in Shaker Ritual." All are examples of early dance history scholarship and give the dance researcher an excellent introduction to dance in the development of American culture. Agnes de Mille's *The Dance in America* devotes sections to parallel developments in American music halls, the history of the social dance scene, and the far-ranging influence of Negro minstrel and folk dance groups. A companion volume is Walter Terry's classic text *The Dance in America*, which traces performance as well as social dance in America. The text has very useful chapters on dance in colonial America, on black dance, and on ethnic dance. Doris Hering's *Twenty-five Years of American Dance* is another invaluable classic introductory history with chapters on social dance and ballroom, exhibition, and ethnic dance. Arthur Todd's "Four Centuries of American Dance" is an excellent series of eight *Dancemagazine* articles that begins with the dance of the American Indian and traces developments through pioneer dances, Negro folk dance, and pertinent trends in theater dance from 1734 to 1900. The scholarship presented in these articles is solid and insightful. A very useful introductory text that takes an anthropological approach to the development of dance in America is Jamake Highwater's *Dance: Rituals of Experience*. The work is useful for its discussion of American society's values as they have shaped the country's dance forms. One of the most pertinent studies in this field is Nancy Lee Chalfa Ruyter's excellent book *Reformers and Visionaries: The Americanization of the Art of Dance*, which traces America's turn-of-the-century acceptance of performance dance as a respectable, serious artistic pursuit. Several general studies of the early history of America's cultural life should be read as background material providing a context for specific treatments of dance history. Several extremely useful works are Russel B. Nye's *The Cultural Life of the New Nation, 1776–1830*; Percy A. Scholes' *The Puritans and Music in England and New England*; Louis B. Wright's *The Cultural Life of the American Colonies, 1607–1763*; and *The Arts in America: The Colonial Period* by Louis B. Wright et al.

Native American dancers. Courtesy of the Denver Public Library

Folk and Ethnic Dance

Among general sources in this area, Cecil J. Sharp's *The Dance: An Historical Survey of Dancing in Europe* is still must reading since the treatment is one of the earliest modern, scholarly discussions of Western folk dance and its applications to American trends. Other valuable general texts are La Meri's early *Dance as an Art Form* and her more recent work, *Total Education in Ethnic Dance*. Both accounts present definitions of ethnic dance by country, with some attention to American ethnic dances. A lesser-known, but valuable, general historical work is J. Tillman Hall's *Folk Dance*, which provides insights into folk dancing as an avenue for social integration and as an educational tool in learning about other American ethnic cultures. Betty Casey's *International Folk Dancing U.S.A.* is an extremely handsome book, complete with a brief history of American folk dancing, descriptions of dance leaders, selected camps and organizations, and dance groups and institutions for various ethnic folk dancers from around the world. A last general source, Richard Nevell's *A Time to Dance: American Country Dancing from Hornpipes to Hot Hash*, is perhaps the most valuable, with its extensive bibliography of contra, round, western square, and southern Appalachian square dancing forms.

A sampling of book-length sources that treat regional dance developments and that also provide historical material as well as instructions includes Betty Casey's *Dance across Texas* and Lucile K. Czarnowski's *Dances of Early California Days*. Two other valuable books are Beth Tolman and Ralph Page's *The Country Dance Book* and Frank Smith's *The Appalachian Square Dance*. Several excellent, shorter-length articles are Lee Ellen Friedland's "Traditional Folkdance in Kentucky," Jennifer

P. Winstead's "Tripping the Light Fantastic Toe: Popular Dance of Early Portland, Oregon, 1800–1864," and Gretchen Schneider's "Pidgeon Wings and Polkas: The Dance of the California Miners." All are well-documented, scholarly treatments.

Square Dance

Two standard works in this area are Samual Foster Damon's *The History of Square Dancing*, which critics have labeled the definitive work, and Martin Rossoff's *Hoedown Heritage: The Evolution of Modern Square Dancing*. Ralph Page's "A History of Square Dancing in America" is an authoritative work by a prominent scholar in the area. Western square dance is treated in *Cowboy Dances* by Lloyd Shaw, the man responsible for reviving interest in western square dancing in the 1930s.

Social Dance

Social dancing, which developed in the urban centers and distinguished itself from country dance forms, is taken up in the classic work of 1885, *Dancing and Its Relation to Education and Social Life* by Allen Dodworth. Rosetta O'Neill's treatment of Dodworth's control over turn-of-the century social dance in New York is especially valuable. Other classic defenses of dancing are Edward Lawson's *On Dancing and Its Refining Influence in Social Life* of 1884 and J. B. Gross' *The Parson on Dancing* of 1879, which relies on a careful use of the Bible to defend the art of fair Terpsichore. These apologies for dance must be read in conjunction with the classic treatises against dancing written by Increase and Cotton Mather, which are very well edited and discussed by Joseph E. Marks III in *The Mathers on Dancing*. Arthur Cole's 1942 account of social dance history in "The Puritan and Fair Terpsichore" is a most valuable piece, especially for its attention to the early development of dancing in education at Harvard and Yale.

The influence of Europe's dance tradition in this country transmitted via dancing masters is the topic of a most useful scholarly article by Ann Barzel, "European Dance Teachers in the United States." A group of well-researched seminal articles on social dance forms in the seventeenth and eighteenth centuries is Chrystelle T. Bond's "A Chronicle of Dance in Baltimore: 1780–1814"; Joy Van Cleef's "Rural Felicity: Social Dance in Eighteenth Century Connecticut"; and Shirley Wynne's "From Ballet to Ballroom: Dance in the Revolutionary Era." In addition, Paul Nettle's discussion of the waltz in "Birth of the Waltz" lets us see precisely how that dance paved the way for a new liberal attitude in social dance forms.

A short, but excellent, study of dance in education is Joseph E. Marks' *America Learns to Dance*, which emphasizes the important place that dance increasingly held in the cultural and educational life of the new country. Arthur Franks takes a scholarly approach in *Social Dance: A Short History*, as does Belinda Quirey in *May I Have the Pleasure? The Story of Popular Dancing*. Popular, but nonetheless very useful, introductory histories are found in Peter Buckman's *Let's Dance: Social, Ballroom and Folk Dancing* and Don McDonagh's *Dance Fever*. A book published by the Metropolitan Museum of Art is *Dance: A Very Social History* by Carol McD. Wallace and others, which nicely brings together discussions of the evolution of social dance, its corresponding costumes or clothing fashions, and the iconography of dance.

Albert McCarthy's *The Dance Band Era: The Dancing Decades from Ragtime to Swing, 1910–1950* traces popular dance forms through the concurrent developments in popular music. A very interesting sociological account of the popularity of the taxi dance hall and dancer is found in Paul Cressey's *The Taxi-Dance Hall*. A later excellent study of the same topic is Russel B. Nye's "Saturday Night at the Paradise Ballroom or Dance Halls in the Twenties." Nye also presents a brief, but useful, treatment of popular dance in the 1930s and 1940s in "The Big Band Era" in *The Unembarrassed Muse*. Frank Calabria very nicely researches the dance marathon phenomenon in "The Dance Marathon Craze," which adds to our knowledge of 1920s dance behavior. No bibliography of social dance would be complete without mentioning *Castles in the Air*, Irene Castle's story of her and her husband, Vernon's, role in popularizing social dance by making it acceptable in high society during the years 1900–1930.

Musical Theater

Any story of American social dance history must take into consideration the early and consistently intimate connections between popular theatrical dance and the social dance taking place in dance schools and balls or "assemblies" across the country. An examination of general histories of American popular musical theater yields valuable insights into the earliest of forms, which were the foundation for later social dance developments. Julian Mates' excellent work on early stage entertainments in *The American Musical Stage before 1800* and *America's Musical Stage: Two Hundred Years of Musical Theatre* describes the pantomime ballets and comic operas that set the stage for the later vaudeville and musical comedy developments that became the signature forms of the American musical stage. Of the valuable general histories of the entire American musical theater, several will serve the dance researcher in providing a basic framework into which dance history properly fits. Stanley Green's *The World of Musical Comedy*, David Ewen's *The Story of America's Musical Theatre*, Tom Vallance's *The American Musical Theatre*, and Richard Kislan's *The Musical: A Look at the American Musical Theatre* and *Hoofing on Broadway: A History of Show Dancing* together cover all phases and developments of American stage dance. Two very important and valuable collections of essays are *American Popular Entertainment*, edited by Myron Matlaw, and *Musical Theatre in America*, edited by Glenn Loney. Pertinent articles in the first volume deal with the popularity of pantomime, minstrel shows, burlesque, and blacks in vaudeville, in addition to treating the influence of Ruth St. Denis on the development of dance as a high art form in the early twentieth century. Two particularly useful articles from the second volume trace the tremendous influence of black dance on choreography in the American musical theater.

The one dance figure whose career greatly influenced developments in social dance is Fred Astaire. Three volumes provide ample information about Astaire's influence and career. Arlene Croce's *The Fred Astaire and Ginger Rogers Book* traces Astaire's approach to dance on film and his creation of a classic American dance style on stage and in film. Croce's valuable insights also target Astaire's profound effect upon popular dance, as he inserted elements of class and elegance that only the best could come near to imitating. Bob Thomas' *Astaire: The Man, the Dancer, the Life of Fred Astaire* is a chatty biography written by a friend of forty years and is most useful when read in conjunction with Astaire's own autobiography, *Steps in Time*.

Another major dance performer whose career has had a great impact upon American popular dance forms is Agnes de Mille. Besides her very useful dance histories mentioned earlier, her series of dance autobiographies gives a full account of her response to dance currents in her own time and ways in which she has emerged as a seminal figure in shaping modern American dance forms. The three pertinent de Mille autobiographies are *Dance to the Piper*, *And Promenade Home*, and *Speak to Me, Dance with Me*.

In the area of jazz dance, two books worth mention as general histories are *Anthology of Jazz Dance*, edited by Gus Giordano, the dean of American jazz dance, and John Shepherd's *Tin Pan Alley*. The Giordano volume offers a fine collection of essays that trace the history of jazz dance as well as developments in performance dance seen in Jerome Robbins' jazz ballets and social dance developments in the popular swing dance period. A brief, but useful, text, *Tin Pan Alley* chronicles the close development between the period's popular music and dance, a phenomenon that we take for granted today.

Black Dance

So powerful an influence has black dance been upon modern American social dance that historians regard it as the true, indigenous precursor of present-day social dance. Two absolutely essential texts covering the entire field are Marshall and Jean Stearns' *Jazz Dance: The Story of American Vernacular Dance* and Lynne Fauley Emery's *Black Dance in the United States from 1619 to 1970*. The Stearns volume draws on extensive fieldwork to document the native African roots of America's vernacular dance forms. Each chapter deals thoroughly with developments, records contributions of particular artists, and puts all information into a larger historical, social context. The book has an extensive bibliography and is an overall scholarly treatment of the highest caliber. Likewise, *Black Dance in the United States* traces African dance roots and influences and ties them to developments in music, poetry, and oral literature. Emery's scholarly approach is impressive yet highly readable and useful. A good companion article to Emery's studies is Helen Armstead-Johnson's "Blacks in Vaudeville: Broadway and Beyond" in *American Popular Entertainment*, along with the much earlier Marian Hannah Winter article "Juba and American Minstrelsy" in *Chronicles of the American Dance*. Hans Nathan's *Dan Emmett and the Rise of Early Negro Minstrelsy* is a solid treatment of the subject and should be read in conjunction with Edith J. Issacs' *The Negro in American Theatre* and Tom Fletcher's *One Hundred Years of the Negro in Show Business*. James Haskins' *The Cotton Club* chronicles the significant 1920s and 1930s era of Harlem's influence upon the development of black music and dance performance.

The life stories of important black performers should also be taken into account in the history of black dance in America. Several performers are seminal, influential figures. The legendary Josephine Baker tells her story in *Josephine*, while Katherine Dunham's *A Touch of Innocence* chronicles her own important life in the development of American black dance forms. Two other important works tracing Dunham's influence are *Kaiso! Katherine Dunham: An Anthology of Writings*, edited by VeVe A. Clarke and Margaret B. Wilkerson, and *Katherine Dunham: Reflections on the Social and Political Contexts of Afro-American Dance*, edited by Joyce Aschenbrenner. The last volume is an excellent monograph that traces Dunham's place at the forefront of the attempt to pioneer a respectful and rightful place for Afro-American dance in America. The last great performance artist whose career should be taken into account is Judith Jamison. Olga Maynard's biography *Judith Jamison: Aspects of a Dancer* details Jamison's rise in the Alvin Ailey company. Maynard nicely portrays Jamison's goals, trials, and accomplishments, along with those of Ailey's troupe, as they chart the hazards and fortunes of black dancers in the contemporary American dance scene.

Periodicals

Periodical literature devoted to popular dance can be found in major scholarly journals and in popular dance magazines. The oldest journals are *Dance Index* and *Dance Perspectives* (later superseded by *Dance Chronicle: Studies in Dance and the Related Arts*). The *Dance Research Journal*, published by the Congress on Research in Dance, is another excellent publication focusing on scholarly dance research in all areas. *Dance Observer* contained useful material and includes book reviews, while *Dance Scope* covered the field of dance education. The *Journal of Physical Education, Recreation and Dance* is an excellent publication that features research on social as well as folk and ethnic dance; it also includes book reviews. A more popular, but extremely useful, publication is *Dancemagazine*, which attempts to cover all dance forms in practice in the United States today, from classical ballet to street break dancing. Several useful journals can be found on folk dancing. *English Dance and Song*, *The English Folk Dance Society Journal*, and *Folk Music Journal* were three successive titles of the major journal covering the folk dance field; they contain reviews, scholarly articles, and notes on research. *American Squares* and *Square Dance* were other magazines covering club and association news and square dance news.

BIBLIOGRAPHY

Computer-Assisted Research

Since the first version of this chapter was published some years ago, the advance in computer technology has added a new level of resources for the dance researcher. The bibliography provided with the first version is still a solid beginning, and I have kept it intact for this new version. However, the Internet has made available such major research resources as the *Dictionary Catalogue of the Dance Collection* at the New York Public Library and the *Bibliographic Guide to Dance*. The beginning researcher in the field of dance would do well to begin a search for materials with a general search of dance resources on the World Wide Web. Some good general Web sites are listed next. They will lead to further and more specific Web sites on individual dance categories. Any good multisearch engine will identify hundreds of sites of possible use in research into dance.

The World-Wide Web Virtual Library at http://artswire.org. This comprehensive Web site lists a wide variety of resources on dance. The Dance Library Resources category lists other sites with information on all categories of dance research.

Cross-Cultural Dance Resources at http://www.ccdr.org

Country Dance and Song Society at http://www.cdss.org

Research in Dance Education at http://www.carfax.co.uk

Society of Dance History Scholars at http://www.sdhs.org

Books and Articles

Andrews, E. D. "The Dance in Shaker Ritual." In *Chronicles of the American Dance*, ed. Paul D. Magriel. New York: Da Capo Press, 1978, 3–14.

Armstead-Johnson, Helen. "Blacks in Vaudeville: Broadway and Beyond." In *American Popular Entertainment*, ed. Myron Matlaw. Westport, Conn.: Greenwood Press, 1979, 77–86.

Art Index. New York: H. W. Wilson, 1929– .

Arts and Humanities Citation Index. Philadelphia: Institute for Scientific Information, 1975– .

Aschenbrenner, Joyce, ed. *Katherine Dunham: Reflections on the Social and Political Contexts of Afro-American Dance. Dance Research Annual XII*. New York: Congress on Research in Dance, 1981.

Astaire, Fred. *Steps in Time*. New York: Da Capo Press, 1979.

Baker, Josephine. *Josephine*. New York: Harper and Row, 1977.

Barzel, Ann. "European Dance Teachers in the United States." *Dance Index* 3 (1944), 56–100.

Bibliographic Guide to Dance. New York: G. K. Hall, 1976– .

Bond, Chrystelle T. "A Chronicle of Dance in Baltimore: 1780–1814." *Dance Perspectives* 17 (Summer 1976), 4–49.

Burchenal, Elizabeth. *Twenty-eight Contra Dances, Largely from the New England States*. New York: G. Schirmer, 1918.

Buckman, Peter. *Let's Dance: Social, Ballroom and Folk Dancing*. New York: Penguin Books, 1979.

Calabria, Frank. "The Dance Marathon Craze." *Journal of Popular Culture* 10 (1976), 54–69.

Casey, Betty. *Dance across Texas*. Austin: University of Texas Press, 1985.

———. *International Folk Dancing U.S.A.* New York: Doubleday, 1981.

Castle, Irene. *Castles in the Air*. New York: Da Capo Press, 1958.

Chujoy, Anatole, ed. *The Dance Encyclopedia*. New York: Simon and Schuster, 1976.

Clarke, VeVe A., and Margaret B. Wilkerson, eds. *Kaiso! Katherine Dunham: An Anthology of Writings*. Berkeley: Institute for Study of Social Change, Women's Center, University of California, 1978.

Cohen, Selma Jeanne, ed. *The International Encyclopedia of Dance*. New York: Oxford University Press, 1998.

Cohen-Stratyner, Barbara Naomi. *Biographical Dictionary of Dance*. New York: Schirmer Books, 1982.

Cole, Arthur. "The Puritan and Fair Terpsichore." *Mississippi Valley Historical Review* 29 (1942).

Completed Research in Health, Physical Education, Recreation and Dance. Washington, D.C.: American Alliance for Health, Physical Education, Recreation and Dance, 1981.

Cressey, Paul. *The Taxi-Dance Hall*. New York: Greenwood Press, 1968.

Croce, Arlene. *The Fred Astaire and Ginger Rogers Book*. New York: Vintage Books, 1972.

Czarnowski, Lucile K. *Dances of Early California Days*. Palo Alto, Calif.: Pacific Books, 1950.

Damon, Samuel Foster. *The History of Square Dancing*. Barre, Mass.: Barre Gazette, 1957.

de Mille, Agnes. *And Promenade Home*. Boston: Little, Brown, 1958.

———. *The Book of the Dance*. New York: Golden Press, 1963.

———. *The Dance in America*. Washington, D.C.: U.S. Information Service, 1971.

———. *Dance to the Piper*. Boston: Little, Brown, 1951.

———. *Speak to Me, Dance with Me*. Boston: Little, Brown, 1972.

Dick's Quadrille Book. New York: Dick and Fitzgerald, 1878.

Dictionary Catalogue of the Dance Collection. 10 vols. New York: New York Public Library and G. K. Hall, 1974.

Dodworth, Allen. *Dancing and Its Relation to Education and Social Life*. New York: N.p., 1885.

Dunham, Katherine. *A Touch of Innocence*. New York: Books for Libraries, 1980.

Emery, Lynne Fauley. *Black Dance in the United States from 1619 to 1970*. New York: Dance Horizons, 1980.

Ewen, David. *The Story of America's Musical Theatre*. Philadelphia: Chilton Book, 1968.

Fletcher, Tom. *One Hundred Years of the Negro in Show Business*. New York: Burdge, 1967.

Franks, Arthur. *Social Dance: A Short History*. London: Routledge and Kegan Paul, 1963.

Friedland, Lee Ellen. "Traditional Folkdance in Kentucky." *Country Dance and Song* 10 (1979), 5–19.

Giordano, Gus, ed. *Anthology of Jazz Dance*. Evanston, Ill.: Orion, 1975.

Green, Stanley. *The World of Musical Comedy*. New York: Da Capo Press, 1980.

Gross, J. B. *The Parson on Dancing*. Philadelphia: J. B. Lippincott, 1879. New York: Dance Horizons, 1979.

Guide to Dance Periodicals. Vols. 1–10. New York: Belknap Press, 1931–1962.

Hall, J. Tillman. *Folk Dance*. Pacific Palisades, Calif.: Goodyear, 1969.

Haskins, James. *The Cotton Club*. New York: Goodyear, 1969.

Hering, Doris, ed. *Twenty-five Years of American Dance*. New York: Rudolf Orthwine, 1951.

Highwater, Jamake. *Dance: Rituals of Experience*. New York: A and W, 1978.

Humanities Index. New York: H. W. Wilson, 1975– .

Isaacs, Edith. *The Negro in American Theatre*. New York: Theatre Arts, 1947.

Kaprelian, Mary H. *Aesthetics for Dancers: A Selected Annotated Bibliography*. Washington, D.C.: American Alliance for Health, Physical Education and Recreation, 1976.

Kislan, Richard. *Hoofing on Broadway: A History of Show Dancing*. New York: Prentice-Hall, 1987.

————. *The Musical: A Look at the American Musical Theatre*. Englewood Cliffs, N.J.: Prentice-Hall, 1980.

La Meri. *Dance as an Art Form*. New York: Scribner's, 1933.

————. *Total Education in Ethnic Dance*. New York: Marcel Dekker, 1977.

Lawson, Edward. *On Dancing and Its Refining Influence in Social Life*. London: N.p., 1884.

Loney, Glenn, ed. *Musical Theatre in America*. Westport, Conn.: Greenwood Press, 1984.

Magriel, Paul D. *A Bibliography of Dancing: A List of Books and Articles on the Dance and Related Subjects*. New York: H. W. Wilson, 1936.

————. *A Bibliography of Dancing: A List of Books and Articles on the Dance and Related Subjects, 4th Cumulated Supplement*. New York: H. W. Wilson, 1936–1940.

————. *Chronicles of the American Dance from the Shakers to Martha Graham*. New York: Da Capo Press, 1978.

Marks, Joseph, III, ed. *America Learns to Dance: A Historical Study of Dance Education in America before 1900*. New York: Dance Horizons, 1957.

————, ed. *The Mathers on Dancing*. New York: Dance Horizons, 1975.

Mates, Julian. *The American Musical Stage before 1800*. New Brunswick, N.J.: Rutgers University Press, 1962.

————. *America's Musical Stage: Two Hundred Years of Musical Theatre*. Westport, Conn.: Greenwood Press, 1985.

Matlaw, Myron, ed. *American Popular Entertainment*. Westport, Conn.: Greenwood Press, 1979.

Maynard, Olga. *Judith Jamison: Aspects of a Dancer*. New York: Doubleday, 1982.

McCarthy, Albert. *The Dance Band Era: The Dancing Decades from Ragtime to Swing, 1910–1950*. Radnor, Pa.: Chilton Book, 1971.

McDonagh, Don. *Dance Fever*. New York: Random House, 1979.

Music Index. Detroit: Information Service, 1949– .

Nathan, Hans. *Dan Emmett and the Rise of Early Negro Minstrelsy*. Norman: University of Oklahoma Press, 1962.

Nettle, Paul. "Birth of the Waltz." *Dance Index* 5 (1946), 208–28.

Nevell, Richard. *A Time to Dance: American Country Dancing from Hornpipes to Hot Hash*. New York: St. Martin's Press, 1977.

Nye, Russel B. "The Big Band Era." In *The Unembarrassed Muse: The Popular Arts in America*. New York: Dial Press, 1970, pp. 326–40.

————. *The Cultural Life of the New Nation, 1776–1830*. New York: Harper and Row, 1960.

————. "Saturday Night at the Paradise Ballroom or Dance Halls in the Twenties." *Journal of Popular Culture* 7 (1974), 14–22.

————. *Society and Culture in America, 1830–1860*. New York: Harper and Row, 1914.

O'Neill, Rosetta. "The Dodworth Family and Ballroom Dance in New York." In *Chronicles of American Dance*, ed. Paul Magriel. New York: Da Capo Press, 1948, pp. 81–100.

Page, Ralph. "A History of Square Dancing in America." In *Focus on Dance: Dance Heritage*. Washington, D.C.: American Association for Health, Physical Education and Recreation, 1977.

Pease, Esther, ed. *Compilation of Dance Research, 1901–1964.* Washington, D.C.: American Association for Health, Physical Education and Recreation, Dance Division, 1964.

Playford, John. *The English Dancing Master or, Plaine and Easie Rules for the Dancing of Country Dances, with the Tune to Each Dance.* Ed. Hugh Mellor and Leslie Bridgewater. London: Dance Books, 1984.

Porter, Evelyn. *Music through Dance.* London: B. T. Batsford, 1937.

Quirey, Belinda. *May I Have the Pleasure? The Story of Popular Dancing.* London: British Broadcasting, 1976.

Raffe, Walter G. *Dictionary of the Dance.* New York: A. S. Barnes, 1964.

Readers' Guide to Periodical Literature. New York: H. W. Wilson, 1890–   .

Research in Dance I: A Supplement to Compilation of Dance Research 1901–1966. Washington, D.C.: American Association for Health, Physical Education and Recreation, Dance Division, 1968.

Research in Dance II: Research Completed and in Progress from 1967–1972. Washington, D.C.: American Association for Health, Physical Education and Recreation, Dance Division, 1973.

Research in Dance III. Washington, D.C.: American Association for Health, Physical Education and Recreation, Dance Division, 1982.

Rossoff, Martin. *Hoedown Heritage: The Evolution of Modern Square Dancing.* Sandusky, Ohio: American Square Dance Magazine, 1977.

Ruyter, Nancy Lee Chalfa. *Reformers and Visionaries: The Americanization of the Art of Dance.* New York: Dance Horizons, 1979.

Sachs, Curt. *World History of Dance.* New York: W. W. Norton, 1937.

Schneider, Gretchen. "Pidgeon Wings and Polkas: The Dance of the California Miners." *Dance Perspectives*, no. 39 (1969), 1–57.

Scholes, Percy A. *The Puritans and Music in England and New England.* London: Oxford University Press, 1934.

Sharp, Cecil J. *The Dance: An Historical Survey of Dancing in Europe.* London: Haltox and Truscott Smith, 1924.

Shaw, Lloyd. *Cowboy Dances.* Caldwell, Ohio: Caxton Printers, 1952.

Shepherd, John. *Tin Pan Alley.* London: Routledge and Kegan Paul, 1982.

Smith, Frank. *The Appalachian Square Dance.* Berea, Ky.: Berea College, 1955.

Stearns, Marshall, and Jean Stearns. *Jazz Dance: The Story of American Vernacular Dance.* New York: Schirmer Books, 1968.

Terry, Walter. *The Dance in America.* New York: Harper and Row, 1971.

Thomas, Bob. *Astaire: The Man, the Dancer, the Life of Fred Astaire.* New York: St. Martin's Press, 1984.

Todd, Arthur. "The Dance of the American Indian." *Dancemagazine* 23 (September 1949), 18–19.

———. "Folk Dance of Our Pioneers." *Dancemagazine* 23 (November 1949), 20–21, 34–35.

———. "Negro American Theatre Dance, 1840–1900." *Dancemagazine* 24 (November 1950), 20–21, 33–34.

———. "The Negro Folk Dance in America." *Dancemagazine* 24 (January 1950), 14–15.

———. "The Rise of Musical Comedy Dance." *Dancemagazine* 24 (December 1950), 23–25, 38–39.

————. "Theatre Dance in America, 1784–1812." *Dancemagazine* 24 (April 1950), 24–25, 40.

————. "Theatre Dance in America, 1820–35." *Dancemagazine* 24 (May 1950), 22–24.

————. "Theatrical Dancing in America before the Revolution, 1734–1775." *Dancemagazine* 24 (March 1950), 20–21, 35.

Tolman, Beth, and Ralph Page. *The Country Dance Book*. Guilford, Vt.: Countryman Press, 1937.

Vallance, Tom. *The American Musical Theatre*. New York: Castle Books, 1970.

Van Cleef, Joy. "Rural Felicity: Social Dance in Eighteenth Century Connecticut." *Dance Perspectives*, no. 65 (1976), 1–44.

Wallace, Carol McD., et al. *Dance: A Very Social History*. New York: Metropolitan Museum of Art, 1986.

Winstead, Jennifer P. "Tripping the Light Fantastic Toe: Popular Dance of Early Portland, Oregon, 1800–1864." In *American Popular Entertainment*, ed. Myron Matlaw. Westport, Conn.: Greenwood Press, 1979, 229–240.

Winter, Marian Hannah. "Juba and American Minstrelsy." In *Chronicles of the American Dance*, ed. Paul Magriel. New York: Da Capo Press, 39–63.

Wright, Louis B. *The Cultural Life of the American Colonies, 1607–1763*. New York: Harper and Row, 1957.

Wright, Louis B., et al. *The Arts in America: The Colonial Period*. New York: Scribner's, 1966.

Wynne, Shirley. "From Ballet to Ballroom: Dance in the Revolutionary Era." *Dance Scope* 10 (1975–1976), 65–73.

Periodicals

American Squares. New York, 1945–1965.
Dance Chronicle: Studies in Dance and the Related Arts. New York, 1977– .
Dance Index. New York, 1942–1948.
Dancemagazine. New York, 1927– .
Dance Observer. New York, 1936–1964.
Dance Perspectives. New York, 1959–1977.
Dance Research Journal. New York, 1974– .
Dance Scope. New York, 1965–1981.
English Dance and Song. London, 1899–1931.
The English Folk Dance Society Journal. London, 1927–1931.
Folk Music Journal. London, 1931– .
Journal of Physical Education, Recreation and Dance. Washington, D.C., 1975– .
Square Dance. Glenview, Ill., 1966– .

DEATH

John P. Ferré

Death has always played a significant part in American popular culture. In the colonial era, lessons from death were preached from the pulpit and taught from the lectern, and every American schoolchild since then has learned Nathan Hale's brave statement before he was hanged, "I regret that I have but one life to give for my country." Death has suffused music, poetry, and prose, and it has always been an essential element in the stories that Americans have written and told, from the earliest novels to the latest movies and television programs. The consistency of death as a theme in popular expression from colonial times to the end of the twentieth century makes it a subject capable of illuminating constants and changes in American values.

HISTORICAL OUTLINE

In 1982, the National Institute of Mental Health reported that by the age of sixteen the typical American had witnessed 18,000 homicides on television. This statistic is remarkable, but whatever the excesses, television in the late twentieth century was not dissimilar from American media of previous centuries, at least in one key way: death has been ubiquitous from the very beginning of the republic. To be sure, the meaning of death has changed. In Puritan America, depictions of death had a didactic function: to teach people the fear of God. In the nineteenth century, death became an occasion for contemplation. In the twentieth century, death was present in every medium of popular culture from humor and holidays to newspapers, movies, and the Internet. But whatever the changes, death has always found popular expression in the United States.

In Puritan America, death was much more than the inevitable end of life: it was the point at which God would decide whether an individual's life was faithful and deserving of eternity in heaven or unfaithful and deserving of eternity in hell. It was true that this world was ruled by Providence—not a sparrow fell that God

Mortuary in Denver, Colorado, early 1900s. Courtesy of the Denver Public Library

didn't permit to fall—but from the very limited human perspective, activities on this earth could only hint at what was to come. The point of life was not to be found in its earthly joys and sorrows but in its eternal desserts. Death was a central presence in Puritan America.

Puritans learned the presence of death as schoolchildren. Here's how their textbook, *The New England Primer*, expressed this point:

> Awake, arise, behold thou hast
> Thy Life a Leaf, thy Breath a Blast;
> At night lye down prepar'd to have
> Thy sleep, thy death, thy bed, thy grave.

Death also appeared in the primer's ABCs:

> Liars shall have their part in the lake
> Which burns with fire and brimstone. . . .
> *Time* cuts down all
> Both great and small. . . .
> *Xerxes* the great did die,
> And so must you & I.

Puritan children learned to hope for salvation from hell, not the promise of rewards on earth or in heaven.

These lessons were a simpler version of what Puritans were preaching in church.

"The heaven I desired was a heaven of holiness; to be with God, and to spend my eternity in divine love," Jonathan Edwards wrote in his *Personal Narrative*. "Heaven appeared exceedingly delightful, as a world of love; and that all happiness consisted in living in pure, humble, heavenly, divine love." However much inspiration could be found in the vagueness of heaven, the motivation for righteous living came from the details of hell. In his famous sermon of 1741, "Sinners in the Hands of an Angry God," Edwards described the dire consequences of succumbing to temptation: "O sinner! Consider the fearful danger you are in: it is a great furnace of wrath, a wide and bottomless pit, full of the fire of wrath, that you are held over by in the hand of that God, whose wrath is provoked and incensed as much against you, as against many of the damned in hell." Puritans lived on an eternal precipice, anxious about the mysteries of divine grace and judgment.

Because the meaning of death resided solely in God's subsequent judgment, Puritan funerals in early New England were austere. Puritans did not embalm corpses for display because with the flight of the soul, the vessel had been purged, leaving only a repulsive reminder of sin and the absence of spirit. According to Puritan expositor Samuel Willard, the loathsome shell was ready "to be commended to the cold and silent Grave where it must be entertained with Worms and Rottenness, and be turned into putrefaction." Burial was quick, funeral services simple, and grave markers plain.

By the eighteenth century, Puritan funerals evolved into services that had begun to recognize the grief (and the social standing) of survivors. Funerals became elaborate and expensive occasions, requiring, in addition to the costs of burial, the purchase of gloves and rings and large quantities of food and drink for invited guests. Life in Puritan New England had changed. The preoccupation with predestination and original sin, which led to the belief that most people were destined for the tortures of hell, had given way to a worldview in which death was not omnipresent and was less threatening.

Death was just as familiar to Americans in the nineteenth century as it had been in the eighteenth, but gone was the predominant fear of eternal damnation. Indeed, the nineteenth century was a period of transition. Less and less would the body be spurned as sinful and putrid and deserving only of immediate burial and decay. Less and less would death be simply the occasion for the soul to begin eternity either in torment or in tranquility. Americans continued to distinguish between body and soul and this life and the next, but as the century progressed, the conceptual distance between the living and the dead decreased. Americans in the nineteenth century had begun to domesticate death.

The rural cemetery was the first place to reflect nineteenth-century Romanticism. Beginning with Mount Auburn in Cambridge, Massachusetts (1831), Laurel Hill in Philadelphia (1836), and Green-Wood in Brooklyn (1838), cemeteries were created as places for contemplation. These were not church or city graveyards where corpses in disease and decay awaited the resurrection of the body. Renamed "cemeteries" from the Greek *koimētērion* (sleeping place), these were bucolic parks with lawn, trees, shrubs, flowers, water, and monuments that appealed to the nineteenth-century ideal of melancholy. In these serene gardens people could stroll, talk, and meditate near loved ones in their final rest. So popular were these cemeteries that when Frederick Law Olmstead's Central Park opened, many people raved that it was just like a cemetery without monuments.

The new craft of arterial embalming also helped to shrink the psychological distance between the living and the dead. First practiced in America after 1840 by medical schools in need of a steady supply of fresh cadavers, embalming became widespread during the Civil War as the only sure way to preserve the bodies of slain soldiers for transportation back home, where they could be displayed before burial, as was customary. True, embalming was pricey, so that it was performed mostly on the bodies of officers and soldiers from wealthy families, but by the end of the war the practice was widely accepted. Embalming not only relieved relatives and neighbors of the burden of preparing corpses for burial but preserved the body with the appearance of peaceful slumber.

Undertakers would later champion embalming as the means of creating "memory pictures," but more tangible memory pictures came from postmortem photography, which became popular in mid-nineteenth century. Jay Ruby reports this photographer's advertisement from the 1846 business directory of Boston:

> We make miniatures of children and adults instantly, and of Deceased Persons either at our rooms or at private residences . . . we take great pains to have Miniatures of Deceased Persons agreeable and satisfactory, and they are often so natural as to seem, even to Artists, in a deep sleep.

Postmortem photographs typically focused on the face or upper body of the corpse and created the illusion of rest or sleep by posing it on a couch, a bed, or a mother's lap. Not until the end of the century did they customarily emphasize grief by showing the deceased in a casket surrounded by flowers and mourners.

Like cemeteries and embalming and postmortem photography, a fascination with spiritualism made the dead seem nearer. In 1847, two sisters living in an old house in Hydesville, New York, claimed to be able to communicate with the dead. Two years later Maggie and Katie Fox were with Barnum and Bailey and receiving great publicity from Horace Greeley's *New York Tribune*. Others improved upon the Foxes' rappings with table-turnings and other acts of clairvoyance, generating tremendous skepticism as well as belief. By 1857, sixty-seven spiritualist periodicals were circulating, and by 1870 spiritualism claimed to have millions of followers. That number had diminished by 1888, when the Fox sisters confessed in 1888 that the rappings were really the sound of their toe joints cracking.

The generation that was intrigued by spiritualism was also the generation that read *The Gates Ajar* by Elizabeth Stuart Phelps. A balm for women who had lost family members in the Civil War, this novel depicted life in heaven as an idealized middle-class America. Not surprisingly, their loved ones were there, taking keen interest in life on earth and waiting for the time when they would be reunited for eternity. The novel's premise is realistic enough: Mary Cabot, the heroine, is unable to find consolation for her brother's death in the Civil War either in religion or in philosophy. But she does find comfort in the way her aunt describes heaven. Heaven is much like earth, Mrs. Forceythe says, only without life's irritations. Homes and friends are in heaven, where there are even ginger snaps in cookie jars for the children. Such was the desire for a close connection between

A "memory photograph" of a deceased baby holding
rosemary to symbolize remembrance. Courtesy of the
Library of Congress

life and afterlife that *The Gates Ajar* became a perennial best-seller that spawned sequels and imitations.

Even though the curtain that separated temporal from eternal existence for Calvinist America was perforated in the nineteenth century, the differences in the ways that Americans in the eighteenth and nineteenth centuries thought of death were minor compared to the changes that would come in the twentieth century. Before the twentieth century, death was an experience common to American households. Death usually occurred at home. There the body was prepared for burial, and there a wake was held. The funeral typically took place at a nearby church, and the body was buried at a local cemetery. Before the twentieth century, death was never far away.

By contrast, the experience of death in the twentieth century steadily became more and more vicarious. Persons at the end of the nineteenth century could expect to live just over forty years, whereas persons at the end of the twentieth century could expect to live well over seventy. Furthermore, increasing mobility in the twentieth century, coupled with professionalized health and funeral industries, meant that the dying were more frequently separated from their families, they were increasingly more likely to die in health-care centers than in their homes, and their bodies would be prepared for disposal by professionals in funeral homes rather than by family and neighbors in their homes. Increasingly, persons in the twentieth century became familiar with death and dying through a medium of communication rather than direct contact. For this reason, understanding the place of death in twentieth-century American culture requires careful attention to oral, print, and electronic channels of communication.

The jokes that people tell one another say a lot about what makes people anxious. Humor has the ability to elicit smiles and laughter about the most disquieting subjects, even death. So it makes sense that death humor was common in the twentieth century because death causes so much anxiety. The observation has been made that the statistics on death are impressive: one out of every one person dies.

But like much of the use of death in American popular culture, humor often uses death as a prop for other subjects. As the sex scandal of President Bill Clinton turned into his impeachment trial, numerous jokes circulated, including the following:

> The pope and President Clinton died at the same time. But a mix-up sent the pope to hell and President Clinton to heaven. When the mistake was corrected, the pope and President Clinton passed on their way to their real eternal homes. "I'm so happy," the pope said. "I've waited all my life to see the Blessed Virgin!" "Sorry," President Clinton replied. "You're about twenty minutes too late."

Jokes like this one use death and dying as a backdrop to highlight a completely different issue, often sexual.

But as Joseph Richman shows in his essay on humor in Robert and Beatrice Kastenbaum's *Encyclopedia of Death*, people do joke about death itself. Some jokes deal with the finality of death:

> A friend came to view Callahan's body in the funeral parlor. He said to Mrs. Callahan, "Look at the beautiful smile on his face." "Yes," she replied. "He died in his sleep. He doesn't know he's dead yet."

Others deal with the definition of death:

> Mr. Jones was lying in bed very ill, when he smelled some delicious food his wife was cooking. He called to his daughter and said, "Could you ask mother if I could have a plate of that delicious meat?" The daughter left, and returned shortly. "Mom says you can't have it. We're saving it for the wake."

Richman illustrates a number of other themes of death humor and finds in such humor a catharsis that allows people to transcend their fear and dread.

Just as death has been a minor, but consistent, presence in American humor, so has it been in two American holidays: Memorial Day and Halloween. Memorial Day began as a day to honor veterans of the Civil War, but it has become a memorial to all U.S. war veterans. For most people it marks the beginning of summer, and it signals another day of sale prices at the malls. But if any day is still used to decorate graves, Memorial Day is it. In *All around the Year*, Jack Santino points out the irony that more people die because of automobile accidents on Memorial Day weekend than during any other weekend. As Memorial Day travelers are dying on America's highways, race-car drivers are trying to set speed records in the Indianapolis 500, a death-defying race held every Memorial Day afternoon.

The other holiday that recognizes death is Halloween. Unlike Memorial Day, Halloween conjures not the deaths of individuals such as soldiers but the death of us all. Halloween is celebrated in mid-autumn as the days shorten and darken and the nights become long. Children who go from door to door trick-or-treating often wear costumes of skeletons or ghosts, and many houses are decorated to receive these symbols of the walking dead with cobwebs, garish carved pumpkins, and even headstones. According to Santino, "Halloween is about death, and it involves people's attempts to understand death and control it. During Halloween, people play with death, mock it, and fear it."

Another avenue for understanding the place of death in American popular culture is through the daily press—specifically, in the obituaries that the press has published since cheap dailies were first published in the nineteenth century. Humor is important, but it is occasional, and holidays are seasonal, but the popular media have produced death stories on a daily basis for a century and a half, more than long enough for their ritual consumption to become second nature.

Obituaries and death notices are both democratic and discriminatory. Although most people who die in this country receive an inch or so of type at the time of death, only a fraction of them receive a full-fledged obituary. "Many are called," says the gospel, "but few are chosen." The *New York Times* obituary writer Alden Whitman listed four characteristics of persons whose death would prompt an obituary in a metropolitan daily newspaper: fame, infamy, eccentricity, and controversy. On the other hand, he said, "The poor, those who work in an occupation not high on the prevailing scale of social values, or who belong to one of the lesser regarded ethnic groups, or have never previously been in the news for good or ill, are unlikely to make it in death." Occasionally, a reporter builds a reputation by writing obituaries of the rank and file, but they are exceptions that prove the rule.

If the past is any type of prologue to the future, then equality on the obituary page may be mostly meaningless by the time it is ever reached. In his study of urban, rural, and black obituaries between 1856 and 1972, Gary Long documented a shift from the personal to the impersonal. Obituaries in the nineteenth century were detailed articles that described individuals in terms of their personalities, friendships, recreations, work life, and volunteerism. By the latter part of the twentieth century, they had become mere accounting records that categorized the deceased according to kin, occupation, death, and funeral arrangements, with very few particularizing details for each formatted life. According to Long, obituaries became "the person-empty cenotaphs of a rationalizing society." Only in circumstances where obituaries are understood in terms of inventory instead of biography could it make sense to report a miscarriage after sixteen weeks of pregnancy, as an obituary, as the *Register-Guard* of Eugene, Oregon, did in 1995.

Dozens of graduate theses and easily as many scholarly articles have analyzed obituaries, and their production shows no sign of abatement. After all, as Janice

Laurel Hill Cemetary, Philadelphia. © Painet

Hume argues in *Obituaries in American Culture*, much can be learned about American culture by paying attention to what and how much are said about whom. But the nature of the record seems to be changing. For generations, daily newspapers have recorded the deaths of persons in their locales, but with fewer daily newspapers, diminished circulation, and the added pressure for space due to an aging population, such publications of record may cease to be widely available. One newspaper after another has begun charging for death notices, a policy certain to diminish the full acknowledgment of the dead. Some channels on cable television have broadcast death notices, and there are numerous obituary sites on the Internet, but however interesting these virtual memorials and worldwide gardens of remembrance are, these sources lack the apparent universality and popular appeal of their daily newspaper forebears.

Of course, death is a primary component of news in general, not just obituaries. Indelible images of death in twentieth-century news include the crash of the *Hindenburg* in 1937, the assassination of President John F. Kennedy in 1963, and the explosion of the *Challenger* in 1986. But despite Walter Cronkite's daily assurance to viewers—"And that's the way it is"—the front page and the nightly newscast are highly selective sources of narratives about death. In "Whose Lives Count?" William Adams showed that nightly television news uses three criteria to determine whether to report foreign natural disasters: the popularity of the country among most U.S. tourists, the number of deaths, and the nearness to New York City. In American news reports, Adams concluded, "the death of 1 Italian would equal those of 3 Romanians, 9 Latin Americans, 11 Middle Easterners, and 12 Asians." Domestic news is equally selective. As Combs and Slovic showed, American news media overemphasize homicide, accidents, and disasters and deemphasize the cause of most deaths in the United States: disease. These features of daily news reporting support Gerbner's contention that the media contribute to the common acceptance of violence as a solution to problems.

Messages about death also come consistently from sympathy cards. As the twentieth century progressed, and direct contact with death diminished, Americans became increasingly hard pressed to convey their condolences to bereaved persons. The greeting card companies that had begun by the early twentieth century added lines of sympathy cards after World War II. Sympathy cards continued to gain market share so that by the 1990s, one out of four Americans bought at least one sympathy card every year.

What prompts so many people to send mass-produced messages of consolation? According to Charles Lippy, who analyzed the content of sympathy cards and interviewed persons who sent or received them, Americans have lost a viable vocabulary that they can use to fulfill their social obligation of expressing condolences. This deficiency becomes more pronounced the less intimate the relationship, which is when people are likely to purchase cards to put their feelings of caring into words for them. Interestingly, the cards that they buy are likely to mention the inadequacy of language ("words cannot express. . . ."), and they are unlikely to mention death at all. Ironically, although people purchased sympathy cards to convey a message that they could not put into words, most people who sent them felt compelled to make them personal by writing a message of their own at the bottom. The personal messages were just as vague as the manufactured ones, but those who received them found that they did provide an extra measure of consolation.

Finding a way to express feelings about death has not been a problem for popular American songwriters. As Michael Kearl pointed out in *Endings*, folk music has dealt with death from violence and war (e.g., "Mountain Meadows Massacre"), work ("John Henry"), disease ("Meningitis Blues"), and accidents ("The Wreck of the Old 97"). Grief pervades "Will the Circle Be Unbroken?" These themes have also worked their way through youth music since the 1950s. Death from violence pervaded hip-hop music of the 1980s and 1990s, just as death from war pervaded rock and roll during the Vietnam War (e.g., Barry Maguire's "Eve of Destruction" and Edwin Starr's "War"). Work continued to kill in songs such as Harry Chapin's "30,000 Pounds of Bananas," and death from disease appears in songs like "Waterfalls," TLC's top-40 song about a girl with AIDS. Accidents also continued to kill, from Jan and Dean's "Dead Man's Curve," to "Ironic," Alanis Morrisette's 1996 song about an airplane crash. Grief pervades James Taylor's "Fire and Rain." John Thrush and George Paulus conclude that popular music portrays death as an unfair and destructive interference, never seeing it as an inevitability of human existence that can encourage us to make the most of the present.

By the late twentieth century, film had become the *media franca* in the United States. Death has been a mainstay in film ever since *The Great Train Robbery* portrayed the violent death of a man in 1903. In most movies, life ends when characters are killed or die naturally, but at least since *Topper* (1937), some characters have been given a reprieve from the finality of death, usually in order to finish unfinished business or to make reparations on earth. In their afterlife, characters frequently deal with life more effectively than they did when they were alive. In *Field of Dreams* (1989), the lead character, who had walked out on his father at the age of seventeen in the heat of an argument, is reunited with his long-dead father for a relationship that he was unable to establish when his father was alive. The main character in *Ghost* (1990) declines entry into heaven so that he can avenge his murder and tell his girlfriend that he loves her, something that he never did when he was alive. *Dead Again* (1991) reincarnates its characters so that they can right the wrongs of their lives. In Hollywood, the afterlife provides the dead with opportunities for self-improvement.

Death has been prominent in American popular culture since well before the American Revolution, but it has seldom been the subject of sustained and systematic scholarship. Research has tended to be episodic and dispersed in such disciplines as anthropology, psychology, history, and sociology, and it says more about the production than about responses to messages about death. But provocative theories and compelling histories have emerged, so as long as mortality remains an inevitability and a preoccupation, raw material and fresh investigations of American ways of death will continue to appear.

REFERENCE WORKS

Numerous reference tools are available for the study of death in popular culture. None have popular culture as their focus, but relevant entries can be found in the available bibliographies and encyclopedias on death. Although most of these reference works are on death in general, a number are devoted to causes of death, children, and such issues as near-death experiences.

A good research library will have well over a dozen bibliographies on death. The earliest go back to 1969: Joel J. Vernick's *Selected Bibliography on Death and Dying* and Kutscher and Kutscher's *A Bibliography of Books on Death, Bereavement, Loss, and Grief: 1935–1968*. The Kutschers' bibliography, together with a supplement that came out in 1974, groups some 2,400 books published in the United States, beginning with ancestor worship and ending with widows' allowances. Martin L. Kutscher et al. subsequently compiled 4,700 citations in *A Comprehensive Bibliography of the Thanatology Literature* in 1975 and published *A Cross-Index of Indices of Books on Thanatology* in 1978.

Other important bibliographies also appeared at that time. In *Death, Grief, and Bereavement: A Bibliography, 1845–1975*, Robert Fulton indexed 4,700 citations by subject and author. Fulton's sequel, *Death, Grief, and Bereavement II: A Bibliography, 1975–1980* contains nearly 4,000 entries that approach death primarily from an empirical perspective; it excludes literary and theological works as well as material on suicide. G. Howard Poteet's *Death and Dying: A Bibliography, 1950–1974* lists 2,000 books and articles on the psychology of death. *Death: A Bibliographical Guide* by Albert Jay Miller and Michael James Acri cites 4,000 scholarly, professional, and popular publications and 200 audiovisual sources. Irene L. Sell's *Dying and Death: An Annotated Bibliography* identifies more than 500 articles, books, and audiovisual sources with an eye toward individual and interpersonal dimensions of death and dying.

Production of reference materials kept pace in the 1980s. Hannelore Wass, Charles A. Corr, Richard A. Pacholski, and Catherine M. Sanders published *Death Education: An Annotated Resource Guide* to provide general information on death studies. Besides evaluating books, articles, and audiovisual materials, this source discusses community resources and organizations that offer assistance. Another evaluative resource is Michael A. Simpson's *Dying, Death, and Grief: A Critical Bibliography*. Simpson not only indexed more than 1,700 books, mostly from 1979–1987, many of which deal with American culture, but also rated the sources from one star (not recommended) to five stars (strongly recommended), with a few zeros thrown in for sources beneath contempt. *Attitudes to Death and Dying: Medical Analysis Index with Reference Bibliography* by Katie Lee Holt and *Death and Dying: A Research Bibliography* by Larry A. Platt appeared in the late 1980s. These were followed in the next decade by Robert and Beatrice Kastenbaum's *Encyclopedia of Death*, a highly readable resource with entries beginning with AIDS and ending with zombie and including discussions of deathbed scenes, vampires, and humor.

Two general bibliographies of note appeared in the 1990s. Robert Kastenbaum and Bert Hayslip compiled *Death and Dying* for the Association for Gerontology in Higher Education. The other is *Death and Dying: A Bibliographical Survey* by Samuel Southard, an eight-chapter annotated survey of more than 2,200 books, articles, chapters, monographs, and reports about counseling and theological aspects of death and dying. Chapter 8, "Bibliographies," lists fifty-four sources.

Several bibliographies have focused on causes of death. The National Institute of Neurological Diseases and Stroke published Andrew Smith and J. Kiffin Penry's *Brain Death: A Bibliography with Key-Word and Author Indexes* in 1972. That same year Norman L. Farberow's *Bibliography on Suicide and Suicide Prevention: 1897–1957 and 1958–1970* appeared with subject and author indexes for more than 4,700 citations. John L. McIntosh published a complement, *Research on Suicide: A Bibliography*, more than ten years later. Most of his 2,300 entries appeared after 1970. In *The Challenge of Euthanasia: An Annotated Bibliography on Euthanasia and Related Subjects*, hospital chaplain Don V. Bailey pores through the literature on medical ethics in search of resolution of issues involving care for the dying. Murder is the subject of Bal and Rajinder Jerath's *Homicide: A Bibliography*, which cites several thousand sources and includes entries on murder mysteries and news stories, and Michael Newton's *Mass Murder: An Annotated Bibliography*, which describes ninety-five general and specialized works and summarizes 620 case histories. Problems with determining cause of death are dealt with in Alan M. Gittelsohn's *Annotated Bibliography of Cause-of-Death Validation Studies, 1958–1980*.

"Death is always and under all circumstances a tragedy," wrote Theodore Roosevelt, but it is doubly so whenever children are concerned. For this reason, several bibliographies that focus on death and children have been published. Sarah Sheets Cook's 1973 book, *Children and Dying: An Exploration and a Selective Professional Bibliography*, was followed by *The Bereaved Child: Analysis, Education, and Treatment: An Abstracted Bibliography* by Gillian S. Mace, Faren R. Akins, and Dianna L. Akins in 1981; *Books and Films on Death and Dying for Children and Adolescents: An Annotated Bibliography* by Eva Murphy in 1985; and *Death and Dying in Children's and Young People's Literature: A Survey and Bibliography* by Marian S. Pyles in 1988. That was the year that Hazel B. Benson published *The Dying Child: An Annotated Bibliography*, which summarizes more than 700 sources and lists children's books and audiovisual (AV) material as well as hospices and various support organizations.

A variety of issues is covered in other death-related bibliographies. In 1976, the National Association of Cemeteries published *An Annotated, Select Bibliography of Books and Materials Relating to the Cemetery Industry. Near-Death Experiences: An Annotated Bibliography* grew out of Terry K. Basford's research for an article on the popular culture dimensions of near-death experiences. His 710 entries on near-death experiences, deathbed visions, and analogues of near-death experiences span the years from 1847 to 1988. Barbara and David Harrah's *Funeral Service: A Bibliography of Literature on Its Past, Present and Future, the Various Means of Disposition and Memorialization* has 2,000 annotated entries on the funeral and includes references to audiovisual materials and lists of cemetery associations, memorial societies, and other funeral-related organizations. Cecile Strugnell's *Adjustment to Widowhood and Some Related Problems: A Selective and Annotated Bibliography* summarizes 450 sources, the largest number dealing with bereavement of children, bereavement of the elderly widowed, and cross-cultural studies of bereavement.

HISTORY AND CRITICISM

Scholars and critics who think about public attitudes toward death have a wealth of publications at their disposal. Death and popular culture are not exactly a bona fide field of study—there are few thanatology programs or certificates in universities, no endemic research methods, no dominant paradigm, and no definitive textbooks—but courses are fairly common in sociology and philosophy departments, and scholarship finds its way into journals in communications, history, literature, sociology, psychology, and anthropology. Over the past forty years, provocative conceptual and historical work has been done, and a number of scholarly publications have been established.

The publication of *The American Way of Death* by Jessica Mitford in 1963 marked the beginning of a ten-year period when much of the foundation for the study of death in popular culture was laid. In irreverent and evocative language, it challenged the comfort of the funeral industry, which had become accustomed to selling unnecessary embalming as well as expensive caskets and grave sites. The exposé decried the commercial exploitation of American funeral customs, what Mitford called a "full-fledged burlesque," and it did so by quoting liberally from the funeral industry's own publications. The book hit home. Memorial societies formed across the country to reduce funeral costs, and in 1984 the Federal Trade Commission established the Funeral Rule, which required funeral homes to itemize all of their charges.

Two years after Mitford questioned funeral traditions and their costs, Geoffrey Gorer's *Death, Grief and Mourning* introduced the concept of "pornographic death" to the study of popular culture. Gorer argued that just as sex turns into pornography when it is portrayed without its natural human emotion, which is affection, so death becomes pornographic when divorced from its natural human emotion, which is grief. Gorer's argument seems to become more powerful as American culture becomes increasingly video-oriented. An ethos of pornographic death seems undeniable given the popularity of *Faces of Death I, II,* and *III*—as well as clones and satires such as *The Many Faces of Death I* and *II* and *The Worst*

Jesse James displayed in coffin after his death. Courtesy of the Library of Congress

of the Many Faces of Death—which purport to show numerous actual deaths, mostly grisly, for their sheer entertainment value.

The third influential book published during the decade was *On Death and Dying* by Elisabeth Kübler-Ross. After interviewing hundreds of dying patients, Kübler-Ross discerned five emotional stages that dying patients undergo: (1) denial, (2) anger, (3) bargaining, (4) depression, and (5) acceptance. Kübler-Ross also described the isolation that dying patients feel and the ineptitude of their physicians, who are trained to save life, not to help their patients with the problems of dying. With the popularity of *On Death and Dying*, "the taboo topic" of death began to be discussed in psychological terms, and the nascent American hospice movement gained momentum.

The fourth influential book to be published in this ten-year period was by cultural anthropologist Ernest Becker: *The Denial of Death*, which won a Pulitzer Prize for nonfiction in 1974. Like Kübler-Ross, Becker dealt with the fear of dying, but not within the confines of U.S. hospitals. Becker argued that the refusal to acknowledge one's own mortality was a universal human trait, that humans embrace myths and illusions that blot out the sense of finitude in order to shield themselves from the devastation of acknowledging human meaninglessness. Becker's thesis seemed to be confirmed just a few years later, with sales figures topping 14 million for *Life after Life* by Raymond Moody, who relayed the stories of numerous persons who had died, been resuscitated, and told of serene consciousness beyond the pale. Of course, the denial of death has a much longer history, as Howard Kerr showed in *Mediums, and Spirit Rappers, and Roaring Radicals: Spiritualism in American Literature 1850–1900*.

Since these four books were published, much of the significant work on culture and death has been historical. The most sweeping histories have been written by the French historian Philippe Ariès, beginning in 1974 with the publication of *Western Attitudes toward Death from the Middle Ages to the Present*. That slim book, which divided Western history into epochs beginning with Tamed Death in the Middle Ages and continuing through the contemporary era of Forbidden Death, became the basis for the much heftier 1981 volume, *The Hour of Our Death*. This history, like its predecessor, combined cultural studies with psychology and theology.

Although Ariès did include American attitudes and practices in his work, other historians have profitably chosen American attitudes and practices as their sole focus. David Stannard's study of death in colonial New England, *The Puritan Way of Death*, is a good starting place for the chronological study of American attitudes toward death. A worthy sequel is *The Sacred Remains* by Gary Laderman, which argues that attitudes toward death changed during the nineteenth century in large part because of the Civil War and the burgeoning funeral industry that followed. *The History of American Funeral Directing* by Robert Habenstein and William Lamers picks up where *The Sacred Remains* leaves off. *The Last Great Necessity* by David Charles Sloane, which shows how Americans' perceptions of death are revealed in their attitudes toward cemeteries, is equally intriguing.

A recent book that deserves mention is *The American Way of Death Revisited*, a second edition of the classic that Jessica Mitford was finishing as she died in 1998. Mitford revised *The American Way of Death* thirty-five years after its publication in order to take into account two significant changes in the funeral industry. Most gratifying to her was the steady rise in cremation, from nearly 4 percent to 21 percent. But she was distressed by the rise of funeral conglomerates such as Service Corporation International, which owns one out of ten funeral homes in the United States and five out of ten in Australia. Mitford's inspiration is very much alive in the Funeral and Memorial Societies of America, headed by Lisa Carlson, whose *Caring for the Dead: Your Final Act of Love* shows families how they can take control of the funerals—and the disposal—of their loved ones.

Although much of the illuminating scholarship on death in American popular culture is to be found in books, one frequently cited journal article deserves mention: George Gerbner's "Death in Prime Time: Notes on the Symbolic Functions of Dying in the Mass Media." "Who can get away with what against whom?" is Gerbner's central question, and the answer on prime-time television is that the perpetrators tend to be white, middle-class men in the prime of life, and the victims tend to be female, lower-class, and old. The effect of this imbalance, according to Gerbner, is support for the political status quo and, for persons who watch an inordinate amount of television, an elevated sense of danger.

Like many scholarly articles that explore themes of death in popular culture, Gerbner's was published in a general social science journal, not one devoted to issues of death and dying. Nevertheless, such journals do exist, and although their usefulness to the study of popular culture varies, their standards tend to be high.

Omega: Journal of Death and Dying, which began publication in 1970, was the first journal to focus on death. Its emphasis is social and psychological, and its articles, such as "Death Concern and Religious Belief among Gays and Bisexuals of Variable Proximity to AIDS" and "Declining Use of Firearms to Commit Suicide in Alabama in the 1980s," are accessible. The following year, the Foundation of Thanatology launched *Advances in Thanatology* as a quarterly academic venue for short articles that range widely in subject matter. One issue alone carried such articles as "Death in Religious Jewish Society" and "A Projective Measurement of Death Anxiety." A third journal, *Death Studies*, was begun in 1977. This interdisciplinary publication focuses on research and education. Articles such as "Meaning Reconstruction in the Experience of Parental Bereavement" and "Dragons as Amulets, Dragons as Talismans, Dragons as Counselors" have appeared in this bimonthly.

Some of the journals are more narrowly focused. *Suicide and Life-Threatening Behavior*, published by the American Association of Suicidology, takes a multidisciplinary approach to its subject. "Adolescent Attitudes about Death" and "The Kurt Cobain Suicide Crisis" are typical articles. *Journal of Near-Death Studies (Anabiosis)* began publication in 1981 to explore such topics as clinical death and out-of-body experiences. This scholarly quarterly publishes articles such as "Why Birth Models Cannot Explain NDEs [Near-Death Experiences]" and "Pathophysiology of Stress-Induced Limbic Lobe Dysfunction: A Hypothesis for NDEs." The Hemlock Society has published *The Euthanasia Review* since 1986 to encourage scholarly debate over issues such as the right to die, physician-assisted suicide, and living wills by publishing articles such as "Theological Reflections on Euthanasia" and "Euthanasia in the Courts."

ANTHOLOGIES AND REPRINTS

Because the study of death in American popular culture is disparate—there are no academic society devoted to the enterprise, no conferences, no specific journal—there are few major collections and reprint projects that bring together primary material.

There is, of course, a lot of research material, but it tends to be spread throughout libraries. Even at the Columbia University Library's repository of materials from the Foundation of Thanatology, materials are dispersed rather than located in one area. Special collections in the traditional sense tend to be quite specialized. The American Antiquarian Society in Worcester, Massachusetts, has a collection of 1,200 funeral sermons delivered between 1656 and 1830 as well as three sets of photographs of New England gravestones. The Center of Intercultural and Folk Studies at Western Kentucky University at Bowling Green has 200 tapes and 2,000 manuscripts about southern folklore involving death. Likewise, the William R. Perkins Library at Duke University has the Frank C. Brown Collection of North Carolina Folklore Frank Clyde Brown Papers, which contains 38,000 folktales, 1,400 recorded songs, and 650 musical scores. Newman Ivey White edited this material in seven volumes, the sixth of which has material on death and afterlife. The Eileen J. Garrett Library at the Parapsychology Foundation in New York has sizable collections on both the history of parapsychology, including early spiritualism and mysticism, and contemporary and experimental parapsychology and related subjects. The Beryl Boyer Library of the National Foundation of Funeral Service in Des Plaines, Illinois, has 250,000 works on funeral customs and the funeral industry.

Edited collections of essays on death have been published since 1959, when *The Meaning of Death* by Herman Feifel came out. This collection, with its overview of death and dying and valuable essays on subjects such as death in modern art, inspired *Death and the Quest for Meaning*, a Festschrift edited by Stephen Strack that includes chapters on grief, care of the sick, children and death, teenagers and death, and thanatology.

A number of worthy anthologies followed Feifel's. *Man's Concern with Death*, Arnold Toynbee's valuable anthology on attitudes toward death and dying, was published in 1968. Three others followed in rapid succession. Arien Mack's *Death in American Experience* included essays on death in American counterculture, poetry, and religion. David Stannard's *Death in America* includes articles about attitudes toward death from the Puritan era to the early twentieth century. Charles Jackson's *Passing* explored responses to death by including essays that discuss attitudes toward death, death rituals, and burial methods one century at a time.

Two anthologies from this period have undergone multiple revisions. John Williamson has helped revise Edwin Shneidman's 1976 collection *Death: Current Perspectives*, an overview of death from individual, interpersonal, and social perspectives. Robert Bendiksen has helped bring Robert Fulton's *Death and Identity* up-to-date. This anthology discusses theoretical and social dimensions of bereavement.

BIBLIOGRAPHY

Books and Articles

Adams, William C. "Whose Lives Count?: TV Coverage of Natural Disasters." *Journal of Communication* 36 (Spring 1986), 113–22.

Ariès, Philippe. *The Hour of Our Death*. Trans. Helen Weaver. New York: Knopf, 1981.

———. *Western Attitudes toward Death from the Middle Ages to the Present*. Trans. Patricia M. Ranum. Baltimore: Johns Hopkins University Press, 1974.

Bailey, Don V. *The Challenge of Euthanasia: An Annotated Bibliography on Euthanasia and Related Subjects*. Lanham, Md.: University Press of America, 1990.

Basford, Terry K. *Near-Death Experiences: An Annotated Bibliography*. New York: Garland, 1990.

Becker, Ernest. *The Denial of Death*. New York: Free Press, 1973.

Benson, Hazel B., comp. *The Dying Child: An Annotated Bibliography*. New York: Greenwood Press, 1988.

Carlson, Lisa. *Caring for the Dead: Your Final Act of Love*. Hinesburg, Vt.: Upper Access, 1998.

Combs, Barbara, and Paul Slovic. "Newspaper Coverage of Causes of Death." *Journalism Quarterly* 56 (Winter 1979), 837–43, 849.

Cook, Sarah Sheets. *Children and Dying: An Exploration and a Selective Professional Bibliography*. New York: Health Sciences, 1973.

Edwards, Jonathan. *Representative Selections*. Ed. Clarence H. Faust and Thomas H. Johnson. New York: Hill and Wang, 1962.

Farberow, Norman L., ed. *Bibliography on Suicide and Suicide Prevention: 1897–1957 and 1958–1970*. Rockville, Md.: National Institute of Mental Health, 1972.

Feifel, Herman, ed. *The Meaning of Death*. New York: McGraw-Hill, 1965.

Ford, Paul Leicester, ed. *The New England Primer: A History of Its Origin and Development with a Reprint of the Unique Copy of the Earliest Known Edition and Many Facsimile Illustrations and Reproductions*. New York: Columbia University Teachers College, 1962.

Fulton, Robert. *Death, Grief, and Bereavement: A Bibliography, 1845–1975*. New York: Arno Press, 1977.

———. *Death, Grief, and Bereavement II: A Bibliography, 1975–1980*. New York: Arno Press, 1981.

Fulton, Robert, and Robert Bendiksen, eds. *Death and Identity*. 3rd ed. Philadelphia: Charles Press, 1994.

Gerbner, George. "Death in Prime Time: Notes on the Symbolic Functions of Dying in the Mass Media." *American Academy of Political and Social Science Annals* 447 (January 1980), 64–70.

Gittelsohn, Alan M. *Annotated Bibliography of Cause-of-Death Validation Studies, 1958–1980*. Washington, D.C.: Government Printing Office, 1982.

Gorer, Geoffrey. *Death, Grief and Mourning*. New York: Doubleday, 1965.

Habenstein, Robert W., and William Lamers. *The History of American Funeral Directing*. Milwaukee: Bulfin, 1955.

Harrah, Barbara K., and David F. Harrah. *Funeral Service: A Bibliography of Literature on Its Past, Present and Future, the Various Means of Disposition and Memorialization*. Metuchen, N.J.: Scarecrow, 1976.

Holt, Katie Lee. *Attitudes to Death and Dying: Medical Analysis Index with Reference Bibliography*. Washington, D.C.: Abbe, 1985.

Hume, Janice. *Obituaries in American Culture*. Jackson: University Press of Mississippi, 2000.

Jackson, Charles O., ed. *Passing: The Vision of Death in America*. Westport, Conn.: Greenwood, 1977.

Jerath, Bal K., and Rajinder Jerath. *Homicide: A Bibliography*. 2nd ed. Boca Raton, Fla.: CRC, 1993.

Kastenbaum, Robert, and Bert Hayslip, comps. *Death and Dying*. Washington, D.C.: Association for Gerontology in Higher Education, 1995.

Kastenbaum, Robert, and Beatrice Kastenbaum, eds. *Encyclopedia of Death*. Phoenix: Oryx Press, 1989.

Kearl, Michael C. *Endings: A Sociology of Death and Dying*. New York: Oxford University Press, 1989.

Kerr, Howard. *Mediums, and Spirit-Rappers, and Roaring Radicals: Spiritualism in American Literature, 1850–1900*. Urbana: University of Illinois Press, 1972.

Kübler-Ross, Elisabeth. *On Death and Dying*. New York: Macmillan, 1969.

Kutscher, Austin H., Jr., and Austin H. Kutscher, eds. *A Bibliography of Books on Death, Bereavement, Loss, and Grief: 1935–1968*. New York: Health Sciences, 1969.

Kutscher, Austin H., Jr., Austin H. Kutscher, and Martin Kutscher. *A Bibliography of Books on Death, Bereavement, Loss, and Grief: Supplement 1, 1968–1972*. New York: Health Science, 1974.

Kutscher, Martin L., et al., eds. *A Comprehensive Bibliography of the Thanatology Literature*. New York: MSS Information, 1975.

———. *A Cross-Index of Indices of Books on Thanatology*. New York: MSS Information, 1978.

Laderman, Gary. *The Sacred Remains: American Attitudes toward Death, 1799–1883*. New Haven, Conn.: Yale University Press, 1996.

Lippy, Charles H. "Sympathy Cards and the Grief Process." *Journal of Popular Culture* 17 (Winter 1983), 98–108.

Long, Gary L. "Organizations and Identity: Obituaries 1856–1972." *Social Forces* 65 (June 1987), 964–1001.

Mace, Gillian S., Faren R. Akins, and Dianna L. Akins. *The Bereaved Child: Analysis, Education, and Treatment: An Abstracted Bibliography*. New York: Plenum, 1981.

Mack, Arien, ed. *Death in American Experience*. New York: Schocken, 1972.

McIntosh, John L. *Research on Suicide: A Bibliography*. Westport, Conn.: Greenwood Press, 1985.

Miller, Albert Jay, and Michael James Acri. *Death: A Bibliographical Guide*. Metuchen, N.J.: Scarecrow, 1977.

Mitford, Jessica. *The American Way of Death*. New York: Simon and Schuster, 1963.

———. *The American Way of Death Revisited*. New York: Alfred A. Knopf, 1998.

Moody, Raymond A., Jr. *Life after Life: The Investigation of a Phenomenon—Survival of Bodily Death*. Harrisburg, Pa.: Stackpole, 1976.

Murphy, Eva, ed. *Books and Films on Death and Dying for Children and Adolescents: An Annotated Bibliography*. Boston: Good Grief Program, 1985.

National Association of Cemeteries Young Executives Committee. *An Annotated, Select Bibliography of Books and Materials Relating to the Cemetery Industry*. Arlington, Va.: National Association of Cemeteries, 1976.

National Institute of Mental Health. *Television and Behavior: Ten Years of Scientific Progress and Implications for the Eighties*. Washington, D.C.: Government Printing Office, 1982.

Newton, Michael. *Mass Murder: An Annotated Bibliography*. New York: Garland, 1988.

Phelps, Elizabeth Stuart. *The Gates Ajar*. Boston: J. R. Osgood, 1869.

Platt, Larry A. *Death and Dying: A Research Bibliography*. Statesboro: Social Gerontology Program, Georgia Southern College, 1986.

Poteet, G. Howard. *Death and Dying: A Bibliography, 1950–1974*. Troy, N.Y.: Whitston, 1976.

Pyles, Marian S. *Death and Dying in Children's and Young People's Literature: A Survey and Bibliography*. Jefferson, N.C.: McFarland, 1988.

Ruby, Jay. *Secure the Shadow: Death and Photography in America*. Cambridge: MIT Press, 1995.

Santino, Jack. *All around the Year: Holidays and Celebrations in American Life*. Urbana: University of Illinois Press, 1994.

Sell, Irene L. *Dying and Death: An Annotated Bibliography*. New York: Tiresias, 1977.

Simpson, Michael A. *Dying, Death, and Grief: A Critical Bibliography*. Pittsburgh: University of Pittsburgh Press, 1987.

Sloane, David Charles. *The Last Great Necessity: Cemeteries in American History*. Baltimore: Johns Hopkins University Press, 1991.

Smith, Andrew J. K., and J. Kiffin Penry, eds. *Brain Death: A Bibliography with Key-Word and Author Indexes*. Bethesda, Md.: National Institute of Neurological Diseases and Stroke, 1972.

Southard, Samuel, comp. *Death and Dying: A Bibliographical Survey*. Westport, Conn.: Greenwood, 1991.

Stannard, David E., ed. *Death in America*. Philadelphia: University of Pennsylvania Press, 1975.

———. *The Puritan Way of Death: A Study in Religion, Culture, and Social Change*. New York: Oxford University Press, 1977.

Strack, Stephen, ed. *Death and the Quest for Meaning: Essays in Honor of Herman Feifel*. Northvale, N.J.: J. Aronson, 1997.

Strugnell, Cecile. *Adjustment to Widowhood and Some Related Problems: A Selective and Annotated Bibliography*. New York: Health Sciences, 1974.

Thrush, John C., and George S. Paulus. "The Concept of Death in Popular Music: A Social Psychological Perspective." *Popular Music and Society* 6:3 (1979), 219–28.

Toynbee, Arnold, et al. *Man's Concern with Death*. New York: McGraw-Hill, 1968.

Vernick, Joel J. *Selected Bibliography on Death and Dying*. Washington, D.C.: Government Printing Office, 1969.

Wass, Hannelore, Charles A. Corr, Richard A. Pacholski, and Catherine M. Sanders. *Death Education: An Annotated Resource Guide*. Washington, D.C.: Hemisphere, 1980–1985.

Whitman, Alden. *The Obituary Book*. New York: Stein and Day, 1971.

Williamson, John B. and Edwin S. Shneidman, eds. *Death: Current Perspectives*. 4th ed. Mountain View, Calif.: Mayfield, 1995.

Specialized Periodicals

Advances in Thanatology. New York, 1971– .

Death Studies. Washington, D.C., 1977– .

The Euthanasia Review. New York, 1986– .

The Hospice Journal. Binghamton, N.Y., 1985– .

Journal of Near-Death Studies (Anabiosis). New York, 1981– .

Omega: Journal of Death and Dying. Westport, Conn., 1970– .

Suicide and Life-Threatening Behavior. New York, 1976– .

DEBATE AND PUBLIC ADDRESS

Robert H. Janke and
Theodore F. Sheckels

Debate and public address in the United States are two distinct, but related, areas within the academic discipline of speech communication. The study of debate is frequently grouped with argumentation or included as a component of forensics, whereas the study of public address is often coupled with rhetoric. In this chapter, however, debate and public address are generally considered as a single area of inquiry, although the section dealing with reference works also treats educational debate and public speaking as separate skills in communication.

Culture in the United States is perceived as a matter of taste, with many factors, primarily economics and education, influencing each individual's preferences. It is pluralistic, ranging from the high to the low, with boundaries loose and ever changing. A treatment of debate and public address as an element of American popular culture could appropriately begin with a frequently quoted statement by William Norwood Brigance from the preface to his celebrated work *A History and Criticism of American Public Address*: "Most of the mighty movements affecting the destiny of the American nation have gathered strength in obscure places from the talk of nameless men, and gained final momentum from leaders who could state in common words the needs and hopes of common people."[1] This momentum might come from the sophisticated Inaugural Address of a patrician president or from the outspoken words of an uneducated civil rights worker. Great speakers through the centuries have shared the ability to move their listeners to action, whether at a political meeting, a religious assembly, an outdoor rally or through broadcasts on radio and television. In the democratic American process, the people, responding either directly or indirectly to these speakers, take action that determines the course of historical events.

This chapter deals with such speakers. It is a survey whose scope is necessarily wide; however, it does not include such related areas as mass communication, interpersonal communication, group discussion, parliamentary procedure, or the issues of freedom of speech or the right to communicate. Space allotted here is limited. The references and bibliographic items are therefore selective and the descriptions brief. The major criterion is usefulness. The intent is to offer a concise guide for the student or general reader to important and practical source material.

HISTORICAL OUTLINE

The history of debate and public address in the United States is, in essence, the religious, political, and social history of the nation. Therefore, an outline of value to the reader should include, in chronological order, a selection of the most significant speakers, popular issues, and contemporary events that have contributed to this history.

The most significant speakers of early New England were the preachers, who exerted considerable influence, for they were also leaders and teachers whose sermons adapted the established theology to everyday application. What many consider to be the first notable speech delivered in America is John Winthrop's speech on liberty. Winthrop, who was chosen the first governor of the Massachusetts Bay Colony, opposed broad democracy. In 1635, he argued that man was not free to do simply as he wished but must submit to civil and lawful authority, an authority that encompassed a moral covenant between God and man, an authority that was looked upon as the "ecclesiastical elect."

This theological approach, known as theocracy, was upheld by four generations of the Mather family, who were predominant in shaping the lives of the colonists during the later seventeenth and early eighteenth centuries. Richard Mather advocated the liberalizing of the means to attain church membership; his son, Increase Mather, assuming the pastorate of Boston's North Church, upheld the Puritan views of church and state. Increase's son, Cotton Mather, became recognized as New England's leading Puritan preacher. He spoke out on the vital issues of the time, for example, advocating inoculation against smallpox; but he is known today largely for his part in the Salem witch trials of 1692.

Changing concepts in religion gradually spread throughout the colonies. Solomon Stoddard, a liberal preacher in Northampton, Massachusetts, espoused a doctrine of predestination. In 1727 he was succeeded in the pulpit by his grandson, Jonathan Edwards. From among Edwards' hundreds of sermons, the best known is "Sinners in the Hands of an Angry God," preached in 1741, which epitomized his theme that all men were sinners facing damnation and could be saved only through God's arbitrary, predestined choice. Traveling evangelist George Whitefield preached more than 18,000 sermons, primarily on New Calvinism, which offered personal salvation through the acceptance of Christ and sanctioned a sense of freedom previously unknown to the colonists.

During this same period the seeds of freedom were also developing in the political sphere. The concept of the town meeting, which took many forms throughout the colonies, gave the colonists the opportunity to air grievances and discuss issues in a democratic manner. Increasingly, these issues centered on British rule and the union of the colonies. As early as 1754, addressing the representatives to the congress at Albany, Benjamin Franklin of Philadelphia advocated a confederation. In Boston, Samuel Adams, a highly effective orator, aroused the citizens to the cause with his fiery speeches, one in particular delivered in Faneuil Hill in

1770 following the massacre of five colonists by British soldiers; at a meeting three years later his heated oratory triggered the dumping of tea into Boston harbor.

While such men as Samuel Adams and his compatriot James Otis were addressing assemblies for the revolutionary cause in Boston, Patrick Henry was arguing for American independence in Virginia. His speech in that state's House of Burgesses in opposition to King George III's Stamp Act of 1765, delivered to shouts of "Treason!," is recognized as a triumph in American oratory. Henry's statement delivered before the second Virginia Convention on March 23, 1775, at St. John's Church in Richmond, is now part of American folklore: "Is life so dear, or peace so sweet, as to be purchased at the price of chains and slavery? Forbid it, Almighty God! I know not what course others may take; but as for me, give me liberty or give me death!"[2] Henry became known as the Voice of the Revolution.

Some of the most intense and significant debates of this period in American history took place in 1787 and 1788 as the various states deliberated the proposed federal Constitution. In Virginia, the opponents were evenly matched. The anti-Federalists, led by Patrick Henry, who thought that Virginia should refrain from immediate ratification, lost by a narrow margin to the Federalists, led by James Madison, who cogently refuted the points made by Henry. In a similar dispute in New York, Alexander Hamilton's oratory in favor of the Federalist cause defeated the anti-Federalists under the leadership of Governor George Clinton. Eventually, the Constitution was ratified, and the fledgling government was launched as George Washington assumed the presidency in 1789. Washington's statement from his Farewell Address of 1797 is frequently quoted in political debate: " 'Tis our true policy to steer clear of permanent alliances with any portion of the foreign world."[3]

The popular issues treated in the debates and public addresses during the first half of the nineteenth century included such matters as tariffs, New England manufacturing, foreign interests, centralization of government, expansion, internal improvements, sectionalism, slavery, nullification, and secession. These issues were debated at thousands of rallies, platforms, and "stumps" across the country, as well as in the famed halls of the nation's Capitol.

Three of America's most distinguished orators, known as the Great Triumvirate, emerged during this early national period, referred to as America's golden age of oratory: the West's Henry Clay, the North's Daniel Webster, and the South's John C. Calhoun. Clay's eloquent speech on the New Army bill, delivered before the House in 1813, rallied the forces necessary to bring the War of 1812 to a successful conclusion. Clay was popularly called the Great Pacificator during the Missouri controversy of 1820 and continued to play this role throughout his long career. Daniel Webster, considered America's foremost public speaker, was known equally for his political, legal, and platform or special occasion speaking. He is best remembered for his debate in the Senate in 1830 with Robert Y. Hayne of South Carolina, who argued for the states' right of nullification, the right to put liberty first and union afterward. Webster's famous reply, concluding with the statement, "Liberty and Union, now and forever, one and inseparable!," has ever since been identified with popular American oratory.[4] Calhoun was the most effective orator from the South, a leading spokesman for states' rights and slavery. But in the final speech of his career, on the Clay Compromise Measures of 1850, he could not persuade his fellow senators to support his stand against Clay and Webster in their combined efforts to preserve the Union.

Other prominent public speakers of the early nineteenth century included John Quincy Adams, known for his compromises on the Treaty of Ghent and arguments for the Monroe Doctrine; Thomas Hart Benton, longtime senator from Missouri whose oratorical skills were directed at western expansion; and Thomas Corwin, political leader from Ohio whose speech "Against War with Mexico," delivered to the Senate in 1847, caused him to be burned in effigy as a traitor.

Some twenty years earlier an era had begun of what was called platform speaking, reflected in the emergence and development of professional orators who addressed themselves, either voluntarily or for a fee, to specific issues, usually concerned with some demand for social reform, such as abolition, women's rights, or Prohibition.

Antislavery spokesmen included William Lloyd Garrison of Massachusetts, who agitated against slavery through the New England Antislavery Society, the American Antislavery Society, and numerous other abolitionist societies that he helped to establish; Wendell Phillips, public orator noted for his speech delivered in 1837 to an overflowing crowd in Boston's Faneuil Hall on the murder of abolitionist Elijah Lovejoy; and Charles Sumner, who is best known for his offensive "Crimes against Kansas" speech, delivered to the Senate in 1856 in opposition to the Kansas-Nebraska bill. (This speech resulted in Sumner's being severely assaulted by his opponents and left unconscious on the floor of the Senate.) Edward Everett was a well-known and highly skilled orator of the time who, as circumstances evolved, was the principal speaker at the ceremony dedicating the cemetery on the battlefield at Gettysburg, Pennsylvania, in 1863, an occasion made famous by the brief address of Abraham Lincoln.

Numerous blacks also spoke in public on the slavery question. Chief among these was Frederick Douglass, an ex-slave whose greatest speeches include "The Meaning of July Fourth for the Negro," delivered in Corinthian Hall, Rochester, New York, on July 5, 1852, and the "West India Emancipation" speech delivered at Canandaigua, New York, on August 4, 1857. Other black speakers prominent during this period were Charles Lennox Remond, Henry Highland Garnet, Samuel Ringgold Ward, James McCune Smith, and Robert Purvis. Some decades later, Booker T. Washington became recognized as the national spokesman for the Negro, largely as a result of his oration before the Cotton States and International Exposition in Atlanta, Georgia. This speech, delivered on September 18, 1895, became known as the "Atlanta Compromise Address." Favoring greater economic opportunity at this time rather than broader societal changes, Washington declared, "In all things that are purely social we can be as separate as the fingers, yet one as the hand in all things essential to mutual progress."[5]

Abraham Lincoln was among the most effective popular orators of the midcentury period. Upon accepting the Republican nomination in Illinois for the U.S. Senate in 1858, he stated: " 'A house divided against itself cannot stand.' I believe this government cannot endure, permanently half *slave* and half *free*."[6] His opponent, Stephen A. Douglas, the Little Giant, refuted Lincoln's statement several weeks later by arguing that the people should have the right to decide for themselves. The stage was thus set for a series of seven debates that attracted audiences numbering into the thousands across the prairies of Illinois. These debates are still the best known in American history. Although Douglas won the Senate seat, the debates provided the path to the presidency for Lincoln only two years later. Lincoln's masterpiece, the Gettysburg Address, delivered on November 19, 1863, and since memorized by millions of schoolchildren, ranks among the world's great speeches.[7] Also considered a special work of oratorical literature is his Second Inaugural Address, delivered March 4, 1865, famed for the words: "With malice toward none, with charity for all, with firmness in the right as God gives us to see the right, let us strive on to finish the work we are in."[8]

Following the Civil War, the issues facing the nation were new and varied, but no popular debate topic was more crucial than that dealing with the reconstruction of the southern states. Robert G. Ingersoll was known for his verbal brilliance while defending the cause of the northern Republicans. Georgia's Henry Grady became known as the spokesman for the new South.

A distinctive feature of this era of platform speaking, a period when the role of women in American society was universally acknowledged as inferior to that of men, was that women, despite resistance and sometimes ridicule, emerged as public speakers on popular issues. With an address on July 4, 1828, in New Harmony, Indiana, Frances Wright was a forerunner among early American women orators, appealing for reforms in education. Other women orators followed, such as Angelina Grimké, a southerner who moved northern audiences to the antislavery cause, and Abbey Kelley Foster, who spoke out fiercely on the issues of woman's rights and temperance, often denouncing her audiences and frequently meeting with public disapproval. The speaking career of Ernestine L. Rose was largely concerned with human rights, particularly the rights of women; and Lucy Stone traveled and spoke extensively for woman's rights. In 1848 in Seneca Falls, New York, Elizabeth Cady Stanton addressed the first Women's Rights Convention, which she and Lucretia Mott had promoted. A leading advocate for the cause of Prohibition was Frances E. Willard, who crusaded widely for temperance, presiding over the National Women's Christian Temperance Union and eventually broadening her advocacy to include labor reform and women's liberation. Pioneer black women orators, concerned mainly with antislavery and woman's rights, included Sojourner Truth, Frances Ellen Watkins Harper, and Sarah P. Remond.

Susan B. Anthony was foremost in the women's movement as a speaker and organizer. She lectured for more than forty-five years, and her influence on popular culture was reflected in 1979, when her likeness was sculptured for the obverse of the one-dollar coin.

During the nineteenth century two uniquely American media concerned with public address were the "lyceums" and the "Chautauquas." Thousands of lyceums, organized and staffed by civic-minded volunteers, flourished in cities across the nation at this time, operating mainly in auditoriums during the winter months. Originally intended to provide a platform for a series of educational lectures by local specialists, the lyceums soon attracted the nation's leading statesmen and scholars. The long list of traveling speakers, who drew large crowds and earned large fees, included such prominent personalities as Henry Ward Beecher, Ralph Waldo Emerson, Horace Greeley, Oliver Wendell Holmes, James Russell Lowell, Theodore Parker, and Daniel Webster. Wendell Phillips' "The Lost Arts," delivered some 2,000 times over a period of forty years, was a major attraction.

The Chautauquas originated and operated in a different manner. At Lake Chautauqua, New York, during the summer of 1874, John H. Vincent offered a program of lecture courses. Based on the success and growth of his project, he acquired a partner, Keith Vawter, and in 1904 organized what became known as "traveling Chautauquas." The Chautauquas, traveling with tents mostly through the rural areas during the summer months, were particularly popular with the masses, and their programs, featuring distinguished speakers on appealing topics, catered to mass tastes. William Jennings Bryan and Russell H. Conwell were audience favorites. Conwell presented his lecture "Acres of Diamonds", to over 6,000 audiences during a period of more than fifty years and with his huge profits founded Temple University. It is estimated that during a single year Chautauqua programs were offered in some 10,000 communities, with a total audience of 4 million.[9]

As the various lyceums either disappeared or merged to form literary societies during the period after the Civil War, newly formed lecture bureaus supplied speakers who gave audiences what they wanted to hear, utilizing local facilities for public address and providing eminent speakers for substantial fees. James B. Pond became a major entrepreneur whose contracted speakers included the best that money could attract: Henry Ward Beecher, Chauncey M. Depew, John B. Gough, Robert G. Ingersoll, and Wendell Phillips, to name only a few. Mark Twain was extremely successful on the lecture circuit, reportedly earning more money from public address than from publication. With the coming of the economic depression of 1929, the traveling Chautauqua phenomenon waned, but through the 1930s and 1940s lecture bureaus continued to supply large and enthusiastic audiences with such speakers as Richard Halliburton, Eleanor Roosevelt, and Lowell Thomas.

From the early days of colonial "theocracy" through the expansion into the many different denominations existing today, the clergy wielded considerable persuasive power. Some of these individuals made significant contributions to American popular culture. Theodore Parker's noteworthy sermon "The Transient and the Permanent in Christianity," delivered in a South Boston church in 1841, established him as an advocate of modernist doctrines and aroused wide criticism. He became known for his sermons against slavery, the most noted being his denunciation of Webster for his speech of March 7, 1850. Henry Ward Beecher, like his father, Lyman Beecher, was a powerful orator for many causes, including the antislavery movement, and is recognized as the greatest American preacher of the nineteenth century. His "Memorial Sermon on Abraham Lincoln," delivered April 23, 1865, is a sublime example of oratorical tribute.

Skillfully organized revivalism became big business during the latter half of the nineteenth century, and the best-known revivalist was Dwight L. Moody. Not ordained, Moody preached in convention halls, warehouses, and theaters to audiences numbering well into the thousands. Following Moody by a generation and addressing audiences into the early decades of the twentieth century, Billy (William A.) Sunday, a former baseball player with the Chicago White Sox, also not ordained, continued in the tradition of Moody in "saving souls." Sunday was an energetic preacher who put sawdust on the floor so that sinners would not make a noise as they walked down the aisle to the foot of his speaking platform, a ritual known as "hitting the sawdust trail." Later, Archbishop Fulton J. Sheen, a Roman Catholic traditionalist with a commanding presence and a sharp intellect, brought his evangelism to a radio and television audience estimated at 30 million at its peak. His television program *Life Is Worth Living*, won an Emmy Award in 1952. In the next decades, eminent Protestant evangelist Billy (William F.) Graham attracted large audiences in major cities largely through his "crusades," some of which were televised. Other popular evangelists, however, relied on television to attract millions of viewers and millions of dollars, mixing religion with social and political issues. The most successful of these preachers include Jerry Falwell, founder of the Moral Majority; Oral Roberts, head of Oral Roberts University; Pat Robertson, former chief of the Christian Broadcasting Network and a U.S. presidential candidate in 1988; and Robert Schuller, builder of the Crystal Cathedral.

As the nineteenth century drew to a close, the Populists were advocating free coinage of silver, agrarian reform, and a graduated federal income tax. Involved in these issues was the most prominent speaker of the period, William Jennings Bryan, a Democrat of Nebraska with Jeffersonian principles. His address to the Democratic convention in Chicago in 1896, "The Cross of Gold," advocating the cause of labor and the farmer, is considered a high point of convention oratory. Bryan had a long and popular career as a proponent for humanity, democracy, and religious orthodoxy, which culminated in 1924 in the world-famous Scopes "Monkey Trial" in Dayton, Tennessee, where he argued eloquently for the cause of the divine creation of humans against Clarence S. Darrow, the lawyer for the defense of the theory of evolution.

The popular hero of the Spanish-American War, New York Republican Theodore Roosevelt, as vice president of the United States, addressed an audience at the Minnesota State Fair, Minneapolis, on September 2, 1901, in which he made a vigorous plea that this nation maintain the principles of the Monroe Doctrine. He illustrated his attitude:

> A good many of you are probably acquainted with the old proverb: "Speak softly and carry a big stick—you will go far." If a man continually blusters, if he lacks civility, a big stick will not save him from trouble; and neither will speaking softly avail, if back of the softness there does not lie strength, power. . . . So it is with the nation.[10]

Assuming the presidency upon the assassination of William McKinley less than two weeks later, Roosevelt spoke extensively and successfully to break the trusts of big business and the railroads and to promote conservation. Roosevelt's well-known speech calling for decency in government, "The Man with the Muck-Rake," delivered in Washington, D.C., in 1906, reflected the tenor of the time. Other progressives noted for public address were also campaigning for reform, including Albert J. Beveridge, Robert M. LaFollette, and William E. Borah.

In the early years of the twentieth century, issues of war and peace, as well as reform, engulfed Democratic president Woodrow Wilson, a crusading, intellectual speaker. Wilson's "Peace without Victory" speech, delivered to the Senate on January 21, 1917, intended to convince the warring European powers to resolve their conflict, was to no avail: three months later, on April 2, Wilson had to appear before a joint session of Congress to ask for a declaration of war. This momentous "War Message" was enthusiastically endorsed, and the nation embarked on its first world war. In an address before a joint session of Congress on January 8, 1918,

Kennedy-Nixon debate. Courtesy of the Library of Congress

Wilson proposed his famous Fourteen Points as a basis for a peace treaty. Following the conclusion of this war, against strong opposition from the Senate led by Henry Cabot Lodge, Wilson traveled to Versailles, and on January 25, 1919, appealed to the international delegates for the formation of a League of Nations as a means to render justice and maintain peace. Although the world was not then ready for Wilson's idealistic vision, his concepts would find realistic expression a generation later in the formation of the United Nations.

Faced with the darkest depression known in this country, Democrat Franklin D. Roosevelt assumed the presidency on March 4, 1933, and the era of the New Deal was launched. His Inaugural Address, transmitted by radio, was heard by more people than any previous public address, and his words brought a renewal of hope and confidence: "This great Nation will endure as it has endured, will revive and prosper. So, first of all, let me assert my firm belief that the only thing we have to fear is fear itself—nameless, unreasoning, unjustified terror which paralyzes needed efforts to convert retreat into advance."[11] A week later, on March 12, Roosevelt gave his first radio "fireside chat," in which he personalized the workings of government. The success of the fireside chat was immediate. Roosevelt continued to bring the problems and solutions of government directly to the people through some thirty of these chats, and the people responded by backing him in his programs for recovery and reform.

Following the Japanese attack on Pearl Harbor in the Hawaiian Islands, Roosevelt addressed a joint session of Congress on December 8, 1941:

Yesterday, December 7, 1941—A date which will live in infamy—the United States of America was suddenly and deliberately attacked by naval and air forces of the Empire of Japan. . . . With confidence in our armed forces—with the unbounding determination of our people—we will gain the inevitable triumph—so help us God.[12]

The peace that came with the "inevitable triumph" ushered in an era known as the Cold War. An "Iron Curtain," a term employed by Winston Churchill in a speech delivered at Westminster College in Fulton, Missouri, on March 5, 1946, was drawn between the forces of communism and the free peoples of the Western world. Democratic president Harry Truman, confronted with a major crisis when the communist army of North Korea invaded South Korea in June 1950, used a radio address to declare a national emergency. Less than a year later, in a historic controversy over military policy, Truman relieved General of the Army Douglas MacArthur of his command of the United Nations Forces in the Far East, and MacArthur was honored with an invitation to address a joint session of Congress. On April 19, 1951, the respected World War II hero, receiving a tremendous ovation, stated his position and bade good-bye:

But I still remember the refrain of one of the most popular barrack ballads of that day which proclaimed most proudly that "Old soldiers never die; they just fade away." And like the old soldier of that ballad, I now close my military career and just fade away—an old soldier who tried to do his duty as God gave him the light to see that duty.[13]

A new type of participatory government, made possible by electronics, was introduced with the debates and public addresses of the two national political conventions and the succeeding presidential campaigns in 1952, when for the first time these proceedings were brought directly to the people coast to coast via television. Never before had so many people witnessed history in the making. The Republicans nominated General of the Army Dwight D. Eisenhower; the Democrats nominated the articulate governor of Illinois, Adlai E. Stevenson. Eisenhower was elected by the largest popular vote ever cast for a presidential candidate, and his Inaugural Address, televised on January 20, 1953, was the first to be seen and heard by millions of people throughout the country.[14] Also noteworthy were his December 8, 1953, address, titled "Atoms for Peace," to the United Nations General Assembly and his January 17, 1961, Farewell Address to the American people.

The power of television as an element in determining the course of political events was dramatically emphasized during the fall of 1960, when the Republican candidate for the presidency, Vice President Richard M. Nixon, confronted the Democratic nominee, Senator John F. Kennedy of Massachusetts, in a series of four debates. Although the original impression of the electorate was that the candidates were equally qualified, Kennedy's fluency and charisma, transmitted to millions of viewers through the medium of television, carried the debates and, ultimately, the election. Kennedy's cause was also aided by his September 12, 1960, address to the Greater Houston Ministerial Association, in which he directly confronted the issue of his Catholic faith. Kennedy's eloquent Inaugural Address, telecast on January 20, 1961, noted for its epigram, "Ask not what your country can do for you—ask what you can do for your country," sought to inspire a new beginning, a New Frontier, in attempts to solve problems both at home and abroad.[15] Perhaps President Kennedy's other most noteworthy speeches were his October 22, 1962, television address to the American people about the Cuban Missile Crisis and his June 26, 1963, address in West Berlin's Rudolph Wilde Platz in which he declared his and the United States' firm commitment to the people of that embattled city.

The major domestic problem facing the nation during this period was civil rights. In the forefront of black protest was the Reverend Martin Luther King Jr., who delivered hundreds of speeches and organized marches, boycotts, and sit-ins to achieve his vision of nonviolent integration. King's "I Have a Dream" speech, delivered on August 28, 1963, from the steps of the Lincoln Memorial to a crowd of more than 200,000 blacks and whites who had marched on Washington, is the most renowned public address of the civil rights movement and, perhaps, the most renowned public address of the century. Advocating an opposing point of view was Malcolm X (Malcolm Little), whose address, "The Ballot or the Bullet," delivered on April 3, 1964, in Cleveland, pressed for black nationalism. Black rhetoric became more militant with Stokely Carmichael, who coined the slogan "black power," and H. Rap Brown, who threatened armed confrontation. The revolutionary public statements of Black Panthers Huey P. Newton, Eldridge Cleaver, and Bobby Seale expressed the ideology of Marx and Lenin. As the struggle continued into the 1970s, the debate and public address of black revolution became less inflammatory. Although most of the public speaking that one associates with the civil rights movement was delivered by black speakers, President Lyndon B. Johnson's March 15, 1965, address to a joint session of Congress should certainly not be neglected. Although not an especially eloquent speaker, Johnson spoke from his heart about the effects of racism that he had seen while growing up in West Texas and joined civil rights activists in declaring "We shall overcome."

Concurrent with black agitation as a vital oratorical issue was the complex problem of the war in Vietnam. Prominent vocal advocates of peace included Senators J. William Fulbright, George McGovern, Eugene McCarthy, and Robert F. Kennedy. The administration's Vietnam policy was openly probed on television by the Senate Foreign Relations Committee. Amid great dissension within the leadership of his own party, Democratic president Lyndon B. Johnson in a historic, nationally televised address on March 31, 1968, announced both the cessation of bombing in Vietnam and his decision not to seek reelection. Unrest in the country was strong. Educators, clergymen, and other groups addressed themselves to the war issue, but young people across the nation became the most potent voice for peace. Hundreds of student demonstrations and protests on college and university campuses, some peaceful, others violent, emphatically expressed opposition to the war. Such public expression undoubtedly contributed greatly to the cease-fire agreement, effective January 28, 1973, with which the Nixon administration brought U.S. involvement in Vietnam to a close.

During this same period, the space age became a popular issue of debate and public address. Astronaut John H. Glenn Jr., following his orbital flight around the earth, declared before a joint session of Congress on February 26, 1962, that "what we have done so far are but small building blocks in a huge pyramid to come."[16] Seven years later, on July 20, 1969, Neil Armstrong became the first human being to set foot on the moon. Millions of people all over the world watched and listened as Armstrong, the first person to address the planet earth from another planetary body, proclaimed: "That's one small step for a man, one giant leap for mankind."[17]

During the 1970s, one of the popular issues debated at length was woman's rights, including a proposed Equal Rights Amendment to the Constitution. This issue was exemplified by the public addresses and activities of Representative Shirley Chisholm, the first black woman elected to Congress, who in 1972 actively sought the Democratic presidential nomination. Other prominent issues of the decade included the energy crisis, culminating in an antinuclear rally in Washington, D.C., in 1979; and homosexual or "gay" rights, whose activists also marched on Washington during that year. In addition, the debate and public address centering on two historic events of the 1970s had great impact on popular culture. First, as part of the aftermath of the Watergate incident, the American public witnessed the televised debate of the Committee on the Judiciary of the House of Representatives in 1974, as members considered the possible impeachment of President Nixon. Less than two weeks later, in an address unprecedented in American history, speaking to the nation via television from the White House, Nixon announced his resignation. The other historic event of major oratorical importance during this period was the celebration of the U.S. Bicentennial during 1976. Students from more than 8,500 high schools, colleges, and universities argued pertinent topics as part of the Bicentennial Youth Debate program, and ceremonial speech activities across the nation involved many thousands.

The 1976 presidential campaign was distinguished by three televised debates between Republican president Gerald R. Ford and Democratic candidate Jimmy Carter of Georgia, marking the first such confrontation since the Kennedy–Nixon debates of 1960. The vice presidential candidates, Democratic senator Walter F. Mondale of Minnesota and Republican senator Robert J. Dole of Kansas, met face-to-face in a single debate, establishing the first such televised encounter. Four years later, in the fall of 1980, presidential candidate John B. Anderson, Illinois Republican congressman turned Independent, faced Republican presidential candidate Ronald Reagan of California in a single debate; and Reagan confronted President Carter, also in a single debate. The 1984 campaign saw President Reagan, dubbed the Great Communicator by the press, meet opponent Mondale in two debates and Vice President George Bush face Democratic vice presidential candidate Geraldine A. Ferraro, New York congresswoman, in one debate. Attracting millions of viewers, these debates, complex in structure and difficult to assess, afforded maximum nationwide mass involvement in debate and public address. Since 1984, debates between (and, in 1992, among) the presidential and vice presidential candidates have become the norm. During the 1988–1996 period, the most noteworthy development was the use of citizen questioners for a debate among Bill Clinton, George Bush, and Ross Perot in 1992 at the University of Richmond.

The 1980s witnessed two of the largest peaceful assemblies ever to take place in this country, reflecting two paramount issues that American speakers have repeatedly addressed during recent decades. On June 12, 1982, a crowd estimated to be more than 500,000 marched through Manhattan and rallied at Central Park to protest the proliferation of nuclear arms. Among the dozens of diverse speakers who exhorted the audience to press for worldwide disarmament were the Reverend William Sloane Coffin Jr., Coretta Scott King, and Orson Welles. On August 27, 1983, a crowd of about 250,000 gathered to observe the twentieth anniversary of the Reverend Martin Luther King Jr.'s "I Have a Dream" speech at the original site, the steps of the Lincoln Memorial in Washington. Some five hours of speeches delivered by Coretta Scott King, Benjamin Hooks, the Reverend Jesse Jackson, and Andrew Young, who, among others, called for jobs, peace, freedom, and a rebirth of the civil rights movement. In more recent years, Washington, D.C., has seen black men and, then, black women convene the "Million Men" and Million Women" marches on the Mall. These marches were not for civil rights but rather were demonstrations of commitment to family and God. Washington, D.C., has also seen annual demonstrations to either celebrate or protest the 1973 Supreme Court decision *Roe v. Wade*. Public oratory played a role in all of these gatherings.

Few speeches during the Nixon, Ford, or Carter presidencies are noteworthy as successes. Critics have, however, devoted a good deal of attention to Nixon's unsuccessful attempts to explain the Watergate situation, Ford's Sunday morning pardon of Nixon, and Carter's July 15, 1979, address to the nation, in which, in the context of a discussion of the nation's energy problem, he discusses the nation's spiritual crisis. A good discussion of the second speech is to be found in Karlyn Kohrs Campbell and Kathleen Hall Jamieson's *Deeds Done in Words: Presidential Rhetoric and the Genres of Governance*; a good discussion of the latter is in Roderick P. Hart's *Verbal Style and the Presidency*.

With Ronald Reagan's election in 1980, eloquence returned to the White House. Many speeches delivered during his eight years in office are memorable. Especially noteworthy is the way that Reagan used the physical setting of an address as part of its rhetoric. This ability to move and persuade visually as well as verbally is noticeable in his addresses at Bitburg and Normandy as well as in his 1980 inaugural. Kathleen Hall Jamieson's *Eloquence in an Electronic Age: The Transformation of Political Speechmaking* does an excellent job of tracing the changes in oratory that Reagan effected. In many ways, Bill Clinton's style is imitative of Reagan's. However, perhaps due to his tendency to speak at greater length than necessary, Clinton, like George Bush before him, has not produced especially memorable public addresses.

What must be considered a preeminent address delivered by an American in modern times was the work not of a great orator but of a great writer. William Faulkner, on accepting the 1949 Nobel Prize in literature at the awards ceremony in Stockholm, Sweden, held December 10, 1950, spoke to the world at a time when the fear of atomic annihilation cast a pall:

> I decline to accept the end of man. It is easy enough to say that man is immortal simply because he will endure: that when the last ding-dong of doom has clanged and faded from the last worthless rock hanging tideless in the last red and dying evening, that even then there will still be one more

sound: that of his puny inexhaustible voice, still talking. I refuse to accept this. I believe that man will not merely endure: he will prevail.[18]

Another noteworthy address upon accepting the Nobel Prize in literature was Toni Morrison's in 1993, in which she celebrated the ability of narrative to reveal the black experience.

From the town meeting to the march on Washington, debate and public address, stimulated and magnified in modern times by radio and television, have been an integral part of American popular culture. Through the power of public speaking the American people have reached the crucial decisions that have governed the country as well as the personal choices by which they have lived. Essentially, the debate and public address of America's past not only have served the immediacy of particular occasions but also have provided a rich heritage of permanent and popular literature.

REFERENCE WORKS

The reference works in debate and public address noted here include not only resources for scholarly inquiry but also means through which communication skills can be learned.

The following three references are practical, introductory works designed to prepare students who are embarking on research projects in speech communication. *Communication Research: Strategies and Sources*, by Rebecca B. Rubin, Alan M. Rubin, and Linda J. Piele, is an elementary guide to the literature available in the major areas of communication, including speech communication. This reference offers basic information on the library research process, design of the research project, and the use of computer search of on-line databases. *Research in Speech Communication*, by Raymond K. Tucker, Richard L. Weaver II, and Cynthia Berryman-Fink, is comprehensive in its coverage. It gives an overview of research procedures and then introduces the three basic methods of problem solving: historical-critical, descriptive, and experimental. Chapters dealing with generating quantitative data and statistical models are clearly presented, and bibliographic listings are extensive. *Communication Research Methods*, by John Waite Bowers and John A. Courtright, is intended for upper-division undergraduate and beginning graduate students. It combines a social science research methods approach with data analysis and statistical concepts. The detailed application of statistics, using case studies and examples, is a major strength of this reference.

The federal government is a principal source of reference material. The U.S. Congress' *Congressional Record* is of inestimable value because it routinely prints more debates and speeches than any other U.S. publication. From the 1st Congress to the present, the proceedings have been reported in four series of publications: *Annals of Congress* (1789–1824); *Register of Debates* (1824–1837); *Congressional Globe* (1833–1873); and *Congressional Record* (1873 to date), issued daily and biweekly and also permanently bound and indexed. Although not a verbatim or complete account of daily congressional proceedings, the *Record* is the official and most authoritative publication of the words spoken on the floor of the two houses. Beginning in 1979 in the House of Representatives and in 1986 in the Senate, proceedings were televised on C-SPAN 1 (House) and C-SPAN 2

(Senate). The televised proceedings are archived by the Public Affairs Video Archives, School of Liberal Arts, Purdue University.

The presidential papers, including public messages, speeches, and statements, as well as transcripts of news conferences, can be found in the U.S. General Services Administration's *Weekly Compilation of Presidential Documents* and annual *Public Papers of the Presidents of the United States*. References have been published for each year of office for Presidents Hoover, Truman, Eisenhower, Kennedy, Johnson, Nixon, Ford, Carter, Reagan, Bush, and Clinton. The *Department of State Bulletin*, issued monthly by the U.S. Department of State's Bureau of Public Affairs, is the official record of this country's foreign policy and includes major addresses and news conferences of the president and the secretary of state as well as statements made before congressional committees by the secretary and other senior Department of State officials.

Joe Morehead's *Introduction to United States Public Documents* presents a contemporary overview of accessing federal government information, in general, including on-line databases and microfilm collections. This work examines the publications, reports, and materials of the legislative, executive, and judicial branches of the government, the independent agencies with regulatory powers, and the advisory committees and commissions. Although the materials cited are not exhaustive, this reference is an appropriate starting point for gaining information from federal publications. *Government Reference Books: A Biennial Guide to U.S. Government Publications*, compiled by LeRoy C. Schwarzkopf, is an annotated guide to bibliographies, catalogs, dictionaries, indexes, and other reference works issued by agencies of the U.S. government. Also of great value as a research tool is *Index to U.S. Government Periodicals: A Computer-Generated Guide to 183 Selected Titles by Author and Subject*. This work provides access to substantive articles published in the periodicals produced by more than 100 federal agencies.

The National Communication Association (NCA), headquartered in Washington, D.C., is a national organization that serves those who are concerned with the principles of communication, particularly speech communication. Its annual *Directory* provides useful current information pertaining to debate and public address. This reference is published in cooperation with the NCA's four regional organizations: Central States Speech Association, Eastern Communication Association, Southern Speech Communication Association, and Western Speech Communication Association. Listed are the names and addresses of the officers of the national association and its divisions, boards, commissions, and committees as well as those heading the regional, state, and various affiliated and related speech organizations and the editorial staffs of the several publications. Alphabetical and geographical listings of the membership and a roster of institutions of higher education that offer programs in speech and the names of appropriate administrative officers are included. The National Communication Association maintains an increasingly useful Web site at http://www.natcom.org.

Abstracts provide a convenient form for surveying contemporary scholarship. *Communication Abstracts*, a quarterly international information service edited by Thomas F. Gordon, presents current summaries of communication-related literature in the various subfields of communication. These abstracts are drawn from close to 200 professional periodicals, including *International Popular Culture* and *Journal of Popular Culture*, as well as recent books and book chapters. *Dissertation*

Abstracts International: The Humanities and Social Sciences, compiled monthly, publishes abstracts of doctoral dissertations offering insight into contemporary research and thought in debate and public address. These abstracts are grouped under the subheading "Speech Communication" in the "Communications and the Arts" section. University Microfilms International, Ann Arbor, Michigan, issues a catalog of doctoral dissertations in the broad field of communications. Citations pertinent to debate and public address can be found under the headings "Argumentation/Persuasion," "Rhetoric," and "Theory/Methods/Research."

The major bibliographies and indexes in the area of debate and public address include the following: *Bibliography of Speech Education*, compiled by Lester Thonssen and Elizabeth Fatherson in 1939, and *Bibliography of Speech Education: Supplement, 1939–1948*, compiled by Thonssen, Mary Margaret Robb, and Dorothea Thonssen. They comprise an authoritative reference of articles, books, and advanced-degree theses from the nineteenth century through 1948. These listings are indexed by the various areas of speech and dramatic art, including public speaking, debate, radio speaking, after-dinner speaking, and pulpit speaking. *Rhetoric and Public Address: A Bibliography, 1947–1961*, compiled and edited by James W. Cleary and Frederick W. Haberman, is a comprehensive and clearly organized listing of articles, books, monographs, and doctoral dissertations that appeared during the period. *Bibliography of Speech and Allied Areas, 1950–1960*, by Dorothy I. Mulgrave, Clark S. Marlor, and Elmer E. Baker Jr., is a selective compilation of doctoral dissertations and books. A major division of the work on public address includes subheadings for debate, history, orators, public speaking, and rhetoric. "A Bibliography of Rhetoric and Public Address for the Year [1947–1969]," compiled by Frederick W. Haberman and others from 1948 through 1969, which appeared initially in *Quarterly Journal of Speech* and subsequently in *Speech Monographs* (now *Communication Monographs*), offers a comprehensive bibliography of contemporary studies in the history, theory, and criticism of public address. From 1970 through 1975, this bibliography was published, together with other selective bibliographies and listings of graduate theses and dissertations in the various areas of speech communication, in *Bibliographic Annual in Speech Communication*, edited successively by Ned A. Shearer and Patrick C. Kennicott. This bibliography was discontinued with the 1975 edition. "A Bibliography of Speech and Theatre in the South for the Year [1954–1982]" (title varies), compiled by Ralph T. Eubanks, V. L. Baker, and others over the years, appeared annually in *Southern Speech Communication Journal*. Significant material relevant to communication literature of the South is listed. This bibliography was discontinued with the 1982 compilation.

Three specialized bibliographies are applicable reference works for research in debate and public address. *Political Campaign Communication: A Bibliography and Guide to the Literature, 1973–1982*, by Lynda Lee Kaid and Anne Johnston Wadsworth, cites more than 2,400 interdisciplinary entries from books, pamphlets, journal articles, dissertations, and theses relevant to American political campaign processes. *Religious Broadcasting, 1920–1983: A Selectively Annotated Bibliography*, by George H. Hill and Lenwood Davis, is a compilation of books, dissertations, theses, and articles. Subject and author indexing includes religious affiliations, networks, organizations, and personalities. The coverage in this reference is mostly of Christian radio and television broadcasting but includes as well Baha'i, Jewish, ecumenical, and interfaith broadcasts. *Women Speaking: An Annotated Bibliography*

Chautauqua tent, Kearney, Nebraska. Courtesy of the Nebraska State Historical Society

of Verbal and Nonverbal Communication, 1970–1980, by Mary E. W. Jarrard and Phyllis R. Randall, is an interdisciplinary guide to published empirical and scholarly research on women's communication during the 1970s. Entries are organized into three divisions of communication: settings, characteristics, and means. A comprehensive subject index that lists works by specific topics, including rhetorical analysis, sex differences, sex-role stereotyping, and style of speaking, is most useful.

The National Communication Association publishes more than forty annotated bibliographies covering various aspects of communication and distributes them for the cost of the postage. Titles include "Argumentation and Debate," "Argumentation Theory," "Black American Rhetorical Studies," "Coaching Debate and Forensics," "Communication and Gender," "Communication and Politics," "Feminist Rhetoric," "Health Communication," "Persuasion," "Political Campaign Debating," "Resources for Public Speaking," "Rhetoric of Gay Liberation," "Video Tape Resources in Speech Communication," and "Voice and Articulation."

A reference highly useful to researchers in debate and public address is *Index to Journals in Communication Studies through 1995*, edited by Ronald J. Matlon and Sylvia P. Oritz. This publication lists primary articles, volume by volume, of fifteen major journals in communication from their inception through 1995. Works are also indexed by contributor and subject matter. The National Communication Association's *COMM Search* is a useful companion to the Matlon and Ortiz bibliography. *COMM Search*, in its second edition, is a CD-ROM index to twenty-four journals with abstracts for six NCA-published journals since 1972 and the full text of articles from these journals since 1991. *COMM Search* is available in many college and university libraries; it is also available for purchase from NCA. *Speech Index: An Index to 259 Collections of World Famous Orations and Speeches for Various Occasions*, composed by Roberta Briggs Sutton in 1966, and a 1966–1980 supplement composed by Charity Mitchell provide a guide to speeches of famous orators from the earliest times to the present. Entries are arranged and cross-referenced by speaker, subject, and type of speech. *Index to American Women Speakers, 1828–1978*, compiled by Beverley Manning, is intended to aid in locating women's speeches, past and present. Indexed by author, subject, and title, the work encompasses the full range of women's interests but concentrates heavily on woman's rights and struggles.

Audio and video recordings are a valuable primary reference. The yearly output of recordings, however, is prolific, and it is difficult to obtain a "complete" directory. *On Cassette, 1986–1987: A Comprehensive Bibliography of Spoken Word Audiocassettes* offers over 20,000 annotated and cross-referenced entries. Indexed by title, author, reader/performer, subject, producer-distributor/title, and producer/distributor, this work is thorough and practical. Also useful is Gerald McKee's *Directory of Spoken-Word Audio Cassettes*, which lists offerings of nearly 700 producers of spoken-word audiocassettes. Among these listings can be found tapes dealing with speaking skills. Such titles as "Effective Public Speaking," "Speak for Success," and "How to Enter the World of Paid Speaking" illustrate available resources. This work includes the names and addresses of the producers/distributors and a subject index. *Video Source Book*, published annually since 1979, contains more than 40,000 videocassette programs available from 850 sources. Entries are classified by title, subject, and wholesaler. Titles listed in the subject index under "Communication" include "How to Make a More Effective Speech" and "Speaking before a Group"; titles listed under "Speech" include "Preparing to Speak" and "Public Speaking." The producers or distributors indexed in the preceding directories usually fill a request free of charge for their brochure or catalog.

Professional speakers who are stimulating or entertaining are always in demand, and prospective audiences can find assistance in locating them. *Speakers and Lecturers: How to Find Them. A Directory of Booking Agents, Lecture Bureaus, Companies, Professional and Trade Associations, Universities, and Other Groups Which Organize and Schedule Engagements for Lecturers and Public Speakers on All Subjects, with Information on Speakers, Subjects and Arrangements, and Biographical Details on Over 2,000 Individuals*, edited by Paul Wasserman, is of considerable use in bringing together speakers and audiences. Howard J. Langer's *Directory of Speakers* contains an alphabetical listing of about 1,300 available speakers. This work is indexed by both geographical area and subject and includes a short biographical sketch of each speaker. The International Platform Association, with executive offices in Winnetka, Illinois, is a nonprofit organization that promotes the professional speaking interests of its approximately 5,000 members. This organization is the successor to the International Lyceum Association, established in 1903, and traces its origins to the American Lyceum Association, which was founded by Daniel Webster and Josiah Holbrook in 1831. Its members are professional lecturers and others who appear before live audiences to inform and entertain, as well as program chairmen, booking agents, and men and women of various fields who are interested in oratory and the power of the spoken word. The International Platform Association sponsors an Orator's Hall of Fame, whose members are such renowned speakers as William Jennings Bryan, John F. Kennedy, Martin Luther King Jr., Abraham Lincoln, Douglas MacArthur, Franklin D. Roosevelt, Adlai Stevenson, and Daniel Webster.

Debating and public speaking are not only an area of interest to the critic or historian but also a skill that can be acquired. Skill in debating and public speaking is probably best learned in the classroom under the guidance of an instructor with the aid of a suitable textbook selected from an abundant supply on the market. Several of the more widely recognized books and sources that offer instruction in speaking in public are presented first; then publications that treat educational or academic debate are considered. Many textbooks, of course, are written so that a person of average intelligence and discipline can use them as references for self-study. *Principles and Types of Speech Communication*, by Douglas Ehninger, Bruce E. Gronbeck, Ray E. McKerrow, and Alan H. Monroe, used on college campuses for more than fifty years and now in its eleventh edition, is a leading basic textbook. The authors are noted for their organizational pattern for persuasive speeches known as the "motivated sequence." Included are chapters detailing the adapting of a speech to an audience, outlining a speech, and the use of visual aids, as well as sample speeches for study and analysis. A very different, but widely used, textbook is James C. McCroskey's *An Introduction to Rhetorical Communication*. Now in its sixth edition, McCroskey's text tries to incorporate relevant advances in theory and empirical research as it offers practical advice. A somewhat different format from the preceding textbooks is offered in *The Speaker's Handbook*, by Jo Sprague and Douglas Stuart. Using a prescriptive approach, this work is cross-referenced, with endpapers, a subject index, and tabbed and numbered running heads. Other useful texts include David Zarefsky's *Public Speaking: Strategies for Success*, second edition, and John J. Makay's *Public Speaking: Theory into Practice*, third edition.

In addition to traditional textbooks, there are numerous books designed for do-it-yourself popular use. These works frequently are written by well-known persons and are anecdotal in format. Examples include Ed McMahon's *The Art of Public Speaking* and Jack Valenti's *Speak Up with Confidence: How to Prepare, Learn, and Deliver Effective Speeches*. A popular offering of this sort, also, is Dale Carnegie's *The Quick and Easy Way to Effective Speaking*. Collections of humorous stories, quotations, epigrams, and unusual facts and illustrations for the speaker are readily available. *The Public Speaker's Treasure Chest* and a companion volume, *The Toastmaster's Treasure Chest*, by Herbert V. Prochnow and Herbert V. Prochnow Jr., are examples of this type of reference.

Instruction in public speaking is offered by both commercial and noncommercial organizations in communities throughout the country. Listings of commercial organizations can be obtained by consulting the classified pages of the local telephone directory under such headings as "Public Speaking Instruction." Probably the most widely known commercial organization engaged in the teaching of public speaking is Dale Carnegie, which is international in scope. The Carnegie method has proven successful for hundreds of thousands of students since 1912. Other commercial programs are competitive.

Among the noncommercial organizations that provide opportunities to develop skills in public speaking is Toastmasters International. The first Toastmasters club was established in 1924; and local Toastmasters groups now number more than 5,600, with a membership of approximately 120,000 in over forty-seven countries. Each local group consists of about twenty to forty persons who meet regularly to learn and practice techniques of public speaking and constructive evaluation. Included in the organization's annual activities are the sponsorship of the World Championship of Public Speaking and the bestowal of the Golden Gavel Award to a prominent communicator. *Toastmaster Magazine*, a monthly publication, is devoted to relevant news and articles. Toastmasters International is affiliated with Gavel Clubs, an organization of sixty local groups with about 2,500 members who cannot participate in the complete Toastmasters club program. Both of these organizations are headquartered in Santa Ana, California. International Training in Communication, formerly International Toastmistress Club, founded in 1938, is an organization of over 1,400 local groups with headquarters in Anaheim, California. This is an association of approximately 27,000 adults who are interested in speech improvement and communication.

Educational debate in this country is conducted under the guidance of both secondary and collegiate institutions. Several formats for educational debating are officially recognized, and each is organized in accordance with established rules and procedures applicable to competitive tournament debating. Austin J. Freeley's *Argumentation and Debate: Critical Thinking for Reasoned Decision Making* is a comprehensive textbook that has been used for the typical undergraduate course in argumentation and debate for a quarter of a century. Chapters dealing with evidence, reasoning, case construction, evaluation, and tournament procedures are clear and authoritative. This work covers national intercollegiate debate practices for the American Forensic Association's National Debate Tournament (NDT) as well as for the programs of the Cross Examination Debate Association (CEDA). *Student Congress and Lincoln–Douglas Debate*, by Maridell Fryar and David A. Thomas, offers insight into the theory and practice of these two specialized high school forensic events. The Lincoln–Douglas format has recently become popular among colleges as well. As of yet, no text adequately treats it. Also popular on college and university campuses are public debate and parliamentary debate. Useful references are Robert O. Weiss' *Public Argument* and Lawrence Galizio and Trischa Knapp's *The Elements of Parliamentary Debate: A Handbook*. An additional reference of interest to academic debaters is the "Opposing Viewpoints" series published by Greenhaven Press, St. Paul, Minnesota. Available in three separate categories—books, pamphlets, and sources—this series offers diverse points of view on a broad spectrum of contemporary issues.

Resource materials pertaining to the annual debate topics are available from various sources: governmental, institutional, and commercial. The superintendent of documents, U.S. Government Printing Office, annually publishes a bibliography applicable to the topics: *Subject Bibliography 043*, which furnishes an annotated listing of government publications relating to the national high school debate topic; and *Subject Bibliography 176*, which furnishes an annotated listing of government publications relating to the college debate topic. Among the leading sources that offer materials on the high school topic are the National Communication Association, Washington, D.C.; the National Forensic League, Ripon, Wisconsin; the American Enterprise Institute for Public Policy Research, Washington, D.C.; and the National Textbook Company, Lincolnwood, Illinois. Sources offering handbooks and other materials relating to the college topic include the Study Group of the Alan Company, Clayton, Missouri, and Springboards, Inc., St. Louis, Missouri. This list is only a sampling. Additional information on debating and debate resources may be obtained by writing to the Secretary of the American Forensic Association, University of Wisconsin-River Falls, River Falls, Wisconsin 54022, or by consulting the National Communication Association, referred to earlier.

Compilations of intercollegiate debates provide useful reference tools for many aspects of debating. Among these compilations are the following two series. *Intercollegiate Debates: Being Briefs and Reports of Many Intercollegiate Debates*, a work of twenty-two volumes edited successively by Paul M. Pearson and Egbert Ray Nichols, presents selective affirmative and negative debates on important topics of the day as argued by various college debate teams from 1909 to 1941. A compilation of thirty-seven volumes, *University Debaters' Annual: Constructive and Rebuttal Speeches Delivered in Debates of American Colleges and Universities during the College Year*, edited successively by Edward Charles Mabie, Edith M. Phelps, and Ruth Ulman, offers representative intercollegiate debates and other forensic activities presented on American campuses from the academic year 1914–1915 through 1950–1951. Selected bibliography and briefs accompany each debate. Debates from these two series as well as numerous other debates, arguments, and briefs are listed by subject in *Debate Index*, compiled by Edith M. Phelps; *Debate Index Supplement*, compiled by Julia E. Johnsen; and *Debate Index Second Supplement*, compiled by Joseph R. Dunlap and Martin A. Kuhn.

Championship Debating—West Point National Debate Tournament Final-Round Debates and Critiques, 1949–60, together with a second volume published six years later, both edited by Russel R. Windes and Arthur N. Kruger, provides a record of the annual National Debate Tournament from its inception at the U.S. Military Academy in 1947 through 1966, when the American Forensic Association assumed responsibility for conducting the tournament. For the years 1967 through 1985, transcripts of the final round of the National Debate Tournament appeared in the *Journal of the American Forensic Association*. The debates since 1986 have been published in an annual series sponsored by the Speech Communication Association and the American Forensic Association with the cooperation of the Cross Examination Debate Association and the National Forensic Association. *Championship Debates and Speeches* edited by John K. Boaz and James R. Brey presents the National Debate Tournament Final Debate, sponsored by the American Forensic Association, and the National CEDA Tournament Final Debate, sponsored by the Cross Examination Debate Association, as well as winning oratorical efforts in national intercollegiate competitions. Critiques of the judges of each event add greatly to the use of these transcripts as a reference work.

An international debate program between teams from the United States and those of foreign countries has been established since the early part of the twentieth century. *Fifty Years of International Debate, 1922–1972*, by Robert N. Hall and Jack L. Rhodes, is a brief documentation beginning with the visit of the Oxford University debating team to Bates College, Lewiston, Maine, in 1922, and concluding with the visit on American campuses of a team from the Soviet Union in the spring of 1972. Current information about international debating can be obtained from the program's sponsor, the Committee on International Discussion and Debate of the National Communication Association.

RESEARCH COLLECTIONS

The researcher in American debate and public address will find it difficult to locate specific collections so designated. Collections are more easily located by the name of the speaker, occasion, or issue.

A logical first reference to research collections is *Research Centers Directory*, edited by Mary Michelle Watkins. The several indexes in this work are of considerable aid to the researcher, but there are no listings in the subject index for debate, public address, or oratory. References to general collections, however, can be found in the subject index under "Communication Arts," "Communication in Management," and "Communication in Organizations."

A second comprehensive reference is Lee Ash and William G. Miller's computerized compilation, *Subject Collections: A Guide to Special Book Collections and Subject Emphases as Reported by University, College, Public, and Special Libraries and Museums in the United States and Canada*. This work presents an alphabetical listing of subjects and persons for whom collections have been established. Again, no listings are offered for debate, public address, or oratory. The only listing under "Public Speaking and Speakers" is that of the Chauncey Mitchell Depew Collection in the library of George Washington University. Entries are included, however, for presidential collections as well as for many individuals well known for their oratory.

A third guide of considerable scope is *Directory of Special Libraries and Information Centers: A Guide to More than 18,000 Special Libraries, Research Libraries, Information Centers, Archives, and Data Centers Maintained by Government Agencies, Business, Industry, Newspapers, Educational Institutions, Nonprofit Organizations, and Societies in the Fields of Science and Technology, Medicine, Law, Art, Religion, the Social Sciences, and Humanistic Studies*, edited by Brigitte T. Darnay. There are no listings for debate, public address, oratory; and the listings under "Speech" are a combination of speech communication and speech science. Among the research collections in speech communication described in this work are those at the following centers: ERIC Clearinghouse on Reading and Communication Skills; National Council of Teachers of English, Urbana, Illinois (annotated later); Humanities Division Library, Southern Illinois University, Carbondale; and Emerson College Library, Boston. This directory also describes numerous collections of sound recordings.

A fourth major source of information pertaining to research collections is the annual *American Library Directory*. The collections of more than 37,000 libraries are listed by geographical communities within each state, the regions administered by the United States, and the provinces of Canada. Among the listings are the libraries and archives of ABC, CBS, and NBC in New York, where each of the three major commercial radio and television networks maintains collections dealing, in part, with current issues and events. *Special Collections in Libraries of the Southeast*, edited by J. B. Howell, smaller in scope than the preceding guides, includes annotations of relevant collections in all types of libraries in the ten states constituting the southeastern part of the country. These collections are listed by person or subject under geographical communities for each state. This guide is especially useful for researching prominent local citizens and regional history. *Library and Reference Facilities in the Area of the District of Columbia*, edited by Margaret S. Jennings, lists holdings in the Washington area. Included are those of the

Democratic National Committee Research/Issues Library and the Republican National Committee Library, both of political interest.

Complementing the preceding directories as a valuable source for researchers of debate and public address in popular culture is the *National Union Catalogue of Manuscript Collections*, compiled by the U.S. Library of Congress. The first twenty-two issues in this ongoing series, which cover the years 1959 through 1984, describe approximately 54,799 collections located in 1,297 repositories in the United States. The cumulative indexes categorize approximately 597,000 references to topical subjects and personal, family, corporate, and geographical names.

The most recent *Directory of Communication Research Centers in North American Universities*, compiled by Barry S. Sapolsky, Jodi S. Hale, and Jayme Harpring, tabulates pertinent data for more than fifty-two communication research centers and institutes affiliated with universities in the United States and Canada. This spiral-bound guide includes the governance structure, staffing, facilities, funding, publications, methodologies, and research pursuits for each listing.

The Educational Resources Information Center (ERIC), sponsored by the Office of Educational Research and Improvement of the U.S. Department of Education, offers access to education-related journal articles as well as hard-to-find unpublished, noncopyrighted documents. ERIC, formed in 1966, consists of a national network of sixteen clearinghouses, each representing a broad educational subject area, integrated through a central computerized facility. Materials related to debate and public address are processed through the ERIC Clearinghouse on Reading and Communication Skills (ERIC/RCS), which is located at the headquarters of the National Council of Teachers of English (NCTE), 1111 Kenyon Road, Urbana, Ill. 61801. Three guides facilitate a search for information from ERIC's bibliographic database. *Thesaurus of ERIC Descriptors* is the source of subject headings and vocabulary for information retrieval from the ERIC collections. The U.S. Department of Education's monthly *Resources in Education*, which originated as *Research in Education*, indexes such "fugitive literature" as speeches, position papers, and research reports. Microfiche or paper copies of most of the listed documents are available from ERIC Document Reproduction Service, Alexandria, Virginia. *Current Index to Journals in Education* (CIJE) is an annotated index to articles from more than 760 publications in the field of education and peripherally related areas, including the major speech journals. Reprints of many of the journal articles can be ordered from University Microfilms International, Article Clearinghouse, Ann Arbor, Michigan. Options for searching the ERIC database also include three on-line vendors: BRS Information Technologies, Latham, New York; DIALOG Information Services, Palo Alto, California; and SDC Information Services, Santa Monica, California.

The presidential libraries and museums, which are maintained by the National Archives and Records Administration, Washington, D.C., are a primary source for rhetorical research. These collections house official public papers pertaining to all aspects of the presidency and include presidential speech texts and voice recordings of speeches: Herbert Hoover Library, West Branch, Iowa (some papers being filed at Stanford University); Franklin D. Roosevelt Library, Hyde Park, New York; Harry S Truman Library, Independence, Missouri; Dwight D. Eisenhower Library, Abilene, Kansas; John F. Kennedy Library, Boston; Lyndon Baines Johnson Presidential Library, Austin, Texas; Gerald R. Ford Library, Ann Arbor,

Michigan (the Ford Museum being located in Grand Rapids); Jimmy Carter Library, Atlanta, Georgia; and Ronald Reagan Library, Simi Valley, California. Presidential materials from the Nixon administration are maintained at the University of Maryland, College Park; materials from the Bush administration at Texas A&M University in College Station. Together these collections span a time period of more than the past fifty years.

Collections of audio and video recordings have reflected the growth of the recording and broadcasting industries as well as the increased recognition of recordings as a primary research source. The researcher will find spoken-word recordings in abundance, including recordings of addresses, debates, newscasts, hearings, readings, lectures, and oral history. "Recorded Sound Collections: New Materials to Explore the Past," an article by Ellen Reid Gold, describes the country's leading sound collections of interest to the researcher in debate and public address.

Two national archives housed in Washington, D.C., are of major importance. The collection of the Motion Picture, Broadcasting, and Recorded Sound Division of the Library of Congress encompasses some 1.5 million sound recordings on disc, tape, wire, and cylinder. Holdings include radio programs from 1924 to the present and television programs on tape and film from 1948 to the present, as well as recordings of the National Press Club luncheon speakers and NBC Radio broadcasts. A substantial collection of recorded sound is also held by the Motion Picture, Sound, and Video Branch of the National Archives and Records Administration. Recordings of speeches, panel discussions, press conferences, court and conference proceedings, interviews, entertainment programs, and news broadcasts have been gathered largely from the various federal agencies but include as well many from private and other sources. Thus, the holdings in this collection are mostly unpublished or not commercially available. These recordings date from the 1890s and include the voices of Presidents Theodore Roosevelt, William Howard Taft, Woodrow Wilson, Warren G. Harding, and Calvin Coolidge. Also included are the special collections of ABC Radio, American Town Meeting of the Air, League of Nations, and National Public Radio.

Among the major collections of sound recordings throughout the country of interest to researchers in debate and public address are the following: Stanford Archive of Recorded Sound, Braun Music Center, Stanford University, Stanford, California; Yale Collection of Historical Sound Recordings, Sterling Memorial Library, Yale University, New Haven, Connecticut, which contains recordings of historical interest in the fields of drama, politics, literature, and documentary from the end of the nineteenth century to the present, with an emphasis on the history of performance practice in the arts; G. Robert Vincent Voice Library, Michigan State University, East Lansing, Michigan, which houses historical sound recordings of voices and events in all fields of human endeavor; Record Collection of the Donnell Library Center, New York Public Library, New York City, which includes recordings of speeches and documentaries; Rodgers and Hammerstein Archives of Recorded Sound, Performing Arts Research Center, New York Public Library, New York City, which holds materials dealing with the performing arts as well as literary, historical, and political events; Audio Archives of the George Arents Research Library for Special Collections, E. S. Bird Library, Syracuse University, Syracuse, New York, which includes among its 250,000 items sound recordings of political leaders, poets, theatrical personalities, singers, and transcriptions of audio broadcasts dating from the earliest of the Thomas Edison cylinder recordings to the present; and the Phonarchive at the University of Washington, School of Communication, Seattle. Holdings in these recorded sound collections are indexed or described in various catalogs, brochures, and articles that are available through the archivists.

A collection of particular interest is Arnold's Archives, 1106 Eastwood, S.E., East Grand Rapids, Mich. 49506, which offers spoken-word recordings by hundreds of figures associated with American popular culture. Available are the recorded voices of such varied personalities as P. T. Barnum, Roberto Clemente, Jack Dempsey, Amelia Earhart, Helen Keller, Fiorello LaGuardia, Joe Louis, Joseph R. McCarthy, Jacqueline Kennedy Onassis, Babe Ruth, Norman Thomas, and Walter Winchell.

A fascinating archive of taped radio and television programs spanning a period from the 1920s to the present is housed in the Museum of Broadcasting, New York City. This collection's audiotapes and videotapes, which can be monitored in console booths, preserve a wide variety of broadcasts, including presidential oratory beginning with Warren G. Harding as well as addresses of the World War II era. The museum issues a subject guide to its collection.

The Vanderbilt Television News Archive, Nashville, Tennessee, contains videotapes of the evening news telecasts of the three major networks as seen in Nashville. This collection dates from August 5, 1968, and now consists of more than 30,000 individual network news broadcasts. In addition, this archive houses approximately 9,000 hours of tapes of special newscasts of such events as presidential speeches and press conferences and presidential and vice presidential debates. These holdings, which are readily accessible and rapidly expanding, include coverage of the Democratic and Republican National Conventions of 1968, 1972, 1976, 1980, and 1984, as well as such diverse historical events as the Nixon impeachment debates of 1974 and the reopening celebration of the Statue of Liberty of July 4, 1986. These tapes are indexed by subject and date in *Television News Index and Abstracts: A Guide to the Video Tape Collection of the Network Evening News Programs in the Vanderbilt Television News Archive*. Other useful archives are that for C-SPAN maintained at the Public Affairs Video Archives, School of Liberal Arts, Purdue University, and that for radio and television political commercials maintained at the Political Communication Center, Department of Communication, University of Oklahoma. The latter archives' holdings date back to 1936 for radio and 1950 for television.

HISTORY AND CRITICISM

American debate and public address emerged as a discrete area of scholarly inquiry in higher education in this country during the early part of the twentieth century. Any contemporary approach to the study of the history and criticism of American debate and public address, however, has its roots in the rhetorical theory of philosophers and scholars dating back to the ancient Greeks.

Among the preeminent classical works that modern critics embrace are Plato's *Gorgias* and *Phaedrus*; Aristotle's *The Rhetoric*, considered to this day the single most thorough and influential philosophical analysis of the art of speaking; Cic-

William Jennings Bryan. Courtesy of the Library of Congress

ero's *De Oratore* (55 B.C.); Quintilian's *Institutio Oratoria* (Education of an Orator, ca. A.D. 93); Longinus' *On the Sublime* (ca. first half of the first century); Francis Bacon's *The Advancement of Learning* (1605); George Campbell's *The Philosophy of Rhetoric* (1776); Hugh Blair's *Lectures on Rhetoric and Belles Lettres* (1783); and Richard Whately's *Elements of Rhetoric* (1828). Complete translations and reprints of these works are readily available. Pertinent excerpts from the preceding writings of Plato, Aristotle, Cicero, Quintilian, and Longinus may be found in translation in *Readings in Classical Rhetoric*, edited by Thomas W. Benson and Michael H. Prosser; and *The Rhetoric of Blair, Campbell, and Whately*, by James L. Golden and Edward P. J. Corbett, offers substantial selections from the works of these three theorists. *The Rhetoric of Western Thought*, by James L. Golden, Goodwin F. Berquist, and William E. Coleman, surveys major theory through the three great periods: the classical period of Greece and Rome, the British period of the seventeenth to the nineteenth centuries; and the contemporary period of the twentieth century. Dividing contemporary rhetorical theory into four areas, "Rhetoric as Meaning," "Rhetoric as Value," "Rhetoric as Motive," and "Rhetoric as a Way of Knowing," the authors explore works of renowned theorists I. A. Richards, Marshall McLuhan, Richard Weaver, Kenneth Burke, Stephen Toulmin, and Chaim Perelman.

An overview recounting the study and practice of rhetorical criticism from the early twentieth century through its development into the 1970s can be found in

Charles J. Stewart's "Historical Survey: Rhetorical Criticism in Twentieth Century America," the lead essay in *Explorations in Rhetorical Criticism*, edited by G. P. Mohrmann, Charles J. Stewart, and Donovan J. Ochs. The following two works serve well as an introduction to rhetorical theory and criticism: *Contemporary Theories of Rhetoric: Selected Readings*, edited by Richard L. Johannesen, which offers relevant essays and selections from the works of contemporary theorists Burke, McLuhan, Perelman, Richards, Toulmin, and Weaver; and Douglas Ehninger's *Contemporary Rhetoric: A Reader's Coursebook*, an anthology of twenty-seven essays, that presents an overview of contemporary rhetorical scholarship grouped by subject areas. A more recent work, *Contemporary Perspectives on Rhetoric*, by Sonja K. Foss, Karen A. Foss, and Robert Trapp, also functions as an introduction to contemporary rhetoric, treating the works of Richards, Weaver, Toulmin, Perelman, and Burke, as well as Ernesto Grassi, Michel Foucault, and Jürgen Habermas. Worthy of note are the synthesis in the final chapter and the well-organized bibliography.

Historical Studies of Rhetoric and Rhetoricians, edited by Raymond F. Howes, offers twenty-two essays by distinguished scholars, including Carroll C. Arnold, Hoyt H. Hudson, Everett Lee Hunt, Wayland Maxfield Parrish, Karl R. Wallace, Herbert A. Wichelns, and James A. Winans. In a work sponsored by the National Communication Association and edited by Lloyd F. Bitzer and Edwin Black, *The Prospect of Rhetoric: Report of the National Developmental Project*, leading rhetoricians attempt to answer the question, What is the essential outline of a conception of rhetoric useful in the second half of the twentieth century? This report concludes in part that, because modern technology has created new channels and techniques of communication, the scope of rhetorical studies should be broadened to explore such contemporary phenomena as popular music, news reporting and interpretation, and film, which have become increasingly influential in American culture. A collection of essays, *Form and Genre: Shaping Rhetorical Action*, edited by Karlyn Kohrs Campbell and Kathleen Hall Jamieson, was published as a result of the 1976 conference on " 'Significant Form' in Rhetorical Criticism," under the auspices of the National Communication Association. The contributors, who include Herbert Simons, Edwin Black, Michael Halloran, Ronald Carpenter, Bruce E. Gronbeck, Ernest G. Bormann, and the editors, explore theoretical perspectives and their possible application to new rhetorical understanding.

Among the many significant essays published during this century of interest to the modern student of rhetorical history and critical theory, three are fundamental. "The Literary Criticism of Oratory" (1925) by Herbert A. Wichelns sets forth the neo-Aristotelian approach, which established the standard for much of the criticism that followed in the 1930s and 1940s. "Public Address: A Study in Social and Intellectual History" (1947) by Ernest J. Wrage urges an idea-centered critical orientation as an alternative to the traditional speaker-centered approach. Both of these essays have been reprinted in *Methods of Rhetorical Criticism: A Twentieth-Century Perspective*, a solid introductory textbook edited by Bernard L. Brock and Robert L. Scott. The third essay, "Rhetoric: Its Function and Its Scope" (1953) by Donald C. Bryant, discusses aspects of rhetoric as instrumental, critical, philosophical, and social disciplines. Bryant's essay has been reexamined in his more recent *Rhetorical Dimensions in Criticism*.

Distinguished collections of essays published in honor of an esteemed colleague, used as textbooks or for reference, have contributed greatly to the whole of speech history and criticism. Several are briefly listed: *Studies in Rhetoric and Public Speaking in Honor of James Albert Winans*, edited by A. M. Drummond, is a volume of eleven scholarly papers, including the aforementioned "The Literary Criticism of Oratory." The seventeen studies offered in *The Rhetorical Idiom: Essays in Rhetoric, Oratory, Language, and Drama Presented to Herbert August Wichelns with a Reprinting of His "Literary Criticism of Oratory"* (1925), edited by Donald C. Bryant, include Karl R. Wallace's "Rhetoric, Politics, and Education of the Ready Man," of political interest, and Bryant's " 'A Peece of a Logician' The Critical Essayist as Rhetorician," of literary interest. *American Public Address: Studies in Honor of Albert Craig Baird*, edited by Loren Reid, presents fifteen critical essays on such speakers as Oliver Wendell Holmes, Clarence Darrow, Ralph J. Bunche, and Edward R. Murrow. *Rhetoric in Transition: Studies in the Nature and Uses of Rhetoric*, edited by Eugene E. White and presented as a tribute to Carroll C. Arnold, offers ten essays by leading scholars, including Lloyd F. Bitzer, Robert L. Scott, Edwin Black, and Douglas Ehninger. The essays included in *Explorations in Rhetoric: Studies in Honor of Douglas Ehninger*, edited by Ray E. McKerrow, provide insights into areas of classical rhetoric.

Textbooks published during the last several decades on the theory and practice of rhetorical criticism offer various theoretical definitions and critical methodologies. These different approaches are not mutually exclusive. In the critical evaluation of debate and public address, it is frequently sound not to rely solely on the work of one critic or one method. Five widely accepted works are discussed here. *Speech Criticism*, by Lester Thonssen, A. Craig Baird, and Waldo W. Braden, is a comprehensive introductory treatise that is grounded in the classics. The authors deal with the nature of rhetorical criticism, development of theory, methods of the critics, and standards of judgment and provide extensive bibliographies for further study. Carroll C. Arnold's introductory textbook, *Criticism of Oral Rhetoric*, clearly written and practical, uses a traditionalist approach to analysis. Two more recent useful texts are Bernard L. Brock, and Robert L. Scott's *Methods of Rhetorical Criticism: A Twentieth-Century Perspective* and Roderick P. Hart's *Modern Rhetorical Criticism*. Both cover the traditional Aristotelian approach as well as dramatistic, narrative, "fantasy theme," Marxist, feminist, and postmodern ways to analyze a "text." The former includes sample theoretical and critical essays from such noteworthy critics as Ernest Bormann, Martha Solomon, Karlyn Kohrs Campbell, and Lawrence Grossberg. Edwin Black's provocative and controversial work, *Rhetorical Criticism: A Study in Method*, is written for the advanced or graduate student and the professional audience. Black attacks the shortcomings of the various approaches to rhetorical criticism, particularly the neo-Aristotelian, as he considers the entire genre of the argumentative process.

Other works deal forthrightly with the process and practice of critical analysis by providing applicable examples of important speeches and by illuminating a particular means by which "to do criticism." Lionel Crocker's *Rhetorical Analysis of Speeches* offers a paragraph-by-paragraph rhetorical analysis of eleven speeches by such orators as Franklin D. Roosevelt, Harry Emerson Fosdick, Wendell L. Willkie, and Lyndon B. Johnson, as well as the famous persuasive speeches of Brutus and Antony in Shakespeare's *Julius Caesar* (act 3, scene 2). L. Patrick Devlin's *Contemporary Political Speaking*, in analyzing the nature of oral politics, presents thirteen topics and speakers of political significance in the 1960s and 1970s, including verbatim transcripts of their speeches. *Critiques of Contemporary Rhetoric*, by Karlyn Kohrs Campbell, discusses the rhetorical process and the traditional, psychological, and dramatistic systems of criticism and includes nine speeches by such leaders as Richard M. Nixon, George Wald, Spiro T. Agnew, Eldridge Cleaver, Jo Freeman, and Emmet John Hughes. In *A Choice of Words: The Practice and Criticism of Public Discourse*, assuming that the student of public address is both a producer and a consumer, James R. Andrews presents six basic principles of rhetoric as guides for both the speaker and the critic and for illustration selects twelve speeches on historical and contemporary issues. Andrews' more recent work, *The Practice of Rhetorical Criticism*, is also intended for undergraduate courses in rhetorical criticism. The first part of this sourcebook submits an overview of the nature of criticism, context and audience, speaker, and analysis; the second part reprints Richard M. Nixon's "Address to the Nation on the War in Vietnam, November 3, 1969," and offers critical analysis of it by Robert P. Newman, Hermann G. Stelzner, Karlyn Kohrs Campbell, and Forbes Hill; and the third part presents studies by contemporary scholars illustrating a variety of critical approaches.

Great Speeches for Criticism and Analysis, by Lloyd E. Rohler and Roger Cook, groups transcripts of speeches, mostly well known, into the two broad categories of deliberative speeches and ceremonial speeches. The initial chapter describes critical theories, and critical examinations accompany some of the speeches. Of particular interest is Lois J. Einhorn's essay, which addresses the issue of ghost-writing. The speeches range chronologically from Franklin D. Roosevelt's First Inaugural Address (1933) through Ronald Reagan's "Tribute to the *Challenger* Astronauts" (1986). Videotapes of most of the speeches included in this collection are available in a series of thirteen volumes, each with five speakers, making this work an especially valuable learning instrument.

History of American Oratory, by Warren Choate Shaw, published in 1928, is recognized as the first comprehensive history of American oratory. Shaw presents descriptive studies of twenty-one representative orators from Patrick Henry to Woodrow Wilson and includes a pertinent bibliography for each. Of greater influence today, however, is *A History and Criticism of American Public Address*, a seminal study published in two volumes in 1943, edited by William Norwood Brigance, and followed twelve years later by a third volume, edited by Marie Kathryn Hochmuth. Brigance's work is divided into two parts: Part 1 presents a historical background of public address from the colonial period through 1930; Part 2 offers twenty-nine analytical studies of leaders from the fields of religion, reform, law, general culture, education, labor, and statecraft, ranging chronologically from Jonathan Edwards to Woodrow Wilson. The analyses vary in style and scope but are uniformly sound. Hochmuth introduces the third volume with a significant essay, "The Criticism of Rhetoric," and presents critical studies of such orators as Alexander Hamilton, Susan B. Anthony, Clarence Darrow, Theodore Roosevelt, William E. Borah, Harry Emerson Fosdick, and Franklin D. Roosevelt. The extensive footnotes, bibliographies, and indexes contribute to the usefulness of these three volumes.

The Rhetoric of Protest and Reform: 1878–1898, edited by Paul H. Boase, presents thirteen essays divided into five parts that deal with labor protest, the agrarian revolt, women speakers, religious issues, and the efforts of intellectuals in the reform movement. Primarily historical or neo-Aristotelian in their critical approach, the essayists together offer a survey of public address from the Gilded Age through the Gay Nineties as orators spoke out against injustice and corruption in their struggle toward democratic reform.

Robert T. Oliver's *History of Public Speaking in America* is an evaluative work of broad scope, which illuminates the influence of public address on the flow of history from the earliest period through the era of Woodrow Wilson. Oliver's style is anecdotal, and the work includes extensive bibliographies. A volume as insightful and utilitarian as Oliver's and more current in coverage is *America in Controversy: History of American Public Address*, edited by DeWitte Holland. While Oliver concentrates largely on individual orators and their contributions, Holland presents an idea- and issue-centered study, an analytic work that traces twenty-four significant debates, beginning with evangelism among the Indians in the Massachusetts Bay Colony, through the peace movement and the Vietnam War. The rhetoric of the polarity of views is developed and supported for such major controversies as the separation of church and state, the Constitution, slavery, imperialism, the agrarian issue, socialism, suffrage and prohibition, the New Deal, internal communism, the black revolution, and freedom of speech in the 1960s. A different approach is taken by Barnet Baskerville in *The People's Voice: The Orator in American Society*. Baskerville examines the changing role of the orator and attitudes toward oratory throughout periods of American history from "The Revolutionary Period: The Orator as Hero," to "The Contemporary Scene: The Decline of Eloquence." This lively work elucidates American's political, social, and intellectual history.

American Orators before 1900: Critical Studies and Sources and its companion volume, *American Orators of the Twentieth Century: Critical Studies and Sources*, both edited by Bernard K. Duffy and Halford R. Ryan, offer critical essays treating public speakers from various fields of endeavor, including presidents, congressional leaders, diverse individuals largely known for their oratory, and significant religious figures. Each essay follows the same format: an introduction that places the speaker in historical perspective, a critical examination of the oratory, information sources (research collections and collected speeches, selected critical studies, and selected biographies), and a chronology of major speeches. Among the fifty-five orators discussed in the work on the earlier period are Susan B. Anthony, John Cotton, Jefferson Davis, Abraham Lincoln, Red Jacket, Sojourner Truth, Booker T. Washington, and George Washington; among the fifty-eight orators discussed in the work on the twentieth century are Cesar Chavez, Clarence S. Darrow, Everett M. Dirksen, Jesse Jackson, Barbara Jordan, Martin Luther King Jr., Ronald Reagan, and Eleanor Roosevelt. Most of the public addresses available in sources reviewed thus far are male-authored. Karlyn Kohrs Campbell, in an important 1991 essay in *Communication Education* entitled "Hearing Women's Voices," noted this male bias and recommended oratory by women that might be profitably studied. Carole Spitzack and Kathryn Carter, in an important 1987 *Quarterly Journal of Speech* essay entitled "Women in Communication Studies," point to some of the ways that public address scholars have defined women's "place" in communication and argue that these conceptualizations have limited the study of women as orators. Campbell's work in the two volumes of *Man Cannot*

Speak for Her serves as an important corrective. The first volume studies women orators; the second presents their speeches. Campbell's work has inspired others to explore women orators. A good example of this more recent work is Cheryl R. Jorgensen-Earp's *"The Transfiguring Sword": The Just War of the Women's Social and Political Union*. A good example of the sparse work that preceded Campbell's is Lillian O'Connor's *Pioneer Women Orators: Rhetoric in the Ante-Bellum Reform Movement*. Both works do a good job contextualizing women's oratory within its historical setting.

More than 200 debates, beginning with those pertaining to the Stamp Act and concluding with those dealing with the repeal of the Silver Purchase Act, are presented chronologically in the fourteen volumes of *Great Debates in American History: From the Debates in the British Parliament on the Colonial Stamp Act (1764–1765) to the Debates in Congress at the Close of the Taft Administration (1912–1913)*, edited by Marion Mills Miller. This is an estimable source containing explanations, the debates themselves, and summaries of how decisions and compromises were reached by the leaders who forged this country. Miller's work discusses the relevant debates leading up to the Revolutionary War as well as the popular Lincoln–Douglas debates of 1858, which prefigured the outbreak of the Civil War. Both of these periods of American history have been treated by contemporary rhetorical scholars.

Richard Allen Heckman's *Lincoln vs. Douglas: The Great Debates Campaign* assesses the role of the Lincoln–Douglas debates in the history of American oratory. The reader is also referred to Lionel Crocker's *An Analysis of Lincoln and Douglas as Public Speakers and Debaters*, which offers the texts of the debates as well as a number of studies reflecting on the speaking effectiveness of the two political leaders. *Anti-Slavery and Disunion, 1858–1861: Studies in the Rhetoric of Compromise and Conflict*, edited by J. Jeffery Auer, presents a solid integration of historical analysis and rhetorical criticism in twenty-three essays relating to the central issues preceding the Civil War.

No series of debates since the Lincoln–Douglas debates has captured the imagination of the American public and the attention of scholars of debate and public address as completely as that between John F. Kennedy and Richard M. Nixon during the presidential campaign of 1960. The foremost book dealing with this clash is *The Great Debates: Background—Perspective—Effects*, edited by Sidney Kraus, later reissued as *The Great Debates: Kennedy vs. Nixon, 1960*. This work is an overview that presents the texts of the four debates as well as insights of various communications experts. Interesting to read, also, is Nixon's account of these debates in his book *Six Crises*. (He writes here, too, about his "Checkers" speech and his debate with Khrushchev.)

The campaign debates in the fall of 1976 between Gerald R. Ford and Jimmy Carter mark the second such series of face-to-face exchanges between presidential candidates, and these debates have been duly described and analyzed. Three relevant efforts are listed here. *The Great Debates: Carter vs. Ford, 1976*, edited by Sidney Kraus, presents studies contributed by a wide range of authorities on the background, perspectives, and analyses of the debates. *The Presidential Debates: Media, Electoral and Policy Perspectives*, edited by George F. Bishop, Robert G. Meadow, and Marilyn Jackson-Beeck, offers essays dealing with the campaign setting, communications context, and cognitive and behavioral consequences of the debates. *Carter vs. Ford: The Counterfeit Debates of 1976*, by Lloyd Bitzer and Theodore Rueter, treats campaign context, argumentation, and format. All three works include transcripts of the debates. Of course, since 1976, debates have become the norm. The debates of 1980, 1988, and 1992, as well as the preceding events in 1960 and 1976, are discussed by several noteworthy scholars in the second edition of *Rhetorical Studies of National Political Debates*, edited by Robert V. Friedenberg. A third edition is planned. Transcripts of the debates discussed in this text can be located at http://www/debates/org/, an Internet site maintained by the Commission on Presidential Debates.

A straightforward foundation for the study of modern political rhetoric is presented in *Handbook of Political Communication*, edited by Dan D. Nimmo and Keith R. Sanders. This work is a collection of twenty-two essays that cover theoretical approaches, modes, and means of persuasive communication, political communication settings, and methods of study. A useful supplement is Mary E. Stuckey's *The Theory and Practice of Political Communication Research*, and a good extended example of one of the several large-scale research projects undertaken in recent years is presented in Marion R. Just et al.'s *Crosstalk: Citizens, Candidates, and the Media in a Presidential Campaign*. Contemporary works of note examine presidential rhetoric. *Essays in Presidential Rhetoric*, edited by Theodore Windt with Beth Ingold, analyzes the rhetoric of six presidents, from John F. Kennedy to Ronald Reagan. Dante Germino's *The Inaugural Addresses of American Presidents: The Public Philosophy and Rhetoric* is a brief study in which the author contends that a public philosophy espousing God and nation is expressed through presidential Inaugural Addresses. Karlyn Kohrs Campbell and Kathleen Hall Jamieson's *Deeds Done in Words: Presidential Rhetoric and the Genres of Governance* examines the inaugural in even more detail. In addition, it scrutinizes many other genres of public address, such as the declaration of war and the Farewell Address.

Critical and historical works of so-called regional oratory illuminate the debate and public address of a particular geographical area and serve as a means of placing it within a meaningful context. Southern oratory from 1828 to 1970 is analyzed and evaluated in Waldo W. Braden's trilogy. *Oratory in the Old South, 1828–1860* presents nine essays ranging from "The Rhetoric of the Nullifiers," to "The Southern Unionist, 1850–1860" and concludes that there is no genre of southern oratory, thereby destroying the myth of the southern orator. Dealing with the post–Civil War years, 1870–1910, in *Oratory in the New South*, Braden refers to the public address of these decades as oratory of "accommodation." The eight essays in this volume include Danny Chapman's "Booker T. Washington versus W.E.B. Du Bois: A Study in Rhetorical Contrasts" and Annette Shelby's "The Southern Lady Becomes an Advocate." Both of these volumes contain useful bibliographies. Completing this definitive trilogy, *The Oral Tradition in the South* presents six essays that include studies of southern demagoguery and the segregationist rhetoric of white supremacy. *The Oratory of Southern Demagogues*, edited by Cal M. Logue and Howard Dorgan, is a collection of nine critical essays, each treating a southern political figure prominent during the first half of the twentieth century. *Landmarks in Western Oratory*, edited by David H. Grover, brings together criticism of the oration of the Plains Indians, the Mormons, Henry Spalding, Thomas Star King, and Upton Sinclair, among others, and suggests that western oratory has an indigenous quality of its own.

Oratory from the pulpit is an integral part of the whole of American debate and public address. *Preaching in American History: Selected Issues in the American Pulpit, 1630–1967*, edited by DeWitte Holland, is a collection of twenty essays that describe and analyze significant issues debated by America's religious leaders over a span of more than three centuries. Much of this work is devoted to modern preaching and issues that are important today. A companion volume, Sermons *in American History: Selected Issues in the American Pulpit, 1630–1967*, also edited by Holland, presents representative sermons on those issues covered in the critical work. (This second collection is noted under Anthologies and Reprints.) Henry H. Mitchell's *Black Preaching* provides a history of black preaching and insights into the black sermon and the role of the black preacher. *Prime Time Preachers: The Rising Power of Televangelism*, by Jeffrey K. Hadden and Charles E. Swann, and *Religious Television: The American Experience*, by Peter G. Horsfield, are thought-provoking studies that examine the increasing influence of television evangelism and the power of religious rhetoric. They are of particular value to those interested in the study of religious communication as well as political and social movements. *Religious Communication Today*, the annual journal published by the Religious Speech Communication Association, offers articles and resources pertinent to the field.

The first history of black oratory in the United States during the twentieth century is Marcus H. Boulware's *The Oratory of Negro Leaders, 1900–1968*. Boulware presents a survey, largely biographical, of prominent black speakers from Booker T. Washington to Martin Luther King Jr. and includes chapters on public addresses of black women, fraternal oratory, and church and pulpit oratory, as well as radio and television speaking. Although the work is not critical, it offers a vital description of black oratory during the period. *The Rhetoric of Black Americans*, a critical study written by James L. Golden and Richard D. Rieke, explores the role of persuasive black rhetoric in achieving the goal of the "good life." Interweaving more than fifty complete texts of addresses, debates, sermons, interviews, essays, and letters from the early period of the struggle to 1970, the work offers a rhetorical analysis by theme. The history and criticism of black oratory are supplemented by two books that offer perspectives and source materials on debate and public address of the 1960s. *The Rhetoric of Black Power*, by Robert L. Scott and Wayne Brockriede, presents public speeches and critical essays on the issues of black power. Included are two different interpretations by Stokely Carmichael, "Stokely Carmichael Explains Black Power to a Black Audience in Detroit" and "Stokely Carmichael Explains Black Power to a White Audience in Whitewater, Wisconsin," in addition to a description of black power by Charles V. Hamilton. *The Black Panthers Speak*, edited by Philip S. Foner, sets forth primary source materials, including official documents of the Panthers and selected essays and speeches of Huey P. Newton, Bobby Seale, Eldridge Cleaver, David Hilliard, Fred Hampton, and some of the Panther women. Foner's work does not offer a critical analysis but serves as a basis for further research in Black Panther rhetoric. A readable study in social and intellectual history that provides background material for an exploration of the contemporary black movement can be found in *Forerunners of Black Power: The Rhetoric of Abolition*, edited by Ernest G. Bormann. This work includes essays in speech criticism and a diverse collection of abolition speeches.

Malcolm X. Courtesy of the National Archives

Some critical attention has been paid to other groups. *Aboriginal American Oratory: The Tradition of Eloquence among the Indians of the United States,* by Louis Thomas Jones, records a descriptive appreciation of the inherent eloquence of native American oratory. This work is interesting and illustrated and, although not a definitive study, includes notes and references. *American Demagogues: Twentieth Century,* by Reinhard H. Luthin, discusses the public career of ten "masters of the masses" who lusted for power during the first half of this century. Easily readable essays with extensive bibliographic notes are devoted to such popular leaders as James M. Curley, Frank Hague, Eugene Talmadge, Huey P. Long, and Joseph R. McCarthy, all highly skilled in the art of political oratory. Donald E. Phillips' *Student Protest, 1960–1970: An Analysis of the Issues and Speeches* functions as an interdisciplinary summary and guide to the student movement, beginning with the sit-in demonstrations in Greensboro, North Carolina, in 1960 and climaxing with the events at Kent State University, Kent, Ohio, in 1970. Its bibliography is particularly comprehensive and well organized. *A War of Words: Chicano Protest in the 1960s and 1970s,* by John C. Hammerback, Richard J. Jensen, and Jose Angel Gutierrez, analyzes the rhetorical discourse of four principal leaders: Reies Lopez Tijerina, Cesar Chavez, Rodolfo "Corky" Gonzales, and Jose Angel Gutierrez. Included is a bibliographic essay that surveys Mexican American rhetoric. *Hispanic Voices,* edited by Robert W. Mullen, offers a collection of thirteen essays as an introduction to the role of Hispanic protest rhetoric as it attempts to encompass a greater concern for global issues. *Gayspeak: Gay Male and Lesbian Communication*, edited by James W. Chesebro under the auspices of the Caucus on Gay Male and Lesbian Concerns of the National Communication Association, presents twenty-five essays treating homosexuality as a social issue or, more specifically, as a communication phenomenon. The chapters entitled "Gay Liberation as a Rhetorical Movement" (Part V) and "Gay Rights and the Political Campaigns" (Part VI) are relevant to debate and public address.

If one stands back and examines evolving public address scholarship, one finds that foci have shifted over the years from individual orators to the rhetorical activities of groups and social movements. Another shift has taken scholars from a narrow definition of "text" to a broader one, for example, treating places as texts. Carole Blair's work exemplifies this trend. In an essay in the *Quarterly Journal of Speech*, she, together with Marsha S. Jeppeson and Enrico Pucci Jr., "reads" the Vietnam Veterans Memorial, and in *At the Intersection: Cultural Studies and Rhetorical Studies*, edited by Thomas Rosteck, she, together with Neil Michel, "reads" the Astronauts Memorial. More generally, Blair discusses places as offering a kind of public address in "Contemporary U.S. Memorial Sites as Exemplars of Rhetoric's Materiality," an essay in *Rhetorical Bodies: Toward a Material Rhetoric*, edited by Jack Selzer and Sharon Crowley.

Finally, the various professional journals are an indispensable source of contemporary scholarship in debate and public address. Two prestigious journals published by the National Speech Communication Association are relevant. *Quarterly Journal of Speech* offers historical, critical, empirical, and theoretical investigations into all areas of human communication. Each issue contains in-depth essays as well as critical reviews of books that have been recently published in the several areas of speech. *Communication Monographs*, issued quarterly, is devoted to all modes of inquiry into communication theory, broadly defined. In addition, journals of a similar nature are also published quarterly by each of the four regional divisions of the National Communication Association: *Communication Quarterly* (Eastern Communication Association), *Southern Speech Communication Journal* (Southern States Speech Communication Association), *Communication Studies* (Central States Speech Association), and *Western Journal of Speech Communication* (Western Speech Communication Association).

Argumentation and Advocacy (formerly *Journal of the American Forensic Association*), published quarterly by the American Forensic Association, presents scholarly studies on argumentation, persuasion, discussion, debate, and other types of forensic activities. *National Forensic Journal* is a biannual publication of the National Forensic Association, an organization that focuses on intercollegiate individual speaking events. This journal offers scholarly inquiry into all aspects of forensics. Additional publications that offer articles, reviews, and commentary relating to forensics include *Speaker and Gavel*, a quarterly publication of Delta Sigma Rho–Tau Kappa Alpha, a national honorary forensic society for college students; *Forensic*, a quarterly publication of Pi Kappa Delta, a national honorary fraternal organization also for those involved in forensic speaking at the college level; and *Rostrum*, published monthly by the National Forensic League, an honorary society for high school students.

ANTHOLOGIES AND REPRINTS

Anthologies of speeches are numerous and are infinitely organized and categorized. In addition to pure anthologies, some volumes dealing with the history or criticism of public address and some designated primarily as speech textbooks contain noteworthy speeches. Many collections have been published, moreover, of the addresses of a well-known individual speaker, for example, Mark Twain, W.E.B. Du Bois, Adlai E. Stevenson, Robert F. Kennedy, Norman Vincent Peale, Billy Graham, Malcolm X. and Ronald Reagan, to name only a few. These are best located by checking the indexing system of any good-sized library, particularly college and university libraries, under the name of the speaker. Some anthologies attempt to give complete and authoritative texts of speeches; others for quite legitimate reasons present edited or abridged versions.

Among those sources that are particularly concerned with contemporary oration, a most respected anthology is *Representative American Speeches*, an annual series compiled since 1938 and successively edited by A. Craig Baird, Lester Thonssen, and Waldo W. Braden and presently by Owen Peterson. Each volume contains about twenty speeches, not necessarily the "best" speeches of each year but rather those most representative. Many of these speeches are from the political arena. Cumulative indexes appear every five years beginning in 1960. A second, highly regarded source of contemporary speeches is the semimonthly publication *Vital Speeches of the Day*. These speeches, delivered by leaders from all fields of endeavor on current problems of national interest, are impartially selected to present both sides of public questions. This periodical is indexed annually in November.

The turn of the twentieth century brought several multivolume anthologies that became standard references and are still highly regarded by scholars and students of oratory. Among them are David J. Brewer's ten-volume compilation *The World's Best Orations from the Earliest Period to the Present Time*, which gives prominence to English and American orators. More than 620 speeches delivered by 383 speakers from the time of Pericles to the late nineteenth century are included. The series is arranged alphabetically by orator, for each of whom a short biographical sketch is given, and is scrupulously indexed in Volume 10. Guy Carleton Lee's ten-volume work *The World's Orators: Comprising the Great Orations of the World's History with Introductory Essays, Biographical Sketches and Critical Notes* is exactly what its title implies, the final three volumes dealing exclusively with orators of America. Volume 8 covers the secular oratory of the eighteenth century, volume 9 presents the classical oratory of the first half of the nineteenth century, and volume 10 is concerned largely with the period of the Civil War and includes a general index. William Jennings Bryan's *The World's Famous Orations* is also a ten-volume work whose last three volumes are devoted to American oratory. These volumes cover public speaking in America for the years 1774 to 1905; volume 10 also contains an index to the series.

Ashley H. Thorndike's work of fifteen volumes *Modern Eloquence: A Library of the World's Best Spoken Thought*, published in 1928, is, indeed, almost a library in itself. The various volumes are devoted to specialized areas: after-dinner speeches, of which more than 300 are presented; speeches dealing with such commercial and professional interests as banking, economics, railroads, law, medicine, engineering, labor, journalism, theater, ministry, and science; public affairs, including citizenship, government, and education; the standard historical masterpieces, one volume being devoted to American history; speeches concerning World War I; plus humorous, inspirational, and scientific lectures. A general index in volume 15 guides by speaker, speech, occasion, subject, or quotation. A diversified collection of speeches, delivered by prominent Americans from the colonial period through the 1960s, is included in *The World's Great Speeches*, a comprehensive, single-volume anthology edited by Lewis Copeland and Lawrence W. Lamm. A section devoted to domestic affairs contains speeches by Fiorello H. LaGuardia, John L. Lewis, Thomas E. Dewey, and Herbert Hoover; a section dealing with World War II presents addresses by Franklin D. Roosevelt, Wendell L. Willkie, Charles A. Lindbergh, Fulton J. Sheen, Dorothy Thompson, Henry A. Wallace, and Norman Thomas; and a section of informal speeches includes those of Ralph Waldo Emerson, Edward Everett Hale, Mark Twain, Irvin S. Cobb, Will Rogers, and John D. Rockefeller Jr. Also included are speeches delivered by Harry S Truman, Adlai E. Stevenson, Dwight D. Eisenhower, John F. Kennedy, Richard M. Nixon, Martin Luther King Jr., and Malcolm X. *The Voices of History: Great Speeches of the English Language*, selected and introduced by Lord George-Brown of Great Britain's House of Lords, is a compilation of oratory of ninety-five well-known speakers, organized chronologically beginning with Sir Thomas More and concluding with President Jimmy Carter. This work comprises largely excerpts from speeches, and it is of interest for those who enjoy reading eloquent discourse.

Companion anthologies edited by Ernest J. Wrage and Barnet Baskerville, *American Forum: Speeches on Historic Issues, 1788–1900* and *Contemporary Forum: American Speeches on Twentieth-Century Issues*, present an issue-centered history of significantly relevant oration. Each issue is illuminated with speeches representing competing points of view, a historical context, and biographical sketches of the speakers. The first compilation contains twenty-six speeches arranged chronologically in relation to basic historic issues, beginning with the speeches of Patrick Henry and James Madison on the ratification of the federal Constitution and concluding with the speeches of Albert J. Beveridge and William Jennings Bryan on U.S. imperialism. The thirty-two speeches of the second anthology deal with issues of the twentieth century: the Progressive era, the League of Nations debate, the questions of modernism versus fundamentalism in religion, the polemics of the New Deal, issues in higher education and social change, isolationism, the Cold War, and desegregation. Especially useful are the bibliographical notes indicating supplementary information and other speeches on the topic. Also issue-centered is *Selected American Speeches on Basic Issues (1850–1950)*, edited by Carl G. Brandt and Edward M. Shafter Jr. Complete texts of nineteen noteworthy public address with appropriate background information are presented in three parts: "Time of Civil Strife: Slavery and States' Rights," "The Dawn of the Twentieth Century: American Nationalism and Expansion," and "World Wars I and II: Crises and Controversies."

Several works that have been compiled primarily for use as textbooks also function as research tools. Glenn R. Capp's *Famous Speeches in American History* contains the eighteen speeches that professors of public address voted the most significant. The speeches range chronologically from Patrick Henry's "Liberty or Death" to John F. Kennedy's Inaugural Address and include orations by George

Washington, Daniel Webster, Ralph Waldo Emerson, Abraham Lincoln, Henry W. Grady, Booker T. Washington, William Jennings Bryan, Theodore Roosevelt, Woodrow Wilson, Franklin D. Roosevelt, Douglas MacArthur, and Adlai E. Stevenson. *American Speeches*, edited by Wayland Maxfield Parrish and Marie Hochmuth, presents twenty-eight classic speeches beginning chronologically with Jonathan Edwards' "Sinners in the Hands of an Angry God" and concluding with Franklin D. Roosevelt's "America Has Not Been Disappointed," in addition to an introductory essay on rhetorical criticism and a thorough analysis of Abraham Lincoln's First Inaugural Address. *Selected Speeches from American History*, edited by Robert T. Oliver and Eugene E. White, presents twenty-two distinguished speeches as case studies in persuasion, ranging from George Whitefield's "Abraham's Offering Up His Son Isaac," to Pope Paul VI's "Address at the United Nations." *Contemporary American Speeches: A Sourcebook of Speech Forms and Principles*, edited by Wil A. Linkugel, R. R. Allen, and Richard L. Johannesen, offers forty-two speeches delivered during the 1960s, 1970s, and 1980s. They are an uncommon mixture of the well known and the little known, selected to illustrate speech forms and principles and to guide the student in speech analysis. Included are Martin Luther King Jr.'s "Love, Law and Civil Disobedience," Douglas MacArthur's "Farewell to the Cadets," and Barbara C. Jordan's "Democratic Convention Keynote Address," as well as seven outstanding speeches presented by college students. Halford Ross Ryan's *American Rhetoric from Roosevelt to Reagan: A Collection of Speeches and Critical Essays* contains thirty-three speeches and ten critical essays. Covering a fifty-year period of American history, the public addresses printed in this anthology center attention on diverse national issues. Included are speeches of, among others, Huey P. Long, Father (Charles E.) Coughlin, Eleanor Roosevelt, Douglas MacArthur, Richard M. Nixon, Adlai E. Stevenson, Shirley Chisholm, Barbara C. Jordan, and Jerry Falwell. James R. Andrews and David Zarefsky's *Contemporary American Voices: Significant Speeches in American History, 1945-Present* covers a comparable period. It is organized around crucial public policy issues, with sections on the Cold War, the civil rights movement, the Kennedy-Johnson domestic public policy agenda, the Vietnam War, and the social protests that erupted in its wake.

John Graham's *Great American Speeches, 1898–1963: Texts and Studies* presents twenty-four significant speeches beginning with William Jennings Bryan's "Naboth's Vineyard" and concluding with Adlai E. Stevenson's "Eulogy: John Fitzgerald Kennedy." The volume includes headnotes and offers critical studies centering on Franklin D. Roosevelt, Douglas MacArthur, and John F. Kennedy. This anthology is singular in that the texts of the speeches are available on recordings edited by Graham and published by Caedmon as part of its series of Great American Speeches. (Caedmon also offers recordings of great women's speeches, black speeches, and American Indian speeches, as well as the Hamilton vs. Jefferson debates and the Lincoln vs. Douglas debates.) Lloyd Rohler and Roger Cook's *Great Speeches for Criticism and Analysis* offers the texts of forty-four speeches as well as sixteen critical essays on some of the addresses. Packaged either with this text or separately by the Educational Video Group is a thirteen-volume series containing some rare footage. This same company produces several other videos of note: Great *Speeches—Today's Women*; *Great Moments from Great Speeches*; *Great Speeches—The Presidents*; *The Golden Age of American Oratory*; and *Canadian*

Great Speeches. The Educational Video Group's catalog also features videos focused on particular orators (Franklin D. Roosevelt, John F. Kennedy, Hubert H. Humphrey, and Barbara Jordan) and videos dealing with presidential campaigns. The five-volume *Modern Presidential Campaigns*, written by Robert E. Denton, is especially noteworthy. A thematic collection of interest to the history and criticism of public address is Charles W. Lomas' *The Agitator in American Society*, which presents thirteen representative speeches, illustrating the rhetoric of violence, socialism and social reform, civil rights, and anticommunism. Two anthologies dealing with the public address of the 1960s exemplify the rhetoric and illuminate the issues of the period. *The Great Society: A Sourcebook of Speeches*, edited by Glenn R. Capp, traces the evolution and analyzes the basic concept of the Great Society in addition to the specific issues of civil rights, education, and poverty. Twenty speeches are included by such leaders as John F. Kennedy, Lyndon B. Johnson, Hubert H. Humphrey, Dwight D. Eisenhower, George W. Romney, Ronald Reagan, Ralph J. Bunche, and Richard M. Nixon. *In Pursuit of Peace: Speeches of the Sixties*, edited by Donald W. Zacharias, offers an informative introduction and ten key speeches, each with headnotes, paired so as to present opposing points of view in five areas: "Scientists and Politics," "Peace and Security," "Religion and War," "Soldiers and Peace," and "Dissent and Vietnam."

Three paperbound anthologies designed for popular reference and enjoyment are Houston Peterson's *A Treasury of the World's Great Speeches*, George W. Hibbitt's *The Dolphin Book of Speeches*, and Stewart H. Benedict's *Famous American Speeches*. Peterson's collection dates from biblical times to the mid-1960s and includes for each speech a foreword and an afterword that give details of the speaker, the setting, and the effect of the speech on the audience. Among the speeches are Elizabeth Cady Stanton's keynote address in 1848 to the first woman's rights convention as well as the Sacco and Vanzetti claims of innocence in 1927. Hibbitt's collection is also comprehensive in scope, dating from the Greeks to the mid-1960s. Included are Clare Boothe Luce's "American Morality and Nuclear Diplomacy," John H. Glenn Jr.'s "A New Era," and several eulogies rendered upon the assassination of John F. Kennedy. Benedict's collection, a slim volume of twenty-three important speeches, includes William Faulkner's "Nobel Prize Speech" and Douglas MacArthur's "Old Soldiers Never Die." Charles Hurd's *A Treasury of Great American Speeches* is also styled for popular taste. A palatable newspaper format presents the "who, what, when, where, and why" as an introduction to each speech. Running the gamut from John Winthrop's "Liberty is the proper end and object of authority," to Richard M. Nixon's "We cannot learn from one another until we stop shouting at one another," this anthology contains addresses delivered by almost 100 speakers, including Alfred E. Smith, Robert C. Benchley, John L. Lewis, George S. Patton, Cornelia Otis Skinner, and Carl Sandburg.

Two recently published anthologies offer an overview of the role of American women speakers in affecting the course of social, cultural, and political history. *We Shall Be Heard: Women Speakers in America, 1828–Present*, by Patricia Scileppi Kennedy and Gloria Hartmann O'Shields, presents twenty-eight speeches arranged chronologically into three periods: "Early Period Pioneers—Pre-Civil War," "Civil War—Turn of the Century," and "World War I—Contemporary." A photograph of the speaker, a bibliographic essay, and a list of references amplify each speech. *Outspoken Women: Speeches by American Women Reformers, 1635–1935*, by Judith Anderson, is a compilation of forty speech texts presented in alphabetical order by the name of the speaker, each accompanied by an abbreviated biographical sketch. This work begins chronologically with Anne Hutchinson's testimony of 1637 and concludes with the speeches of notable reformers of the early twentieth century: Emily Greene Balch, Mary McLeod Bethune, Carrie Chapman Catt, Crystal Eastman, Elizabeth Gurley Flynn, Charlotte Perkins Gilman, Emma Goldman, Mary Harris "Mother" Jones, Florence Kelley, Carry Nation, Kate Richards O'Hare, Leonora O'Reilly, Alice Paul, Margaret Sanger, Rose Schneiderman, Ida Tarbell, Mary Church Terrell, and Lillian Wald. To these must, of course, be added the second volume of Karlyn Kohrs Campbell's *Man Cannot Speak for Her*, discussed in an earlier section of this chapter.

Compilations of presidential rhetoric are important sources for debaters, speakers, and those concerned with political communication. *The President Speaks: The Inaugural Addresses of the American Presidents from Washington to Nixon*, edited by Davis Newton Lott, offers for each speech a capsule description of "The President," "The Nation," and "The World," as well as a perspective on the speaking occasion, but does not attempt to analyze the addresses. Michael J. Lax's *The Inaugural Addresses of the Presidents of the United States, 1789–1985*, published in celebration of the fiftieth inaugural, is an impressive-looking volume that presents the speeches without description or comment. *The State of the Union Messages of the Presidents, 1790–1966* is a three-volume work edited by Fred L. Israel. The addresses are not annotated, but the usefulness of the anthology is enhanced by the inclusion of a comprehensive index of significant events and policy in U.S. history. *Presidential Rhetoric: 1961 to the Present*, edited by Theodore Windt, covers the period of the six presidencies from John F. Kennedy to Bill Clinton. Presented are texts of important speeches, together with a very brief description of the term in office and a bibliography.

Public address from the pulpit has played a significant role in the evolution of American history and culture and has been duly anthologized. A comprehensive anthology encompassing Christian preaching in America from the early period of Jonathan Edwards to the modern era of Billy Graham and Martin Luther King Jr. can be found in the thirteen volumes of *Twenty Centuries of Great Preaching: An Encyclopedia of Preaching*, edited by Clyde E. Fant Jr., and William M. Pinson Jr. Among other preachers whose sermons the editors considered relevant to the issues and needs of their day are George Whitefield, Lyman Beecher, John Jasper, Henry Ward Beecher, John A. Broadus, Phillips Brooks, Dwight L. Moody, Sam Jones, Billy Sunday, Henry Sloane Coffin, Harry Emerson Fosdick, Walter Maier, Fulton J. Sheen, Norman Vincent Peale, and Peter Marshall. This work includes biographies of the preachers and is thoroughly indexed in volume 13. *Sermons in American History: Selected Issues in the American Pulpit, 1630–1967*, edited by DeWitte Holland, presents brief analyses of twenty selected issues and sermons representing various points of view on these issues. Included are the sermons of noted preachers as well as those not well known, speaking on such topics as "The Ecumenical Movement," "The Thrust of the Radical Right," and "The Pulpit and Race Relations, 1954–1966." (This work is a companion volume to Holland's *Preaching in American History: Selected Issues in the American Pulpit, 1630–1967*, noted under History and Criticism.) Contemporary sermons are published in *Pul-*

pit Digest, an ecumenical bimonthly periodical devoted to religious issues, and in *Master Sermon Series*, a monthly periodical. A three-volume collection, *Outstanding Black Sermons*, edited in order by J. Alfred Smith Sr., Walter B. Hoard, and Milton E. Owens Jr., offers the work of prominent Christian preachers of the contemporary black community. Volume 3 includes additional resources for sermons and preaching.

Greater public awareness of minority oratory came with the civil rights issues and the arousing of black consciousness during the past several decades. The most comprehensive of the anthologies devoted exclusively to the black speaker is Philip S. Foner's *The Voice of Black America: Major Speeches by Negroes in the United States, 1797–1971*. Divided into six chronological sections beginning with "The Antebellum Period, 1797–1860" and concluding with "Civil Rights to Black Power, September 1963–1971," Foner presents scores of important speeches, many of which have never appeared in book form, each with a brief historical setting. Among the more contemporary speeches are "The Third World and the Ghetto" by H. Rap Brown, "It's Time for a Change" by Shirley Chisholm, and "The Legacy of George Jackson" by Angela Davis. Other voices include those of Paul Robeson, Langston Hughes, Martin Luther King Jr., Lorraine Hansberry, Dick Gregory, Malcolm X, Ossie Davis, Adam Clayton Powell Jr., Kenneth B. Clark, Eldridge Cleaver, Julian Bond, and Huey P. Newton. Supplementing Foner's work is his and Robert James Branham's *Lift Every Voice: African American Oratory, 1787–1900*. Not as broad in scope as Foner's work are three anthologies worth noting: *Rhetoric of Racial Revolt*, by Roy L. Hill; *The Negro Speaks: The Rhetoric of Contemporary Black Leaders*, edited by Jamye Coleman Williams and McDonald Williams; and *The Voice of Black Rhetoric: Selections*, edited by Arthur L. Smith and Stephen Robb. Hill's work is a collection of almost fifty speeches dealing with racial relations, the speeches ranging from those of Booker T. Washington to Malcolm X and including those of Elijah Muhammad, Marian Anderson, James Baldwin, Martin Luther King Jr., Thurgood Marshall, and A. Philip Randolph. This study provides biographical sketches, introductions, commentaries, and some analyses, but these are brief and at random. The Williamses' book reprints a cross-section of twenty-three speeches, many of them abridged, beginning with William L. Dawson's "Race Is Not a Limitation" in 1945 and extending chronologically to Edward W. Brooke's "Address to the National Convention of the NAACP [National Association for the Advancement of Colored People]" in 1967. Other speakers include Patricia Roberts Harris, Ralph J. Bunche, Carl T. Rowan, Roy Wilkins, Sadie T. M. Alexander, Whitney M. Young Jr., Constance Baker Motley, Edith S. Sampson, and Howard Thurman. A portrait of each speaker brightens the text. Smith and Robb present an anthology of significant speeches of twenty orators spanning in time from David Walker (1828) to H. Rap Brown (1967). This work includes an appropriate introduction, headnotes, and a pertinent bibliography.

Two vintage anthologies, historically significant and readily available, are Alice Moore Dunbar's *Masterpieces of Negro Eloquence: The Best Speeches Delivered by the Negro from the Days of Slavery to the Present Time*, published in 1914 on the occasion of the fiftieth anniversary of the Proclamation of Emancipation and reissued in 1970 as part of the Basic Afro-American Reprint Library; and Carter G. Woodson's *Negro Orators and Their Orations*, published in 1925 and reprinted in 1969.

Dunbar presents without introduction or commentary the public addresses of forty-nine speakers ranging from Prince Saunders to W.E.B. Du Bois. Woodson's work is wider in scope and includes early protest speeches by such pseudonymous orators at "Othello" and "A Free Negro," as well as "The Negro's First Speech in Congress" by John Willis Menard and orations by Frederick Douglass and Booker T. Washington. A short sketch of each orator is presented, and an effort is made to publish the complete, unaltered text.

Popular interest in minority oration encompasses a sympathetic understanding of the Native American. W. C. Vanderwerth's *Indian Oratory: Famous Speeches by Noted Indian Chieftains* offers an interesting, illustrated collection with authoritative headnotes. The speeches range from Teedyuscung's "I Gave the Halloo" in 1758, to Quanah Parker's "Some White People Do That, Too" in 1910. Chief Joseph's "An Indian's Views of Indian Affairs," one of the most widely quoted speeches delivered by a Native American, is reprinted in full. Four centuries of Native American oratory, arranged chronologically, can be found in *I Have Spoken: American History through the Voices of the Indians*, compiled by Virginia Irving Armstrong. A total of 251 speeches, parts of speeches, and statements, each with a very brief introduction, together with notes on the original sources of the speeches, are presented in a simple, highly readable format. Both collections include sizable bibliographies of works pertaining to the Native American. These two anthologies offer valuable insight into the events of American history and the contribution of Native American oratory to the whole of American debate and public address.

Increasingly, print anthologies are being replaced by Web sites. Many sites make available the speeches delivered by a particular speaker, living or dead. These sites are easily located using any search engine and entering the speaker's name as the subject descriptor. A more general site is the archives of American Public Address at http://douglass.speech.nwu.edu, at which a growing anthology of oratory can be searched by speaker as well as by the controversy or movement in which she or he might be involved when speaking. Internet sites will undoubtedly continue to proliferate through the years. *Spectra*, the National Communication Association's monthly newsletter, attempts to update its members on new sites as they emerge.

In conclusion, it should be remembered that a debate or public address is delivered orally to a specific audience at a particular time and place. The message is *heard*. Part of the joy and satisfaction that come from analyzing and evaluating a debate or pondering a speech is in hearing the sound of the words. Debate and public address should be read aloud to appreciate its full impact and beauty.

NOTES

1. William Norwood Brigance, ed., *A History and Criticism of American Public Address*, 2 vols. (New York: McGraw-Hill, 1943; reprint, New York: Russell and Russell, 1960), 1: vii.

2. Patrick Henry, "Liberty or Death," in *American Speeches*, ed. Wayland Maxfield Parrish and Marie Hochmuth (New York: Longmans, Green, 1954), 94. Many of the popular speeches from which brief passages are quoted in this chapter can be found in more than one of the bibliography sources.

3. George Washington, "Farewell Address," in *Famous Speeches in American History*, ed. Glenn R. Capp (Indianapolis: Bobbs-Merrill, 1963), 40.

4. Daniel Webster, "Second Speech on Foote's Resolution—Reply to Hayne," in Parrish and Hochmuth, *American Speeches*, 229.

5. Booker T. Washington, "Atlanta Exposition Address," in *The Voice of Black America: Major Speeches by Negroes in the United States, 1797–1971*, ed. Philip S. Foner (New York: Simon and Schuster, 1972), 581.

6. Abraham Lincoln, "A House Divided," in *American Forum: Speeches on Historic Issues, 1788–1900*, ed. Ernest J. Wrage and Barnet Baskerville (New York: Harper and Brothers, 1960; reprint, Seattle: University of Washington Press, 1967), 180.

7. On the occasion of its 150th anniversary, the International Platform Association (IPA) conducted a survey among more than 200 members of Congress, journalists, speakers, and speech professionals to determine "What Is the Best Speech Given in the English Language during the 150 Years' Existence of the IPA?" Lincoln's "Gettysburg Address" was the first choice, followed in order by Winston Churchill's "Blood, Toil, Tears and Sweat" and Martin Luther King Jr.'s "I Have a Dream."

8. Abraham Lincoln, "Second Inaugural Address," in Capp, *Famous Speeches in American History*, 94.

9. The Chautauqua concept is now more than 100 years old. Information pertaining to current programs in the arts, education, religion, social and political affairs, and recreation can be obtained by writing to Chautauqua Institution, Chautauqua, N.Y. 14722.

10. Theodore Roosevelt, "National Duties: Address at Minnesota State Fair, September 2, 1901," in *The Strenuous Life: Essays and Addresses* (New York: Century, 1901, 1928), 288.

11. Franklin D. Roosevelt, "First Inaugural Address," in *Contemporary Forum: American Speeches on Twentieth-Century Issues*, ed. Ernest J. Wrage and Barnet Baskerville (New York: Harper and Brothers, 1962; reprint, Seattle: University of Washington Press, 1969), 157.

12. Franklin D. Roosevelt, "The President's War Address: We Will Gain the Inevitable Triumph—So Help Us God," in *Vital Speeches of the Day*, Vol. 8, no. 5, 130.

13. Douglas MacArthur, "American Policy in the Pacific," in *Representative American Speeches; 1951–1952*, ed. A. Craig Baird, vol. 24, no. 3 of the Reference Shelf Series (New York: H. W. Wilson, 1952), 30.

14. There had been a limited television coverage for Harry Truman's Inaugural Address on January 20, 1949. For a brief historical overview of radio and television broadcasting in presidential campaigns from 1924 through 1960, see Samuel L. Becker and Elmer W. Lower, "Broadcasting in Presidential Campaigns," in *The Great Debates: Kennedy vs. Nixon, 1960*, ed. Sidney Kraus, reissued (Bloomington: Indiana University Press, 1977), 25–55; and updated by the same authors in "Broadcasting in Presidential Campaigns, 1960–1976," in *The Great Debates: Carter vs. Ford, 1976*, ed. Sidney Kraus (Bloomington: Indiana University Press, 1979), 11–40.

15. John F. Kennedy, "Inaugural Address," in *Representative American Speeches: 1960–1961*, ed. Lester Thonssen, vol. 33, no. 3 of the Reference Shelf Series (New York: H. W. Wilson, 1961), 39.

16. John H. Glenn Jr., "Address before the Joint Meeting of Congress," in *Representative American Speeches: 1961–1962*, ed. Lester Thonssen, vol. 34, no. 4 of the Reference Shelf Series (New York: H. W. Wilson, 1962), 206.

17. Neil Armstrong, quoted by John Noble Wilford, "Astronauts Land on Plain; Collect Rocks, Plant Flag," *New York Times*, July 21, 1969: 1. See also Wernher Von Braun and Frederick I. Ordway III, "The First Men on the Moon," in *Encyclopedia Americana*, international ed., vol. 25 (Danbury, Conn.: Grolier, 1982), 357–63.

18. William Faulkner, "Address upon Receiving the Nobel Prize for Literature," in *William Faulkner: Essays, Speeches and Public Letters*, ed. James B. Meriwether (New York: Random House, 1965), 120.

BIBLIOGRAPHY

Books and Articles

American Library Directory. 39th ed. 2 vols. New York: R. R. Bowker, 1986.

Andrews, James R. *A Choice of Words: The Practice and Criticism of Public Discourse.* New York: Harper and Row, 1973

———. *The Practice of Rhetorical Criticism.* New York: Macmillan, 1983.

Arnold, Carroll C. *Criticism of Oral Rhetoric.* Columbus, Ohio: Charles E. Merrill, 1974.

Ash, Lee, and William G. Miller, comps. *Subject Collections: A Guide to Special Book Collections and Subject Emphases as Reported by University, College, Public, and Special Libraries and Museums in the United States and Canada.* 6th ed., rev. and enl. 2 vols. New York: R. R. Bowker, 1985.

Auer, J. Jeffery, ed. *Anti-Slavery and Disunion, 1858–1861: Studies in the Rhetoric of Compromise and Conflict.* New York: Harper and Row, 1963.

Baskerville, Barnet. *The People's Voice: The Orator in American Society.* Lexington: University Press of Kentucky, 1979.

Benson, Thomas W., and Michael H. Prosser, eds. *Readings in Classical Rhetoric.* Boston: Allyn and Bacon, 1969.

Bishop, George F., Robert G. Meadow, and Marilyn Jackson-Beeck, eds. *The Presidential Debates: Media, Electoral, and Policy Perspectives.* New York: Praeger, 1980.

Bitzer, Lloyd F., and Edwin Black, eds. *The Prospect of Rhetoric: Report of the National Developmental Project.* Englewood Cliffs, N.J.: Prentice-Hall, 1971.

Bitzer, Lloyd F., and Theodore Rueter. *Carter vs. Ford: The Counterfeit Debates of 1976.* Madison: University of Wisconsin Press, 1980.

Black, Edwin. *Rhetorical Criticism: A Study in Method.* New York: Macmillan, 1965. Reprint. Madison: University of Wisconsin Press, 1978.

Blair, Carole. "Contemporary U.S. Memorial Sites as Exemplars of Rhetoric's Materiality." In *Rhetorical Bodies: Toward a Material Rhetoric,* ed. Jack Selzer and Sharon Crowley. Madison: University of Wisconsin Press, 1999.

Blair, Carole, Marsha S. Jeppeson, and Enrico Pucci Jr. "Public Memorializing in Postmodernity: The Vietnam Veterans Memorial as Prototype." *Quarterly Journal of Speech* 77 (1991), 263–88.

Blair, Carole, and Neil Michel. "Commemorating in the Theme Park Zone: Reading the Astronauts Memorial." In *At the Intersection: Cultural Studies and Rhetorical Studies,* ed. Thomas Rosteck. New York: Guilford, 1998.

Boase, Paul H., ed. *The Rhetoric of Protest and Reform: 1878–1898.* Athens: Ohio University Press, 1980.

Boaz, John K., and James R. Brey, eds. *Championship Debates and Speeches.* Vol. 1– . Annandale, Va.: Speech Communication Association and American Forensic Association, 1986– .

Bormann, Ernest G., ed. *Forerunners of Black Power: The Rhetoric of Abolition.* Englewood Cliffs, N.J.: Prentice-Hall, 1971.

Boulware, Marcus H. *The Oratory of Negro Leaders, 1900–1968.* Foreword by Alex

Haley. Contributions in Afro-American and African Studies, No. 1. West-port, Conn.: Negro Universities Press, 1969.

Bowers, John Waite, and John A. Courtright. *Communication Research Methods*. Glenview, Ill.: Scott, Foresman, 1984.

Braden, Waldo W. *The Oral Tradition in the South*. Baton Rouge: Louisiana State University Press, 1983.

———, ed. *Oratory in the New South*. Baton Rouge: Louisiana State University Press, 1979.

———. *Oratory in the Old South, 1828–1860*. Baton Rouge: Louisiana State University Press, 1970.

Brigance, William Norwood, ed. *A History and Criticism of American Public Address*. 2 vols. New York: McGraw-Hill, 1943. Reprint. New York: Russell and Russell, 1960.

Brock, Bernard L., and Robert L. Scott, eds. *Methods of Rhetorical Criticism: A Twentieth-Century Perspective*. 3rd ed., rev. Detroit: Wayne State University Press, 1989.

Bryant, Donald C. "Rhetoric: Its Function and Its Scope." *Quarterly Journal of Speech* 39 (December 1953), 401–24. In *Rhetoric: A Tradition in Transition. In Honor of Donald C. Bryant*, ed. Walter R. Fisher. East Lansing: Michigan State University Press, 1974, 195–246.

———. *Rhetorical Dimensions in Criticism*. Baton Rouge: Louisiana State University Press, 1973.

———, ed. *The Rhetorical Idiom: Essays in Rhetoric, Oratory, Language, and Drama Presented to Herbert August Wichelns with a Reprinting of His "Literary Criticism of Oratory"* (1925). Ithaca, N.Y.: Cornell University Press, 1958. Reprint. New York: Russell and Russell, 1966.

Campbell, Karlyn Kohrs. "Hearing Women's Voices." *Communication Education* 40 (1991), 33–48.

———. *Critiques of Contemporary Rhetoric*. Belmont, Calif.: Wadsworth, 1972.

———. *Man Cannot Speak for Her*. 2 vols. New York: Greenwood Press, 1989.

Campbell, Karlyn Kohrs, and Kathleen Hall Jamieson. *Deeds Done in Words: Presidential Rhetoric and the Genres of Governance*. Chicago: University of Chicago Press, 1990.

———, eds. *Form and Genre: Shaping Rhetorical Action*. Falls Church, Va.: Speech Communication Association, 1978.

Carnegie, Dale. *The Quick and Easy Way to Effective Speaking*. Revision by Dorothy Carnegie of *Public Speaking and Influencing Men in Business*, by Dale Carnegie (1962). New York: Pocket Books/Simon and Schuster, 1977.

Chesebro, James W., ed. *Gayspeak: Gay Male and Lesbian Communication*. New York: Pilgrim Press, 1981.

Cleary, James W., and Frederick W. Haberman, comps. and eds. *Rhetoric and Public Address: A Bibliography, 1947–1961*. Madison: University of Wisconsin Press, 1964.

Crocker, Lionel. *An Analysis of Lincoln and Douglas as Public Speakers and Debaters*. Springfield, Ill.: Charles C. Thomas, 1968.

———. *Rhetorical Analysis of Speeches*. Boston: Allyn and Bacon, 1967.

Current Index to Journals in Education. Vols. 1–11, no. 2. New York: Macmillan

Information, January 1969–February 1979; Vol. 11, no. 3–   . Phoenix: Oryx Press, March 1979–   .

Darnay, Brigitte T., ed. *Directory of Special Libraries and Information Centers: A Guide to More than 18,000 Special Libraries, Research Libraries, Information Centers, Archives, and Data Centers Maintained by Government Agencies, Business, Industry, Newspapers, Educational Institutions, Nonprofit Organizations, and Societies in the Fields of Science and Technology, Medicine, Law, Art, Religion, the Social Sciences, and Humanistic Studies.* 10th ed. 3 vols. Detroit: Gale Research, 1987.

Denton, Robert E. *Modern Presidential Campaigns.* 5 videocassettes. Greenwood, Ind.: Educational Video Group, 1990.

Devlin, L. Patrick. *Contemporary Political Speaking.* Belmont, Calif.: Wadsworth, 1971.

Dissertation Abstracts International: The Humanities and Social Sciences. Ann Arbor, Mich.: University Microfilms International, 1938–   .

Drummond, A. M., ed. *Studies in Rhetoric and Public Speaking in Honor of James Albert Winans.* By pupils and colleagues. New York: Century, 1925. Reprint. New York: Russell and Russell, 1962.

Duffy, Bernard K., and Halford R. Ryan, eds. *American Orators before 1900: Critical Studies and Sources.* Westport, Conn.: Greenwood Press, 1987.

———. *American Orators of the Twentieth Century: Critical Studies and Sources.* Westport, Conn.: Greenwood Press, 1987.

Dunlap, Joseph R., and Martin A. Kuhn, comps. *Debate Index Second Supplement.* Vol. 36, no. 3 of the Reference Shelf Series. New York: H. W. Wilson, 1964.

Ehninger, Douglas. *Contemporary Rhetoric: A Reader's Coursebook.* Glenview, Ill.: Scott, Foresman, 1972.

Ehninger, Douglas, Bruce E. Gronbeck, Ray E. McKerrow, and Alan H. Monroe. *Principles and Types of Speech Communication.* 11th ed. Glenview, Ill.: Scott, Foresman, 1994.

Eubanks, Ralph T., et al. "A Bibliography of Speech and Theatre in the South for the Year [1954–1982]." Title varies. *Southern Speech Communication Journal* (formerly *Southern Speech Journal*) 20–49 (1955–1984).

Foner, Philip S., ed. *The Black Panthers Speak.* Preface by Julian Bond. Philadelphia: J. B. Lippincott, 1970.

Foss, Sonja K., Karen A. Foss, and Robert Trapp. *Contemporary Perspectives on Rhetoric.* Prospect Heights, Ill.: Waveland Press, 1985.

Freeley, Austin J. *Argumentation and Debate: Critical Thinking for Reasoned Decision Making.* 8th ed. Belmont, Calif.: Wadsworth, 1996.

Friedenberg, Robert V., ed. *Rhetorical Studies of National Political Debates, 1960–1992.* 2nd ed. Westport, Conn.: Praeger, 1994.

Fryar, Maridell, and David A. Thomas. *Student Congress and Lincoln–Douglas Debate.* Skokie, Ill.: National Textbook, 1981.

Galizio, Lawrence, and Trischa Knapp. *The Elements of Parliamentary Debate: A Handbook.* New York: Longman, 1999.

Germino, Dante. *The Inaugural Addresses of American Presidents: The Public Philosophy and Rhetoric.* Preface and Introduction by Kenneth W. Thompson.

Vol. 7, White Burkett Miller Center Series on the Presidency and the Press. Lanham, Md.: University Press of America, 1984.

Gold, Ellen Reid. "Recorded Sound Collections: New Materials to Explore the Past." *Central States Speech Journal* 31 (Summer 1980), 143–51. "Errata." *Central States Speech Journal* 31 (Fall 1980), n.p.

Golden, James L., Goodwin F. Berquist, and William E. Coleman. *The Rhetoric of Western Thought*. 3rd ed. Dubuque, Iowa: Kendall/Hunt, 1983.

Golden, James L., and Edward P. J. Corbett. *The Rhetoric of Blair, Campbell and Whately*. New York: Holt, Rinehart, and Winston, 1968.

Golden, James L., and Richard D. Rieke. *The Rhetoric of Black Americans*. Columbus, Ohio: Charles E. Merrill, 1971.

Gordon, Thomas F., ed. *Communication Abstracts*. Beverly Hills, Calif.: Sage, 1978– .

Grover, David H., ed., *Landmarks in Western Oratory*. Laramie: University of Wyoming and Western Speech Association, 1968.

Haberman, Frederick W., et al. "A Bibliography of Rhetoric and Public Address for the Year [1947–1969]." *Quarterly Journal of Speech* 34–36 (1948–1950); *Communication Monographs* (formerly *Speech Monographs*) 18–36 (1951–1969), Falls Church, Va.: Speech Communication Association, 1948–1969.

Hadden, Jeffrey K., and Charles E. Swann. *Prime Time Preachers: The Rising Power of Televangelism*. Introduction by T. George Harris. Reading, Mass.: Addison-Wesley, 1981.

Hall, Robert N., and Jack L. Rhodes. *Fifty Years of International Debate, 1922–1972*. New York: Speech Communication Association, 1972.

Hammerback, John C., Richard J. Jensen, and Jose Angel Gutierrez. *A War of Words: Chicano Protest in the 1960s and 1970s*. Westport, Conn.: Greenwood Press, 1985.

Hart, Roderick P. *Modern Rhetorical Criticism*. Glenview, Ill.: Scott, Foresman/Little, Brown, 1990.

———. *Verbal Style and the Presidency: A Computer-Based Analysis*. Orlando, Fla.: Academic Press, 1984.

Heckman, Richard Allen. *Lincoln vs. Douglas: The Great Debates Campaign*. Washington, D.C.: Public Affairs Press, 1967.

Hill, George H., and Lenwood Davis. *Religious Broadcasting, 1920–1983: A Selectively Annotated Bibliography*. New York: Garland, 1984.

Hochmuth, Marie Kathryn, ed. *A History and Criticism of American Public Address*. Vol. 3. New York: Longmans, Green, 1955. Reprint. New York: Russell and Russell, 1965.

Holland, DeWitte, ed. *America in Controversy: History of American Public Address*. Dubuque, Iowa: William C. Brown, 1973.

———. *Preaching in American History: Selected Issues in the American Pulpit, 1630–1967*. Nashville, Tenn.: Abingdon Press, 1969.

Horsfield, Peter G. *Religious Television: The American Experience*. New York: Longman, 1984.

Howell, J. B., ed. *Special Collections in Libraries of the Southeast*. Introduction by Frances Neel Cheney. Jackson, Miss.: Howick House, 1978.

Howes, Raymond F., ed. *Historical Studies of Rhetoric and Rhetoricians*. Ithaca, N.Y.: Cornell University Press, 1961.

Index to U.S. Government Periodicals: A Computer-Generated Guide to 183 Selected Titles by Author and Subject. Chicago: Infordata International, 1970– .

Jamieson, Kathleen Hall. *Eloquence in an Electronic Age: The Transformation of Political Speechmaking.* New York: Oxford University Press, 1988.

Jarrad, Mary E.W., and Phyllis R. Randall. *Women Speaking: An Annotated Bibliography of Verbal and Nonverbal Communication, 1970–1980.* New York: Garland, 1982.

Jennings, Margaret S., ed. *Library and Reference Facilities in the Area of the District of Columbia.* 11th ed. White Plains, N.Y.: Knowledge Industry, 1983.

Johannesen, Richard L., ed. *Contemporary Theories of Rhetoric: Selected Readings.* New York: Harper and Row, 1971.

Johnsen, Julia E., comp. *Debate Index Supplement.* Vol. 14, no. 9 of the Reference Shelf Series. New York: H. W. Wilson, 1941.

Jones, Louis Thomas. *Aboriginal American Oratory: The Tradition of Eloquence among the Indians of the United States.* Los Angeles.: Southwest Museum, 1965.

Jorgensen-Earp, Cheryl R. *"The Transfiguring Sword": The Just War of the Women's Social and Political Union.* Tuscaloosa: University of Alabama Press, 1998.

Just, Marion R., et al. *Crosstalk: Citizens, Candidates, and the Media in a Presidential Campaign.* Chicago: University of Chicago Press, 1996.

Kaid, Lynda Lee, and Anne Johnston Wadsworth. *Political Campaign Communication: A Bibliography and Guide to the Literature, 1973–1982.* Metuchen, N.J.: Scarecrow Press, 1985.

Kennicott, Patrick C., ed. *Bibliographic Annual in Speech Communication.* Falls Church, Va.: Speech Communication Association, 1973–1975.

Kraus, Sidney, ed. *The Great Debates: Background—Perspective—Effects.* Introduction by Harold D. Lasswell. Bloomington: Indiana University Press, 1962. Reprint. Gloucester, Mass.: Peter Smith, 1968. Rev. ed. *The Great Debates: Kennedy vs. Nixon, 1960.* Bloomington: Indiana University Press, 1977.

———. ed. *The Great Debates: Carter vs. Ford, 1976.* Bloomington: Indiana University Press, 1979.

Langer, Howard J., ed. *Directory of Speakers.* Phoenix, Ariz.: Oryx Press, 1981.

Logue, Cal M., and Howard Dorgan, eds. *The Oratory of Southern Demagogues.* Baton Rouge: Louisiana State University Press, 1981.

Luthin, Reinhard H. *American Demagogues: Twentieth Century.* Introduction by Allan Nevins. Boston: Beacon Press, 1954. Reprint. Gloucester, Mass.: Peter Smith, 1959.

Mabie, Edward Charles, ed. *University Debaters' Annual: Constructive and Rebuttal Speeches Delivered in Debates of American Colleges and Universities during the College Year.* Vols. 1–2 (1914/1915–1915/1916). New York: H. W. Wilson, 1915–1916.

Makay, John J. *Public Speaking: Theory into Practice.* 3rd ed. Dubuque, Iowa: Kendall/Hunt, 1998.

Manning, Beverley. *Index to American Women Speakers, 1828–1978.* Metuchen, N.J.: Scarecrow Press, 1980.

Matlon, Ronald J., and Sylvia P. Oritz, eds. *Index to Journals in Communication Studies through 1995.* Annandale, Va.: Speech Communication Association, 1997.

McCroskey, James C. *An Introduction to Rhetorical Communication.* 6th ed. Englewood Cliffs, N.J.: Prentice-Hall, 1993.

McKee, Gerald. *Directory of Spoken-Word Audio Cassettes.* New York: Jeffrey Norton, 1983.

McKerrow, Ray E., ed. *Explorations in Rhetoric: Studies in Honor of Douglas Ehninger.* Glenview, Ill.: Scott, Foresman, 1982.

McMahon, Ed. *The Art of Public Speaking.* New York: Putnam's, 1986.

Miller, Marion Mills, ed. *Great Debates in American History: From the Debates in the British Parliament on the Colonial Stamp Act (1764–1765) to the Debates in Congress at the Close of the Taft Administration (1912–1913).* 14 vols. New York: Current Literature, 1913. Reprint. 3 vols. Metuchen, N.J.: Mini-Print, 1970.

Mitchell, Charity. *Speech Index: An Index to Collections of World Famous Orations and Speeches for Various Occasions, Fourth Edition Supplement, 1966–1980.* Metuchen, N.J.: Scarecrow Press, 1982.

Mitchell, Henry H. *Black Preaching.* Philadelphia: J. B. Lippincott, 1970.

Mohrmann, G. P., Charles J. Stewart, and Donovan J. Ochs, eds. *Explorations in Rhetorical Criticism.* University Park: Pennsylvania State University Press, 1973.

Morehead, Joe. *Introduction to United States Public Documents.* 3rd ed. Littleton, Colo.: Libraries Unlimited, 1983.

Mulgrave, Dorothy I., Clark S. Marlor, and Elmer E. Baker Jr. *Bibliography of Speech and Allied Areas, 1950–1960.* Philadelphia: Chilton, 1962. Reprint. Westport, Conn.: Greenwood Press, 1972.

Mullen, Robert W., ed. *Hispanic Voices.* Lexington, Mass.: Ginn Custom, 1984.

National Communication Association Directory, [1935–   ] (formerly *Speech Association of American Directory, Speech Communication Association Directory and Speech Communication Directory*). Annandale, Va.: Speech Communication Association, 1935–   .

New York Times Index: A Book of Record. New York: New York Times, 1851–   .

Nichols, Egbert Ray, ed. *Intercollegiate Debates.* Subtitle varies. Vols. 2–22. New York: Noble and Noble, 1910–1941.

Nimmo, Dan D., and Keith R. Sanders, eds. *Handbook of Political Communication.* Beverly Hills, Calif.: Sage, 1981.

Nixon, Richard M. *Six Crises.* New York: Doubleday, 1962.

O'Connor, Lillian. *Pioneer Women Orators: Rhetoric in the Ante-Bellum Reform Movement.* New York: Columbia University Press, 1954.

Oliver, Robert T. *History of Public Speaking in America.* Boston: Allyn and Bacon, 1965. Reprint. Westport, Conn.: Greenwood Press, 1978.

On Cassette, 1986–1987: A Comprehensive Bibliography of Spoken Word Audiocassettes. New York: R. R. Bowker, 1986.

Pearson, Paul M., ed. *Intercollegiate Debates: Being Briefs and Reports of Many Intercollegiate Debates.* Vol. 1. New York: Hinds, Hayden, and Eldredge, 1909.

Phelps, Edith M., comp. *Debate Index.* Rev. ed. Vol. 12, no. 9 of the Reference Shelf Series. New York: H. W. Wilson, 1939.

———, ed. *University Debaters' Annual: Constructive and Rebuttal Speeches Delivered in Debates of American Colleges and Universities during the College Year.* Vols. 3–33 (1916/1917–1946/1947). New York: H. W. Wilson, 1917–1947.

Phillips, Donald E. *Student Protest, 1960–1970: An Analysis of the Issues and Speeches. Revised Edition with a Comprehensive Bibliography*. Lanham, Md.: University Press of America, 1985.

Prochnow, Herbert V., and Herbert V. Prochnow Jr. *The Public Speaker's Treasure Chest*. 4th ed. New York: Harper and Row, 1986.

———. *The Toastmaster's Treasure Chest*. New York: Harper and Row, 1979.

Reid, Loren, ed. *American Public Address: Studies in Honor of Albert Craig Baird*. Columbia: University of Missouri Press, 1961.

Rohler, Lloyd E., and Roger Cook. *Great Speeches for Criticism and Analysis*. Greenwood, Ind.: Alistair Press, Educational Video Group, 1988.

Rubin, Rebecca B., Alan M. Rubin, and Linda J. Piele. *Communication Research: Strategies and Sources*. Belmont, Calif.: Wadsworth, 1986.

Sapolsky, Barry S., Jodi S. Hale, and Jayme Harpring, comps. *1988 Directory of Communication Research Centers in North American Universities*. Tallahassee, Fla.: Communication Research Center, Florida State University, 1988.

Schwarzkopf, Leroy C., comp. *Government Reference Books 84/85: A Biennial Guide to U.S. Government Publications*. 9th biennial vol. Littleton, Colo.: Libraries Unlimited, 1986.

Scott, Robert L., and Wayne Brockriede. *The Rhetoric of Black Power*. New York: Harper and Row, 1969.

Shaw, Warren Choate. *History of American Oratory*. Indianapolis: Bobbs-Merrill, 1928.

Shearer, Ned A., ed. *Bibliographic Annual in Speech Communication*. Falls Church, Va.: Speech Communication Association, 1970–1972.

Spitzack, Carole, and Kathryn Carter. "Women in Communication Studies: A Typology for Revision." *Quarterly Journal of Speech* 73 (1987), 401–23.

Sprague, Jo, and Douglas Stuart. *The Speaker's Handbook*. 2nd ed. San Diego: Harcourt Brace Jovanovich, 1988.

Stuckey, Mary E., ed. *The Theory and Practice of Political Communication Research*. Albany: State University of New York Press, 1996.

Superintendent of Documents. *Monthly Catalogue of United States Government Publications*. Washington, D.C.: Government Printing Office, 1895– .

———. *Subject Bibliography 043: Publications Relating to the [1975/76-] National High School Debate Topic*. Washington, D.C.: Government Printing Office, 1975– .

———. *Subject Bibliography 176: Publications Relating to the [1975/76-] College Debate Topic*. Washington, D.C.: Government Printing Office, 1975– .

Sutton, Roberta Briggs. *Speech Index: An Index to 259 Collections of World Famous Orations and Speeches for Various Occasions*. 4th ed., rev. and enl. New York: Scarecrow Press, 1966.

Television News Index and Abstracts: A Guide to the Videotape Collection of the Network Evening News Programs in the Vanderbilt Television News Archive. Nashville, Tenn.: Jean and Alexander Heard Library, Vanderbilt University, 1972– .

Thesaurus of ERIC Descriptors. 11th ed. Phoenix: Oryx Press, 1986.

Thonssen, Lester, A. Craig Baird, and Waldo W. Braden. *Speech Criticism*. 2nd ed. New York: Ronald Press, 1970. Reprint. Melbourne, Fla.: Krieger, 1981.

Thonssen, Lester, and Elizabeth Fatherson, comps. *Bibliography of Speech Education*. New York: H. W. Wilson, 1939.

Thonssen, Lester, Mary Margaret Robb, and Dorothea Thonssen, comps. *Bibliography of Speech Education: Supplement, 1939–1948*. New York: H. W. Wilson, 1950.

Tucker, Raymond K., Richard L. Weaver II, and Cynthia Berryman-Fink. *Research in Speech Communication*. Englewood Cliffs, N.J.: Prentice-Hall, 1981.

Ulman, Ruth, ed. *University Debaters' Annual Reports of Debates and Other Forensic Activities of American Colleges and Universities during the Academic Year*. Vols. 34–37 (1947/1948–1950/1951). New York: H. W. Wilson, 1948–1951.

U.S. Congress. *Annals of Congress*. 1st–18th Cong., 1st sess., 1789–1824. Washington, D.C.: Gales and Seaton, 1934–1956.

———. *Congressional Globe*. 23rd–42nd Cong., 1833–1873. Washington, D.C.: Globe Office, 1934–1973.

———. *Congressional Record: Containing the Proceedings and Debates of the 43rd Congress 1873–   *. Washington, D.C.: Government Printing Office, 1874–   .

———. *Register of Debates*. 18th Cong., 2nd sess.–25th Cong., 1st sess., 1824–1837. Washington, D.C.: Gales and Seaton, 1925–1937.

U.S. Department of Education. Office of Educational Research and Improvement. *Resources in Education*. Washington, D.C.: Government Printing Office, 1966–   .

U.S. Department of State, Bureau of Public Affairs. *Department of State Bulletin*. Washington, D.C.: Government Printing Office, 1939–   .

U.S. General Services Administration. *Public Papers of the Presidents of the United States*. Washington, D.C.: Government Printing Office, 1958–   .

———. *Weekly Compilation of Presidential Documents*. Washington, D.C.: Government Printing Office, 1965–   .

U.S. Library of Congress. *National Union Catalogue of Manuscript Collections*. Washington, D.C.: Library of Congress, 1962–   .

Valenti, Jack. *Speak Up with Confidence: How to Prepare, Learn, and Deliver Effective Speeches*. New York: William Morrow, 1982.

Video Source Book. 7th ed. Syosset, N.Y.: National Video Clearinghouse, 1985.

Wasserman, Paul, ed. *Speakers and Lecturers: How to Find Them. A Directory of Booking Agents, Lecture Bureaus, Companies, Professional and Trade Associations, Universities, and Other Groups Which Organize and Schedule Engagements for Lecturers and Public Speakers on All Subjects, with Information on Speakers, Subjects, and Arrangements, and Biographical Details on over 2,000 Individuals*. 2nd ed. 2 vols. Detroit: Gale Research, 1981.

Watkins, Mary Michelle, ed. *Research Centers Directory*. Foreword by Erich Bloch. 11th ed. 2 vols. Detroit: Gale Research, 1987.

Weiss, Robert O. *Public Argument*. Lanham, Md.: University Press of America, 1995.

White, Eugene E., ed. *Rhetoric in Transition: Studies in the Nature and Uses of Rhetoric*. University Park: Pennsylvania State University Press, 1980.

Wichelns, Herbert A. "The Literary Criticism of Oratory." In *Studies in Rhetoric and Public Speaking in Honor of James Albert Winans*, ed. A. M. Drummond. By pupils and colleagues. New York: Century, 1925, 181–216. Reprint. New York: Russell and Russell, 1962. In *The Rhetorical Idiom: Essays in*

Rhetoric, Oratory, Language, and Drama Presented to Herbert August Wichelns with a Reprinting of His "Literary Criticism of Oratory" (1925), ed. Donald C. Bryant. Ithaca, N.Y.: Cornell University Press, 1958, 5–42. Reprint. New York: Russell and Russell, 1966. Also in *Methods of Rhetorical Criticism: A Twentieth-Century Perspective*, ed. Bernard L. Brock and Robert L. Scott. 2nd ed., rev. Detroit: Wayne State University Press, 1980, 40–73.

Windes, Russel R., and Arthur N. Kruger, eds. *Championship Debating—West Point National Debate Tournament Final-Round Debates and Critiques, 1949–60*. Portland, Maine: J. Weston Walch, 1961.

———. *Championship Debating*. Vol. 2 (1961–1966). Portland, Maine: J. Weston Walch, 1967.

Windt, Theodore, ed., with Beth Ingold. *Essays in Presidential Rhetoric*. Rev. printing. Dubuque, Iowa: Kendall/Hunt, 1984.

Wrage, Ernest J. "Public Address: A Study in Social and Intellectual History." *Quarterly Journal of Speech* 33 (December 1947), 451–57. In *Methods of Rhetorical Criticism: A Twentieth-Century Perspective*, ed. Bernard L. Brock and Robert L. Scott. 2nd ed., rev. Detroit: Wayne State University Press, 1980, pp. 116–24.

Zarefsky, David. *Public Speaking: Strategies for Success*. 2nd ed. Needham Heights, Mass.: Allyn and Bacon, 1999.

Anthologies and Reprints

Anderson, Judith. *Outspoken Women: Speeches by American Women Reformers, 1635–1935*. Dubuque, Iowa: Kendall/Hunt, 1984.

Andrews, James R., and David Zarefsky, eds. *Contemporary American Voices: Significant Speeches in American History, 1945–Present*. New York: Longman, 1992.

Armstrong, Virginia Irving, comp. *I Have Spoken: American History through the Voices of the Indians*. Intro. Frederick W. Turner III. Chicago: Sage Books/Swallow Press, 1971.

Baird, A. Craig, ed. *Representative American Speeches*. Vols. 11–31 (1937/1938–1958/1959) of the Reference Shelf Series. New York: H. W. Wilson, 1938–1959.

Benedict, Stewart H., ed. *Famous American Speeches*. New York: Laurel/Dell, 1967.

Braden, Waldo W., ed. *Representative American Speeches*. Vols. 43–52 (1970/1971–1979/1980) of the Reference Shelf Series. New York: H. W. Wilson, 1971–1980.

Brandt, Carl G., and Edward M. Shafter Jr., eds. *Selected American Speeches on Basic Issues (1850–1950)*. Boston: Houghton Mifflin/Riverside Press, 1960.

Brewer, David J., ed. *The World's Best Orations from the Earliest Period to the Present Time*. 10 vols. St. Louis: Ferd. P. Kaiser, 1900. Reprint. 2 vols. Metuchen, N.J.: Scarecrow Press, 1970.

Bryan, William Jennings, ed. *The World's Famous Orations*. Vols. 8–10. New York: Funk and Wagnalls, 1906.

Capp, Glenn R. *Famous Speeches in American History*. Indianapolis: Bobbs-Merrill, 1963.

————, ed. *The Great Society: A Sourcebook of Speeches*. Belmont, Calif.: Dickenson, 1967.

Copeland, Lewis, and Lawrence W. Lamm, eds. *The World's Great Speeches*. 3rd enl. ed. New York: Dover, 1973.

Dunbar, Alice Moore, ed. *Masterpieces of Negro Eloquence: The Best Speeches Delivered by the Negro from the Days of Slavery to the Present Time*. New York: Bookery, 1914. Reprint. New York: Johnson Reprint, 1970.

Fant, Clyde E., Jr., and William M. Pinson Jr., eds. *Twenty Centuries of Great Preaching: An Encyclopedia of Preaching*. 13 vols. Waco, Tex.: Word Books, 1971.

Foner, Philip S., ed. *The Voice of Black America: Major Speeches by Negroes in the United States, 1797–1971*. New York: Simon and Schuster, 1972. Reprint. 2 vols. New York: Capricorn Books, 1975.

Foner, Philip S., and Robert James Branham, eds. *Lift Every Voice: African American Oratory, 1787–1900*. Tuscaloosa: University of Alabama Press, 1998.

George-Brown, George Alfred Brown, Baron, ed. *The Voices of History: Great Speeches of the English Language*. New York: Stein and Day, 1980. Orig. pub. as *The Voice of History: Great Speeches of the English Language*. London: Sidgwick and Jackson, 1979.

Graham, John, ed. *Great American Speeches, 1898–1963: Texts and Studies*. New York: Appleton-Century-Crofts, 1970.

Hibbitt, George W., ed. *The Dolphin Book of Speeches*. Garden City, N.Y.: Dolphin/Doubleday, 1965.

Hill, Roy L. *Rhetoric of Racial Revolt*. Denver: Golden Bell Press, 1964.

Hoard, Walter B., ed. *Outstanding Black Sermons*. Vol. 2. Valley Forge, Pa.: Judson Press, 1979.

Holland, DeWitte, ed. *Sermons in American History: Selected Issues in the American Pulpit, 1630–1967*. Nashville, Tenn.: Abingdon Press, 1971.

Hurd, Charles, comp. *A Treasury of Great American Speeches*. New and rev. ed. by Andrew Bauer. New York: Hawthorn Books, 1970.

Israel, Fred L., ed. *The State of the Union Messages of the Presidents, 1790–1966*. Intro. Arthur M. Schlesinger. 3 vols. New York: R. R. Bowker and Chelsea House, 1967.

Kennedy, Patricia Scileppi, and Gloria Hartmann O'Shields. *We Shall Be Heard: Women Speakers in America, 1828–Present*. Dubuque, Iowa: Kendall/Hunt, 1983.

Lax, Michael J., ed. *The Inaugural Addresses of the Presidents of the United States, 1789–1985*. Atlantic City, N.J.: American Inheritance Press, 1985.

Lee, Guy Carleton, ed. *The World's Orators: Comprising the Great Orations of the World's History with Introductory Essays, Biographical Sketches and Critical Notes*. Vols. 8–10. New York: Putnam's/Knickerbocker Press, 1900–1901.

Linkugel, Wil A., R. R. Allen, and Richard L. Johannesen. *Contemporary American Speeches: A Sourcebook of Speech Forms and Principles*. 5th ed. Dubuque, Iowa: Kendall/Hunt, 1982.

Lomas, Charles W. *The Agitator in American Society*. Englewood Cliffs, N.J.: Prentice-Hall, 1968.

Lott, Davis Newton, ed. *The President Speaks: The Inaugural Addresses of the Amer-*

ican Presidents from Washington to Nixon. 3rd ed. New York: Holt, Rinehart, and Winston, 1969.

Oliver, Robert T., and Eugene E. White, eds. *Selected Speeches from American History*. Boston: Allyn and Bacon, 1966.

Owens, Milton E., Jr., ed. *Outstanding Black Sermons*. Vol. 3. Valley Forge, Pa.: Judson Press, 1982.

Parrish, Wayland Maxfield, and Marie Hochmuth, eds. *American Speeches*. New York: Longmans, Green, 1954.

Peterson, Houston, ed. *A Treasury of the World's Great Speeches*. Rev. and enl. ed. New York: Fireside/Simon and Schuster, 1965.

Peterson, Owen, ed. *Representative American Speeches*. Vols. 53– (1980/1981–) of the Reference Shelf Series. New York: H. W. Wilson, 1981– .

Ryan, Halford Ross. *American Rhetoric from Roosevelt to Reagan: A Collection of Speeches and Critical Essays*. 2nd ed. Prospect Heights, Ill.: Waveland Press, 1987.

Smith, Arthur L., and Stephen Robb, eds. *The Voice of Black Rhetoric: Selections*. Boston: Allyn and Bacon, 1971.

Smith, J. Alfred, Sr., ed. *Outstanding Black Sermons*. Vol. 1. Valley Forge, Pa.: Judson Press, 1976.

Thonssen, Lester, ed. *Representative American Speeches*. Vols. 32–42 (1959/1960– 1969/1970) of the Reference Shelf Series. New York: H. W. Wilson, 1960– 1970.

Thorndike, Ashley H., ed. *Modern Eloquence: A Library of the World's Best Spoken Thought*. 15 vols. New York: Modern Eloquence, 1928.

Vanderwerth, W. C. *Indian Oratory: Famous Speeches by Noted Indian Chieftains*. Foreword William R. Carmack. Norman: University of Oklahoma Press, 1971.

Williams, Jamye Coleman, and McDonald Williams, eds. *The Negro Speaks: The Rhetoric of Contemporary Black Leaders*. New York: Noble and Noble, 1970.

Windt, Theodore, ed. *Presidential Rhetoric: 1961 to the Present*. Fourth ed. Dubuque, Iowa: Kendall/Hunt, 1999.

Woodson, Carter G., ed. *Negro Orators and Their Orations*. Washington, D.C.: Associated, 1925. Reprint. New York: Russell and Russell, 1969.

Wrage, Ernest J., and Barnet Baskerville, eds. *American Forum: Speeches on Historic Issues, 1788–1900*. New York: Harper and Brothers, 1960. Reprint. Seattle: University of Washington Press, 1967.

———. *Contemporary Forum: American Speeches on Twentieth-Century Issues*. New York: Harper and Brothers, 1962. Reprint. Seattle: University of Washington Press, 1969.

Zacharias, Donald W., ed. *In Pursuit of Peace: Speeches of the Sixties*. New York: Random House, 1970.

Periodicals

Argumentation and Advocacy (formerly *Journal of the American Forensic Association*, formerly *The Register*). Falls River, Wis., 1964– .

Communication Monographs (formerly *Speech Monographs*). Annandale, Va., 1934– .

Communication Quarterly (formerly *Today's Speech*). Upper Montclair, N.J., 1953– .

Communication Studies (formerly *Central States Speech Journal*). Detroit, 1949– .

Forensic, Portales, N. Mex., 1915– .

Master Sermon Series. Royal Oak, Mich., 1970– .

National Forensic Journal. Mansfield, Pa., 1983– .

Pulpit Digest (formerly *New Pulpit Digest*, a merger of *Pulpit Digest* and *Pulpit Preaching*). Louisville, Ky., 1972– .

Quarterly Journal of Speech (formerly *Quarterly Journal of Public Speaking* and *Quarterly Journal of Speech Education*). Annandale, Va., 1915– .

Religious Communication Today. Manhattan, Kans., 1978– .

Rostrum (formerly *Bulletin*). Ripon, Wis., 1934– .

Southern Speech Communication Journal (formerly *Southern Speech Bulletin* and *Southern Speech Journal*). Boone, N.C., 1935– .

Speaker and Gavel (merger of *Speaker* and *Gavel*). Lawrence, Kans., 1964– .

Toastmaster Magazine. Santa Ana, Calif., 1932– .

Vital Speeches of the Day. Mount Pleasant, S.C., 1934– .

Western Journal of Speech Communication (formerly *Western Speech* and *Western Speech Communication*). Pullman, Wash., 1937– .

DO-IT-YOURSELF, HOME REPAIR, AND REMODELING

Elizabeth S. Bell

In 1991, television brought to American homes a new kind of role model with comedian Tim Allen's lead role in the ABC series *Home Improvement*. Inspired by the success of PBS' *This Old House* home remodeling series, which premiered in 1978, hosted by then-small-time contractor Bob Vila, the new television comedy spotlighted Allen as a somewhat bumbling Vila-ish television host, complete with Richard Karn in a comedic version of *This Old House*'s master carpenter, Norm Abram, also known as the host of PBS' *New Yankee Workshop*. In a clear case of comedy following real life, this bit of programming announced that the do it yourself home remodeler had become an American archetype.

Americans have been confirmed do-it-yourselfers virtually from the first European settlements on the North American continent. From earliest colonial days, self-reliance and a talent for improvisational constructions and repair provided the settler with the staples of frontier life. The technological and mercantile centers for the colonies hugged the eastern seaboard well into the eighteenth century, expanding slowly westward as the Europeans moved deeper into the North American wilderness and carved from it colonial replicas of the country villages of England and Europe. Distances between settlements could be vast, and established supply lines were virtually nonexistent. Necessity required that settlers should be adept at building their own shelters and repairing any tools or pieces of equipment that were broken or lost. The hapless settler totally dependent on others for materials and replacements paid dearly for his or her ineptitude. Frontier lifestyles following the movement west across the continent, with their emphasis on beginning anew with whatever one could carry, defined the emerging national character. Especially on the frontier, divisions of labor along gender lines remained fluid. Both men and women, then, of necessity had to become skilled at construction and repair of needed items. Manual dexterity counted as a definite virtue. The accompanying habit of inventive, do-it-yourself repairs and construction innova-

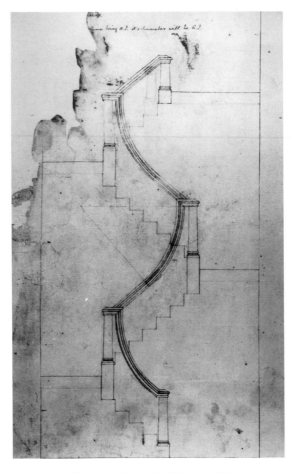

Thomas Jefferson's sketch for Monticello's staircase.
Courtesy of the Library of Congress

tions even produced a label of its own—Yankee ingenuity—even though the trait was not confined to one region of the country alone.

By the mid-1700s, the picture changed somewhat, especially in the more established areas of the eastern seaboard and the urban centers of the older colonies. Especially for the well-to-do, doing it oneself became more a matter of choice than of necessity, immortalized in the images of Benjamin Franklin puttering around to improve the heating capability of his stove and Thomas Jefferson creating new gadgets, such as prototype double-hung storm windows, for Monticello. If they didn't exactly do it themselves, they at least legitimated the idea of utilitarian hobbies, not to mention home workshops.

Ironically enough, these early developments in the history of the United States define the two major interwoven trends in the current concept of do-it-yourself home remodeling. Part of the success of doing-it-yourself is tied inexorably to the economy, both as a response to its fluctuations and as a contributor to its growth and health. When the economy is tight and costs of labor are high, homeowners find remodeling and repairing their current homes more feasible than purchasing new ones. But at the same time, the interest in do-it-yourself feeds the economy by encouraging the development of new building products and tools, new avenues for disseminating information, and new supporting technologies and services. The other part of the success of doing-it-yourself resides firmly in our changing concept of leisure time. During times of financial prosperity, the emphasis shifts from thrift to considerations of status and recreation, and do-it-yourselfing provides both creative and utilitarian outlets for leisure time. The combination of these factors made the do-it-yourself home remodeling movement big business at the end of the twentieth century. The Home Improvement Research Institute noted in 1994 that Americans increased their spending on home improvement products by 15 percent over 1992 and estimated that by 1998, we would spend over $157 billion on do-it-yourself home remodeling (Anderson 40). In addition to expanding already existing areas of the economy, such as tool and equipment manufacturing and construction supplies, consumer interest in home improvement has actually developed new areas of the economy by spawning innovative and popular "how-to" television programming, a focused home and garden television network, and, in addition to its burgeoning print media dissemination of information, increasing experimentation in the use of video- and Web-based avenues for providing up-to-date information to the home repair and remodeling aficionado. Indeed, the do-it-yourself home remodeling megaindustry was an economic and recreational success story to mark the end of the twentieth century.

Ingrained in our conceptions of who we are as Americans, the do-it-yourself movement has grown from humble beginnings into a major factor in the economic and psychological health of the United States. Although taken very much for granted, its emergence in the twentieth century signaled a reaffirmation of the individualism and self-reliance that have been endemic in the development of our society. It permeates not only the business of the country but the leisure as well.

HISTORICAL OUTLINE

Not until the twentieth century was do-it-yourselfing seen as anything other than normal behavior. Furthermore, as long as the United States had remained basically an agrarian nation with an open frontier, people needed to develop a wide range of mechanical and design skills. The Industrial Revolution in the late nineteenth and early twentieth centuries changed this. As the population clustered in urban manufacturing centers and the economy evolved into an assembly-line industrial base, people began developing more specialized skills. The concept of a master craftsman lost its appeal as industrial production quotas and profit margins began to rise. Furthermore, as the population became more prosperous with a growing middle class during the first decades of the twentieth century, status was associated with being able to hire professionals to do household construction and repairs. Little, if any, interest was paid beyond trade and vocational training to the concept of mechanical dexterity or competence.

Nevertheless, a handful of articles appeared in the first decade of the twentieth century that showed the beginnings of a renewed interest in crafts. In 1907, for example, D. H. Culyer showed readers of *The Circle* that "Making a Magazine Stand" was within their range of carpentry skills. Publications such as *Craftsman* had published articles prior to 1910 showcasing the "workroom" as an innovative part of the home, while other publications extolled the values of remodeling and redecorating existing houses. Generally speaking, these articles emphasized the efficient use of space and money, as well as enjoyment, as foundations for such activities. As early as 1910, however, Ira S. Griffith, supervisor of manual training in Oak Park, Illinois, began to see another use for developing these skills. In an article published in *Suburban Life*, he spotlighted the virtues of woodworking as a form of recreation separate from the daily work of the average male homeowner. Its attraction was the physical and mental balance that it provided by bringing respite from the stresses of one's daily employment. His article focused on the beginning amateur woodworker, and among the hints he gave for setting up a home workshop, he advised that one of the most valuable assets that the amateur woodworker can have at hand is a good how-to manual, for appreciation and relaxation are greatly enhanced if one turns out a successful product. Griffin became a repeat contributor to *Suburban Life* during 1910 and 1911, with useful articles about carpentry crafts that the homeowner could complete in his home workshop, while in 1912, Agnes Athol reminded the publication's readers of "What a Woman Can Do with a Paintbrush."

With the growth of the arts and crafts movement in the early twentieth century, however, the idea of crafts as legitimate fields of endeavor began to attract notice. By the early 1920s, delicate crafts as in M. T. Priestman's "Home-Made Novelties for the Country Home" in *American Home* from 1909 had been augmented with a more robust idea of what the homeowner could accomplish, as such articles as F. L. Wright's "Evolution of a Woodshed," in *Woman's Home Companion* (1924) and W. P. Eaton's "Handy Man around the House," in *Country Life* (1920) indicate. At the same time, articles appeared that indicated the ongoing commitment and benefit of these projects, as A. Bennett's "Home as Hobby" in the June 1924 *Woman's Home Companion* implies. Once the home itself becomes a source of recreation, the homeowner's relationship to it drastically changes. One does not merely repair what is broken; one updates, improves, renovates, and remodels, opening new areas to do-it-yourself projects. A handful of related articles appeared over the next decade in such publications as *American Home*, *Craftsman*, *House Beautiful*, and *Delineator*, published by Butterick, but, by and large, consumers were still more interested in having someone else do it for them, and they were willing to pay for these services.

Nevertheless, authors were beginning to create books devoted to home projects. In 1924, Henry H. Saylor solidified the idea of doing-it-yourself with his *Tinkering with Tools*, published by Popular Science. Popular Mechanics Press followed in 1927 with *Make It Yourself. . . . 900 Things to Make and Do*, which consisted of directions written by individual experts showing how to do a variety of projects, some of which involved home repair or remodeling ideas. By the end of the decade, the do-it-yourself concept was well-known and popular enough for Arthur Wakeling to edit a book drawing its title from consumer recognition of the movement: His *Fix It Yourself* appeared in 1929, followed the next year by a more pragmatic-sounding volume entitled *Home Workshop Manual*, both published by Popular Science.

By the 1920s, another significant shift had taken place in the focus of do-it-yourself projects. More and more of the so-called women's magazines began carrying articles aimed at the "handywoman." She even had a name: "Meet Mrs.

Fixit" by K. H. Hunting, appearing in *Illustrated World* in December 1922. There were two dominant patterns in the content of these articles. First, most of them in one way or another, usually in a humorous tone, acknowledged that men scoffed at the efforts of women to be involved in home repair projects. Still largely defined as men's work, home repair as it would later be defined by the do-it-yourself movement was considered far too complex and difficult to be tackled by women. Nevertheless, men writers as well as women began actively to solicit women for home repair projects. Significantly, the women's magazines themselves became the leading source of how-to articles, whether aimed at the handywoman or the handyman.

The other pattern that emerged for handywomen in the 1920s can be found in the kinds of projects that these articles discussed. Most of them covered such repairs as frayed cords on appliances, burned-out fuses, stopped-up drains, and silent doorbells. Mildred Braddocks Bentley in *Ladies' Home Journal* (January 1926), for example, pointed out that even if men ridicule women's efforts at such trivial repairs, those repairs, even if temporary, are of value to the household. Henry H. Saylor wrote a two-part series for *Delineator* that same year that he entitled "Woman as Handy Man." These articles were written to encourage women to try elementary home repair projects. The first, dealing with swollen doors and clogged drains, begins with a gentle laugh at the expense of *Godey's Lady's Book*, circa 1851, which saw women's usefulness limited to the genteel crafts such as making bracelets from loved ones' hair. Saylor portrays the 1920s as an enlightened time in which women can practice more pragmatic skills. As he discusses repairing electric doorbells and changing fuses in the second article, he reassures his reader that the task is no more complex than the "intricacies that our children so readily grasp in the domain of the radio" (69), oddly reminiscent of the 1990s discussion of children's computer and VCR programming skills.

Women writers in the 1920s and 1930s quite frequently began their articles with personal accounts of unexpectedly having to repair an appliance that their husbands did not have time for. Martha Wirt Davis, for example, writing for *American Home* in 1936, tells of having to repair an iron, using information that she remembered from high school physics about how electricity works. From there, she goes on to discuss other appliance repair projects. Interestingly enough, at the same time that these publications defined the rather rigid limits of what women could repair, many of them also advertised how-to booklets, covering such expansive topics as building a fireplace and buying a house. By the 1940s, second-generation handywomen found a voice in Sabrina Ormsby Dean's "It Didn't Take a War to Make a Carpenter Out of Mother" (*House Beautiful* 1943). In this memoir, she describes the many carpentry and plumbing projects that her mother enjoyed and, in so doing, acknowledges that while she hated them at the time, now she has succumbed to her mother's enthusiasm for doing it herself. Not the major component of the movement, women, nevertheless, held a vocal and significant part of it even in the first half of the twentieth century.

The home workshop became very popular in the 1930s, even though the depression was in full swing. Oddly enough, the appeal was not exclusively economic. Do-it-yourself hobbies provided a form of escape from the worries of depression and the impending war in Europe. The National Homeworkshop Guild, established in 1933 with the sponsorship of *Popular Science* and with an estimated constituency of 400 clubs nationally in 1937, conducted a survey to profile the average home workshop owner. They found him to be a male under thirty-five, more than likely a college graduate not engaged in a skilled trade, and claiming recreation as his primary reason for owning the workshop ("Millions," 29). In part, the catalyst and in part the response to the development of more power tools designed for home use, in the 1930s approximately 1 million homes contained a workshop, primarily for woodworking but offering a core of resources for do-it-yourself projects. Delta Manufacturing Company spearheaded the marketing of home-use power tools with a handheld drill and in the thirteen years between 1924 and 1937 grew from a small mail-order company to a large national retailer ("Millions" 28). Other manufacturers followed suit, producing an expanding, but still limited, line of home-use tools.

During the war years, the focus of the do-it-yourself movement was pragmatic and based almost entirely on economic factors. Building materials and supplies, as well as trained labor, were channeled toward military needs. While huge resources were being expended on the war effort, people "back home" were urged to learn to repair instead of replace and to become adept at making their own repairs. How-to manuals took on a new importance. *House and Garden's Wartime Manual for the Home* (1943) focused on typical practical repairs that the inexperienced amateur might have to complete. Hearst Magazines published the *House Beautiful Maintenance and Postwar Building Manual* in 1944, with a cover reminder to homeowners: "Your present home will have to do for the duration." To a large extent, doing-it-yourself became a patriotic duty.

The real growth of the do-it-yourself movement, however, took place in the 1950s as the postwar United States settled into a period of prosperity and expanded leisure time. In 1952, *Business Week* ran an extensive article on "The New Do-It-Yourself Market," offering several reasons for the expanding popularity of the movement. Population growth and the corresponding need for new housing formed a major reason. Veterans returning from the war and the corresponding baby boom encouraged young families to become first-time homeowners. Thus, with more demand for it, labor was difficult to hire, and the costs were high. Furthermore, in 1940, only 44 percent of houses were occupied by owners. By 1950, this percentage had grown to 51 percent. The marketing and design of standardized, small, low-cost housing, made famous by William and Alfred Levitt, met an immediate need, but homeowners with growing families and a developing sense of pride in homeownership rapidly began to want more individual houses. Owners have a different relationship with housing than tenants, so more people were involved in repairing and remodeling their houses. Another factor identified by this article was the large number of veterans and war plant workers, both male and female, who had developed high levels of comfort in working with power tools. Thus, more people were willing to take on complex repairs or construction that formerly would have been handled by professionals. Finally, rural electrification, which had mushroomed during the previous decade, made power tools useful to more households than ever before. Manufacturers had analyzed these trends and produced to meet them. In 1940, only 25 different kinds of home-use power tools had been available on the market. By 1952 that had jumped to 100 kinds with over 4,000 accessories.

Business Week also discussed the kinds of do-it-yourself jobs homeowners were willing to take on. It reported a survey by *Popular Homecraft Magazine*, which noted that 85 percent of readers whose houses were being remodeled were doing it themselves. In part, this growth in do-it-yourselfers resulted from the efforts of manufacturers to redesign their products for the home market. By the mid-1950s, both floor tiles and wall paneling, for example, were being manufactured in squares and sizes more friendly to amateur remodelers. In addition, as more people found do-it-yourself repairs more possible, they actively pursued more knowledge about how to do them. *Publishers Weekly* reported a corresponding growth in how-to titles. From 1950 to 1951, while the overall growth in the publishing industry was 2 percent, the growth in how-to titles was 18 percent.

Unlike earlier decades, however, that drew on a complex of benefits in do-it-yourself home projects, home repairing that was both simple and timely captured the attention of homeowners in the 1950s. How-to manuals addressed these concerns in several ways. Some claimed to be complete repositories of home repair information. Prentice-Hall issued the first of these, *Complete Home Repair Handbook*, by Emanuele Stieri, in 1950. This volume covered both interior and exterior repairs and improvements, discussed effective techniques for completing these projects, and even covered tools and equipment. In 1951, *Better Homes and Gardens Handyman's Book* offered homeowners practical and thorough information on a wide variety of home repair and remodeling projects. It was loose-leaf in design and would lie flat to stay open, allowing for convenience on the job site. It also provided room for remodelers to add their own notes or project descriptions. This was the most complete manual to date for the home do-it-yourselfer, and it became an immediate best-seller. Other large mainstream publishers soon followed with manuals of their own. Houghton Mifflin published the *Homeowner's Complete Guide to Remodeling* in 1953, and McGraw-Hill issued an impossibly long title edited by Charles Flato, *Complete Home Improvement Handbook; A Guide to Material, Tools, Equipment and Do-It-Yourself Techniques,* in 1957.

Other manuals suggested that simple was better for the amateur, and they marketed the concept of easy-to-do projects. Popular Mechanics, though not the first to publish a guide to simple repairs, made a bold play for this category with *125 Simple Home Repairs* (1954), clearly basing its appeal on simple tasks for the disinterested or the unskilled. Homemaker's Encyclopedia had published *Home Repair Simplified*, edited by Miriam Reichl, in 1952, while the editors of *Family Handyman* magazine compiled *400 Quick Answers to Home Repair and Improvement Problems* in 1955. Another kind of manual stressed timely repairs, suggesting that with periodic examination of areas where repairs were likely to be needed, homeowners could ensure the health of their investments. *The Calendar Guide to Home Repair* by Henry Lionel Wiliams appeared in 1952 and was reissued in 1953. Again, Popular Mechanics Press entered the market with *How to Winterize Your Home* (1954). Clearly, in the 1950s the do-it-yourself movement was becoming more diversified and more focused on the individual homeowner's interests and range of abilities. It was becoming a recognizable element in the economic climate of the time.

By 1953, the do-it-yourself home remodeling movement was pronounced enough to be somewhat controversial. Roger Babson, writing for *Commercial and Financial Chronicle*, raised an unexpected objection to the growing do-it-yourself industry, an objection that he then argued against. To some, the trend toward doing-it-yourself seemed to undercut the professional builder or repairman. This led, he charged, to manufacturers' and newspapers' refusing to advertise construction and maintenance products for home use, especially, he added, by the housewife. Yet the movement also led to new products, such as the paint roller and rubber-based paint, which revolutionized homeowners' ability to do their own painting. He praised doing-it-yourself as a hobby but also as an effective bonding activity for fathers and sons. In a stroke of farsightedness, he saw the movement continuing to grow and even admitted that if he were starting a new business, it would be in this field. He perhaps provided the most articulate statement of dissonance at a time when doing-it-yourself was poised to redefine the home marketplace.

Ready to help with this redefining, New York expositioner William Orkin saw 1953 as a perfect time to organize the first-ever do-it-yourself exhibition. He focused on practical exhibits of kits and plans for projects, as well as user-friendly tools, equipment, and products from a total of fifty-five exhibitors ("Do-It-Yourself Idea"). Many of the publications and manufacturers most likely to profit from the exposure declined to attend, but the consumer response was significant, with more than 13,000 in attendance over the exhibition's two days. By the next year, 125 exhibitors were on hand to welcome the 11,000 attendees on the first day ("Sap"). Later that year, *Independent Woman* carried Lenore Hailparn's article "She Did It Herself" about Iowa housewife Marianne Shay, who, having read about the upcoming exhibition, wrote Orkin Exposition Management telling them about her own experiences tiling showers, laying linoleum, and other projects. She became a highlight of the exhibition as "Miss Do-It-Yourself," demonstrating many of the products and projects. Orkin featured her in other exhibitions around the country.

Ironically, even though Marianne Shay represented a growing reality among American women do-it-yourselfers, advertisers still portrayed the division of labor for do-it-yourself projects in rigidly stereotyped patterns. In her book, *Do-It-Yourself: Home Improvement in 20th-Century America* (1998), Carolyn Goldstein reports an early 1950s survey showing that "women not only initiated more home improvement projects than men but actually took on more of the 'muscle work'" (71). Yet women were consistently portrayed in passive roles in product advertising and in magazine articles. More so than in the 1930s, women were urged to see their roles as domestic, whether in the aesthetic realm of decorating or the health realm of cleanliness and sanitation in the home. It would take another decade or two to demonstrate to manufacturers and advertisers that recognizing the role of women do-it-yourself remodelers was smart business.

The 1960s brought a period of turmoil to the United States. Fueled by mounting displeasure in the United States' growing involvement in the Vietnam War and a more jaundiced view of 1950s materialism, many people sought to live a more "natural" lifestyle. For many, this meant a move "back to nature" and consequently more interest in a variety of do-it-yourself projects, from organic gardening to home building. How-to guides proliferated.

In the 1960s several trends emerged in both manuals and magazine articles. A great deal of emphasis in the do-it-yourself movement was placed on the rising costs of professional home repair. Articles in several magazines urged readers to avoid paying more than necessary for home repairs, even to the point of providing tips on how to recognize unscrupulous repairmen. By the end of the decade, *House Beautiful* even covered the contingency of what to do "When the Repairman Won't Come" (Watkins). Clearly emphasizing the element of homeowner choice in how necessary repairs should be carried out, R. H. Ingersoll published an article in *Better Homes and Gardens* directed toward helping homeowners decide, "Does It Really Pay to Do Your Own Home Repairs?" (1965). The temper of the times urged homeowners to be educated and responsible consumers of services, if necessary, or of home repair tools and materials, if desired. Other articles touted the financial benefits of making repairs oneself. To aid the amateur do-it-yourselfer or the one more advanced but trying new projects, many magazines began running regular question-and-answer columns devoted to real home repair issues raised by their readers. Most of these columns appeared under several titles, but *Popular Science* ("Fixit File"), *Better Homes and Gardens* ("Home Upkeep"), *American Home* ("Home Maintenance Clinic"), and *Popular Mechanics* ("Homeowner's Clinic") all provided informative, reader-friendly advice to their readers. Such columns have since become a regular feature of contemporary do-it-yourself publications. *Consumer Bulletin* also indexed a series of booklets about home repairs in its October 1965 issue.

Keeping up with the burgeoning flow of information—manuals, articles, products, and technology—began to be a concern. Out of their own frustration at not being able to locate needed information for their own projects, Betty and Herb Shugar founded a bookstore in 1967 that has become an institution in its own right as a source of how-to publications. Catering to the customer needing clear, specific directions for projects, the How-to Do It Book Shop in Philadelphia makes finding those resources much more pleasant. Bought by John Wiley in 1984, the bookstore's inventory contains a full range of do-it-yourself topics, only some of which cover home remodeling and repair. Nevertheless, the bookstore maintains a knowledgeable staff and steady clientele. It also features a mail order catalog (Bragg). Other bookstores have followed suit. For example, Builder's Booksource in Berkeley, more focused on professional home remodeling than on crafts, finds approximately a third of its business belonging to do-it-yourselfers (Anderson).

The 1950s had marked the first organized attempts to distribute guidelines about how to sort through the growing amount of how-to information. *Publishers Weekly*, in cooperation with R. R. Bowker Company, published *How-to-Do-It Books: A Selected Guide* by Robert Kingery in 1950 and created a whole new category of publication connected to the movement. Covering a wide range of topics, among them house repair and remodeling groupings, this volume indexed and briefly annotated do-it-yourself books published in the late 1940s. Later updates, in 1954 and 1963, included the 1950s as well. Norman Lathrop's *Index to How to Do It Information*, first compiled in 1963 and continuing to be updated annually, was a major development in managing the growing body of print manuals and encyclopedias, articles, and books linked to do-it-yourself. The regularity of its annual supplements assures its continuing value to the do-it-yourselfer. As information about how-to projects proliferated, more attention to systematized means of retrieving it meant that more information could become more available to more people.

The next decades brought sweeping changes to the face of the marketplace. A major development during the 1970s, 1980s and 1990s was the growth of home centers, large superstores with a wide inventory of products channeled toward both professional builders and home amateurs. Generally born of the old-time hardware store, they redesigned both the image and the substance of building supply outlets. Goldstein reports that True Values Stores had originated in 1948 as Cotter and Company, a cooperative of independent hardware and lumber dealers. Not only did combining their products provide consumers with more convenient shopping, but also the volume purchasing that the cooperative was able to afford resulted in lower prices for consumers. Lowe's, second only to Home Depot as a home center, began in 1921 as North Wilkesboro (North Carolina) Hardware Store, founded by L. S. Lowe very much as a traditional country store with little to no self-service. Twenty-five years later, the existing two Lowe's stores were bought by H. Carl Buchan, and, although expanded rather dramatically, the company still remained relatively small-scale and not a factor in most major urban marketplaces. This did not change until 1987, when Lowe's expanded into larger urban centers with larger stores. Between 1987 and 1997, stock in the company grew by over 900 percent, and it continues to grow ("Lowe's Borrows"). Meanwhile, Home Depot, a latecomer that captured the market, opened its first store in Atlanta, Georgia, in 1979. Eighteen years later, it had more than 500 stores. Home centers are growing, literally. The top 100 companies expanded square footage of individual stores (50.8 percent), while holding the number of stores virtually steady with only 3.7 percent growth over the same period of time (Anderson). They've also upscaled marketing concepts with designer lines of remodeling and decorating products. For example, Lowe's carries a line of Laura Ashley products, while Home Depot markets Ralph Lauren.

Many do-it-yourself manuals and videos are marketed virtually exclusively through home centers. Ortho Books, for example, which began its home improvement focus in the late 1970s and adds titles every year, gets 75–80 percent of its sales through home centers and hardware stores (Anderson). So successful has it been that Ortho adds to its list of publications several new titles each year, focusing generally on a specific kind of project for each volume. Dean Johnson markets his popular series of home videos, based on his television program *Hometime*, through home centers and direct mail. Although Sunset Books, a division of Time Warner since 1990, has begun to market its manuals through large bookstore chains, its staple has been the home center/hardware store venue. Time Warner, however, still relies heavily on television and direct sales for its popular Home Repair and Improvement series of amateur manuals established in 1976 and its second series of manuals, Fix-It Yourself, begun in the late 1980s.

Both individual authors and publishing companies have become associated with the do-it-yourself movement. One of the most prolific of the do-it-yourself authors, Tom Philbin, began writing in the 1970s, producing eleven different titles before 1980. His topics covered everything from plumbing to patios, with *Home Repairs Any Woman Can Do* (1973) and *The Nothing Left Out Home Improvement Book* (1976) being important items for Prentice-Hall. In the 1980s, he began to do revisions of older texts, mostly for T. Audel Publishers. By the 1990s, he was writing for Consumer Report Books, Warner, St. Martin's, and Wiley. As this 1992 Warner title indicates, his status and expertise were well recognized in the

Buying tools at Home Depot. © Painet

industry: *Tom Philbin's Do-It-Yourself Bargain Book: How to Save 50%—and More—Buying Products and Materials by America's # 1 Expert.*

Also in the 1970s, Stanley Schuler held a unique place in the do-it-yourself book trade. Quite prolific during the decade, sometimes with as many as four books a year, he covered gardening topics for Macmillan, along with home improvement ideas for Reston Publishing and Collier Books. More than merely describing how-to-do-it projects, Schuler focused also on aesthetics. His books could be read for enjoyment, as much as for practical advice and instruction.

In the 1980s and 1990s, Katie and Gene Hamilton established a name for themselves by publishing two to three books every few years. Their subject matter was aimed at the amateur hobbyist interested in projects both simple and short-term. Yet, while they sometimes detailed projects that could be called novelties, such as *Wooden Toys* (1984), they also dealt with pragmatic repair projects that the homeowner might need. Their *Fix It Fast, Fix It Right: Hundreds of Quick and Easy Home Improvement Projects* (1991) for Rodale Press describes the focus of most of their publications.

By the early 1990s, Betterway Publications made a concerted bid for the do-it-yourself market, and, from 1990 to 1994, Gary D. Branson produced eight home repair and remodeling titles for them, in addition to two for *Popular Mechanics* under the auspices of Hearst Books. His books covered topics from quick and budget-conscious repairs to building one's own log cabin.

In 1978, the do-it-yourself movement hit television as a direct result of the vision of Russell Morash, producer for the Public Broadcasting System's Boston affiliate, WBGH. *This Old House*, television's first home remodeling and repair program, still retains its position as the nation's most recognized and followed home renovation program, available to an amazing 98 percent of homes with televisions in the United States (Prescott). Morash, who also produces such programs as *Julia Child, the French Chef* (1963), *The Victory Garden* (1975), and *The New Yankee Workshop* (1988), is credited with originating the concept of a televised series of programs following real homeowners' experiences renovating their homes. Bob Vila, an unknown South Floridian and small-time house remodeler who, by his own admission, happened to be at the proverbial right place at the right time doing the right thing, was chosen as host of *This Old House*. In a 1987 interview in *Playboy*, he claims that he had just returned from the Peace Corps and with his wife was remodeling a run-down house in an upscale Boston neighborhood. A newspaper reporter happened by and wrote a feature article about him that a television producer happened to see. The producer interviewed him, shot some video of the project, and six months later hired him for *This Old House*, using Vila's own home as the location for the pilot episode.

The program originally focused on a more do-it-yourself approach to home remodeling, incorporating the homeowner's "sweat equity" as a major component of the program. As the show developed, however, its focus changed to more of a showcase for state-of-the-art tools and materials. In addition to Bob Vila, who was clearly the star of the program, it introduced the viewing public to master carpenter Norm Abram and, on an irregular basis, heating and plumbing expert Richard Trethewey and builder-contractor Tom Silva. In 1988, Morash fired Vila from the program over a dispute with one of the program's underwriters, Home Depot, Inc., which had called for Vila to end his endorsement of Rickel Home Centers. Vila refused, and in October 1989 he was replaced by Steve Thomas as host for *This Old House*.

Thomas was a natural for PBS. He had studied philosophy in college but had also had experience as a sailor, about which he had written a book, had made two documentaries, and had remodeled his own home (Giffels). Under his leadership, *This Old House* has become less of the star vehicle that it was in Vila's day and more of an ensemble program featuring Thomas, Norm Abram, Richard Trethewey, and Tom Silva as a team. The personal and professional interaction among these regulars has become one of the more noteworthy features of the program in recent years. While the program spotlights local builders and contractors, it still retains some effort to demonstrate do-it-yourself renovation techniques to homeowners, even though "sweat equity" is no longer a requirement of the program. Nevertheless, one of its messages remains that some things are better left in the hands of professionals. As the program has developed, it has also focused on more expensive renovation projects requiring specialized skills not typically within the expertise or tool collections of amateurs. Topics covered in individual episodes range from initial inspections and designs, to infrastructure considerations, to landscaping and interior decoration. Episodes are supplemented with trips to factories and studios supplying the materials for the program or to historic houses and museums in the area.

As a spin-off of the television program, in 1995 Steve Thomas, Norm Abram, and Russell Morash established *This Old House Magazine*, published by Time Inc. Ventures, also responsible for *Martha Stewart Living* and *Southern Living*. The magazine follows the on-screen projects of the television program, but also contains unrelated features such as a home-repair advice column by Norm Abram and articles on topics of interest to the do-it-yourselfer, as well as a directory of suppliers and specialists.

As a result of their exposure on national television, both Steve Thomas and Norm Abram have written books aimed at the do-it-yourselfer. Thomas' books, written with Philip Langdon, *This Old House Baths* (1993) and *This Old House Kitchens* (1992), deal with the two most prevalent remodeling projects in which homeowners engage in and are unabashedly connected to *This Old House* itself. Abram's books are slightly different and less directly tied to the television program. His *Norm Abram's New House* (1995) details the building of his own dream house, the role that his family played in the process, the work of craftsmen and builders in the process, and the reasons behind each of the decisions that he made during its building. His *Measure Twice, Cut Once: Lessons from a Master Carpenter* (1996) combines personal memoir beginning with Abram's childhood and continuing through his adult years with practical advice culled from his own experience about everything from how to carry tools to how to use design in a project. It has a rare personal flavor, for his father, who was also a master carpenter and who died shortly before the book was finished, played a significant role in both the memoir and the informative parts of the book. In addition, Abram has created a multitude of publications around *The New Yankee Workshop* projects that he has demonstrated on that program.

Again under the guidance of friend and producer Russell Morash, in 1988 Norm Abram became the host and master carpenter on *The New Yankee Workshop*, also for PBS. Morash and Abram had first met when Abram worked on the renovation of Morash's own house. Morash was so impressed that he hired Abram for *This Old House* (Heavens). Ten years later, *The New Yankee Workshop* was developed as a perfect showcase for Abram's talents. Its focus is on woodworking and carpentry projects for the home workshop. Abram takes the viewer on a step-by-step demonstration of how to build the project, discussing techniques and potential problems as he works. Many of the projects spotlighted on this program are results of location work that Abram does for *This Old House* (Prescott 1966).

In 1984, Dean Johnson premiered a home improvement program geared more directly to the do-it-yourselfer. *Hometime*, created for PBS and syndicated on the Learning Channel, features Johnson and a female cohost actually doing a great deal of the hard work of building and remodeling houses, although they are careful to point out which jobs should be left to professionals. With a background in cost accounting and construction, Johnson serves as executive producer of *Hometime* and as president of Hometime Video Publishing, Inc. Robin Hartl, his current cohost, joined the program in 1993, bringing with her experience in real estate, insurance, and part-time home renovation. The Hometime Internet Web site was established in December 1995 and provides a listing of current programs, as well as pertinent information about the program, its products, and its hosts.

After his departure from *This Old House*, Bob Vila's syndicated *Home Again with Bob Vila* premiered on the Arts and Entertainment cable network. Its format mirrors almost exactly that of *This Old House*, again focusing on renovation projects beyond the skills and tools of do-it-yourselfers. Vila spotlights local contractors and builders, often counting on them to provide the plans and scheduling of construction and to discuss the kinds of adaptations that must be made to local building codes and construction practices.

Through the 1970s, 1980s, and 1990s, women became much more significant economically to the movement than ever before. Amateur manuals directed specifically at women proliferated. As women became more involved in the public arenas of American life, their purchasing power increased, and the definitions of appropriate behavior expanded. In 1972, Kay Ward published *The Feminine Fix-It Handbook: Everything You Need to Know to Do-It-Yourself* for Grosset and Dunlap. It was followed by an increasing number of titles for women, such as Florence Adams' *I Took a Hammer in My Hand: The Woman's Build-It and Fix-It Handbook* (1973) and Bernard Gladstone's *New York Time Guide to Home Repairs without a Man* (1973). Within the last decade or so, that number has expanded geometrically, producing writers recognizable for creating complete guides and manuals directed toward women do-it-yourselfers. Lyn Herrick led the way with *Anything He Can Fix, I Can Fix Better* (1990) and the later *Woman's Hands-On Home Repair Guide* (1997). Karen Dale Dustman touched on two trends in the market by combining an emphasis on women with an emphasis on easy-to-accomplish repairs in *The Woman's Fix-It Book: Incredibly Simple Weekend Projects and Everyday Home Repair* (1998). The most telling example of women's place in the do-it-yourself marketplace belongs, however, to Beverly DeJulio, who copyrighted her signature designation, Handyma'am, and turned it into a line of home repair books, including *Handyma'am: Home Improvement, Decorating, and Maintenance Tips and Projects for Your Family* (1999) and a television program, *Homewise*, cohosted with her daughter Chris, on the cable Home and Garden Television Network.

The do-it-yourself movement is even developing a sense of humor directed at itself. While cartoonists and comedians have long laughed at the bumbling efforts of unskilled amateur handymen (Goldstein), manuals aimed at those amateurs took themselves very seriously and, by and large, presented mainstream, descriptive titles to consumers. Not so today. Eric Tyson and Ray Brown played on the success of the IDG Books Worldwide computer manuals with *Home Repair for Dummies* (1996), and Katie and Gene Hamilton joined in with *Home Improvement for Dummies* (1998). In addition, in 1999, the Hamiltons published *Carpentry for Dummies*. David J. Tenenbaum published *The Pocket Idiot's Guide to Home Repair* in 1998. TAB Books even began a line of how-to manuals in an All Thumbs Guide series in the early 1990s, several of which deal with home repair topics. As the century closed, it became trendy to be somewhat bumbling, à la Tim Allen. This trend, however, may have its roots in the changing nature of our interest in do-it-yourself home remodeling.

While advertising, product design, sales, and venues have grown dramatically, a corresponding decline has occurred in actual numbers of people who want to do it themselves. A 1993 Roper survey found that while 19 percent of adults enjoy reading about do-it-yourself topics, this represents a drop from 28 percent in 1984 (Crispell). Robert Berkstrom, former contractor and managing editor of Ortho

Scene from the television sitcom *Home Improvement*.
Kobal Collection/Buena Vista TV/Touchstone TV

Books, also senses a change in the do-it-yourself audience, "away from the die-hard do-it-yourselfer, to the more sophisticated audience who are more than likely not doing the work themselves but hiring somebody, yet they want to know what is being done so they can talk the language and be sure they are getting a good job" (quoted in Anthony). The popularity of home repair manuals, products, and television programs suggests that he is correct. While the typical homeowner may not want to grapple with the nuts and bolts of home repair, he or she seems to recognize a need to know the language of repair well enough to communicate with contractors and professionals. Several books dealing with that subject appeared in the late 1980s and throughout the 1990s. Hugh Howard sounded an almost desperate introduction to this trend with *I'm Not Doing It Myself: The Comprehensive Guide to Managing a Home Construction or Renovation Project* for Noonday Press in 1987. Perennial do-it-yourself author Tom Philbin's *How to Hire a Home Improvement Contractor without Getting Chisled* (1991) was the most clearly pointed, but it was joined by Homeowner's Library's *How to Hire the Right Contractor* (1991) by Paul Bianchina. Two years later Steve Gonzalez published

Ready, Set, Build: A Consumer's Guide to Home Improvement Planning and Contracts (1993). Books such as these focused on pragmatic issues that homeowners need to consider when deciding on a remodeling or repair project and on what expectations they should have about the contractor's role and responsibility, as well as their own, in the project. Another helpful source of information for the homeowner not doing all of it himself or herself is Monroe Speigel and Robert Berko's *Consumer Guide to Home Repair Grants and Subsidized Loans* (1990). One of the appeals of the do-it-yourself movement has always been economic, as this title suggests, but it also leads to another popular trend of the 1990s. Fed by the success of home remodeling television programs, especially in the variety found on PBS and the new Home and Garden Television cable network, house restoration and preservation have found a nook in the home improvement industry. The National Trust for Historic Preservation in Washington, D.C., established Preservation Press to publish books detailing various periods and styles in American building and decorating. A number of journals and magazines, such as *Old House Journal*, specialize in the topic. These items typically are not focused on doing-it-yourself but may identify specialized areas of construction or remodeling for which expert professionals are essential.

Attitudes toward house and leisure changed dramatically during the course of the century. In some ways, it appears that we have returned to the perceptions that marked pre–World War I American society. Then, the house was shelter, its repair the province of professionals. Gradually, homeowners developed a more involved relationship with their houses, first through the twin necessities of economy and of practical use of growing leisure time. The euphoria that accompanied the end of World War II, coupled with the material expansion and prosperity that many young homeowners felt, fed the effort to individualize and personalize the family's dwelling. Products that made do-it-yourselfing easier, manuals that made projects more manageable, more leisure time than ever before, and an increasing attention to consumer education made the latter half of the twentieth century a dream period for the movement. Yet, at century's close, while sales were still high and new technology was making both products and information more available than ever before, more and more Americans were content to contract out projects once the mainstay of the movement. One conclusion that may be drawn from this is that, rather than returning to the attitudes defining the early part of the century, we've redefined once again the nature of do-it-yourself. It has become for us as much entertainment as activity. Home repair and improvement television programs that follow a project from start to finish over a period of several episodes add something that the print manuals did not—a narrative story line. Those manuals were strictly sources of how-to information. The television programs take us into the lives of homeowners, contractors, and television hosts as they wage battle with termites, cracked foundations, historical societies, and dry rot. As the season of programs progresses, the plot becomes more complex, and the people involved—and the houses—take on more personality. With the likes of Bob Vila, Steve Thomas, Norm Abram, Dean Johnson, and Beverly DeJulio, we have anointed new superstars who invite us to watch them work on tasks both practical and attractive. With computer technology, we have adapted the concept of the interactive computer game to the matters of home repair and remodeling. Home centers offer attractive, mall-like structures in which to browse or shop. Consumer education insists that we learn all that we can about new products and services. More consumer-oriented than ever before, do-it-yourselfing encapsulates the changing face of twenty-first-century America.

REFERENCE WORKS

Various indexes and guides to how-to books prove useful to the scholar trying to locate important books from the 1950s to the 1990s. *How-to-Do-It Books: A Selected Guide* by Robert E. Kingery appeared in 1950 and was revised and reissued in 1954 and again, without Kingery's name, in 1963 by R. R. Bowker Company. Although only a fraction of its listings deal with home remodeling or repair, it was the only index to that time dealing with how-to publications. Its listing is by topic with useful cross-referencing, and its annotations, while brief, convey pertinent information about each book. Intended for use by the then-current do-it-yourselfer, it also includes for many of its entries the price of the publication.

R. R. Bowker Company also issued *How-To: 1400 Best Books on Doing Almost Everything* by Bill and Linda Sternberg Katz. Appearing in 1985, this index follows the same format as *How-to-Do-It Books* and covers the years 1980–1984. The annotations are more detailed than in the previous books but provide the same kind of supporting information about page length, current price, and cross-references. As in the previous volumes, a full range of how-to topics is included, a portion of which deal with home repair and remodeling.

The *Index to How-to-Do-It Information*, originally compiled by Mary Lou and Norman Lathrop in 1963 as a mimeographed listing of how to materials on a range of topics and revised annually thereafter, was updated and expanded in 1990 as a comprehensive index covering 1963–1989 for a subscription list of 1,500. During the years 1991–1993, supplements were not issued, but those years were included in the 1997, 1998, and 1999 supplements as "backfile indexing" at the rate of one-third of the titles each year. Each annual supplement indexes approximately 180 magazine titles and over 150,000 entries. Approximately one-fourth of its entries deal with home repair and remodeling. Its annotations identify, where possible, the level of expertise that the item assumes and note whether specialized or professional tools are needed. The editors avoid professional product reviews and focus on home repair magazines. The 1999 supplement also contains a complete listing of the magazines indexed since 1963 and the years in which they have been included. According to Norman Lathrop, the editors plan a CD-ROM option for the index that will allow full-text searching of the index, as well as a union list of public libraries that permanently retain copies of magazines.

The Carnegie Public Library in Pittsburgh, which maintains a Special Collection in Science and Technology, in 1986 published *Index to Handicraft Books: 1974–1984* from the University of Pittsburgh Press. While the index covers many kinds of handicrafts, some topics (i.e., furniture, tiles, floors) touch on the do-it-yourself home remodeling movement. Its entries are cross-referenced by type and annotated. A second volume covering the years 1985–1995 is under preparation.

Library Journal periodically updates information on the do-it-yourself movement with annotated bibliographic articles. "Fixing Up Your Home Repair Collection" by Bill Demo appeared in September 1991, briefly discussing the appeal of the do-it-yourself movement and providing guidelines for what effective publications on the topic should include. Its annotated listing of titles is subdivided into closely related kinds of manuals—"Basic Homeowner Guides," "Common Repair Projects," "Comprehensive Guides," "Material Guides," and the like. Each category contains five or six titles with photographs of the covers and useful information about the item. Peter C. Leonard's "Remodeling a Home Renovation Collection" appeared in February of the next year, covering a slightly different focus. In addition to general guides, this article deals with titles for "Contracting Out Projects," "Historic Preservation," and, on a much more limited basis, specific room projects. Within each category, items are arranged by Leonard's analysis of their usefulness to a library collection. Jonathan Hersey's "Getting a Fix on Your Home Repair Collection" (February 1997) subdivides into categories such as "Basic Guides and Sources," "Repair Manuals/Series," "Specialized Skills and Areas," and several additional ones. His article also contains a listing of CD-ROMs and World Wide Web sites. Annotations, as in all these articles, include descriptions of the item, its ISBN, the number of pages, and its publication retail price. "Home Repair Best Sellers" (March 1997) simply lists the top book titles as identified by Baker and Taylor Books for the past six months. Adapting to the changing how-to market, "CD-ROM Review" (April 1996) by Harvard librarians Cheryl LaGuardia and Ed Tallent provides extensive annotations on the top CDs in the home maintenance and remodeling area. It describes screens and menus and special features of each CD and includes an analysis of each item's strengths and weaknesses. To date, it is one of the best indexes to the developing CD-ROM how-to technology.

In May 1995, *Publishers Weekly* also published an annotated bibliography of do-it-yourself home remodeling and CD-ROM titles. "Plugging into the 'DIY' Market," by Heather Vogel Frederick provides background on the role of CDs in the market, including comment by publishers and chief executive officers (CEOs) in the software field. Among the advantages that Frederick cites for this product are the graphics and technical advances impossible to show in books. Among the disadvantages are cost and lack of mobility to job site or hammock. Her article concludes that, generally speaking, CD-ROMs marketed through computer dealers fare better in retail sales than those marketed through bookstores. She annotates several of the most important items in a somewhat limited listing.

In keeping with the expansion of technological development in the 1990s, a new source of information about do-it-yourself home repair and remodeling must be addressed. World Wide Web sites abound with both useful and arcane information on the topic. The astute consumer must be adept at distinguishing one type from the other. In addition, Web sites tend to be temporary, appearing and disappearing with the rapidity commensurate with computer technology. Nevertheless, several Web sites appear to be more stable and more informative than many. Reader's Digest Web site contains links to several useful sites, including "Ask the Family Handyman," which features a weekly response to one reader's questions, and "Reader's Digest World," which offers advice and product information on a number of kinds of home repair projects. HomeArts Web site also contains links to a wide variety of other sites, such as "Handy Home Advisor," an interactive House Beautiful page, Bob Vila's American Home, and "BTW: Home Repair Encyclopedia." The HomeIdeas Web site allows access to *Today's Homeowner* archives and bills itself as an "ultimate research tool" for home repair and remodeling ideas. Hometime's Web draws from the PBS television program of the same name. It has its own Web site but can also be accessed through the PBS home page at pbs.org. The PBS site also allows access to home pages for their programs, such as *This Old House* and Bob Yapp's *About Your House*. Do It Yourself.com covers a multitude of topics dealing with maintenance and home repair. *Home Improvement Encyclopedia*, as useful as its title implies with diagrams and animation, can be accessed through the *Better Homes and Gardens* Web site. The new Home and Garden Television Web provides links to its numerous program homepages, as well as a wide variety of useful information for the do-it-yourselfer. In addition, various home centers have their own Web sites with information about products and, to varying extent, how-to projects. These Web sites are generally the name of the home center followed by the commercial site designator ".com." Any of the currently popular search engines, such as Yahoo!, can identify additional or new sites.

HISTORY AND CRITICISM

Scholarship on the do-it-yourself home remodeling movement takes two different forms. Traditional scholarly articles, limited in number, deal mostly with the historical overview of the movement, defined subjectively by individual authors. The most thorough of these histories, Carolyn M. Goldstein's *Do It Yourself: Home Improvement in 20th-Century America* (1998), covers the history and other topics relating to the marketplace for the do-it-yourselfer, gender roles within the movement, and nostalgia for the past. She provides detailed information about the development of tools and supplies that fed the do it yourself movement, for example, noting that such things as latex paints, laminated wood products, and plywood panels appeared on the market in the 1950s, but PVC plastic piping did not appear until the late 1960s, thus making home plumbing a later part of do-it-yourself remodeling than wiring and carpentry. She draws on advertisements, contemporary news and magazine articles, product brochures, and business reports to provide a well-rounded, thorough discussion of the movement in the twentieth century. Lavishly illustrated with period cartoons, advertisements, and photographs, the book provides a visual treat, as well as well-presented information on the subject.

Steven M. Gelber's "Do-It-Yourself: Constructing, Repairing and Maintaining Domestic Masculinity," in the March 1997 *American Quarterly*, argues that the twentieth-century do-it-yourself movement developed mainly as a way to restore a feeling of masculinity to the generations of men separated from manual skills— and hence, traditional definitions of manhood—by the Industrial Revolution. He incorporates sociological theories of leisure and recreation, as well as contemporary magazine articles, for his information. The article contains a brief historical rendition of pre-1900 craftsmanship but focuses predominantly on a theoretical interpretation of the do-it-yourself movement in the 1900s to the 1970s. The bibliography contains primary books and articles dating from early in the twentieth century, as well as book and article discussions of related subjects, such as leisure activity and recreation. In addition, his article "A Job You Can't Lose: Work and Hobbies in the Great Depression," published in *Journal of Social History* (Summer 1991), focuses more specifically on the 1930s and discusses the popularity of hobbies as both didactic and creative activities during the depression.

While it provides useful theoretical background for the do-it-yourself movement, its focus is broader.

Roland Albert's "Do-It-Yourself: A Walden for the Millions" in *American Quarterly* (1958) offers a contemporary analysis of the movement in the decade of its real emergence. Roland categorizes do-it-yourselfers into three groups: artisan/craftsmen, fix-it repairers, and true do-it-yourselfers. His premise that the current interest in do-it-yourself projects signals a turn toward consumerism, rather than development of skill or production, is borne out by his contention that the kits and simplified products accompanying the movement both militate against artisanship and enhance the economy in useful ways. In addition, they make possible individuals' sense of accomplishment and identity. Unlike advertisements and marketing articles from the 1950s that portray women in passive roles, however, Roland contends that do-it-yourselfers are frequently married couples working as a unit.

Joseph J. Corn's "Educating the Enthusiast: Print and the Popularization of Technical Information," in John L. Wright's *Possible Dreams: Enthusiasm for Technology in America* (1992), offers related information on the growth and evolution of technical how-to manuals. While it deals mainly with manuals describing how to operate machinery and coexist with expanding technology, it includes an expanded section on *Popular Mechanics*, which in 1910 changed its focus from the professional to the amateur handyman and housewife. It provides useful background information on the history of the how-to manual.

Another important type of scholarship devoted to the do-it-yourself home remodeling movement targets the professional librarian and archivist as audience. Mostly in the form of annotated bibliographies designed to aid in the development and maintenance of special collections and holdings, this type of scholarship also provides useful guidance to the researcher.

Managing the How-To Collection and Learner's Advisory Services: A How-to-Do-It Manual for Librarians by Sy Sargent (1993) offers guidance on selecting appropriate how-to materials and developing learner-based advisory expertise for using the collection, in addition to a theoretical discussion of the assumptions underlying library how-to collections in general, as well as specific guides to locating periodical information about specific items, including videos and, to a lesser extent, computer software. Included in its bibliography are items specifically devoted to home repair and remodeling.

To date there are no traditional scholarly collections or archives dealing with the do-it-yourself home remodeling movement. Public libraries, the natural repositories of these publications, approach the subject from the perspective of building collections that are useful to current users. Many public libraries, particularly in larger urban areas, have extensive holdings in current user manuals and encyclopedias, but since much of the home improvement literature becomes dated as new products and building materials are developed, individual libraries regularly cull their collections, basing decisions of what to keep on such considerations as available shelf space, user interest, and general applicability to current practices. The Carnegie Public Library in Pittsburgh, which maintains a Special Collection in Science and Technology, published through the University of Pittsburgh Press in the mid-1980s *Index to Handicraft Books: 1974–1984* and still holds most, but not all, of the books and articles contained in that index, a proportion of which deal with home remodeling and repair. In addition, the library has continued to index relevant volumes.

University libraries, operating on the principle of archiving materials for scholarly study, have shown little interest in the do-it-yourself home remodeling movement. Even the Popular Culture Library at Bowling Green State University in Bowling Green, Ohio, maintains only a sporadic holding on the subject. According to Allison Scott, head librarian, their collection is not systematic, but its listing can be accessed via the library's on-line catalog.

The National Building Museum in Washington, D.C., although focusing more on architectural holdings, maintains a collection of materials relating more to professional building than to do-it-yourself projects; however, it is not fully cataloged. Research in their collection is by appointment only.

ANTHOLOGIES AND REPRINTS

For the do-it-yourself home improvement movement, with very few exceptions, traditional anthologies and reprints have been supplanted by technology. The most useful updates of old standards appear as CD-ROMs. The two most important pioneering electronic publishers in this area to date are Books That Work and Broderbund Software, although other companies are rapidly developing their own products. Dean Johnson has released a CD entitled *Hometime Weekend Home Projects*, which draws heavily on his *Hometime* television program, even to the point of including clips from several programs in the series. Manuals offer a ready and useful source for CD format. For example, *The Stanley Complete Step-by-Step Book of Home Repair and Improvement* (1993) found new life as the CD, *Simply House* (1995). *The Reader's Digest Compete Do-it-Yourself Guide* (Microsoft, 1996) retains all the advantages of the printed version, *Reader's Digest New Complete Do-It-Yourself Manual* (1991), which itself updates the 1973 original title but adds graphics and menus, including a program to help estimate costs and amounts of materials. For Macintosh users, *Home Depot's Home Improvement 1–2–3* (Multicom 1995) provides one of the best comprehensive guides and updates *Home Improvement 1–2–3: Expert Advice from the Home Depot* (1995).

BIBLIOGRAPHY

Abram, Norm. *Measure Twice, Cut Once: Lessons from a Master Carpenter.* Boston: Little, Brown, 1996.

———. *Norm Abram's New House.* Boston: Little, Brown, 1995.

Adams, Florence. *I Took a Hammer in My Hand: The Woman's Build-It and Fix-It Handbook.* New York: William Morrow, 1973.

Albert, Roland. "Do-it-Yourself: A Walden for the Millions?" *American Quarterly* 10 (Summer 1958), 154–64.

Allen, Benjamin W., ed. *Home Improvement 1–2–3: Expert Advice from the Home Depot.* Des Moines: Meredith Books, 1995.

Anderson, Evy Herr. "Flourishing with the Fixits." *Publishers Weekly* 43 (October 24, 1994), 40–44.

Anthony, Carolyn. "A Book in Every Toolbox." *Publishers Weekly* 237: 44 (November 2, 1990), 25–29.

Athol, Agnes. "What a Woman Can Do with a Paintbrush." *Suburban Life* 15 (November 1912), 268.

Babson, Roger W. " 'Do It Yourself'—A New Industry." *Commercial and Financial Chronicle* 177 (March 5, 1953), 1012.

Bennett, A. "Home as Hobby." *Woman's Home Companion* 51 (June 1924), 4.

Bentley, Mildred Braddocks. "Substituting for the Service Man." *Ladies' Home Journal* (January 1926), 104, 113.

Better Homes and Gardens Handyman's Book. Des Moines, Iowa: Meredith Books, 1951.

Bianchina, Paul. *How to Hire the Right Contractor.* New York: Consumer Reports Books, 1991.

Bragg, Malara. "Just Do It: Where to Get Directions for Anything." *Mother Earth News* 162 (June–July 1997), 14.

Brinley, Maryann. "Do-It-Yourself Takes Over." *McCall's* (January 1955), 24.

———. "Stores That Help You to Be Handy." *McCall's* 110 (March 1983), 82–83.

Cadoree, Michelle. *Home Maintenance, Repair and Improvement.* LC Tracer Bullet. Washington, D.C.: Library of Congress, 1995.

Corn, Joseph J. "Educating the Enthusiast: Print and the Popularization of Technical Knowledge." In *Possible Dreams: Enthusiasm for Technology in America*, ed. John L. Wright. Dearborn, Mich.: Henry Ford Museum and Greenfield Village, 1992, 18–33.

Crispell, Diane. "Virtual Reality Meets Do-It-Yourself." *Folio: The Magazine for Magazine Management* 22: 9 (May 15, 1993), 25–26.

Culyer, D. H. "Making a Magazine Stand." *The Circle* 2 (July 1907), 48.

Davis, Martha Wirt. "Some Tips for Mrs. Fixit." *American Home* 15 (1936), 44, 98–99.

Dean, Sabrina Ormsby. "It Didn't Take a War to Make a Carpenter Out of Mother." *House Beautiful* 85 (October 1943), 118–19, 127.

DeJulio, Beverly. *Handyma'am: Home Improvement, Decorating and Maintenance Tips and Projects for Your Family.* Chicago: Real Estate Education, 1999.

Demo, Bill. "Fixing Up Your Home Repair Collection." *Library Journal* (September 1, 1991), 161–65.

"Do-It-Yourself Idea—On Parade." *Business Week* (March 21, 1953), 33.

Dustman, Karen Dale. *The Woman's Fix-It Book: Incredibly Simple Weekend Projects and Everyday Home Repair.* Worchester, Mass.: Chandler House Press, 1998.

Eaton, W. P. "Handy Man around the House." *Country Life* 30 (April 1920), 60–62.

Flato, Charles, ed. *Complete Home Improvement Handbook; A Guide to Material, Tools, Equipment and Do-It-Yourself Techniques.* New York: McGraw-Hill, 1957.

400 Quick Answers to Home Repair and Improvement Problems, by the Editors of Family Handyman Magazine. New York: Harper, 1955.

Frederick, Heather Vogel. "Plugging into the 'DIY' Market." *Publishers Weekly* 242: 18 (May 1, 1995), 28–29.

Gelber, Steven M. "Do-It-Yourself: Constructing, Repairing and Maintaining Domestic Masculinity." *American Quarterly* 49: 1 (March 1997), 66–112.

————. "A Job You Can't Lose: Work and Hobbies in the Great Depression." *Journal of Social History* (Summer 1991), 741–66.

Giffels, David. "Steve Thomas Retains Regular-Guy Image despite Success of *This Old House*." Knight-Ridder/Tribune News Service (February 22, 1996), 222. *Infotrac SearchBank*. On-line. Discus. 3/8/99.

Gladstone, Bernard. *New York Times Guide to Home Repairs without a Man*. New York: Quadrangle, 1973.

Goldstein, Carolyn. *Do-It-Yourself: Home Improvement in 20th-Century America*. New York: Princeton Architectural Press, 1998.

Gonzalez, Steve. *Ready, Set, Build: A Consumer's Guide to Home Improvement Planning and Contracts*. Fort Lauderdale, Fla.: Women's Publications, 1993.

Griffith, Ira S. "Cabinet Making as Handcraft." *Suburban Life* (September 1910), 346.

————. "Recreation with Tools." *Suburban Life* (June 1910), 22.

————. "Three Things to Make in Your Home Workshop." *Suburban Life* (November 1911), 269.

Hailparn, Lenore. "She Did It Herself." *Independent Woman* 32 (June 1953), 203.

Hamilton, Gene, and Katie Hamilton. *Carpentry for Dummies*. Foster City, Calif.: IDG Books Worldwide, 1999.

————. *Fix It Fast, Fix It Right, Hundreds of Quick and Easy Home Improvement Projects*. Emmaus, Pa: Rodale Press, 1991.

————. *Home Improvement for Dummies*. Foster City, Calif.: IDG Books Worldwide, 1998.

————. *Wooden Toys*. (1984). New York: Sedgewood Press, 1987.

Heavens, Alan J. "Preparation, Precision Key to Success of Norm Abram and *The New Yankee Workshop*. Knight-Ridder/Tribune News Service, January 16, 1997. 116. *Infotrac SearchBank*. On-line. Discus. 3/8/99.

Herrick, Lyn. *Anything He Can Fix, I Can Fix Better: A Comprehensive Guide for Home and Auto Repair*. Valle Crucis, N.C.: Quality Living, 1990.

————. *Woman's Hands-On Home Repair Guide*. Pownal, Vt.: Storey Communications, 1997.

Hershey, Jonathan. "Getting a Fix on Your Home Repair Collection." *Library Journal* 122: 2 (February 1, 1997), 51–55.

"Home Repair Best Sellers." *Library Journal* 122: 4 (March 1, 1997), 61.

Homeowner's Complete Guide to Remodeling. New York: Houghton Mifflin, 1953.

House and Garden's Wartime Manual for the Home. New York: Simon and Schuster, 1943.

House Beautiful Maintenance and Postwar Building Manual. New York: Hearst Magazines, 1944.

How to Winterize Your Home. Chicago: Popular Mechanics Press, 1954.

Howard, Hugh. *I'm Not Doing It Myself: The Comprehensive Guide to Managing a Home Construction or Renovation Project*. New York: Noonday Press, 1987.

Hufnagel, James A. *The Stanley Complete Step-by-Step Book of Home Repair and Improvement*. New York: Simon and Schuster, 1993.

Hunting, K. H. "Meet Mrs. Fixit." *Illustrated World* (December 1922), 597–99.

Index to Handicraft Books: 1974–1984. Pittsburgh: University of Pittsburgh Press, 1986.

Ingersoll, R. H. "Does It Really Pay to Do Your Own Home Repairs." *Better Homes and Gardens* 42 (July 1965), 14.

Katz, Bill, and Linda Sternberg Katz. *How-To: 1400 Best Bookss on Doing Almost Everything*. New York: R. R. Bowker, 1985.

Kingery, Robert E. *How-to-Do-It Books: A Selected Guide*. Rev. ed. New York: R. R. Bowker, 1954.

LaGuardia, Cheryl, and Ed Tallent. "CD-ROM Review." *Library Journal* (April 1, 1996), 128, 130.

Lathrop, Norman, Ed. *Index to How-to-Do-It Information*. (1963–). Annual.

Leonard, Peter C. "Remodeling a Home Renovation Collection." *Library Journal* (February 1, 1992), 53–56.

"Lowe's Borrows the Blueprint." *Fortune* (November 23, 1998), 212.

Make It Yourself. . . . 900 Things to Make and Do. Chicago: Popular Mechanics Press, 1927.

"Millions in Power Tools for Craftsman Hobbies." *Steel* 100 (May 1937), 28–29.

"The New Do-It-Yourself Market." *Business Week* (June 14, 1952), 60–76.

125 Simple Home Repairs. Chicago: Popular Mechanics Press, 1954.

Philbin, Tom. *Home Repairs Any Woman Can Do*. Englewood Cliffs, N.J.: Prentice-Hall, 1973.

———. *How to Hire a Home Improvement Contractor without Getting Chisled*. New York: St. Martin's Press, 1991.

———. *The Nothing Left Out Home Improvement Book*. Englewood Cliffs, N.J.: Prentice-Hall, 1976.

———. *Tom Philbin's Do-It-Yourself Bargain Book: How to Save 50%—and More— Buying Products and Materials by America's #1 Expert*. New York: Warner, 1992.

Prescott, Jean. "Norm Abram and *The New Yankee Workshop* Begin Their 8th Season on PBS." Knight-Ridder/Tribune News Service. January 11, 1966. 111. *Infotrac SearchBank*. On-line. Discus. 3/8/99.

———. "Steve Thomas Continues His Role as Host, Skeptic as *This Old House* Begins 17th Season." Knight-Ridder News Service, September 28, 1995. 92. *Infotrac SearchBank*. On-line. Discus. 3/8/99.

Priestman, M. T. "Home-Made Novelties for the Country Home." *American Home* 6 (April 1909), 148–49.

Reader's Digest Complete Do-It-Yourself Manual. Pleasantville, N.Y.: Reader's Digest Association, 1973.

Reader's Digest New Complete Do-It-Yourself Manual. New York: Putnam, 1991.

Reichl, Miriam, ed. *Home Repair Simplified*. New York: Homemaker's Encyclopedia, 1952.

"The Sap Is Running in Do-It-Yourself." *Business Week* (March 27, 1954), 122.

Sargent, Sy. *Managing the How-To Collection and Learner's Advisory Services: A How-To-Do-It Manual for Librarians*. New York: Neal-Schuman, 1993.

Saylor, Henry H. *Tinkering with Tools*. New York: Popular Science, 1924.

———. "Woman as Handy Man, I." *Delineator* 108 (March 1926), 60–62.

———. "Woman as Handy Man, II. Be Your Own Electrician." *Delineator* 108 (April 1926), 69–70.

Speigel, Monroe, and Robert Berko. *Consumer Guide to Home Repair Grants and*

Subsidized Loans. South Orange, N.J.: Consumer Education Research Center, 1990.

Stieri, Emanuele. *Complete Home Repair Handbook*. Englewood Cliffs, N.J.: Prentice-Hall, 1950.

Tenenbaum, David J. *The Pocket Idiot's Guide to Home Repair*. New York: Alpha Books, 1998.

Thomas, Steve and Philip Langdon. *This Old House Baths*. Boston: Little, Brown, 1993.

————. *This Old House Kitchens*. Boston: Little, Brown, 1992.

Tyson, Eric, and Ray Brown. *Home Repair for Dummies*. Foster City, Calif.: IDG Books, 1996.

Vila, Bob. "Interview." *Playboy* 34 (March 1987), 122–25.

Wakeling, Arthur. *Fix It Yourself*. New York: Popular Science, 1929.

————. *Home Workshop Manual*. New York: Popular Science, 1930.

Ward, Kay. *The Feminine Fix-It Handbook: Everything You Need to Know to Do-It-Yourself*. New York: Grosset and Dunlap, 1972.

Williams, Henry Lionel. *The Calendar Guide to Home Repair*. New York: Simmons-Boardman Books, 1953, ca. 1952.

Wright, F. L. "Evolution of a Woodshed." *Woman's Home Companion* 51 (May 1924), 50.

CD-ROM Computer Software

Home Depot's Home Improvement 1-2-3. CD-ROM. Seattle: Multicom/Multimedia 2000, 1995.

Hometime Weekend Home Projects. CD-ROM. Chaska, Minn., 1995.

Reader's Digest Complete Do-It-Yourself Guide. CD-ROM. Redmond, Wash.: Microsoft, 1996.

Simply House. CD-ROM. Islandia, N.Y.: 4Home Productions, 1995.

Periodicals

American Home. 1928– .

American Craftsman. 1965– .

American Woodworker. 1994– .

Better Homes and Gardens. 1922– .

Building Supply Home Centers. 1917.

Chilton's Hardware Age: For the Do-It-Yourself Hardware/Home Center Market. 1855.

Craftsman. 1901–1916.

Decorating Remodeling: The Magazine of Style and Design. 1986– .

Do-It-Yourself Retailing. 1984– .

Family Handyman: The Do-It-Yourself Home Improvement Magazine. 1951– .

Good Housekeeping. 1885– .

Historic Preservation. 1949– .

Home: The Magazine of Remodeling and Decorating. 1955– .

Home Craftsman. 1932–1966.

Home Mechanix. 1985–1996.

Homecraft. 1930–1955.

HomeOwner. 1976–   .
House and Garden. 1901–   .
House Beautiful. 1896–   .
Ladies Home Journal. 1883–   .
Mechanix Illustrated. 1928–1984.
Mother Earth News. 1970–   .
Old House Journal. 1973–   .
Popular Mechanics. 1902–   .
Popular Science. 1872–   .
Repair and Remodel Quarterly. 1995–   .
This Old House. 1995–   .
Today's Homeowner. 1996–   .
Workbench. 1957–   .

Selected Web Sites

Home and Garden Television. hgtv.com
Home Improvement Encyclopedia. www.bhglive.com/homeimp
HomeArts. http://homearts.com
HomeIdeas. www.homeideas.com
Hometime. www.hometime.com
Public Broadcasting Systems. pbs.org
Reader's Digest. www.readersdigest.com